TAMING CAPITALISM BEFORE
ITS TRIUMPH

KOJI YAMAMOTO is a historian of early modern England. He has spent twelve happy years in the UK, taking master's and doctoral degrees in York, and subsequently working at universities in London (King's College London), St Andrews, Edinburgh, and Cambridge. He was a British Academy Postdoctoral Fellow between 2012 and 2014. He went back to Japan in 2016, and since October 2018, he has been an Associate Professor in Business History at the Faculty of Economics, the University of Tokyo.

More praise for *Taming Capitalism before its Triumph*

'Koji Yamamoto's much-awaited book addresses how the impact of economic change upon society can be accommodated. It is a highly challenging work in both senses of the word, taking aim at several established lines of argument by bringing economic, social, political, and cultural approaches together into a wider synthesis. . . . it deserves to find a very wide readership.'

Aaron Graham, *Economic History Review*

'I recommend this book to anyone interested in early modern England's road to financial capitalism.'

Amy Froide, *English Historical Review*

'[An] ambitious and yet meticulously researched book . . . Yamamoto's willingness to tackle head on the grandest of narratives about early modern England signifies the extent of his ambitions. However, this is not at the expense of close contextualised reading of the early modern evidence, resulting in an impressive balance between detailed case studies and striking generalisations. . . . an impressive and indeed agenda setting work.'

Thomas Leng, *Seventeenth Century*

Taming Capitalism before its Triumph

Public Service, Distrust, and 'Projecting' in Early Modern England

KOJI YAMAMOTO

OXFORD
UNIVERSITY PRESS

OXFORD
UNIVERSITY PRESS

Great Clarendon Street, Oxford, OX2 6DP,
United Kingdom

Oxford University Press is a department of the University of Oxford.
It furthers the University's objective of excellence in research, scholarship,
and education by publishing worldwide. Oxford is a registered trade mark of
Oxford University Press in the UK and in certain other countries

© Koji Yamamoto 2018

The moral rights of the author have been asserted

First published 2018
First published in paperback 2021

Published in the United States of America by Oxford University Press
198 Madison Avenue, New York, NY 10016, United States of America

British Library Cataloguing in Publication Data
Data available

Library of Congress Cataloging in Publication Data
Data available

ISBN 978–0–19–873917–3 (Hbk.)
ISBN 978–0–19–284833–8 (Pbk.)

Preface

By pursuing his own interest he frequently promotes that of the society more effectually than when he really intends to promote it. I have never known much good done by those who affected to trade for the public good.

Adam Smith, *An Inquiry into the Nature and Causes of the Wealth of Nations*, vol. 1, p. 456 (bk IV, ch. ii, 9)

Adam Smith thus set aside promises of the public good as extraneous, even contrary, to the wealth of nations. Upon this premise rests a powerful classical vision of the market overseen by an invisible hand, something that is often believed to be self-regulating. Milton Friedman quoted this very passage to argue that 'the social responsibility of business is to increase its profit'.[1] In this book I wish to present a history of enterprise and society to which neither the Glasgow professor of political economy nor the Nobel laureate paid much attention: a history of countless *visible hands* exercised by promises of doing good through business.

I have written this book with two goals in mind. First, by recovering the story of countless early modern actors little known except among specialist historians, I wanted to suggest that the well-known story of British economic development needs to be accompanied by a parallel story in which numerous actors contributed to what we might call the taming of incipient capitalism. The word 'taming' has been chosen to highlight *processes* of taming and *human agency* in these processes, two things that I suggest merit closer attention in our understanding of England's culture of improvement, a crucial ingredient for its economic development. As we shall see, the story of taming cannot be reduced to opposition to capitalism or obstruction of its development. Rather, in early modern England incipient capitalism ensured its survival and gathered strength by containing its destructive tendencies and by drawing on human desire in new ways. I would argue that the kind of economic vision that culminated in Smith's invisible hand—a conviction that the benign pursuit of private interests could accelerate economic development—became intellectually plausible, and politically advisable, thanks to this collective process of taming. Accidents or positive externalities alone cannot adequately explain this.

Second, by approaching the process of taming through the early modern concept of *projecting*, I wish to propose one way of making early modern historical research relevant to our lives without falling into dire anachronism or the whiggish celebration of England's fortuitous success. The concept provided early modern actors with a vital framework for understanding and grappling with the precarious relationship

---

[1] Milton Friedman, 'The Social Responsibility of Business is to Increase its Profit', *New York Times Magazine*, 13 September 1970, 32–3, 122–6, at p. 124.

between enterprise and society. When early modern actors spoke about projects and their promoters, they spoke not only of their hopes of enrichment, abundance, and betterment in life, but also of their anxieties about the impending danger of failure, avarice, deception, and even social upheaval. Their engagement with these 'projects' was rarely abstract, unfolding in markets, Westminster, Whitehall, and the Royal Society, in and outside London, mediated by petitions, letters, pamphlets, and periodicals, and even through songs, theatre plays, rumours, and riotous protests. Close attention to the notion of projecting enables us to follow these processes and thereby unravel how early modern promoters and stakeholders shaped and reshaped England's collective pursuits of wealth and abundance. Their experience testifies to the arduous processes of taming incipient capitalism, a kind of challenge that we have since inherited, and may for this reason resonate even among audiences outside Anglophone countries, in places like Japan where I live and teach at present. My Japanese origins may have done me some favour on this count. Studying British history as an East Asian has forced me to think hard about how we might approach the early modern English past in ways that can engage readers on both sides of Eurasia and beyond. This book is my tentative answer.

In writing this book, I have incurred more debts than I can properly express here. The book originates from a doctoral thesis submitted to the University of York. My first, and foremost, intellectual debt is to Mark Jenner who supervised the thesis and has been a constant source of advice ever since. I also wish to thank Natasha Glaisyer for first introducing me to Defoe's 'Projecting Age', and acting subsequently as an examiner of the thesis, and Chris MacLeod for examining the thesis and supporting my career well beyond the call of duty.

My postdoctoral years were blessed with a wide range of scholars and colleagues. I thank my successive mentors and colleagues, including Anne Goldgar, Ludmilla Jordanova, Rab Houston, the late Susan Manning, Liliane Hilaire-Pérez, and Craig Muldrew. For timely encouragements and advice, I am grateful to Martin Bauer, John Brewer, Laurence Fontaine, Steve Hindle, Julian Hoppit, Rob Iliffe, Sandra Jovchelovitch, Mark Knights, Peter Lake, Anne Murphy, Simon Schaffer, Timon Screech, and Nuala Zahedieh. My intellectual outlook would have been much narrower were it not for their generosity.

I have also been fortunate to work alongside a wonderful range of colleagues who have helped enrich this project. They are too numerous to be fully listed here, and many are acknowledged in subsequent pages. Yet for commenting on various parts of this book in its early forms, I thank David Alff, Adam Fox, Julian Hoppit, Michael Hunter, David Magliocco, Craig Muldrew, Shinji Nohara, and Sir Keith Thomas. For illuminating conversations and suggestions, I also wish to thank Will Cavert, Vlad Glăveanu, Yuichi Hiono, Shusaku Kanazawa, Yukiko Kawamoto, Vera Keller, Ted McCormick, Noah Millstone, Will Pettigrew, Valentina Pugliano, Yuichiro Sakamoto, David Chan Smith, Edmund Smith, Toshiaki Tamaki, Hélène Vérin, and Brodie Waddell. Chris MacLeod has read the entire manuscript and has helped me to improve the text. Any remaining shortcomings are, of course, mine.

Equally crucial to the making of this book has been a host of seminars and conferences. I wish to thank the organizers of and participants in these meetings, especially 'British History in the Seventeenth Century' and 'Economic and Social History of the Early Modern World', both hosted by the Institute of Historical Research, the University of London. At a time when humanities subjects are coming under increasing pressure, the institute has been able to provide us with indispensable, welcoming communities in which to test ideas, learn, and collaborate. Equally vital to this study have been the research libraries, archives, and record offices listed in the bibliography. I am grateful to the archivists and librarians in these places, but I would like to thank Colin Harris at the Bodleian Library in particular for his exemplary professionalism. My sincere thanks also go to two anonymous referees, and to members of staff at Oxford University Press, including Stephanie Ireland and Cathryn Steele for patiently taking me through the production process, and Dan Harding for copy-editing. Chapters 3 and 6 are partially based on earlier journal articles. I thank Cambridge University Press and Oxford University Press for allowing me to adopt passages from Koji Yamamoto, 'Reformation and the Distrust of the Projector in the Hartlib Circle', *Historical Journal*, 55 (2012), 375–97; Koji Yamamoto, 'Piety, Profit, and Public Service in the Financial Revolution', *English Historical Review*, 126 (2011), 806–34.

I also wish to acknowledge the institutions that made my postdoctoral research possible: the Economic History Society (UK); the School of History at St Andrews; the Institute for Advanced Studies in the Humanities, University of Edinburgh; the City of Paris and Université Paris 7 Diderot. In Cambridge Subha Mukherji and her excellent team at the 'Crossroads of Knowledge in Early Modern England' project (ERC grant 617849) gave me a rewarding setting for engaging with literary scholarship. Jesus College, Cambridge, provided me with an ideal base for cross-disciplinary dialogue and hospitality. Above all, I must single out and express my gratitude to the British Academy for awarding me a postdoctoral fellowship. The award boosted my confidence and gave me the freedom with which to pursue my projects. To all these institutions I am deeply grateful.

Since April 2016, the University of Tokyo has provided me with a welcome academic home. On this count I thank my colleagues at the Faculty of Economics, especially Satoshi Baba, Makoto Kasuya, Hitoshi Matsushima, Tetsuji Okazaki, Tomoji Onozuka, and Masayuki Tanimoto. I also thank Masashi Haneda and Lisa Hellman at the Institute for Advanced Studies in Asia (Tobunken) for welcoming me. My undergraduate teachers Ken Tsutsumibayashi and Noboru Notomi have also welcomed me back to Tokyo. I look forward to discussing this book and other topics with them.

This project would have been impossible without the moral and personal support of my friends and family. For this let me thank Helen Birkett, Konrad Burchardi, Stefano Costantini, Barbara Gribling, Yoshinori Imamura, Kumiko Jin, Bronach Kane, Yohei Kawakami, Yuka Kitayama, Yanagi and Yuzuki Matsushita, Ena and Ryosuke Motohashi, Hiroko Namba, Kei Numao, Ruth Puig-Peiró, Mireia Raluy i Callado, Simon Sandall, Kunio Shin, Wanchen Tai, Hiroto Tanaka, and Niels and Vidhi van Manen. Some of these friends have been kind enough to ask me the toughest of questions: why study early modern England; so what? Responding to them has been a uniquely rewarding experience. Finally, I wish to record my gratitude to Kaoru and Shigeko Yamamoto for being wonderful parents, and to Sakiko Kaiga for love and support. This book is dedicated to them.

Contents

List of Figures and Illustrations

Abbreviations

A&O	*Acts and Ordinances of the Interregnum*, ed. C. H. Firth and R. S. Rait (3 vols., London: Wyman, 1911)
AHEW Vii	Joan Thirsk (ed.), *The Agrarian History of England and Wales, Volume Vii, 1640–1750: Agrarian Change* (Cambridge: Cambridge University Press, 1985)
AHR	*American Historical Review*
APC	*Acts of the Privy Council of England*
BJHS	*British Journal for the History of Science*
BL	British Library, London
BM	British Museum, London
Bodl.	Bodleian Library, Oxford
Boyle Correspondence	Robert Boyle, *The Correspondence of Robert Boyle*, ed. Michael Hunter, Antonio Clericuzio, and Lawrence M. Principe (6 vols., London: Pickering & Chatto, 2001)
CJ	*Journals of the House of Commons*
Constitutional Documents	*The Constitutional Documents of the Puritan Revolution, 1625–1660*, ed. Samuel Rawson Gardiner (3rd edn, Oxford: Clarendon, 1906)
CSPD	*Calendar of State Papers, Domestic*
CTB	*Calendar of Treasury Books*
CTP	*Calendar of Treasury Papers*
'Culpeper Letters'	Cheney Culpeper, 'The Letters of Sir Cheney Culpeper (1641–1657)', ed. M. J. Braddick and M. Greengrass, *Camden Miscellany*, 33, 5th ser., 7 (1996), 105–402 [references given in parentheses are to *The Hartlib Papers*]
Culture and Cultivation	Michael Leslie and Timothy Raylor (eds.), *Culture and Cultivation in Early Modern England* (Leicester and London: Leicester University Press, 1992)
EcHR	*Economic History Review*
EHR	*English Historical Review*
HEH	Henry E. Huntington Library, San Marino
HJ	*Historical Journal*
HMC	*Historical Manuscripts Commission*
HP	Sheffield University, *The Hartlib Papers* (2 CD-ROMs, 2nd edn, Sheffield: HR Online, 2002)
JBS	*Journal of British Studies*
Leng, *Worsley*	Thomas Leng, *Benjamin Worsley (1618–1677): Trade, Interest and the Spirit in Revolutionary England* (Woodbridge: Boydell, 2008)

LJ	*Journals of the House of Lords*
LMA	London Metropolitan Archives, City of London
McCormick, *Petty*	Ted McCormick, *William Petty and the Ambitions of Political Arithmetic* (Oxford: Oxford University Press, 2009)
MacLeod, *Patent*	Christine MacLeod, *Inventing the Industrial Revolution: The English Patent System, 1660–1800* (Cambridge: Cambridge University Press, 1988)
NLW	National Library of Wales, Aberystwyth
NRRS	*Notes and Records of the Royal Society*
OED	*Oxford English Dictionary Online*, 4th edition
Oxford DNB	H. C. G. Matthew and Brian Harrison (eds.), *Oxford Dictionary of National Biography* (60 vols., Oxford: Oxford University Press, 2004)
PA	Parliamentary Archives, London
P&P	*Past & Present*
PT	*Philosophical Transactions*
RS	Royal Society Archives, London
Scott, *Joint-Stock*	William Robert Scott, *The Constitution and Finance of English, Scottish and Irish Joint-Stock Companies to 1720* (3 vols., Cambridge: Cambridge University Press, 1910–12)
Slack, *Invention of Improvement*	Paul Slack, *The Invention of Improvement: Information and Material Progress in Seventeenth-Century England* (Oxford: Oxford University Press, 2015)
Slack, *Reformation to Improvement*	Paul Slack, *From Reformation to Improvement: Public Welfare in Early Modern England* (Oxford: Clarendon, 1998)
Staff.RO	Staffordshire Record Office, Stafford
T&C	Joan Thirsk and J. P. Cooper (eds.), *Seventeenth-Century Economic Documents* (Oxford: Clarendon, 1972)
Thirsk, 'Crown as Projector'	Joan Thirsk, 'The Crown as Projector on its Own Estates, from Elizabeth I to Charles I', in R. W. Hoyle (ed.), *The Estates of the English Crown, 1558–1640* (Cambridge: Cambridge University Press, 1992), 297–352
Thirsk, *Economic Policy and Projects*	Joan Thirsk, *Economic Policy and Projects: The Development of a Consumer Society in Early Modern England* (Oxford: Clarendon, 1978)
TNA	The National Archives, Kew
TRHS	*Transactions of the Royal Historical Society*
Universal Reformation	Mark Greengrass, Michael Leslie, and Timothy Raylor (eds.), *Samuel Hartlib and Universal Reformation: Studies in Intellectual Communication* (Cambridge: Cambridge University Press, 1994)
VCH	Victoria County History

Webster, *Great Instauration*   Charles Webster, *The Great Instauration: Science, Medicine and Reform 1626–1660* (2nd edn, with new preface, Oxford: Peter Lang, 2002)

Wrightson, *Earthly Necessities*   Keith Wrightson, *Earthly Necessities: Economic Lives in Early Modern Britain, 1470–1750* (London: Penguin, 2002)

Yamamoto, 'Thesis'   Koji Yamamoto, 'Distrust, Innovation and Public Service: "Projecting" in Early Modern England' (PhD thesis, University of York, 2009)

Conventions

I have given all the dates in the old style, but with the year taken to have started on 1 January. Dates in the new style are additionally given where the discussion concerns the European Continent as well as the British Isles. When citing early modern manuscript sources, I have replaced 'y' with 'th', and 'v' with 'u' where appropriate. I have otherwise retained the original spelling and punctuation. Acts of parliament are cited from *Statutes of the Realm* (11 vols., London: George Eyre and Andrew Strahan, 1810–28). All quotations from the Bible are taken from *The Bible: Authorized King James Version*, ed. Robert Carroll and Stephen Prickett (Oxford: Oxford Paperbacks, 2008). Patent numbers given in the text and in footnotes refer to those given in Bennet Woodcroft, *Titles of Patents of Invention, Chronologically Arranged, from March 2, 1617 (14 James I) to October 1, 1852 (16 Victoriae), Part I. Nos. 1 to 4,800* (London: Queen's Printing Office, 1854). When discussing figures, decimals are rounded to the nearest whole number. Place of publication of primary sources published prior to 1800 is London unless otherwise stated.

Introduction
Projecting and Capitalism: A Reappraisal

England in the early eighteenth century was a society that was fascinated by wealth-creating, profit-yielding innovations, but remained strikingly sceptical about the morality of would-be promoters. Consider the experience of John Cary, a Bristol merchant and a friend of the philosopher John Locke. Cary's *An essay on the state of England* (1695) discussed whether the competitive price of commodities such as sugar, spirits, glass bottles, and silk stockings depended on the lowering of wages. His answer was negative. Prices could be, and ought to be, reduced without cutting wages. An alternative factor that Cary identified for achieving lower prices was 'the ingenuity of the manufacturer'. Another—the theme of this study—was 'projects', which in this context meant the commercial exploitation of useful knowledge and techniques. 'New projections are every day set on foot to render the making [of] our manufactures easy'; thanks to these initiatives, 'Tobacco is cut by Engines instead of Knives'; 'Pits are drained and Land made Healthy by Engines and Aquaducts instead of Hands'. Likewise the '*Glass-maker* hath found a quicker way of making it out of things which cost him little or nothing'.[1] Daniel Defoe agreed. In 1697, he declared the arrival of a 'Projecting Age', an age teeming with schemes at best capable 'of publick Advantage, as they tend to Improvement of Trade, and Employment of the Poor, and the Circulation and Increase of the publick Stock of the Kingdom'.[2] In Cary's view, these projects made it possible to produce items for export and home consumption without suppressing wages. Seen from an economic perspective, Cary's observation contains 'a classic statement about productivity-increasing investments, lowered prices, and higher real wages'.[3] His treatise proved influential. It was subsequently translated into French (1755), Italian (1757–8), and German (1788). England's economy, which in 1550 was still adopting continental practices, came two centuries later to provide a model to be studied and emulated.[4] Projects were closely associated with England's fateful economic transformation that struck Cary's European readers.

---

[1] John Cary, *An essay on the state of England in relation to its trade, its poor, and its taxes for carrying on the present war* (Bristol, 1695), pp. 145–7.

[2] Daniel Defoe, *An essay upon projects* (1697), pp. 1, 10–11.

[3] D. C. Coleman, *The Economy of England, 1450–1750* (Oxford: Oxford University Press, 1977), p. 157. Cf. Robert C. Allen, *The British Industrial Revolution in Global Perspective* (Cambridge: Cambridge University Press, 2009), pp. 42–6, 56, 138–44.

[4] Sophus A. Reinert, *Translating Empire: Emulation and the Origins of Political Economy* (Cambridge, MA: Harvard University Press, 2011), pp. xiii, 11, 84–5; Slack, *Invention of Improvement*, pp. 45–6, 242.

We might expect that promoters of those wealth-generating projects were warmly received by society at the time. They had a bad reputation, however. This simple fact provides us with the departure point for this study. In the year Cary published *An essay*, the anonymous pamphlet *Angliae tutamen* in fact offered a very different 'ACCOUNT OF THE *Banks, Lotteries, Mines, Diving, Draining, Lifting,* and *other Engines,* and many pernicious *Projects* now on foot'. The author claimed that they were 'tending to the Destruction of *Trade* and *Commerce,* and the Impoverishing [of] this REALM'.[5] The promoters of new schemes were aware of their bad name. Dalby Thomas was a Gentleman of the Privy Chamber and one of the promoters of the Hampstead Aqueduct Company and the 'General Fishery' scheme. When Defoe dedicated his '*Book of Projects*' to him, he made a revealing qualification:

> Your having a Capacity to Judge of these things, no way brings You under the Despicable Title of a Projector, any more than knowing the Practices and Subtleties of Wicked Men, makes a Man guilty of their Crimes.[6]

This concern was not just a public posture. In a letter to Locke, Cary in fact confided that he had omitted from *An essay* some of the proposals for levying tax and improving industries. It was because, Cary explained, including them in this 'Treatise designed for a publique use...might bringe me under the name of a Projector, which I carefully endeavour to avoyd'.[7] Those self-appointed purveyors of improvement and progress had some reasons to operate with utmost caution.

Crucially, we are not dealing with clear-cut oppositions between virtuous proponents of improvement and anxious defenders of the status quo refusing economic progress. While praising beneficial schemes, Defoe attacked the 'meer Projector' as a 'Contemptible thing, driven by his own desperate Fortune'.[8] The vociferous author of *Angliae tutamen* declared that his intention was not to 'discountenance Ingenuity, but quite the contrary, to support and advance it' by exposing chicanery.[9] Jonathan Swift, who disparaged dubious 'projects' of all kinds in his *Gulliver's Travels,* nonetheless approved of 'a projector' working on agricultural improvement; even a pack of playing cards mocking commercial 'projects' acknowledged that some of them could be beneficial.[10] These commentators would

---

[5] *Angliae tutamen: or, the safety of England* (1695), title page.
[6] Defoe, *Essay upon projects*, pp. i, ii. For Dalby Thomas, see J. H. Thomas, 'Thomas Neale, A Seventeenth-Century Projector' (PhD thesis, University of Southampton, 1979), p. 395.
[7] John Locke, *Correspondence of John Locke*, ed. E. S. de Beer (8 vols., Oxford: Clarendon, 1976–89), vol. 5, pp. 633–4. For background, see Jonathan Barry, 'The "Great Projector": John Cary and the Legacy of Puritan Reform in Bristol', in Margaret Pelling and Scott Mandelbrote (eds.), *The Practice of Reform in Health, Medicine and Science, 1500–2000* (Aldershot: Ashgate, 2005), 185–206.
[8] Defoe, *Essay upon projects*, p. 33   [9] *Angliae tutamen*, pp. 23, 25, 30, at p. 30.
[10] Jonathan Swift, *The Prose Writings of Jonathan Swift, Vol. 11: Gulliver's Travels, 1726*, ed. Herbert Davis (Oxford: Blackwell, 1941), p. 180; BM, Schreiber Collection, English 66, 'English Bubble Companies Playing Cards', ace of hearts, two of hearts, and ace of diamonds. This qualifies the suggestions that Swift and others might have been unequivocally against projects. See Simon Schaffer, 'Defoe's Natural Philosophy and the Worlds of Credit', in John Christie and Sally Shuttleworth (eds.), *Nature Transfigured: Science and Literature, 1700–1900* (Manchester: Manchester University Press, 1989), 13–44, p. 37; Christine MacLeod, *Heroes of Invention: Technology, Liberalism and British Industry, 1750–1914* (Cambridge: Cambridge University Press, 2007), pp. 36–7.

have agreed with Cary that some projects for improvement had been, and *could be*, beneficial to society as well as to their promoters.

At stake is therefore a profound ambivalence. Could economic initiatives, which involved elements of profit, be relied upon as a means to serve the public? Like today's entrepreneurs, projectors were all too fond of highlighting their originality. Yet in reality, emulation and the adoption of existing practices in new contexts were central to early modern projects as well as to modern entrepreneurship. As David Edgerton has put it, 'there is a remarkable lack of originality in innovation policies'.[11] This holds true also for the projectors' claim of novelty. Yet another problem was even more troubling. Would promoters and their backers not abuse the slogan of public service in order to pursue their private ends at the public's expense? Such concerns help us to understand why Cary gratefully received Locke's comment that Cary's *An essay* was written 'without partiality'. From Cary's perspective, the philosopher's approval confirmed that he stood above common projectors who aired schemes 'fitted for their private Interests under the splendid name of the Publique Good'.[12] Then, as now, there was a great concern about whether the public good and private interests could be reconciled when it came to the promotion of new initiatives. As Francis Bacon put it pithily in his essay 'On Innovations', 'the novelty, though it be not rejected, yet be held for a suspect'.[13]

The concept of projecting lies at the heart of this study because it encapsulated early modern hopes and, crucially, anxieties about improvement and enrichment. A brief foray into its etymology proves the point, and establishes the conceptual thrust of this book. In classical Latin, *proicere* meant primarily to 'throw forth', 'put out', and 'cast out', and *proiectum*, something thrown forth, extended, or cast out. Their post-classical and medieval descendants acquired the range of meanings that Defoe and Swift would have readily recognized.[14] Translators of Arabic texts such as Robert of Ketton (*fl.* 1141–1157) and Michael Scot (d. in or after 1235) used *projectio* in medicinal and alchemical contexts to denote the 'casting of a substance into a crucible' and the transmutation of base metals into gold.[15] The alchemist George Ripley (d. *c.*1490) drew on this tradition when he intimated that 'projection' was the final step (or 'gates') in the elusive process of transmuting base metals into gold.[16] This explains why the much sought-after 'Philosopher's Stone' was also

[11] David Edgerton, *The Shock of the Old: Technology and Global History since 1900* (London: Profile Books, 2006), p. 209.

[12] Locke, *Correspondence*, vol. 5, pp. 633–4.

[13] Francis Bacon, *The Essayes or Counsels, Civill and Morall*, ed. Michael Kiernan (Oxford: Clarendon, 1985), p. 76.

[14] In addition to those cited later, the dictionary entries I have consulted include R. E. Latham, D. R. Howlett, and R. K. Ashdowne (eds.), *Dictionary of Medieval Latin from British Sources* (2 vols., Oxford: British Academy, 1975–2013) [hereafter cited as *DMLBS*], fascicule XII, pp. 2499–500 (s.vv. *proicere* 1a, 1c; *projectio* 1a, 1b); Albert Blaise, *Dictionnaire latin-français des auteurs chrétiens* (Paris: Librairie des Méridiens, 1954), p. 671 (s.v. *prōicio*); Takeshi Matsumura, *Dictionnaire du français médiéval* (Paris: Les Belles Lettres, 2015), p. 2720 (s.v. *projeccion*).

[15] *DMLBS*, fascicule XII, pp. 2499 (s.v. *proicere* 1c).

[16] Jennifer M. Rampling, 'The Catalogue of the Ripley Corpus: Alchemical Writings Attributed to George Ripley (d. ca. 1490)', *Ambix*, 57 (2010), 125–201, pp. 151–8, 197–9. See also Lawrence M. Principe, *The Secrets of Alchemy* (Chicago: University of Chicago Press, 2013), p. 125; Stanton J. Linden,

called the 'powder of projection' in early modern Europe, a powder 'supposed to have the Virtue of changing any quantity of' base metals 'into a more perfect one, as Silver or Gold', as an eighteenth-century 'universal dictionary' explained.[17] By the fifteenth century, the term *projectio* was also used more metaphorically to designate 'planning', as in the Franciscan Statutes of 1451 that spoke against 'the composition or projecting [i.e. planning] of an infamous libel'.[18] A cognate word in medieval French was also used figuratively, as in 'pourjeter une embusque'—or 'to plot an ambush'.[19] In Middle English, the noun *proiect* could mean 'a design or pattern according to which something is made'.[20] In sixteenth-century French, we find the noun *project* (often spelt *pourget*) being used to designate a map or an architectural draft, as in 'la figure et pourget...des rivieres'—the plan and (geometrical) scheme of rivers.[21]

The notion of projecting thus boasted a rich semantic heritage by the time Bacon wrote 'On Innovation'. By then the alchemical connotations had a particularly rich lineage of more than three centuries, with the geometric ones probably being a more recent vintage.[22] As we shall see, under the influence of Renaissance humanism,

---

Darke Hierogliphicks: Alchemy in English Literature from Chaucer to the Restoration (Lexington, KY: University Press of Kentucky, 1996), p. 6.

   [17]   Ephraim Chambers, *Cyclopaedia: or an universal dictionary of art and science* (2 vols., 1728), vol. 2, p. 887. See also Walther von Wartburg et al., *Französisches Etymologisches Wörterbuch* (25 vols., Bonn: Schroeder, 1922–2002) [hereafter cited as *FEW*], vol. 9, p. 439 (s.v. projectio 1). Cf. Pamela H. Smith, *The Business of Alchemy: Science and Culture in the Holy Roman Empire* (Princeton, NJ: Princeton University Press, 1994), p. 269; Jan Lazardzig, '"Masque der Possibilität": Experiment und Spektakel barocker Projektemacherei', in Helmar Schramm, Ludger Schwarte, and Jan Lazardzig (eds.), *Spektakuläre Experimente: Praktiken der Evidenzproduktion im 17. Jahrhundert* (Berlin: de Gruyter, 2006), 176–212, pp. 179–80.

   [18]   *DMLBS*, fascicule XII, p. 2500 (s.v. *projectio* 4); J. S. Brewer and Richard Howlett (eds.), *Monumenta Franciscana* (2 vols., Cambridge: Cambridge University Press, 1858–82), vol. 2, p. 98 'composicionis vel projectionis libelli famosi'. See also Charles du Cange et al., *Glossarium Mediae et Infimae Latinitatis* (10 vols., Niort: L. Favre, 1883–7), vol. 6, p. 527 (*s.v.* projestum).

   [19]   *FEW*, vol. 5, p. 21 (s.v. jactare k.β). See also Frédéric Godefroy, *Dictionnaire de l'ancienne langue française et de tous ses dialectes du IXe au XVe siècle* (10 vols., Paris: F. Vieweg, 1891–1902), vol. 6, p. 293 (s.v. porgeter).

   [20]   Hans Kurath (ed.), *Middle English Dictionary* (128 parts, Ann Arbor, MI: University of Michigan Press, 1955–2001), pt. P.7, p. 1379 (s.v. *project* c); *OED*, s.v. project n. 1.a (quotation). The medieval romance *The Wars of Alexander* (*c*.1400) used the term this way when it depicted the sumptuous crown given to Alexander the Great as being made according to the most befitting 'proiecte' (i.e. design) for a magnificent conqueror like him. See *The Wars of Alexander: An Alliterative Romance*, ed. Walter W. Skeat (London: Early English Text Society, 1886), p. 198: 'coron...þe propurest of proiecte þat euire prince bere'.

   [21]   Edmond Huguet, *Dictionnaire de la langue française du seizième siècle* (7 vols., Paris: E. Champion, 1925–73), vol. 6, p. 211 (s.v. project 1). See p. 43 n. 56 for an example drawn from Rabelais.

   [22]   The evidence presented here corrects the recent suggestion that 'the term [project] first appeared in the context of architectural drafting' rather than in relation to 'the alchemical step of "projection"'. Vera Keller and Ted McCormick, 'Towards a History of Projects', *Early Science and Medicine*, 21 (2016), 423–44, at p. 426. To support this particular statement, the article cites a book chapter by Stefan Brakensiek that discusses the use of the terms 'project' and 'projection' in the *Oekonomische Encyklopädie* (published from 1773 onwards). In the cited passage, Brakensiek notes that the concept of projection carried mathematical and cartographic meanings, but does not discuss their precedence over alchemical ones. The brief entry on 'Projection' in the German encyclopaedia defines the term in relation to cartography, optics, and alchemy, but without establishing chronology. Keller and McCormick—astute scholars of my generation—may have accidentally omitted to substantiate their

crafts, engineering, architecture, mining, and metallurgy came by that time to be promoted as something at best capable of enhancing the honour and the wealth of polities. Used in this context, the terms 'project' and 'projecting' highlighted the confidence in human art's ability to conquer nature. The project was a promise of alchemy-like transformation, turning untapped resources (such as human ingenuity, dormant legislation, or idle labour) into wealth, a process fuelled by another transmutation, of private desires into public benefits. Such alchemical confidence, coupled with the metaphor of a draughtsman capable of designing and project-ing a complex plan for a better future, gave rise to the sixteenth-century English definition of the project: 'a planned and proposed undertaking'. This is the def-inition that Defoe's age (and ours) inherited.[23] At the same time, the concept of a project was capacious, even slippery. Jeremy Bentham defined its promoters as those who 'strike into any channel of invention'; who pursued 'the cultivation of any of those arts which have been by way of eminence termed *useful*'; who 'aim at any thing that can be called *improvement*'.[24] If we take a closer look, projects included the kind of process innovations that Cary spoke of, and also schemes that fall under Defoe's 'true definition of a Project'—'a vast Undertaking, too big to be manag'd', that required large overheads or legal assistance, or both. The pro-motion of new projects mostly required something beyond 'business as usual'.[25] Projects were things yet to be materialized, and many of them produced few tangible results. In Defoe's and Cary's positive use of the term, we can discern 'the belief'—we might say the presumptuous belief—'that human thought and action *could* transform society'.[26]

Crucial to our story are the underlying negative overtones—that the prospect of alchemical transmutation was too good to be true. The Latin verb *iactare* could indeed mean to 'discuss, to boast of' and to 'make an ostentatious display'.[27] These shades of meaning were not lost when Samuel Butler satirized the projector as 'a Man of *Forecast*', whose 'Talent consists in Quacking and Lying, which he calls

---

statement. See Stefan Brakensiek, 'Projektemacher: Zum Hintergrund ökonomischen Scheiterns in der Frühen Neuzeit', in Stefan Brakensiek and Claudia Claridge (eds.), *Fiasko—Scheitern in der Frühen Neuzeit: Beiträge zur Kulturgeschichte des Misserfolgs* (Bielefeld: Transcript, 2015), 39–58, pp. 42–3; Johan Georg Krünitz et al. (eds.), *Oekonomische Encyklopädie* (242 vols., Berlin, 1773–1858), vol. 117, p. 720 (s.v. Projection).

[23] *OED*, s.v. project, n.   [24] Jeremy Bentham, *Defense of usury* (1790), pp. 138–9.

[25] Defoe, *Essay upon projects*, p. 20. Bentham likewise defined projecting as the 'application of the human powers, in which ingenuity stands in need of wealth for its assistant'. Bentham, *Defence of usury*, pp. 138–9. Accordingly, the expansion of merchants' portfolios was rarely construed as a project if it took place within well-established trading networks. Plans to augment the corporate privilege of trading companies could be scrutinized as harmful 'projects', but their routine trading activities were not usually discussed as such in the early modern period.

[26] Maximillian E. Novak, 'Introduction', in Maximillian E. Novak (ed.), *The Age of Projects* (Toronto: University of Toronto Press, 2008), 3–25, p. 7 (italics added). Positive and neutral definitions were not uncommon. See Robert Cawdry, *A table alphabeticall contayning and teaching the true writing and vnderstanding of hard vsuall English wordes* (1609), s.v. proiect; Henry Cockeram, *The English dictionarie: or, An interpreter of hard English words* (1623), s.v. proiect; Elisha Coles, *An English dictionary explaining the difficult terms* (1692), s.v. projection; Samuel Johnson, *A Dictionary of the English Language* (2 vols., 1756), vol. 2, s.v. projector, *n*.

[27] *OED*, s.v. project, *v*., jactation, *n*.

answering of Objections, and convincing the Ignorant', or when Joseph Addison identified a projector in a coffeehouse by 'the Extravagance of his Conceptions, and the Hurry of his Speech'.[28] Thomas Fuller suggested that 'disaffected' readers of the alchemist Ripley's tracts 'demand whether these *gates* [i.e. the twelve alchemical operations] be to let in, or let out the *Philosophers Stone*, seeing *Projection* the last of all, proves but a *Project*, producing nothing in effect'.[29] Any discussions of early modern projecting should be alert to the duality of its negative and more descriptive connotations. We shall accordingly speak of *projects for improvement* and *schemes for innovations and improvement* in a descriptive sense, without neglecting the underlying elements of suspicion that troubled Defoe and Cary alike.

This element of suspicion is significant. It even affected one of the best-known observers of the pre-industrial economy, Adam Smith. Presumptuous projectors in his view did little good to the economy. 'Projects of mining' stood as 'the most disadvantageous lottery in the world'. 'Every injudicious and unsuccessful project in manufacture, mines, fisheries, trade, or manufactures, tends...to diminish the funds destined for the maintenance of productive labour.'[30] For the philosopher, it was the private interests of numerous economic actors, not the projectors' presumptuous promises of public service, that ultimately mattered:

> By preferring the support of domestick to that of foreign industry, he intends only his own security; and by directing that industry in such a manner as its produce may be of the greatest value, he intends only his own gain, and he is in this, as in many other cases, led by an invisible hand to promote an end which was no part of his intention.[31]

We need not suppose that Smith celebrated unbridled greed, or that his analysis focused so closely on private interests as to leave no role for the state. Smith was well aware that the saving of capital was vital for facilitating productive investment, and that diligence and 'self-command' (rather than promiscuous consumption) were the key. Smith also admitted that the government was to play a critical, if circumscribed, role in areas such as education, banking, and the usury laws that would prevent projectors from wasting money on impractical schemes.[32] Yet the case

---

[28] Samuel Butler, *Samuel Butler 1612–1680: Characters*, ed. Charles W. Daves (Cleveland, OH: Press of Case Western Reserve University, 1970), p. 167; *Spectator*, ed. Donald F. Bond (5 vols., Oxford: Clarendon, 1965), vol. 1, no. 31, p. 127. The gendered references were not incidental, as female projectors were rare, albeit not unknown. See pp. 82–3 below; Thirsk, 'Crown as Projector', p. 343.

[29] Thomas Fuller, *The history of the worthies of England* (1662), p. 204.

[30] Adam Smith, *An Inquiry into the Nature and Causes of the Wealth of Nations*, ed. R. H. Campbell and A. S. Skinner (2 vols., Indianapolis, IN: Liberty Fund, 1976), vol. 2, p. 562 (bk IV, ch. vii, pt. a, 18); vol. 1, p. 341 (bk II, ch. iii, 26).

[31] Ibid., vol. 1, p. 456 (bk IV, ch. ii, 9). See also, Adam Smith, *The Theory of Moral Sentiments*, ed. D. D. Raphael and A. L. Macfie (Indianapolis, IN: Liberty Fund, 1976), p. 184 (pt. IV, sec.i, 10). Smith is known to have used the phrase 'invisible hand' only three times. On his usage and the intellectual history behind the concept, see Emma Rothschild, 'Smith and the Invisible Hand', *American Economic Review*, 84 (1994), 319–22; Peter Harrison, 'Adam Smith and the History of the Invisible Hand', *Journal of the History of Ideas*, 72 (2011), 29–49.

[32] On the importance of 'self-command' for facilitating savings, see Craig Muldrew, 'Self-Control and Savings: Adam Smith and the Creation of Modern Capital', in James Shaw and Simon Middleton (eds.), *Market Ethics and Practices, 1300–1850* (Abingdon: Routledge, 2017), 63–86. For Adam Smith on the role of the state, see Donald Winch, *Adam Smith's Politics: An Essay in Historiographic Revision*

remains. It was the vested interests of social and occupational groups (rather than their public utterances) that were to be examined alongside other factors such as land, capital, and the division of labour. Within this grand scheme, Smith used the figure of the patient 'undertaker' to discuss functional aspects of the projector's activities, such as capital accumulation, investment, and inventions. Like his idealized notion of the 'prudent man', that of the undertaker was conveniently stripped of undesirable characteristics often associated with the projector.[33] Accordingly, the anxieties felt by promoters such as Defoe and Cary were given little systematic attention in Smith's account of political economy, of ways and means to 'enrich both the people and sovereign'.[34]

In this book, I want to tell the story of projectors and their tempestuous relationship with society that Smith did not write because of his inherited preconceptions about them. This is an exercise in writing a history of early capitalism that is not primarily about a chosen industrial sector, means of production, economic region, or socio-occupational group, or about vital time-series indicators such as real wages, prices, and gross domestic product (GDP). Thanks to recent work on these topics, we now know that the two centuries following 1550 saw the emergence of England's culture of material improvement and progress. By 1750, numerous rivers had been made more navigable, more patents granted to promote technology transfer and protect specific inventions, new urban and rural industries set up, and numerous schemes were enhancing productivity in various sectors such as textiles, agriculture, and mining. By the time Defoe and Cary were writing, per capita GDP and living standards were rising; having recovered at last from the demographic shock of the Black Death, England was transforming itself into the first industrial nation. England's culture of improvement was central to this piecemeal, yet decisive, 'transition to capitalism'.[35]

(Cambridge: Cambridge University Press, 1978), pp. 119, 159–60, 170–2; Donald Winch, 'Adam Smith's Problems and Ours', *Scottish Journal of Political Economy*, 44 (1997), 384–402; Istvan Hont and Michael Ignatieff, 'Needs and Justice in the *Wealth of Nations*: An Introductory Essay', in Hont and Ignatieff (eds.), *Wealth and Virtue: The Shaping of Political Economy in the Scottish Enlightenment* (Cambridge: Cambridge University Press, 1983), 1–44, pp. 14–15, 21; Emma Rothschild and Amartya Sen, 'Adam Smith's Economics', in Knud Haakonssen (ed.), *The Cambridge Companion to Adam Smith* (Cambridge: Cambridge University Press, 2006), 319–65, pp. 337, 346–7.

[33] On the prudent man, see Smith, *Theory of Moral Sentiments*, p. 215 (pt. VI, sec. i, 12); Enzo Pesciarelli, 'Smith, Bentham, and the Development of Contrasting Ideas on Entrepreneurship', *History of Political Economy*, 21 (1989), 521–36. Cf. Winch, 'Adam Smith's Problems', pp. 392–3; Istvan Hont, *Jealousy of Trade: International Competition and the Nation-State in Historical Perspective* (Cambridge, MA: Harvard University Press, 2005), pp. 358–62, 381–4.

[34] Smith, *Wealth of Nations*, vol. 1, p.428 (bk iv, introduction). Cf. Nicholas Phillipson, *Adam Smith: An Enlightened Life* (New Haven, CT: Yale University Press, 2010), pp. 105–6.

[35] An overview is provided by Slack, *Invention of Improvement*, *passim*; Wrightson, *Earthly Necessities*, pp. 108–12, 227–48; E. A. Wrigley, *Poverty, Progress, and Population* (Cambridge: Cambridge University Press, 2004), pp. 44–5; Stephen Broadberry et al., *British Economic Growth, 1270–1870* (Cambridge: Cambridge University Press, 2015), ch. 5 (esp. pp. 206, 210–11). Rich historiographies related to agrarian and merchant capitalism are ably surveyed by David Ormrod, 'Agrarian Capitalism and Merchant Capitalism: Tawney, Dobb, Brenner and Beyond', in Jane Whittle (ed.), *Landlords and Tenants in Britain, 1440–1660: Tawney's Agrarian Problem Revisited* (Woodbridge: Boydell, 2013), 200–15.

Explaining England's economic success leading to the Industrial Revolution has arguably been one of the most prominent themes in economic history. The very best of scholars have devoted themselves to solving this question.[36] Early modern England demands our attention, however, not only because of its precocious economic development or its putatively 'growth-friendly culture', as Joel Mokyr puts it.[37] It demands our fresh attention in the twenty-first century all the more because it is a society that was, like ours, deeply concerned about the societal implications of economic forces.

Instead of using modern theoretical accounts of capitalist economy to define the direction of research, then, this study tactically sets them aside and revisits England's economic development through the early modern lens of projecting in both the neutral and pejorative senses of the term that actors such as Defoe, Cary, and Swift would have readily understood: as concrete economic initiatives at best capable of *public service*; and as a negative public understanding of these activities that exposed promoters to enduring *distrust*. *Taming Capitalism* argues that there is a rich history of broken promises of public service and ensuing public scepticism. By the early eighteenth century, this history could go back at least a century. Defoe's caution and Cary's frustration belong to this story we are yet to discover.

This book begins by surveying how ambitious projects for economic improvement and innovation emerged in large numbers from the sixteenth century. Lofty slogans such as the 'commonweal' and the 'public good' helped make otherwise shady business initiatives more socially and morally attractive, drawing more money, manpower, and knowledge from across social strata.[38] Bold enterprises were put forward under Elizabeth I and early Stuart monarchs in ways that anticipated Joseph A. Schumpeter's notion of 'creative responses', some enjoying royal backing. Yet, as we shall see, courtiers (who were not skilled artisans) began to advance projects of dubious legality under the colour of serving the commonwealth. By making ostensible claims to technical mastery and new inventions, some secured monopolistic patents that enabled them to suppress competitors; others tightened economic regulations or pushed for controversial 'improvement' of rivers, forests, and fenlands. Most promised revenues to the Crown while securing profits to themselves. By the end of Elizabeth I's reign, many projects in effect induced *rent-seeking* behaviours— the exploitation of regulatory mechanisms for private gain 'as if it were part of the market sphere'.[39] As the terminology was absent, even those schemes that had little or nothing to do with production were construed as 'improvement' in the original

---

[36] In addition to the works already cited, see also Simon Smith, 'Determining the Industrial Revolution', *HJ*, 54 (2011), 907–24; E. A. Wrigley, *The Path to Sustained Growth: England's Transition from an Organic Economy to an Industrial Revolution* (Cambridge: Cambridge University Press, 2016).

[37] Joel Mokyr, *A Culture of Growth: The Origins of the Modern Economy* (Princeton, NJ: Princeton University Press, 2017), p. 223.

[38] Arthur B. Ferguson, *The Articulate Citizen and the English Renaissance* (Durham, NC: Duke University Press, 1965), esp. p. 363; Thirsk, *Economic Policy and Projects*, p. 1; Slack, *Reformation to Improvement*, pp. 1, 5–7.

[39] Linda Levy Peck, *Court Patronage and Corruption in Early Modern England* (London: Unwin Hyman, 1990), p. 136.

sense of the term, to raise rents.[40] Like Schumpeter's enterprises, projects for economic improvement were promoted as something at best capable of bringing about discontinuous change in the economy. Yet they were prone to perversion, with grave implications not only for subjects' rights and liberty, but also for social and political stability. *Taming Capitalism* explores the ways in which the worst of such perversions came to be avoided. Because it focuses on one aspect of incipient capitalism—projects for economic improvement—and because these projects bear a certain similarity to Schumpeter's entrepreneurship (as will be seen in Chapter 1), alternative titles for this book would include *Taming Early Modern Projects* and *Taming Schumpeterian Enterprises in Early Modern England*.

After establishing the historical context and contours of England's culture of projecting (Chapter 1), the study explores how controversial projects caused grievances under the early Stuarts, and gave rise to the pejorative notion of the projector (Chapter 2). Reconstructing the social circulation of this image, it investigates in what ways the public distrust of the projector influenced the mundane promotion of enterprises in the crucial eight decades from the 1640s to the 1710s, from the end of Charles I's Personal Rule to Defoe's Projecting Age (Chapters 3–6). A close look at these eight decades is useful. England's political economy began to diverge visibly from the continental models during this period. If we pay attention to numerous, often forgotten historical actors contributing to the processes of taming during this period, we will then be able to see very clearly how seventeenth-century foundations paved the way for the emergence of Defoe's Projecting Age, a commercializing society in which Smith's vision of the market became politically advisable and intellectually plausible. Even the South Sea Bubble of 1720—something often described as an essentially *modern* stock price bubble— will begin by the end of this book to look more like an essentially *early modern* project unfolding in the transformative environment of the emerging stock market. This rethinking of the bubble will serve as the end point of our discussion.

HISTORIOGRAPHY: BETWEEN HOPES AND SUSPICION

Projectors and their projects have drawn scholars' attention ever since the early days of economic history as an academic discipline. Yet the possibility that there is a rich history about projectors' promises and public responses to them has been something of a blind spot. Like Smith, some earlier accounts developed their analyses by reproducing, rather than scrutinizing, the early modern biases towards the projector. William Hyde Price viewed Charles I's Personal Rule and the controversial 'projects' that thrived under him as antithetical to economic growth. The '"projecting" spirit gave birth to some monstrous and artificial schemes' and

---

[40] Useful surveys include Paul Warde, 'The Idea of Improvement, 1520–1720', in Richard Hoyle (ed.), *Custom, Improvement and the Landscape in Early Modern Britain* (Farnham: Ashgate, 2011), 127–48; Slack, *Invention of Improvement*, pp. 4–8; Slack, *Reformation to Improvement*, pp. 80–1.

'culminated in failure'.[41] But their demise 'taught the crown the necessity of finding other forms of bounty for favorites'. The 'permanent outcome', argued Price, 'was the triumph of [economic] freedom'.[42] Studying the salt industry, Edward Hughes likewise suggested that 'the first condition of healthy industrial growth was the exclusion of the parasitic entourage of the Court'.[43] Speaking of controversial monopoly grants to London corporations under Charles I, George Unwin argued that 'If such a system could have been maintained, the Industrial Revolution would never have happened', a view Christopher Hill found convincing as late as 1980.[44]

Others portrayed early modern projects according to their interpretations of modern capitalism, in effect endorsing the projectors' confidence in their ability to transform the society. H. M. Robertson looked at the 'plantations, fen drainage, mining operations and projects of all sorts' that flourished from the late Elizabethan reign.[45] Although many of them 'were fraudulent or piratical' and 'all' driven by 'the spirit of gain', he argued, the 'business projector... brought into being a new philosophy of business and paved the way for modern large-scale capitalistic enterprise'.[46] The image of the projector and his nefarious 'wiles' were read as signs of the emerging spirit of capitalism.[47] 'The profit motive', J. W. Gough disagreed, 'has never been more than part of the incentive of the entrepreneur'. But Gough too highlighted the historical contribution of innovators, this time by celebrating individual talent: the early modern entrepreneur—though stigmatized as the 'projector'—was 'the individual whose energy, and willingness to assume risks and responsibilities enabled an enterprise to be launched'. He was thus 'a typical leader of the Industrial Revolution'.[48] A more recent study by Richard Grassby has drawn on this tradition, and concludes that the English business community in the seventeenth century was 'committed to change and oriented towards growth'.[49] This line of interpretation thus treated projecting activities, not their demise, as the embodiment of economic modernity.

[41] William Hyde Price, *English Patents of Monopoly* (Boston, MA: Houghton, Mifflin & Co., 1906), pp. 129 (quotation), 131.

[42] Price, *Monopoly*, p. 132. See also George Unwin, *Industrial Organization in the Sixteenth and Seventeenth Centuries* (2nd edn, London: Frank Cass, 1957), p. 194.

[43] Edward Hughes, *Studies in Administration and Finance, 1558–1825* (Manchester: Manchester University Press, 1934), p. 36.

[44] George Unwin, *The Guilds and Companies of London* (London: Methuen, 1908), p. 328; Christopher Hill, *The Century of Revolution 1603–1714* (2nd edn, London: Routledge, 1980), pp. 21–8, at p. 28.

[45] H. M. Robertson, *Aspects of the Rise of Economic Individualism: A Criticism of Max Weber and his School* (New York: Kelley Millman, 1959), [first published in 1933], p. 190.

[46] Robertson, *Rise of Economic Individualism*, pp. 192–3, 189–90. See also H. M. Robertson, 'Sir Bevis Bulmer: A Large-Scale Speculator of Elizabethan and Jacobean Times', *Journal of Economic and Business History*, 4 (1932), p. 100.

[47] Robertson, *Rise of Economic Individualism*, p. 192.

[48] J. W. Gough, *The Rise of the Entrepreneur* (London: Batsford, 1969), pp. 289, 15. See also B. A. Holderness, *Pre-Industrial England: Economy and Society 1500–1750* (London: Dent, 1976), ch. 6.

[49] Richard Grassby, *The Business Community of Seventeenth-Century England* (Cambridge: Cambridge University Press, 1995), pp. 411–12. Perceptive readers may now be thinking about Schumpeter's discussion of the entrepreneur. On this, see pp. 52, 66–7.

Earlier scholarly accounts were hardly monolithic, therefore. Yet we can almost hear distant echoes of early modern hopes and anxieties: in developing competing accounts of economic modernity, these accounts portrayed projectors as parasitic monopolists obstructing free trade or as capitalists emblematic of an emerging 'acquisitive society' or as bold entrepreneurs breaking out of the beaten path. Coleman issued one of the most powerful critiques: 'The temptation to resort to hyperbole...to detect in sixteenth- and seventeenth-century England an "industrial revolution"; or to feel oneself present at the unearthing of the roots of modern, materialistic industrial civilization: such delights need to be resisted.'[50] England under Elizabeth I and the early Stuarts was catching up with economically more advanced continental rivals; the criticism of early Stuart patent policies 'came not from doctrines of free trade but from the opposition' of those whose livelihood was threatened by patentees.[51]

The most important revision, offered by Joan Thirsk's Ford Lectures, published in 1978, prompted the reader to acknowledge, but crucially move beyond, the public outcries against projectors. She admitted that there was a shift in about the 1580s from a 'constructive phase' to a 'scandalous phase' of projecting. 'Scandals about projects, however, were but the scum on the surface of a healthy current of water...and it is this current which we must follow.'[52] She followed this current by drawing attention to rich evidence, found in local archives, of emerging rural industries such as pin-making and the cultivation of new commercial crops like woad, many of which began as modest projects of doubtful feasibility.[53] These eventually took root in far corners of the country so that knitted stockings, caps, pins, glass bottles, and other such commodities that had been imported in bulk under the late Tudors came to be produced in large quantities by the end of the seventeenth century. By then, these schemes helped redistribute wealth 'geographically...and socially' to such an extent that even humble folks were able to earn enough to start consuming some of the semi-luxuries produced by these emerging local rural industries. Thirsk thereby reappraised the long-term contribution of otherwise dubious projects for the eventual rise of a consumer society, a society with the thriving, diversified industries that Cary discussed in the 1690s. She did so without resorting to the hyperbole of preceding generations.[54]

Two competing impulses may now be detected in the historiography since Thirsk's Ford Lectures: the advancement, on the one hand, of focused case studies which, while rich in details, accelerates the fragmentation of the field; the aspiration, on the other hand, to offer a broad synthesis that nevertheless borders on the

---

[50] Coleman, *Economy of England*, p. 88.   [51] Peck, *Court Patronage*, p. 159.
[52] Thirsk, *Economic Policy and Projects*, p. 11.   [53] Ibid., pp. 27–50.
[54] Ibid., pp. 2 (quotation), 8, 141–8. Aspects of her argument have now been challenged. See David Harris Sacks, 'The Countervailing of Benefits: Monopoly, Liberty, and Benevolence in Elizabethan England', in Dale Hoak (ed.), *Tudor Political Culture* (Cambridge: Cambridge University Press, 1995), 272–91, pp. 273–4; Keith Fairclough, 'A Successful Elizabethan Project: The River Lea Improvement Scheme', *Journal of Transport History*, 3rd ser., 11 (1998), 54–65; Lien Bich Luu, *Immigrants and the Industries of London, 1500–1700* (Aldershot: Ashgate, 2005), ch. 3; Sebastian A. J. Keibek and Leigh Shaw-Taylor, 'Early Modern Rural By-Employments: A Re-Examination of the Probate Inventory Evidence', *Agricultural History Review*, 61 (2013), 244–81.

revival of the whiggish, celebratory narrative of England's economic progress. We should follow this double movement at some length now, as it is rarely examined despite its profound implications for the way the fields are evolving.

Early modern projects continue to draw scholarly attention, especially in relation to mercantilism, the fiscal state, and the so-called financial and scientific revolutions—many of them closely related to the process of state-formation. Projects for improving domestic trade and industries came to attract statesmen's attention during the sixteenth century because England's prowess was believed to hinge not only upon its military might, but also upon the favourable 'balance of trade', something to be achieved and maintained through measures such as tariffs, trade bans, navigation acts, and projects for substituting imports with new (or revived) domestic industries. This policy orientation to enhance both 'power and profit' has often been studied under the key analytic concept of *mercantilism*.[55] As recent studies have shown, mercantilism cannot be conceived of as a coherent doctrine imposed from above. In early modern London (as in other European cities such as Venice and Paris), natural philosophers, merchants, and skilled craftsmen rubbed shoulders with patrons and statesmen interested in mobilizing their expertise.[56] Policy options often came from merchants, courtiers, and many others (often dubbed projectors); their proposals were subsequently pondered in Privy Councils, presented to civic assemblies, and often disseminated and debated in print.[57] Many of these proposals hinged upon the commercial exploitation of knowledge and technique. What we nowadays call 'science' and 'technology', or 'inquiry' and 'invention', or 'knowledge' and 'technical ingenuity' were closely intertwined during this period. Promoters tried not only to mobilize state authority, but also to tap into such *useful knowledge*—technical knacks, ingenuities, know-how, observations, and more 'scientific' hypotheses, many of them concerned with 'natural phenomena that potentially lend themselves to manipulation'.[58] Many promoters thereby offered projects that promised to enrich the public, the monarch, and themselves—but in reality not necessarily in that order. Here is one reason why historians interested in revisiting aspects of mercantilism and the scientific revolution have been turning to projectors and their proposals.[59]

[55] The most useful overviews are D. C. Coleman, 'Mercantilism Revisited', *HJ*, 23 (1980), 773–91; Philip J. Stern and Carl Wennerlind, 'Introduction', in Philip J. Stern and Carl Wennerlind (eds.), *Mercantilism Reimagined: Political Economy in Early Modern Britain and its Empire* (New York: Oxford University Press, 2014), 3–22.

[56] Lissa Roberts, Simon Schaffer, and Peter Dear (eds.), *The Mindful Hand: Inquiry and Invention from the Late Renaissance to Early Industrialisation* (Amsterdam: Koninklijke Nederlandse Akademie van Wetenschappen, 2007); Deborah E. Harkness, *The Jewel House: Elizabethan London and the Scientific Revolution* (New Haven, CT: Yale University Press, 2007).

[57] In addition to Stern and Wennerlind's overview cited in note 55, see also Tristan Stein, 'Passes and Protection in the Making of a British Mediterranean', *JBS*, 54 (2015), 602–31, esp. pp. 615–20, 630–1; Corey Tazzara, 'Managing Free Trade in Early Modern Europe: Institutions, Information, and the Free Port of Livorno', *Journal of Modern History*, 86 (2014), 493–529, at pp. 521–7.

[58] Joel Mokyr, *The Gifts of Athena: Historical Origins of the Knowledge Economy* (Princeton, NJ: Princeton University Press, 2002), p. 3.

[59] Leng, *Worsley*; Stern and Wennerlind, *Mercantilism Reimagined* (especially chapters by Wennerlind, Leng, and Jonsson); Vera Keller, *Knowledge and the Public Interest, 1575–1725* (Cambridge: Cambridge University Press, 2015), pp. 25–7, 65–7, 131–5, 336; Keller and McCormick,

The underlying proximity between private and public interests—an enduring feature of early modern projects—was symptomatic of the broader process of *state-formation*. The functioning of the early modern English state was highly dependent upon a plethora of local actors. It was what Patrick Collinson called the 'monarchical republic', a highly dispersed embryonic empire, dependent upon the active contributions and initiatives of local actors ranging from landed gentry, municipal corporations, and churchwardens to London merchants, their partners stationed in factories abroad, and sea captains on voyages.[60] As Steve Hindle puts it, the early modern state can be understood as 'a reservoir of authority on which the populace might draw, a series of institutions in which they could participate, in pursuit of their own interests'.[61] Projectors formed similar symbiotic relationships with the government, procuring political support and privileges under the slogans of 'commonweal' and the 'public good'.

This explains why early modern projecting has been studied in relation to another aspect of state-formation, what Schumpeter once described as the evolution of the *demesne state* into the *tax state*. During the medieval and Renaissance periods, the raising of revenue depended upon demesne (pronounced *di-mayn*), 'the "patrimonial" concept of the rights of the prince' encompassing feudal dues and privileges arising from the *personal* prerogative of the monarch.[62] Many a project launched under Elizabeth I and the early Stuart monarchs operated within this rubric, offering the 'improvement' of the royal coffer; all too often they ended up becoming desperate attempts to raise demesne revenues by delegating royal authority to favourite courtiers, private syndicates, and corporations. Projectors thus operated at the intersection of mercantilist and fiscal imperatives of the fledgling state. It is in this broad context that their activities have also drawn critical attention from historians interested in early Stuart law, finance, patronage, politics, and corruption, and also from historians studying their evolution in the

---

'Towards a History of Projects', esp. pp. 424–6, 442–3; Aurélien Ruellet, *La Maison de Salomon: Histoire du patronage scientifique et technique en France et en Angleterre au XIIIe siècle* (Rennes: Presses Universitaires de Rennes, 2016), pp. 22–6, 254–9, 268–75; Mordechai Feingold, 'Projectors and Learned Projects in Early Modern England', *Seventeenth Century*, 32 (2017), 63–79.

[60] Key works include Patrick Collinson, *Elizabethan Essays* (London: Hambledon, 1994), ch. 1; Jonathan Barry, 'Civility and Civic Culture in Early Modern England: The Meanings of Urban Freedom', in Peter Burke, Brian Harrison, and Paul Slack (eds.), *Civil Histories: Essays Presented to Sir Keith Thomas* (Oxford: Oxford University Press, 2000), 181–96, pp. 181, 186–7; Mark Goldie, 'The Unacknowledged Republic: Officeholding in Early Modern England', in Tim Harris (ed.), *The Politics of the Excluded, c. 1500–1850* (Basingstoke: Palgrave, 2001), 153–94; Phil Withington, *The Politics of Commonwealth: Citizens and Freemen in Early Modern England* (Cambridge: Cambridge University Press, 2005).

[61] Steve Hindle, *The State and Social Change in Early Modern England, 1550–1640* (Basingstoke: Palgrave, 2000), p. 16. Private and civilian actors continued to play a vital role in the functioning of the emerging British state. See Aaron Graham and Patrick Walsh, 'Introduction', in Aaron Graham and Patrick Walsh (eds.), *The British Fiscal-Military States, 1660–c.1783* (Abingdon: Routledge, 2016), 1–25, pp. 9–10, 21, 25.

[62] Joseph A. Schumpeter, 'The Crisis of the Tax State', in Schumpeter, *The Economics and Sociology of Capitalism*, ed. Richard Swedberg (Princeton, NJ: Princeton University Press, 1991), 99–140, at p. 108.

subsequent decades.[63] As James I put it in 1609, all lawful sovereigns were '*to be bound themselves within the limits of the Lawes, and they that perswade them to the contrary, are…Projectors, Vipers, and Pests*'.[64]

The political turmoil of the mid-century gave rise to what Schumpeter called a tax state, in which revenues were raised increasingly by more regularized taxes, *publicly authorized* by parliament and levied by the burgeoning bureaucracy of tax collectors answerable to the Treasury, which was reformed in the 1660s.[65] Dominant forms of projecting evolved alongside this evolution from the demesne state to the tax state (later dubbed the fiscal state). Projects for raising revenues and facilitating their levy continued to emerge. Yet, by the late seventeenth century, they became less answerable to the Crown than to parliament, which started sitting annually from 1688. This is the context in which projects related to the financial revolution—the concept proposed by P. G. M. Dickson—have attracted much scholarly attention. Drawing on future tax income, the complex system of deficit financing began to emerge in the decades after the Restoration of Charles II in 1660. The immediate aftermath of the Glorious Revolution of 1688 saw competing proposals for setting up a national bank, which led to the establishment of the Bank of England in 1694. As Carl Wennerlind and Seiichiro Ito have shown, the proposals for securing easy public access to credit were projects *par excellence* in that institutions such as the land bank and land registry were believed to have the potential to unlock unlimited growth potential.[66] Thanks to wider economic change and the developments of public subscriptions and the law of trusts, promoters came by the 1690s to adopt the joint-stock company and public subscription as dominant forms for organizing improvement schemes—hence, finally, the ongoing scholarly interest in Defoe's Projecting Age.

---

[63] John Cramsie, *Kingship and Crown Finance under James VI and I, 1603–1625* (Woodbridge: Boydell, 2002); Christopher W. Brooks, *Law, Politics and Society in Early Modern England* (Cambridge: Cambridge University Press, 2008), pp. 136–40, 193–200, 387; Vera Keller, 'Air Conditioning Jahangir: The 1622 English Great Design, Climate, and the Nature of Global Projects', *Configurations*, 21 (2013), 331–67; D'Maris Coffman, *Excise Taxation and the Origins of Public Debt* (Basingstoke: Palgrave, 2013), ch. 5; David Chan Smith, *Sir Edward Coke and the Reformation of the Laws* (Cambridge: Cambridge University Press, 2014), pp. 91–9, 109–10; Simon Healey, 'Crown Revenue and the Political Culture of Early Stuart England' (PhD thesis, Birkbeck, University of London, 2015); Noah Millstone, *Manuscript Circulation and the Invention of Politics in Early Stuart England* (Cambridge: Cambridge University Press, 2016), pp. 1, 21, 216–18, 282–3, 290–4, 303–5. See also Jason Peacey, 'Print, Publicity, and Popularity: The Projecting of Sir Balthazar Gerbier, 1642–1662', *JBS*, 51 (2012), 284–307; Mark S. R. Jenner, 'Print Culture and the Rebuilding of London after the Fire: The Presumptuous Proposals of Valentine Knight', *JBS*, 56 (2017), 1–26.

[64] James's speech is in William Prynne, *An humble remonstrance to his maiesty, against the tax of ship-money* (1641), p. 39 [*recte* p. 65].

[65] Schumpeter, 'The Crisis of the Tax State', p. 108. See also Michael J. Braddick, *The Nerves of State: Taxation and the Financing of the English State, 1558–1714* (Manchester: Manchester University Press, 1996), pp. 10–14, 17.

[66] Carl Wennerlind, *Casualties of Credit: The English Financial Revolution, 1620–1720* (Cambridge, MA: Harvard University Press, 2011), pp. 68–75; Seiichiro Ito, 'Registration and Credit in Seventeenth-Century England', *Financial History Review*, 20 (2013), 137–62, pp. 138, 146. See also Anne L. Murphy, *The Origins of English Financial Markets: Investment and Speculation before the South Sea Bubble* (Cambridge: Cambridge University Press, 2009), 45–7, 50–3; Steven Pincus and Alice Wolfram, 'A Proactive State? The Land Bank, Investment and Party Politics in the 1690s', in Perry Gauci (ed.), *Regulating the British Economy, 1660–1850* (Farnham: Ashgate, 2011), 41–62.

Early modern projectors and their projects, in short, have now been discussed not just in a single subdiscipline, but *across* a striking range of subfields and topics, in relation to alchemy, inventions, patents, patronage, and the advancement of learning in the history of science and technology, Crown finance, land registry, banking proposals, and joint-stock companies in economic and financial history, subjects' liberty and the rule of law in legal history, manuscript circulation, petitioning, and public politics in political history, and finally plays and pamphlets in literary history, to mention some of the most notable.[67] This efflorescence of specialist literature has been assisted by the so-called 'linguistic turn'. Historians now prefer to speak of projectors and their projects in their variegated historical contexts just as social historians have turned their attention to the early modern concept of 'middling sorts of people' rather than the anachronistic 'middle class', as historians of science now study early modern 'natural philosophers' instead of scientists, as religious historians examine popery and Puritanism without collapsing them into any preconceived religious identities.[68] What used to be an obscure early modern terminology thus turns out to be a fruitful keyword connected with several of the larger themes in early modern historiography. Yet these specialist studies have often been undertaken separately; some studies casually equate projectors with entrepreneurs, or do little more than acknowledge their negative reputation.[69] Accordingly, we still know relatively little about the larger history to which these richly varied accounts of projecting belong. Why were projects launched across so many different spheres of life? To what kind of history does Defoe's and Cary's circumspection belong? Paul Slack's magisterial account of England's culture of improvement has provided one possible answer from a perspective that is at once impressive and problematic.

Slacks' *The Invention of Improvement* (2015), like his earlier *From Reformation to Improvement* (1998), documents how England's ideology of improvement evolved in early modern England. The broad claim of his works is that England underwent a profound transformation during the seventeenth century, moving away from a

[67] For recent literary discussions, see, for example, Aaron Kitch, *Political Economy and the States of Literature in Early Modern England* (Farnham: Ashgate, 2009), pp. 75, 80–90, 96; Jessica Ratcliff, '"Art to Cheat the Common-weal": Inventors, Projectors, and Patentees in English Satire, ca. 1630–70', *Technology and Culture*, 53 (2012), 337–65; David Alff, 'Swift's Solar Gourds and the Rhetoric of Projection', *Eighteenth-Century Studies*, 47 (2014), 245–60; Natalie Roxburgh, *Representing Public Credit: Credible Commitment, Fiction, and the Rise of the Financial Subject* (Routledge: Abingdon, 2016), pp. 31, 51–6.

[68] A perceptive reflection on the linguistic turn is Judith Surkis, 'When Was the Linguistic Turn? A Genealogy', *AHR*, 117 (2012), 700–22, esp. pp. 706, 709–12. Seminal works on the middling sort include Keith Wrightson, '"Sorts of People" in Tudor and Stuart England', in Jonathan Barry and Christopher Brooks (eds.), *The Middling Sort of People: Culture, Society and Politics in England, 1550–1800* (Basingstoke: Macmillan, 1994), 28–51; H. R. French, *The Middle Sort of People in Provincial England, 1600–1750* (Oxford: Oxford University Press, 2007). For the history of science, see Adrian Johns, 'Identity, Practice, and Trust in Early Modern Natural Philosophy', *HJ*, 42 (1999), 1125–45; Pamela H. Smith, 'Science on the Move: Recent Trends in the History of Early Modern Science', *Renaissance Quarterly*, 62 (2009), 345–75. See pp. 85 n. 83, 86 n. 89 for relevant works on the religious politics of post-Reformation England.

[69] On this point, see a perceptive comment in Keller and McCormick, 'Towards a History of Projects', p. 425 n. 5.

culture of speedy reformation towards that of gradual improvement. Slack portrays projects under the early Stuarts by building upon Thirsk's assessment of the 'scandalous phase': 'most of the attempts by [Charles I's] absolute government to regulate the economy were blatantly self-interested'; accordingly, 'Crown manipulation of projects for profit had given improvement a bad name'.[70] Particularly remarkable is the discussion of improvement's subsequent career. Combining the impressive array of recent research into demographic pressure, prices, wage rates, urbanization, and expanding consumer behaviour, Slack convincingly argues that by the last third of the seventeenth century England came to enjoy 'ideal conditions for the diffusion of improvement culture', so much so that it was able to accommodate elements of Epicurean philosophy that viewed private passions and interests as potentially beneficial to society.[71] This is how happiness acquired new connotations, becoming more like an attainable 'common mixture of physical well-being and psychological content' rather than a 'rare experience' in a life of strict piety and suffering without becoming altogether secularized.[72] Slack shows us that the precocious vision of political economy driven by the individual pursuit of profit and comfort was already emerging in late seventeenth-century England.

His analysis is richly nuanced and superbly well documented, incorporating much of the recent specialist literature, including those works cited earlier. My own debts to his scholarship will be recorded in subsequent footnotes. Yet herein lies the greatest challenge of current historiography: as it stands, we face an imminent danger of reverting to whiggish grand narratives of English exceptionalism. Slack in fact suggests that England—and no other rivals—was able to cultivate 'the collective conviction that material progress for a state and its citizens could be infinitely prolonged'.[73] In this view England was unique in nurturing 'a pervasive attachment to improvement [that] encouraged the accumulation of skills and appetites necessary for innovations and investment in them'. This in turn set in motion 'the "positive-feedback" effect of an improvement culture on economic growth well before the industrial revolution'.[74] In this regard, Slack's recent account is becoming similar to the celebratory position long held by Joel Mokyr. In his view, 'the cultural beliefs that had been slowly ripening in the sixteenth and seventeenth centuries affected technology and eventually output, productivity, and economic performance, even if sometimes through roundabout mechanisms'.[75] Mokyr's account of England's 'culture of growth' portrays England in a more glowing light. Like Slack's, it gives a prominent role to 'a culture of practical improvement, a belief in social progress, and the recognition that useful knowledge was the key to their realization'. This culture is then depicted more explicitly

---

[70] Slack, *Invention of Improvement*, pp. 89, 61. See also Slack, *Reformation to Improvement*, pp. 68–76 (esp. p. 74).

[71] Slack, *Invention of Improvement*, pp. 151–64 (at p. 161).

[72] Ibid., pp. 111–13, 150–1 (quotation from p. 113). Cf. Keith Thomas, *The Ends of Life: Roads to Fulfilment in Early Modern England* (Oxford: Oxford University Press, 2009), pp. 266–7.

[73] Slack, *Invention of Improvement*, pp. 252–3.   [74] Ibid., pp. 240–52 (at p. 240).

[75] Mokyr, *Culture of Growth*, p. 276.

(than by Slack) as 'an elite phenomenon', related essentially to a 'literate educated minority' such as physicians, philosophers, engineers, industrialists, and instrument makers.[76] The wall separating these influential minorities was so thin that their 'scientific ideas and methods penetrated other intellectual discourses', with transformative implications for inventive activities on the ground.[77] This he calls the Industrial Enlightenment. The European Enlightenment is said to have paved the way forward by planting growth-friendly institutions such as 'the rule of law, checks and balances on the executive, and severe sanctions on more blatant and harmful forms of rent-seeking'.[78] The concepts of cultural evolution and biases in evolutionary processes are used to explain the functioning of the European 'Republic of Letters' as a competitive 'market for ideas', a market through which ideas of influential 'cultural entrepreneurs' such as Bacon and Newton fuelled the culture of improvement and 'helped organize and standardize the work of many'.[79] In this account of England's evolutionary success, there is little room to consider Bacon's role in authorizing controversial monopolies, or Newton's interest in alchemy and unorthodox Christian doctrines, which equipped him with analytical methods for revolutionizing physics and mathematics.[80]

Going further than Mokyr is Deirdre McCloskey, whose works have sung the praises of projectors. The 'real engine' of growth and betterment, in her view, was 'Liberty and dignity for ordinary projectors', which in turn yielded what she calls 'the Bourgeois Deal':

> 'You accord to me, a bourgeois projector, the liberty and dignity to try out my schemes in voluntary trade, and let me keep the profits, if I get any, in the first act—though I accept, reluctantly, that others will compete with me in the second act. In exchange, in the third act of a new, positive-sum drama, the bourgeois betterment provided by me...will make *you* all rich.' And it did.[81]

If Mokyr highlights institutional variables such as the rule of law and a well-oiled 'market for ideas' that helped reduce the 'access cost' to useful knowledge, in McCloskey's view a 'new dignity for the bourgeoisie in its dealings and a new liberty...to innovate in economic affairs' were the two comparable 'positive

---

[76] Ibid., pp. 267, xiii.   [77] Ibid., p. 276.   [78] Ibid., p. 315.

[79] Ibid., pp. 60, 67 (quotation), 70–116, 208, 216. Mokyr developed many of these ideas over the decades. See Joel Mokyr, *The Lever of Riches: Technological Creativity and Economic Progress* (Oxford: Oxford University Press, 1990), pp. 176–8, 179–81, 243–4; Joel Mokyr, 'Editor's Introduction: The New Economic History and the Industrial Revolution', in Joel Mokyr (ed.), *The British Industrial Revolution: An Economic Perspective* (2nd edn, Boulder, CO: Westview Press, 1999), 1–127, pp. 45–8, 58–9, 127; Joel Mokyr, *Gifts of Athena*, pp. 284–97.

[80] Peck, *Court Patronage*, pp. 10, 186; Cesare Pastorino, 'The Mine and the Furnace: Francis Bacon, Thomas Russell, and Early Stuart Mining Culture', *Early Science and Medicine*, 14 (2009), 630–60; Rob Iliffe, *Newton: A Very Short Introduction* (Oxford: Oxford University Press, 2007), pp. 57–8, 61–2, 98–9, 115–18; Rob Iliffe, *Priest of Nature: The Religious Worlds of Isaac Newton* (Oxford: Oxford University Press, 2017). Cf. Sean Bottomley, 'Mansell v Bunger (1626)', in Jose Bellido (ed.), *Landmark Cases in Intellectual Property Law* (London: Bloomsbury, 2017), 1-20, p. 11 n. 48.

[81] Deirdre Nansen McCloskey, *Bourgeois Equality: How Ideas, Not Capital or Institutions, Enriched the World* (Chicago: University of Chicago Press, 2016), p. 21. See also Deirdre Nansen McCloskey, *Bourgeois Dignity: Why Economics Can't Explain the Modern World* (Chicago: University of Chicago Press, 2010), pp. 70, 365–8.

externalities' vital for the making of the modern world.[82] The former invites us to take Cary's favourable depiction of 'new projection' as convincing evidence of England's precocious industrial enlightenment; the other encourages us to reproduce (rather than scrutinize) the most daring of hopes that the likes of Defoe expressed. McCloskey characterizes her enterprise as 'an "apology" for the modern world', in the sense of 'a defense at a trial, and in the theological sense, too, of a preachment to you'.[83] Such an ideological position has begun to attract searching scrutiny over the last couple of years.[84] While specialist studies are recovering rich details in their respective fields, then, the earlier celebrations of entrepreneurs by Gough and Grassby are being refashioned and reproduced. The anxiety felt by Defoe and Cary has virtually no significance for such triumphant narratives of capitalist modernity and infinite enrichment.

These works of synthesis cannot be considered a unified whole, of course. Unlike Mokyr and McCloskey, Slack has long been a master of archival sources; his account is alert to the richly varied experience of historical actors and to internal contradictions of the improvement culture.[85] Yet these accounts all celebrate England's culture of progressive improvement, which, they argue, provided indispensable stimuli to its precocious economic development. Herbert Butterfield was right: 'it is over large periods and in reference to the greatest transitions in European history that the whig view holds hardest and holds longest'.[86] Being an exceptional historian, Slack is mindful of his position, and has issued a disclaimer: 'The history of improvement is by definition a whiggish story of progress and I make no apology for the fact that this book is consequently a piece of Whig history.'[87] This specific judgement needs firm qualification, however. The ideology of improvement aided not only the expansion of enclosure in the countryside (which reduced poor workers' access to the commons), but also British imperial expansion abroad. Programmes of evangelical preaching, public hygiene, and sanitation came to be promoted as 'improvement', and thereby lent themselves to British control over colonial India and beyond.[88] Recent studies thus make it clear that histories

---

[82] McCloskey, *Bourgeois Dignity*, p. 394 (quotation); McCloskey, *Bourgeois Equality*, pp. 285–91.

[83] McCloskey, *Bourgeois Dignity*, p. 42.

[84] See Andre Wakefield, 'Butterfield's Nightmare: The History of Science as Disney History', *History and Technology*, 30 (2014), 232–51, pp. 239–44; William J. Ashworth, 'The Ghost of Rostow: Science, Culture and the British Industrial Revolution', *History of Science*, 46 (2008), 249–74, esp. pp. 256–60; William J. Ashworth, *The Industrial Revolution: The State, Knowledge and Global Trade* (London: Bloomsbury, 2017), pp. 2, 193, 244–5.

[85] For example, see Slack, *Reformation to Improvement*, pp. 51–2, 88, 112, 168.

[86] Herbert Butterfield, *The Whig Interpretation of History* (New York: Norton, 1965) [originally published in 1931], p. 6. This small book can still serve as a critical guide to the 'growth' literature that highlights the role of European culture. See ibid., pp. 28, 35, 42, 52. Equally instructive is David Cannadine, 'The Present and the Past in the English Industrial Revolution 1880–1980', *P&P*, 103 (1984), 131–72, esp. pp. 149–58.

[87] Slack, *Invention of Improvement*, p. 263.

[88] E. P. Thompson, *Customs in Common: Studies in Traditional Popular Culture* (New York: New Press, 1993), pp. 134, 138; Craig Muldrew, 'The "Middling Sort": An Emergent Cultural Identity', in Keith Wrightson (ed.), *A Social History of England, 1500–1750* (Cambridge: Cambridge University Press, 2017), 290–309, at pp. 299–300; Nicholas Thomas, 'Sanitation and Seeing: The Creation of State Power in Early Colonial Fiji', *Comparative Studies in Society and History*, 32 (1990), 149–70,

of improvement can never *by definition* be reduced to accounts of progress. It follows that the broad conclusion that Slack has drawn from his magisterial synthesis may well be less than the sum of its parts. Butterfield's warning cannot be more pertinent to anyone wishing to go further: 'this whig tendency is so deep-rooted that even when piece-meal research has corrected the story in detail, we are slow in re-valuing the whole and reorganizing the broad outlines of the theme in the light of these discoveries'.[89] A history built around the period concept of projecting is especially useful, as it enables us to throw light on elements of distrust so often pushed aside in accounts of progress. Yet correcting whiggish narratives through article-length case studies is no longer sufficient. We need a book-length reappraisal of the broad outline. Exciting work is being undertaken on this subject from different angles.[90] *Taming Capitalism* contributes to this work of reorganization.

METHODS AND APPROACHES

We can start this work of reorganization by aligning the analysis of early modern economic development more explicitly with two separate bodies of historical research. One is concerned with what we might call the political economy of capitalism. Spurred by the financial crisis of 2008, historians of nineteenth- and twentieth-century America have been reappraising capitalism as a crucial analytical prism for combining a wide range of research agendas such as political history, social history, labour history, and economic history. 'Historians of capitalism', as Sven Beckert calls them,

> study the particular ways in which the market and the state interact, how this inter-action is influenced by the shifting power relations of various social groups, and how the rules of exchange are set politically. In short, they do not study capital as such, but instead the political economy of capitalism, and this political economy is not exclusively constituted by capital and capitalists.[91]

Notice that works of grand synthesis often lack precisely this sort of sustained attention to the local negotiation of power that may have given rise to some of the

---

pp. 156, 160; Richard Drayton, *Nature's Government: Science, Imperial Britain, and the 'Improvement' of the World* (New Haven, CT: Yale University Press, 2000); Sujit Sivasundaram, *Nature and the Godly Empire: Science and Evangelical Mission in the Pacific, 1795–1850* (Cambridge: Cambridge University Press, 2005), pp. 69–71, 117–18, 212–13.

[89] Butterfield, *Whig Interpretation*, pp. 5 (quotation), 6, 28, 33–5, 41.

[90] As this book goes to press the following works have appeared. Eric H. Ash, *The Draining of the Fens: Projectors, Popular Politics, and State Building in Early Modern England* (Baltimore, MD: Johns Hopkins University Press, 2017); David Alff, *The Wreckage of Intentions: Projects in British Culture, 1660–1730* (Philadelphia, PA: University of Pennsylvania Press, 2017). Other work currently in progress includes Martin Giraudeau and Frédéric Graber (eds.), *Les Projets: Une histoire politique (17e-21e siècles)*, which seeks to historicize the notion of projecting from the early modern period onward; Igor Fedyukin, *The Enterprisers: The Politics of School in Early Modern Russia*, which explores projects in Peter the Great's Russia.

[91] Sven Beckert, 'History of American Capitalism', in Eric Foner and Lisa McGirr (eds.), *American History Now* (Philadelphia, PA: Temple University Press, 2011), 314–35, at p. 319.

conditions conducive to economic improvement. Such an integrated approach would explore 'markets in historical contexts', as Mark Bevir and Frank Trentmann have put it, throwing light on 'a politics beyond the formal institutions of the modern nation state, a politics located at the boundaries of the state and civil society, a politics in which power operates in and through a vast network of organizations, actors and systems of knowledge'.[92] The business historian Patrick Fridenson has also urged colleagues to pursue a comparable investigation: 'How does the embeddedness of markets in society make them permeable to forces present in the public space', such as science, media, culture, associations, and governments?[93] Their perspectives chime with social history studies of early modern social conflict and popular politics.[94] *Taming Capitalism* draws inspiration from their studied attention to processes of negotiation.

We can combine the political economy of capitalism with another emerging body of literature, one that revisits and revises traditional grand narratives about the early modern period. William Bulman has shown that early modern representations of Puritanism and popery provided conceptual underpinnings for the subsequent enlightened understanding of Islam and Judaism.[95] William Pettigrew has argued that the perceived liberty of Englishmen played a pivotal role in the 'freedom to enslave', that is, in the parliamentary deregulation of the transatlantic slave trade, thereby escalating the largest organized human trafficking operation in history.[96] Historians of science such as William Newman and Lawrence Principe have demonstrated the central role that alchemical pursuits played in the experimental practices of Robert Boyle, and more broadly in the unfolding of the scientific revolution; the advancement of learning and the institutionalization of natural philosophy were likewise driven not just by rational thinking, traditionally associated with the scientific revolution, but also, as Vera Keller has argued, by human passions, desires, and even ideas about the 'reason of state'.[97] These works by no means form a coherent body of scholarship. Yet they force us to recognize the

---

[92] Mark Bevir and Frank Trentmann, 'Markets in Historical Contexts: Ideas, Practices and Governance', in Mark Bevir and Frank Trentmann (eds.), *Markets in Historical Contexts: Ideas and Politics in the Modern World* (Cambridge: Cambridge University Press, 2004), 1–24, p. 8.

[93] Patrick Fridenson, 'Is there a Return of Capitalism in Business History?', in Jürgen Kocka and Marcel van der Linden (eds.), *Capitalism: The Reemergence of a Historical Concept* (London: Bloomsbury, 2016), 107–31, at p. 124. See also Philip Scranton and Patrick Fridenson, *Reimagining Business History* (Baltimore, MD: Johns Hopkins University Press, 2013), pp. 3, 14–15, 79–80.

[94] The most important collection remains Michael J. Braddick and John Walter (eds.), *Negotiating Power in Early Modern Society: Order, Hierarchy and Subordination in Britain and Ireland* (Cambridge: Cambridge University Press, 2001). See also Steve Hindle, Alexandra Shepard, and John Walter, 'The Making and Remaking of Early Modern English History', in Steve Hindle, Alexandra Shepard, and John Walter (eds.), *Remaking English Society: Social Relations and Social Change in Early Modern England* (Woodbridge: Boydell, 2013), 1–40, pp. 30–2.

[95] William J. Bulman, *Anglican Enlightenment: Orientalism, Religion and Politics in England and its Empire, 1648–1715* (Cambridge: Cambridge University Press, 2015), pp. 117–28, 233–7.

[96] William A. Pettigrew, *Freedom's Debt: The Royal African Company and the Politics of the Atlantic Slave Trade, 1672–1752* (Chapel Hill, NC: University of North Carolina Press, 2013), 6.

[97] Lawrence M. Principe, *The Aspiring Adept: Robert Boyle and his Alchemical Quest* (Princeton, NJ: Princeton University Press, 1998); William R. Newman and Lawrence M. Principe, *Alchemy Tried in the Fire: Starkey, Boyle, and the Fate of Helmontian Chymistry* (Chicago: University of Chicago Press, 2002); Keller, *Knowledge and the Public Interest*, pp. 14–15, 44–5, 62, 219–21.

remarkable extent to which seemingly 'modern' or 'progressive' elements derived from early modern beliefs and practices, and the degree to which even seemingly progressive beliefs conversely often lent themselves to stereotyping and even to human atrocities. Similar perspectives are being applied to economic themes. As is well known, the German émigré Samuel Hartlib, his allies, and many others argued that 'infinite progress was possible through the continuous pursuit of knowledge, innovation, and industry'. While this may appear to be an appealingly progressive world view, we now know that ideas about alchemical transmutation—what looks rather archaic and extraneous to modernity—provided key conceptual underpinnings for England's financial revolution in general and for the discussion in particular of the infinite economic potential of banks, land registration, and public credit.[98] These wide-ranging studies therefore urge us to use the sources and analytical tools at our disposal to revisit larger historical transformations without resorting to whiggish progressive narratives. These studies, in short, invite us to a post-whiggish rethinking of grand narratives.

What, then, might a comparable reappraisal of the political economy of early modern projects look like? It will throw fresh light on the emergence of both Defoe's Projecting Age and the attendant vision of improvement that eventually culminated in that of Smith. The recognizably *modern* forms of improvement (promoted in the emerging stock market) and its ideological underpinnings will be shown to have evolved out of *early modern* processes of taming incipient capitalism, processes of negotiation mediated by the *post-medieval* understanding of projecting.[99] In the absence of economics and management studies as autonomous intellectual disciplines, talking about projectors and their projects provided a powerful, pervasive framework for grappling with what I think is one of the enduring questions of capitalism: how would it be possible to mobilize creativity and business acumen for public benefit while generating profits, and to do so without descending into mere profiteering or into the infringement of citizens' rights, liberties, and properties? A history of projecting helps us to move beyond learned opinions and explore mundane responses of early modern petitioners, promoters, and statesmen to this fundamental question.[100]

We can start retracing their responses if we attend to the experience of public distrust exemplified by the cases of Cary and Defoe. If the rise of projecting in the

---

[98] Wennerlind, *Casualties*, pp. 44, 59, 62 (quotation at p. 44). See also Webster, *Great Instauration*, p. 355; Jackson Lears, *Fables of Abundance: A Cultural History of Advertising in America* (New York: Basic Books, 1994), pp. 26–34; Stern and Wennerlind, 'Introduction', in Stern and Wennerlind (eds.), *Mercantilism Reimagined*, p. 9; Fredrik Albritton Jonsson, 'The Origins of Cornucopianism: A Preliminary Genealogy', *Critical Historical Studies*, 1 (2014), 151–68, pp. 155–60.

[99] In addition to the works already cited, I find the following particularly inspiring: Phil Withington, 'Public Discourse, Corporate Citizenship, and State Formation in Early Modern England', *AHR*, 112 (2007), 1016–38, esp. pp. 1036–7.

[100] Thus this study complements the intellectual history of political economy that is based primarily on published statements. See Joseph A. Schumpeter, *History of Economic Analysis* (New York: Oxford University Press, 1954), ch. 7; Joyce Oldham Appleby, *Economic Thought and Ideology in Seventeenth-Century England* (Princeton, NJ: Princeton University Press, 1978); Andrea Finkelstein, *Harmony and the Balance: An Intellectual History of Seventeenth-Century English Economic Thought* (Ann Arbor, MI: University of Michigan Press, 2000). But see Wennerlind, *Casualties*, ch. 6.

late sixteenth century engendered literary representations of the projector, the image, once in circulation, in turn came to shape and reshape England's culture of improvement. Lorraine Daston and other historians of science have studied how a range of 'scientific personae', from the diligent botanist to the polite scientist, shaped emerging modern science. We are concerned with their obverse, pejorative personae, which may have *negatively conditioned* the promotion of economic innovations and improvement.[101] Like the versatile figures of the quack, the charlatan, and the alchemist, I argue, the image of the projector was among the negative personae— something from which actors sought to distance themselves.[102] The topic is consequential. Mokyr, Margaret Jacob, and others have suggested that economic growth owed much to the development of the knowledge economy, that is, to the cultural and institutional frameworks such as the republic of letters, the Royal Society, and joint-stock companies through which useful knowledge was exchanged, refined, funded, and put to use.[103] A history of projecting complements these studies of *enabling factors* by exploring the pervasiveness of distrust, an element that *constrained* promoters and backers by inducing (and often even compelling) them to behave in ways that would prevent them from being rejected as unreliable projectors. Such constraining factors are important for those wishing to understand the mechanics of economic development. For even sound proposals could fail to attract sustained investment and support if stigmatized as unreliable projects; their economic potential could be lost, and as a result the diffusion of 'new projections' (which Cary and Coleman linked to economic development) could be hindered.[104]

Yet our chief concern is not the early modern equivalent of reputational management conducive to growth-friendly entrepreneurial success. Crucially, repercussions of public distrust went far beyond *episodic* cases of certain promoters like Cary and Defoe suffering from bad names. Local experience of distrust had far-reaching repercussions that we are yet to understand. As promoters and their backers responded to the pervasive distrust of the projector, the practices of economic

[101] Lorraine J. Daston and H. Otto Sibum, 'Introduction: Scientific Personae and their Histories', *Science in Context*, 16 (2003), 1–8.

[102] Roy Porter, *Quacks: Fakers and Charlatans in English Medicine* (Stroud: Tempus, 2000), pp. 15–17; David Gentilcore, *Medical Charlatanism in Early Modern Italy* (Oxford: Oxford University Press, 2006), ch. 2; See also Tara E. Nummedal, *Alchemy and Authority in the Holy Roman Empire* (Chicago: University of Chicago Press, 2007), pp. 168–75.

[103] Mokyr, *Gifts of Athena*; Maxine Berg, 'The Genesis of "Useful Knowledge"', *History of Science*, 45 (2007), 123–33; Larry Stewart, 'Experimental Spaces and the Knowledge Economy', *History of Science*, 45 (2007), 155–77; Joel Mokyr, 'Knowledge, Enlightenment, and the Industrial Revolution: Reflections on *The Gifts of Athena*', *History of Science*, 45 (2007), 185–96; Margaret C. Jacob, *The First Knowledge Economy: Human Capital and the European Economy, 1750–1850* (Cambridge: Cambridge University Press, 2014).

[104] For the diffusion of inventions and new techniques, see, for example, Christine MacLeod, 'The Paradoxes of Patenting: Invention and its Diffusion in Eighteenth- and Nineteenth-Century Britain, France, and North America', *Technology and Culture*, 32 (1991), 885–910; Liliane Hilaire-Pérez and Catherine Verna, 'Dissemination of Technical Knowledge in the Middle Ages and the Early Modern Era: New Approaches and Methodological Issues', *Technology and Culture*, 47 (2006), 536–65, pp. 540–59. For the diffusion of new crops, see Frank Emery, 'The Mechanics of Innovation: Clover Cultivation in Wales before 1750', *Journal of Historical Geography*, 2 (1976), 35–48; Joan Thirsk, *Alternative Agriculture: A History* (Oxford: Oxford University Press, 1997), pp. 139–43 (esp. p. 140).

improvement and innovation started moving away from the early Stuart model. By the late seventeenth century, England's culture of improvement came to incorporate private desire for gain, comfort, emulation, and consumption as the vital ingredient for increasing national power and profit. Transmutation for generating wealth was not to be effected by the projector's genius alone, but also by adeptly mobilizing people's desires. Despite increasing scholarly interest in the history of projecting, few accounts have explored this development in depth.

This study pursues this line of inquiry by drawing eclectically on a range of approaches available across historical and social science research, including the analysis of manuscript circulation and stereotyping, what French economists call economic conventions, and the analysis of trust and credibility pioneered by economic historians and historians of science and technology. The purpose here is neither to promote a particular set of methodologies nor to impose theoretical assumptions upon historical evidence, but to combine analytic tools so that we can start bringing together different types of sources that are needed for developing a post-whiggish account of the early modern projects to which Defoe and Cary belonged.

In order to develop this perspective in a manageable fashion, this study pays special attention to the promotion of useful knowledge related to what we may call natural resource management, a set of domestic primary industries such as agriculture, horticulture, river navigation, and mining, all concerned with the exploitation of nature. A recent estimate suggests that, in 1600, 71 per cent of the male working population (aged between 15 and 64) served the primary sector such as agriculture and mining; the proportion is 50 per cent for the early eighteenth century.[105] If negative images about the projector affected schemes related to this largest, most reputable sector, then the problem would have been conceivably greater in those other sectors that were held in lower repute such as manufacturing, trading, and banking. Schemes concerning natural resource management may therefore serve as a prima facie representative for projecting activities more broadly, as samples from which a more exhaustive survey of early modern projects may be developed.[106] Similarly, I have chosen to focus on schemes promoted in London, leaving aside schemes like water distribution that were often promoted locally and

---

[105] Leigh Shaw-Taylor and E. A. Wrigley, 'Occupational Structure and Population Change', in Roderick Floud, Jane Humphries, and Paul Johnson (eds.), *The Cambridge Economic History of Modern Britain* (2 vols., Cambridge: Cambridge University Press, 2014), vol. 1, 53–88, at p. 59.

[106] The relationship between England's projecting culture and its expanding global trade and empire remains to be fully explored. The topic is partially addressed in J. D. Alsop, 'The Age of the Projectors: British Imperial Strategy in the North Atlantic in the War of Spanish Succession', *Acadiensis*, 21 (1991), 30–53; Thomas Leng, '"A Potent Plantation Well Armed and Policeed": Huguenots, the Hartlib Circle, and British Colonization in the 1640s', *William and Mary Quarterly*, 66 (2009), 173–94; Vera Keller, 'The "Framing of a New World": Sir Balthazar Gerbier's "Project for Establishing a New State in America," ca. 1649', *William and Mary Quarterly*, 70 (2013), 147–76; Koji Yamamoto, 'Medicine, Metals and Empire: The Survival of a Chymical Projector in Early Eighteenth-Century London', *BJHS*, 48 (December 2015), 607–37; William A. Pettigrew, 'The Failure of the Cloth Trade to Surat and the Internationalisation of English Mercantilist Thought, 1614–1621', in William A. Pettigrew and Mahesh Gopalan (eds.), *The East India Company, 1600–1857: Essays on Anglo-Indian Connection* (Abingdon: Routledge, 2017), 21–43.

authorized by municipal corporations.[107] It is hoped that the processes of taming reconstructed in this book will soon be contextualized by local and global comparisons, and its main findings cross-examined and refined by experts of particular periods, industries, regions, and countries in and outside Europe.

These limitations notwithstanding, I am hopeful that the stake is not altogether trivial. The pervasiveness of promises, disappointments, and ensuing suspicion indicates that the 'first industrial nation' emerging in England exhibited striking preoccupations about the social responsibilities of private businesses. Corporate social responsibility with its conceptual variables now forms a rich subfield of its own among business and management scholars, but this important topic is rarely discussed in the light of historians' findings about topics such as mercantilism, improvement, and business enterprise in the pre-industrial period. Yet, as Christine Meisner Rosen has suggested, an important strand of business history has been concerned about 'societal impacts [of businesses] and society's efforts to control those impacts'.[108] Early modernists could open up a new dialogue by furnishing useful long-term perspectives for those concerned about the societal impact of business enterprises today.[109]

Another broad implication has to do with the relationship between different scales of analysis. In exploring the local experience of distrust and its repercussions, we face a broader analytical challenge of linking 'the microsocial with the macrosocial, experiences with structures, face-to-face relationships with the social system or the local with the global'.[110] Drawing on the global to explain local variations might be easier than the task at hand: that of surveying the broad process of state-formation to contextualize the local experience of distrust, *and then* moving from these micro case studies *back* to the account of long-term economic development. Here, then, is one of the methodological problems that many historians face after the cultural turn. Being critical of modernization theories and of 'grand narratives', humanity disciplines in general, and cultural historians in particular, are often said to have poured tremendous energy into understanding subjective experience and historical actors' values and assumptions in the ways in which these actors understood them. This book pays close attention to actors' experience too. Yet being too

---

[107] Useful starting points are given by Paul Slack, 'Great and Good Towns, 1540–1700', in Peter Clark (ed.), *The Cambridge Urban History of Britain, Volume II, 1540–1840* (Cambridge: Cambridge University Press, 2000), 347–76. On London's social and economic significance, see E. A. Wrigley, 'A Simple Model of London's Importance in Changing English Society and Economy 1650–1750', *P&P*, 37 (1967), 44–70; William M. Cavert, *The Smoke of London: Energy and Environment in the Early Modern City* (Cambridge: Cambridge University Press, 2016), pp. 13–14.

[108] Christine Meisner Rosen, 'What is Business History?', *Enterprise and Society*, 14 (2013), 475–85, at p. 483.

[109] On this point, see p. 232; Koji Yamamoto, 'Early Modern Business Projects and a Forgotten History of Corporate Social Responsibility', in André Spicer and Grietje Baars (eds.), *The Corporation: A Critical, Multi-disciplinary Handbook* (Cambridge: Cambridge University Press, 2017), 226–37.

[110] Peter Burke, 'The Microhistory Debate', in Burke (ed.), *New Perspectives on Historical Writing* (2nd edn, University Park, PA: Pennsylvania State University Press, 2001), 115–17, p. 116. See also Filippo de Vivo, 'Prospect or Refuge? Microhistory, History on the Large Scale', *Cultural and Social History*, 7 (2010), 387–97, p. 390–2; Hindle, Shepard, and Walter, 'Making and Remaking', p. 28.

fond of such microscopic 'thick descriptions', humanity scholars are said to have abandoned sustained effort to study long drawn-out processes of change; unlike their social science siblings, they are deemed to have grown incapable of offering robust 'explanations'.[111] I suggest we need not be too pessimistic. Historians of various stripes have begun, as we have seen, to revisit larger narratives in the light of their context-sensitive scholarship; historians of early modern social relations, too, have long been concerned with the account of long-term change that pays close attention to micro-scale experience.[112] As Jan de Vries judiciously accepts, while 'material structures...ordinarily shape people's practices, it is also, under certain conditions, people's practices that constitute, reproduce and alter structures'.[113] This is the possibility that this study pursues in the pages that follow. Sustained attention to the local experience of distrust is indispensable in this regard because it enables us to unravel precisely such 'structure-modifying acts',[114] local evidence of *visible hands* engaging with emergent capitalism with macro-scale implications.

It is worth repeating that the pages that follow revolve around the early modern concept of projecting, and do not rest upon any preconceived definitions of capitalism. Butterfield has a point once again: 'it is better to assume unlikeness at first and let any likenesses that subsequently appear take their proper proportions in their proper context'.[115] We shall accordingly come back to competing definitions of capitalism at the very end of the book in order to unpack the wider implications.

---

[111] Such is the judgement of Jan de Vries, *The Return from the Return to Narrative* [Max Weber Lecture No. 2013/01] (Badia Fiesolana: European University Institute, 2013), pp. 9–10. See also rather pessimistic assessments by William H. Sewell Jr, *Logics of History: Social Theory and Social Transformation* (Chicago: University of Chicago Press, 2005), pp. 40–53, 62, 77–80; Lynn Hunt, *Writing History in the Global Era* (London: Norton, 2014), ch. 1, esp. pp. 39–40. For a more positive assessment, see Hindle, Shepard, and Walter, 'Making and Remaking', pp. 32–8. Cf. Surkis, 'Linguistic Turn', pp. 718–20; James W. Cook, 'The Kids Are All Right: On the "Turning" of Cultural History', *AHR*, 117 (2012), 746–71, pp. 756–7.

[112] The best introduction to this tradition remains Keith Wrightson, *English Society 1580–1680* (London: Routledge, 1982); Wrightson, *Earthly Necessities*.

[113] De Vries, *Return from the Return to Narrative*, p. 11.　　　[114] Ibid., p. 11.

[115] Butterfield, *Whig Interpretation*, pp. 38 (quotation), 62–3.

1

Contexts and Contours

By the early eighteenth century the bold promotion of business schemes and the attendant public suspicion had a history going back at least a century, as the poet and entrepreneur Aaron Hill recognized. Having obtained a patent for a method of extracting oil from beechnuts in 1713, Hill launched a joint-stock company for oil production. The idea was to produce high-quality oil suitable for cooking and manufacturing that could compete with foreign imports from Spain, Italy, and Portugal. Yet the business struggled due to organizational problems and bad harvests. In 1715, desperate to keep sceptical investors on board, Hill published a long tract calling for more investment.[1] The book contained an episode about King James I's attempt to establish silk manufacture in Britain. Hill quoted extensively from the letter James sent in 1607 to lord lieutenants, deputy lieutenants, and local justices of the peace. James told them 'to persuade and require' prominent local inhabitants 'to buy and distribute in that County [where they resided] the Number of Ten thousand Mulberry-Plants' at 3 farthings a plant or 6 shillings a hundred. Distribution of plants was to be accompanied by the publication of 'a plain Instruction and Direction' for cultivating mulberry trees and raising silkworms. These measures would, the king declared, help to establish domestic production of silk to rival their French counterparts, advance the nation's 'Arts and Trades', give jobs to poor families, and hence be conducive to 'the Welfare of our People', 'so great a publick Utility to our Kingdom and Subjects in general'.[2] Hill quoted this royal command for four pages in order to draw a lesson for his contemporary readers:

> You see here a King, endeavouring by the Force of promised Rewards and threatened Punishments, to make his People only sensible of their own Interest...And what do you think was the Effect of all his Reasons?...the merry Creatures laugh'd immoderately at their good old Sovereign's being turn'd *Projector*, while they universally neglected and despised the Excellence of his Intention.[3]

The public derision of the king's command is probably Hill's fiction, yet a revealing one nonetheless. The king's letter was sent to his regional office-holders in the context of patronage and the pursuit of import substitution. In Jack Fisher's view,

---

[1] Patent no. 393. For background, see Christine Gerrard, *Aaron Hill: The Muse's Projector, 1685–1750* (Cambridge: Cambridge University Press, 2003), pp. 42–5.

[2] Aaron Hill, *An account of the rise and progress of the beech-oil invention* (1715), pp. 19–21. A version of this letter is at TNA, SP 14/26, fols. 16–17.

[3] Hill, *Rise and progress*, p. 22.

this and other early Stuart projects to which we shall turn represented 'the nearest approach to national planning and state capitalism ever made in England', anticipating 'some of the most grandiose ideas of Colbert'.[4] By contrast, Hill was operating in an emerging stock market in London, appealing to his current and potential investors via print. Like Cary, Hill too was a denizen of Defoe's Projecting Age, which could be described as a different kind of capitalism: 'that form of private property economy in which innovations are carried out by means of borrowed money which in general... implies credit creation'.[5] Despite the difference in time and institutional settings, James's episode stood for Hill as a pertinent precedent. It captured the nature of his own pursuit and the challenge that he faced: enterprises of 'publick Utility', undermined by the pervasive 'Practice of discountenancing' such endeavours. In his desperate attempt to persuade his sceptical investors, Hill spotted a rich undercurrent of promises and public distrust that ran through the early modern period.[6] How did James I's world evolve by the end of the seventeenth century into Defoe's Projecting Age, which was to become the envy of Europe? More theory-minded readers might rephrase the question: what is the historical process through which one kind of embryonic capitalism overseen by a monarch came to be replaced by another based in the emerging stock market—one that seems more recognizably modern? Our task is to develop an answer that is non-whiggish and based on early modern actors' perspectives.

A history of projecting suggests that the rich undercurrents of promises and public distrust that Hill detected played a crucial role in this evolution. Yet if we are to explore this undercurrent of suspicion (which brought many historical actors into the collective taming of embryonic capitalism), it is vital that we first establish what it was that gave rise to the kind of derision that Hill thought he and James alike encountered. It was, I suggest in this chapter, the pervasive symbiosis between private and public interests embedded in the process of early modern state-formation. The private–public partnership has, of course, received some comments from historians. Joan Thirsk suggested that 'Englishmen found that they did well by doing good.... The motives of every projector mixed public and private in different proportions.'[7] Studies in early modern political history, social history, and the history of science and technology have likewise acknowledged that England's culture of economic innovations and improvement hinged upon a kind of 'partnership of public business and personal gain', or upon 'the unification of the public good with private interest'.[8]

---

[4] F. J. Fisher, 'Some Experiments in Company Organization in the Early Seventeenth Century', *EcHR*, 4 (1933), 177–94, at p. 186.

[5] J. A. Schumpeter, *Business Cycles: A Theoretical, Historical and Statistical Analysis of the Capitalist Process* (2 vols., New York: McGraw-Hill, 1939), vol. 1, p. 223.

[6] During the seventeenth century, James's letter became a common point of reference. See Samuel Hartlib, *Samuel Hartlib his legacie* (1651), pp. 69, 74–7. See p. 216 below for Beale's reference to James.

[7] Thirsk, *Economic Policy and Projects*, p. 18.

[8] John Cramsie, *Kingship and Crown Finance under James VI and I, 1603–1625* (Woodbridge: Boydell, 2002), p. 36; Margaret C. Jacob and Larry Stewart, *Practical Matter: Newton's Science in the Service of Industry and Empire, 1687–1851* (Cambridge, MA: Harvard University Press, 2004), p. 82.

Note, however, that the point has often been made in passing. Specialist accounts do often acknowledge that early modern contemporaries accused projectors of feigning public service. These studies usually focus on particular industries, decades, or reigns (for good reasons). To give but one example, studies of early Stuart political culture and finance often consider projects and monopolies together as a problem of royal patronage, but tend to end their discussions with the outbreak of the Civil Wars.[9] Consequently, we do not know how the concept of projecting provided an enduring framework for engaging with the problematic proximity of public and private interests in the context of early modern improvement. Grand syntheses usually acknowledge the symbiosis between private interests and political authority, but rarely dwell upon the remarkable extent to which early modern contemporaries were worried about its perversions. Mokyr, for example, suggests 'the pre-existence of certain social norms' that in turn 'led to cooperative behavior and a voluntary willingness to forego opportunistic behavior'.[10] Unless we first chart the evolution of projecting activities, unless we establish the underlying elements of public service and distrust across time, it is likely that we will end up reinforcing the current division of labour between specialist inquiries and broad, triumphant syntheses.

This chapter, therefore, sketches the broader contexts and contours of the history of projecting as a concrete activity and discourse, and paves the way for Chapter 2, which focuses on perversion, public anger, and distrust. We start from a macroscale discussion so that we can historicize a micro-level experience of distrust before turning to consider the long-term repercussions. Because projecting neither as a concrete economic activity nor as public discourse remained static across the period, we shall begin by charting their evolution in tandem by combining the results from the *English Short Title Catalogue* and a database of patents for invention. Once we establish the overview, we shall then go on to specify the elements of continuity that Hill found, despite the significant change in institutional settings between the early seventeenth century and the early eighteenth century. To do so, it is vital that we place the seventeenth century in a longer chronology. We shall therefore consider a range of antecedents in medieval and Renaissance Europe, survey their convergence in sixteenth-century England, and plot its transformation during the seventeenth century. Be they schemes for technical innovation or economic improvement, backed by the Crown or by parliament or floated in the stock market,

---

See also Slack, *Reformation to Improvement*, p. 161; Leng, *Worsley*, p. 144; Joel Mokyr, *The Enlightened Economy: Britain and the Industrial Revolution, 1700–1850* (London: Penguin, 2011) [originally published in 2009], pp. 382–3.

 [9] See Thirsk, *Economic Policy and Projects*, chs. 3–4; Linda Levy Peck, *Court Patronage and Corruption in Early Modern England* (London: Unwin Hyman, 1990); Cramsie, *Kingship*; Michael Zell, 'Walter Morrell and the New Draperies Project, c. 1603–1631', *HJ*, 44 (2001), 651–75; Stephen Pumfrey and Frances Dawbarn, 'Science and Patronage in England, 1570–1625: A Preliminary Study', *History of Science*, 42 (2004), 137–88.

 [10] Mokyr, *Enlightened Economy*, p. 369 (quotation); Joel Mokyr, *A Culture of Growth: The Origins of the Modern Economy* (Princeton, NJ: Princeton University Press, 2017), pp. 18, 296. It is hoped that forthcoming studies of corruption by Mark Knights and David Chan Smith will correct whiggish perspectives on this count.

projects were, it will be argued, promoted as solutions to the problem of early modern governance. Projecting in early modern England can be considered an early modern antecedent of Schumpeterian entrepreneurship, one that operated symbiotically with the fledgling English state. Only by repositioning early modern projects in this historical context can we begin to recover the rich history of taming incipient capitalism that Adam Smith did not write, a story of ambitious promises and ensuing public suspicion to which Hill, James I, and many others like Defoe and Cary belonged.

PATENTS AND THE *ENGLISH SHORT TITLE CATALOGUE*: AN INITIAL OVERVIEW

How many projectors were there in early modern England? How many projects did they launch across the period between England under James I and that of Defoe, Cary, and Hill? These are difficult questions to answer. Ideally, we would have liked to count the number of projectors active within a given period, but the projector was never an occupation associated with a set of trades or training, as in the case of clothiers or ironmongers. Nor was the projector a social status mentioned regularly in wills or in probate inventories. Therefore, no institutional record exists to which we might turn to ascertain their number during the early modern period. Counting the number of projects is equally problematic. Given the breadth of activities that fell under the notion of projecting, and given also that projects were proposals and not things done, we should do well to accept the impossibility of counting them in a totally satisfactory way. Yet long-term trends of projecting as activity and as discourse can be rendered visible if we attend to two key channels: the patent system, which often provided legal backing, and printed pamphlets, which helped promote schemes to wide (or sometimes more targeted) audiences. I therefore propose to juxtapose two data sets drawn respectively from the *Chronological Index* of patents for invention and the *English Short Title Catalogue*.

As with all other data sets, we need to use them with caution. *Titles of Patents of Invention, Chronologically Arranged*—also known as the *Chronological Index*—was published in 1854 by Bennet Woodcroft of the Patent Office. It contains many errors in the dates of grants; it only covers grants related to inventions conferred after 1617; most crucially, it tells us little about unpatented innovations or about projects concerned primarily with poor relief or taxation.[11] The *English Short Title Catalogue* (*ESTC*) is by far the most comprehensive bibliography of printed books

---

[11] Bennet Woodcroft, *Titles of Patents of Invention, Chronologically Arranged, from March 2, 1617 (14 James I) to October 1, 1852 (16 Victoriae), Part I. Nos. 1 to 4,800* (London: Queen's Printing Office, 1854). For the nature of the *Index* and the context of its production, see MacLeod, *Patent*, p. 2; Christine MacLeod, *Heroes of Invention: Technology, Liberalism and British Industry, 1750–1914* (Cambridge: Cambridge University Press, 2007), pp. 251–64. Woodcroft selected grants related to inventions from 'docket books' (TNA, C 233) which summarized grants that resulted in actual patent rolls (TNA, C 66). Woodcroft's *Index*, hence my patent data, accordingly leaves out some grants. A new database based on the original patent rolls has been compiled by the French research project, *Les Privilèges économiques en Europe, XVe–XIXe siècles*. Its data set includes all the grants that conferred privileges

and pamphlets published in the English language or in Britain and its colonies up to 1800. Title pages of printed publications admittedly represent just the tip of the iceberg of the early modern discursive landscape. There are some printed bills and petitions about projects not listed in the *ESTC* (such omissions will be noted in footnotes). The coverage of the *Chronological Index* and *ESTC* is therefore by no means flawless. Nor did they reveal long-term trends of stable categories. Institutional forms of concrete projects never remained static, as we have seen; accordingly, the usage of the terms 'project' and 'projector' was hardly static either. It is therefore best to handle these terms as representations that were 'always in the making'—each invocation by turns reinforcing, extending, and altering the existing range of usage.[12]

We can turn these challenges into an advantage, for the title pages of this period were crammed with lines describing the contents; more publications appeared with terms such as 'project' and 'projector' in times of crisis and profound social change; the *ESTC* can therefore tell us which aspects of their connotations became more prominent than others in different historical junctures. Likewise, even if the patent data do not tell us much about the long-term trend of a single well-defined activity, it still remains that patenting provided a major channel for launching new economic initiatives throughout the early modern period. Thus, the data enable us to add precision to Hill's observation, and reveal how institutional arrangements of projecting activities evolved over the period. If corroborated with other sources, the two data sets should at least give us useful indications about the long-term development of both projecting activities and public discourse about them.[13]

Following the deft use of the *ESTC* by social and cultural historians, I have therefore counted publications whose title pages contained the words 'project', 'projector', and other derivatives.[14] I have left out the small number of publications that dealt with geometric 'projection' of the sphere and similar mathematical and cartographic topics. The remaining results include titles that used words like 'project' and 'projector' in either neutral or negative senses. The decade-by-decade total of these publications, shown in Figure 1.1, suggests that there were clear surges during the 1640s and from the later seventeenth century. The number of patents

for implementing economic and technological undertakings. Interim results from this exciting project will be noted where appropriate.

[12] Serge Moscovici, 'Notes towards a Description of Social Representations', *European Journal of Social Psychology*, 18 (1988), 211–50, p. 219. See also pp. 84–5 below.

[13] Here we shall draw on the patent database I have created, consisting of all 410 patents for inventions known to have been granted between 1617 and 1716. For a sector-by-sector analysis, see Yamamoto, 'Thesis', pp. 64–74, 360–1.

[14] Slack, *Reformation to Improvement*, p. 96 n. 89; Kei Nasu, 'Heresiography and the Idea of "Heresy" in Mid-Seventeenth-century English Religious Culture' (PhD thesis, University of York, 2000), pp. 55–9; Sarah Tarlow, *The Archaeology of Improvement in Britain, 1750–1850* (Cambridge: Cambridge University Press, 2007), pp. 13–20; Phil Withington, *Society in Early Modern England: Vernacular Origins of Some Powerful Ideas* (Cambridge: Polity, 2010), chs. 3–5. Technical challenges of using the *ESTC* for statistical analysis are discussed in Withington, *Society*, p. 7; Michael F. Suarez, 'Towards a Bibliometric Analysis of the Surviving Record, 1701–1800', in Michael F. Suarez and Michael L. Turner (eds.), *The Cambridge History of the Book in Britain, vol. V, 1695–1830* (Cambridge: Cambridge University Press, 2009), 39–65. It will not be long before we can analyse early modern English printed texts in their virtual entirety as one 'very large textual object'. For a test case on Shakespeare's First Folio as a textual corpus, see Jonathan Hope and Michael Whitmore, 'The Very Large Textual Object: A Prosthetic Reading of Shakespeare', *Early Modern Literary Studies*, 9 (2004), 1–36.

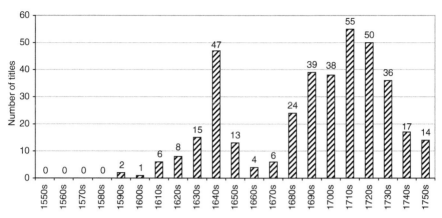

Figure 1.1. 'Project' and 'projector' in the *ESTC*

Source: *English Short Title Catalogue* (accessed July 2015)

Search words = project* OR proiect*

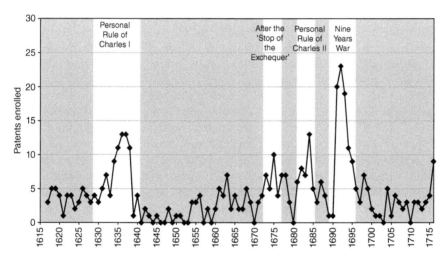

Figure 1.2. Annual totals of patents for invention enrolled, 1617–1716

Sources: Bennet Woodcroft, *Titles of Patents of Invention, Chronologically Arranged, from March 2, 1617 (14 James I) to October 1, 1852 (16 Victoriae), Part I. Nos. 1 to 4,800* (London: Queen's Printing Office, 1854), pp. 1–74; idem, *Alphabetical Index of Patentees of Invention* (2nd edn, London: Evelyn, Adams & MacKay, 1969), pp. viii–xv; Rhys Jenkins, 'The Protection of Inventions during the Commonwealth and Protectorate', *Notes & Queries*, 11th ser., 12 (1913), 162–3; Christine MacLeod, 'Patents for Invention and Technical Change in England, 1660–1753' (PhD thesis, University of Cambridge, 1983), Appendix I; Arnold Hunt, 'Book Trade Patents, 1603–1640', in Arnold Hunt, Giles Howard Mandelbrote, Alison E. M. Shell (eds.), *The Book Trade and its Customers, 1450–1900* (Winchester: St Paul's, 1997), 27–54, pp. 40–54

for inventions granted yearly, shown in Figure 1.2, suggests that the two peaks visible in the *ESTC*—an indicator for the realm of public discourse—were related to two different periods, with higher levels of patenting, first during the 1630s, and then later at the end of the century. We shall look at these two peaks first before considering the intervening decades.

The earlier peak of the 1630s indicates the fullest and most controversial exploitation of the patent system alongside other branches of royal prerogative (Fig. 1.2). Fifty-seven patents for inventions were enrolled between 1634 and 1638, a five-year total that was not to be matched until the 1690s. They represented just the tip of the iceberg. As the master of the Charterhouse, George Garrard, noticed in 1637, 'Discontinuance of Parliaments brings up' a surge in schemes by which 'Profit may come to the King'.[15] Under Charles I's Personal Rule, which began in 1629, claims for having 'invented' a new production method were used to justify monopolies over a range of industries. Because such monopolies were granted in order to raise revenues for the Crown, the patent system served as a means of introducing prerogative taxation, de facto taxation without parliamentary approval. Many of these patents are not listed in Woodcroft's *Index*, which focuses on inventions;[16] for this reason, it is likely that the use (and abuse) of the patent system was greater in the 1630s than in the 1690s. The social and political disturbances triggered by these schemes by the end of the 1630s will be considered in Chapter 2. The first surge in the *ESTC* in the 1640s represents critical printed responses to patents granted under Charles I for revenue purposes.

This can be corroborated if we draw on the etymology of projecting (discussed in Introduction), and divide the results of the *ESTC* search further into neutral and negative uses of the concept. The first category includes all the titles that used words like 'project' in proposing, or commenting on, all sorts of proposals. Here, I include titles like 'A project much desired, & of singular use for all sorts of Christians' and 'A project for the kingdoms or cities speedy prosperity'.[17] Within the second category fall all the works that spoke of projects and projectors in explicitly negative tones. This includes such phrases as 'the moderne projectors. Divulged for the pretended good of the kingdoms of England' and 'strange and wonderful plots, projects, policies and stratagems'.[18] The results, shown in Figure 1.3, reveal that the sudden surge of texts related to project and projector in the 1640s was due almost entirely to the negative use of the words 'project' and 'projector', attacking Caroline projects. In 1695, Defoe would declare his age to be the 'Projecting Age'; the rise of patenting in the 1630s and the ensuing explosion of printed responses would certainly deserve a similar name.

We see something rather different in the second peak towards the end of the century. While it is somewhat difficult to explain the relative decline of the usage

---

[15] Thomas Wentworth, *The Earl of Strafforde's letters and dispatches*, ed. W. Knowler (2 vols., 1739), vol. 2, p. 55, Garrard to Wentworth, 23 March 1636.

[16] While my data set based on Woodcroft contains only seventy-seven grants for the 1630s, the French *Privilèges* project reports 256 grants, 114 of which confer monopolies. As for the 1690s, there is little difference between the two data sets—my database reporting 105 grants, the French one 109. See Isabelle Bretthauer and Yohann Guffroy, 'Patents and Exclusivity in Seventeenth-Century England: Was Invention at Stake?', a conference paper presented at the World Economic History Congress, Kyoto, 3–7 August 2015.

[17] Nicholas Byfield, *Paterne of wholsome words* (1618); Samuel Kem, *The king of kings his privie marks for the kingdoms choyce of new members* (1646).

[18] Thomas Heywood, *Machiavel. As he lately appeared to his deare sons, the moderne proiectors* (1641); *The French rogue: or the life of Monsieur Ragour de Versailles* (1694).

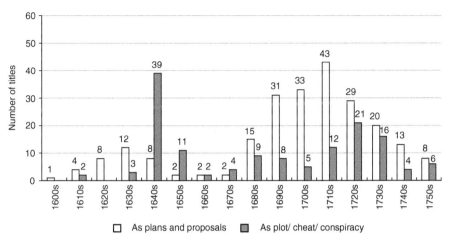

Figure 1.3. 'Project' and 'projector' in the *ESTC* (detail)
Source: English Short Title Catalogue

of terms related to project from the mid-eighteenth century, the boom from the 1680s is clearly linked with the onset of Defoe's Projecting Age. These publications reflected waves not of monopolies, but of business enterprises and joint-stock companies promoted via print, as shown in the greater amount of pamphlets appearing with the neutral use of terms related to project. These included those schemes that drew on patented inventions launched in large numbers, especially during the first half of the 1690s, as captured by the patent data. As Figure 1.3 shows, the three decades from 1690 saw an average of thirty-six pamphlets in each decade using the term in a neutral sense of 'plans' and 'proposals', almost a sixfold increase compared to the decadal average of 6.3 titles in the preceding three decades.[19] The increase in project-related literature in this period (and also in the 1640s) was comparatively greater than the overall expansion or contraction of publishing activities; the rises related to the notion of projecting were also sharper compared to those of other related keywords such as 'improvement', 'adventure', and 'undertaking' (Fig. 1.4).

The rise of projecting as a keyword helps us to account for the salience of project-related language for Hill's contemporaries, who began their adult lives in the final decades of the seventeenth century, such as Defoe (1660–1731), Swift (1667–1731), and Steele (1672–1729). In contrast, authors born a few decades earlier, such as Robert Boyle (1627–91) and Samuel Pepys (1633–1703), lived through the unfolding of the Civil Wars and the Interregnum; the notion of projecting is less visible in their writings, and hence in studies of these authors. If important at all, as we shall see, it was as the dark memory of the earlier 'age of projects' in the 1630s that the

---

[19] We also need to exercise caution in treating a relative rise in the 1680s; seven out of twenty-four pamphlets that used terms like 'project' on their title-pages were concerned either with the unification of Christians or with the repeal of certain penal laws. This means that the terms related to projecting perhaps became more dramatically salient from the 1690s than indicated by the figures.

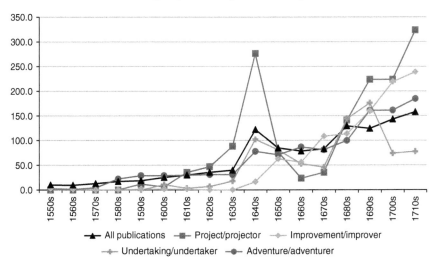

Figure 1.4. 'Project' and 'projector' compared with other keywords and publishing activities, 1550–1719

Source: English Short Title Catalogue; base=100=AVG(1650–99)

Search words: project* OR proiect*; improvement* OR improuement* OR improver* OR improuer*; undertaking* OR vndertaking* OR undertaker* OR vndertaker*; adventure* OR aduenture*

notion of projecting carried weight in the post-Civil War England in which they lived. The two peak periods in the history of projecting are therefore qualitatively different. This substantiates the impression with which we began this chapter—that the nature of projecting evolved significantly in the intervening decades.

In fact, the collapse of Charles I's Personal Rule did not put an end to projecting activities. If lower numbers of patents were recorded after the outbreak of the Civil Wars (Fig. 1.2), it was because the Chancery mechanism by which patents had been enrolled was discontinued, and the legal protection of economic innovations and improvement took place only intermittently through the Council of State and parliament.[20] However, the overturning of the Caroline government provided renewed religious impetus, as well as fresh opportunities, for trying new schemes. Half of the eighteen patents issued without royal assent between 1643 and 1659 were backed by the German émigré Samuel Hartlib.[21] (We shall examine the activities of Hartlib and his reforming circle in Chapter 3.) The negative images of projects

---

[20] Rhys Jenkins, 'The Protection of Inventions during the Commonwealth and Protectorate', *Notes & Queries*, 11th ser., 12 (1913), 162–3. It is unclear whether the sources Jenkins drew upon represent the majority of legal protection during this period. These are *CJ, LJ, CSPD*, reports of the HMC, Scobell's 'Collection of Acts', and nine extant patent rolls for the Protectorate.

[21] Mark Greengrass, 'The Projecting Culture of Samuel Hartlib and his Circle' (unpublished conference paper for 'Publicists and Projectors in Seventeenth-Century Europe', Wolfenbüttel, 1996), no pagination.

and projectors continued to circulate as well. Daniel Noddel published a pamphlet in 1654, 'setting forth the plot and design of Mr. John Gibbon, and his fellow-projectors, to gain a possession of the said free-holders ancient inheritance'.[22] Shortly after the Restoration, an anonymous broadsheet, *The new projector; or the priviledged cheat*, was published, announcing that 'I Am a projector that alwaies have thriv'd'—hinting that vexatious projecting did not die with Charles I.[23]

Unlike the boom in the 1630s, the next peak in patents for inventions—forty patents enrolled between 1673 and 1678 (Fig. 1.2)—was not so much linked to royal fiscal policy as to a spell of economic prosperity. Here the patent data reveal how the history of projecting is related to the better-known narratives of economic development, state-formation, and constitutional change. In the seventeenth century, regional economies were becoming better connected by extending navigable rivers and turnpikes. (Chapter 4 considers a project for river navigation that facilitated the integration of different economic regions.) Relatively stable prices of basic commodities and the fall in rents during the 1660s and 1670s meant that people below the middling strata could now afford more consumer goods than before, especially if they were willing to work for longer hours. Commentators often complained of the decay of trade, the fall in rents, and the dislocation of foreign trade by war and by French imports. Yet expanding consumer behaviour is confirmed by the increasing returns in excise and a sales tax levied on consumer goods such as beer, cider, tea, and coffee during the 1670s.[24] Patentees accordingly sought to take advantage of the rising purchasing power of consumers—hence patents granted in this decade for an improved beehive, paper-making, and the production of point-lace.[25] Although the Third Anglo-Dutch War ended in 1673, some of the patents granted shortly thereafter are still indicative of the perennial Anglo-Dutch rivalry of this period. A patent for a desalination engine, which William Walcot obtained in 1675, was intended to help naval ships as well as merchant vessels making long voyages.[26] Two patents granted in 1675 and 1676 were related to dyestuffs and earthenware that had been produced and imported from Holland.[27]

These economic and international factors are crucial; they highlight that the rise in patenting was no longer driven by the government's attempts to raise revenues as in the 1630s. Figure 1.5 graphically demonstrates the point, revealing the annual total of patents for invention that promised to pay fees to the Crown. Whereas the increase in the annual total of patents during the 1630s accompanied a surge in the

---

[22] Daniel Noddle, *To the parliament of the commonvvealth of England, and every individual member thereof* (1654).

[23] *The new projector; or the priviledged cheat* [1662?].

[24] Jeremy Boulton, 'Food Prices and the Standard of Living in London in the "Century of Revolution", 1580–1700', *EcHR*, 53 (2000), 455–92, pp. 469–70; Gregory Clark, 'The Condition of the Working Class in England, 1209–2004', *Journal of Political Economy*, 113 (2005), 1307–40, pp. 1311, 1324; Margaret Priestley, 'Anglo-French Trade and the "Unfavourable Balance" Controversy, 1660–1685', *EcHR*, 4 (1951), 37–52; Henry Roseveare, *The Financial Revolution* (Harlow: Longman, 1991), p. 23; John Spurr, *England in the 1670s: 'This Masquerading Age'* (Oxford: Blackwell, 2000), pp. 122–3.

[25] Patent nos. 180, 178, 182.

[26] Patent no. 184. His patent was revoked eight years later, when Richard Fitzgerald, a nephew of Robert Boyle, obtained a similar patent. See MacLeod, *Patent*, p. 36. See also my discussion in Chapter 5.

[27] Patent nos. 181, 191.

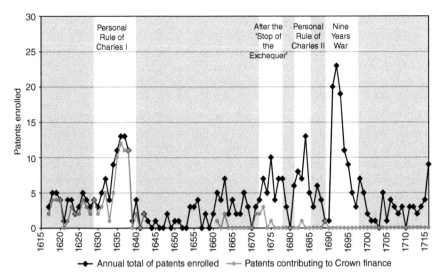

Figure 1.5. Patents for invention and Crown finance, 1617–1716
Sources: See Figure 1. 2

grants that promised to pay fees to the Exchequer, the boom during the 1670s had little to do with fiscal policy.[28] This is significant, especially since the liability of the Crown had risen from £925,000 in 1660 to nearly £3 million by 1670. Charles II's government could have raised much-wanted revenues as his father had done by granting monopolies. The fiscal pressures were handled instead by parliamentary taxation. By the 1670s, 90 per cent of the revenue in fact came to be controlled by parliament, a significant shift from 24 per cent during Charles I's reign.[29] By then the Crown's fiscal instruments had been replaced by a set of assessments such as customs, excise, and stamp duties that were authorized by parliament and levied on the consumption of goods and services. From 1665, designated revenue streams were in turn used as securities for borrowing money from private lenders in return for Treasury Orders, an assignable credit instrument bearing interest.[30] By the end of 1671, the Third Anglo-Dutch War (which would be declared in the following March) was imminent, and a great deal of military expenditure was expected. The fiscal pressure was managed not by returning to the granting of monopolies, but by defaulting on outstanding Treasury Orders. This was the so-called 'Stop of the

---

[28] This confirms MacLeod, *Patent*. See also my discussion in Chapter 3.

[29] Michael J. Braddick, *The Nerves of State: Taxation and the Financing of the English State, 1558–1714* (Manchester: Manchester University Press, 1996), p. 9; Michael J. Braddick, *State Formation in Early Modern England c. 1550–1700* (Cambridge: Cambridge University Press, 2000), pp. 233–4.

[30] Patrick O'Brien, 'Fiscal Exceptionalism: Great Britain and its European Rivals from Civil War to Triumph at Trafalgar and Waterloo', in Donald Winch and Patrick O'Brien (eds.), *The Political Economy of British Historical Experience, 1688–1914* (Oxford: Oxford University Press, 2002), 245–65, p. 261; C. D. Chandaman, *The English Public Revenue, 1660–1688* (Oxford: Clarendon, 1975), pp. 295–300; Christine Desan, *Making Money: Coin, Currency, and the Coming of Capitalism* (Oxford: Oxford University Press, 2014), pp. 245–51.

Exchequer' declared in December 1671.[31] By the 1670s, therefore, England's fiscal state came to hinge heavily upon parliamentary taxation, its local collection, and the use of these revenue streams as securities for borrowing from the public—early signs of the financial revolution. The patent database confirms this trend, and suggests that by the 1670s the granting of patents no longer served as a fiscal instrument of the Crown.[32] As we shall see in Chapter 5, projects for improvement evolved during this period in tandem with the decoupling of public finance from prerogative and court patronage, and did so in ways that could take advantage of the expanding consumer base.

The same trend continued. A wide range of patents was issued between 1681 and 1685, including ones for strong liquor (no. 231), earthenware (no. 234), and the finishing of cloth (nos. 237, 241). While the reason for the modest increase is unclear, we know that only one patent offered to pay fees to the Crown.[33] James II was the last king of England who raised revenue independently of parliament. But as Figure 1.5 suggests, even in his reign, between 1685 and 1688, patents for inventions did not become an instrument of Crown finance.[34]

The revolution of 1688 and the ensuing Nine Years War against France brought a dramatic change in the economy and public finance, and thereby ushered in a new 'age of projects'. The war obstructed overseas trade and diverted capital to domestic industries; as evidenced in Figure 1.5, this led to a spectacular, if short-lived, boom of patents for inventions. An unprecedented total of sixty-two patents were enrolled between 1691 and 1693, nearly half the patents granted during the whole of Charles II's and James II's reigns combined (138 patents). Many of the grants were concerned with domestic industries such as mining, water supply, and the making of items including brass, calicoes, paper, and tapestry.[35] Several promised to improve weaponry, while others were concerned with the production of saltpetre, pitch, and tar, all of them useful for the military and naval contest with the French.[36]

The prospective benefits of patented inventions were divided into shares, and schemes were now floated as joint-stock companies. As John Houghton observed:

> a great many *stocks* have arisen since this war with *France*; for trade being obstructed at sea, few that have money were willing it should lie idle, and a great many that

---

[31] Roseveare, *Financial Revolution*, p. 21; Chandaman, *Public Revenue*, pp. 224–7, at p. 227.

[32] On this point, see also Yamamoto, 'Thesis', pp. 82–3.

[33] Patent no. 225 granted to Richard Maudrell and John Williams in 1683 for the making of hollow pewter and block tin buttons, which promised to pay the Exchequer 'according to such reasonable rates as they shall see meet'.

[34] Roseveare, *Financial Revolution*, pp. 29–30; Chandaman, *Public Revenue*, pp. 256–61. We await focused studies that examine fiscal 'projects' under James II.

[35] For example, patent nos. 273, 276, 284, 296. For the impact of the war on the economy, see Christine MacLeod, 'The 1690s Patents Boom: Invention or Stock-Jobbing?', *EcHR*, new ser., 39 (1986), 549–71, p. 559; Samuel Jeake, *An Astrological Diary of the Seventeenth Century: Samuel Jeake of Rye 1652–1699*, ed. Michael Hunter and Annabel Gregory (Oxford: Clarendon, 1988), p. 233; Anne L. Murphy, 'Lotteries in the 1690s: Investment or Gamble?', *Financial History Review*, 12 (2005), 227–46, p. 230; D. W. Jones, *War and Economy in the Age of William III and Marlborough* (Oxford: Blackwell, 1988).

[36] Patent nos. 266, 274, 303, 316, 329, 330. See also MacLeod, 'The 1690s Patents Boom', pp. 558–9.

wanted employment studied how to dispose of their money...which they found they could more easily do in *joint-stock*, than in laying out the same in lands, houses or commodities[.][37]

Joint-stock companies increased in number, from eleven companies before 1688 to ninety-three in 1695. They became an important form of projecting, as will be seen in Chapter 6.

Meanwhile, the war increased governmental expenditure to £4.9 million per year, more than double its average annual expenditure during the 1680s. From 1702, England fought the War of Spanish Succession for thirteen years. By the end of it, expenditure had risen to a staggering £7.8 million, nearly three-quarters of which went to military purposes. None of the patents obtained either during or after the 1690s boom paid fees to the Exchequer (Fig. 1.5). While in the early 1680s financial exigencies were met primarily by retrenchment, the renewed financial necessity now begot fiscal inventions. A series of experiments were contrived to raise revenues: lotteries, recoinage, and the most famous of all, the founding of the Bank of England and the establishment of long-term national debt underpinned by future revenues from (mostly indirect) taxation. These fiscal experiments comprise what P. G. M. Dickson famously called the 'financial revolution'.[38] Notably, these schemes were also dubbed 'projects' because of their promises to advance the public interest as well as that of promoters and shareholders.

The patent record thus renders visible the long-term evolution in projecting activities, something that remains implicit in the *ESTC* records: the changing relationship between projects and the Crown. The difference between the two short-term peaks of patenting, one in the 1630s and the other in the 1690s, captures the underlying constitutional change: the royal prerogative, which had authorized controversial projects under the early Stuarts, lost much of its grip upon projecting by the end of the seventeenth century. While improvement schemes concerned with primary and secondary industries had lost any direct obligation to enrich the Crown's coffers, other more explicitly fiscal novelties, such as the Bank of England, emerged to meet the rising expenditure. These financial projects concerning taxation and public debts did remain closely aligned with the interests of the state, but they now became less answerable to the Crown than to parliament, which began sitting annually from 1688. Meanwhile, the promotion of domestic economic improvement—the focus of this study—became more closely aligned with the emerging stock market.

Public discourse about projects and projectors evolved in tandem. As unprecedented numbers of patents for inventions were granted and joint-stock companies

---

[37] John Houghton, *A collection for improvement of husbandry and trade* (4 vols., 1727–8), vol. 1, no. 98, p. 261.

[38] P. G. M. Dickson, *The Financial Revolution in England: A Study in the Development of Public Credit, 1688–1756* (London: Macmillan, 1967); Roseveare, *Financial Revolution*; John Brewer, *Sinews of Power: War, Money and the English State, 1688–1783* (London: Unwin Hyman, 1989), esp. ch. 4. These financial experiments were complemented by efforts to improve, albeit patchily, the efficiency of the bureaucracy and of local tax collection. Colin Brooks, 'Taxation, Finance and Public Opinion, 1688–1714' (PhD thesis, University of Cambridge, 1971), chs. 7–8; Colin Brooks, 'Projecting, Political Arithmetic and the Act of 1695', *EHR*, 97 (1982), 31–53.

launched calling for subscribers in the 1690s, more pamphlets emerged using the terms 'project' and 'projector' in the context of promoting (and responding to) new fiscal and economic projects. So the number of pamphlets with this descriptive usage increased to thirty-one pamphlets in the 1690s, and reached the height of forty-three titles in the 1710s, as revealed by Figure 1.3. The increase is due to the greater use of the term 'project' in descriptive contexts rather than the term 'projector'.[39] Negative connotations of the projector remained; but unlike in the 1640s it became more of an undercurrent of suspicion running beneath the strong flow of new business schemes calling for subscriptions. As Thomas Baston complained, the 'weak and unthinking Part of Mankind' had been deceived 'by *knavish* and *ridiculous Projects* and *Stock-jobbing*'.[40] His *Thoughts on Trade* in fact singled out Hill's beech oil scheme for a scathing satire:

> the *Devil* was resolv'd for the future to appear more like a Gentleman, and now has begun to *liquor his Boots*, and sets up for an *Oil Projector*, and has writ several learn'd Treatises on this Subject, and very modestly calls every Man a *Fool* or *Knave* that has not a mind to let him finger their Money.[41]

By the time Hill, Defoe, and Cary were writing, therefore, the project was no longer about courtiers and monopolies drawing on prerogative. Projecting was now about new enterprises that were driving England to become the first industrial nation. The figure of the projector accordingly represented the pervasive concern that these schemes might fail to live up to their exalted expectations.[42]

The *ESTC* data also throw light on early uses of the terms 'project' and 'projector'. They indicate that these terms began to gain currency in print only from the end of the sixteenth century. One of the earliest publications that used the term 'project' on its title page is *An apologie for sundrie proceedings* (1593) by the Cambridge-trained lawyer Richard Cosin, a three-volume work, 'much enlarged aboue the first priuate proiect'. The next one is William Stoughton's *An assertion for truee and Christian church-policie*, containing 'sundrie projectes' of spreading 'the discipline by pastors & elders' (1604). This was followed by an irrigation scheme described in 1610 as 'a project, for the great benefit of the common-wealth generally'. It was in 1614 that a printed proclamation first bore a phrase like a 'project of dying and dressing of broad cloathes within the kingdome'.[43] As we shall see in Chapter 2, the social circulation of these terms had important consequences for the self-identity of promoters of new schemes.

Yet this is not to suggest that projects for improvement came into being only at the end of the sixteenth century. Far from it—projecting activities became well

---

[39] The difference in the *ESTC* results between the 1680s (twenty-four titles) and the 1690s (thirty-nine titles) is almost entirely due to the greater neutral use of the term 'project' and its derivatives, which grew from fifteen titles to twenty-nine in the 1690s.

[40] Thomas Baston, *Thoughts on trade and a publick spirit* (1716), pp. 12–13.

[41] Ibid., p. 11.   [42] See also pp. 241–2.

[43] William Stoughton, *An assertion for truee and Christian church-policie* (1604); Rowland Vaughan, *Most approued, and long experienced water-workes* (1610); *By the King. A proclamation conteyning his Maiesties royall pleasure, concerning the proiect of dying and dressing of broad cloathes within the kingdome, before they be exported* (1614).

established in England by the mid-sixteenth century, well before the terms made their way into the titles of books and pamphlets. The project's characteristic ambitions to serve the public in fact derived from the rise of political economy in late medieval and Renaissance Europe, the protracted blurring of the boundary between *oikos* and *polis* at a time of profound social and economic transformations, whereby key components of economic life, such as manual labour, technical ingenuity, and practical knowledge, came to be reappraised as strategic elements in the governing of polities, something at best capable of advancing the common good of rulers and inhabitants. The differences between projects in the 1630s and the 1690s of course remain significant. Yet their commonalities—something Hill recognized in 1715—would stand out if we now bring earlier, European counterparts into perspective. It is for this purpose that we now undertake a brief, selective survey of European antecedents.

PROJECTING AND THE BACKGROUND OF ITS EMERGENCE

Projects' characteristic promises of public service would not have existed without the increasing appreciation, from the late medieval period onwards, of merchants, craftsmen, and inventors—appreciation that their skills and knowledge could help bring abundance, achieve comfort, and even transform nature as well as society. We need not assume that merchants were universally condemned by medieval commentators. In his *Colloquy*, the Benedictine abbot Ælfric of Eynsham (*c.*955–*c.*1010) already had a merchant argue that 'I am useful both to king and ealdormen, and to the wealthy and to all people' because he helped circulate goods by boarding ships with cargoes, sailing to overseas destinations, and selling goods there in return for other items for import.[44] Deeper analyses would soon be undertaken in response to economic changes. As European populations tripled from the eleventh to the early fourteenth century in the run-up to the Black Death, urban populations grew and interregional trade increased. To the south we find the introduction and then the spread of partnerships such as *commenda* and *societas* from Venice and then Genoa; to the north we see Cologne, Hamburg, and Lübeck being united in 1281 into one German Hansa. Trading centres like Venice, Genoa, Avignon, Montpellier, Barcelona, Valencia, and northwards to Paris, Bruges, and London, were being connected by extensive networks of roads, navigable rivers, and sea routes; by 1300 bills of exchange underwritten by bankers became widespread, lowering transaction costs and accelerating trade between entrepôts.[45]

---

[44] Michael Swanton (ed.), *Anglo-Saxon Prose* (London: Dent, 1975), pp. 111–12.
[45] Kathryn L. Reyerson, 'Commerce and Communications', in David Abulafia (ed.), *The New Cambridge Medieval History Volume V, c.1198–1300* (Cambridge: Cambridge University Press, 1999), 50–70, pp. 51, 61, 64; Peter Spufford, 'Trade in Fourteenth-Century Europe', in Michael Jones, *The New Cambridge Medieval History, Volume VI, c. 1300–1415* (Cambridge: Cambridge University Press, 2000), 155–208, pp. 170–1, 178. Cf. Mark Bailey, 'The Commercialisation of the English Economy, 1086–1500', *Journal of Medieval History*, 24 (1998), 297–311.

It was in the midst of this 'commercial revolution' that theologians started elucidating the nature of commodities, exchange, and value. At stake was the civic and ethical status of mercantile wealth within the body of Christian believers.[46] It thus became common among theologians to examine how merchants might serve the common good by performing duties of their stations, and especially by observing 'just price'.[47] Within this rubric the influential Dominican friar, Thomas Aquinas (1225–74), suggested that 'commerce can become justifiable' in the case of such a merchant

> who uses moderate business profits to provide for his household, or to help the poor; or in order to ensure that the country does not run short of essential supplies, and who makes a profit as it were to compensate for his work and not for its own sake.

Note that the underlying justification is a negative one, in that mercantile activities were deemed neither inherently sinful nor contrary to virtue.[48] A bolder justification came from the Franciscan Peter John Olivi (1248–98). Olivi highlighted merchants' capacity to appraise the market value of goods and their readiness to hazard capital in order to buy goods where they were plentiful and sell them where they were scarce. Such merchants were not just spared from damnation; their labour could at best bring 'proper advantage' (*lucrum competens*) to both communities. The profits the merchants made in the process, Olivi suggested, were justifiable because they were an integral part of the just price.[49] The underlying notion of diligence and industry (*sollicitudo* and *industria* in Latin) were repeatedly employed by Olivi and subsequent generations of theologians and preachers, and later taken up by merchants themselves when writing memoirs as 'honorable citizens and good merchants'.[50]

In the century after the outbreak of the Black Death in the 1340s, writers moved beyond cautious defence of merchants and their role in evaluating and circulating commodities. Some writers, as Martha Howell has shown, went beyond the usual

---

[46] Giacomo Todeschini, *I mercanti e il tempio: la società cristiana e il circolo virtuoso della ricchezza fra Medioevo ed età moderna* (Bologna: Il Mulino, 2002), pp. 311–12, 318–20, 335–6.

[47] Joel Kaye, *Economy and Nature in the Fourteenth Century: Money, Market Exchange and the Emergence of Scientific Thought* (Cambridge: Cambridge University Press, 1998), pp. 87–101. A brief overview is provided by Jacques Le Goff, *Money and the Middle Ages* (Cambridge: Polity, 2012) [French original published in 2010], pp. 77–9; for a fuller treatment, see Odd Inge Langholm, *Economics in the Medieval Schools: Wealth, Exchange, Value, Money, and Usury according to Paris Theological Tradition 1200–1350* (Leiden: Brill, 1992). I thank James Davis and Sylvain Piron for discussing medieval markets and morality with me.

[48] Thomas Aquinas, *Summa Theologiae: Latin Text and English Translation*, ed. T. Gilby et al. (61 vols., London, 1964–80), vol. 38, p. 229 (2a2ae, 77, 4).

[49] Pierre de Jean Olivi, *Traité des contrats*, ed. and tr. Sylvain Piron (Paris: Les Belles Lettres, 2012) [Latin and French parallel text], pp. 135–43 (at p. 140, paragraph 73); Joel Kaye, *A History of Balance, 1250–1375: The Emergence of a New Model of Equilibrium and its Impact on Thought* (Cambridge: Cambridge University Press, 2014), pp. 118–22. See also Todeschini, *I mercanti e il tempio*, pp. 343–5, 355; Giacomo Todeschini, *Ricchezza francescana: dalla povertà volontaria alla società di mercato* (Bologna: Il Mulino, 2004), pp. 95, 100, 131; Germano Maifreda, *From Oikonomia to Political Economy: Constructing Economic Knowledge from the Renaissance to the Scientific Revolution* (Farnham: Ashgate, 2012), pp. 52–3.

[50] Giacomo Todeschini, 'Theological Roots of the Medieval/Modern Merchants' Self-Perception', in Margaret C. Jacob and Catherine Secretan (eds.), *The Self-Perception of Early Modern Capitalists* (New York: Macmillan, 2008), 17–46, pp. 29–32.

advice (for male heads of household) to work honestly and diligently; their wives were now urged to complement the masculine virtue by establishing the habit of modest consumption for the comfort and reputation of the household.[51] Meanwhile, as mercantile classes increased their influence in cities across the Italian peninsula, more confident praise of merchants' civic contribution emerged. In his *On commerce and the perfect merchant*, originally composed in 1458, Benedetto Cotrugli declared that merchants

> through their work enable the poor to live by; through their initiative in tax-farming they promote the activity of estate stewards; by exporting and importing their goods they enrich the customs and excise of the lords and republics; and consequently they enlarge the public and common treasury.[52]

Believers in modern capitalism and its efficacy might as well be delighted to find such an early indication of the emerging 'bourgeois dignity'. Be that as it may, it is important to note that Cotrugli's argument for mercantile dignity and social contribution was destined for wealthy merchants operating on a grand scale, men of the rank of Francesco di Marco Datini (*c.*1335–1410), who had eight factories across the Mediterranean region. Cotrugli excluded humble pedlars and artisans from his praise.[53]

By the end of the fifteenth century, however, artisans, craftsmen, and engineers joined merchants in asserting their utility and virtue, vigorously promoting their knowledge to powerful patrons. Treatises on technical matters had existed since antiquity; yet their techniques and useful knowledge—ranging from carpentry, fortification, hydrostatics, and mining to fencing, painting, and the preparation of medicine—had often remained unwritten, passed down in workshops and in construction sites from masters to apprentices. Now, thanks partly to the introduction of the printing press, greater proportions of related skills, know-how, observations, and theories came to be codified, printed, and 'reduced to order and method' for the advantage of the prince and his people.[54] By the mid-sixteenth century, mathematics, which had been associated with the mechanical arts and

---

[51] Martha C. Howell, *Commerce before Capitalism in Europe, 1300–1600* (Cambridge: Cambridge University Press, 2010), pp. 289–97. For background, see Peter Spufford, *Power and Profit: The Merchant in Medieval Europe* (London: Thames & Hudson, 2002), ch. 2; Steven A. Epstein, *An Economic and Social History of Later Medieval Europe, 1000–1500* (Cambridge: Cambridge University Press, 2009), pp. 215–21.

[52] Benedetto Cotrugli, *Della mercatura et del mercante perfetto* (Brescia, 1602) [composed originally in 1458], p. 125 ('fanno campare li poueri, mediante il loro essercitio. Fanno essercitar li massari mediante l'industria dell'loro arendamenti. Fanno valer le doane, & le gabelle de Signori & delle Republiche, mediante l'estrationi, & immissioni delle loro mercantie, & conseguentemente accrescono l'erario publico & com[m]une'). Cf. Diana Wood, *Medieval Economic Thought* (Cambridge: Cambridge University Press, 2002), p. 119; Todeschini, 'Theological Roots', pp. 23, 35–7.

[53] Cotrugli, *Della mercatura*, p. 124. Datini's *Palazzo Datini* in Prato still houses an enormous archive of his business operations across factories in Avignon, Prato, Pisa, Florence, Genoa, Barcelona, Valencia, and Majorca, a documentary treasure exploited ably by Giampiero Nigro (ed.), *Francesco di Marco Datini: The Man the Merchant* (Florence: Firenze University Press, 2010).

[54] Hélène Vérin, 'Rédiger et réduire en art: Un Projet de rationalisation des pratiques', in Pascal Dubourrg Glatigny and Hélène Vérin (eds.), *Réduire en art: La Technologie de la Renaissance aux Lumières* (2008), 17–58, esp. pp. 22–3, 53.

held in lower repute in Aristotelian philosophy, also came to acquire a higher status.[55] It was in this context that the term 'project' came to mean a geometric plan or architectural drafting.[56] Negative connotations of manual and mechanic labour did survive well into the seventeenth century; yet craft knowledge was no longer mere labour. It began to acquire something of a higher epistemic and symbolic status, at least in the eyes of promoters and their fickle backers (at least while in need of expertise).[57]

Such an upward mobility of crafts and technical knowledge took place alongside, and owed much to, deliberate policies by the public authorities to encourage innovations and technology transfer. As early as the thirteenth century, princely and city authorities in the Italian peninsula encouraged the immigration of skilled migrants into their domain. One of the earliest examples took place between 1230 and 1231. The commune of Bologna offered loans and subsidies to induce more than 150 skilled artisans specializing in silk and woollen textiles to settle there, along with their families and dependent workforce.[58] During the fourteenth century, written contracts and deals for encouraging the immigration of a skilled workforce became frequent; by the latter half of the fifteenth century, patents for protecting specific inventions and techniques came into being initially in Venice, a trend that was 'soon followed by the Hapsburg and Spanish Empires, the Netherlands, and England'.[59] Such patents granted privileges to skilled individuals because of the multiple benefits they would bring to the state. A petition, submitted by the city of Verona to the Venetian government in December 1554, made it plain that the introduction of velvet manufacture would tend not only to profit established merchants, but also to give jobs to poor

[55] Pascal Brioist, "'Familiar Demonstrations in Geometry': French and Italian Engineers and Euclid in the Sixteenth Century', *History of Science*, 47 (2009), 1–26.

[56] In the following example from Rabelais, we can almost visualize the project as a two-dimensional architectural drawing: 'The work of this round chapel was in such an exact symmetry that the diameter of its drawing [*proiect*] was equal to the height of the vault.' See Edmond Huguet, *Dictionnaire de la langue française du seizième siècle* (7 vols., Paris: E. Champion, 1925–1973), vol. 6, p. 211 (s.v. project 1). The source is François Rabelais, *Le cinquiesme et dernier livre... du bon Pantagruel* ([Lyons], 1564), ch. 43, sig. [Miii v] 'l'ouvrage d'icelle chapelle ronde estoit en telle symmetrie compassé, que le diametre du proiect, estoit la hauteur de la voute'.

[57] Pamela O. Long, *Openness, Secrecy, Authorship: Technical Arts and the Culture of Knowledge from Antiquity to the Renaissance* (Baltimore, MD: Johns Hopkins University Press, 2001), pp. 15, 247, 250. Long's emphasis has shifted towards the analysis of the 'trading zone' in which skilled artisans and their patrons mingled. See Pamela O. Long, *Artisan/Practitioners and the Rise of the New Sciences, 1400–1600* (Corvallis, OR: Oregon State University Press, 2011), pp. 95–6, 103–4, 120–5, 127–8. For the comparable elevation of husbandry as a noble art, see Joan Thirsk, 'Making a Fresh Start: Sixteenth-Century Agriculture and the Classical Inspiration', in *Culture and Cultivation*, 15–34.

[58] Maureen Fennell Mazzaoui, 'The Emigration of Veronese Textile Artisans to Bologna in the Thirteenth Century', *Atti e memorie dell'Accademia di Agricoltura, Scienze e Lettere di Verona*, 6th ser. 19 (1967–68), 275–319, at pp. 277, 279–80.

[59] Philippe Braunstein, *Travail et entreprise au Moyen Âge* (Brussels: De Boeck, 2003), pp. 45–54; Luca Molà, *The Silk Industry of Renaissance Venice* (Baltimore, MD: Johns Hopkins University Press, 2000), pp. 186–9; Luca Molà, 'State and Crafts: Relocating Technical Skills in Renaissance Italy', in Michelle O'Malley and Evelyn Welch (eds.), *The Material Renaissance* (Manchester: Manchester University Press, 2007), 133–53; Mario Biagioli, 'From Print to Patents: Living on Instruments in Early Modern Europe', *History of Science*, 44 (2006), p. 140 (quotation).

children and women, while raising revenues through taxes on raw materials.[60] Thus, the praise that Cotrugli had earlier only reserved for great merchants—their contribution to job creation, to the domestic economy, and to public finance—was now replicated in the promotion of inventions and industries. Thriving domestic industries, as well as their merchandise at home and abroad, came to be seen as foundational to political greatness and advantage.

Related to the reappraisal of technical skills and knowledge was the rethinking of labour and poor relief—another element that would resurface in early modern England. Attitudes to labour were never uniform within society, or across what would become Catholic and emerging Protestant regions. Yet more positive attitudes to manual labour became commonplace by the fourteenth century.[61] William Langland's *Piers Plowman* (composed *c.*1360–87) revolved around the ploughing of the God-given Half-Acre, wherein diligent labour was a prerequisite for both the good Christian community and its members' salvation. Thomas Wimbledon's Paul's Cross sermon of 1387 or 1388 likewise highlighted, as David Sacks puts it, 'the virtue of hard work performed in one's calling for the common good'.[62] Such virtues were often negatively construed: if peasants' labour was deemed worthy, it was not so much because their hard work conferred spiritual potency as because the sweat on their forehead signalled their penitence, a recompense of Adam's sin.[63] These texts proved influential in post-Reformation England. Wimbledon's sermon, for example, came to be repackaged as an early text prophesying the coming of the Protestant Reformation in England; at least twenty editions are known to have been published between 1540 and 1640.[64] It is these intellectual currents that subsequently made 'putting the poor to work' such a powerful slogan in early modern England.

Another stream to flow into sixteenth-century England was what we might call market solutions to poor relief. Important initiatives are again to be found in Italy. Inspired by Franciscans like Bernardino of Siena (1380–1444), fifteenth-century preachers and reformers argued that benevolent forms of lending could be more befitting for the relief of the poor than the alms and benefactions that had been predominant. For, if wisely regulated, the lending of small sums could undercut rampant usury and facilitate borrowers' economic survival through their own labour. The underlying appreciation of the charitable potential of both diligent labour and

---

[60] Molà, *Silk Industry*, pp. 36–7, 342 n.15.

[61] Christopher Dyer, 'Work Ethics in the Fourteenth Century', in James Bothwell, P. J. P. Goldberg, and W. M. Ormrod (eds.), *The Problem of Labour in Fourteenth-Century England* (Rochester, NY: York Medieval Press, 2001), 21–41.

[62] Derek Pearsall, '*Piers Plowman* and the Problem of Labour', in Bothwell, Goldberg, and Ormrod (eds.), *Problem of Labour*, 123–32; David Harris Sacks, 'The Greed of Judas: Avarice, Monopoly, and the Moral Economy in England, ca. 1350–ca. 1600', *Journal of Medieval and Early Modern Studies*, 28 (1998), 263–307 (at p. 295).

[63] Paul Freedman, *Images of the Medieval Peasant* (Stanford, CA: Stanford University Press, 1999), pp. 32–5.

[64] Alexandra Walsham, 'Inventing the Lollard Past: The Afterlife of a Medieval Sermon in Early Modern England', *Journal of Ecclesiastical History*, 58 (2007), 628–55, pp. 649, 654–5. For the early modern afterlives of *Piers Plowman*, see Andrew McRae, *God Speed the Plough: The Representation of Agrarian England, 1500–1660* (Cambridge: Cambridge University Press, 1996), 28–9, 85–6, 96–7.

credit provision underpinned the subsequent establishment of *monti di pietà*, church-supervised pawnshops.[65] From the establishment of the first one in Perugia in 1462, *monti* spread to other Italian cities like Orvieto (1463), Siena (1472), and Bologna (1473), and subsequently other parts of Europe. In 1515 Leo X gave a further impetus by giving general papal approval to the taking of interest on loans against pawned goods. By the time the Perugian *monte* celebrated a centenary in 1562, there were more than 200 *monti* within the Italian peninsula alone, complementing existing forms of charity such as almsgiving and hospitals for the sick and the old.[66]

While Italian-style *monti* were not firmly established in England until the nineteenth century,[67] confidence in economic solutions to poor relief proved highly consequential. One form of relief that embodied such confidence was the provision of work in houses of correction and workhouses, institutions that spread across western Europe during the sixteenth century, including London's Bridewell of 1552.[68] Local practices varied, but the employment of the poor became a 'political priority' and an important dimension of relief from Rome to London; in April 1590, for example, Pope Sixtus V ordered the architect Domenico Fontana to transform the Colosseum into a large-scale woollen factory, creating jobs for the poor and thereby boosting local industry while reducing begging in the Roman streets.[69] While the Roman plan never materialized, it is worth noting that the relief of individual beggars now carried wider socio-economic implications. By producing vendible commodities that could at best compete with foreign equivalents, paupers' (forced) manual labour became the means not only for their social discipline and spiritual salvation, but also for generating wealth for society.

If workhouses spread across western Europe as a part of the Catholic renewal, the call for reformation was spreading in emerging Protestant nations, giving religious overtones to poor relief and even to economic improvement. In his celebrated letter

[65] Laurence Fontaine, *L'Économie morale: Pauvreté, crédit et confiance dans l'Europe préindustrielle* (Paris: Gallimard, 2008), pp. 164–5, 194–5. For the intellectual background and promotional efforts, see John T. Noonan, *The Scholastic Analysis of Usury* (Cambridge, MA: Harvard University Press, 1957), pp. 70–81; Léon Poliakov, *Jewish Bankers and the Holy See: From the Thirteenth to the Seventeenth Century*, tr. Miriam Kochan (London: Routledge, 1977) [French original published in 1965], pp. 146–59. More recent work tells us that Renaissance Christian communities rarely unconditionally rejected the lending of money upon interest. Franco Mormando, *The Preacher's Demons: Bernardino of Siena and the Social Underworld of Early Renaissance Italy* (Chicago: University of Chicago Press, 1999), pp. 164–91, 217 (esp. pp. 185, 189, 217); Giacomo Todeschini, 'Usury in Christian Middle Ages: A Reconsideration of the Historiographical Tradition (1949–2010)', in Francesco Ammannati (ed.), *Religion and Religious Institutions in the European Economy, 1000–1800* (Florence: Firenze University Press, 2012), 249–60, esp. pp. 254–6.

[66] Vittorino Meneghin, *I monti di pietà in Italia dal 1462 al 1562* (Vicenza: LIEF Edizioni, 1986), pp. 56, 67–72; Noonan, *Scholastic Analysis*, pp. 299–300; Carol Bresnahan Menning, *Charity and State in Late Renaissance Italy: The Monte di Pietà of Florence* (Ithaca, NY: Cornell University Press, 1993), pp. 28–9, 104.

[67] Fontaine, *L'Économie morale*, pp. 170–1, 183–4. See also p. 234 below; Seiichiro Ito, 'The Making of Institutional Credit in England, 1600–1688', *European Journal of the History of Economic Thought*, 18 (2011), 487–519, pp. 494–5, 499–500.

[68] Henry Kamen, *The Iron Century: Social Change in Europe 1550–1660* (London: Cardinal, 1976), pp. 446–56; Slack, *Reformation to Improvement*, p. 20.

[69] Molà, 'State and Crafts', pp. 141–2. I am grateful to Professor Molà for drawing my attention to the episode.

to Paul Volz written in August 1518, Erasmus declared that even great monasteries, which had once sought true Christian life through isolation, now 'spend all their time in the very heart of worldly business'. Not only monks but also city merchants, professionals, and craftsmen were in need of reformation; they were all to aspire to live a pious, virtuous life. '[W]hat else, I ask you, is a city than a great monastery?'[70] Like monastic piety and prayer, the exercise of urban trade and professions, the mobilization of craft skills and commercial knowledge could at best be a path to godliness and salvation. Variations on this religious theme, closely interwoven with concerns about the common good, would be found repeatedly well into the eighteenth century. The other side of reformation carried a more disturbing implication. As Erasmus' remark suggests, reform presupposed rampant corruption in social and spiritual life that urgently needed discovery and correction. As we shall see in Chapter 2, the legacy of the Protestant Reformation was multifaceted, lending itself to the vexatious 'reformation' of alleged abuses in markets under Elizabeth and the early Stuarts, as well as to the more spiritual initiatives for improvement led by Samuel Hartlib that soon followed.

By the sixteenth century, then, knowledge, skills, and even manual labour related to industries came to be vested with great potential to serve God and the commonwealth. This amounted to a profound change. It had long been considered commendable for wealthy freemen to disburse their money for the building of public infrastructures. Cicero, for example, commended private generosity 'bestowed upon citiewalles, shippedockes, havens, conduites, and all, that appertein to the use of the Com[m]onweale'.[71] Aquinas later wrote of the virtue of magnificence as the generous spending of private wealth for anything 'which brings honour to the whole community; for example one *for which the whole community is enthusiastic*'.[72] These sensibilities proved influential well into the eighteenth century. In 1733, John Thomas alluded precisely to these passages of Cicero and Aquinas in order to celebrate the passage of an act for making the River Dee navigable. The scheme, Thomas suggested, was conducive to 'the desirable Increase of Trade and Commerce . . . and consequently to the sure Promotion of the Common Good and Interest of the Publick'. Invoking the learned authorities, Thomas preached that bestowing private money upon such a scheme would be a great service to the community, a sign of one's magnificence and liberality.[73]

[70] Erasmus, *Collected Works of Erasmus, Vol. 66, Spiritualia. Enchiridion, de Contemptu Mundi, de Vidua Christiana*, ed. John W. O'Malley (Toronto: University of Toronto Press, 1988), p. 22.

[71] Cicero, *Marcus Tullius Ceceroes thre bokes of duties to Marcus his sonne*, tr. Nicholas Grimalde (1556), fol. 87. Cicero was careful not to endorse endowments upon buildings such as theatres, which were deemed less 'useful' at the time. See Paul Veyne (ed.), *A History of Private Life I: From Pagan Rome to Byzantium*, tr. Arthur Goldhammer (Cambridge, MA: Harvard University Press, 1987), 107–10. A useful overview of Paul Veyne's influential analysis of Roman generosity is Peter Garnsey, 'The Generosity of Veyne', *Journal of Roman Studies*, 81 (1991), 164–8.

[72] Aquinas, *Summa Theologiae*, vol. 42, p. 177 (2a2ae, 134, 3). Italics in original.

[73] John Thomas, *Liberality in promoting the trade and interest of the publick display'd: A sermon preach'd at St. Mary's in Chester September 16 1733 on occasion of obtaining an act of parliament for making the river Dee navigable* [1733?], pp. 11–12 (quotation from p. 11).

By the end of the sixteenth century, however, not only private generosity, but also the skills and expertise needed for realizing such an improvement scheme, also came to be reappraised as evidence of one's public-spiritedness. Giving jobs to the poor through these schemes could likewise testify to one's charity and godliness. These were the variegated traditions that were brought together in sixteenth-century England. The grandiloquence of subsequent promoters like Defoe, Cary, and Hill was rooted in this rich layer of historical precedents. The convergence of these traditions had taken place by the sixteenth century, as promoters (some of them European immigrants) offered to put their knowledge and expertise to public ends, and thereby began to 'form symbiotic relationships with authority and co-opt the state just as the state is co-opting' them.[74] This dynamic symbiosis between the political and the economic, which was to have transformative consequences, set the early modern period apart from its late medieval antecedents. How did it come about? The dynamic symbiosis came to emerge as England responded to a set of interlocking geopolitical transformations, to which we shall now turn.

THE EMERGENCE OF PROJECTING IN TUDOR ENGLAND

Colonial expansion and the development of long-distance trade brought into Europe an unprecedented amount of silver from the mines of Potosi in modern-day Bolivia; this, coupled with silver from the mines of central Europe and the coining of existing silver plates, triggered unprecedented inflation from the mid-sixteenth century onward. The price of wheat in southern England, for example, rose by more than 360 per cent between the 1490s and the 1570s; yet because population was rising during the same period, wage rates lagged behind the pace of inflation. Various estimates suggest that in real terms wage rates declined—especially sharply in the second half of the sixteenth century.[75] Climatic conditions may have made the situation worse. Some estimates suggest that glaciers expanded and that cold summers were frequent during the later sixteenth century—with a succession of crop failures.[76] Meanwhile, England was embroiled in a series of wars from the mid-sixteenth century, including those with France from 1557 to 1559 and 1562

---

[74] Ethan Shagan, *Popular Politics and the English Reformation* (Cambridge: Cambridge University Press, 2003), p. 14.

[75] Wrightson, *Earthly Necessities*, pp. 116–17, 120–31 (at p. 117); Gregory Clark, 'The Long March of History: Farm Wages, Population, and Economic Growth, England 1209–1869', *EcHR*, 60 (2007), 97–135, pp. 132–3; Robert C. Allen, *The British Industrial Revolution in Global Perspective* (Cambridge: Cambridge University Press, 2009), pp. 42–3; N. J. Mayhew, 'Prices in England, 1170–1750', *P&P*, 219 (2013), 3–39, p. 37; Stephen Broadberry et al., *British Economic Growth, 1270–1870* (Cambridge: Cambridge University Press, 2015), pp. 252–9.

[76] J. M. Grove, 'The Initiation of the "Little Ice Age" in Regions round the North Atlantic', *Climatic Change*, 48 (2001), 53–82; Christian Pfister and Rudolf Brázdil, 'Climatic Variability in Sixteenth-Century Europe and its Social Dimension: A Synthesis', *Climatic Change*, 43 (1999), 5–53; Braddick, *State Formation*, p. 119 nn. 64, 66. Note that the precise dating of the Little Ice Age and the measuring of its socio-economic impact are at best speculative. On this point, see Paul Warde, 'Global Crisis or Global Coincidence?', *P&P*, 228 (2015), 287–301, pp. 289–90.

to 1564 as part of the French Wars of Religion, then with Spain, first from 1585 to 1604, and then after the succession of Charles I, between 1625 and 1630. These wars were symptomatic not only of England's remaking as a Protestant nation, but also of its growing imperial ambition. In fact, the latter half of the sixteenth century saw waves of expeditions, followed by the establishment of trading companies, including that of the Muscovy Company (chartered 1555), the Levant Company (1581), the Barbary Company (1585), the Senegal Adventurers (1588), and the famous East India Company (1600).[77] Establishing overseas factories was to help take lucrative trades away from other European powers. Doing so would create new markets for domestic commodities in return for silver, spices, and raw materials that could be finished in England for home consumption and re-exporting abroad.

The combination of demographic pressure, economic hardship, and imperial ambition gave rise to pressing problems with welfare, revenue, and industries. First, inflation and stagnant wages, combined with bad harvests and food scarcity, exacerbated the miserable condition of the poor. The latter half of the sixteenth century was indeed the period in which the existence of the labouring poor—those who were healthy and capable of labour and yet not able to earn a livelihood for their families—was identified as a policy problem to be tackled by the state.[78] Second, successive wars put great pressure on Crown finances, despite a windfall profit from the dissolution of the monasteries and the subsequent sales of church lands that exceeded £1 million between 1539 and 1554.[79] Third, imperial prowess was to be established by riches as well as by might. Voyages to the Americas, trading with the Turks, and privateering were undertaken in order to take riches away from continental rivals. During the late sixteenth century, England's export of traditional woollen broadcloth, which had so far dominated English overseas trade, went into decline, while the import of foreign luxuries continued.[80] The import of consumer goods was to be avoided as much as possible; the encouragement of new domestic industries was urgently called for.

One of the best-known responses to these interlocking challenges is Sir Thomas Smith's *Discourse of the Commonweal of This Realm of England*, which circulated first as a manuscript in 1549. This was before the collapse of the traditional woollen export trade, and the timing of its composition helps us to clarify its chief concerns. The exporting of English woollens, which hinged heavily on Antwerp, was at its height in the 1540s. Customs accounts suggest that annual English cloth exports more than doubled, with short-term fluctuations, between the 1440s and 1540s

[77] Kenneth R. Andrews, *Trade, Plunder and Settlement: Maritime Enterprise and the Genesis of the British Empire, 1480–1630* (Cambridge, 1984); John C. Appleby, 'War, Politics, and Colonization, 1558–1625', in Nicholas Canny (ed.), *The Oxford History of the British Empire, Volume 1: The Origins of Empire* (Oxford, 1998), 55–78; T. S. Willan, *Studies in Elizabethan Foreign Trade* (Manchester: Manchester University Press, 1959), pp. 183–7.

[78] Steve Hindle, *On the Parish? The Micro-Politics of Poor Relief in Rural England, 1550–1750* (Oxford: Clarendon, 2004), pp. 2–3; Paul Slack, *Poverty and Policy in Tudor and Stuart England* (London: Longman, 1988), pp. 27–9.

[79] Joan Thirsk (ed.), *The Agrarian History of England and Wales, Volume iv 1500–1640* (Cambridge: Cambridge University Press, 1967), p. 263; Patrick K. O'Brien and Philip A. Hunt, 'The Rise of a Fiscal State in England 1485–1815', *Historical Research*, 66 (1993), 129–76, p. 144.

[80] Ralph Davis, *English Overseas Trade 1500–1700* (London: Macmillan, 1973), pp. 11–15.

(from 60,000 to 130,000 packs of cloths); the flow of these English cloths and kerseys into Antwerp in the 1540s was so great that their re-export occupied nearly 60 per cent of the total value of the city's export trade between 1544 and 1545.[81] It was only from the 1550s, *after* the composition of Smith's *Discourse*, that the export trade with Antwerp began to be seriously disrupted, first by the financial defaults of the Spanish Crown, and subsequently by the Spanish army that sacked the trading entrepôt in 1577.[82]

The crucial background for Smith's *Discourse* was, therefore, not so much the collapse of England's traditional woollen export trade as the strong inflow of imported luxuries and their consumption among those above the middling station, who benefitted from rising prices and lower wages of labour. Whereas in the 1520s there were only a dozen or so haberdashers that sold 'French or Milan caps, glasses, daggers...and such like', now, Smith tells us, streets 'from the Tower to Westminster along' were full of such shops that 'glitter and shine of glasses, as well looking as drinking', alluring even a 'temperate man to gaze on them and to buy somewhat though it serve to no purpose necessary'.[83] Indeed, the membership of the London Haberdashers' Company grew almost threefold between 1501 and 1537/8 (from 41 to 120). Evidence from probate inventories also suggests that consumer behaviour was spreading well beyond the metropolis. The average number of movable goods found in houses of provincial towns such as Boston, Chesterfield, and Lincoln was increasing during the middle decades of the sixteenth century, testifying to a greater flow into provinces of consumer items, some of them no doubt imported from the continent.[84]

The consumption of foreign luxuries, Smith declared, had significant consequences: 'not so little as a hundred thousand pounds a year is fetched of our treasure for things of no value of themselves but only to the workers of the same which are set awork [abroad] all on our charges'. Thus he brought the point home: 'Were it not better for us that our own people should be set to work with such things than strangers?'[85] This was a dangerous situation. 'For we must always take heed that we buy no more of strangers than we do sell them; for so we should impoverish ourselves and enrich them. For he were no good husband...that would buy more in the market than he sells again.'[86] Here we have the paradigmatic analogy between household and national economies, lending itself to the diagnosis of excessive importation of foreign-manufactured goods. We shall repeatedly encounter the

[81] E. M. Carus-Wilson and Olive Coleman, *England's Export Trade, 1275–1547* (Oxford: Clarendon, 1963), pp. 138–9; Jeroen Puttevils, '"Eating the Bread Out of their Mouth": Antwerp's Export Trade and Generalized Institutions, 1544–5', *EcHR*, 68 (2015), 1339–64, at pp. 1349–50.

[82] Davis, *Overseas Trade*, pp. 14–16; Peter Spufford, 'From Antwerp and Amsterdam to London: The Decline of Financial Centres in Europe', *De Economist*, 154 (2006), 143–75, pp. 156–8.

[83] Thomas Smith, *A Discourse of the Commonweal of This Realm of England*, ed. Mary Dewar (Charlottesville, VA: University Press of Virginia, 1969), p. 64.

[84] Sylvia L. Thrupp, *The Merchant Class of Medieval London* (Ann Arbor, MI: University of Michigan Press, 1962) [first published in 1948], p. 43; Craig Muldrew, *Economy of Obligation: The Culture of Credit and Social Relations in Early Modern England* (London: Macmillan, 1998), pp. 25–6.

[85] Smith, *Discourse of the Commonweal*, pp. 65, 122.   [86] Ibid., p. 63.

two problems identified here—the decay of domestic industries and the adverse balance of payment.

Import substitution, Smith argued, could remedy the trade imbalance while creating jobs for the poor. His vision was never confined to a single industry or commodity. The vast range of commodities capable of enhancing the comfort and conveniences of life was to be produced at home, rather than imported: 'all kind of cloth' including kerseys, worsted, hats, caps; 'all kind of leather ware as gloves, points, girdles' among others; 'and also all kinds of vessels, earthen pots, tennis balls, tables, cards, chests'. These articles, Smith argued, 'might be wrought here not only sufficient to set so many to work and serve the realm but also to serve other parts' of the realm.[87] One key solution was technology transfer through the immigration of skilled artisans. Note that Smith wrote *Discourse* only seven years after the completion of his grand tour to the continent, on which he visited Paris, Padua, and possibly Venice.[88] This explains why Smith looked to Italian city states to find examples to emulate. Speaking of Venice, 'that most flourishing city at these days of all Europe', he pointed out that 'if they may hear of any cunning craftsman in any faculty, they will find the means to allure him to dwell in their city; for it is a wonder to see what deal of money one good occupier does bring in to a town though he himself do not gain to his own commodity but a poor living'.[89]

This policy of attracting a skilled workforce was precisely what William Cecil, Smith's student at Cambridge, took further by granting letters patent. Patents, of course, had long been used by English monarchs for conferring privileges. Skilled foreigners had long been involved in English government too: Italian families such as the Ricciardi and the Frescobaldi played an important role in English mints in 1279–1311, and again after the introduction of an English gold coinage in 1344; in 1496, Henry VII issued a patent for the Genoese of Venetian citizenship John Cabot to authorize his expedition to discover islands unknown to Christians—the beginning of English participation in overseas expansion; in the 1520s German miners such as Petrus Filius were given commissions to search, dig, and refine ores of 'gold Silver Lead Iron Stele Tynne and Cooper'.[90] Yet, shortly after Smith's *Discourse*, the English government started granting patents in larger numbers in order to encourage the immigration of foreign workers, first those skilled in glassmaking in 1552, and then others versed in searching out and working metals in 1554.[91] After Elizabeth succeeded to the throne in 1558, Cecil, whom she appointed as a secretary of state, encouraged the denization of immigrants in London, and further promoted the use of patents. By the end of her reign, at least sixty-seven grants were made to promote the domestic production of items such as white soap, window glass, ovens, furnaces, and Spanish leather, and to introduce new skills in draining mines,

[87] Ibid., pp. 122–3.

[88] Ian W. Archer, 'Smith, Sir Thomas (1513–1577)', *Oxford DNB*, vol. 51, 324–30 (at p. 324). An informed discussion of the text is provided by Thirsk, *Economic Policy and Projects*, pp. 13–18, 24.

[89] Smith, *Discourse of the Commonweal*, p. 124.

[90] Martin Allen, *Mints and Money in Medieval England* (Cambridge: Cambridge University Press, 2012), pp. 192–3, 214–15; S. B. Chrimes, *Henry VII* (New Haven, CT: Yale University Press, 1972), pp. 28–9; TNA, SP 1/59, fol. 60 (quotation); SP 1/236, fol. 38.

[91] Thirsk, *Economic Policy and Projects*, pp. 33–4.

dredging rivers, and grinding corn. Of these more than one-third (twenty-six grants) included aliens and naturalized foreigners among patentees; others were granted to native subjects, but often in order to protect immigrants and their skills.[92]

Projects could also be pursued outside the channel of patenting. An interesting example is Bridewell Hospital, established as a 'house of labour and occupations' in 1552. It promised to provide workshops for the 'making of featherbed ticks, wool-cards, drawing of wire, spinning, carding, knitting, and winding of silk, and other profitable devices'.[93] Echoing Smith's blueprint for import substitution, the hospital also promised to produce 'cap...as well dressed and died' as 'any [that] are made in France'. Thus, not only poor children, the sick, and the weak, but also vagabonds would be set to work and 'to live profitably to the commonwealth', a godly scheme that would 'increase' the 'charity of the good citizens' who had promoted it.[94] Just as schemes for import substitution could prove charitable by setting the poor to work, charitable institutions might contribute to import substitution and hence to the commonwealth. A similar agenda for import substitution was soon picked up in the Parliament of 1559; it discussed plans for encouraging the cultivation of dye plants such as madder and woad, and for reviving dormant statutes for prohibiting import of items such as 'caps, pins, points, dice, gilt stirrups' and other items, for whose production 'the people might be better employed' within the realm.[95]

Underlying these initiatives for import substitution was the embryonic notion of the balance of trade, anticipated in the fifteenth century, and given sophisticated expression later by Thomas Mun and others in the first decades of the seventeenth.[96] Robert Cotton's advice of 1612 to a privy councillor repeated the analogy, used earlier by Smith, between household and international economy, and highlighted the importance of 'restrain[ing] the mighty indraught of Forraine Manufactures and unnecessary wares [so] that the outward trade might overbalance the inward w[hi]ch otherwise' would lead to 'desperate Consumption of the Com[m]onwealth'.[97]

[92] I have arrived at the figures by comparing and combining the two lists of patents, G. D. Duncan, 'Monopolies under Elizabeth I, 1558–1585' (PhD thesis, University of Cambridge, 1976), pp. 340–6; E. Wyndham Hulme, 'The History of the Patent System under the Prerogative and at Common Law. A Sequel', *Law Quarterly Review*, 16 (1900), 44–56, pp. 48–52. Duncan's list incorporates grants not listed by Hulme, but ends at 1585. Thus, for the period between 1586 and 1603, I have relied on Hulme's list. In order to make a conservative estimate, I have excluded grants for regulating import and export. For patenting under Elizabeth, see also E. Wyndham Hulme, 'The History of the Patent System under the Prerogative and at Common Law', *Law Quarterly Review*, 12 (1896), 141–54, esp. pp. 145–9; Thirsk, *Economic Policy and Projects*, pp. 30–49, 52; Ian W. Archer, *The History of Haberdashers' Company* (Chichester: Phillimore, 1991), p. 61; Lien Bich Luu, *Immigrants and the Industries of London, 1500–1700* (Aldershot: Ashgate, 2005), p. 64.
[93] R. H. Tawney and Eileen Power (eds.), *Tudor Economic Documents* (3 vols., London: Longmans, 1924), vol. 2, pp. 311, 308; Marjorie Keniston McIntosh, *Poor Relief in England 1350–1600* (Cambridge: Cambridge University Press, 2011), pp. 126, 206.
[94] Tawney and Power, *Tudor Economic Documents*, vol. 2, pp. 307–9; Slack, *Reformation to Improvement*, pp. 20–1.
[95] Tawney and Power, *Tudor Economic Documents*, vol. 1, pp. 327, 329.
[96] Wood, *Medieval Economic Thought*, pp. 126–7. For antecedents in the thirteenth and fourteenth centuries, see Kaye, *History of Balance*.
[97] BL, Cotton MS, Cleopatra F VI, 'Means to repayr the Kings Estate collected by Sr Robert Cotton for the Earl of Northampton', 1612, fols. 49v–50.

Import substitution was, of course, not just about restoring the balance of payments. Domestic industries strong enough to reverse the flow of goods were deemed to be as consequential as the discovery of silver mines. Invoking the economic prowess of Italian city states, Smith declared:

> What need they beyond [the] sea to travel to Peru or such far countries…to dig the deep bowels of the earth for the mine of silver or gold when they can…make good gold and silver more than a great many of silver and gold mines would make?

Even more, if imported goods could be successfully replaced by those produced at home, Smith argued, 'twenty thousand persons might be set to work'.[98] Such was the global potential of local industries that fascinated Smith and others in subsequent generations.

The disparate arguments that had long existed for the public utility of labour, craft skills, and merchandise thus converged by the mid-sixteenth century as England pursued its imperial ambitions under demographic, fiscal, and economic pressures. It is not too much to suggest that, facing such setbacks, early modern state-formation boosted entrepreneurship as much as entrepreneurs drove its machinery on the ground. Indeed, early modern projects, especially those concerned with trade and industries, exhibit unexpected similarity to one of the most influential definitions of entrepreneurship and innovation—one proposed by Joseph Schumpeter. Like innovative schemes promoted by Schumpeter's entrepreneur, early modern projects were very often attempts to generate wealth through 'the carrying out of new combinations'. They include schemes for introducing 'new' commodities never produced or hitherto only produced abroad; schemes for introducing technological novelties into the production of 'old' commodities to achieve higher quality or lower costs; schemes for opening up new markets for products or new sources of supply of materials; and schemes for reorganizing an industry by, for example, setting up a monopoly based on it.[99] Projects that emerged in early modern England thus stand as unacknowledged antecedents of Schumpeterian entrepreneurship.

By the early years of James I's reign, diverse entrepreneurial schemes that incorporated elements of technology transfer, import substitution, and poor relief came to be discussed and ordered under the category of the project. This probably marked the first rise of the concept in the context of administration. Among the papers of statesmen such as Julius Caesar, Robert Cecil, and Robert Cotton, we

---

    [98] Smith, *Discourse of the Commonweal*, pp. 122, 65. This qualifies the suggestion that Botero was the first author to argue that riches greater than Spanish mines could be extracted from untapped 'above ground mines', i.e. market activities. On this point, see the otherwise excellent discussion of Vera Keller, 'Mining Tacitus: Secrets of Empire, Nature and Art in the Reason of State', *BJHS*, 45 (2012), 189–212, at p. 191.

    [99] Joseph A. Schumpeter, *The Theory of Economic Development: An Inquiry into Profits, Capital, Credit, Interest, and the Business Cycle*, tr. Redvers Opie (Cambridge, MA: Harvard University Press, 1961) [first published in German in 1911], pp. 65–6; Joseph A. Schumpeter, 'The Creative Response in Economic History', *Journal of Economic History*, 7 (1947), 149–59, at p. 153; Joseph A. Schumpeter, *Capitalism, Socialism, and Democracy* (3rd edn, New York: Harper, 1950), p. 132. We can add to the list schemes for applying existing techniques on a larger scale, or applying them to a new frontier.

find a number of manuscripts listing and documenting examples of 'suits' and 'projects'.[100] Strong emphasis was placed upon the revenue implications of these schemes, partly because Crown finance was under unprecedented pressure after the accession of James. Commissioned by his master the Earl of Southampton, for example, Cotton composed and circulated in manuscript form a treatise giving an overview as to 'How Kinges of England have from tyme to tyme supported and repared their Estates', giving examples of sixteen avenues for fiscal retrenchment and improvement.[101] The historical precedents were systematically collected and studied in order to inform policy-making in the present. Elsewhere, Cotton tabulated different avenues for fiscal improvement as 'A short view of all such courses as precedent times have practics'd, or theis present have projected for supply & support of the Soverainge Ma[jes]tie in wants & extremity'.[102] Portions of Cotton's voluminous manuscripts were circulated, copied, and later relaunched as William 'Noyes Projects: Being a Declaration or Description of how the King of England may Support and increase his annual Revenues'.[103] The social and political disturbances triggered by such projects by the end of the 1630s will be examined in Chapter 2. It now suffices to point out that the projector's promise of public service that Aaron Hill recognized in James I was rooted in rich layers of historical precedents, going back at least to the late medieval period. Ambitious schemes emerged in large numbers by the mid-Tudor period, and were surveyed, ordered, and discussed during James I's reign as 'projects' for informing future political actions.

WELFARE, REVENUE, AND THE PUBLIC GOOD: PROJECTING AND EARLY MODERN GOVERNANCE

By the early eighteenth century the promotion of ambitious schemes became more integrated into the fledgling stock market. Yet, crucially, schemes for economic innovation and improvement hardly became *private* business enterprises detached from societal concerns. Instead they retained their ambition, or pretention, to serve the public. In order to understand this resilience, we must consider these schemes within the broad context of early modern state-formation and its limits, especially officialdom's limited capacity to provide for the poor and to raise revenues.

[100] Thirsk, 'Crown as Projector', pp. 298–300; Cramsie, *Kingship*, pp. 29–30.

[101] BL, Cotton MS, Cleopatra F VI, 'Means to repayr the Kings Estate collected by Sr Robert Cotton for the Earl of Northampton', 1612, fols. 41–51. The quotation is taken from the title page of another presentation copy at University of London Special Collection, MS308, Robert Cotton, 'A declaration how kinges of England have from tyme to tyme supported and repared their estates, collected out of the records remaining in the Tower of London', [1611 or 1612].

[102] BL, Cotton MS Cleopatra F VI, fols. 65v–67v, at 65v.

[103] Ibid., fols. 41–51. Two copies attributed to the attorney general Noy have been found: University of London Library, Special Collection, MS 581; Baker Library, Kress MS 106. It is unclear whether Noy actually adopted the material from Cotton or whether his authorship was erroneously attributed to a treatise outlining means of financial exaction. This treatise was subsequently published as [Robert Cotton], *An abstract out of the records of the Tower, touching the Kings revenue* (1642); and as part of Robert Cotton, *Cottoni posthuma: divers choice pieces of that renowened antiquary Sir Robert Cotton* (1651) [subsequent editions in 1671 and 1679].

Labour discipline featured prominently in the Elizabethan poor law (39 Eliz. 1, c. 3), the early Stuart Books of Orders, and in other related decrees and proclamations.[104] This owed much to the emerging tradition surveyed earlier, in which labour was hailed as a God-given duty; as Thomas Becon put it in 1551, 'thy godly pleasure is no man be idle, but everyman labour according to his vocation and calling'.[105] Such sentiments persisted. By the end of the seventeenth century, the number of the poor who suffered near starvation (or *deep* poverty) declined and living standards generally improved, thanks in part to demographic stability, declining grain prices, and the specialization and integration of regional economies. Yet the number of those who suffered *shallow* poverty, those who were on the verge of requiring poor relief and doles, did not decline. The proportion of wage labourers to farmers in fact increased, especially in south-eastern England.[106] Despite the overall economic improvement, its pace and impact varied considerably depending on regions and occupational groups; hence the persistent concern for relieving the poor.[107] Promoters often brushed aside these variations with a sweep of the pen, calling instead for relief by discipline: 'after all, the truest and best Charity is to set People a Work, where they are able, and if they will not, to get 'em Whipt out of their Laziness'.[108]

Local poor relief schemes were rarely successful, however, chiefly because many of them hinged heavily on money raised locally. An Elizabethan act of 1572 demanded that local paupers insufficiently relieved by parishes be housed in certain designated 'abiding places' and compelled to undertake whatever work they could; the money for their support was to be collected from neighbouring parishes. If implemented, the statute was to lead to the establishment of local workhouses across England.[109] By the end of the Elizabethan reign, only a quarter of the counties had set up such 'abiding places'. Even where similar schemes were put into practice for many years, as in the parishes of Cowden (Kent), Kempton (Bedfordshire), and Frampton (Lincolnshire) in the early seventeenth century, many of them ultimately failed to run at a profit and thus ended up burdening local ratepayers.[110] Anthony Fletcher has concluded that parochial work schemes were 'the most impractical aspect of the whole corpus of Tudor legislation'. Even a more modulated assessment

---

[104] Hindle, *On the Parish?*, p. 172. See also Thirsk, *Economic Policy and Projects*, p. 51.

[105] Thomas Becon, *The flower of godly prayers* (1551), quoted in Sacks, 'Greed of Judas', p. 295.

[106] In Bedfordshire, for example, nearly three farm labours worked for every farmer in the early eighteenth century, indicating the increasing proletarian nature of the workforce in the region. See Leigh Shaw-Taylor, 'The Rise of Agrarian Capitalism and the Decline of Family Farming in England', *EcHR*, 65 (2012), 26–60, at p. 52.

[107] Slack, *Poverty and Policy*, pp. 38–40, 53–5. For the concomitant fear of downward mobility, see Michael Mascuch, 'Social Mobility and Middling Self-Identity: The Ethos of British Autobiographers, 1600–1750', *Social History* [Hull], 20 (1995), 45–61.

[108] *Athenian gazette or casuistical mercury*, 23 June 1694, issue 10.

[109] McIntosh, *Poor Relief*, pp. 22, 148, 168, 228, 281.

[110] Hindle, *On the Parish?*, pp. 178–9, 183–4. For similar difficulties encountered in the later seventeenth century, see Stephen Macfarlane, 'Social Policy and the Poor in the Later Seventeenth Century', in A. L. Beier and Robert Finlay (eds.), *London 1500–1700: The Making of the Metropolis* (London: Longman, 1986), 252–77.

by Steve Hindle concurs that they 'appear to have been successful only intermittently, if at all' during the seventeenth and early eighteenth centuries.[111]

The widespread shallow poverty and the pressure to relieve the poor were only partially met, therefore. This is why even schemes for economic innovations and improvements (which were not poor relief based on local assessments) frequently claimed to help relieve the poor by putting them to work. In 1586, Robert Payne, a yeoman of Buckinghamshire, promoted a scheme for planting woad in Wollaton (Nottinghamshire) with the backing of Sir Francis Willoughby:

> the two hundered thowsande poundes a yere in wares and mony whiche is bestowed beyonde the Seas upon the saide woade, might rather be heare imployed to the releeffe of our poore native people[.][112]

Walter Morrell's 'New Drapery' scheme, though ultimately abortive, promised to employ the 'many thousands which now live in idleness' in Hertfordshire.[113] In 1660, Thomas Bushell promised Charles II that his Welsh mining scheme would relieve 'many whole families' now 'starving for want' of bread and alms. His scheme would 'now be most gratefull and acceptable to all good men' because 'such poor Souls may be completely relieved, without any charge at all to the publick'.[114] Sir Edward Ford publicized in a broadsheet in 1666 that he was ready to propose a 'Herring Trade...to the Breeding up and Maintaining Plenty of Mariners... employ[ing] our Poor from their Childhood'.[115] Cressy Dymock claimed in 1668 that 'I know divers honest, beneficial and not enslaving ways which...may set [to work] not only all the Poor in *England*, but five times more', and even raise several millions of pounds within several years.[116] Applicants for patents, too, often stated in their petitions that their inventions would help employ the poor.[117] Hill's beech oil project with which we began this chapter stemmed from this tradition. In 1714, he reassured his investors that his beech mast oil extraction business would 'supply all *Europe* with *Oil*', raise vast profits for shareholders, and, crucially, tend to 'a general Good to the *Poor*' by giving them employment.[118]

Underlying these promises was the enormous potential of economic improvement for complementing poor relief. This prospect was put eloquently by an agricultural improver, Gabriel Plattes, the author of a husbandry manual befittingly

[111] Anthony Fletcher, *Reform in the Provinces: The Government of Stuart England* (New Haven, CT: Yale University Press, 1986)?, p. 213; Hindle, *On the Parish?*, pp. 173, 191, at p. 191.

[112] R. S. Smith, 'A Woad Growing Project at Wollaton in the 1580s', *Transactions of the Thoroton Society of Nottinghamshire*, 65 (1961), 27–46, pp. 40–1.

[113] Zell, 'Walter Morrell', p. 665 (quoting from HEH, MS 53654, p. 99).

[114] Thomas Bushell, *An extract by Mr. Bushell of his late abridgment of the lord chancellor Bacons philosophical theory of mineral prosecutions* (1660), sig. A2, p. 3.

[115] Edward ford, 'Experimented Proposals how the King may have Money to pay and maintain his Fleets, with Ease to his People' [1666], in *Harleian Miscellany*, ed. William Oldys (8 vols., 1744–6), vol. 4, p. 187.

[116] Cressy Dymock, *The new and better art of agriculture* (1668), one-page handbill.

[117] See, for example, patent nos. 89, 225, 246. Labour-saving inventions existed, but as MacLeod finds, there was 'an overwhelming capital-saving bias in the goals evinced by patentees'. MacLeod, *Patent*, pp. 159–73 (quotation from p. 159).

[118] Aaron Hill, *Proposals for raising a stock of one hundred thousand pounds; for laying up great quantities of beech-mast for two years* (1714), pp. 19, 10.

entitled *A discovery of infinite treasure* (1639). Those promoting new and improved methods of crop cultivation could do

> a more charitable deed in publishing thereof: then if he had built all the Hospitalls in *England:* for the one feedeth and cloatheth a few hungry and naked persons, the other enableth an infinite number both to feed and clothe themselves and others[.][119]

Plattes was by no means a saintly philanthropist selflessly serving the public at his own expense; as we shall find in Chapter 3, he was adeptly selling his expertise in a marketplace of knowledge. His ambition is still emblematic: the employment of the poor became one of the enduring promises amid the pervasive shallow poverty and the relative inadequacy of municipal and parish welfare provision.

In addition to contributions to poor relief, promoters of improvement also promised fiscal contributions, and continued to do so well into the age of the financial revolution. After the 1640s, the total amount of government spending increased dramatically largely because of rising military spending for the succession of domestic and international wars. Money had to be found somewhere. Parliamentary taxation, which came to play a dominant role in the second half of the seventeenth century, was not without its problems. Local administration remained highly controversial and its rapidly expanding apparatus was often slow to realize its full fiscal potential. It was also difficult to achieve proportional and equitable taxation due to evasion and the lack of compliance. The broadening of taxation—necessary for meeting the demands of wars and other exigencies— continued to be difficult as well. MPs after the Restoration often feared that setting up too autonomous a revenue source, such as a general excise, might allow the Crown to be fiscally independent from parliament, thereby precipitating the emergence of an 'arbitrary government'.[120] Moreover, although tax collection became more professional and standardized towards the later seventeenth century, few commentators or administrators raised 'questions of [effective] administration'.[121] As Baxter has suggested, there was little sustained effort to improve 'the functioning of a department or of a profession from day to day', or to set specific revenue boards for individual taxes.[122] At least until the mid-eighteenth century, the imperial ambitions of the British fiscal-military state, and its ensuing demand for money, probably grew faster than its capacity to provide it.

This is why, even after the Restoration (let alone the early Stuart period), the governmental apparatus left a considerable 'vacuum into which external, unofficial, [fiscal] advice poured'.[123] Because the aggressive use of the prerogative caused much stir under Elizabeth and the early Stuarts by imposing fines and assessments

---

[119] Gabriel Plattes, *A discovery of infinite treasure, hidden since the worlds beginning* (1639), sig. [(a)v] (quotation), sig. [C4]. Compare this with p. 246 n. 90 below.

[120] Braddick, *Nerves of State*, pp. 99, 115, 148.

[121] Braddick, *State Formation*, pp. 263, 285; Stephen B. Baxter, *The Development of The Treasury, 1660–1702* (London: Longman, 1957), p. 171 (quotation).

[122] The observation is based on Treasury Papers and later seventeenth-century writings on the Exchequer. Baxter, *Development of The Treasury*, p. 171. A similar observation for the post-1688 period can be found in Brooks, 'Taxation, Finance and Public Opinion', pp. 225–7.

[123] Brooks, 'Taxation, Finance and Public Opinion', p. 223.

upon ordinary subjects, raising revenues 'without imposition' became a common slogan. As early as 1604, for example, Richard Fiennes, seventh Baron Saye and Sele, proposed to raise money by taxing theatregoers. This, he argued, constituted 'no monopole, noe nor imposition' because watching fashionable shows, like smoking tobacco, was an act of luxury which was 'as unnecessary & yet yelde noe penny to his Maiesty' (unlike tobacco).[124] During the 1640s and the 1650s, Hartlib and Dury were attracted to an ambitious 'universal trade' scheme that would raise £300,000 'without any tributarie taxation'.[125] In the 1670s, promoters of a fishery scheme promised to reveal to the Lord High Treasurer Thomas Osborne how to raise money 'without taking any thing out of his Coffers or forceing the Subject to any thing against their wills'.[126] In 1693, Sir Edward Harley was informed that 'Many Projectors are preparing proposals, for raiseing vast Summs without Burdening the people'.[127] Defoe fumed in 1712 that 'our Projectors Heads are full of fancy'd Funds, and many a fine Castle in the Air they build every year', obsessed as they were with the prospect of 'raising Taxes without Burthening the People'.[128] Swift, on the other side of the political spectrum, also found it worth mocking. In the Kingdom of Lagado, Gulliver learned about a proposal for levying taxes upon female beauty and male politeness according to their own evaluation; this, Gulliver was told, was 'the most . . . effectual ways and means of raising money without grieving the subject'.[129]

Projects concerned primarily with economic improvement often promised to raise revenues as well. In his new fishing scheme published in 1615, one J. R. ostentatiously promised to present a 'sweete fountaine of profite' of more than £50,000 per annum, which 'runneth into the sea of the Kings custome'.[130] The similarly grandiose promise of mid-seventeenth century 'universal trade', with its fishing and agricultural fronts, has already been mentioned. Another fishery proposal, promoted under Charles II, suggested that the Crown might even be able to lower tonnage and poundage significantly, because depriving the Dutch of their cod and herring 'alone is able to make the king great, and more enrich the people then all the mines . . . (yea cloth and wooll put together) can doe'.[131] John Smith suggested in 1670 that, if his readers planted timber across the nation according to his advice, 'his Majesty might be readily furnished with . . . a considerable sum paid

---

[124] Peter R. Roberts, 'The Business of Playing and the Patronage of Players at the Jacobean Courts', in Ralph Houlbrooke (ed.), *James VI and I: Ideas, Authority, and Government* (Aldershot: Ashgate, 2006), pp. 95–102 (quotation from p. 96).

[125] HP 25/8/1A-2B. See the discussion in Chapter 2.

[126] BL, Egerton MS 3352, Danby Papers Vol. 29, Smith Watson, Memoranda relating to fisheries [1677?], fol. 41v.

[127] Brooks, 'Taxation, Finance and Public Opinion', p. 258 (quoting BL, Loan MS 29/187, fol. 185, 17 October 1693).

[128] Daniel Defoe, *Defoe's Review*, ed. John McVeagh (9 vols., London: Pickering & Chatto, 2003–11), vol. 8, pt. 2, p. 815.

[129] Jonathan Swift, *The Prose Writings of Jonathan Swift, Vol. 11: Gulliver's Travels, 1726*, ed. Herbert Davis, (Oxford: Blackwell, 1941), pp. 189–90.

[130] J. R. *Trades increase* (1615), p. 46. For background, see John Cramsie, 'Commercial Projects and the Fiscal Policy of James VI and I', *HJ*, 43 (2000), pp. 345–64.

[131] BL, Egerton MS 3352, Danby Papers Vol. 29, fol. 40, 'The Incomparable Benefitt that the Fishery would be to this Nation', n.d. [1677?].

into his Exchequer' by means of a sales tax.[132] It was reported in 1679 that Yarranton's proposal for 'Methodising of the fleet a new way' would 'save in the standing expenses 60,000*l* per an[num]'.[133] Sir Robert Southwell suggested in 1675 that his canal scheme would save nearly £2 million in the long run by lessening the amount of Newcastle coal shipped to London.[134] Richard Haines obtained a patent for his method of strengthening 'cider, perry, and the juice or liquors of wildings, crabbs, cherries, goosberries, currants, & mulberries' in 1684. Like many others, his patent made no formal arrangements to pay fees to the Exchequer. Significantly, however, Haines claimed that, if widely practised under his supervision, his patented cider production would 'raise hereby 800,000 Pounds *per Annum*...to the Publique Exchequer', without 'Raising any Burthensome Taxes, or putting their Subjects to heavy Charges'.[135]

If projects for introducing new taxes or improving tax levies were primarily and directly concerned with the raising of revenues, then those concerned with primary and secondary sectors—ranging from a fishing scheme, husbandry manuals, and the exploitation of patents for inventions to joint-stock companies and a secret method of organizing naval fleets—indirectly shared the same concern. Projects for encouraging domestic economic improvements were therefore promoted as great solutions, not only for encouraging home industries and thereby contributing to a favourable balance of trade, but also for relieving the poor while raising revenues to fund the emerging fiscal-military state.

This explains why, throughout the early modern period, promoters of those schemes variously highlighted their public service. In 1586, Robert Payne argued that his woad cultivation scheme would put the poor to work, prevent money being siphoned away in exchange for imports, and thus 'maie do goode to a great number without hurte to any'.[136] Some put more emphasis on the maintenance of a divinely appointed social order. In his manuscript treatise for introducing flax cultivation and other agrarian improvements, John Stratford argued that his schemes successfully employed the poor and thus enabled them to live 'according to God's ordinance by the sweat of their face in a more religious order'.[137] Thomas Trollop was even more explicit about divine and temporal benefits when promoting his hemp-manufacturing scheme in the 1560s:

> by the lawes of god, humanity, and reason, governours ought to procure their owne people to be vertuousely occupied and inryched by theyr travaile, rather then straungers, for therby they winne the love of the pore nedy people, & therby the blessing of

---

[132] John Smith, *England's improvement reviv'd* (1670), p. 104.

[133] Bodl., Carte MS 233, fol. 293v, Goodwin [Wharton] to [Thomas Wharton?], 9 July 1679.

[134] RS, MS/238, 'Sir Robert Southwell's Lecture at the Royal Society about Water', pp. 35–6. See also T. S. Willan, *River Navigation in England, 1600–1750* (London: Frank Cass, 1964), p. 12.

[135] Patent no. 231; Richard Haines, *Aphorisms upon the new way of improving cyder* (1684), sig. [Bv], pp. 8, 14 (quotations from p. 14, sig. [Bv]). He proposed, however, to impose a penny excise tax upon a quart of his patented cider. See ibid., p. 9.

[136] Smith, 'Woad Growing', p. 41. See also Thrisk, *Economic Policy and Projects*, pp. 18–20, 22, 38; Andrew McRae, 'Husbandry Manuals and the Language of Agrarian Improvement', in *Culture and Cultivation*, 35–62, pp. 54–6.

[137] Thirsk, *Economic Policy and Projects*, p. 104.

god to them and their posteritie, they also encourage the subjectes to love their prince and magestrates.[138]

Thus, he argued, his scheme would be 'inriching…our realme and common weale'.[139]

The conservation of the existing, divinely appointed social order was not the only way of invoking religious values. Under the influence of millenarianism, Samuel Hartlib and his allies aspired to act as instruments of the second coming of Christ, promoting radical reforms, including economic ones. Nor was the definition of the public monolithic. The meaning of terms like commonwealth was often ambiguous.[140] Some promoters under the early Stuarts in fact conflated the interests of the commonwealth and those of the Crown. Tobias Gentleman claimed that his 1614 fishery scheme 'will bring plenty unto his Majesties kingdoms, and be for the generall good of the Common-wealth, in setting of many thousands of poore people on worke' and 'the bringing in of gold, and money' from abroad. Benefits both to the Crown and to the commonwealth were mentioned, but it is not clear which was to come first.[141] Walter Morrell's abortive New Drapery project, to take another example, was expected to bring 'the great benefit…unto your highness and the commonwealth'. Here, in a very literal sense, the Crown's interests were placed before those of the commonwealth.[142] Asking for a monopoly over the manufacturing of ovens and a privilege to license maltsters who would use the ovens, Nicholas Halse assured the king that his supervision of the whole industry would prevent 'deceitful' maltsters from producing cheap, low-quality ovens dangerous to health and houses, and thereby raise £200,000 yearly. This would be 'for yo[u]r Ma[jes]t[ie]s owne honour and private good, & for the generall good of all the kingdome'.[143] Contemporary critics would have had no hesitation in suggesting that public service degenerated into the advancement of the king's (or his ministers') private good.

The idea of serving the monarch did not completely disappear.[144] After the execution of Charles I in 1649, however, the concept of the commonwealth became tied more closely to a republican polity; thus, certainly by the Restoration of

[138] Lynn Muchmore, 'The Project Literature: An Elizabethan Example', *Business History Review*, 45 (1971), 474–87, pp. 477, 480 (at p. 480). Trollop was urging influential London citizens to take up his scheme and promote it to the Privy Council. The article gives a transcription of the pamphlet (pp. 480–7). See also Felicity Heal and Clive Holmes, 'The Economic Patronage of William Cecil', in Pauline Croft (ed.), *Patronage, Culture and Power: The Early Cecils* (New Haven, CT: Yale University Press, 2002), 199–229, pp. 203, 225 n. 24.

[139] Muchmore, 'Project Literature', p. 481.

[140] Early Modern Research Group, 'Commonwealth: The Social, Cultural, and Conceptual Contexts of an Early Modern Keyword', *HJ*, 54 (2011), 659–87, p. 667.

[141] Tobias Gentleman, *Englands vvay to vvin vvealth, and to employ ship and mariners* (1614), pp. 7–8. See also Trinity College Dublin Special Collections, MS 842, 'Advertisements for Ireland' [n.d. temp. Jac.1], fols. 175–206, suggesting 'trade' and 'trafique' as the means 'to make them happie & to advance highly his Majties Revenuewe' (fol. 181).

[142] Zell, 'Walter Morrell', p. 659.

[143] BL, Egerton MS 1140, Sir Nicolas Halse, 'Great Britains Treasure', 1637, fols. 43–58v (at fol. 50v).

[144] See, for example, Samuel Weale's petitions to Queen Anne, Bodl., Rawl. D 808, fols. 19–20v, 35–36v; Nehemiah Grew's proposals dedicated to the same, Julian Hoppit (ed.), *Nehemiah Grew and England's Economic Development: The Means of Most Ample Increase of the Wealth and Strength of England 1706–7* (Oxford: Oxford University Press, 2012), pp. 3–5.

Charles II, notions such as the public good and the common good became more palatable as a denominator of public service when promoting innovative schemes. In 1655 Francis Mathew dedicated his river navigation scheme to Cromwell for '*the true advancement of the Publick good*'.[145] The Royal Lustring Company similarly claimed that it would 'promote the said Work to the Honour and Common Good of this Nation, by Imploying many Thousands of Poor People...as also by saving the vast Expences of Money that used to be sent Yearly into *France* for [importing] the said Commodities'.[146] The Company of the Mine Adventurers of England was promoted as '*An* Undertaking Advantagious for the *Publick Good*, Charitable *to the* Poor *and* Profitable *to every Person who shall be concerned therein*', although it ended in one of the most sensational business frauds to happen before the South Sea Bubble.[147]

Neither the 'godly' nor the 'public' components of the claim were monolithic or uncontested, therefore. Yet assertions of religious duty and public service survived well into the eighteenth century. This was an enduring feature of projecting as a category of action: be they policy proposals or business proposals for the emerging stock market, new schemes underlined their contribution to solving the persistent social, fiscal, and economic problems that were not fully resolved by the machinery of the state. Playing a role in governance was a fundamental characteristic of the economic project in early modern England.

CONCLUSION: PROJECTING—A UNIQUE HERITAGE OF EARLY MODERN ENGLAND?

The culture of projecting changed its institutional outlook from predatory monopolies and fiscal experiments under the early Stuarts to business partnerships under the later Stuarts and joint-stock companies in Defoe's Projecting Age. If we were to follow earlier accounts, this could be described as an evolution from state capitalism in which the Crown acted as a key stakeholder (rather than arbitrator) to another that is closer to modern corporate capitalism based on public offerings, stock trading, and financial journalism.[148] In tandem with the transformation of concrete projects, the discourse about them evolved too. Charting the joint evolution of projecting as activity and representation, we have thereby seen how this strand of incipient capitalism and its evolution were implicated in the fortunes of quasi-absolutism and wars, both domestic and international, and in long-term social, economic, and administrative developments. As we have covered many areas that are often studied separately, it is worth bringing together our findings once again. The following

---

[145] Francis Mathew, *Of the opening of rivers for navigation: the benefit exemplified by the two Avons of Salisbury and Bristol* (1655), sig. [A2v].

[146] *The charter of the Royal Lustring Company* (1697), p. [3]. For a general account, see Scott, *Joint-Stock*, vol. 3, pp. 73–89.

[147] [The Mine-Adventurers of England], *A new abstract of the mine-adventure* (1698). See Chapter 6.

[148] Fisher, 'Company Organization', p. 186; Larry Neal, *The Rise of Financial Capitalism: International Capital Markets in the Age of Reason* (Cambridge: Cambridge University Press, 1990).

paragraphs do so first by reflecting upon the *social reach* of both projecting activities and their promotional language, and then by juxtaposing the English trajectory with those of European counterparts.

The idea of the common good was already prominent in the discussions of market activities during the thirteenth century, as we have seen in the writings of theologians such as Aquinas and Olivi. Writers like Cotrugli reappraised the beneficial implications of mercantile activities for social welfare, trade balance, and public revenue. Yet, by the sixteenth century, the discussion was no longer restricted to normative or regulatory pronouncements upon market activities; nor was the invocation of the commonwealth ideal limited to the discussion of existing market routines. The idea was now invoked in the context of identifying problems and thereby promoting new, unrealized solutions for improving the status quo, schemes that drew on useful knowledge and expertise as potentially capable of solving society's problems, restoring lost glory, and even creating new realities. Visions of piety and public service were, furthermore, not just expounded in learned treatises or voiced in cautious appreciation of merchants' and craftsmen's stations, but came to be presented and co-opted by a dazzling array of actors across social and economic strata. In the first decade of the eighteenth century, for example, Samuel Weale, a former tax collector from Cornwall, now bankrupt and confined to the Rules of Fleet Prison in London, asked the archbishop of Canterbury to support his plan to launch a mining company to raise money for a charitable mission at home and across the colonies. This, the ageing projector approaching his eighties prayed, illustrated his readiness to 'make the best Improvem[en]t I can of my little time that remains for publick good'.[149]

That grandiose promoters like Weale came from across the social hierarchy is another striking feature of the projecting culture that emerged in early modern England. Take water management, for example. According to John Aubrey, William Englebert, who worked under Hugh Myddelton for the New River scheme to bring drinking water from Hertfordshire to London, was a 'poore-man' and 'projector'.[150] William Sandys, who made the Warwickshire Avon navigable after obtaining a patent in 1636, was an MP who sat in the Long Parliament (but was expelled as a monopolist).[151] Robert Southwell, who in 1675 offered a scheme for building canals to bring water to London, was a Fellow of the Royal Society and was a civil servant under the patronage of the Duke of Ormond, Lord Lieutenant of Ireland, whereas Andrew Yarranton, the projector for the Stour river navigation scheme, was a Presbyterian yeoman who fought against the king during the Civil Wars. William Squire and Thomas Steers submitted a bill for making the River Douglas

---

[149] Bodl., Ralw. D 808, fol. 88. The Rules of Fleet was an area outside the prison walls; debtors like Weale were able to take a lodging within the Rules upon paying a fee to prison keepers.

[150] John Aubrey, *Brief Lives, with an Apparatus for the Lives of our English Mathematical Writers*, ed. Kate Bennett (2 vols., Oxford: Oxford University Press, 2015), vol. 1, p. 606. Edmund Colthurst, who also worked on the same scheme, was an army veteran. See J. W. Gough, *Sir Hugh Myddelton: Entrepreneur and Engineer* (Oxford: Clarendon, 1964), p. 27, 32–7.

[151] Willan, *River Navigation*, pp. 26–7; Mary Frear Keeler, *The Long Parliament, 1640–1641: A Biographical Study of its Members* (Philadelphia, PA: American Philosophical Society, 1954), pp. 333–4.

navigable in 1719 and profited handsomely from the investment boom during the South Sea Bubble. Squire was an ex-mayor of Liverpool, Steers an engineer and a freeman and a town bailiff of the same city.[152]

Although a detailed prosopography of projectors across the period is beyond the scope of this study, these limited examples are enough to suggest that projectors cannot be seen as a well-defined socio-economic class.[153] We can instead compare projecting to local officeholding. There were approximately 9,700 parishes in seventeenth-century England; if each had a constable, two churchwardens, and two overseers for the poor, then there would have been more than 48,000 parish officers at any one time. According to Mark Goldie, this amounts to roughly one-twentieth of adult males contributing to local governance in any given year. To this picture we must add the growing number of incorporated cities and boroughs. While there were only forty-two of them in 1560, by 1640 the number more than quadrupled to 181, each an 'unacknowledged republic' overseen by the mayor, the recorder, clerks, justices of the peace, and other officers. While these local offices were open more frequently to prosperous middling sorts than to humble labourers, ideas relating to self-government, language about 'commonwealth' and the 'common good' were deeply embedded in local hierarchy.[154] The projecting of ambitious new proposals was likewise not readily open to the very humble. Yet the underlying promises of public service were never alien to inhabitants of England's city commonwealths.

Early modern commentators accordingly saw projectors as coming from diverse social and occupational groups. Thomas Heywood depicted the projector as a kind of chameleon who 'can change himselfe into as many shapes as Painters can doe colours, either a decayed Merchant, a broken Citizen, a silent Minister, an old maym'd Captaine, a foorejudged Atturney, a busie Soliciter, a crop-ear'd Informer, [or] a pick-thanke Pettyfogger'.[155] The occupation of the projector seemed so malleable that John Wilson declared that a character in his drama, the 'projecting knight' Sir Gudgeon Credulous, 'past all mens understanding':

> I have known him A Mathematician, a Pol, a Star-gazer, a Quack, a *Chaldean* [occult astrologer], a Schoolman, a Philosopher, an Asse, a broken grammarian, and most abominable Poet, and yet sick of all, but the Asse: and now at last (if I mistake him not) a most confident, ignorant Projectour.[156]

Projecting was not tied to any single economic class or occupational group, therefore. A publicly useful scheme could, if successful, become a sign of one's public virtue despite underlying elements of profit and attendant suspicion. In an important

---

[152] Willan, *River Navigation*, p. 59; Alec W. Skempton, et al. (eds.), *Biographical Dictionary of Civil Engineers in Great Britain and Ireland: 1500–1830* (2 vols., London: Thomas Telford, 2002), vol. 1, p. 653.

[153] See also projectors discussed in Webster, *Great Instauration*, ch. 5; Lindsay Sharp, 'Timber, Science, and Economic Reform in the Seventeenth Century', *Forestry*, 48 (1975), 51–79.

[154] See Mark Goldie, 'The Unacknowledged Republic: Officeholding in Early Modern England', in Tim Harris (ed.), *The Politics of the Excluded, c. 1500–1850* (Basingstoke: Palgrave, 2001), 153–94, p. 161; Withington, *Politics of Commonwealth*, pp. 8–9, 18–19.

[155] Heywood, *Machiavel*, sig. B2.4–5. See also James Shirley, *Triumph of peace* (1634), pp. 2–3.

[156] John Wilson, *The projectors. A comedy* (1665), p. 5.

study of medieval English markets and morality, James Davis has suggested that 'a development of a distinct entrepreneurial ethic among the mercantile and middling classes of England' would have been a piecemeal process that did not see 'dramatic shifts in general attitudes until the late eighteenth century'.[157] From a different angle, Jürgen Kocka has also suggested that the 'first far-reaching enhancement of capitalism's reputation came out of the spirit of the Enlightenment', because 'a disposition that was either skeptical of or hostile towards capitalism was dominant in Europe's theologies, philosophies, and theories of the state' well into the seventeenth century.[158] I hope that we can now qualify these suggestions with some confidence: by the late sixteenth century at the very latest, antecedents of Schumpeterian entrepreneurship emerged in England with a fanfare that paraded civic pride and moral rectitude. At best capable of complementing the fledgling early modern state, projects were pursued as a form of collective action oriented towards the public good, a course of action pursued by citizens from across social and economic strata.[159]

We have already seen that England's culture of projecting owed much to European antecedents. How unique was the English trajectory if we set it against continental rivals of the same period? This is a crucial question given that grandiose proposals for economic and fiscal reform abounded across sixteenth- and seventeenth-century Europe. Our knowledge on this count is still limited, but for the purpose of future comparative analysis we can briefly juxtapose English projecting culture with its European counterparts.

The rise of a tax state, the decoupling of public finance from prerogative, court patronage, and predatory fiscal extraction, unfolded in England under the influence of continental practices. The Spanish Netherlands revolted against the Hapsburg Crown partly because of its fiscal policies. The experience after the revolt varied across the Provinces, but Holland, the financial powerhouse of the Republic, moved away from fiscal impositions and developed a centralized system of taxation by the end of the sixteenth century; more than half of its tax revenue now derived from excise taxes levied on key consumer items such as wine, beer, peat, cattle, salt, and soap.[160] In France, by contrast, the so-called 'fisco-fianciers' backed by the Crown boasted large-scale syndicates of tax collectors, and

---

[157] James Davis, *Medieval Market Morality: Life, Law and Ethics in the English Marketplace, 1200–1500* (Cambridge: Cambridge University Press, 2012), pp. 30, 415 (quotation).

[158] Jürgen Kocka, *Capitalism: A Short History* (Princeton, NJ: Princeton University Press, 2016) [German original published in 2014], pp. 88, 87.

[159] In his *Der moderne Capitalismus* (first published in 1902) Werner Sombart noted the symbiosis between the state and emerging capitalism. On this point, see Philipp R. Rössner, 'New Inroads into Well-Known Territory? On the Virtues of Re-Discovering Pre-Classical Political Economy', in Rössner (ed.), *Economic Growth and the Origins of Modern Political Philosophy* (Abingdon: Routledge, 2016), 3–25, pp. 10–11.

[160] A useful survey is Marjolein 't Hart, *The Dutch Wars of Independence: Warfare and Commerce in the Netherlands, 1570–1680* (London: Routledge, 2014), ch. 7 (esp. pp. 150–1, 157). See also Wantje Fritschy, 'The Efficiency of Taxation in Holland', in Oscar Gelderblom (ed.), *The Political Economy of the Dutch Republic* (Farnham: Ashgate, 2009), 55–84, pp. 66, 68–9; Oscar Gelderblom and Joost Jonker, 'Public Finance and Economic Growth: The Case of Holland in the Seventeenth Century', *Journal of Economic History*, 71 (2011), 1–39.

their local operation attracted widespread public resentment during the seventeenth century. In Holland the collection of taxes was auctioned off to humbler collectors covering only small parts of a given municipality; their operation accordingly proved less socially divisive, and the resulting revenues provided a powerful security for raising money from local investors through voluntary loans, a marked contrast given that wealthy fisco-financiers were major lenders to the French Crown.[161] Borrowing from P. G. M. Dickson, Dutch financial historians have called this trajectory in Holland an earlier 'financial revolution'. England's public finances probably evolved under the successive influence of the French and Dutch models. Under Charles I, Thomas Wentworth in fact considered the French system of salt monopoly, *les gabelles*, as an important example to emulate. Just three decades later, George Downing, under the restored monarch, drew on the Dutch example when introducing Treasury Orders—an assignable instrument with annual interest.[162] Continental fiscal practices, therefore, provided vital contexts for the English trajectory.

Elements of divergence as well as emulation can be observed when it comes to poor relief, especially if we look into its proximity to domestic economic improvement. As noted earlier, market solutions to relief had been widespread at least since the emergence of Italian *monti di pietà* in the fifteenth century. In time of military exigency and severe dearth, these pawn-broking institutions made contingency loans to local rulers. Cosimo I de Medici was a cunning ruler, and he did something different from the late 1540s. Taking advantage of the excellent liquidity of the Florentine *monte di pietà*, he started using it as a major lender to the duchy.[163] The operation of these pawn-broking bodies was, however, rarely specifically geared towards the diffusion or commercial exploitation of useful knowledge. If we turn to sixteenth-century Hapsburg Castile, we find reformers such as Domingo de Soto and Miguel Giginta who proposed schemes for setting up hospitals and reforming poor relief. Their schemes contained elements of work discipline. Overall, however, their schemes were rarely linked expressly with import substitution or mercantile competition. The impression is confirmed by Castilian legal evidence. Under the royal sanction of 1552, any wanderers found begging without authorization were subjected to coerced labour, not in industrial production, but

---

[161] 't Hart, *Dutch Wars*, pp. 150, 165; Daniel Dessert, *Argent, pouvoir et société Grand Siècle* (Paris: Fayard, 1984), pp. 319–24, 365–6.

[162] For French and English comments on the unpopular *gabelles*, see Bibliothèque Nationale, Paris, Français 23355, Recueil de pièces relatives au règne de Louis XIII, fols. 198v–199; Roland Mousnier (ed.), *Lettres et mémoire adressés au Chancelier Séguier (1633–1649)* (2 vols., Paris: Presses Universitaires de France, 1964), vol. 1, pp. 264, 274, 345; Wentworth, *Strafforde's letters*, vol. 1, p. 193, Wentworth to Richard Weston, 31 January 1634. On the powerful Bonneau brothers, and the role their kinship networks played in the French salt monopoly and royal finance, see Daniel Dessert, *L'Argent du sel: Le Sel de l'argent* (Paris: Fayard, 2012), pp. 33, 42–7, 274–8. For Downing's role in emulating the Dutch financial revolution, see Desan, *Making Money*, pp. 249–51; Jonathan Scott, '"Good Night Amsterdam." Sir George Downing and Anglo-Dutch Statebuilding', *EHR*, 118 (2003), 334–56.

[163] See Menning, *Charity and State*, pp. 178–9, 259–61; Richard A. Goldthwaite, *The Economy of Renaissance Florence* (Baltimore, MD: Johns Hopkins University Press, 2009), pp. 469–79, 503, 526.

in the galley service.[164] The able-bodied poor in the Dutch Republic, by contrast, were put to work, for example on rasping imported Brazil woods to make dyestuff that was in turn needed for finishing cloths.[165] English debts to the Dutch experience, therefore, seem unmistakable, not only in the sphere of public finance, but also in the relative proximity between poor relief and mercantile priorities.

England's divergence seems even more pronounced when it comes to the relative significance conferred upon the improvement of *domestic* industries as opposed to the shipping of goods overseas. During the 1570s and 1580s, Venice's rulers received a number of proposals for reversing its economic decline, but these tended to focus less on industrial developments than on how to bring competent merchants to settle in the entrepôt, and how to channel the flow of taxable commodities away from rival ports into the Venetian harbour.[166] More broadly, Maria Fusaro has recently suggested that the Venetian Republic, England's competitor in the Mediterranean, 'remained paralysed' well into the late seventeenth century 'by its vision of Venice as an emporium whose role was that of middleman and whose revenue was derived mainly from customs and taxation on imports, exports and re-exports'.[167] Similar assessments have been passed down to the Dutch Republic. As soon as it broke away from the Hapsburg Empire in the 1580s, the Republic started using its legal privileges not so much for fiscal extraction as for encouraging technology transfer and product imitation. Yet the Republic is said to have lost its commercial rivalry against England partly due to its focus on entrepôt trade and processing, 'rather than primary production and manufacture'.[168] This was in

[164] Linda Martz, *Poverty and Welfare in Habsburg Spain: The Example of Toledo* (Cambridge: Cambridge University Press, 1983), pp. 5, 24, 26–8, 30, 67–70, 87–8; Michel Cavillac, 'Miquel Giginta et la délinquance urbaine', in Alexandre Pagès (ed.), *Giginta: de la charité au programme social* (Perpignan: Presses Universitaires de Perpignan, 2012), 107–22, pp. 107, 114, 117–19. Cf. David E. Vassberg, *The Village and the Outside World in Golden Age Castile: Mobility and Migration in Everyday Rural Life* (Cambridge: Cambridge University Press, 1996), pp. 157–8. An important exception to this rule was a proposal of Cristóbal Pérez de Herrera, which, though never put into practice, viewed the poor vagabonds as an able labour force capable of processing raw materials (wool) hitherto exported without processing at home. See Anne J. Cruz, *Discourses of Poverty: Social Reform and the Picaresque Novel in Early Modern Spain* (Toronto: University of Toronto Press, 1999), pp. 69–71.

[165] For an overview, see Jan de Vries and Ad van der Woude, *The First Modern Economy: Success, Failure, and Perseverance of the Dutch Economy, 1500–1815* (Cambridge: Cambridge University Press, 1997), pp. 656–9. On earlier examples before the revolt, see Paul Spicker (ed.), *The Origins of Modern Welfare: Juan Luis Vives, De Subventione Pauperum, and City of Ypres, Forma Subventionis Pauperum* (Oxford: Peter Lang, 2010), pp. 74, 78.

[166] See Benjamin Ravid, 'A Tale of Three Cities and their *Raison d'État*: Ancona, Venice, Livorno, and the Competition for Jewish Merchants in the Sixteenth Century', *Mediterranean Historical Review*, 6 (1991), 138–62, pp. 148–51, 153–4, 156–7. For similar policies in Genoa, see Thomas Allison Kirk, *Genoa and the Sea: Policy and Power in an Early Modern Maritime Republic, 1559–1684* (Baltimore, MD: Johns Hopkins University Press, 2005), pp. 185, 198.

[167] Maria Fusaro, *Political Economies of Empire in the Early Modern Mediterranean: The Decline of Venice and the Rise of England, 1450–1700* (Cambridge: Cambridge University Press, 2015), pp. 302, 339, 350 (quotation). For the centrality of maritime trade to the Venetian empire during the fourteenth and fifteenth centuries, see Noel Malcolm, *Agents of Empire: Knights, Corsairs, Jesuits and Spies in the Sixteenth-Century Mediterranean World* (London: Penguin, 2016) [originally published in 2015], pp. 17–19.

[168] Marius Buning, 'Between Imitation and Invention: Inventor Privileges and Technological Progress in the Early Dutch Republic (c. 1585–1625)', *Intellectual History Review*, 24 (2014), 415–27; David Ormrod, *The Rise of Commercial Empires: England and the Netherlands in the Age of Mercantilism,*

marked contrast to the English trajectory, in which burgeoning colonial settlements came to provide a ready market for cheap goods manufactured at home across increasingly specialized regional industries, some of which began as modest projects that Thirsk has studied.

Taken separately, therefore, few components in the English experience were altogether unprecedented. Yet taken together, the particular bricolage of fiscal, welfare, and mercantile practices that emerged in England by the late seventeenth century turned out to be distinct from those of its continental rivals (as much as they differed among themselves). In early modern England, projects for domestic economic improvement were pursued as means not only to enrich individual entrepreneurs and to fill the royal coffers, but also to advance welfare provision while improving the balance of trade and enriching the kingdom through the circulation of raw materials and semi-finished and finished goods, especially within the emerging empire. This is why Cary deemed '*England* and all its plantations to be one great Body', an economic circuit by which England was to 'become the Centre of Trade, and standing like the Sun in the midst of its Plantations [that] would not only refresh them, but also draw Profits from them'.[169] A suggestive list of English 'peculiarities' could of course be extended to include more structural factors, ranging from demography, resource endowment, and urbanization rate to real wage and occupational structure. Yet even this necessarily limited comparison suggests that England underwent such an evolution that Cary's *An essay* of 1695 soon became an influential source for continental rivals intent on emulating the English.

Can we go on to assert, with Slack, that England's inhabitants were more successful because they cultivated nothing less than a 'powerful "morality of cooperation" ', a unique cultural foundation that facilitated 'the "positive-feedback" effect of an improvement culture on economic growth'?[170] Early modern promoters from Hartlib to Hill would have recognized this buoyant vision to be similar to theirs: by God's providence or otherwise, England is destined to rule and excel.[171] The question of England's divergence is only tangentially relevant to this study; but it still beckons us to make sure that our analysis 'becomes something more than a beauty contest in which the winner always looks rather like the judge'.[172]

Schumpeter's conception of entrepreneurship is worth revisiting once again. In his view, entrepreneurs could in fact be as dubious as the projector in Jonsonian or

---

1650–1770 (Cambridge: Cambridge University Press, 2003), p. 337 (quotation); Arthur Westeijn, *Commercial Republicanism in the Dutch Golden Age: The Political Thought of Johan and Pieter de la Court* (Leiden: Brill, 2012), pp. 219–24; Slack, *Invention of Improvement*, p. 259.

[169] John Cary, *An essay on the state of England in relation to its trade, its poor, and its taxes for carrying on the present war* (Bristol, 1695), pp. 66–7, 70. Conversely, Cary believed New England to 'bring least Advantage' because its intra-colonial, inter-imperial trade took commodity flows and profits away from England. I thank Yuichi Hiono for conversation on this point.

[170] Slack, *Invention of Improvement*, pp. 240–1 (quotations), 253–4, 262. See also Mokyr, *Culture of Growth*, pp. 16, 18, 260, 296.

[171] Slack, *Invention of Improvement*, p. 243.

[172] James Belich, John Darwin, and Chris Wickham, 'Introduction: The Prospect of Global History', in James Belich et al. (eds.), *The Prospect of Global History* (Oxford: Oxford University Press, 2016), 3–22, p. 5.

Swiftian satire: 'a man, realizing the possibility of producing acceptable caviar from sawdust, sets up the Excelsior Caviar concern and makes it a success'. This is not from Swift, but from Schumpeter.[173] He even acknowledged (in a footnote) that 'Whether a given entrepreneurial success benefits or injures society . . . is a question that must be decided on the merits of each case.'[174] So it was also in early modern England. Individual success based on promises of public service did in fact undermine social cohesion by the end of Charles I's reign. Given that Schumpeter was well versed not only in 'canonical' authors such as Cantillon, Smith, Malthus, and Ricardo, but also in a broad range of what he called 'pamphleteers' and 'projectors', it is probable that his balanced assessment of entrepreneurship owed something to his reading of early modern project literature.[175] (His younger colleagues would soon 'discover' the concept of the projector as an antecedent of the Schumpeterian 'creative entrepreneur', who had a mixed reputation.)[176] More importantly for the central theme of this book, the history of projecting serves as a useful antidote to the whiggish narratives because it forces us to recognize that promises of moral action and positive feedback were then—as now—all too often prone to perversion and even abuse. Without *taming* ensuing abuses and negative feedback, any developmental potential of improvement culture and favourable structural conditions might well have been unsustainable. If we now pay closer attention to the negative undertones of the notions of project and projector, we can begin to unravel the taming of incipient capitalism as early modern contemporaries experienced it.

---

[173] Schumpeter, 'Creative Response', p. 154. Compare this with the projectors in Jonson's *The Devil is an Ass* or Swift's kingdom of Lagado. See pp. 82–3 below; Swift, *Gulliver's Travels*, pp. 180–1.

[174] Schumpeter, 'Creative Response', p. 153 n. 9.

[175] His discussion included the writings of Gerard Malynes, William Potter, William Petty, Andrew Yarranton, Nicholas Barbon, John Bellers, and John Cary. See Joseph A. Schumpeter, *Economic Doctrine and Method: An Historical Sketch*, tr. by R. Aris (London: Unwin, 1954) [German original published in 1914], pp. 24–32, 106; Joseph A. Schumpeter, *History of Economic Analysis* (New York: Oxford University Press, 1954), pp. 160, 284, 294, 347, 350, 363–4 and *passim*.

[176] Fritz Redlich, 'The Origin of the Concepts of "Entrepreneur" and "Creative Entrepreneur"', *Explorations in Entrepreneurial History*, 1(2) (1949), 1–7, pp. 3–6; Bert F. Hoselitz, 'The Early History of Entrepreneurial Theory', *Exploration in Entrepreneurial History*, 3 (1951), 193–220, pp. 200–4.

2

Broken Promises and the Rise
of a Stereotype

> If there had been no projects,
> Nor none that did great wrongs...
> How should we do for songs?
>
> *Witt's recreations augmented*
> (1641), sig. [X6v]–X7

One of the 'nonsense songs' published in 1641 thus juxtaposed projects with 'great wrongs', hinting that projects stood for all that had gone wrong under Charles I's Personal Rule.[1] Some five decades later, songs against Jacobite 'plots' could still tap into pejorative connotations of the term project. 'There is a cursed Project, grown common in the town, | As plaguy an invention as ever yet was known: | By the *Jacobitish* Crew and the Devil else knows who, | That try their tricks, the Land to vex, and Nation to undo'.[2] These songs remind us that the term 'project', something that only came into wider circulation towards the end of Elizabeth's reign, became a part of common parlance by the mid-seventeenth century; it became something that could be used, without much explanation, to comment on contemporary events in jocular or polemical fashion.

That the precarious private–public partnership gave rise to these negative overtones has been noted by historians of various stripes. As J. M. Treadwell suggests, an 'eccentric' like Defoe 'might still plead for the existence of the "honest" projector who aimed only at a just profit for his schemes; but for the public generally the projector was a simple fraud whose projects were cheats and whose profits came from preying upon unwary investors'.[3] 'The term Project... possessed connotations of fantasy and unfulfillability', John Christie has noted.[4] MacLeod has shown that until at least the later eighteenth century the reputation of the inventor was very much tainted by the negative image of projectors as 'calculating swindlers and cheats'.[5]

---

[1] For nonsense songs, see Noel Malcolm, *The Origins of English Nonsense* (London: Fontana Press, 1998).

[2] *Conscience by scruples, and money by ounces; or, new fashioned scales for old fashioned money* (1697). See also *Sport upon sport; or, the Jacobite tos'd in a blanket* [1692].

[3] J. M. Treadwell, 'Jonathan Swift: The Satirist as Projector', *Texas Studies in Literature and Language*, 17 (1975), p. 444.

[4] John Christie, 'Laputa Revisited', in John Christie and Sally Shuttleworth (eds.), *Nature Transfigured: Science and Literature, 1700–1900* (Manchester: Manchester University Press, 1989), p. 58.

[5] Christine MacLeod, *Heroes of Invention: Technology, Liberalism and British Industry, 1750–1914* (Cambridge: Cambridge University Press, 2007), p. 39. See also Julian Hoppit, *The Land of Liberty? England 1689–1727* (Oxford: Clarendon, 2000), p. 337.

In a similar way, Maximillian Novak has acknowledged that 'the word "project"…had a distinctly unsavoury connotation' during the long eighteenth century, 'being associated with unscrupulous schemes for getting money'.[6] These were the pejorative overtones that troubled the likes of Defoe, Cary, and Hill at the turn of the seventeenth century.

We thus know enough about the negative undertones *in general*. We know relatively little, however, about a more *specific*, yet richer social history behind the nonsense song of 1641: how the discourse about projects emerged and came to circulate widely in response to the parallel developments in concrete projects that we charted in Chapter 1; how, as built-in assumptions, negative connotations of the term came in turn to condition the promotion of economic improvement. The collective taming of capitalism cannot be reconstructed unless we tackle these topics.

Neither literary studies nor the analysis of project proposals can handle these tasks on their own. Over the last few decades, we have seen the emergence of the so-called 'new economic criticism' among literary scholars; it has turned critical attention to economic themes explored in Renaissance dramas; the literary qualities of mercantilist treatises have also been investigated.[7] The main goal of these studies has been to offer fresh interpretations of the texts under investigation, to relate literary genres to wider socio-economic developments, and ultimately to throw new light on the nature of the English Renaissance. Our next task, then, is to draw on this literature and start exploring the *social repercussions* of literary engagements with incipient capitalism.

To do this, I propose to combine the analysis of literary texts with that of manuscripts and rumours and their circulation that has been put to excellent use by historians of early Stuart politics.[8] If we trace early literary depictions of the projector and their reappropriations in letters, petitions, songs, and manuscript copies of parliamentary speeches, we can then begin to understand how the image of the projector came to circulate as a kind of literary character, and how it was quickly taken up by a striking range of actors, from petitioners and members of parliament to London Puritans and even rural protestors. We can, in other words, start investigating what we might call the *social circulation* of distrust, and what it did (and

---

[6] Maximillian E. Novak, 'Introduction', in Maximillian E. Novak (ed.), *The Age of Projects* (Toronto: University of Toronto Press, 2008), 3–25, p. 3.

[7] Important works include Theodore Leinwand, *Theatre, Finance and Society in Early Modern England* (Cambridge: Cambridge University Press, 1999); Ceri Sullivan, *The Rhetoric of Credit: Merchants in Early Modern Writing* (Madison, NJ: Fairleigh Dickinson University Press, 2002); Jonathan Gil Harris, *Sick Economies: Drama, Mercantilism, and Disease in Shakespeare's England* (Philadelphia, PA: University of Pennsylvania Press, 2003); Valerie Forman, *Tragicomic Redemptions: Global Economics and the Early Modern English Stage* (Philadelphia, PA: University of Pennsylvania Press, 2008); David Landreth, *The Face of Mammon: The Matter of Money in English Renaissance Literature* (Oxford: Oxford University Press, 2012). Useful overviews include Barbara Sebek, 'Global Traffic: An Introduction', in Barbara Sebek and Stephen Deng (eds.), *Global Traffic: Discourses and Practices of Trade in English Literature and Culture from 1550 to 1700* (Basingstoke: Palgrave, 2008), 1–15; Peter F. Grav, 'Taking Stock of Shakespeare and the New Economic Criticism', *Shakespeare*, 8 (2012), 111–36.

[8] See, for example, Thomas Cogswell, '"The Symptoms and Vapors of a Diseased Time": The Earl of Clare and Early Stuart Manuscript Culture', *Review of English Studies*, new ser., 57 (2006), 310–36, pp. 321–8; Noah Millstone, *Manuscript Circulation and the Invention of Politics in Early Stuart England* (Cambridge: Cambridge University Press, 2016). See also works cited on p. 83 n. 74 below.

what it did not do) to the practices of improvement. As we shall see, analytical tools drawn from sociology and social psychology turn out to be useful when assessing the impact of social circulation. Promises of public service were so badly and repeatedly broken under the early Stuarts that they gave rise to the powerful stereotype about projecting that could be taken up even by the nonsense song of 1641 with which we began this chapter.

REFORMATION AND PROJECTING
UNDER THE LATE TUDORS

A good starting point is the immediate aftermath of England's break with Rome. Some of the underlying problems of projecting had already manifested themselves in the ensuing dissolution of the monasteries and subsequent waves of schemes for 'discovering concealed Crown lands'.

The dissolution of the monasteries and the Crown's takeover of church lands, made possible by a succession of statutes between 1536 and 1547, led to the unprecedented transfer of church lands to the Crown. This extraordinary measure was justified in terms of the 'reformation' of alleged abuses. As the statute of 1536 put it, this was an act of rectifying 'manifest synne, vicious carnall and abhomynable lyvyng' allegedly committed in monasteries and chantries, whereby corrupt monks 'maye be compelled to lyve relygyously for *Reformac[i]on* of ther lyves'.[9] The idea of discovering and reforming abuses, and the practice of expropriating land for the 'common good', both predated the break with Rome.[10] Yet their economic implications now took on new significance. As much as two-thirds of the monastic properties were confiscated and disposed of by the end of Henry VIII's reign. Yet at the time of dissolution, numerous church lands and smaller endowments were left unrecorded or deliberately concealed. Local resistance, driven as much by financial as by religious motives, was ubiquitous.[11] Still quietly enjoyed by churches or discreetly sold to private owners for profit, these lands in principle owed arrears to the Crown. These 'concealed Crown lands' thus later became targets of the waves of detective campaigns, launched by entrepreneurial patentees close to the court. These hunts, the 'discovery of concealed lands', emerged in large numbers from the early years of Elizabeth's reign. Between 1559 and 1561, six grants

---

[9] 27 Hen. VIII, c. 28, section 1 (my italics). See also Joyce Youings, *The Dissolution of the Monasteries* (London: Allen, 1971), pp. 42–9, 191; Wrightson, *Earthly Necessities*, pp. 141–5.

[10] On expropriation, see Susan Reynolds, *Before Eminent Domain: Toward a History of Expropriation of Land for the Common Good* (Chapel Hill, NC: University of North Carolina Press, 2010), pp. 34–42. For earlier calls for 'reforming' abuses, see, for example, Simon Fish, *A supplicacyon for the beggers* ([Antwerp?], [1529?]), sig. [5v]. I thank Debora Shuger for drawing my attention to this. The broader issue of pre-Reformation anticlericalism is a hotly debated topic. See Peter Marshall, 'Anticlericalism Revested? Expressions of Discontent in Early Tudor England', in Clive Burgess and Eamon Duffy (eds.), *The Parish in Late Medieval England* (Donington: Shaun Tyas, 2006), 365–80; P. R. Cavill, 'Anticlericalism and the Early Tudor Parliament', *Parliamentary History*, 34 (2015), 14–29.

[11] Wrightson, *Earthly Necessities*, pp. 141–2; Ethan Shagan, *Popular Politics and the English Reformation* (Cambridge: Cambridge University Press, 2003), ch. 7.

for searching for concealed lands were made to the master of the royal armoury, Sir George Howard. More grants followed in the subsequent decades.[12] Enterprising individuals thus pursued opportunities, promising revenue for the Crown while also seeking their private gain. This was the parasitic relationship of private and public interests that would characterize a broader range of projects in the coming generations.

Not all the projects that emerged subsequently were couched as the reformation of alleged abuses. But it is important to highlight the proximity between such fiscal devices and schemes primarily concerned with economic improvement. As one promoter so eloquently advised the monarch later in 1612:

> Whatsoever you abate...at home comes out of yo[u]r Subjects purse[,] and be it never so just is hardly drawn from them w[i]thout clamo[u]r or murmure[;] but what you catch or winne out of the Seas, or worke & fetch out of the earth, and so therew[i]th gaine by pollicie of entercourse [i.e. international trade]...magnifies the glorie and wisdome of the State and infinitly inriches yo[u]r kingdome and people, who will then be as readie as able to requite [i.e. repay] this yo[u]r gratious care w[i]th full handes.

Here we have a clear picture of interconnection between fiscal exaction, on the one hand, and the generation of wealth achieved through economic improvement, on the other hand. They were construed as complementary means for advancing the kingdom's glory.[13] If the long-term benefits of import substitution did not answer the short-term fiscal needs of the Crown, then the fiscal exploitation of prerogative could accelerate accordingly. The breakdown of such desperate fiscal experiments would, in turn, invite fresh attention to economic means as a way of enriching the nation.

Such dynamics played out under the later Tudors as well. In his *Discourse of the Commonweal*, Thomas Smith commended import substitution as a remedy for the 'decay of the good towns of this realm'; yet he was quick to add another dimension by asking, 'Might not the King's Highness be glad of any aid whereby he might find a thousand persons [employed] through the whole year and burden his treasure with never a penny thereof?'[14] Elizabethan administration of patents likewise embraced competing priorities. When establishing and reviving an industry to reduce imports, the custom receipts from foreign imports of the same commodities often decreased. Promoters of new schemes accordingly tried to 'forestall criticism' by offering fees or 'a percentage of their profits to offset any loss that might be incurred in custom revenues'.[15] Herein lay the possibility that the granting of patents could in itself become a financial aid to the Crown, not just a means for developing domestic industries.

---

[12] Thirsk, 'Crown as Projector', pp. 307–8; C. J. Kitching, 'The Quest for Concealed Lands in the Reign of Elizabeth I', *TRHS*, 5th ser. 24 (1974), 63–78, at p. 66.

[13] TNA, SP 14/71, fol. 164. See also Robert Cotton's policy documents in BL, Cotton MS, Cleopatra F VI, *passim*.

[14] Thomas Smith, *A Discourse of the Commonweal of This Realm of England*, ed. Mary Dewar (Charlottesville, VA: University Press of Virginia, 1969), pp. 121, 122.

[15] Thirsk, *Economic Policy and Projects*, pp. 57–8.

The Crown's financial interest in fact lent itself to something rather more dubious. Examination was frequently undertaken to test the feasibility of proposed inventions and projects; but, under English law, the administration of patents was a matter of registration.[16] Scrutiny could be thorough; but it was selective rather than codified and compulsory, so it could give way to other considerations. The demands of court politics and patronage further complicated the problem. Obtaining a patent was neither cheap nor easy;[17] courtiers with power and purse accordingly came in to play the role of intermediaries. Because issuing potentially lucrative patents cost little to the Crown, the granting of such patents came to serve as a ready method for rewarding courtiers and royal servants to whom the sovereign was indebted, financially or otherwise. After all, rewarding courtiers was a backbone of Tudor and early Stuart political life. Grants were expected to benefit these men as well as the population.[18] Patenting was thus embedded in the politics of patronage as well as in the political economy of the emerging empire.

This was how, under Elizabeth, patents were granted for 'inventions' and 'mysteries' of dubious technical credibility. We know that the London Goldsmiths' Company and the Pewterers' Company enjoyed the power to monitor quality standards and to conduct searches nationwide much earlier. Yet they did not have a monopoly over production; nor did they generally use their authority to suppress non-members.[19] By contrast, in order to recoup profits, Elizabethan courtier patentees and their syndicates vigorously prosecuted the force of their patents. Instead of pursuing technology transfer or industrial revival to achieve import substitution, some patentees were therefore permitted to monopolize a whole industry with the power to levy fines from producers or vendors or both. Echoing the ostensible reformation of monastic abuse that permitted Henrician dissolution, Elizabethan and early Stuart promoters obtained grants 'on the basis of allegations of abuses in existing industries which would receive regulation by the patentee'.[20] The colour of reforming abuses lent itself to the de facto devolution of economic regulation and the indirect taxation of commodities and business operations. These regulatory schemes were joined by financial schemes that had little or nothing to do with production processes. Some, like a tonnage duty for ships passing through the

---

[16] MacLeod, *Patent*, p. 41.

[17] Procuring a patent cost approximately £70 and various gratuities to officials and lawyers concerned. Yet enforcing the privilege often proved even more costly. See ibid., p. 76; Sean Bottomley, *The British Patent System during the Industrial Revolution: From Privilege to Property* (Cambridge: Cambridge University Press, 2014), pp. 44–6, 59–65.

[18] David Harris Sacks, 'The Countervailing of Benefits: Monopoly, Liberty, and Benevolence in Elizabethan England', in Dale Hoak (ed.), *Tudor Political Culture* (Cambridge: Cambridge University Press, 1995), pp. 277–91.

[19] Ian Anders Gadd and Patrick Wallis, 'Reaching beyond the City Wall: London Guilds and National Regulation, 1500–1700', in S. R. Epstein and Maarten Prak (eds.), *Guilds, Innovation and the European Economy, 1400–1800* (Cambridge: Cambridge University Press, 2008), 288–315, pp. 293–4, 298.

[20] Ian Archer, 'The London Lobbies in the Later Sixteenth Century', *HJ*, 31 (1984), p. 32. Promoters also proposed to reform abuses in governmental institutions such the Exchequer and the Navy. See M. W. Beresford, 'The Common Informer, the Penal Statutes and Economic Regulation', *EcHR*, new ser. 10 (1957), 221–38; National Maritime Museum, SER/77, 'Abuses and Disorders in Her Majesties Navy', January 1598 [non-foliated section of the volume].

English Channel and the new licensing of inns, taverns, and alehouses, were devised in the 1570s in order to fund the state-led rebuilding of Dover Harbour. In order to raise revenues directly for the Crown, other schemes were promoted that cunningly, and controversially, redefined taxable lands and levied 'arrears' from their proprietors.[21]

Elizabethan England thus witnessed a variety of projects. Some, such as the discovery of concealed Crown lands, were primarily about the increase of Crown revenue. Others were concerned with the relief of the poor and the suppression of vagrancy, yet with the potential for benefitting the realm by producing items that could at best reduce imports. Virtually all of them purported to advance the public good and the commonweal, by setting up new industries, by employing the poor, by reducing alleged abuses, or by raising revenues for the Crown.

These late Tudor initiatives also speak of the institutional arrangement and its problems that would characterize the early Stuart experience. All of these depended on the initiatives and supervision of a group of promoters and their subcontractors who would slice profit out of the venture. If prudently undertaken, these schemes were expected to satisfy all those parties involved, uniting them in the advancement of royal glory and material welfare without unlawful damage to any good subjects. Not only were the global priorities of these schemes at best ambiguous, but there was a profound mixing of the public and the private: public interests as well as those of the Crown were closely allied with, and depended upon, the will of private undertakers. What is crucial here is not only that competing goals were often pursued simultaneously through a single scheme, but also that the royal prerogative could be fiscally exploited for the Crown's or courtiers' benefits at the expense of public welfare. This was precisely what happened under the early Stuart kings, which caused grievances and occasioned complaints about evil projectors.

THE ESCALATION OF FISCAL EXPLOITATION UNDER THE EARLY STUARTS

The promotion of controversial projects escalated after the accession of James I to the English throne, partly due to the worsening of Crown finance, and partly due to his difficult relationship with parliament. James's larger, more costly royal household, and his liberal patronage of Scottish as well as English subjects, exacerbated the royal debts that he had inherited from Elizabeth; within five years of his reign, the total debt grew almost six times to £597,337.[22] The Crown's relationship with parliament was hardly straightforward; the 1610 Great Contract, by which the Commons was to offer an annual subsidy of £200,000, foundered. James being unwilling to summon parliament again, his government sought ways of raising

---

[21] See Frederick C. Dietz, *English Public Finance, 1558–1641* (2nd edn, London: Frank Cass, 1964), pp. 44–7; Thirsk, 'Crown as Projector', pp. 312–14.

[22] Menna Prestwich, *Cranfield: Politics and Profits under the Early Stuarts* (Oxford: Clarendon, 1966), p. 16; Diana Newton, *The Making of the Jacobean Regime: James VI and I and the Government of England* (Woodbridge: Boydell, 2005), pp. 35–6.

money independently. Thus, various grants and monopolies were considered by ministers such as Robert Cecil as a dual solution for patronage and for public finance, with potential benefits even to the wider economy. In fact, one-fifth of all the 'petitions for grace' that sought James's discretion and patronage in the first thirteen years of his English reign were projects of some kinds.[23] This was the context in which the notion of the project gained currency as a heuristic concept for ordering precedents and policy recommendations.

Another aspect had to do with penal statutes that defined criminal offence. Virtually every imaginable aspect of economic life was touched by penal statutes, and enterprising promoters proposed to 'discover abuses' by suing defaulters at courts of record. A manuscript list of 'all generall Penall Statutes now in force', compiled under James, suggests that many of these regulations had become obsolete 'through the alteration of tymes and change of mens Manners' and were now 'very hard to be Kept and observed'. Yet, due to the vigorous prosecution of the same, the 'Kinges Ma[jes]t[ie]s subjects daily doe incurre' fines and forfeiture of goods, with proceeds split between the Crown and the informer. If an informer decided to go to a fair or a market pretending to buy cheese and meat, and stopped for a restorative pint at an alehouse on the way back, that brief tour would have allowed him to inspect cheesemongers and others—and potentially persecute them—at least under thirty-one active penal statutes.[24]

No parliament was held between 1610 and 1621, except for two months in 1614. By 1620, James had issued no fewer than fifty proclamations. Some were concerned with economic 'improvement' and the regulation of trade, and others with the production of goods such as tin wares, starch, tobacco, and gold threads.[25] Claims to introduce new inventions and novelties, or to prevent abuse in industries served as pretexts for raising revenues without parliament. So, John Chamberlain complained in 1620 that 'proclamations and patents' had 'become so ordinary that there is no end, every day bringing forth some new project or other'.[26] Some of them caused a national scandal. By the force of the inns patent of 1617, Sir Giles Mompesson compelled some 1,200 innkeepers to purchase licences priced between £5 and £10 each, suing 4,000 of them who refused to comply. One of Mompesson's agents allegedly pretended to be an innocent traveller, tricked an alehouse keeper

---

[23] The figures are based on Richard Hoyle, 'The Masters of Requests and the Small Change of Jacobean Patronage', *EHR*, 126 (2011) 544–81, pp. 564–5, and are corroborated by John Cramsie's extensive survey of the papers of Robert Cecil, Julius Caesar, Robert Cotton, Thomas Egerton, and Lionel Cranfield. See John Cramsie, *Kingship and Crown Finance under James VI and I, 1603–1625* (Woodbridge: Boydell, 2002), pp. 108–50. For background, see also Cramsie, *Kingship*, pp. 29–35, 50–61.

[24] Butchers were under four statutes (4 Hen. VII, c. 3; 24 Hen. VIII, c. 9; 4 Ed. VI c. 19; 1 Jac. I, c. 22); cheesemongers under three (3 Ed. VI, c.21; 1 et 2 Phi. et Mar. c. 5; 1 Jac. I, c. 25); the sale of ale under three of them (1 Jac. cap 9; 4 Jac. c. 4, 5); fairs and markets under seven statutes, and weights and measures under fourteen. See full details at Beinecke Library, Osborn fb158, Miscellaneous Parliamentary Manuscripts, item 1, 'A Briefe Collection of all generall Penall Statutes now in force', n.d. [*c*.1607]. See also Beresford, 'The Common Informer'.

[25] Cramsie, *Kingship*, p. 165 n. 89.

[26] William Hyde Price, *The English Patents of Monopoly* (Boston, MA: Houghton, Mifflin & Co., 1906), p. 30 n. 4). Cf. Cramsie, *Kingship*, pp. 165–6, 177; Thirsk, *Economic Policy and Projects*, p. 100.

into sheltering him and his horse for the night, and later forced the manager to pay for a licence for inn-keeping.[27]

There was a backlash once James summoned a parliament in 1621. A group of MPs led by Sir Edward Coke scrutinized a wide range of monopolies upon receiving petitions against almost 100 projects; many of them were declared illegal or inconvenient and James issued a proclamation against them. Mompesson fled to the continent to escape apprehension; his knighthood and membership of parliament were rescinded.[28] Mompesson's associate in the inn patent, Sir Francis Michell, was ordered by the Commons in 1621 'to ride on a lean jade backward through London'; here is an example of a shaming ritual being meted out to an odious projector, by parliament, in a way that would be readily understood even by humbler sorts of inhabitants.[29] Little wonder that only one patent for invention, presumably an uncontroversial one, was granted that year.[30] Exeter merchants had been able to obtain a de facto monopoly of overseas trade in 1606; in contrast, Bristol's Society of Merchant Venturers failed to do the same in 1621.[31] The Commons debate in 1621 led to the famous Statute of Monopolies of 1624, which confirmed the existing common law position that all monopolies were contrary to the ancient and fundamental laws of the realm (21 Jac. 1, c. 3).[32]

This, however, did not terminate the granting of monopolies or the fiscal exploitation of royal prerogative more broadly. Due to provisos added by the Lords, the 1624 statute neither invalidated existing grants nor prohibited prospective grants of monopolies in sectors such as printing, the licensing of taverns, and the production of saltpetre, gunpowder, alum, and glass. Monopolies for specific inventions of up to fourteen years (not extending to a whole industry) also remained legal, and so were, crucially, grants for new offices and corporations. These were to be permitted in so far as they would 'not [be] contrary to law, nor mischievous to the State...or hurt of trade, or generally inconvenient'.[33] A war against

---

[27] John P. Ferris and Andrew Thrush (eds.), *House of Commons, 1604–1629* (6 vols., Cambridge: Cambridge University Press, 2010), vol. 5, p. 350; HEH, HA, Parliament Box 2(11), a conference of both houses about Mompesson, 8 March 1621. William Cockayne's project for dyed cloth was another notorious project. See Astrid Friis, *Alderman Cockayne's Project and the Cloth Trade: The Commercial Policy of England in its Main Aspect* (Copenhagen: Levin & Munsgaard, 1927); B. E. Supple, *Commercial Crisis and Change in England, 1600–1642: A Study in the Instability of a Mercantile Economy* (Cambridge: Cambridge University Press, 1959), pp. 32–51, 247–8.

[28] Linda Levy Peck, *Court Patronage and Corruption in Early Modern England* (London: Unwin Hyman, 1990), p. 34; Elizabeth Read Foster, 'The Procedure of the House of Commons against Patents and Monopolies', in W. A. Aiken and B. D. Henning (eds.), *Conflict in Stuart England* (New York: Jonathan Cape, 1960), 59–85; Cramsie, *Kingship*, pp. 168–79.

[29] Martin Ingram, 'Ridings, Rough Music and Mocking Rhymes in Early Modern England', in Barry Reay (ed.), *Popular Culture in Seventeenth-Century England* (London: Croom Helm, 1985), 166–97, pp. 171, 173.

[30] Patent no. 19. This grant to Hugh Myddelton for a draining engine was probably intended to aid the New River Company under his supervision. For background, see J. W. Gough, *Sir Hugh Myddelton: Entrepreneur and Engineer* (Oxford: Clarendon, 1964), esp. pp. 20–1.

[31] David Harris Sacks, *The Widening Gate: Bristol and the Atlantic Economy, 1450–1700* (Berkeley, CA: University of California Press, 1991), pp. 216–17.

[32] Derek Hirst, *Authority and Conflict: England 1603–1658* (London: Edward Arnold, 1986), p. 128; Chris R. Kyle, '"But a New Button to an Old Coat": The Enactment of the Statute of Monopolies, 21 James I cap.3', *Journal of Legal History*, 19 (1998), 203–23, p. 216–19.

[33] 21 Jac. I, c. 3 (sections 5 to 12).

Spain broke out in the same year, ushering in the prospect of fiscal breakdown. Charles I dissolved the 1626 parliament without being able to procure the funds that he badly needed. Then 'a whole world of projectors offered themselves', as one member of parliament put it.[34] The infamous 'forced loan' of 1626–7 emerged in this context.[35] Within four weeks of the dissolution, a new Privy Council committee was appointed for reducing government expenditure and increasing revenues, which considered a monopoly over tobacco imports among many other schemes.[36] As it was later recalled with anger during the Long Parliament, projectors were now able to 'shelter themselves under the Name of a Corporation', 'a Vizard [i.e. a mask worn in theatre plays] to hide the Brand made by that good Law in the last Parliament of King James', a reference no doubt to the 1624 statute.[37] In the end, the Statute of Monopolies did little to curb controversial projects.

This was how England entered the 1630s—a decade that saw probably the fullest and most controversial fiscal exploitation of the patent system alongside other branches of royal prerogative. As we noted in Chapter 1, fifty-seven patents for inventions were granted between 1634 and 1638. The increase of projects relating to primary and secondary industries was unmistakable for the master of the Charterhouse, George Garrard: 'Here are abundance of new Projects on Foot upon Sea-Coal, Salt, Malt, Marking [*sic*] of Iron, Cutting of Rivers, Setting up a new Corporation in the Suburbs of *London*' and many others.[38] Among these was the Westminster Soap Company, to which we shall turn shortly. Monopolistic patents were also granted to raise revenue from such commodities as tobacco, beer, and wine. Custom farms and other kinds of economic regulation were devolved to courtiers to raise revenues.[39] An Elizabethan statute against cottages without four acres of ground (31 Eliz. 1, c. 7) was enforced vigorously. By the 1630s, even prisoners were allegedly mobilized 'as principal Commissioners to call the People before them...and compound with them'.[40] The conspicuous rise in patents for invention was a part of this broader exercise of prerogative, including the levying of ship money, forced loans, and the vigorous exploitation of forest laws.[41]

---

[34] Millstone, *Manuscript Circulation*, p. 222.

[35] Richard Cust, *The Forced Loan and English Politics, 1626–1628* (Oxford: Oxford University Press, 1987); Millstone, *Manuscript Circulation*, pp. 119–21.

[36] University of London Library Special Collection, MS 195, A journal book of the proceeding of his majesty's commissioners for...increasing of the revenue, fols. 11, 13; G. E. Aylmer, 'Buckingham as an Administrative Reformer?', *EHR*, 105 (1990), 355–62; Thomas Cogswell, '"In the Power of the State": Mr Anys's Project and the Tobacco Colonies, 1626–1628', *EHR*, 123 (2008), 35–64.

[37] John Rushworth, *Historical collections* (8 vols., 1721), vol. 4, p. 34. See also Thirsk, *Economic Policy and Projects*, pp. 99–100; Cramsie, *Kingship*, p. 178.

[38] Wentworth, *Strafforde's letters*, vol. 2, p. 55, Garrard to Wentworth, 23 March 1636. See a list of industrial and agricultural patents excerpted from the papers of Charles's attorney general, Sir John Bankes (Bankes MS) at the Bodleian, in Peck, *Court Patronage*, pp. 266 n. 18, 267 n. 19.

[39] Ronald G. Asch, 'The Revival of Monopolies: Court and Patronage during the Personal Rule of Charles I, 1629–40', in Ronald G. Asch and Adolf M. Birke (eds.), *Princes, Patronage, and the Nobility: The Court at the Beginning of the Modern Age* (Oxford: Oxford University Press, 1991), 357–92, pp. 370–4.

[40] Thirsk, 'Crown as Projector', pp. 345–6, 348; Wentworth, *Strafforde's letters*, vol. 2, p. 117 (quotation). Cf. Valerie Pearl, *London and the Outbreak of the Puritan Revolution: City Government and National Politics, 1625–43* (Oxford: Oxford University Press, 1961), p. 21.

[41] See Dietz, *Public Finance*, pp. 234–45, 242, 262–5, 282–4; Kevin Sharpe, *The Personal Rule of Charles I* (New Haven, CT: Yale University Press, 1992), pp. 120–4, 249–62. For ship money and the

We need not assume that the king and his counsellors suffered from myopia, leading the king's claim of prerogative 'to land beyond the limits of reason and credibility'.[42] It is true that Charles ordered the seizing of libraries of eminent individuals such as Robert Cotton and Edward Coke, lest their manuscripts of legal precedents and commentaries should cause 'inconveniences' for royal policies. Yet we must also remember that privy councillors such as Sir Robert Heath and Sir John Coke expressed considerable reservations and scepticism when discussing potentially lucrative, yet controversial schemes such as the tobacco monopoly proposed by the grocer William Anys.[43] More broadly, the early Stuart monarchs did issue proclamations in 1603, 1610, 1621, 1623, and 1639 in order to cancel certain monopolies and projects that had proved controversial.[44] Their advisors, too, expressed considerable reservations towards the very idea that made so many controversial projects possible, 'That absolute pr[e]rogative...maie be exercised and executed by any Subjecte to whome power may be given by the King'. A year before the commencement of his Personal Rule, Charles had in fact been asked to declare that 'everie free Subjecte of the Kingdome hath a fundamentall proprietie in his goods and a Fundamentall libertie of his p[er]son'.[45] Thomas Wentworth even sought to reform some prevailing abuses of prerogative.[46] Yet even such initiatives had to be devolved to commissioners. As one proposal put it, projects' ills were to be remedied by 'Certayne spetiall projects for the discovery of abuses'.[47] There was much complaint about enclosures; the ensuing decay of tillage and depopulation were handled in a similar fashion, by commissioners authorized to levy fines.[48] Caroline attempts at administrative reform thus reinforced, rather than replaced, the institutional and rhetorical practices that caused grievances in the first place. Reforming attempts did exist, but they did little to stop further grievances.

forest laws, see Dietz, *English Public Finance*, p. 274; Michael J. Braddick, *The Nerves of State: Taxation and the Financing of the English State, 1558–1714* (Manchester: Manchester University Press, 1996), pp. 83–4, 140–3; Thirsk, 'Crown as Projector', pp. 339–47.

[42] Thirsk, 'Crown as Projector', p. 310.

[43] Sharpe, *Personal Rule*, p. 655–7; Cogswell, 'Anys's Project', p. 46.

[44] *Stuart Royal Proclamations*, ed. James F. Larkin and Paul L. Hughes (2 vols., Oxford: Clarendon, 1973, 1983), vol. 1, pp. 11–14, 511–19, 568–70, vol. 2, pp. 673–6; *Commons Debates 1621*, ed. Wallace Notestein, Frances Helen Relf, and Hartley Simpson (7 vols., New Haven, CT: Yale University Press, 1935), vol. 7, Appendix B, pp. 491–6. See also Elizabeth's 'golden speech', in T. E. Hartley (ed.), *Proceedings in the Parliaments of Elizabeth I* (3 vols., Leicester: Leicester University Press, 1981), vol. 3, pp. 288–97, 412–14.

[45] Harvard Law School, Small Manuscript Collection, 'A coppie of a wrytten discourse by the Lord Chauncellor Elsemere, concerning the Royal Prerogative', n.d. [April 1628], non-foliated. See also *Commons Debates 1628*, ed. Robert C. Johnson et al. (4 vols., New Haven, CT: Yale University Press, 1977–8), vol. 3, pp. 74–5, 81, 85, 87, 90–1.

[46] Asch, 'Revival of Monopolies', pp. 378–88.

[47] Baker Library, Kress MS 85, 'Certayne spetiall projects for the discovery of abuses', n.d. See also G. E. Aylmer, 'Attempts at Administrative Reform', *EHR*, 72 (1957), 229–59, p. 232; Peck, *Court Patronage*, p. 141.

[48] Record Office for Leicestershire, Leicester, and Rutland, 11D53/XIII/6, 'The Coppie of Articles to be enquried of conc[e]rning deceaie [i.e. decay] of Tillage, and depopulation', 1635; Sharpe, *Personal Rule*, pp. 472–3.

THE 'PROJECTOR': THE CHARACTER
AND ITS SOCIAL CIRCULATION

The unprecedented rise of printed attacks against the projector, captured in the *ESTC* (Fig. 1.3 and Fig. 1.4), was a direct response to the numerous controversial projects discussed above. The Long Parliament abolished the Star Chamber in July 1641. This in effect ended censorship by the Stationers' Company, and led to an outburst of printing.[49] During the 1640s, the total number of publications increased threefold (18,247 titles) from the average of the previous two decades (6,015 titles).[50] In contrast, forty-seven titles appeared in the 1640s with the titular words 'project' and 'projector', a fivefold jump (as opposed to threefold) from the average of 9.5 titles in the previous two decades. As parliamentarians reintroduced a de facto control of the press in 1643 to curb the torrent of polemical writing, a substantial proportion of pamphlets appeared during 1641 and 1642.[51] Within these two years 31 per cent (5,700 titles) of the total publication appeared; as for project-related publication, thirty-one were published within this two-year window, representing 66 per cent (as opposed to 31 per cent) of the decade's total number. Thus, the boom in the 1640s, as seen in the *ESTC*, owed much to the great explosion between 1641 and 1642, and the surge of pamphlets with titular words like 'projects' and 'projectors' was proportionally greater, and more intensive, than the general boom in printing activities at the time.

Three subgenres are noticeable within the booming anti-project literature. The first is targeted attacks on the wine monopoly concentrating on 1641 and 1642. 'What effect their Project took, is known to all', declared a printed attack on the 'Projectors for Wine' monopoly, Alderman Abell and Richard Kilvert: 'with what power (without pitty) they executed the force of their Patent, what charge & trouble divers of the best Vintners…were put too both by fines and commitments [i.e. imprisonment]'.[52] The second is the satirical denunciation of the projector. Some described him as a ridiculous, deceitful, and evil promoter pretending public service. As Thomas Heywood declared in his pamphlet Machiavel: 'he is every thing but what he should bee, *Honest*'.[53] At the same time, the controversial imposition of prerogative was singled out for criticism. Thomas Brugis suggested in his *The discovery*

---

[49] See Joad Raymond, *Pamphlets and Pamphleteering in Early Modern Britain* (Cambridge: Cambridge University Press, 2003), chs. 5–6. George Thomason's monthly acquisition of prints from 1640 is discussed in Michael J. Braddick, *God's Fury, England's Fire: A New History of the English Civil Wars* (London: Allen Lane, 2008), p. 153.

[50] John Barnard and D. F. McKenzie (eds.), *The Cambridge History of the Book in Britain, vol. IV, 1557–1695* (Cambridge: Cambridge University Press, 2002), Appendix 1, Statistical tables, Table 1. Annual book production 1475–1700, pp. 782–3.

[51] Limits of this press control are examined by Michael Mendel, 'De Facto Freedom, De Facto Authority: Press and Parliament, 1640–1643', *HJ*, 38 (1995), 307–32, pp. 327–32.

[52] *A dialogue or accidental discourse betwixt Mr. Alderman Abell, and Richard Kilvert, the two maine projectors for wine* (1641), p. 7.

[53] Thomas Heywood, *Machiavel. As he lately appeared to his deare sons, the moderne proiectors* (1641), sig. [Bv].

of a proiector (1641) that the typical projector would endeavour 'to propose the faire outside of a reformation':

> this he begins with a Petition to his Majestie, with such mighty pretences of enriching the Kingdome, that he dares most impudently to affirme that it shall bring to his Majestie... many thousands yearely; yea, and imployment for all the poore people of the Realme (which how well all those late *Projects* have effected, I leave to judicious censures).[54]

Another printed attack against projectors highlighted their alleged encroachment upon others' right to pursue their trade: 'It was not well done of you to undo | So many poore men, of your owne trade too.'[55]

The third component of the sharp rise of the terms 'project' and 'projector' in the 1640s is as a political and polemical weapon. Whereas one pamphlet spoke of 'devilish designes and killing projects of the Society of Jesuites', John Wildman warned his readers of the danger of 'Putney proiects... the serpentine deceit of their [readers] pretended friends in the Armie'.[56] As these polemical uses remind us, the negative connotations of the terms 'project' and 'projector' penetrated society by impinging upon different aspects of social and political life.

We should now go beyond title pages and start exploring the birth and the initial circulation of the image of the projector. After all, the explosion of anti-project literature between 1641 and 1642 owed much to existing patterns of complaints that had already been aired under Elizabeth. The promoter of woad-growing, Robert Payne, whom we encountered in Chapter 1, was accused by his neighbours of being 'a slanderer, and a stirrer up of many and great contentions':

> That he wold arrest men in sundrie Courtes upon false suggestions: That he made himselfe a promoter, and tooke at one tyme tenne clothes in her Majesties name, as supposed to be forfeyted, & sold them to his owne use, without triall whether the sayd Clothes were forfeyted or not.

Payne was also said to have sued his neighbour in the Star Chamber; the promoter here meant a professional accuser or informer.[57] Sometimes complaints were couched more explicitly as deviations from Christian, as well as commonwealth, ideals. The Speaker, Robert Bell, urged the queen in 1571 to 'prohibit the evill practises of purveiors [for woods],... takeinge under pretence of her Majestie's service what they woulde at what price they themselves like'.[58] The same parliamentary session also debated a de facto monopoly of Bristol's overseas trade by the

---

[54] Thomas Brugis, *The discovery of a proiector* (1641), sig. B2–[B2v].
[55] *The copie of a letter sent from the roaring boyes in Elizium* (1641), sig. [A3].
[56] *Camiltons discoverie, of devilish designes and killing projects of the Society of Jesuites of later yeares* (1641); John Wildman, *Putney proiects. Or the old serpent in a new forme* (1647).
[57] Nottingham University Manuscripts and Special Collections, Mi 5/165/124, 'The copie of the Testimonie of the men of Wicomb against Payne', 2 March 1592. See also R. S. Smith, 'A Woad Growing Project at Wollaton in the 1580s', *Transactions of the Thoroton Society of Nottinghamshire*, 65 (1961), 27–46, p. 38.
[58] Hartley (ed.), *Proceedings*, vol. 1, p. 202. For a similar complaint under James I, see Surrey History Centre, Loseley MSS, LM/1777, 'Grievances by Patents', [n.d., after 1603].

city's Society of Merchant Venturers. Mr Young of Bristol argued that the grant had been made 'without the consent of the Major or Commons' of the town.[59] The underlying criticism of monopoly, which Thomas More had discussed earlier in his *Utopia*, went back to Aristotle's *Politics*; the critique of avarice or 'covetousness', which had been dealt with extensively by Tudor commentators such as Thomas Becon and Richard Morison, drew upon rich traditions of medieval poems and sermons that explored the question of morality in the community of Christians.[60] The underlying notions of the common good and its perversion were never a monopoly of prominent statesmen, scholars, and clergy; as Phil Withington has shown, this language had long been used to designate the common good of local communities or *communitates*—the vibrant nurseries of civic, participatory politics. By the mid-fifteenth century, urban communities such as Coventry and Bristol had in fact already spoken of the 'weal of the Commune', and 'prejudice of common weal'.[61] Such was the depth of England's associational culture upon which rested both projectors' promises and public responses to their perversions.

Tudor writers tended, however, to focus far less on those seeking patents for setting up new industries or introducing new ways of raise revenues than on themes such as enclosure and 'depopulation'.[62] When complaints about patents were voiced, as they were in the 1571 parliamentary session, their arguments were not yet based on established literary personae of the abuser. Instead, the idea of the commonwealth and its perversion by greed, ambition, and covetousness was often invoked to denounce the actions that were deemed to be against public interests. During the final Elizabethan parliament in 1601, for example, MPs launched unprecedented criticisms of monopolies and other grants, and disparaged 'monopolists' and other 'bloodsuckers of the commonwealth'.[63] The earliest biography of William Cecil, written by an anonymous author close to him sometime between

---

[59] Hartley (ed.), *Proceedings*, vol. 1, pp. 160, 202, 207, 209–11, 238, 245, 436, at p. 160; Sacks, *Widening Gate*, pp. 201–4.

[60] Andrew McRae, *God Speed the Plough: The Representation of Agrarian England, 1500–1660* (Cambridge: Cambridge University Press, 1996), pp. 25–8; David Harris Sacks, 'The Greed of Judas: Avarice, Monopoly, and the Moral Economy in England, ca. 1350–ca. 1600', *Journal of Medieval and Early Modern Studies*, 28 (1998), 263–307, esp. pp. 264–9.

[61] Phil Withington, *Society in Early Modern England: Vernacular Origins of Some Powerful Ideas* (Cambridge: Polity, 2010), pp. 139–40; Withington, *Politics of Commonwealth*, pp. 10–11, 65–7.

[62] For criticisms of enclosure and covetousness, see respectively Thomas More, *A fruteful, and pleasant worke of the beste state of a publyque weale, and of the newe ysle called Vtopia*, tr. Ralphe Robynson (1551) sig. [C8v], [D1v]; Thomas Becon, *The Catechism of Thomas Becon*, ed. John Ayre (Cambridge: Cambridge University Press, 1844), pp. 115–16. For general discussions of Tudor literature on economic issues, see Arthur B. Ferguson, *The Articulate Citizen and the English Renaissance* (Durham, NC: Duke University Press, 1965); Whitney R. D. Jones, *The Tudor Commonwealth, 1529–1559: A Study of the Impact of the Social and Economic Developments of Mid-Tudor England upon Contemporary Concepts of the Nature and Duties of the Commonwealth* (London: Athlone Press, 1970); Laura Caroline Stevenson, *Praise and Paradox: Merchants and Craftsmen in Elizabethan Popular Literature* (Cambridge: Cambridge University Press, 1984); Neal Wood, *Foundations of Political Economy: Some Early Tudor Views on State and Society* (Berkeley, CA: University of California Press, 1994).

[63] Hartley (ed.), *Proceedings*, vol. 3, pp. 370–8, 381–6, at p. 375.

May 1599 and March 1603, noted that Cecil wanted to support only 'reasonable' and 'lawful' 'suits to Her Majesty':

> he would never recommend their suit: as some would sue for monopolies, some for concealments [of Crown lands], some for innovations against law, all which he protested against, terming them cankers of the commonwealth[.][64]

By the end of Elizabeth's reign, then, promoters of new controversial schemes of all kinds were gaining a bad reputation. Some of them, those who obtained monopoly grants, had been singled out for criticism as monopolists.[65] The deep-rooted notions like commonwealth and the common good served to censure deviations from these amorphous ideals. Yet there was not yet an overarching typology capable of depicting and mocking a wide range of promoters (including monopolists) who perverted the promise of using economic initiatives to public ends.

The figure of the projector emerged, and captured many of these existing concerns when the powerful image of alchemical projection was combined with the revived tradition of character writing. Literary depictions of the alchemist and the alchemical transmutation of base metals into gold were widespread during the sixteenth century, in England as in Europe. The subject found its way into satirical verse and prose, in comedy and tragedy, in didactic prose, rogue literature, and in prose fiction; they were 'present in nearly every genre that gained prominence' at the time.[66] This powerful image was then adapted for *character writing*, a genre of writing that was being revived from the classical, Theophrastian tradition at the turn of the sixteenth century. The first English printed 'character book', Joseph Hall's *Characters of vertves and vices* (1608), alluded to the courtier projector in the figures of 'The Distrustfull' and 'the Ambitious': the former 'full . . . of strange projects, and far-fetched constructions', who 'loves no payments but reall', while the latter 'hath projected a plot to rise' but 'never cares how to come downe'.[67] The elaboration of literary characters was never unique to early modern England. Promoters of proposals to reverse the fortune of the declining Spanish Empire were satirized by writers such as Cervantes and Quevedo as *arbitristas*; in France, tax-farmers who lent to the Crown were denounced as the *laquais-financier* or the servile financier.[68] As Hall put it, these character types were often presented as

---

[64] *The Anonymous Life of William Cecil, Lord Burghley*, ed. Alan G. R. Smith (Lewiston, NY: Edwin Mellen, 1990), p. 108.

[65] The first citation of the term 'monopolist' in the *OED* is in 1601. See *OED*, s.v. monopolist, *n*.

[66] Stanton J. Linden, *Darke Hierogliphicks: Alchemy in English Literature from Chaucer to the Restoration* (Lexington, KY: University Press of Kentucky, 1996), pp. 62–71, 103, at p. 103. For European sources of inspiration, see Tara E. Nummedal, *Alchemy and Authority in the Holy Roman Empire* (Chicago: University of Chicago Press, 2007), ch. 2, esp. 50, 55–62.

[67] Joseph Hall, *Characters of virtues and vices in two bookes* (1608), pp. 150–1, 153–4. For background and closer analysis of the genre, see Richard A. McCabe, *Joseph Hall: A Study in Satire and Meditation* (Oxford: Clarendon, 1982), pp. 53–61, 110–30; Benjamin Boyce, *The Theophrastan Character in England to 1642* (Cambridge, MA: Harvard University Press, 1947). I thank Professor McCabe for advice on the topic.

[68] Steven Hutchinson, 'Arbitrating the National *Oikos*', *Journal of Spanish Cultural Studies*, 2 (2001), 69–80, pp. 69–70; Jean Vilar Berrogain, *Literatura y economía: la figura satírica del arbitrista en el Siglo de Oro* (Madrid: Revista de Occidente, 1973); Daniel Dessert, 'Le "Laquais-financier" au Grand Siècle: Mythe ou réalité?', *Dix-Septième Siècle*, 122 (1979), 21–36; Françoise Bayard, 'L'Image littéraire du

'image[s] without the offence', images that would leave desirable impressions on readers' minds. The ultimate goal was to induce readers by the pleasure of reading to 'abjure those vices' hitherto permitted, to seduce them to 'fall in love with...goodly faces of vertue', and to let them dust off 'anie little touch of these evils'.[69] Sharing such reforming ambitions, theatre plays also began to feature the projector. In Ben Jonson's play *Volpone*, performed in 1607, Sir Would-be Politick was poised to launch 'certaine projects' on 'tinder-boxes', marine insurance, and 'water-workes', which would make 'a fortune'.[70] Jonson soon elaborated the theme in *The Alchemist* (1610) and *The Devil is an Ass* (1616).

A brief look at the latter illustrates how early Stuart writers invested the character with rich meanings and invited the audience to learn to abjure vices, as Hall put it. One of the protagonists, the projector Merecraft, was depicted as a relentless schemer. He declared, 'Sir, money's a whore, a bawd, a drudge...I'll have her!'[71] He proposed to set up, inter alia, monopolies for 'making wine of raisins' (2.1, ll.97–110) and toothpicks (4.2, ll.39–54). Merecraft set up a bogus 'academy for women' to teach them fashionable Spanish deportment (2.8, ll.26–8), and proposed to erect the 'Office of Dependancy', which would help gentlemen avoid duels (3.3, ll.62–88). He also tried to swindle the main character of the play, the gullible Fizdottrel, by drawing him and others into a bogus drainage scheme. He thus declared that he would 'drive his patent for him. | We'll take in citizens, commoners, and aldermen, | To bear the charge, and blow 'em off again' (2.1, ll.41–3).[72]

Embedded within what we might call the generic image of the projector as the greedy conman were more specific critiques about those who would pervert legal privileges for their own advantage while pretending to serve the public. One revealing example is Lady Tailbush in the same play. Tailbush and Merecraft were 'on a project for...venting | Of a new kind of fucus—paint, for ladies— | To serve the kingdom: wherein she...hopes to get the monopoly | As the reward of her invention' (3.4, ll.48–54). When asked 'What is her end in this?', Merecraft replied:

---

fincancier dans la première moitié du XIIe siècle', *Revue d'Histoire Moderne et Contemporaine*, 33 (1986), 3–20.

[69] Hall, *Characters*, sig. [A5v], [A6v]. John Earle's celebrated character book, *Microcosmographie* (first published in 1628) does not seem to contain the character of the projector. Some others did, for example, Brugis, *Discovery* and Heywood, *Machiavel*. See also Benjamin Boyce, *The Polemic Character 1640–1661* (Lincoln, NE: University of Nebraska Press, 1955), esp. pp. 82–6.

[70] Ben Jonson, *The Cambridge Edition of the Works of Ben Jonson*, ed. David Bevington et al. (7 vols., Cambridge: Cambridge University Press, 2012), vol. 3, pp. 130 (4.1, ll.40–126). The close link between character writing and early Jacobean plays is discussed in Richard A. McCabe, 'Ben Jonson, Theophrastus, and the Comedy of Humours', *Hermathena*, 146 (1989), 25–37.

[71] Jonson, *Works of Ben Jonson*, vol. 4, p. 510 (2.1, l.1–6). In this and the paragraphs that follow in the main text, particular acts, scenes, and lines are cited in round brackets.

[72] Some of these schemes may have alluded to actual schemes promoted in the period. See R. C. Evans, 'Contemporary Contexts of Jonson's "*The Devil is an Ass*"', *Comparative Drama*, 26 (1992), 140–76. See also Julie Sanders, *Ben Jonson's Theatrical Republics* (Basingstoke: Macmillan, 1998), p. 113–20; Richard Dutton, 'Jonson's Satiric Styles', in Richard Harp and Stanley Stewart (eds.), *The Cambridge Companion to Ben Jonson* (Cambridge: Cambridge University Press, 2000), 58–71, pp. 68–9; Jonson, *Works of Ben Jonson*, vol. 4, pp. 469, 471–3.

'Merely ambition, | Sir, to grow great, and court it with the secret, | Though she pretend some other' (3.4, ll.55–7).[73] Indeed she declared to her friend that 'If we once see it [the patent] under the seals…we will live, I' faith, | The examples o' the town, and govern it' (4.2, ll.10–14). But when Tailbush was paid compliments by a stranger about her 'great undertakings', she replied with an air of modesty: 'If I can do my sex by 'em any service | I've my ends, madam' (4.3, ll.14–17). A striking contrast was therefore drawn between her greed and pretended willingness to serve the public. Lurking beneath this exploitation was the abuse of royal patents, something, as we have seen, that caused a great stir in the early Stuarts' reigns.

Even before the explosion of printed literature against the projector in the 1640s, however, this emerging character reached far beyond London theatres and printed pages, permeating both the upper and the lower social strata. In recent decades, social, political, and literary historians have shown how closely print, manuscript, and oral media were knitted together, permeating court, cities, and countryside.[74] The image of the projector gained currency in this vibrant culture of multifarious communication. The dynamic process of social circulation is well captured by the case of Sir Giles Mompesson. A client of the powerful Duke of Buckingham, Mompesson was one of the most active patentees under James I, amassing more than five grants, including controversial ones concerned with the licensing of inns and a monopoly over the production of silver wires. When the parliament of 1621 was opened, Sir Dudley Digges declared that 'wee are not now sicke of diseases of former tymes, but we are sicke of new diseases Projects, unworthy to trample upon the ground of this famous kingdome, but the kinge that is famous pater & our Jupiter, loves huntinge, but not such grounds'.[75] First to be hunted down was Sir Giles Mompesson, to whom substantial time was devoted. '[N]one more doth plague the Cuntrye then Projects and Monopolies,' Thomas Crewe continued the discussion, but 'Sir Giles Mompesson's Patents was [*sic*] the first…of all grievances'.[76] Note that the notion of the nefarious projector—still about twenty years old—served in Westminster as a byword for those causing grievances; two parliamentary diaries also recorded the same discussion over Mompesson, who 'amongst others was a principal projector', epitomizing 'a new disease called proiectors, who have robbed the subiects and trampled the lawes of the kingdome'.[77]

---

[73] The term 'ambition' carried pejorative connotations. See *OED*, s.v. ambition, *n.* 1: 'The ardent (in early usage, inordinate) desire to rise to high position, or to attain rank, influence, distinction or other preferment'.

[74] Adam Fox, *Oral and Literate Culture in England, 1500–1700* (Cambridge: Cambridge University Press, 2000), pp. 302–7; Alastair Bellany, *The Politics of Court Scandal in Early Modern England: News Culture and the Overbury Affair, 1603–1660* (Cambridge: Cambridge University Press, 2002), pp. 94, 102–11, 117; Andrew McRae, *Literature, Satire and the Early Stuart State* (Cambridge: Cambridge University Press, 2004), pp. 36–44; Arnold Hunt, *The Art of Hearing: English Preachers and their Audiences, 1590–1640* (Cambridge: Cambridge University Press, 2010), p. 118; Andy Wood, *The Memory of the People: Custom and Popular Senses of the Past in Early Modern England* (Cambridge: Cambridge University Press, 2013), pp. 247–56.

[75] HEH, HA, Parliament Box 2(11), speeches at the conference regarding the business concerning Sir Giles Mompesson, 8 March 1620 [no foliation].

[76] Ibid.

[77] *Commons Debates 1621*, vol. 2, p. 180, vol. 6, p. 40. See also another manuscript report on 'the Censure' of both houses, BL, Add. MS. 22,587, fol. 20.

Also significant for the present discussion is the resilient memory of his wrongdoings, and the way it continued to circulate outside the metropolis. By 1631, Mompesson (who had fled England) had come back, resuming his business of projecting. Now acting as an agent of his sister-in-law Lady Villiers, he enclosed part of the Forest of Dean and dug coal pits there. When Mompesson embarked on the work, however, he reportedly faced revealing local opposition. 'The foresters grieved with this attempt of his…whom they termed to be an odious projector'. The protest developed into a 'rough music' of a sort; 'by sound of drum and ensigns in most rebellious manner, carrying a picture or statue apparelled like Mompesson and with great noise and clamour [they] threw it into the coalpits which the said Sir Giles had digged'.[78] By 1630, within a quarter of a century after the publication of Hall's *Character*, the image of the projector thus became an integral part of common parlance, something that could be picked up even by angry rural inhabitants. Assertions of public service could at best lend legitimacy to profit-bearing enterprises despite their medieval association with avarice, ambition, and sin; yet promises of advancing the public good and reformation all too often lent themselves to the aggrandizement of the Crown's and others' interests at the public's expense. The character of the projector enabled England's inhabitants to engage with this fundamental problem of England's culture of improvement.

Seen from a modern analytic perspective, it is of course possible to suggest that the underlying problem owed much to the lack of conceptual distinction that scholars would take for granted today. Elizabethan and early Stuart statesmen often promoted measures that permitted rent-seeking alongside what we would today recognize as Schumpeterian enterprises underpinned by genuine technical skills or business innovations.[79] Yet the problem was not conceptualized in terms of the choice between 'harmful' rent-seeking and more 'constructive' enterprises. The character of the projector, which began to serve as a powerful frame of reference, was hardly neutral or descriptive. Rather, the concept operated more like 'a form of symbolic knowledge intrinsic to public life', what social psychologists would now call 'social representations'.[80] Social representations, in order 'to make the unfamiliar familiar, connect to everyday experience and established belief'. So, for example, a study of the public understanding of genetically modified food across Europe in the 1990s found that the public understood modified tomatoes according to the familiar trope of the 'contagious and monstrous'.[81] The resulting trope did not have to be 'correct' or 'accurate', but 'just needs to be *good*

---

[78] HMC, *Manuscripts of the Earl Cowper* (3 vols., London: HMSO, 1888–9), pp. 429–30. Cf. Ingram, 'Ridings', pp. 171, 173.

[79] For the definitions of rent-seeking and Schumpeterian innovation, see pp. 8, 52.

[80] Sandra Jovchelovitch, 'Social Representations, Public Life, and Social Construction', in Kay Deaux and Gina Philogène (eds.), *Representations of the Social: Bridging Theoretical Traditions* (Oxford: Blackwell, 2001), 165–82, p. 165.

[81] Wolfgang Wagner and Nicole Kronberger, 'Killer Tomatoes! Collective Symbolic Coping with Biotechnology', in Deaux and Philogène (eds.), *Representations of the Social*, 147–64, pp. 148, 150–1, 161. Public understanding of satellite space technology in the 1950s and nuclear energy in the 1960s are also mentioned as parallel examples.

to think'.[82] Similarly, 'all of the church's enemies, atheists, Dissenters and papists, were associated in sin' in the later seventeenth century. Intricate politics of religious toleration could thus be presented with polemical, often comforting clarity.[83] The notions of project and projector likewise explained grievances—something that resulted from a close symbiosis of public and private interests in the early modern political economy and state-formation—primarily through the familiar alchemical metaphor, comparing the perpetrators to promoters of alchemical projection.

Decrying the sinful papist or the fraudulent projector served a variety of purposes. It made it possible to stigmatize certain individuals or groups as unreliable, enhance the credibility of those who offered counsel, and give comforting clarity in a complex society, drawing the line between the sinful and the virtuous, the deceitful and the credible.[84] Somewhat like scientists who can claim to understand the intricacy of biotechnology, for example, Francis Bacon examined petitions and suits concerned with inventions and industries as attorney general and later as lord chancellor. Thus he remarked: 'Many ill Matters and Projects are undertaken; And Private *Sutes* doe Putrifie the Publique Good. Many Good Matters are undertaken with Bad Mindes...that intend not Performance.'[85] Disapproving of the projector's moral deficiencies would have helped to enhance his own credibility as a legal advisor. As recently as 2014, Lynn Hunt suggested that 'the "iron curtain" between historians and psychology...remains standing'.[86] The curtain has begun to be lifted. Medieval and early modern historians are now drawing on social psychological studies of social representations while interrogating their theoretical assumptions.[87] I build on this strand of research, and use the projector stereotype as a shorthand for the multifaceted, evolving, social representation of the projector. Beyond the *ESTC* and the patent records lies a rich social history of early modern actors *engaging with* the emerging stereotype, which was predominantly pejorative.[88]

---

[82] Wagner and Kronberger, 'Killer Tomatoes', p. 150. See also Sandra Jovchelovitch, *Knowledge in Context: Representation, Community and Culture* (London: Routledge, 2007), esp. pp. 59, 111, 119.

[83] John Spurr, *The Restoration Church of England, 1646–1689* (New Haven, CT: Yale University Press, 1991), p. 235. For the earlier period, see Peter Lake, 'Anti-Popery: The Structure of a Prejudice', in Richard Cust and Ann Hughes (eds.), *Conflict in Early Stuart England: Studies in Religion and Politics, 1603–1642* (London: Longman, 1989), 72–106, at pp. 81–2, 90–2; Peter Lake, 'Anti-Puritanism: The Structure of a Prejudice', in Kenneth Fincham and Peter Lake (eds.), *Religious Politics in Post-Reformation England* (Woodbridge: Boydell, 2006), 80–97.

[84] Cf. Spurr, *Restoration Church of England*, pp. 236, 277–8.

[85] Francis Bacon, *The Essayes or Counsels, Civill and Morall*, ed. Michael Kiernan (Oxford: Clarendon, 1985), p. 150 (cf. p. 75 'Of Innovations'). See also Cramsie, *Kingship*, p. 215; Peck, *Court Patronage*, p. 161.

[86] Lynn Hunt, *Writing History in the Global Era* (London: Norton, 2014), pp. 101–7 (quotation from p. 107).

[87] See, for example, Bronach Kane, 'Social Representations of Memory and Gender in Later Medieval England', *Integrative Psychological and Behavioural Science*, 46 (2012), 544–58; Mark Knights, 'Historical Stereotypes and Histories of Stereotypes', in Christian Tileagă and Jovan Byford (eds.), *Psychology and History: Interdisciplinary Explorations* (Cambridge: Cambridge University Press, 2014), 242–67. Cf. Vlad Glăveanu and Koji Yamamoto, 'Bridging History and Social Psychology: What, How and Why', *Integrative Psychological and Behavioural Science*, 46 (2012), 431–9 (an introduction to a special issue on 'Bridging History and Social Psychology').

[88] My case study of projecting contributes to emerging comparative studies of stereotypes in early modern England. Some of the parallel case studies will be published in Peter Lake and Koji Yamamoto

The social circulation of the projector stereotype had one consequence of great importance: the shaping of the self-identity of promoters. The process is somewhat analogous to the way in which 'Puritan' identity was forged. Like the character of the Puritan whom Patrick Collinson studied, the projector as a social identity came to exist 'by virtue of being perceived to exist, most of all by their enemies, but eventually to themselves and to each other'.[89] So in the absence of established stereotypes, few Tudor promoters guarded themselves against the danger of being perceived as a projector. Thomas Trollop, who authored the earliest surviving English printed proposal for setting up a new industry (*c.*1563), said nothing of the suspicion that his audiences (the London mayor, aldermen, and the privy councillors) might have had of promoters like him. He instead anticipated the criticism that making the poor work in linen manufacturing could end with the neglect of 'plowe & tyllage'.[90] Neither the 1549 manuscript version nor the 1581 printed edition of Thomas Smith's *Discourse of the Commonweal* dealt at any length with pre-existing stereotypes of the projector. Nor does Richard Hakluyt's propaganda literature for colonial plantations indicate any effort to distance itself from negative stereotypes.[91]

By contrast, from the middle of James's reign, and certainly by Charles's Personal Rule, the negative stereotype of the projector had clearly begun to affect the self-identity and conduct of promoters. In 1616, William Cockayne, the promoter of dyeing and dressing cloth, dedicated to James a (lost) play in which cloth dressers and others 'spake such language as Ben Jonson put in theyre mouthes'.[92] In 1623, the godly reformist Thomas Scott published a pamphlet titled *The proiector*. This was an ironic title, as the book was about godly humanist reform. Playing with the growing public antipathy towards projectors, Scott declared that 'I propound a Project more profitable, more gainefull, more necessarie': 'if now I should propound some admirable project, how to raise great summes of mony, filling the Exchequer...without drayning the Country bogges below, I should be welcome to Court'.[93] This awareness separated the projecting culture after the early Stuarts' reign from its Tudor predecessors. Following Erving Goffman and medical sociologists after him, I would suggest that the emerging projector stereotype gave rise to clear *stigma consciousness* among those who were exposed to the danger of being stereotyped.[94] This is a key finding in that it urges us to move beyond the analysis

---

(eds.), *Papists, Puritans and Projectors: Stereotypes and Stereotyping in Early Modern England* (Manchester: Manchester University Press, under contract).

[89] Patrick Collinson, 'Ben Jonson's *Bartholomew Fair*: The Theatre Constructs Puritanism', in David L. Smith, Richard Strier, and David Bevington (eds.), *The Theatrical City: Culture, Theatre and Politics in London, 1576–1649* (Cambridge: Cambridge University Press, 1995), 157–69, at p. 158.

[90] Lynn Muchmore, 'The Project Literature: An Elizabethan example', *Business History Review*, 45 (1971), 474–87, at p. 487.

[91] Smith, *Discourse of the Commonweal*. I wish to thank David Sacks for this information based on his research for David Sacks, 'Richard Hakluyt's Navigation in Time: History, Epic, and Empire', *Modern Language Quarterly*, 67 (2006), 31–62.

[92] *CSPD 1611–1618*, p. 373.   [93] Thomas Scott, *The proiector* (1623), pp. 18, 19, 21 (at p. 18).

[94] The concept is adopted from Erving Goffman, *Stigma: Notes on the Management of Spoiled Identity* (Englewood Cliffs, NJ: Prentice Hall, 1963). Cf. Bruce G. Link and Jo C. Phelan, 'Conceptualizing Stigma', *Annual Review of Sociology*, 27 (2001), 363–85, esp. pp. 373–4. Note that

of representations and their circulation, via the close attention to self-fashioning, to the analysis of promotional strategies, conventions, and their evolution. Examples of stigma consciousness prompt us to combine lines of inquiry too often pursued separately.

The projector stereotype was probably the first established vernacular stock character of entrepreneurs and would-be innovators in English history. The image was capacious; it was capable of ridiculing those who perverted the assertion of public service by abusing political authority, or simply by their sheer greed and ambition. It captured the prevalent perversion of public interests by private ambitions, something that became conspicuous under the Elizabethan reign and occurred repeatedly in different forms when ingenuity, innovation, and private interests were put to use to complement early modern governance, to improve the welfare of the poor, or to buttress imperial ambitions by raising revenues. This flexibility helps to explain the longevity of the concept well into the eighteenth century.

THE COMFORTING *TRIUMPH OF PEACE*: TRIVIALIZING THE 'GREAT WRONGS' UNDER THE PERSONAL RULE

If we accept that projectors' notoriety became so well established as to affect their own identity, it may be tempting to suppose that the social circulation of distrust amounted to critical scrutiny of quasi-absolutism, a critical voice coming from outside the royal government.[95] Those who first elaborated the satirical character were close to the corridors of power, however. Francis Bacon, who called for the revival of character writing in his *The Advancement of Learning* (1605)—two years ahead of Hall's *Characters*—authorized Mompesson's inn patent in 1617 as the attorney general.[96] While producing *The Alchemist* and *The Devil is an Ass*, Ben Jonson wrote masques for the Jacobean court. Nor was he unfamiliar to courtiers who benefitted from the lucrative grants of monopolies. When Jonson travelled north to Edinburgh in 1618, he in fact visited Sir Robert Mansell and Sir Arthur Ingram, respectively patentees for controversial glass and alum monopolies. Responsible for Jonson's local reception, Ingram even conveyed the playwright in a coach to meet the archbishop of York.[97] Such was the striking proximity among those who encouraged, produced, and ultimately became the target of, satirical attacks and edification.

Goffman's influential work, and the medical sociology of stigma inspired by it, are less about moral deviance (our concern) than about problems such as deformity, for which persons being stigmatized carried little or no perceived culpability. Despite the difference, I find the conceptual vocabularies developed in this field very good to think with.

[95] Cf. David Zaret, *Origins of Democratic Culture: Printing, Petitions, and the Public Sphere in Early-Modern England* (Princeton, NJ: Princeton University Press, 2000).

[96] McCabe, *Hall*, p. 130; *House of Commons, 1604–1629*, vol. 5, p. 350.

[97] James Loxley, Anna Groundwater, and Julie Sanders (eds.), *Ben Jonson's Walk to Scotland: An Annotated Edition of the 'Foot Voyage'* (Cambridge: Cambridge University Press, 2015), pp. 40, 67–8, 70. I thank James Loxley for discussion. For Mansell, Ingram, and their respective industrial patents, see *House of Commons, 1604–1629*, vol. 5, pp. 244–6, vol. 4, p. 853; Price, *Monopoly*, pp. 72–81, 84–96.

The emerging image of the projector was never simply an oppositional discourse for scrutinizing the government.

Here we have begun to approach what I think is the defining feature of the image of the projector before the Civil Wars: more and more actors began to speak ill of the projectors; promoters became aware of their bad name; yet the repeated invocations of the image did not necessarily alter the structure of arguments and counterarguments, the existing patterns of self-fashioning and suspicion. Here the French experience provides us with a useful parallel. Daniel Dessert has shown that the literary depiction of the *humble*, rustic, *laquais-financier* during the seventeenth century tended to trivialize the centrality of *wealthy* fisco-financiers to the French Crown. If anything, the image provided a convenient scapegoat for popular resentment; its invocations did little to alter the Bourbon monarchs' dependence on wealthy lenders like the Bonneau brothers.[98] In early Stuart England, as in France, the image of the wrongdoer initially did little to change the status quo. Promoters who faced criticism co-opted the image of the projector, and in effect suggested that 'this time is different' because only greedy ones were causing grievances.

Accordingly, those who presented themselves as 'real' reformers of allegedly rampant abuses continued to perpetrate what the nonsense song called 'great wrongs'. Instructive here are the connected stories of the projector Thomas Bushell, the playwright James Shirley, the attorney general William Noy and the royal couple Charles I and Henrietta Maria. The series of episodes has never been brought together. Retracing their connections will help us to understand what became of the rhetoric of reformation by the 1630s, and what the consequences were for the future of England's improvement.

Bushell was from a minor gentry family of Cleeve Prior in Worcestershire (b. before 1600, d. 1674). He started his career as an usher to Francis Bacon before his impeachment and, during the 1630s, expanded his portfolio widely, ranging from the regulation of silk production and a national monopoly of soap boiling to the monopoly of silver mines in Wales, the management of a royalist mint, and the monopoly of the carriage of ore in England and Wales.[99] The so-called Silk Office, of which Bushell was one of the two patentees, was authorized from 1638 to impose a duty of 8 pence per pound upon all 'broad silk' produced by native weavers, and 12 pence for those produced by aliens.[100] Bushell was also one of the fifteen original members of the notorious Westminster Soap Company, incorporated in January 1632 with exclusive rights for fourteen years to produce hard and soft soaps and to make potash—a key ingredient of soap hitherto relying on import— out of vegetables.[101] Over the next five years, its corporate privileges were extended by a series of grants and proclamations; by the end of 1636, in order to stamp out

---

[98] Dessert, 'Le "Laquais-financier"', pp. 32, 34. See aso Dessert, *L'Argent du sel*, p. 185.

[99] For an overview of his career, see J. W. Gough, *The Superlative Prodigall: A Life of Thomas Bushell* (Bristol: Bristol University Press, 1932).

[100] Bushell's involvement in the Silk Office, TNA, SP 16/535, fol. 267. See also Price, *Monopoly*, pp. 39–40.

[101] TNA, SP 17/C, no. 17.

evasion and unlicensed producers, the company became authorized 'to search for in all suspected places and to seize and carry away all [unauthorized] Soaps', and 'destroy all panns[,] Tubs[,] Cisternes[,] and other Vessells imployed' in such premises. Mayors, justices of the peace, constables, and other officers across the kingdom were commanded to assist the company 'in breaking or forcing open the doores or houses when they cannot otherwise enter', and in case of 'violent opposic[i]on … to take and use such power and strength as shalbee needfull' and 'to apprehende', i.e. to arrest, 'wilfull Offenders'.[102] A soap barrel was one of the monopolized commodities that were symbolically worn by Wenceslaus Hollar's 'Patenty'—a 'Wolfe like devourer of the Common Wealth' (see Illustration 2.1).[103] At a glance, therefore, Bushell does appear little better than an aggressive monopolist who caused outrage and controversies. Yet something more complex begins to emerge if we move to the world of court patronage and pay close attention to his careful display of piety and technical expertise.

In August 1636, four months before the Privy Council's draconian warrant against unauthorized soaps, Bushell received Charles and the queen consort, Henrietta Maria, at his manor in Enstone, Oxfordshire. There he showed them an underground rock formation with a stream of natural water running through it like a waterfall. This natural curiosity was adorned with Bushell's irrigation works and other devices.[104] Bushell dedicated this to the queen, naming it 'Henrietta's Rock'. By beautifying the natural curiosity with appropriate hydro-static devices, Bushell presented himself as capable of handling greater subterranean riches that bore her husband's name—the *mines royal* in Cardiganshire. Bushell styled himself as the philosophical successor of Bacon, and that was how he impressed Charles upon his visit. As Bushell later recalled, the king, 'upon a discourse in commemoration of my old Master [Bacon], conceived me capable (with the help of that Lords Philosophy) to do him some more acceptable service in Mineral discoveries'.[105]

Bushell combined his Baconian inheritance with an emphasis on Christian piety and reformation. In his first venture into print, *The first part of youths errors* (1628), Bushell presented himself as a prodigal reformed. Having spent a few years as a recluse on the Isle of Man meditating, he came back to Caroline London, he tells us, thoroughly repentant of his former 'pride, bribing, drinking, and wenching'. 'My God,' he exclaimed, 'was not I made thy image to serve and glorifie none other but thy selfe?'[106] The appreciation of God's providence filled pages.[107] Bushell

---

[102] TNA, SP 16/338, fols. 83–83v, Privy Council Warrant, 31 December 1636.

[103] BM, 1856, 0815.48, Wenceslaus Hollar, 'The Picture of a Patenty', [n.d., 1641?].

[104] A detailed textual analysis of the reception, on which my account draws, is C. E. McGee, 'The Presentment of Bushell's Rock: Place, Politics, and Theatrical Self-Promotion', *Medieval and Renaissance Drama in England*, 16 (2003), 31–80.

[105] Thomas Bushell, *An extract by Mr Bushell of his late abridgement of the Lord Chancellor Bacons philosophical theory in mineral prosecutions* (1660), postscript, p. 22. See also Thomas Bushell, *A iust and true remonstrance of his maiesties mines-royall in the principality of Wales* (1641), sig. A2.

[106] Thomas Bushell, *The first part of youths errors* (1628), pp. 121, 40.

[107] Bushell, *Youths errors*, pp. 44, 100, 102.

drew precisely on this pious self-portrait during the royal reception at Enstone, as the songs performed there reveal:

> His only care, his studie is, but how
> He may redeeme the yeares he lost in sinne...
> And to that end he purchas'd at a price
> This field, then sterill, now his Paradise;
> Where he as man of old, by God being bound
> With Adam, wrought, and dig'd, and drest the ground[.]

The royal couple was thus being invited into a paradise. Fruits on the banqueting table were accordingly 'the first fruits...that grewe | in this Eden, and are throwne | On this Altar as your owne'.[108] The rhetoric bordered on a sort of millenarianism: 'Shall I not thinke the world on'[it]s death-bed lyes...when thus I see Nature unlocke her richest treasurie'?[109] The king was encouraged to see himself regaining the lost paradise on earth, the rocks in Oxfordshire and Cardiganshire signifying the abundant riches and marvels promised at Christ's resurrection, riches now within his reach thanks to a reformed, pious servant with Baconian expertise. To a subsequent visitor Bushell's spectacle seemed little better than a fanciful invention by one of 'these Hermiticall and Projecticall Undertakers'.[110] Yet, as Charles' letter makes clear, the royal patron did not miss Bushell's godly self-portrait, or the parallel between the 'Enston rocke and the rocks in Wales, [both of] which your own industrie and Gods providence hath helped you unto'. Neither pious outlook nor providentialism was a monopoly of hot Puritans against the court and popish prelates.[111] Bushell's deft use of a pious, royal outlook, coupled with the display of the Bacon-inspired waterworks, did much to impress his royal patron.

Within months of the Royal reception at Enstone, Bushell successfully became a farmer of the Welsh mines royal, and in July 1637 obtained a grant to set up a mint in Aberystwyth so that the locally extracted silver could be minted and speedily distributed among the miners.[112] Bushell soon went on to expand his operation by alleging common abuse and proposing a remedy—a typical move of early Stuart projectors. In October the same year, Bushell alleged that from the Welsh mines some malefactors 'attempt[ed] secretly to transporte great quantities of Oare' rich in silver.[113] A year later, suggesting an ongoing abuse and its detrimental effect upon 'poor miners' serving the mines, Bushell proposed an ostensible solution: to place the transportation of all unwrought ores within the realm under his control.

---

[108] McGee, 'Bushell's Rock', pp. 55, 58.   [109] McGee, 'Bushell's Rock', pp. 56–7.
[110] 'A Relation of a Short Survey of the Western Counties', ed. L. G. Wickham Legg, in *Camden Miscellany*, 3rd ser., vol. 52 (1936), p. 83.
[111] Henry Ellis (ed.), *Original Letters, Illustrative of English History*, 2nd ser. (4 vols., London, 1827), vol. 3, pp. 312–13. See also Richard Cust, 'Charles I and Providence', in Fincham and Lake (eds.), *Religious Politics*, 193–208, p. 195.
[112] TNA, SP 16/363, fols. 169–169v. For the mint's operation, see George C. Boon, *Cardiganshire Silver and the Aberystwyth Mint in Peace and War* (Cardiff: National Museum of Wales, 1981), pp. 46–81.
[113] TNA, SP 16/393, fol. 148; TNA, PC 2/48, p. 296.

Bushell was immediately granted the monopoly, and instructed to inform the attorney general of anyone 'repugnant' of the king's pleasure. The council 'not only trusted your integrity with our Mynes and Mynt', but was also 'willinge upon yo[u]r Request hereby to Authorize you & none other, to transporte all Refuse oare' not worth refining to extract silver.[114] In principle, this was to enable Bushell to detect any unauthorized movements of silver-rich ores in the kingdom. Yet, within half a year, we find the grant of this de facto monopoly causing a stir on the other side of the British Isles, in Hull. Three tonnes of unwrought Derbyshire lead ore were seized before a ship left the port. Two London merchants who suffered the seizure petitioned the Privy Council with a sense of frustration: 'it is well knowne that never any one gayned by takeing silver' out of Derbyshire ore. Yet their goods were seized and the transaction disrupted 'to the great loss' because of Bushell's nationwide monopoly recently put in place. Probably the merchants refused to purchase a licence for transporting ores.[115] Here, then, we see how the trust reposed in Bushell as a seemingly competent, royal servant lent itself to a grant of a monopoly that could be controversial.[116]

Bushell maintained his reforming outlook throughout. The monopoly for carrying ore was ostensibly conducive to 'the publique good in the silver Mynes or honor to their Nation', and to 'speedy payment of the poore Myners' too.[117] Even the Silk Office and the Westminster Soap monopoly were justified respectively as a step towards an 'absolute Reformation' of 'notable Abuses in the false Dying of Silk', and 'the reformation of abuses in making soap'—reformation to be carried out by credible royal servants.[118] The soap monopoly promised to pay £20,000 yearly to the Exchequer, and was promoted as something capable of 'setting on worke great nombers of the poore natives', while 'preserving at home much of the Treasure' formerly spent 'in fetching materials from forraigne p[ar]ts', such as potash.[119] Far from being monstrous, as in the picture of 'Pattenty', this projector managed to impress his royal patrons, win their trust, and expand his portfolio at the public's expense—all with a striking display of religiosity and public-spiritedness (compare Illustrations 2.1 and 2.2).

The case warns us against accepting narratives of progress at face value. In his account of England's 'culture of growth', Mokyr has drawn on the distinction between 'general' and 'limited' morality. China under the Tang and the Song dynasties is said to have operated with 'limited' morality—limited in the sense that moral obligations usually extended only to kinsmen, friends and close partners,

---

[114] TNA, SP 16/393, fol. 152, 30 June 1638, 'Mr Bushell's Warrant for Transportation of Oare'.

[115] TNA, SP 16/409, fols. 79–79v, 4 January 1639, complaints against the monopoly of carriage Bushell had obtained. See also HP 63/41B.

[116] For further evidence of grievance caused by Bushell, see PA, HL/PO/JO/10/1/58, fols. 27–8; Gough, *Bushell*, p. 21.

[117] TNA, SP 16/393, fols. 148, 152.

[118] Rushworth, *Collections*, vol. 2, p. 186 (silk); *CSPD, 1634–5*, p. 144 (13 July 1634, on soap). For similar claims, see BL, Egerton MS 1140, Sir Nicolas Halse, 'Great Britains Treasure', 1637, fols. 50v–51; Michael Zell, 'Walter Morrell and the New Draperies Project, c. 1603–1631', *HJ*, 44 (2001), 651–75, at p. 671.

[119] Scott, *Joint-Stock*, vol. 1, p. 212; TNA, SP 16/260, fol. 243.

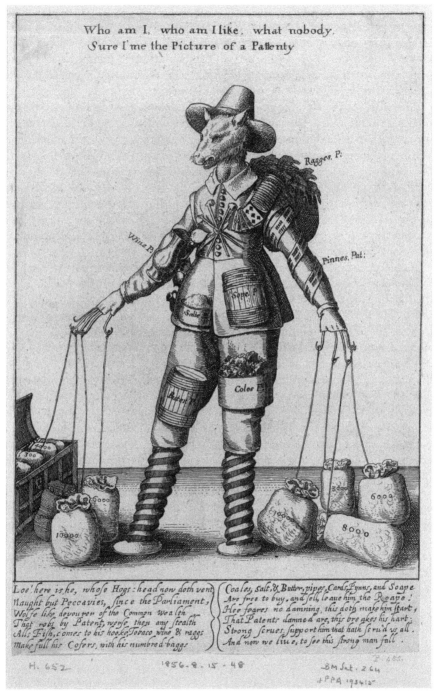

Who am I, who am I like, what nobody,
Sure I'me the Picture of a Patenty

Illustration 2.1. BM, 1856, 0815.48, Wenceslaus Hollar, 'The Picture of a Patenty' [n.d., 1641?]

Note this very visual depiction of a wolf-like patentee with his pet monopolies such as coal and salt all over his attire. Was it based on an actual stage set, as the horizontal line seems to indicate? The visual element is accompanied by a short rhyme on his vices, ensuring oral as well as literate transmission. Copyright The Trustees of the British Museum

Illustration 2.2. Bodl., (OC) 1 g.101, Thomas Bushell, *The first part of youths errors* (1628), frontispiece

The title page facing this image quotes Luke 15.18: 'I will arise and goe to my Father, and say unto him, Father, I have sinned against heaven and before thee, and am no more worthy to be called thy sonne &c.' The reality of early modern entrepreneurship often lay somewhere between this pious self-presentation and the monstrous image of Pattenty (Illustration 2.1). Yet in extreme cases it was precisely through the posture of piety and godliness that the worst of abuses were perpetrated. Such was the case of the Westminster soap monopoly, of which Bushell was a part. Courtesy of The Bodleian Libraries, The University of Oxford

making members of society care 'much less about the larger society in which they live, so that they tend to be more opportunistic when they deal with unknown persons'. Early modern England, by contrast, is said to have enjoyed 'general morality', which, he argues, was more conducive to innovations of general social utility because in such a society moral obligations were often directed towards the generality of the population at large.[120] This is an intriguing conceptual distinction. Yet it does us little service in so far as it invites us to assume that societies based on 'general morality' may have been less prone to rent-seeking and opportunistic behaviours.

Bushell's career indeed forces us to recognize that claims of reformation and morality could in fact lend legitimacy to the most damaging forms of rent-seeking. It follows that we cannot dismiss men like Bushell according to the image of the

---

[120] Joel Mokyr, *A Culture of Growth: The Origins of the Modern Economy* (Princeton, NJ: Princeton University Press, 2017), pp. 16, 18 (quotations), 296. Cf. Slack, *Invention of Improvement*, pp. 89, 241.

wolf-like projector, an opportunistic rent-seeker who would soon be weeded out by the regular working of a reputation mechanism enforcing general morality. Far from it. This aggressive patentee had his piety and reforming zeal prominently on display, and that was how he went on to win royal trust and cause grievances. In his own estimation, Bushell nearly lived up to the aspiration 'that I was not borne for my selfe, but for the service of God, your Majestie, and my Countrie'; yet, from another point of view, he ended up being precisely the kind of hypocrite whom he himself vilified, one who would 'sin wilfully' and hence deserve divine 'judgment and fiery indignation'.[121] The reformation of alleged abuses thereby turned into oppression; legal enforcement of such reformation turned into an instrument of injustice. This was the troubled England that Richard Brome exposed in his *The Antipodes* (first performed in 1636), in which statesmen, by backing spurious projects for reformation, found 'relief for Cheaters, Bawdes, and Thieves'.[122] Herein lay the enormous difficulty of the task set upon the religious reformers of the mid-century that we will encounter in Chapter 3. If promises of reformation had so often exacerbated the status quo rather than reformed it, on what grounds could future calls for reformation be trusted? Would reformation have a future?

Yet such questions were probably all too often swept aside under Charles I's reign, as we can see in the staging of James Shirley's *Triumph of Peace*. One of 'the most spectacular instances of "street theatre" in the Caroline period', *Triumph* was twice performed in February 1634 by men of the four Inns of Court in the presence of Charles and Henrietta Maria.[123] Led by personifications of Confidence and Opinion, Phansie (or Fancy) conjured up amid the procession an antimasque of six projectors, each dancing to beg a patent. One of them, who carried a bellow under each arm, had a 'new project, | A Case to walke you all day underwater'; another was a projector capable of building 'a most strong castle' upon sand, while 'melt[ing] huge Rockes to jelley'.[124] Yet another was a physician, 'on his head a Hat with a bunch of Carrots, a Capon perched on his fist', who studied 'a new way to fatten Poultry | With scrapings of a Carrot, a great benefit | To th' Commonwealth'.[125] As Bulstrode Whitelocke later recalled, this antimasque may have 'pleased the Spectators the more, because by it an Information was covertly given to the King, of the unfitness and ridiculousness of these Projects against the Law'.[126]

The elements of criticism were indeed tactfully conveyed. Seen in the context of the entire masque, this grotesque antimasque was presented as a momentary flight of Fancy; the rest of the performance was assuredly played by masquers who were

---

[121] Bushell, *Iust and true remonstrance*, sig. [A2v]; Bushell, *Youths errors*, p. 101, citing Hebrews 10:26–7 (quotation from the Bible).

[122] Martin Butler, *Theatre and Crisis, 1632–1642* (Cambridge: Cambridge University Press, 1984), pp. 214–16, at p. 216.

[123] Julie Sanders, *The Cultural Geography of Early Modern Drama, 1620–1650* (Cambridge: Cambridge University Press, 2011), p. 221. While the bulk of the performance was held indoors, the masque also included an extravagant street procession.

[124] James Shirley, *Triumph of peace* (1634), pp. 7, 8.

[125] Shirley, *Triumph of peace*, pp. 2–3, 8.

[126] Bulstrode Whitelocke, *Memorials of the English affairs* (1682), p. 20.

members of the Inns of Court, 'the sonnes of Peace Law and Justice'.[127] Thus, both the brevity of the projectors' antimasque and the professional background of the masquers created an impression that, in reality, as in the performance, projectors were little more than brief interruptions of mere fancy in the otherwise orderly realm. The comical antimasque of the projector, seen in this light, was to work just like character writings:

> to ANATOMIZE the Secrets of the HEART, and what VICE soever is found LURKING there ought to be DISCLOSED and brought upon the STAGE in its nakednesse... So by displaying the UGLINES of SINNE in its proper COLOUR, it doth not onely BEGET a LOATHING in the SPECTATORS, but allso CREATETH an HAPPIE Ambition of HABITUATING in themselves the NOBLER opposites of those BASER vices.[128]

Ridiculous, grotesque, and trifling, the figure of the projector would have been something that the royal couple and most courtiers were all too pleased to dismiss.[129] The masque in fact proved a great success; the queen found it so agreeable that she was even said to have danced with some of the performers.[130] Shirley's antimasque reminds us that depictions of the projector could stir the fertile middle ground between criticism and compliment. Such depictions had the potential of edifying the royal spectators about what to detest—or so, perhaps, hoped some spectators. Therein lay a faint possibility of redress short of revolution.

A closer look behind the scenes reveals more disturbing dimensions, however. Following its establishment in 1631, the Westminster Soap Company (of which Bushell was a part) had been pushing for greater control over the production of soaps. We have seen that it achieved a de facto monopoly over the industry by 1636. This campaign to 'reform' alleged abuses in fact reached a critical juncture in the run-up to the performance of *Triumph of Peace* in February 1634.[131] The attorney general, William Noy, played a crucial role in both. A proclamation of June 1632 had prohibited the use of fish oil and whale oil in soap production.[132] During 1633, Noy pressed Star Chamber cases against sixteen London soap-boilers for the use of fish oil and for refusing the assay by the Westminster company, and imprisoned them as 'Delinquents' who 'oppose[d] the Reformation of their owne former abuses, and the prospering of this new Manufacture, which will be so profitable for the

---

[127] Shirley, *Triumph of peace*, p. 17.

[128] Houghton Library, MS Eng 243.50, John Reresby, 'Characterismes... to refresh myself' [1653?], 'To the Reader', non-foliated.

[129] Here I build on a nuanced reading of *Triumph of Peace* by Martin Butler, *The Stuart Court Masque and Political Culture* (Cambridge: Cambridge University Press, 2008), pp. 298–310, esp. p. 304. Cf. Christopher W. Brooks, *Law, Politics and Society in Early Modern England* (Cambridge: Cambridge University Press, 2008), p. 223.

[130] Whitelocke, *Memorials*, p. 21; Brent Whitted, 'Street Politics: Charles I and the Inns of Court's *Triumph of Peace*', *Seventeenth Century*, 24 (2009), 1–25, p. 17.

[131] Price, *Monopoly*, pp. 120–1; W. Cunningham, *The Growth of English Industry and Commerce in Modern Times, Part 1, Mercantile System* (6th edn, Cambridge: Cambridge University Press, 1925), p. 306; Scott, *Joint-Stock*, vol. 1, pp. 210–18.

[132] *Stuart Royal Proclamations*, vol. 2, pp. 356–9, at p. 358.

Publique'.[133] Upon further complaints from London soap-boilers, a public trial was held in December to establish the quality of Westminster soap (often called 'new soap'). At a Privy Council meeting of 29 December 1633, the new soap was confirmed to be superior to common soap; on the strength of this evidence, with Charles I presiding, Noy was 'prayed & required' to draft a proclamation 'as he shall thinke fitt'.[134] The proclamation, dated 26 January 1634, just a week before the first performance of *Triumph of Peace*, reproduced the report of the public trial, and condemned 'divers Soapeboylers' who continued to refuse compliance. None except those authorized by the Westminster company were now to sell any soap, with the company given the power to search houses and seize all unauthorized vessels of soap offered for sale without corporate approval. All soap-boilers were 'from henceforth [to] be under the Survay, Rule, Order, and Government' of the Westminster company.[135]

Strikingly, Noy not only busied himself establishing the monopoly, but also 'had a great hand in this Antimasque of the *Projectors*', drawing on his 'knowledge of them'.[136] Shortly after the performance, thirteen of the soap-boilers who had been imprisoned the previous year were released, perhaps in a display of leniency. The tightening of monopolistic control continued as a matter of reformation, however. Local justices of the peace were commanded in the same month (February 1634) to watch out for any deceitful chandlers who might raise the retail price of soap 'out of a covetuous desire of gaine'; further orders were given to search and seize vessels of unauthorized soap. Two soap-boilers died while in prison; others who acquiesced and sought authorization from the Westminster company were reportedly refused permission to work; a further proclamation of July 1634 then prohibited the production of all kinds of soap, even for private use.[137] The legal declaration ended with a threat of legal action for defaulters; the Star Chamber prosecutions that Noy had pursued earlier thus remained worryingly palpable.[138] City authorities likewise assisted in the tightening of the corporate monopoly. Lord Mayor Ralph Freeman, who organized the performance of *Triumph*, had earlier overseen the crucial public trial regarding the new soap, discrediting petitions against it as being 'clamorous' and signed by persons of 'meane condic[i]on' or by those who 'had noe experience in the said Sope'.[139] We know that Freeman was a major importer of whale oil who would have stood to lose by the rigorous prohibition of its use in soap production.[140] Yet either for fear or favour, even the London mayor who

---

[133] Price, *Monopoly*, p. 120; *Stuart Royal Proclamations*, vol. 2, pp. 400, 402 (quotations).

[134] TNA, PC 2/43, fol. 210 (quotation), 211–211v (a copy report of the public trial).

[135] *Stuart Royal Proclamations*, vol. 2, pp. 396–408 (at p. 404).

[136] Whitelocke, *Memorials*, p. 20.

[137] *A short and trve relation concerning the soap-busines* (1641), pp. 10, 16; TNA, SP 16/260, fols. 243–243v (quotation at fol. 243v); SP 16/267, fol. 157; *Stuart Royal Proclamations*, vol. 2, pp. 429–33, esp. p. 432.

[138] The proclamations discussed here conclude with prominent threats of legal persecution. See *Stuart Royal Proclamations*, vol. 2, pp. 408, 433.

[139] TNA, PC 2/43, 211–211v.

[140] C. E. McGee, '"Strangest Consequence from Remotest Cause": The Second Performance of *The Triumph of Peace*', *Medieval and Renaissance Drama in England*, 5 (1991), 309–42, p. 315; Martin Butler, 'Politics and the Masque: *The Triumph of Peace*', *Seventeenth Century*, 2 (1987), 117–41, pp. 126–7.

contributed to the masque's staging was implicated in the vexation emblematic of early Stuart projects, something that would come to haunt pursuits of improvement well into the latter half of the century.

The episode thus reminds us that theatrical depictions of the projector were in fact presented and performed even in front of a royal audience—highlighting the far-reaching circulation of that image. More importantly, however, Noy's and others' involvement both in the play *and* in the legal persecution indicates what satirical depictions might have achieved, and what they did not. A century earlier, Erasmus declared that, while 'kings do dislike the truth', its veracity and even open reproaches may be accepted if they were received 'with positive pleasure'.[141] True, the antimasque in Shirley's *Triumph of Peace* might well have won royal pleasure; yet, clearly, it did little to stop the machinery of enforcement. The courtly entertainment thus concealed, rather than revealed, the truth about projecting: far from being trifling products of fancy, the projects of controversial projectors like Bushell and their enforcement lay at the heart of Caroline government and its quest for revenues. To the extent that the antimasque downplayed the centrality of projecting to the early Stuart royal policy, and to the extent that hopeful observers found mild criticism in the caricature and others the comforting triumph of peace over trifling projectors—to that extent the royal entertainment and its participants were *complicit* in the grievous state of affairs.[142]

It is precisely this kind of complicity that was soon picked up and exposed in various forms. Noy died in August 1634, six months after the production of the antimasque. Soon afterwards the now lost comedy entitled *A Projector lately Dead* was reportedly performed in London, wherein the attorney general was dissected on the stage and found with a hundred 'Proclamations in his head, a bundle of old motheaten records in his maw, halfe a barrell of new white sope in his belly...and yet, say they, he is still very black & foule within'. Noy became an object of 'publike disgrace on the Stage', as Henry Burton put it.[143]

The episode of Noy's death was later included in Rushworth's *Collections* among 'principal matters' of state.[144] The London Puritan Nehemiah Wallington (1598–1658) soon copied Burton's passage about Noy in his own listed 'Examples of God fearefull Judgements'.[145] For Wallington this was not an isolated issue: 'As wee in great misery in regard of the Church So we were in greate misery in regard of our Corrupted Judges...As also projectors with their Letter pattens for all Stabel

---

[141] Erasmus, *Collected Works of Erasmus, Vol. 27, Panegyricus, Moria, Julius Exclusus, Institutio Principis Christiani, Querela Pacis*, ed. A. H. T. Levi (Toronto: University of Toronto Press, 1986), p. 110.

[142] Studies of the early Stuart dramas would do well to explore further the elements of complicity reconstructed here. Cf. Jessica Ratcliff, '"Art to Cheat the Common-weal": Inventors, Projectors, and Patentees in English Satire, ca. 1630–70', *Technology and Culture*, 53 (2012), 337–65, pp. 346–7; Jessica Dyson, *Staging Authority in Caroline England: Prerogative, Law and Order in Drama, 1625–1642* (Farnham: Ashgate, 2013), pp. 194–5; James Knowles, *Politics and Political Culture in the Court Masque* (Basingstoke: Palgrave, 2015), pp. 176–7, 206.

[143] [Henry Burton], *A divine tragedie lately acted* (1636), p. 45. Burton used the episode to make a polemical argument against ungodly 'prelates' around Charles such as William Laud.

[144] Rushworth, *Collections*, vol. 2, title page (quotation), p. 213.

[145] BL, Add. MS 21935, fol. 47. I thank Kei Nasu for suggesting that I read the diary.

Commoditites: As also Shipp mony & new corprorations even to the undoing of many thousands.'[146] Comical depictions of the projector, as represented in Shirley's antimasque, may well have provided a comforting scapegoat for royal displeasure; yet the same trope of theatrical dissection of vices was turned upon its head to reveal what had gone wrong under Charles's Personal Rule.

This was how public distrust of the projector came to build up by the end of the 1630s. In 1637 John Taylor complained that his effort to gather information about coach services to and from London 'was suspected for a projector, or one that had devised some tricke to bring the Carrriers under some new taxation'.[147] Under the Silk Office held by Bushell, the London Weavers' Company was required to collect duties 'throughout the whole kingdome'. In June 1640, the company petitioned the secretary of state Sir Francis Windebank, and complained that by this measure they did 'find themselves much impoverished & the whole Trade much declined'.[148] Then came the opening of the Long Parliament, in November 1640. Within four weeks, a committee was set up to retrieve Coke's papers; they would soon be found and printed, including his commentaries on the Magna Carta and the 1624 Statute of Monopolies.[149] Yet, as early as 9 November, members of the Commons offered a series of speeches against monopolists and projectors. Among these was one by Sir John Culpeper that condemned monopolists and projectors with a vividness comparable to Noy's anatomical dissection on stage:

> These, like the *Frogs of Egypt* have gotten possession of our Dwellings, and we have scarce a Room free from them: They sup from our *Cup*, they dip in our *Dish*, they sit by *our Fire*...they have *marked and sealed* us from Head to Foote.

The speech was soon copied in manuscripts and circulated in print.[150] It was by drawing on the prevalent images of the projector and the monopolist that the Commons reached a sweeping condemnation of Caroline fiscal policy on the same day. It was resolved:

> That all Projectors and Monopolists whatsoever; or that have any Share, or lately have had any Share, in any Monopolies; or that do receive, or lately have received, any Benefit from any Monopoly or Project; or that have procured any Warrant or Command, for the Restraint or Molesting of any that have refused to conform themselves to any such Proclamations or Projects; are disabled, by Order of this House, to sit here in this House: And if any Man here knows any Monopolist, that he shall nominate him[.][151]

---

[146] Ibid., fol. 127.

[147] John Taylor, *The carriers cosmographie* (1637), sig. [A2v], [A direction to the Reader]. See also Wentworth, *Strafforde's letters*, vol. 2, p. 71, the earl of Northumberland to Wentworth, 28 April 1637.

[148] TNA, SP 16/456, fol. 7, the London Company of Weavers petition, 2 June 1640.

[149] *CJ*, vol. 2, pp. 45–6, 85, 144. The printing of Coke's *Institutes* was to have fateful repercussions after the Restoration. See pp. 200–1 below.

[150] Rushworth, *Collections*, vol. 4, i, p. 3. For the speech's afterlife, see also John Culpeper, *Sir Iohn Cvlepeper his speech in Parliament concerning the grievances of the Church and common-wealth* [1641?], p. 4; Heywood, *Machiavel*, sig. [Bv]; BL, Stowe MS 354, fol. 80; Chetham's Library, MUN Mun.A.6.17, p. 35.

[151] *CJ*, vol. 2, p. 24.

The exact unfolding of investigations in the Long Parliament and their consequences upon the accused individuals are beyond the scope of our discussion. To say the least, we should be careful not to suppose that those who now petitioned the Commons were innocent victims seeking redress. The London Weavers' Company petitioned it on 24 February 1641 to complain about their suffering under the Silk Office; soon they approached the Long Parliament once again, this time for introducing an act for preventing diverse 'abuses' in their trade. In a manner that was strikingly reminiscent of Caroline projectors, they now (abortively) sought a nationwide monopoly over the production of silk.[152] In any case, the Commons' indictment clearly shows that the figure of the projector was no longer what Hall once called an 'image without the offence'. The witty pleasure of character writing morphed into an instrument of public denunciation. The soap patent in which Bushell was implicated was singled out for blame in the Grand Remonstrance of 1641.[153] The ensuing collapse of press control, as well as parliament's readiness to denounce projectors even among members of parliament, 'took the lid off' a decade of grievances under Charles's Personal Rule.[154] This was what is so aptly captured by the sharp rise in the *ESTC* results for the 1640s.

An important element of continuity from the preceding decades was the close interplay across print, manuscript, and oral media. As is well known, Charles's decision to impose the new Anglican Prayer Book of 1637 upon Presbyterian Scotland triggered armed resistance (the Bishops' War); the ensuing fiscal pressure upon the English Crown necessitated the calling of parliament—an occasion for profound change. One of the printed songs produced towards the end of 1640 attacked monopolists and projectors, sardonically thanking Scottish Presbyterians for invading England:

> You Jollie projectors, why hang you the head?
> Promoters, informers, what? are you all dead?
> Or will you beyond-sea to frolick and play,
> With Sir *Giles Monpoison*, who led you the way?...
> The tide is now turn'd let us drink th' other pot,
> And merrily sing; gra[nd]-mercie good Scot.[155]

Note that the song was packaged as a 'New Carrell for Christmasse made and sung at *Londone*'. It is possible that it was printed in the run-up to Christmas 1640. Printed songs like this one were widely distributed by 'the petty traders who carried them amongst their wares along the country's economic

---

[152] PA, HL/PO/JO/10/1/52, fol. 187, 24 February 1641; Guildhall Library, MS 4655/1, Court Minutes of Weavers Company, fols. 15v, 106–8; *CJ*, vol. 2, pp. 197, 202 (the bill was sent to a committee, but was not mentioned again); Alfred Plummer, *The London Weavers' Company 1600–1970* (London: Routledge, 1972), pp. 152, 174. Cf. D'Maris Coffman, *Excise Taxation and the Origins of Public Debt* (Basingstoke: Palgrave, 2013), p. 125.

[153] *Constitutional Documents*, p. 212. The wine monopoly of Abell and Kilvert was also condemned. See also BL, Harley MS 4931, fols. 84–86v, 'The Universall Scourge of the Times', February 1641 (at fol. 85), in which the wine monopolists were mocked.

[154] Butler, *Theatre and Crisis*, pp. 214–48, at p. 233.

[155] National Library of Scotland, Adv. MS 33.1.1 [Denmilne], vol. 13, no. 69, *A New-Carrell for Christmasse sung at Londone* (Edinburgh, [n.d., 1640?]).

(69)

A New Carrell for Christmasse made and sung at *Londone*.

1.

Ou jollie projectors, why hang you the head?
Promoters, informers; what? are you all dead?
Or will you beyond-sea to frolick and play,
With Sir *Giles Monpoison* who led you the way?
If *Empson* and *Dudley* have left you their lot
A twist's readie spun; *gra-mercie good Scot:*

2.

O how high were they flown in their floorishing hope
With their patents for pinnes, tobacco and sope
False dyce and false cardes, besides the great fyne
They yearly receiv'd by enhaunting of wyne.
The tide is now turn'd let us drink th'other pot
And merrily sing; *gra-mercie good Scot.*

3.

Shall one man alone all trading engrosse,
To build up his fortunes with other mens losse?
And that he may jet in dancing and whooring,
The sillie poore subject evermore goring
The titles and honours these gallents have got
May fall in the fire; *gra-mercie good Scot.*

4.

To play at bo-pip our Catholickes strive
Who of late with the devil a bargon did drive
The peace of the kingdome for ever to marre
To change our past plenty to famine and warre
But now it is hoped they'll pay the whole shot,
When the reckning is made; *gra-mercie good Scot.*

5.

What? is there no help at such a dead lift?
To break up the Parlament, is there no shift?
Nor dare they repose any faith in their Creed,
Since their *Ave Maries* do faill them at need?
The house is acquainted with every fine plot
Their mines are blown up; *gra-mercie good Scot.*

6.

Where are our proud Prelats that stridled so wide
As if they had meant the Moon to bestride,
To trad on the Nobles, to trample them down
To set up their Miter above the Kings crown
That e're they were Clerks or Priests have forgot
Which now they'll be taught; *gra-mercie good Scot.*

7.

With Scripturees divine they play fast and loose
And turne holy write to fat Capon and Goose,
Their gut is their god, Religion their mock
To pampher their flesh they famish their flock,
To preach and to pray they have quite forgot,
Which now they'll be taught; *gra-mercie good Scot.*

8.

Although this fair Jsland abound with foule crimes
The Parliament saith we shall see better times
Then let us not fant as men without hope
An halter for *Traitours* an hemp for the *Pope.*
Let *Spaine* and the *strumpet of Babylon* plot
Yet we shall be safe; *gra-mercie good Scot.*

9.

The miser shall give away all to the poore
The City shall coosen the Countrey no more
Oppression shall down, and Justice shall smile;
Force, ryot and Poperie be banisht this Jsle,
Religion shall floorish without any spot
If this come to passe; *gra-mercie good Scot.*

FINIS.

Printed at *London* by E. T.

Illustration 2.3. NLS, Adv. MS 33.1.1 [Denmilne], vol. 13, no. 69, *A New Carrell for Christmasse made and sung at Londone* [n.d., 1640?]
Courtesy of The National Library of Scotland

networks'.[156] Was the subversive song actually sung? It very probably was. We in fact have two manuscript versions of the same song. Their lyrics are slightly different.

[156] Mark Hailwood, *Alehouses and Good Fellowship in Early Modern England* (Woodbridge: Boydell, 2014), pp. 126–30, at p. 126.

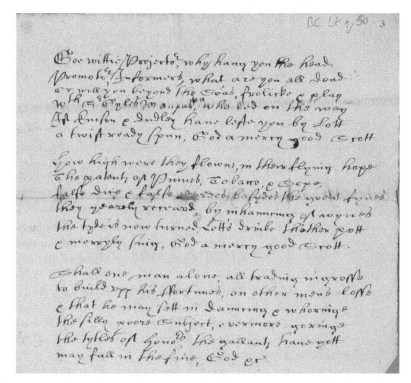

Illustration 2.4. Brotherton Library Special Collection, University of Leeds, MS Lt q 50, fol. 3, a manuscript copy of a ballad, 'Goe wittie projectour' [n.d., Dec. 1640?]

This manuscript version begins thus: 'Goe wittie Project[o]r, why hang you the head | Promoto[u]r, Informers, what, are you all dead? Or will you beyond the Seas, frolicke & play | w[i]th Sir Gyles Monpasson, who led on the way?' The other manuscript version (BL, Harley MS 4931, fols. 80–1) is: 'Yo[u] wily Projectours, why hang yo[u] yo[u]r head?' Notice minor differences in the three versions—an indication of vibrant oral transmission or the existence of other printed, or manuscript, versions on which the Leeds and Harley manuscripts would have been based. The Harley version is extensively quoted and discussed by Millstone, *Manuscript Circulation*, pp. 303–4. Courtesy of The Brotherton Library Special Collection, University of Leeds

The two manuscript versions did not misspell his name deliberately as 'Mon*poison*', as did the printed version; the opening stanza of the manuscript versions begins and ends slightly differently, as illustrated by the manuscript copy found in the Leeds Brotherton Library (compare Illustrations 2.3 and 2.4). It is possible that these manuscripts were copied from another lost version that had been circulating in print or in manuscript, or were recorded from what had been sung in the street or in taverns. In any case, all versions made a clear, political point by thanking the Scots and relishing the projectors' downfall. As Adam Fox has noted, such a 'combination of oral and literate dissemination was deployed in almost all instances of public ridicule by lyric and song', penetrating the social hierarchy 'even down to the level of scurrilous entertainment in provincial alehouses'.[157] Note also that the reference to Mompesson was lost in neither oral nor literate transmission. As in the case of the

---

[157] Fox, *Oral and Literate Culture*, pp. 315–18, 398–400 (quotation at p. 316).

'rough music' against Mompesson in the Forest of Dean, we are once again reminded that his fame as the arch-projector reached well beyond the realms of print and parliamentary politics, inciting derisive laughter in the culture of libellous ballads and irreverent sociability.[158]

CONCLUSION

Thomas Smith would have been startled had he been able to witness what became of the culture of projecting by the end of the 1630s. A certain range of projects had existed for some decades when he wrote *Discourse of the Commonweal of This Realm of England* for private circulation in 1549. In subsequent decades more and more projects came to emerge in response to the interlocking challenges of population growth, inflation, bad harvest, poor relief, and imperial rivalry. Yet the unintended repercussions of England's break from Rome and the dissolution of the monasteries were such that the notion of reformation became a powerful, deeply problematic tool for permitting policies of fiscal exaction.

Mokyr has recently suggested that 'Vested interests of incumbents protecting the rents generated by status quo techniques and fear of the unknown and novel create strong incentives to resist innovation. If groups committed to these beliefs control the formal apparatus of the state, they can thwart innovative efforts.'[159] Bushell is mentioned briefly in the discussion as one of the 'admirers of Bacon who felt inspired by his writings', a 'mining engineer who helped introduce adits (a drainage device based on horizontal tunnels) into British mines'. Bushell is, therefore, placed on the side of innovation and progress, pitted against those supposedly protecting the status quo. Mokyr's book develops this perspective with great theoretical sophistication.[160] Yet the findings of this chapter question how well it applies to the political economy of improvement in early seventeenth-century England. If anything, grievances were created not by declared *opponents* of progress protecting the status quo, but instead by self-appointed *promoters* of new projects for 'improvement' and 'reformation'—by professors of the so-called 'general morality'. Even odious projectors like Bushell peddled their schemes with a compelling reforming outlook, and contributed to technological development (as Mokyr rightly points out). We cannot easily collapse such historical actors into the handy categories of heroes and villains.

Jacobean plays and character writings did not leave the issue untouched. They offered edifying critiques; the image of the projector soon came to enjoy wider social circulation. Projectors were thereby not only mocked in London theatres, but also featured prominently in royal entertainment and were spoken of in rural protests; their vices were exposed in print, sung in a subversive Christmas carol, and their demise recorded in manuscripts, including a list of divine punishments. Yet, on balance, such commentaries did as much to trivialize as to scrutinize

---

[158] On the memory of Mompesson's abuse after the Restoration, see p. 200.
[159] Mokyr, *Culture of Growth*, pp. 16–17.   [160] Ibid., pp. 87 (quotation), 165, 260.

the centrality and malfunctioning of projecting under the early Stuart regimes. The projector stereotype came to reach different sections of society without altering the fundamental pattern of governance and patronage. The Long Parliament echoed and fuelled such criticisms that had built up for more than three decades, something that exploded even further after the collapse of press censorship. By 1641, less than a century after Smith's *Discourse*, writings against the projector came to spell out what had gone wrong in court politics, patronage, and the fiscal exploitation of prerogative. The explosion of printed attacks and the unfolding political crisis at last broke down the existing patterns of criticism, compliment, and complicity. For decades to come, the image of the projector could never be purely jocular again. It now became a byword for the ills of early Stuart rule, a catalyst in the unfolding political crisis, even a symbol of all 'great wrongs' as proclaimed by the nonsense song of 1641 that opened this chapter.

Now we are ready to investigate the process of taming, whereby the culture of projecting began to move away from its early Stuart antecedents. Early Stuart promoters of domestic economic improvement and innovations shared *stigma consciousness*, but their ensuing actions did not at this point amount to 'structure-modifying acts', as Jan de Vries has put it. Yet individual actions—and ultimately collective conventions underlying the projecting culture—began to evolve as promoters continued to launch ambitious projects amid unfolding the political crises of the 1640s, haunted by the memory of early Stuart projectors and grievances. This is the subject of Chapter 3.

3

Reformation and Distrust

I find by experience that if any mans particular forewardnesse transporte him from all privat endes to such purposes as these bee [i.e. reforming the Church and the State]…hee becommeth for the most part a publick object of worldly mens derision & contempt…of many hee is counted a subtill projector & practitioner & of some an inconsiderate & presumptuous foole.

John Dury to ?, 31 March 1634, HP 1/9/5A

Defoe and Hill would have extended their full sympathy to Dury. Pursuing ambitious reform of church and state made Dury and others also look like a company of fools, or of 'projectors'. Yet that did not deter them. On the contrary, the breakdown of Charles I's regime stimulated attempts at comprehensive, universal reform of mankind. An important rallying cry for reform came in late 1641: an anonymous tract entitled *A description of the famous kingdome of Macaria*. Its main author was Gabriel Plattes, who had published two books respectively on husbandry and mining in 1639. He promised to 'doe good to the publick', and depicted an ideal kingdom in order to inspire a campaign for religious moderation and social and economic reform.[1] Religious sectarianism was said to be virtually absent in Macaria. The imaginary kingdom had five councils that supervised and regulated husbandry, fishing, domestic and overseas trade, and plantations; it boasted a 'College of Experience' to support those who could 'demonstrate any experiment for the health or wealth of men'.[2] Thanks to these, 'King and the Governours doe live in great honour and riches, and the people doe live in great plenty, prosperities, health, peace, and happinesse, and have not halfe so much troubles as they have in these European Countreyes'.[3] The pamphlet called for reforms after Macaria: 'let us pursue our good intentions, and bee good instruments in this worke of Reformation'.[4] Thus began the arduous task of rescuing the call for reformation from decades of vexatious abuses. In fact, *Macaria* was followed by a flood of new projects for improvement—the subject of this chapter.

The central figures in these initiatives were Dury and, above all, the German Calvinist émigré Samuel Hartlib, who assisted the publication of Plattes's

---

[1] Gabriel Plattes, *A description of the famous kingdome of Macaria* (1641), sig. [A2v]. The authorship of the tract has been established by Charles Webster, 'The Authorship and Significance of *Macaria*', *P&P*, 56 (1972), 34–48.
[2] Plattes, *Macaria*, p. 5.   [3] Ibid., p. 2.   [4] Ibid., p. 13.

Macaria.[5] Drawing upon his extensive correspondence network, Hartlib set himself to become a 'conduit-pipe' to the public, circulating numerous manuscripts, editing and publishing some of them for wider audiences, while applying for patents and petitioning parliament to press for particular schemes. The underlying religious vision that informed this initiative has been well explored.[6] A passage from Daniel 12 suggested that 'a time of trouble' would be followed by a divine deliverance whereby 'many shall run to and fro, and knowledge shall be increased'. The opening of the Long Parliament, which scrutinized the ills of early Stuart rule, appeared to mark the arrival of such deliverance, a sign of the imminent arrival of the millennium and the restoration of the abundance and innocence that mankind had lost after the Fall. Within this millenarian framework, Hartlib and his associates adopted Francis Bacon's programme for developing experimental knowledge with enthusiasm. These sources of inspiration did not generate a single, well-defined movement, but stimulated a multitude of reforming initiatives covering virtually every aspect of social life, including religious and lay education, medicine, alchemy, poor relief, and innovations in industry and agriculture. In this complex web of correspondence and activities, we find close allies like Cheney Culpeper and the Scottish irenicist John Dury, but also a whole range of men and women, from the relatively humble, such as Plattes and William Wheeler, to the wealthy Robert Boyle and Lady Katherine Ranelagh, from French Huguenot Peter Le Pruvost to Catholic Richard Weston and the royalist Anglican John Evelyn.

Chapter 2 combined the analysis of plays, songs, and other literary texts with the scrutiny of state papers and a wider range of manuscripts in order to trace the rise of the projector stereotype and its subsequent social circulation under the early Stuarts. This chapter proceeds to explore the repercussions of the pervasive distrust, and does so by revisiting the activities of the so-called Hartlib circle—one of the most prolific reformers in early modern Europe. This is a vital topic for the purpose of this book. Joan Thirsk's Ford Lectures did much to highlight projects' contribution to England's economic development during the seventeenth century. Yet, for all its virtues, her magnificent work portrayed the outcries against projectors as something peripheral to the story:

> If London sometimes appears to command most attention in the history of projects because the scandal of monopolies made most noise there, it is in distant regions of the country that we must look for the more impressive evidence of their constructive economic consequences.[7]

---

[5] It is impossible to do adequate justice to the rich historiography on Hartlib and his circle. But see G. H. Turnbull, *Hartlib, Dury and Comenius: Gleanings from Hartlib's Papers* (London: University Press of Liverpool, 1947); Webster, *Great Instauration*; *Culture and Cultivation*; *Universal Reformation*; Slack, *Reformation to Improvement*, ch. 4; Slack, *Invention of Improvement*, pp. 91–117, 126–8.

[6] Webster, *Great Instauration*, ch. 1. See also Michael Walzer, *Revolution of the Saints: A Study in the Origins of Radical Politics* (Cambridge, MA: Harvard University Press, 1965), chs. 2, 5; H. R. Trevor-Roper, 'Three Foreigners: The Philosophers of the Puritan Revolution', in H. R. Trevor-Roper, *Religion, the Reformation and Social Change and Other Essays* (New York: Harper, 1968), 237–93.

[7] Thirsk, *Economic Policy and Projects*, pp. 105, 154, 160, at p. 105.

The reader was therefore invited to move away from the scandal triggered by early Stuart projects. Thirsk's subsequent works did note that Caroline projectors were so notorious as to attract vehement criticisms from the Long Parliament, an acknowledgement that projectors' notoriety may have exacerbated political tensions in the run-up to the Civil Wars. Since her work, numerous accounts have also taken notice of projectors' bad reputations. Yet concrete repercussions of the pervasive public distrust of the projector have rarely been explored in detail. The analysis of literary representations and their social circulation, such as we undertook in Chapter 2, is yet to enrich our accounts of England's culture of improvement and especially its evolution over time.

We can start pushing our analysis further if we draw upon the analysis of trust and creditworthiness that has been developed across a spectrum of early modern historiography. Steven Shapin and Simon Schaffer have shown that natural philosophers could not verify, share, or circulate knowledge about nature as reliable 'matters of fact' without establishing a degree of trust among collaborators and audiences.[8] In the sphere of the medical marketplace too, Jonathan Barry has shown that provincial medical practitioners publicized previous successes of their innovative cures. They thereby tried to have 'their claims validated' in order to fend off 'public scepticism'.[9] Studying the promotion of natural philosophy in the emerging financial markets of the early eighteenth century, Larry Stewart has suggested that 'revealing false projects' and disapproving 'the farce of the bubble' became an important strategy for natural philosophers like John Theophilus Desaguliers to lend credibility to their textbooks, public lectures, and ultimately to the application of natural philosophy in the commercial sphere.[10] Even more striking, Colin Brooks has conjectured that promoters of new wartime taxation schemes during the 1690s 'had not only to deny the fact of projecting; but also to cleanse themselves and others of guilt by association'.[11] Paying close attention to the underlying issue of trust is particularly useful here because it enables us to move from the social circulation of distrust to how it affected promoters' practices of collaboration and exclusion. In other words, we can start exploring how pervasive distrust gave rise to conflicting *coping strategies* in the Hartlibean reformation of mankind.[12] This analytic move, if combined with other complementary approaches, should enable us to go

---

[8] Steven Shapin, *A Social History of Truth: Civility and Science in Seventeenth-Century England* (Chicago: University of Chicago Press, 1994); Steven Shapin and Simon Schaffer, *Leviathan and the Air-Pump: Hobbes, Boyle, and the Experimental Life* (Princeton, NJ: Princeton University Press, 1985).

[9] Jonathan Barry, 'Publicity and the Public Good: Presenting Medicine in Eighteenth-Century Bristol', in W. F. Bynum and Roy Porter (eds.), *Medical Fringe and Medical Orthodoxy, 1750–1850* (London: Croom Helm, 1987), 29–39, p. 35.

[10] Larry Stewart, *The Rise of Public Science: Rhetoric, Technology, and Natural Philosophy in Newtonian Britain, 1660–1750* (Cambridge: Cambridge University Press, 1992), pp. 39, 393.

[11] Colin Brooks, 'Taxation, Finance, and Public Opinion, 1688–1714' (PhD thesis, University of Cambridge, 1970), p. 221.

[12] The concept is adopted from medical sociology inspired by Erving Goffman. See Miriam Heijnders and Suzanne Van Der Meij, 'The Fight against Stigma: An Overview of Stigma-Reduction Strategies and Interventions', *Psychology, Health & Medicine*, 11 (2006), 353–63, esp. p. 354.

beyond the analysis of literary representations, and start developing a fuller account of England's culture of improvement and its evolution with actors' varied experience put back in.

Even a cursory look into Plattes's *Macaria* in fact alerts us to the potential analytic significance of distrust. Crown lands in Macaria were 'improved to the utmost' so that its king 'seldome needeth to put impositions upon his Subjects'. Alluding to Caroline rule, the author sardonically asked: 'Who can but love and honour such a Prince, which...useth no pretences for realities, like to some Princes, in their Acts of State, Edicts, and Proclamations?' When Plattes made a fresh call for 'reformation', he therefore did so by implicitly, but firmly, rejecting the kind of practices that had proliferated under the early Stuarts.[13] After all, the tract was dedicated in October 1641 to the Long Parliament, which had earlier denounced monopolists and projectors.[14]

In matters of political economy, as in those of religion, however, rejecting the undesirable in favour of reformation was easier than delineating concrete programmes for reform. We know that notions such as 'popery' provided a comforting clarity when debating complex matters of church and state in the run-up to, and during, the Civil Wars; cooperation among parliamentarians was driven more by the rejection of 'prelates' and 'evil counsels' than by a positive vision of the reformed religion.[15] Likewise, many would have agreed that monopolies had exacerbated social divisions. Such a broad agreement, however, required little precision as to the specific measures that were to be taken to eradicate monopolies, or as to what exactly constituted reformation in the style of Macaria and what steps might be taken to achieve it.

The rich body of letters, proposals, petitions, and printed sources that Hartlib and others left gives us a rare glimpse of mid-century projecting amid the pervasive distrust of the projector. The well-known proposals for setting up an Office of Address will be examined in this context, alongside hitherto neglected informal negotiations with William Wheeler. Evidence drawn from outside Hartlib's circle will also be considered. Many shared the pursuit of reformation as a slogan, and the distrust of the projector as a practical problem. Their responses to the problem of distrust had far-reaching implications for the development of natural philosophy. As Hartlib and his allies took differing approaches to this common set of experience, however, their promotion of useful knowledge gave rise to strikingly ambivalent, even incoherent practices of collaboration and exclusion. Projecting during the mid-century, it will be argued, was characterized by distancing from aspects of the Caroline model, but did not arrive—at least in the short term—at any viable, widely shared alternative. In this thicket of activities, we shall detect early signs of the long-term evolution of England's projecting culture.

[13] Plattes, *Macaria*, pp. 8–9.   [14] Plattes, *Macaria*, sig. [A2v].
[15] Michael J. Braddick, *God's Fury, England's Fire: A New History of the English Civil Wars* (London: Allen Lane, 2008), pp. 177, 282 (see also pp. 9, 50, 53, 143–4, 152).

SOLUTIONS TO DISTRUST: AVOIDING
MONOPOLIES AND IMPOSITIONS

Hartlib and others had to state the case for reformation and improvement once again, something that had gone so badly wrong under Charles I's Personal Rule. One, perhaps predictable, way forward was to avoid seeking monopolistic patents and avoid imposing fines and confiscation—something reminiscent of early Stuart monopolists and projectors. Even in this respect, however, it took some cautious pitching and probing for Hartlib and his allies to settle into a degree of shared response. When a London-trained barber-surgeon Benjamin Worsley promoted a scheme for producing saltpetre (potassium nitrate) in 1645, for example, he began by laying out several proposals to test the ground. Saltpetre was a constituent of gunpowder, and, as Sir Edward Coke put it, its production was deemed vital 'for the necessary defence and safety of the realm'.[16] As the chemical process was not fully understood, its domestic production depended on searching and digging the floors of stables and dovecots where saltpetre occurred naturally.[17] Under royal authority, the licensees, so-called saltpetremen, were permitted this intrusion. Even Robert Boyle had to pay bribes to stop 'those undermining two-legged moles' from digging his cellar and stables. Indeed, the 1641 Grand Remonstrance highlighted their 'vexation and oppression' upon 'the liberties of the subjects in their habitation' alongside those of other monopolists and projectors.[18] Worsley was promoting his scheme at a time when the procurement of this material, urgently needed for the ongoing war efforts, had a problematic association with the imposition of royal authority during the previous decades.

His proposal was to set up workhouses for the poor in London in which residents would oversee production using their own waste. Worsley wrote some draft proposals anonymously. One of them asked that 'none' but he and his associates 'maie make [saltpetre] their waye or with their materials'. Another went even further, seeking a monopoly over saltpetre production itself once the poor houses began to produce it sufficiently.[19] As these proposals resembled early Stuart monopolies, they were probably not well received by Hartlib and his associates, to whom Worsley had just been introduced.[20] As if these anonymous proposals were there to gauge responses without risking his own reputation, Worsley carefully dropped the requests for monopoly when submitting another version of the proposal to London aldermen. Unlike unscrupulous projectors, he now declared, 'I goe not about to establish my owene good by injury, or with Carelessenesse to the good of others'. That is, 'by a new way of making . . . Salt Peter, I will . . . free the whole

---

[16] *The English Reports* (178 vols., Edinburgh: W. Green & Son, 1900–32), vol. 77, p. 1294 (12 Co. Rep. 14).

[17] A. R. Williams, 'The Production of Saltpetre in the Middle Ages', *Ambix*, 22 (1975), 125–33, at pp. 125–8.

[18] *Boyle Correspondence*, vol. 1, p. 43; *Constitutional Documents*, p. 212. For local grievances and their wider repercussions, see J. P. Ferris, 'The Saltpetreman in Dorset, 1635', *Proceedings of the Dorset Natural History and Archaeological Society*, 85 (1963), 158–63; David Cressy, *Saltpeter: The Mother of Gunpowder* (Oxford: Oxford University Press, 2013), p. 123.

[19] HP 53/26/2B, 3A.   [20] Leng, *Worsley*, p. 23.

Common-wealth of the trouble or injury susteyned in haveing their Houses Cellers yards and other places digged up and spoiled by Salt-Peter-Men'. In all, he promised 'not to intrench upon the libertie or infringe the just priviledges of any subject whatsoever'.[21]

Although Worsley went on to submit a petition to the Lords, his scheme ultimately did not materialize; it is alleged that Worsley did not have the technical knowledge he claimed to possess.[22] Importantly, however, avoiding imposition and thereby distancing himself from monopolistic projectors and saltpetremen enhanced the credibility of the scheme. The committee of London aldermen reported that the scheme would advance 'the publique good' without being 'prejudiciall (in the least) unto any, hee being neither desirous to debarr any to import the said Commodity, or to make it after the way that is now used'.[23]

Equally revealing is the case of William Petty, who obtained a patent in 1648 for what he called the 'double-writing' engine, an invention for producing 'two resembling copies of the same thing at once'.[24] He had originally proposed 'to move the State to lay an additionall taxe upon writing paper', appointing himself as a tax collector who would take a fee as a reward for his invention. This ambitious proposal, Petty admitted, was dropped and a more conventional patent procured instead, because imposing a new tax seemed to have 'cross[ed] too much the nature of the times, when men complain enough already of impositions'.[25]

Promoters did not, however, always agree on precisely what these 'impositions' were. A case in point is the promotion of the ambitious 'universal trade' scheme. First developed by a Huguenot, Hugh L'Amy, and later promoted by Peter Le Pruvost, the scheme was intended to introduce fishery and agricultural innovations in England in order to fund the state-led plantation of a Calvinist colony in North America.[26] When promoting the scheme, Hartlib's allies were acutely aware of the need to avert comparison with the early Stuart projector. Culpeper suggested that the scheme might be tried by getting a patent for the inventions, although, he added, doing so would make it look 'eyther folly or knavery'.[27] Dury agreed. Patents were understood 'not to bee beneficiall to the public'; getting one would make the scheme 'seeme a project indeed and a kind of Monopolie'. It would bring 'soe much opposition of Envie & jeallousie against' the promoter that he 'hardly should be ever able to proceed'. Instead of a patent, Dury thus argued, Le Pruvost would need the state's full support via parliamentary ordinance.[28]

[21] HP 71/11/10A, 8A-B.
[22] *LJ*, vol. 8, p. 574; William R. Newman and Lawrence M. Principe, *Alchemy Tried in the Fire: Starkey, Boyle, and the Fate of Helmontian Chymistry* (Chicago: University of Chicago Press, 2002), pp. 239–40.
[23] HP 71/11/1A–1B. The same report was presented to the Lords. *LJ*, vol. 8, p. 574. See also Boyle's favourable comment in *Boyle Correspondence*, vol. 1, pp.42–3.
[24] *CJ*, vol. 5, p. 481; William Petty, *The advice of W. P. to Mr. Samuel Hartlib for some particular parts of learning* (1647 [1648]), sig. A2.
[25] William Petty, *A declaration concerning the newly invented art of double writing* (1648), p. 3. My account complements McCormick, *Petty*, pp. 58–60.
[26] Thomas Leng, '"A Potent Plantation Well Armed and Policeed"': Huguenots, the Hartlib Circle, and British Colonization in the 1640s', *William and Mary Quarterly*, 66 (2009), 173–94.
[27] 'Culpeper Letters', p. 239, n.d. [late 1645?] (13/279–83).
[28] 'Culpeper Letters', pp. 235–6, Dury to Culpeper, n.d. [autumn 1645] (55/10/11–14).

The debate continued among the reformers because Le Pruvost demanded the imposition of fines and confiscation of properties for offenders so that 'none practise or cause to be practised' his ways of husbandry and fishing except under his authorization.[29] Dury argued parliamentarians could still be persuaded, because discouraging free-riders was reasonable, and because the promoter neither drew upon 'any inventions, which looke like projects', nor 'demands any special priviledge as Monopolists or projectors use to doe' under the early Stuarts.[30] Note that the feasibility of the scheme was measured against the image of the projector and the monopolist. Yet Culpeper disagreed. He claimed that the Frenchman would first have to 'quitte that resolution of takinge mens estates & disposing of them without theire consente'. This, Culpeper wrote, was 'an inseparable companion of moste former monopolies'.[31]

Culpeper's position was more in line with the strong hostility to monopolists and projects that remained. L'Amy and Le Pruvost visited London between 1645 and 1646 in order to have their proposal examined by a parliamentary committee. At the time, the Long Parliament in fact faced vehement opposition to a proposed excise tax on soap and potash. The proposal was denounced as a nefarious plot of 'projecting Monopolers', who would, 'now by the Authority of Parliament, as heretofore they have done, by the Authority of the Kings Majesty', oppress other soapboilers by forcefully collecting taxes, even 'breaking open' their houses, 'taking away their goods', and by 'imprisoning their persons'.[32]

Culpeper's view went along with parliament's cautious attitude. For even where governmental interventions could have been a viable option, the Long Parliament did take pains to avoid direct imposition of its authority, as in the case of the London Corporation of Shipwrights. Shortly after the collapse of Charles I's Personal Rule, 'the Yard keepers and others' started 'taking occasion to w[i]thhold their duties, & to renounce their obedience' to the corporation. Consequently, the 'Corporation become indebted, [and] Meetings & Surveys discontinued'; it could no longer pay a full salary to its clerk, Edward Keling—his salary and the rent due for the hall where he resided as the officer.[33] By the time Dury and others were busy promoting Le Pruvost's scheme in late 1645, the arrears and rent due to Keling had soared above £150.[34] No doubt upon his urging, the corporation petitioned the parliamentary Committee of the Admiralty. Would it be possible

---

[29] HP 53/14/4B. Other versions are HP 55/10/18A, HP12/62B.   [30] HP 53/14/8A, 9B.

[31] 'Culpeper Letters', pp. 307–8 (13/194–5).

[32] *A looking-glasse for sope-patentees* (1646), pp. 4–5. See also *The soap-makers complaint for the losse of their trade* (1650). For background, see D'Maris Coffman, *Excise Taxation and the Origins of Public Debt* (Basingstoke: Palgrave, 2013), pp. 119–21.

[33] Houghton Library, MS Eng 600, Corporation of Shipwrights of England, 'Constitution and Bylaws', 1646, p. 1.

[34] *LJ*, vol. 8, p. 232. The account book of the company is laconic, and the agreed salary and rent are not known. But it suggests that the company paid Kerling only £2 10s a year (£1 for the hall and £1 10s for the salary). This annual salary was worth just thirty days of work by a porter who worked for the Salters' Company (who was paid 1s a day in 1656). See LMA, CLC/L/SD/D/001/MS04597/001, Shipwrights Company Account Book 1621–1726, pp. 30–1; Joseph P. Ward, *Metropolitan Communities: Trade Guilds, Identity, and Change in Early Modern London* (Stanford, CA: Stanford University Press, 1997), p. 70.

to restore corporate discipline in the dockyards, and collect arrears from shipwrights under its regulation? Decisive political intervention might well have been a viable option given that England's naval strength as well as Keling's welfare hinged upon the smooth operation of the corporation. Yet this was no easy task for the Long Parliament, which had been fighting against Charles I and his supporters, a regime that had used corporations in order to sidestep the Statute of Monopolies. The committee's report to the House of Lords reveals the extreme caution with which the case was handled:

> this Committee conceives it most just that the Wages and Rent so due should be satisfied and secured, yet that they have not Power to compel the Members [of the corporation] thereunto: This Committee doth therefore specially recommend it to the House of Peers, to give Order to the said Corporation, to pay the Petitioner [Keling] his said Wages, and to secure him of the said House Rent; as also to authorize the Master, Wardens, and Assistants, to compel the several Members of the Corporation to contribute proportionably thereunto[.][35]

Even in this 'just' cause calling for redress, then, the Long Parliament found it prudent to avoid direct intervention that involved the levying of money. The underlying concern was made explicit in the short manuscript that records the unfolding of the event from the corporation's perspective: the company was obliged to answer the allegation from its dissident members that the tighter enforcement of discipline, including the levying of arrears, 'trenches upon the Subj[ec]t libertie'.[36]

Given the parliamentary committee's cautious response, Dury was probably too optimistic about the prospect of procuring governmental support for Le Pruvost's scheme, which hinged upon the stiff punishment of free-riders in the form of fines and confiscation. Dury soon came to adopt Culpeper's more moderate approach, and with Hartlib went on to revise the draft ordinance to drop draconian elements. But the French promoter rejected this revised proposal, and the scheme reached a deadlock.[37] The caution exercised by the Admiralty Committee therefore suggests that the protection of precarious English liberties was a moot point that exercised not only the religious reformers around Hartlib, but also those sitting in the Admiralty Committee and even yardkeepers.[38] Within that broad context developed England's culture of projecting during the Civil War period. It was by no means easy for the reformers to agree on what exactly made a proposal look like repressive early Stuart projects, especially whether stiff penalties could be permitted if judiciously administered. Nonetheless, the efforts of Worsley, Petty, Dury, and

[35] *LJ*, vol. 8, p. 232. See also HMC, *Sixth Report, Part 1 (Report and Appendix)* (London: HMSO, 1877), p. 113; *LJ*, vol. 8, p. 286.

[36] Houghton Library, MS Eng 600, p. 8. This manuscript throws valuable light on the issue, as shipwrights' court minute books at the Guildhall Library survive only from 1693 onwards. Cf. LMA, CLC/L/SD/A/003/MS04600, Shipwrights Company Ordinance and memorandum book.

[37] Leng, ' "A potent Plantation" ', p. 188.

[38] The privileges of the East India Company were also challenged as 'a monopoly & repugnant to the lawes of the kingdome, & liberty of the subject'. See University of London Special Collection, MS 260, fol. 189.

Culpeper reveal that encroachment upon people's rights and properties was an underlying concern when putting useful knowledge to public use, and that the image of the early Stuart monopolist and projector provided a benchmark for negotiation.

SOLUTIONS TO DISTRUST: OPT-OUT STRATEGIES

A promoter of reform and improvement thus might avoid breaching others' rights and liberties, but he could still resemble an unreliable projector in a more generic sense, profiting himself by airing impractical or fraudulent 'inventions' and 'secrets'. What strategies enabled such men to avoid comparison with the image of the projector as a fool or conman? One way was to renounce rewards for divulging useful knowledge, and to communicate them by publishing pamphlets so that readers might try and adopt them for themselves. It was something of an opt-out strategy, to reject elements of the secrecy and profiteering associated with ostentatious projectors in favour of financial independence and open communication.

This opt-out strategy was adopted by some promoters such as Plattes, the author of the 1641 utopian tract *Macaria*. His ambition in publishing mining and agricultural tracts in 1639 was no less than making 'this Countrey the Paradise of the World'.[39] He was no stranger to the world of early Stuart projecting; he was at pains to distance himself from it. During his master William Englebert's illness in the early 1630s, Plattes in fact promoted 'the realitie of the worke' that could be achieved by his master's invention for 'the makinge of pence & halfe pence'.[40] He must have encountered other would-be promoters in Caroline London. Alluding perhaps to these projectors, Plattes's mining tract of 1639 indicated that 'many people of indifferent vertuous dispositions' pursued 'actions which were not laudable'.[41] Not surprisingly, mindful of projectors' ostentatious claims, Plattes repeatedly stressed the limitations of his knowledge. '[N]o certaine rule can be given for so variable a worke' as husbandry, he argued. Acknowledging that different environmental factors, such as soil and weather conditions, affected the success of these ventures, Plattes kept himself from requesting the investment of others as projectors would do. In his words, he chose to 'part with my money, rather than to suffer another to be oppressed with extreme want and miserie'. He therefore communicated his findings through print for the profit and use of many. Finally, rather than promising quick and substantial returns as typical projectors would do, Plattes issued repeated cautions against taking his advice for granted, and urged 'every man' first to 'trie the truth [of his relations] in a few Perches of Land...then

---

[39] Gabriel Plattes, *A discovery of infinite treasure, hidden since the worlds beginning* (1639), sig. [A3v]–[A4].

[40] HP 71/4A, Plattes's petition to the committee for the Mint [n.d., 1643 or 1644]; Webster, *Great Instauration*, p. 400; G. E. Aylmer, *The King's Servants: The Civil Service of Charles I, 1625–1642* (New York: Columbia University Press, 1961), p. 376. See also Thomas Fuller, *The history of the worthies of England* (1662), p. 284, which notes Englebert's death in Westminster to have been in 1643.

[41] Gabriel Plattes, *A discovery of subterraneall treasure* (1639), sig. [Bv].

to goe to worke in greater quantities'.[42] Similar caveats were issued repeatedly in his pamphlets.[43]

The farmer and inventor Walter Blith, who probably did not develop a sustained collaboration with Hartlib, positioned himself against the stereotype even more explicitly:

> That some Pretending great things…and held forth Wonders, but ever upon the Charge and Expence of others. And have produced little but to themselves.…Others also pretend great Discoveries they can make, if they might have a Publique Stock to worke it, and a Patent for it, otherwise the Publique shall not share of their Inventions[.]

In order to distance himself from such a 'naughty generation of men', this son of a Warwickshire yeoman emphasized the limitations of his knowledge and refrained from seeking investments, instead publishing books about improved cultivation methods.[44] He was acutely aware that this would enhance his credibility. His cultivation techniques, Blith argued, were 'Experimented at the onely and proper cost of the Author'; they 'are therefore somewhat the more Credible'.[45] Thus, instead of asking for money in return for revealing secrets, Plattes and Blith stressed their financial independence and commitment to open communication, while emphasizing the potential limitation of the knowledge they possessed. These measures were to set them apart from what Plattes called men 'of indifferent vertuous dispositions' pursuing 'for very want of meanes' the kinds of projects that had been thriving under Charles's Personal Rule.[46]

Not everyone could afford to opt out of profit and patronage, however. Worsley, for example, declared to 'discharge his Conscience and Duty to the publicke' by submitting his saltpetre scheme to the London aldermen.[47] Yet he never elaborated where exactly the knack of his new 'invention' lay. The promoter of the 'Universal trade', Le Pruvost, too, concealed particulars; he did little more than hint that his scheme would somehow unite subjects' 'owne advantages' and 'the Rules of Righteousnes for a public aime'.[48] Cressy Dymock, a landless inventor from a Lincolnshire family, also refused to reveal his secrets, while at the same time confidently claiming to serve God and the public.[49] Although it is rarely noted in the secondary literature, even Plattes tacitly concealed his seed-setting engine. His 1639 agricultural tract made only passing references to the engine upon the pretext that the labour-saving invention 'might doe more hurt than good' by taking jobs

---

[42] Plattes, *Discovery of infinite treasure*, sig. D.

[43] See Plattes, *Discovery of subterraneall treasure*, sig. [B2v]–B3, pp. 47–9; Samuel Hartlib (ed.) *Chymical, medicinal, and chirurgical addresses* (1655), esp. pp. 51, 65, 86.

[44] Walter Blith, *The English improver* (1649), sig. [av] (block quotation); Walter Blith, *English improver improved* (1652), sig. [c4v], c2. Blith's name does not seem to appear in Hartlib's surviving correspondence or in his work diary, *Ephemerides*.

[45] Blith, *English improver*, sig. [a2v]–a. See also Blith, *English improver improved*, sig. [c4v–c5].

[46] Plattes, *Discovery of subterraneall treasure*, sig. [Bv]. For background, see ch. 2 above; Thirsk, 'The Crown as Projector'.

[47] HP 71/11/9B.   [48] HP 53/14/24A–B.

[49] HP 58/9A; [Samuel Hartlib and Cressy Dymock], *The reformed husband-man, or, A brief treatise of the errors, defects, and inconveniences of our English husbandry* (1651), pp. 6, 9, 10.

away from the poor.[50] In reality, he had been applying for a patent for the engine and a handbill to advertise it.[51] Having obtained the grant in February 1640, he now defied his previous reservations about the invention, and declared in a handbill: 'Those that love themselves or the common good, are invited and desired to learn the knowledge of this new invention for the expeditious setting of corne, against the time of dearth and scarcitie'.[52] Neither technical details nor the intention to disclose them gratis were indicated, suggesting that Plattes probably expected some payment in return for imparting his ingenuity. The Oxford-based Ralph Austen pressed Hartlib hard in the 1650s to lobby for introducing a law to force land-owners to plant apple and other fruit trees. This large producer of apple trees admitted that the scheme 'will be very effectuall, not only for my particuler advantage, but the Publiques also'.[53] Partial concealment of one's skill was no novelty, of course; inventors and ingenious artisans, including Plattes's master Englebert, displayed their prowess without divulging details vital for replication.[54] But it is notable that, unlike monopolies and other fiscal 'impositions', partial concealment and private gain remained more readily compatible with assertions of one's public service.[55] Just like the parliamentarian military officers Ann Hughes has studied, many promoters continued to attach 'their personal ambitions to particular versions of the public interest'.[56]

The problem can be better understood if we juxtapose the negotiations of would-be reformers with what Phil Withington has called the 'politics of common-wealth'. Historians of science and technology have tended to discuss the identity of practitioners by linking it to the notion of a hierarchical polity. Hence the analytical importance often given to the supposed civility and disinterestedness of the wealthy gentleman, and against those virtues, the problematic identities of the scholar, the merchant, the artisan, and the mechanic.[57] Yet historians of politics and religion have shown that the growth of the seemingly stratified church and state hinged heavily upon active participation of (local male) subjects from wider

---

[50] Plattes, *Discovery of infinite treasure*, p. 76.

[51] This has been overlooked in studies of the Hartlib circle. Bodl., Bankes MS 11/39; TNA, C 66/2842/1.

[52] Gabriel Plattes, *Certaine new inventions and profitable experiments* (1640), non-paginated handbill.

[53] HP 41/1/104B, Austen to Hartlib, 10 December 1655. In 1659, Austen declined to leave Oxford to plant fruit trees upon a 'free offer of some barren wasteland' because he did not 'understand how it might be profitable, either to my selfe, or to the Common Wealth, if I should leaue my Plantations heare' (HP 41/1/125A, Austen to Hartlib, 3 May 1659).

[54] For Englebert, see University of Nottingham Manuscripts and Special Collections, Pw2 Hy 164, 'The effects of a certaine Engine devised by Wm Engelbert Gentleman', n.d.

[55] Cf. Pamela O. Long, *Openness, Secrecy, Authorship: Technical Arts and the Culture of Knowledge from Antiquity to the Renaissance* (Baltimore, MD: Johns Hopkins University Press, 2001), pp. 90, 95, 101, 141.

[56] Ann Hughes, 'Men, the "Public" and the "Private" in the English Revolution', in Peter Lake and Steve Pincus, *Politics of Public Spheres in Early Modern England* (Manchester: Manchester University Press, 2007), 191–212, at p. 194.

[57] See earlier formations by Steven Shapin, 'Who was Robert Hooke?', in Michael Hunter and Simon Schaffer (eds.), *Robert Hooke: New Studies* (Woodbridge, 1989), 253–85; Steven Shapin, ' "A Scholar and a Gentleman": The Problematic Identity of the Scientific Practitioner in Early Modern England', *History of Science*, 29 (1991), 279–327.

social strata. Although many of them earned their living through trade and agriculture, they were nonetheless capable of asserting their public virtue, thereby legitimating the roles they played in municipal and ecclesiastical governance.[58]

Seen in this broader context, it is hardly surprising to find the compatibility of profits, proprietary attitudes, and the assertion of public service in the pursuit of useful knowledge. Both of these commonwealths, of politics and of learning, were oriented towards the public good, and united in principle against unregulated pursuits of private gain. Subjects often obeyed the Crown and social mores, and yet they were capable of contributing to the polity as virtuous citizens. Likewise, middle-sort participants in the promotion of useful knowledge were not entirely immune from the accusation of peculation or base labour. Yet they were capable of contributing to the early modern process of governance, and hence of asserting their public service.

Here then was a profound challenge to Hartlib and his close allies. Few promoters would have been unaware of the detrimental effects of being compared to early Stuart projectors. Yet relatively few could escape the damaging comparison because there was little clear-cut distinction between profiteering under the veneer of public service and receiving just reward for divulging useful knowledge.[59] To that extent, then, even after distancing themselves from monopolistic grants, Hartlib and others still had to face the question of how to collaborate with projector-like schemers in the noble pursuit of reformation.

THE OFFICE OF ADDRESS AND THE 'ACCOMMODATION' OF PROJECTORS

Perhaps surprisingly, the Bacon-inspired proposals for encouraging ingenuity and the 'Advancement of Learning', for which the circle is perhaps best known, reveal a tortuous process of negotiation with projector-like promoters seeking rewards. When the scheme was first proposed in print by Dury in May 1647, the aspiration of open communication was featured prominently. The so-called Office of Address had two branches, 'One for Bodily, the Other for Spirituall Matters'.[60] The bodily part was to give jobs to the poor by gathering information concerning demand for, and supplies of, labourers. The branch was named the Office of Address for *Accommodation*. The spiritual branch was to handle 'matters of Religion, of Learning, and', crucially, of 'all Ingenuities' as well. It was to become 'a Center and Meeting-place of Advices, of Proposalls, of Treaties... *freely to bee given and received*,... by and for all such as may think themselves concerned' with 'the most Profitable Undertakings, Discoveries, and Occurences'. Designed to serve as a 'communion'

---

[58] On this point, see works cited earlier, pp. 13 n. 60, 62 n. 154.

[59] See also Kevin Dunn, 'Milton among the Monopolists: *Areopagitica*, Intellectual Property and the Hartlib Circle', in *Universal Reformation*, 177–92, at p. 178.

[60] [John Dury], *Considerations tending to the happy accomplishment of Englands reformation in Church and State* (1647), p. 42.

of noble minds, this upper branch was named the Office of *Communication*, and was deemed 'far beyond that of Accommodations in Usefulnesse'.[61]

This aspiration to free and open communication is the image most commonly associated with the Office of Address.[62] Yet a more complex picture begins to emerge if we consider how well Hartlib and his close allies managed to put this ideal into practice. The underexplored case of the obscure inventor William Wheeler (?–1653) is particularly revealing, as the circle sought to bring him into collaboration at a time when the idea of the Office of Address was taking shape.[63]

Little is known about Wheeler. He seems to have moved to the Netherlands in the 1630s, working on a broad range of inventions, but especially on fen drainage and related inventions under the auspices of the English ambassador to The Hague, Sir William Boswell.[64] Wheeler obtained a patent there for his draining engine in 1639, and an English one in 1642 covering multiple inventions including his water-raising engine—an invention useful not only for Dutch lowlands but also for English fens and mines. He had become known to Hartlib and his associates by 1644, and Culpeper was soon asked to arrange a meeting with Wheeler's associate in England.[65] In October 1645, Culpeper commented on Wheeler's patent for his draining engine, which conferred on him 'the full preiveledge of either sellinge the use of this invention to others or of using it himselfe'.[66]

It seems that Wheeler asked for a rather exorbitant compensation for 'selling' his patented inventions. Yet Culpeper initially expected Wheeler to be a like-minded Christian willing to impart useful knowledge voluntarily and freely. He proposed that Wheeler should surrender his invention to trustees so that they could first invest in building a model of the mill, and subsequently utilize the invention more widely for the public's benefit.[67] Culpeper acknowledged the need to reward inventors and investors who would initially 'undergoe that disbursemente & hazarde', but only by granting them 'concurrent use' of the invention for 'particular

---

[61] Ibid., pp. 42, 48, 45–6.

[62] Webster, *Great Instauration*, pp. 32, 70, 422–4; William Eamon, *Science and the Secrets of Nature: Books of Secrets in Medieval and Early Modern Culture* (Princeton, NJ: Princeton University Press, 1994), pp. 327–8; Dunn, 'Milton', p. 186; Mark Greengrass, 'Samuel Hartlib and the Commonwealth of Learning', in John Barnard and D. F. McKenzie (eds.), *The Cambridge History of the Book in Britain, vol. IV, 1557–1695* (Cambridge: Cambridge University Press, 2002), 304–22, pp. 315–16, 318.

[63] What follows complements recent studies that pay closer attention than hitherto allowed to the prevalence of partial concealment at the time of the Office's promotion. See also Stephen Clucas, 'Samuel Hartlib: Intelligencing and Technology in Seventeenth-Century Europe', in Robert Kretzschmar and Sönke Lorenz (eds.), *Leonardo da Vinci und Heinrich Schickhardt: Zum Transfer technischen Wissens im vormodernen Europa* (Stuttgart: Verlag W. Kohlhammer, 2010), 58–75, at pp. 59–63; Michelle DiMeo, 'Openness vs Secrecy in the Hartlib Circle: Revisiting "Democratic Baconianism" in Interregnum England', in Elaine Leong and Alisha Rankin (eds.), *Secrets and Knowledge in Medicine and Science, 1500–1800* (Farnham: Ashgate, 2011), 105–21, at pp. 119–20.

[64] Webster, *Great Instauration*, pp. 372–3.

[65] 'Culpeper Letters', p. 246 (13/114). We do not know whether the meeting took place. A summary of the inventions and schemes Wheeler could offer survives in the Hartlib Papers. The full list is HP 67/6/3A–10B.

[66] HP 13/119A.

[67] HP 13/119A; 'Culpeper Letters', pp. 247, 31 October 1645 (13/115–16); ibid., p. 249, 12 November 1645 (13/121–2). It is unclear whether Wheeler was meant to reveal his secrets to the trustees.

under takings of their owne'. Hartlib's editorial intervention suggests that he preferred to permit private use only after public interests were first met;[68] Worsley
reportedly proposed to induce disclosure by paying the inventor.[69]

Culpeper's and others' responses were, therefore, not monolithic. Importantly,
however, the 'official' line presented in the first printed proposal for the Office of
1647 indicated little about the need for rewards. When Culpeper commented on
a draft proposal of the Office in 1646, he in fact made no mention of Wheeler,
with whom the circle was negotiating at that time. At this point his concern was
simply that no one but Hartlib would have 'suche a stocke of forreine relation,
intelligence & ingenuities'.[70]

Culpeper had been too optimistic. By February 1646, it emerged that a trial of
Wheeler's engine would not take place in England. Culpeper accordingly told
Hartlib that he 'did not open' himself to a call for investment—a reluctance he
repeated in October 1647, just five months after the publication of the first printed
proposal for the Office of Address.[71] Wheeler probably remained unwilling to agree
to the terms of cooperation. If the overblown narrative in *Mr William Wheeler's case*
(1645) is to be believed, he feared that patrons such as Boswell were plotting to
deprive him of God-given secrets. His expertise, Wheeler alleged, 'drew upon me
infinite enmities, and oppositions', but 'the mercy of God most admirably fortified
me: so that I did conceal my chief skill'.[72] Meanwhile, in December 1647, Petty
performed his 'double-writing' engine before witnesses and soon began seeking a
patent for it.[73] He did not reveal the secret to the circle. Having given up the idea
of introducing a new tax on writing paper (as we saw earlier), Petty went on proposing to take fees of seven shillings and twopence for licensing, asking parliament
to pay £1,000 for fully revealing the technology behind the invention.[74]

Culpeper's view began to change. In January the following year, Culpeper called
for a parliamentary committee for purchasing inventions. He admitted that he had
been 'exceedingly taken with Mr Petit & Mr Wheelers' inventions. Yet, because
'they cannot parte with them without some rewarde, & that noe private purse'
or public authorities as they stood would answer their demands, Culpeper suggested that parliament 'appoint a Committee for the examininge & rewardinge of
Ingenuities & purchasinge them for publike use'. It was now envisaged that the
Office of Address would serve this committee.[75]

The promotion of useful knowledge began to look more like a trade in marketable goods. Culpeper argued that men like Wheeler had shown just 'howe many
ingenuities ar[e] loste & buried because Selfe cannot be advanced'. The 'exchange
and merchandiz of it is & will be between mechanique disposition' who would 'not

[68] 'Culpeper Letters', p. 248 (13/117–18). Hartlib's preference is revealed in another copy of the
letter with his editorial intervention. See HP 13/119A.

[69] 'Culpeper Letters', p. 248–9 (13/121–2).

[70] Ibid., p. 264, 17 February 1646 (13/127–8).   [71] Ibid., pp. 263, 309.

[72] William Wheeler, *Mr William Wheeler's case from his own relation* (1645), pp. 3, 10.

[73] HP 71/7/3A. See also 'Culpeper Letters', p. 320 n. 12.

[74] William Petty, *Double writing* [1648], handbill with no pagination; TNA, SP 18/2, fos. 156–9.

[75] 'Culpeper Letters', p. 318–19, 18 January 1648 (13/180–1).

forgoe their commodities of ingenuity but by way of barter'.[76] The Office of Address
had to be modified accordingly. Commenting on the 1647 proposal, Culpeper argued
that 'the care of rationall ingenuities showlde be annexed to that parte which you
call the office of Accommodation'.[77]

These considerations were echoed in the second publication on the Office, *A
further discoverie of the office of publick addresse for accommodations* (1648). This
striking, yet hitherto underused pamphlet explicitly relegated the status of useful
knowledge to the rank of 'Outward Things concerning this present life' to be handled by the lower Office of Accommodation.[78] Allusions to the possibility of
remuneration must have been unmistakable to contemporary readers. The Office
was to offer 'sensible Inducements towards all Enterprises'; those who had such
things as 'a new discovery of a Truth, or an Experiment in Physick, Mathematicks,
or Mechanicks...shall be able to receive satisfaction therein so far as it is attainable'.[79]
This was because 'most men will not intend any Publick Ayme till they can secure
their own Interests'.[80] Spiritual aspirations did not disappear, of course. In a manuscript sequel to the *Further discoverie*, aptly titled 'A further discoverie of the Office
of Addresse in matter, of *communication*', we find the ideal of free, unimpaired
communication powerfully reiterated:

> The only Meanes to gaine this End [i.e. God's glory] is, that every one as he hath
> received any gift from God...should communicat the same unto others as having
> it for none other use but to bee a steward therof for the good of all...without the
> exercise thereof...wee beleeve that there can bee noe perfection attained, nor any
> Reformation...advanced[.][81]

The ideal was clear, but giving the Office a concrete shape must have been particularly
difficult, now that they had been struggling to negotiate with needy collaborators.
The manuscript tract did not speak explicitly of inventions and business proposals. What it did instead was to discuss in abstract terms 'Arts' and 'Science'
alongside other 'fruites of Reason' such as 'Learning', 'Experience', 'Prudencie', and
'Wisedome'. The final section of the treatise, regarding the 'manner' of implementing
the office 'in an Orderly Way by Faithfull Agents', was never written.[82] Meanwhile,
in the published *Further discoverie*, the purchasing of useful secrets was characterized
as a 'momentary' means for achieving the 'Work of Communication...towards the
Advancement of Pietie, Vertue, and Learning'.[83] Note that the rewarding of inventors was construed here as an explicitly temporary measure. This is confirmed by
Hartlib's scribal intervention elsewhere. When Culpeper called for the introduction
of a parliament committee in January 1648, he depicted it as 'an Accommodation

---

[76] Ibid., p. 287, n.d. [January 1648?] (13/284/5). This dating is based on Culpeper's paying his
Michaelmas rent, which is also mentioned ibid., p. 297.

[77] Ibid., p. 287.

[78] [Samuel Hartlib], *A further discoverie of the office of publick addresse for accommodations* (1648);
Considerations, p. 42 (quotation).

[79] [Hartlib], *Further discoverie*, pp. 3, 24.   [80] Ibid., p. 2.

[81] HP 47/10/2–55B (quotation at HP 47/10/17B).   [82] HP 47/10/22A, 39A.

[83] [Hartlib], *Further discoverie*, sig. [D4]. See also John Dury, *A seasonable discourse written by
Mr John Dury* (1649), sig. [D2v], [D4v].

in this point. Hartlib soon created an abstract of this letter for circulation, but he changed the phrase so that the purchasing of inventions was now presented as an 'accommodation *in this present*', something to be adopted temporarily until individual spiritual reformation fully took root among collaborators.[84] Unless such individual renewal was first accomplished, it would have been futile for Hartlib and his colleagues to publish further details about their idealistic Office of Communication. Indeed, the manuscript sequel about this upper branch was most likely never printed. Its absence in print form thus speaks volumes about the magnitude of reformers' ambitions; its printed counterpart (*Further discoverie*) by contrast testifies to their grudging effort to 'accommodate' those who could not abandon worldly needs for compensation. Subsequent publications on the subject adopted this line.[85]

More broadly speaking, the desire to offer reward and thereby expand the ring of collaborators was probably rooted in the advent of international Calvinism itself. Based on the doctrine of election, zealous Calvinists in the Netherlands, for example, saw themselves as the chosen few, or 'the children of God'. Yet there was also a desire to cast 'the "evangelical net" to catch as many as possible' for the propagation of the Gospel.[86] Like a comprehensive church, then, the Office of Address was to open its door widely. No longer just for public-spirited individuals, the published proposal came to look more like a means for accommodating unreformed brethren into the pursuit of useful knowledge and reformation.

The tension between parliamentarians and royalists remained high, and the state-backed system of testing and purchasing inventions never materialized. Hartlib probably understood this to be God's redirection. As Culpeper once stated approvingly, he had a 'resolution to persiste in your office of address' and 'ever to labor with those materials which God affoords & to leave the successee to him'.[87] 'Men must adjust to God's will, not prescribe to it' by their own devices, as Blair Worden has put it.[88] Hartlib thus started the Office of Address as an unofficial institution drawing on the money parliament had granted him.[89] Unfortunately, however, imitators soon began to set up their own offices of address, and Hartlib argued for suppressing them so that such a useful institution 'may not be left at Random to bee abused'—a measure to be swiftly adapted by parliament for the public good.[90] This must have made him look like the former monopolists encroaching upon

---

[84] Compare the original letter (HP 13/180A) with the abstract (HP 53/35/1A). Italics are mine.

[85] Dury, *Seasonable discourse*, sig. [Dv], [D3v]; [Cressy Dymock], *An essay for advancement of husbandry-learning; or propositions for the erecting a colledge of husbandry* (1651), pp. 6, 10.

[86] Alastair Duke, 'The Ambivalent Face of Calvinism in the Netherlands, 1561–1618', in Menna Prestwich (ed.), *International Calvinism, 1541–1715* (Oxford: Clarendon, 1985), 109–34, at p. 132.

[87] 'Culpeper Letters', p. 269, 4 March 1646 (13/136–7).

[88] Blair Worden, 'Providence and Politics in Cromwellian England', *P&P*, 109 (1985), 55–99, at p. 93.

[89] Hartlib was granted a parliamentary fund of £300 in March 1647, two months before the first publication on the Office. He was also to receive an annuity of about £100, but the payment proved irregular. *CJ*, vol. 5, p. 131; Charles Webster, *Samuel Hartlib and the Advancement of Learning* (Cambridge: Cambridge University Press, 1970), p. 49.

[90] HP 63/7/3B, Hartlib's Petition to the Council of State, n.d. (quotation); Webster, *Great instauration*, p. 74; Turnbull, *Hartlib, Dury and Comenius*, pp. 83–6.

other people's rights and liberties; for (as we saw in Chapter 2) under the early
Stuarts projectors such as Bushell promoted their punitive measures by presenting
them as necessary steps to prevent abuse. Neither introspective nor state-led reform
proved forthcoming in the end. Hartlib and his close allies had to keep negotiating
informally. It would have been easier for them had public distrust of the project
subsided with the execution of Charles I in 1649. This was not the case. On
1 January 1651, Charles II was formally crowned king of Scotland at Scone; a
flurry of pamphlets swiftly appeared to remind the public of early Stuart misrule,
hinting what the royal succession might entail. One such pamphlet described how
'our Estates and Liberties...were impoverished and enthralled, by multitudes of
projects', with William Noy, 'the most hatefull man that ever lived', being 'the sole
Author of all'.[91] Another, purportedly 'published by authority', defamed the executed
Charles I more directly:

> the first resolution [of this king] was, to fall out with his owns good People... [and to]
> wash them in their blood;...he began by the imprisoning of his most faithful sub-
> jects...by his introducing of Idolatry, by Pressures, by Monopolies, by his exacting of
> Ship-money, and all such grievances, whereby he might best settle his Ravenous minde
> at worke[.]

Thanks to such 'dynastic defamation', bitter memories of early Stuart grievances
never died away.[92] If anything, they kept coming back in the tense climate of the
1650s. The problem of distrust therefore remained, and the would-be reformers
began from the end of the 1640s to take a strikingly wide range of actions under
the slogan of reformation. It is to this that the next section turns.

FRAGMENTED DREAMS OF REFORMATION

In the absence of a state-backed office of address, Culpeper grew increasingly
unsympathetic to projector-like promoters unwilling to share knowledge without
monetary rewards. In April 1648, for example, he warned Hartlib against meddling
with the Cambridge-educated Robert Child, should he turn out to be 'not...of a
communicative disposition'.[93] In July, in reference to Wheeler, Culpeper declared
that he would not 'deceive my selfe, in valewinge what lyes buried in another mans
bosome'; in November, he further lamented that Petty and the German alchemist
inventor Johann Glauber were likely 'to turne a Wheeler'. He now resolved 'not to
trowble my thowghts any farther' with them, because their 'ingenuity consistes in

---

[91] Anthony Weldon, *The court and character of King James whereunto is now added the court
of King Charles* (1651), pp. 195–6. See also Anthony Weldon, *A cat may look upon a king* (1652),
pp. 65–6.

[92] Balthazar Gerbier, *The none-such Charles his character* (1651), pp. 119, 158–9 (quotation), 171.
Thomas Cogswell is currently undertaking research into what he calls dynastic defamation and the
creation of the 'Stuart Black Legend' in the 1650s. This episode would tell us much about the ongoing
social circulation of distrust. I thank him for conversation on the subject.

[93] 'Culpeper Letters', p. 331 (13/215–6).

other mens purses and theire owne interestes'.[94] Culpeper learned in March the following year that Wheeler had run away from the United Provinces 'without sending or writing after, to any of his Creditors'.[95] He declared in response:

till every particular person be wrowght on by Gods Spirite, to knowe, & to acknowledge, that the talentes he hath received... are not given, but entrusted onely... not to our owne onely, but to others good[,] till this (I say) be woorckte into the Spirites of men, the divell will hinder the worlde, of a great parte of the happiness,... of that abundance which more communication of ingenuities wowld produce, & of that innocence, which abundance of all thinges wowld bringe into the worlde[.][96]

For Culpeper the sins of unreformed brethren now seemed a profound obstacle to the arrival of the Second Coming.

Speaking unfavourably of 'Mr Pettys zeal for experiments', Henry More also declared that 'great projectes' were nothing but the wasteful 'building of Babell against a second expected deluge' unless accompanied by 'sincerity, and untainted morality'.[97] Where prospective collaborators appeared covetous or unscrupulous, the need for spiritual renewal could be invoked to reject them as unreformed brethren who were wasting God-given talents.

Paradoxically, however, the Calvinist doctrine that underlay the pursuit of reformation simultaneously enjoined to give the benefit of the doubt. For example, by alluding to Ecclesiastes 11:6, Dury advised Culpeper not to be too sceptical about Le Pruvost's scheme: 'wee are bid sow our seed in the morning, and not [to] withhold our hand in the Evening, because wee know not whither shall prosper whether this or that, or both'. It was important 'to resign ourselves up to God by depending upon his providence for a blessing, and not trusting to much to our owne prudencie to doe thinges'.[98] Receiving the letter, Culpeper agreed and confessed his 'hopes... to inlarge my thowghts' and depend on God's providence and guidance.[99] The success of certain enterprises was to be entrusted to divine, rather than human, judgement.

More than religion was at work as well. Hartlib had been interested in the patent system from the 1630s, and later helped various inventors and technologists at home and abroad to obtain patents for specific inventions (i.e. not monopolistic patents).[100] In order to help his wife earn a living, Dury solicited from Worsley a recipe for cordials and ciders; Worsley replied with 'the most luciferous secrett' that was to be 'kept privatt'.[101] Culpeper was probably interested in using

[94] Ibid., p. 338–9 (13/231–2); ibid., p. 348 (13/246–7). For subsequent negative comments on Wheeler, see ibid., pp. 355, 358.

[95] HP 36/8/3A–4A.   [96] 'Culpeper Letters', p. 324 (13/209–11).

[97] HP 18/1/2B–3A. See also McCormick, *Petty*, p. 59.

[98] 'Culpeper Letters', p. 235, Dury to Culpeper, n.d. [autumn 1645] (55/10/11–14).

[99] 'Culpeper Letters', p. 244 (13/294–5).

[100] Clucas, 'Hartlib', pp. 61–3; Mark Greengrass, 'The Projecting Culture of Samuel Hartlib and his Circle' (unpublished conference paper for 'Publicists and Projectors in Seventeenth-Century Europe', Wolfenbüttel, 1996), no pagination; John T. Young, 'Utopian Artificers: Hartlib's Promotion of German Technology in the English Commonwealth' (unpublished paper).

[101] HP 33/2/19A, 26/33/1B.

others' inventions on his estate or elsewhere.[102] Though aspiring to holiness, these reformers were therefore never altogether removed from the monetary concerns that they occasionally censured. After all, Hartlib and his close allies could not promote useful knowledge without drawing on a wider ring of collaborators. Too readily dismissing them as base and unreformed would have been as untenable as it was presumptuous for those aspiring to become instruments—however weak and imperfect—of God's providence.

The aspiration to follow the divine will, bound up with more pragmatic concerns, helps us understand the otherwise puzzling fluctuation of reformers' attitudes towards collaborators.[103] Culpeper, who had once accused Glauber and Petty of mercenary attitudes, for example, came to 'wonderfully approve' of Glauber while arranging to pay for Petty's agricultural inventions, only to become dismissive of them again later. Even then, Culpeper wished that somehow Hartlib might 'give a change to these my thowghts' on them.[104] It is therefore hardly surprising that Hartlib and his allies went on extending support to otherwise dubious inventors such as Dymock. Although details of his experiments in arable cultivation were kept secret, Boyle, Culpeper, and others invested in them the total of fifty pounds in May 1649.[105] In March the following year, Hartlib and one Alexander Tracye of London paid Dymock a 'competent sum of money' so that under their direction Dymock would build the mills that he claimed approached a perpetual motion engine.[106] Some of Dymock's letters and manuscripts were subsequently printed in order to call for more investment.[107] Support was not unconditional. It seems that by 1654, a year after his three-year contract with Hartlib and Tracye on the perpetual motion engines had expired, Dymock had fallen out of favour. In February that year, Hartlib wrote to Boyle: 'Mr. *Dymock* . . . is forsaken, in a manner, by all'. 'Honest Mr. *Dymock* is blamed almost by every body', Hartlib added three months later. Even he admitted that 'I cannot any longer assist either his person, family, or inventions'.[108]

Aspiration to reformation, however, did not allow the reformer completely to ignore dubious promoters like Dymock. As Howard Hotson has shown, Hartlib, Comenius, and his teacher Johann Heinrich Alsted aspired to regain the extent of knowledge mankind had lost after the Fall. As Alsted put it, 'man approaches God as closely as possible when he knows Him and His works and when he forms and conforms all

---

[102] 'Culpeper Letters', pp. 335–7, 340–1, 343–4.

[103] See Charles Webster, 'Benjamin Worsley: Engineering for Universal Reform from the Invisible College to the Navigation Act', in *Universal Reformation*, 213–46, at p. 223 n. 26; John T. Young, *Faith, Medical Alchemy and Natural Philosophy: Johan Moriaen, Reformed Intelligencer, and the Hartlib Circle* (Aldershot: Ashgate, 1998), p. 202.

[104] 'Culpeper Letters', pp. 340–1, 344, 347, 348. For details of Glauber's reception among reformers in England, see Young, *Moriaen*, ch. 6.

[105] HP 62/48/1B. This corrects 'Culpeper Letters', p. 134.

[106] HP 58/8A, While a 'model' of this engine had been erected in Lambeth, access to the engine's mechanical details was tightly controlled (HP 58/8B–9A).

[107] [Hartlib and Dymock], *Reformed husband-man*, p. 10. See also Cressy Dymock, *An invention of engines of motion lately brought to perfection* (1651), p. 2, sig. [A2v].

[108] *Boyle Correspondence*, vol. 1, pp. 159, 178.

his works and deeds to goodness and virtue'.[109] This was not a purely intellectual concern. For, argued Hartlib, 'it is nothing but the Narrownes of our Spirits that makes us miserable'; mankind would indeed obtain 'infinite Meanes of Reliefe and Comfort' if 'that which God hath given them' was put to use 'to serve the Glory of his Goodness'.[110] Despite his frustration, Hartlib in fact never completely dismissed Dymock, urging Boyle that Dymock's 'publick and private usefulness' be reappraised and some of his schemes be further 'supported, than hither it hath been'.[111] Even after a correspondent concluded that Wheeler was nothing less than a charlatan,[112] Hartlib kept noting in his work diary *Ephemerides* Wheeler's numerous inventions until the inventor's death in 1652.[113] Although there was no sign of sustained collaboration, Hartlib also took note of the chequered career of the royalist projector Bushell well into the Interregnum, from his conciliatory approach to the House of Commons in 1649 to his new proposal for developing Scottish mines.[114] Hartlib took a similar inclusive approach to Glauber, stressing the need to 'note whatever was true and good in all his writings' even if the inventor was by some 'count[ed] no better than a moun-tebank, one that continues to cheat all sorts of people by his specious artifices'.[115] '[Y]our rule is goode', acknowledged Culpeper, 'to passe by the woorste of every man soe as the infirmities hinder not the use of what good is [in] him'.[116] Even where collaboration proved untenable, therefore, the impulse towards collecting God-ordained knowledge prompted the gathering of information even from the dubious.

If different facets of the reforming ideal prevented the Hartlib circle from pur-suing a coherent method of promoting useful knowledge, the persistent distrust of the projector led collaborators to take diverging courses of action. In September 1649, when Dymock was busy promoting his schemes for agriculture and perpetual motion, he complained of 'the exceeding antipathy that almost all men have in them against engenuitye which causes them to reject all new inventions... under the name & notion of projects'.[117] This explains why Dymock carefully played to the sensibilities of his prospective patrons. Unlike Wheeler, who did not build mills in England, Dymock set up a 'model' of his engine in Lambeth to prove his technical competence. Although he could drop pious language and highlight forthcoming profits when the occasion suited,[118] Dymock's letters to

---

[109] Quoted in Howard Hotson, *Johann Heinrich Alsted, 1588–1638: Between Renaissance, Refor-mation, and Universal Reform* (Oxford: Clarendon, 2000), p. 70. The tradition of cataloguing divine wisdom and judgement goes well beyond Hartlib's immediate predecessors. See Matthew McLean, *The Cosmographia of Sebastian Münster: Describing the World in the Reformation* (Aldershot: Ashgate, 2007), pp. 105–26, 332; Alexandra Walsham, *Providence in Early Modern England* (Oxford: Oxford University Press, 1999), chs. 2–3.

[110] [Dymock], *Husbandry-learning*, sig. 2A, [2Av], preface by Hartlib.

[111] *Boyle Correspondence*, vol. 1, pp. 160, 178.

[112] HP 62/17/1B, W. Rand to Hartlib, 14 February 1652.

[113] HP 28/2/2A, 14B, 35B, 39B, 45A, 46B, 50A, 52B, 53A.

[114] Relevant entries in Hartlib's *Ephemerides* include HP 28/1/19A (1649); 28/2/75B–76A (1653); 29/4/24B (1654); 29/5/26B, 30A (1655).

[115] HP 7/7/3B, Hartlib to Winthrop, 16 March 1660.

[116] 'Culpeper Letters', p. 312 (13/202–3).

[117] HP 62/50/5A, Dymock to Hartlib, 29 September 1649.

[118] Dymock's letter to Worsley, transcribed in RS, RB/3/7/1, Worsley to Hartlib, 18 May 1649 ('nothing is wanting to make you...rich').

Hartlib constantly emphasized his desire to serve 'ever Gratious God' and 'the universall good of Mankind' by perfecting God-ordained inventions.[119] Alluding to the very passage from Ecclesiastes that Dury mentioned, Dymock even assured Hartlib that 'of this seed you will reap abundant Harvest in due time'—a superb metaphor for promoting engines to be used in agriculture.[120] Even though he did not abandon proprietary attitudes, as Plattes and Blith did, in this way Dymock managed to solicit a degree of support from Hartlib and his associates.

Others in the circle stopped promoting schemes to private backers. Worsley provides the most striking example. In 1649, while staying in the United Provinces, he declared 'the vanity of proposing' new schemes: 'unlesse I may have a place or settled imployment in England, I shall have no heart at all to come over, for I am much convinced of the vanity of proposing any invention to the world of any kind'.[121] This was a clear change from 1646. He had then hoped that schemes like his own, 'propounded even but by strangers' like him, would be capable of winning 'favour and acceptance' from parliament and elsewhere.[122] His interest in saltpetre remained, and Worsley continued to propose ways to achieve the better 'Imploiment of the poor', the 'bringing in of Bullion' from abroad, or 'the augmenting of the Revenue to the State' for the 'Commonwealth's service'.[123] But his activities were increasingly channelled into the government, for example, the commission for the parliamentary settlement in Virginia, and the Council of Trade set up in 1650.[124] Petty pursued a similar path. During 1648, he was busy publicizing the double-writing engine and dabbling in agricultural inventions, including a corn-setting engine, perhaps in an attempt to improve the engine patented by Plattes. Yet after a brief foray into the University of Oxford, he started serving as a government official in Cromwellian Ireland for the famous Down Survey.[125] If Dymock continued to seek support through Hartlib's informal network and by printing some of his writings, Worsley and Petty opted to pursue careers in government to exploit their talents in what must have appeared a more favourable environment. If anything, the unresolved problem of distrust and the ambivalence of reforming ideals fragmented the circle's pursuit of useful knowledge.

LEGACIES: TESTIMONIES, SERIAL PUBLICATION, AND EXPERIMENTS

Just as the problem of distrust influenced how mid-century reformers formed and re-formed projects, it also shaped their knowledge-making practices—how they

---

[119] HP 62/60/9A, *passim*.

[120] A now lost letter to Hartlib on 10 March 1652, printed in Dymock, *An invention*, pp. 2–3.

[121] HP 26/33 2B, Worsley to Hartlib, 22 June 1649.   [122] HP 71/11/9A.

[123] Benjamin Worsley, *Free ports, the nature and necessitie of them stated* (1652), p. 4; [Benjamin Worsley], *The advocate: or, a narrative of the state and condition of things between the English and Dutch nation, in relation to trade* (1651), sig. B2v. For background, see Leng, *Worsley*, pp. 77–9.

[124] Leng, *Worsley*, pp. 55–70.

[125] 'Culpeper Letters', pp. 335–48; McCormick, *Petty*, pp. 73–4, ch. 3.

sought to lend credibility to the knowledge they claimed to possess by mobilizing experiments, direct observations, testimonies, serial publications, and critical empirical reasoning. In the fragmented pursuits of projects in the 1640s and 1650s, we thus find the incipient practices of experimental philosophy that would soon be cherished by the Royal Society, which began its activities in the 1660s.

To begin with, in an attempt to establish credibility amid distrust, Plattes highlighted the role of credible witnesses. No stranger to the world of projecting and patenting, Plattes was scarcely immune to the public suspicion cast upon projectors. After publishing *Macaria* in 1641, Plattes had been preparing a large book called *The treasure house of nature unlocked*, which was to supersede his previous writings in scale and scope. His ideal was the familiar one: 'knowledge that concernth the publick good, ought not to be concealed in the breasts of a few'. Upon publication, he told Hartlib, a copy of the book would be donated to 'every publick Library in the Kingdome'.[126] Yet in May 1644, just a few months before his death, Plattes announced to Hartlib that he had postponed the publication of his magnum opus. 'The reason why it is not printed' was because his relations would 'seem so strange, and incredible to most men, that they will be likely to slight it, to the great prejudice of the Common-Wealth'.[127] What Plattes had done in the tracts of 1639—conducting experiments at his own expense and giving the reader both details of his knowledge and caveats about its limitations—seemed no longer sufficient. The rising tide of anger and criticism of Caroline projectors that exploded in print after the collapse of press censorship in late 1641 probably made it even harder to persuade the reading public to try experiments themselves. Plattes had no hesitation in identifying the problem:

> Projectors have cast so many bitter things into the publick Fountain, whereof all have drunk, and their minds are so poysoned, that there is no other way to unpoyson them, but to win their beleef and willingness to practise [recommended methods of cultivation], by such depositions of Gentlemen of qualities, which know the same as well as I my self.[128]

There was, he thus argued, 'no thinking of publishing of it, till we have obtained a [Parliamentary] Committee to examine witnesses, and to print their Deposition in it'. Testimonies of credible gentlemen, backed up by authority, were called upon as a potential solution for the problem of distrust, in order to 'yeeld unanimous consent' of the reader upon the 'truth thereof' contained there.[129] The tactical use of gentlemanly witnesses would later be taken up by the Royal Society and its Fellows in the post-Restoration period.

The solution adopted by Plattes went against his own recommendations, however. He had earlier warned his reader not to assume that results derived

---

[126] Gabriel Plattes, *The profitable intelligencer, communicating his knowledge for the generall good of the common-wealth and all posterity* (1644), sig. [Av], A2. He also planned to sell copies for five shillings each and make it available for one-week loans for twopence, ibid., sig. A2.
[127] Ibid., sig. A2.   [128] Ibid., sig.[Av].   [129] Ibid., sig.[Av], A2.

from local experiments would be 'unpossible ever to fail' elsewhere. If so, gentlemen's testimonies could not guarantee that a set of successful experiments would be equally successful elsewhere. Worse, if testimonies of failed experiments were to be taken as indicating that the same procedure would be abortive elsewhere, then such testimonies would hinder the progress of knowledge by preventing others from finding out whether or not the same procedure might yield better outcomes under different circumstances. *The treasure house of nature unlocked* was never published despite the author's wish to do so; Plattes died towards the end of 1644, reportedly 'in the street for want of food'.[130] The absence of Plattes's magnum opus is, then, a testimony to the persistent distrust of the projector, distrust that drove him to contradict his own belief in experiment and its limited validity.

Unlike Plattes, who looked to parliamentary authority to command consent upon his recommendations, Blith invited readers to contribute their knowledge and discoveries. The underlying theme was that of collaborative research, experiment, and communication, all aiming at the gradual improvement of useful knowledge. For Blith, differences, rather than unanimity, was the driving force. By exposing his experiments 'to publique view' by print, Blith hoped

> to give either Incouragement to some deeper and solid Practitioners to hold out their Experienced Principles, or else to Exasperate or provoke the offended, or Gaine-sayer, rather to reprove it...desiring a most Cleare, Plaine, and Cordiall Information, to himselfe and Kingdome, by whom soever.[131]

His discussion of drainage was, for example, meant to reveal 'the open face of that Experience I have made, be it beautifull or deformed; in pitty to move others to cover the deformities thereof, or put more beauty thereon'.[132] Blith used the subsequent editions of *The English Improver* precisely for this purpose of collaboration. Interestingly, in the third edition, Blith withdrew the earlier attack upon the fen-projectors that he had made in the first.[133] Reporting that 'a Gentleman of art and worth' had told him of a new way of sowing corn, Blith announced to the reader that 'I hope to have brought into substantiall experience upon my own lands by the next edition, and then expect the faithfull communication thereof'.[134] His plan for publishing successive editions was cut short by his death in 1652, the year in which *The English improver improved*—the third edition—appeared. But by proposing something similar to an evolutionary vision of useful knowledge, facilitated by serial publication of different outcomes, Blith prefigured the Royal Society's *Philosophical Transactions*, and distinguished his writings both from the

---

130 Samuel Hartlib et al., *Samuel Hartlib his legacy of husbandry* (3rd edn, 1655), p. 183.

131 Blith, *English improver*, sig. a2, a. See also Blith, *English improver improved*, p. 187.

132 Joan Thirsk, 'Plough and Pen: Agricultural Writers in the Seventeenth Century', in T. H. Aston et al. (eds.), *Social Relations and Ideas: Essays in Honour of R. H. Hilton* (Cambridge: Cambridge University Press, 1983), 295–318, pp. 309–10; Blith, *English improver improved*, p. 45.

133 Blith, *English improver improved*, sig. [C4v]   134 Ibid., pp. 220–1.

pretension of infallible knowledge and from Plattes' problematic equation of gentlemanly testimony with the 'truth'.[135]

Promoters' efforts went beyond social practices such as the mobilization of witnesses and multiple editions. Responding to the problem of distrust, promoters of useful knowledge also found themselves giving greater emphasis to verification, empirical testing, and experiment. Where technical inventions were concerned, one common method was to demonstrate their technical feasibility by producing a prototype or a (smaller) model, as in the cases of Petty's 'double-writing engine' and Dymock's perpetual motion machine.[136] Blith spoke for many others when he explained why models and experiments mattered. '[T]hose men that now cry down all devices or ingenious discoveries, as projects' tended to 'thereby stifle, and choak Improvement'.[137] This was because there had been 'so much Abuse offered by many, in holding forth strange Affirmations proving but Conjectures, and Heare-sayes, as hath brought Ingenuity under greatest Scandall'. But, he continued, 'None dare scorne when they are made Experiments'.[138]

Yet such experiments could prove inconclusive, or even misleading. In husbandry and silviculture, for example, a small-scale experiment—on a model farm—was often recommended as the first step towards trying it out on a larger scale. Yet the successful cultivation in one location of a crop, such as clover, may not be replicated elsewhere under different soil and climatic conditions. A hypothesis for explaining particular success may fail to predict results obtained elsewhere. As Blith told his reader, 'thou wilt finde it in the Practise more Ambiguous then in the discourse, notwithstanding all my applications to my owne Experiences'.[139] Unexpectedly, therefore, the danger of incurring public distrust led some to call for further cross-examination, controlled experiments, and the refining of hypotheses—some of the defining features of the emerging experimental philosophy. As Plattes put it, old maxims, received theories, and even one's own hypotheses were 'subject to failings...which was the cause that I...addicted myselfe so strongly to experiments, judging no knowledge perfect till it was thereby confirmed'.[140]

Robert Wood of Dublin was one such practitioner addicted to experiments, especially on clover cultivation. Hartlib found Wood's manuscript on the subject to be 'very fit', and asked him in 1656 to publish it in order to dispel 'prejudice that is of late against' it. The 'generall Complaint' was that the plant 'eats out the Heart of the Ground, & leaves it barren'. In his manuscript 'answer', Wood argued that the complaint came from those who 'had no triall of it at all themselves' or from those who tried for less than two years, with 'so little time as...to make a perfect &

---

[135] Publication of scientific periodicals was also fraught with difficulties, including piracy. See Adrian Johns, *The Nature of the Book: Print and Knowledge in the Making* (Chicago: University of Chicago Press, 1998), pp. 498–503, 535–40; Adrian Johns, 'Miscellaneous Methods: Authors, Societies and Journals in Early Modern England', *BJHS*, 33 (2000), 159–86; N. Moxham, 'Fit for Print: Developing an Institutional Model of Scientific Periodical Publishing in England, 1665–ca. 1714', *NRRS*, 69 (2015), 241–60.

[136] See pp. 117, 123.   [137] See Blith, *English improver improved*, p. 234 [recte p. 236].

[138] Blith, *English improver*, sig. [a3v]. See also Blith, *English improver improved*, sig. c2.

[139] Blith, *English improver*, sig. [a3v]–[a4].

[140] Plattes, *Discovery of infinite treasure*, sig. [B3v].

deciding experiment'.[141] Yet Wood declined to publish his manuscript upon his return from north-western Ireland; this was because Wood could not confirm his 'conjectures' against the experience of the other successful cultivators whom he had recently encountered. Thus, he told Hartlib, 'till I have further satisfied myself, I thought it better to leave men to their own experience, than to endeavour to persuade them unto that which might possibly mislead and betray them'. Wood was fearful of publishing mere 'conjectures of mine' about clover cultivation that might not 'hold water in every particular'.[142] Thus, instead of publishing 'Some pretty-devised Hypothesis', Wood kept gathering information, experimenting, and reporting on the matter to Hartlib.[143] It was not easy, as he put it, to pass information for 'the strict Commerce of Right Reason; especially when the thing in question is not seconded, but perhaps contradicted by matter of fact & a practicable Experiment'.[144] Wood was clearly following the kind of disciplined reasoning that Plattes had recommended: 'I did first profoundly dispute with my selfe *pro & contra*...but objected and accused the worke as strongly, as if my enemie had done it'.[145] Direct observations, experiments, and cross-examination of results were given prominence, and their adoption a sense of urgency, as potential solutions to the problem of public distrust. Rigorous repetition of trial and error thereby became something more than a bundle of mere know-how, and the use of reasoning and hypotheses something more than uncritical inferences from old maxims. The permeation of distrust, something that was accelerated by the breakdown of early Stuart rule and boosted again by the tactical defamation of the early Stuart rulers from 1651, had some profound, epistemic implications for the rise of experimental philosophy soon to be enshrined by the Royal Society.[146]

CONCLUSION

The fierce denunciation of Caroline projectors in plays, songs, pamphlets, and in the Long Parliament hardly put an end to projecting activities. On the contrary, a multitude of schemes for economic innovations and improvement continued to emerge, many imbued with religious aspirations. Under Charles I's Personal Rule,

---

[141] His tract is at HP 26/67/1A–2B (quotations from 26/67/1A, 1B). For background, see *AHEW Vii*, pp. 554–5; A. R. Michell, 'Sir Richard Weston and the Spread of Clover Cultivation', *Agricultural History Review*, 22 (1974), 160–1.

[142] HP 33/1/7A, Wood to Hartlib, 23 November 1656.

[143] For example, see HP 33/1/20A (Wood to Hartlib, 8 July 1657), 33/1/56A (Wood to Hartlib, 11 May 1659).

[144] HP 26/67/1B.

[145] Plattes, *Discovery of infinite treasure*, sig. [B3v]. 'My reason hath deceived me so many times, that I will trust it no more, unlesse it be confirmed and made manifest by experience'. Ibid., sig. [B2v.].

[146] The evidence presented in this section complements the discussion in Koji Yamamoto, 'Reformation and the Distrust of the Projector in the Hartlib Circle', *HJ*, 55 (2012), 375–97, pp. 385, 396–7. For recent discussions of Hartlibean legacies, see Richard Yeo, *Notebooks, English Virtuosi, and Early Modern Science* (Chicago: University of Chicago Press, 2014), pp. 135–150; Vera Keller, *Knowledge and the Public Interest, 1575–1725* (Cambridge: Cambridge University Press, 2015), pp. 195–8, 213–19. Cf. Mordechai Feingold, '"Experimental Philosophy": Invention and Rebirth of a Seventeenth-Century Concept', *Early Science and Medicine*, 21 (2016), 1–28.

the social circulation of the image of the projector ultimately did little to change the existing pattern of vexatious projecting. If anything, the image helped trivialize the matter. After the collapse of the Personal Rule, by contrast, it was no longer possible to maintain the status quo either by laughing at the projector or by having recourse to the well-tried rhetoric of reforming abuses. Projects for improving England now had to be organized and promoted differently. Students of Erving Goffman might suggest that, after the collapse of the Caroline regime, *role-distancing* became an indispensable component of promoters' *coping strategies*. Promoters were 'denying not the role [of promoting improvement] but the virtual self that is implied in the role'. Distancing from the early Stuart monopolists and projectors became an important part of England's culture of improvement.[147]

Like the images of the sinful papist or atheist, however, the character of the projector did not do much to define positively how economic innovation and improvement could be pursued without descending into the worst of abuses. By adding the history of science approach to trust to our analytical toolkit, this chapter has shown that the problem of distrust instead divided their initiatives over two fundamental questions. First, there was the delicate question of political economy: how to promote useful knowledge and economic improvement without depriving others of their property and rights to trade. As the cases of Worsley and Petty have shown, there was an emerging agreement that one should avoid behaving like early Stuart projectors, imposing authority purportedly for the public good. Yet, equally importantly, Dury and Culpeper disagreed as to whether Le Pruvost might be permitted to use state authority to impose stiff penalties—including confiscation of private property—to deter free-riders. The second point raised by the distrust of the projector was the question of money and credibility. There was a deep-seated fear that the promotion of useful knowledge might be undermined by elements of profit. Plattes and Blith distanced themselves from monetary rewards and the search for investors in order to lend credibility to themselves and the knowledge they claimed to possess. Yet because many promoters did not adopt such an opt-out strategy, the Office of Address eventually had to allow for the remuneration of men like Wheeler.

The loosely shared concept of religious reformation proved an inadequate guide for action. When discussing the Office of Address proposals, the reformers initially had different views as to what forms of reward should be offered to the inventor, and only reluctantly 'accommodated' what they called men of 'mechanic' dispositions. In the absence of an official Office of Address, commentators like Culpeper and More disparaged inventors like Petty and Wheeler for mercenary attitudes and for lacking inward reformation. Yet avid reformers like Dury were quick to point out that they ought not fully trust their own judgement lest God's will manifest itself through seemingly dubious collaborators—the scenario that Dymock skilfully underlined to solicit continual support. Even if financial support proved untenable (as in the cases of Dymock and Wheeler), Hartlib felt obliged to gather

---

[147] Erving Goffman, 'Role Distance', in Goffman, *Encounters: Two Studies in the Sociology of Interaction* (London: Penguin, 1961), 75–134 (quotation from p. 95).

information from them in order to restore the knowledge lost after the Fall. These varying positions were probably not mutually exclusive. Religiously committed reformers such as Hartlib, Culpeper, and Dury seem to have embraced these reforming impulses, each taking diverging actions drawing differently upon their loosely shared ideals. That the mid-century reformers did not develop a coherent set of measures is hardly surprising. After all, they were operating in an era of unprecedented political upheavals, when articulating unequivocal ideological positions could provoke dissent and controversies.[148] The circle's untidy pursuit of useful knowledge emerged, in short, as differing responses to, and interpretations of, a shared frame of reference: the distrust of the projector and the pursuit of reformation.

There were moments, of course, where the mid-century promoters of renewed reformation did not quite live up to their ideals. When Hartlib lobbied for preventing others from running competing offices of address 'for the public good' and for preventing 'abuses', his rhetoric was disturbingly similar to that of early Stuart projects such as the Silk Office and the Westminster soap monopoly, both of which were justified as the reformation of abuses. More broadly, despite all the calls for godliness and spiritual reform, financial rewards and material interests were never too far away from the mid-century promoters. Even Plattes, who prominently advertised his willingness to give away his knowledge, did obtain a patent to protect his seed-setting engine, and probably accepted fees. Despite their efforts, then, the distinction between profit-hungry projectors and public-spirited reformers remained at times all too indistinct.

If the mid-century reforming initiatives had certain limitations, they were not without some lasting legacies either. In an attempt to dissociate themselves from early Stuart projectors' spurious promises of skills and profits, greater attention was given to the virtue of one's own experience derived from first-hand observations and experiments. Studies of the rise of experimental philosophy have tended to suggest that *philosophical* objections derived from Aristotelianism and Scholasticism presented the chief obstacles to the use of experiments.[149] The findings of this chapter enable us to broaden our perspective to include *political* factors. The collapse of Charles's Personal Rule and the ensuing denunciation of the early Stuart projectors deeply affected knowledge-making practices in the mid-century, especially when it came to the practical application of useful knowledge. This was why Blith and others highlighted the importance of conducting experiments and publishing results to call for further research and cross-examination, why Plattes desperately

---

[148] On the avoidance of explicit 'position-taking', see Mark S. R. Jenner, '"Another *Epocha*"? Hartlib, John Lanyon and the Improvement of London in the 1650s', in *Universal Reformation*, 343–56, at p. 351; Timothy Raylor, 'Samuel Hartlib and the Commonwealth of Bees', in *Culture and Cultivation*, 91–129 (esp. pp. 116–18).

[149] Peter Dear, *Discipline and Experience: The Mathematical Way in the Scientific Revolution* (Chicago: University of Chicago Press, 1995); Shapin, *Social History of Truth*, p. 124. But see Jessica Ratcliff, '"Art to Cheat the Common-Weal": Inventors, Projectors, and Patentees in English Satire, ca. 1630–70', *Technology and Culture*, 53 (2012), 337–65, pp. 342, 357; Keller, *Knowledge and Public Interest*, pp. 124–6, 208–9; Vera Keller and Leigh T. I. Penman, 'From the Archives of Scientific Diplomacy: Science and the Shared Interests of Samuel Hartlib's London and Frederick Clodius's Gottorf', *ISIS*, 106 (2015), 17–42.

called for gentlemanly witnesses, and why Wood chose not to publish his manuscripts on clover cultivation lest he should 'mislead and betray' the sceptical audience.

Can we go on to suggest that the distrust of the projector profoundly affected the promotion of improvement across the intersection between the political and economic spheres? Was public distrust not limited to the likes of Hartlib, whose grand visions far outweighed their capacity for implementation? These questions are vital for the purpose of this book. For the social impact of distrust can be said to have been profound if—but only if—we can ascertain that even those who had a successful career of turning projects into reality suffered from pervasive suspicion. The former Parliamentarian soldier Andrew Yarranton and his river navigation scheme provide us with an ideal test case, as he was one of the best-known, if not respected, promoters of improvement in the later seventeenth century. To these we shall turn in Chapter 4.

4

Turning a Project into Reality

There is one Capt[ain] Yarington a very honest person & extreamly well known, who since the late troubles hath upon the request of several gentlemen of qualitie betaken himselfe to travell both abroad and att home, to observe what improvement may be made in our manufactures & trade: in which he hath made so great a profitiency ass that about a yeare or sow since most of the curious and ingenious people of qualitie in town went to heare his weekly lectures which he made upon that subject[.]

Bodl., Carte MS 233, fols. 293–3v,
Goodwin [Wharton] to [Thomas Wharton?], 9 July 1679

In the 1670s, in his fifties, Andrew Yarranton (1619–84) rose to fame. '[A]t Garways [coffeehouse] met with one Yarrington', Robert Hooke wrote in his dairy on 26 December 1673. Yarranton had, Hooke noted, 'seen the Latten making works neer Leipsick [i.e. Leipzig]'. They exchanged 'much discourse', among which was the discussion of 'many plates beat under the Hammer at once like leaf gold or tinfoyle'—the kind of productivity-enhancing invention that John Cary would soon approve of in his *An essay on the state of England* (1695).[1] Thereafter, Hooke continued to meet Yarranton at London coffeehouses.[2] Hooke, the Gresham Professor of Geometry and the Curator of Experiments at the Royal Society, must have been impressed by Yarranton's expertise. The Society's *Philosophical Transactions* soon celebrated his treatise on national economic improvements, *England's improvement by sea and land* (1677). The book was found to be persuasive, particularly because it was based on the author's actual 'Imployment', ranging from ironworks to inland navigation:

Where Iron-Mills, and Iron-Works, may for General profit be promoted, himself having been long practiced in that Imployment? What Rivers, in *England* and *Ireland*, may be made Navigable; himself having surveyed them, and made some considerable Rivers Navigable?[3]

---

[1] Robert Hooke, *Diary of Robert Hooke, 1672–1680*, ed. Henry W. Robinson and Walter Adams (London: Taylor and Francis, 1935), pp. 76–7. For Cary's comment, see p. 1 above.
[2] Hooke, *Diary*, p. 79, 247, 248, 249, 251, 252, 255.
[3] *PT*, vol. 11, no. 131, 29 January 1677, p. 797. Yarranton's proposal to connect navigable rivers, contained in this book, was more detailed than Petty's comparable proposal in the same period. See Sue Dale, 'Sir William Petty's "Ten Tooles": A Programme for the Transformation of England and Ireland during the Reign of James II' (PhD thesis, Birkbeck, 2014), p. 200 n. 109.

The former associate of Hartlib, John Beale, in fact urged the Society's Fellows 'to cast y[ou]r eye upon' the review and the treatise; John Aubrey did read the book, and mentioned it in his manuscript on natural history.[4] By the end of the 1670s, then, Yarranton had become 'extreamly well known', as Goodwin Wharton reported from London. Wharton sent a copy of Yarranton's book—probably *England's improvement*—and even suggested that the author was being approached by the future James II to discuss naval matters.[5] Given Yarranton's humble origins this was a remarkable rise. A native of the parish of Astley, Worcestershire, Yarranton was apprenticed to a Worcester linen draper in about 1632. Being a Presbyterian, he fought in the Civil Wars as a captain in the New Model Army. By the time Wharton wrote in 1679, however, Yarranton had become one of the most celebrated promoters of improvement in Restoration London—well received among London savants, with his book favourably reviewed and sent around, his expertise even attracting royal attention.

Having looked closely into Hartlibean hopes and frustrations, we might wonder whether paying close attention to their abortive schemes and broken promises of infinite abundance might lead us to exaggerate the seriousness of the distrust—whether, after all, the image of the projector had much at all to do with men of proven experience such as Yarranton. Was distrust reserved for the deservingly dubious? If it were, Yarranton should then be treated differently as a credible expert, capable (unlike common projectors) of translating ambitious 'projects' into tangible 'improvement'. The purpose of this chapter is to test this hypothesis through the well-documented case of the Stour river navigation scheme, one of the large-scale schemes that Yarranton supervised, launched in the immediate aftermath of the Restoration of Charles II.

Studies in the history of science and technology suggest that competent experts played a crucial role in executing large-scale undertakings such as canal building, mining, and fen drainage. Studying the role that the MP and mathematician Thomas Digges played in the rebuilding of Dover Harbour under Elizabeth I, Stephen Johnston has suggested that the privy councillors trusted Digges as one of the 'particularly valued and expert advisors' because of his noble birth, connections, education in mathematics and geometry, and above all because of his skilful self-presentation as a superior, public-spirited gentleman. An important study by Eric Ash has also suggested that the success of the Dover scheme was 'in large part because the former [Privy Council] found an expert whom they trusted'.[6] Business history accounts seem to agree, for early modern England is said to have been blessed

---

[4] RS, EL/B1/72, John Beale to [?], 10 February 1677; RS, MS/92, John Aubrey, 'Memoirs of Naturall Remarques in the County of Wilts[hire]', 1685, fol. 64: 'Consider the sheme in Captain Yarrington's Book entitled Englands Improvement as to the establishing of Granaries at severall Townes on the Thames, and Avon'.

[5] Bodl., Carte MS 233, fol. 293v, Goodwin [Wharton] to [Thomas Wharton?], 9 July 1679 ('I have sent you one of his books if you are pleas[e]d to accept of it'). See also p. 224 below.

[6] Stephen Johnston, 'Making Mathematical Practice: Gentlemen, Practitioners and Artisans in Elizabethan England' (PhD thesis, University of Cambridge, 1994), p. 268; Eric H. Ash, *Power, Knowledge, and Expertise in Elizabethan England* (Baltimore, MD: Johns Hopkins University Press, 2004), pp. 74, 82, 85, at p. 85. See also Eric H. Ash, *The Draining of the Fens: Projectors, Popular*

with entrepreneurs committed to improvement and economic growth, willing 'to invest in new concepts and techniques and to expand both extensively and intensively'. Such prudent actors perhaps 'just knew' whom to trust, to echo Steven Shapin.[7] Projects may have been turned into reality, and robust economic improvement accomplished, thanks to those credible experts and prudent backers, both standing above the unreliable projectors who deserved just mockery.

Coordination between experts and investors was certainly vital for implementing projects. Yet we can arrive at a more nuanced picture if we take a closer look at the case of the Stour river navigation scheme. The trust bestowed upon Yarranton was hardly unconditional. In this regard, he was little better than the less successful promoters like Cressy Dymock and William Wheeler that we encountered in Chapter 3. The suspicion of impractical or, worse, destructive projecting indeed echoed across different stages of the Stour scheme—planning, lobbying, and implementation. It affected an initial contract between Yarranton and his backers; it rendered the safeguarding of local stakeholders urgent in Westminster, and the maintenance of credit lines almost impossible in the West Midlands.

If we are to understand how Yarranton helped turn the inland navigation project into reality, despite underlying caution and suspicion, then we must move beyond the flowery language of promotional self-fashioning, and probe the processes of *proposing*, *negotiating*, and *implementing* the project—protracted processes that involved pitching arguments in parliament, answering criticisms, conceding ground, milking money from cautious backers, compensating grudging landlords, and paying sceptical merchants, carpenters, and labourers. This chapter does this by drawing on sources typically used in parliamentary history and local economic history, ranging from parliamentary minutes and bills, petitions for and against the scheme, articles of agreements, business letters, and financial accounts.

The next two sections introduce river navigation in general and the Stour scheme in particular. This is followed by a brief discussion of inland navigation under the early Stuarts and the controversies that it provoked. Once we place inland navigation schemes firmly within the history of projecting, we shall proceed to the parliamentary debate between 1661 and 1662, and examine how the Commons ensured the protection of regional stakeholders. Moving from Westminster to the West Midlands, we then reconstruct the difficult task of implementing the scheme in Staffordshire and Worcestershire.

We will assess the remarkable extent to which doubts and scepticism about projects influenced both parliamentary debate and local implementation, and affected even promoters like Yarranton whom contemporaries deemed competent. In so doing the chapter will also reveal a little-known interface between the culture of projecting and the world of everyday financial credit. Equally important for this

---

Politics, and State Building in Early Modern England (Baltimore, MD: Johns Hopkins University Press, 2017), pp. 10, 12, 153–4, 262–3.

[7] Richard Grassby, *The Business Community of Seventeenth-Century England* (Cambridge: Cambridge University Press, 1995), pp. 412–13; Steven Shapin, *A Social History of Truth: Civility and Science in Seventeenth-Century England* (Chicago: University of Chicago Press, 1994), p. 241.

book, close attention to the parliamentary debate will enable us to explore how, due to local opposition to the potentially harmful 'project', MPs took measures to protect some of the local stakeholders, rather than suppress them as the Caroline government too often had done. The case of the Stour navigation scheme thereby set an important legislative precedent for subsequent inland navigation bills, about how to promote inland navigation without exacerbating social divisions or undermining the legitimacy of the regime.

RIVER NAVIGATION AS ECONOMIC IMPROVEMENT

The strategic importance of navigable rivers was well established by the seventeenth century.[8] As early as 1424, a statute (3 Hen. 6, *c.* 5) was passed to authorize work on the River Lea; later in the century a twelve-mile waterway was made navigable for the Nene.[9] Inland navigation was given close attention because of its lower cost and because land carriage was more easily affected by rain and damage. For example, the road from Tonbridge, Kent, to London often became impassable during the rainy winter, even though carts carrying timbers and iron were charged under an Elizabethan statute to pay for its maintenance.[10] Transporting a ton of salt for seven miles from Droitwich to Worcester cost five shillings by land; the same amount of money would pay for seventy-seven miles of water transport from Worcester to Bristol.[11] Timber was crucial material for building ships, but on land it could not be hauled more than twenty miles a day. The clear advantage of water over land carriage explains why an Elizabethan statute prohibited making charcoal from large trees within fourteen miles of the sea and navigable rivers.[12] In 1649 it was likewise ordered that timber forests within fifteen miles of navigable rivers were to be exempted from the sales of Crown lands 'for the use and service of the Publique Navy'.[13] The Council of Trade in 1650 and 1668 was ordered to consider the possibilities of extending inland navigation.[14]

The expansion of navigable rivers played a pivotal role in economic development in the early modern period. Barges passing up and down navigable rivers could carry a vast range of commodities produced in different areas. They included not only coal, metal wares, ores, pot clay, grain, salt, and timber, but also 'semi-durables'

---

[8] There is a body of literature on inland navigation before the canal age. General surveys include W. T. Jackman, *The Development of Transportation in Modern Britain* (3rd edn, London: Frank Cass, 1966), pp. 157–210; T. S. Willan, *River Navigation in England, 1600–1750* (London: Frank Cass, 1964); David Hussey, *Coastal and River Trade in Pre-Industrial England: Bristol and its Region, 1680–1730* (Exeter: Exeter University Press, 2000).

[9] Willan, *River Navigation*, p. 28; Alec W. Skempton et al. (eds.), *Biographical Dictionary of Civil Engineers in Great Britain and Ireland: 1500–1830* (2 vols., London: Thomas Telford, 2002), vol. 1, p. 142.

[10] The statute is 39 Eliz. I, *c.* 19, section 2. See Ernest Straker, *Wealden Iron* (London: Bells and Sons, 1931), p. 185.

[11] Willan, *River Navigation*, p. 38, citing more examples of price comparison from the late seventeenth century onward.

[12] 1 Eliz. I, *c.* 15. See also Willan, *River Navigation*, p.133 n. 2.

[13] *A&O*, vol. 2, p. 189.   [14] *T&C*, pp. 501–2, 524–8.

like glassware and ceramics, and consumables such as soap, spices, citrus fruits, and dyewoods.[15] Few of these goods were produced or purchased in port towns themselves, an indication that the economic effects of navigable rivers went far beyond the riverbanks. During the seventeenth century, the River Severn, the longest navigable river in England, 'provided a direct connection between the port of Bristol and a set of interconnected subregions' from 'south Lancashire to the Forest of Dean in one direction and from Birmingham to the Plynlimon range in the other'.[16] By 1660 about 685 miles of rivers were navigable across England, but only ninety miles of them were man-made extensions of 'naturally' navigable rivers. Over the next forty years, however, nearly 200 miles were made navigable in addition.[17] Along with the improvement of highways, therefore, the remarkable extension of navigable rivers in the later seventeenth century was instrumental in the interconnected processes of 'agricultural specialisation, urbanisation, expanding trade, industrial agglomeration and regional differentiation' towards the creation of a single nationwide economy.[18] The Stour navigation scheme is significant because it stands at the beginning of this crucial juncture as the first scheme that received government backing after the Restoration of Charles II in 1660.

YARRANTON AND THE STOUR NAVIGATION: A RELIABLE EXPERT IN A ROBUST SCHEME?

The bill for authorizing the Stour navigation scheme was submitted to the Lords on 11 May 1661, only three days after the opening of the Cavalier Parliament. Other forms of governmental support available, such as patents and commissioners of sewers, will be discussed later. It now suffices to point out that the Stour bill received royal assent at the end of the session, on 19 May 1662.[19] The River Stour originates as a little stream in south Staffordshire. After passing through the coal-producing Black Country, it runs into the longest river in England, the Severn, which flows through Worcester and Tewkesbury into the Bristol Channel. The scheme's initial plan was to make the Stour navigable from the Severn to Stourbridge within two years of the passing of the bill (see Illustration 4.1).[20] In order to

[15] Hussey, *Coastal and River Trade*, p. 199.

[16] Malcolm Wanklyn, 'The Severn Navigation in the Seventeenth Century: Long-Distance Trade of Shrewsbury Boats', *Midland History*, 13 (1988), 34–58, p. 34; Malcolm Wanklyn, 'The Impact of Water Transport Facilities on the Economies of English River Ports c. 1660–c.1760', *EcHR*, 2nd ser., 49 (1996), 20–34, p. 26.

[17] For the figures and the difficulties involved in such estimates, see Willan, *River Navigation*, p. 133; Alec W. Skempton, 'Engineering on the English River Navigations to 1760', in M. Baldwin and A. Burton (eds.), *Canals: A New Look* (Chichester: Phillimore, 1984), 23–44, pp. 23–4.

[18] Wrightson, *Earthly Necessities*, p. 245.

[19] *LJ*, vol. 11, pp. 250, 473. Although much activity should have preceded the introduction of the bill, little evidence has survived. For the parliamentary procedure as 'midway in the course of an economic enterprise', see Willan, *River Navigation*, pp. 30–1.

[20] Staff.RO, D(W)1788/P43/B10, 'Article for the River Stower &c', 10 May 1661.

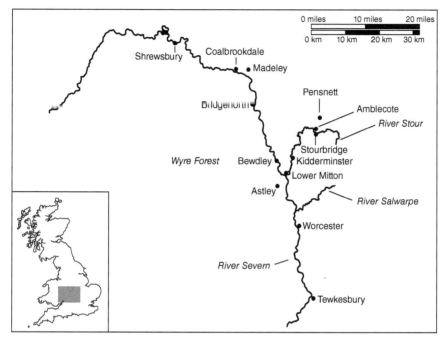

Illustration 4.1. River Stour and other key locations
Courtesy of Stefano Costantini

maximize the benefit of water transport, wooden railways were to connect nearby coal pits to the river.[21] The proprietors of the navigation work hoped to profit by levying tolls from barges passing through the river, and by selling coals down the Stour in Severn-side towns like Worcester. The promoters also developed an interest in establishing a tinplate industry along the Stour, using cheap coal from the region to smelt and process tin ores brought upstream from Cornwall for foreign export and for sale in larger towns—an example of regional specialization that drew on interregional trade.[22] No overall accounts of the navigation scheme survive, but sporadic references to charges and profit estimates suggest that the enterprise was expected to be large. The sale of coal alone was expected to raise more than £3,000 yearly.[23]

At centre stage in this project stood Andrew Yarranton, who played a key managerial and supervisory role. He had experience in inland navigation and hydrostatics. He applied (unsuccessfully) for a patent from the Cromwellian government for the

---

[21] Staff.RO, D(W)1788/P3/B78, [Andrew Yarranton?], A map of the Stour navigation work [n.d.]. Stour was often spelt Stower. The word 'stour' simply means a stream, and there are several other rivers with the same name.

[22] Staff.RO, D(W)1788/P61/B7(f), Reasons wherefore the River Stower is the best place in Europe for the p[er]fecting of the Tynn manufacture [n.d.].

[23] Staff.RO, D(W)1788/P59/B3, An account of the value of Stower [n.d.]. See also the same calculation given at D(W)1788/P61/B7(f), An estimate of the profits that may arise from the River Stower when the same is made navigable & locks finished with brick and stone [n.d.].

navigation of the Salwarpe, another tributary of the Severn.[24] His native parish, Astley, had blast furnaces and watermills; archaeologists suggest that Yarranton helped construct them and make a local stream navigable down to the Severn.[25] After the Civil Wars, Yarranton served as a Worcestershire Commissioner for Sequestrations of royalist lands; having received £500 from the Interregnum parliament 'for his good service', Yarranton then purchased coppice woods in places such as the Wyre Forest west of Bewdley.[26] Then, in about 1661, Yarranton discovered 'a vast quantity of Roman *Cinder*' near Worcester, waste dross 'thrown out of the foot-blasts by the Romans' that still contained iron.[27] Making the Stour navigable would make it possible to carry the Roman cinder up the river and smelt it with coal from the Black Country. The navigation work would also make it easier for him to carry bulky coppice wood from the Wyre Forest for sale upstream in Kidderminster or Stourbridge. It is therefore not surprising to find that Yarranton claimed in 1677 that the Stour navigation scheme was 'my projection'.[28] While we do not have evidence to verify this, Yarranton had both the expertise and clear reasons to promote the scheme.

Yarranton's network, like those of mid-century reformers, cut across contemporary political and ideological divisions. Thomas Smyth, a Middle Temple lawyer of Norfolk origin, probably played the middleman, forging links between Yarranton and two aristocrats Thomas Lord Windsor and George Digby, earl of Bristol.[29] Windsor and Bristol were primarily financial backers, a role they could afford to play thanks partly to the lucrative grants they had received on the Restoration of Charles II.[30] These two were committed 'att their proper Costs and Charges to procure an Act' for the scheme, and also paid for its implementation.[31] Unlike Yarranton, Windsor, the future earl of Plymouth, fought for the royalist cause during the Civil Wars. At Charles II's return, he was made a Justice of the Peace for Worcester, and lord lieutenant of Worcestershire thereafter. Windsor had local reasons to fund the scheme: he had a house near Kidderminster, and extensive

[24] T. Russell Nash, *Collections for the history of Worcestershire* (2 vols., 1781–2), vol. 1, p. 306. The Salwarpe was often spelt Selwerpe.

[25] Thomas Crosbee Cantrill and Marjory Wight, 'Yarranton's Works at Astley', *Transactions of the Worcestershire Archaeological Society*, 2nd ser., 7 (1929), 92–115; Peter J. Brown, 'The Early Industrial Complex at Astley, Worcestershire', *Post-Medieval Archaeology*, 16 (1982), 1–19, p. 7.

[26] *CJ*, vol. 5, p. 642; Peter J. Brown, 'The Military Career of Andrew Yarranton', *Transactions of Worcestershire Archaeological Society*, 3rd ser., 13 (1992), 193–202, pp. 196–7.

[27] Staff.RO, D(W) 1788/P59/B3, *Reasons wherefore the making the rivers of Stower and Salwerp navigable, in the county of Worcester, will be of great advantage unto the Country of Salop, but especially to Shrewsbury, Bridgenorth, Wenlock, Wellington, and all the Towns adjoining to the River of Severn* [1661], p. 1. See also Andrew Yarranton, *England's improvement by sea and land. The second part* (1681), pp. 162–3; Brown, 'The Early Industrial Complex at Astley', pp. 4–5.

[28] Andrew Yarranton, *England's improvement by sea and land* (1677), p. 66.

[29] Smyth was admitted to the Middle Temple in 1652 and was the son and heir of his namesake Thomas Smyth of Walsoaken, Norfolk, 'gent.'. H. A. C. Sturgess (ed.), *Register of Admissions to the Honourable Society of the Middle Temple* (3 vols., London: Middle Temple, 1949), vol. 1, p. 151. At least by 1665, Samuel Whyle, 'gent.' of Oldswinford, Worcestershire, took over Smyth's role. See Staff. RO, D(W)1788/P59/B3, a note on agreements, 1665.

[30] See p. 182.

[31] Staff.RO, D(W)1788/P43/B10, 'Article for the River Stower &c', May 1661. We shall later discuss the funding arrangements in detail.

estates in different parts of Worcestershire, including a property by the River Stour.[32] Bristol's role in the project seems to have been rather limited. He may have invested during the first few years of the project, for which little evidence survives; according to Smyth, Bristol intended to solicit the 'Kings Comendac[i]on ... by his greatnes'.[33] But, by the end of 1665, Bristol rented out his proprietorship to another, the Inner Temple lawyer Samuel Baldwyn of Shropshire.[34] Baldwyn had held Stokesay Castle for Charles I during the first Civil War, and was subsequently elected in 1658 as an MP for Ludlow. Although he seems to have spent much time in London after the Restoration, Baldwyn possessed 1,500 acres of forest in Worcestershire, which may explain why he became a partner.[35] The core players in the scheme—Yarranton, Windsor, and Baldwyn—thus came from different political backgrounds, and yet shared similar local interests.

The promoters failed to realize the initial goal of constructing a navigable route between the Severn and Stourbridge in two years; yet there were some concrete achievements.[36] By December 1665, a wooden railway was laid between the river to coal pits at Pensnett, 2.5 miles north-east of Stourbridge, but the navigation was only finished for the twelve-mile section from Stourbridge down to Kidderminster; the final 4.5 miles to the Severn were still impassable.[37] At this point, all the previous accounts were settled, presumably for the first time, and Samuel Baldwyn joined as a major backer.[38] He paid the rent of £300 to the earl of Bristol, and invested about £1,500 within a year and half.[39] This new partnership, however, could not finish the project either. In February 1670, Yarranton proposed to complete it in two years. This attempt again failed to materialize. The final downstream section, where the Stour flows into the Severn (currently Stourport), was populated by the mills of Worcester clothiers, which presumably made it particularly

[32] J. W. Willis Bund et al. (eds.), *VCH, Worcestershire* (4 vols., London: Constable, 1901–24), vol. 3, pp. 23, 225, 282, 570 n. 80; S. Kelsey, 'Windsor [formerly Hickman], Thomas, first earl of Plymouth (c. 1627–1687)', *Oxford DNB*, vol. 59, 709–10.

[33] TNA, SP 29/44/21, Thomas Smyth to Andrew Yarranton, 7 November 1661. For Bristol's chequered career, see R. Hutton, 'Digby, George, second earl of Bristol (1612–1677)', *Oxford DNB*, vol. 16, 143–6.

[34] For Bristol's relation to Baldwyn, see Staff.RO, D(W)1788/P59/B3, Mr Baldwyns Case as to his lease & Farme Of the Navigation upon ye Stower and Salworp under ye right ho[noura]ble George Earle of Bristoll & Proposals thereupon [February–July 1667?].

[35] Evelyn H. Martin, 'History of Several Families Connected with Diddlebury. I. The Baldwyns: Part III', *Transactions of the Shropshire Archaeological and Natural Historical Society*, 4th ser., 2 (1912), 327–47, esp. pp. 334, 339; Yarranton, *England's improvement by sea and land. The second part*, p. 71.

[36] Staff.RO, D(W)1788/P43/B10, 'Article for the River Stower &c', 10 May 1661. They also hoped to, but failed to, make the Salwarpe navigable. Little evidence seems to survive about this plan. HMC, *Manuscripts of the House of Lords, 1692–1693* (London: HMSO, 1894), p. 387.

[37] M. J. T. Lewis, *Early Wooden Railways* (London: Routledge, 1970), p. 245; *VCH, Worcestershire*, vol. 2, p. 252.

[38] Baldwyn was one of the witnesses of the May 1661 article of agreement. See Staff.RO, D(W)1788/P43/B10, 'Article for the River Stower &c'. Staff.RO, D(W)1788/P37/B8 contains indentures and recognizances bearing the date 14 December 1665. More papers seem to survive for the years after 1666, partly because most of the papers regarding the Stour navigation are kept as part of the family papers of the Baldwyn family in the Aqualate Estate Collection.

[39] Staff.RO, D(W)1788/P59/B3, 'Mr Baldwyns Case as to his lease & Farme Of the Navigation upon ye Stower and Salworp under the right ho[noura]ble George Earle of Bristoll & Proposals thereupon' [February–July 1667?].

difficult to complete the work, and it was still going on in the summer of 1673. Yarranton sold some forestlands to raise £500, and engaged his son Robert to continue the work. Yarranton seems to have become active elsewhere from about this period. In July 1674 he surveyed the River Dee, and later that year he also surveyed the Enniscorthy Ironworks and the River Shane in Ireland. In January 1678, Robert Yarranton and William Farnolls were appointed as the main undertakers; their task was to finish the navigation work down to north of Lower Mitton and to build a 'waggon Rayle of one hundred and forty yards or thereabouts' down to the Severn, presumably in order to bypass a difficult section.[40] At this point, Andrew Yarranton gave up all his interest in exchange for a life annuity of thirty pounds from the scheme's profits. He died in 1684, and Windsor in 1687; the enterprise probably soon died out too.

Did the Stour navigation scheme achieve what it did because investors trusted Yarranton's expertise and competence? This might seem plausible, given his extensive concerns with coppice wood, Roman cinder, local rivers, and furnaces, and also given his subsequent reputation in London. Upon closer inspection, however, Yarranton's *England's improvement* suggests that Yarranton's credibility was not quite so impeccable. In a section where he discussed the possibility of connecting the Thames and the Severn based on his and his son's surveys, Yarranton was careful to forestall criticism from the reader: 'I hear some say you projected the making Navigable the River *Stoure* in *Worcestershire*, what is the reason it was not finished?' Carefully highlighting his goodwill, Yarranton blamed the 'want of Money':

> I was not willing it should be Abortive; therefore I made offers to perfect it…made it completely Navigable from *Sturbridge* [Stourbridge] to *Kederminster* [Kidderminster]…and laid out near one thousand pounds, and there it was obstructed *for want of Money* which by Contract was to be paid.[41]

Yarranton's defensive remark betrays the difficulty of securing timely investment. This was a serious problem, especially when it came to schemes such as river navigation or mining that required large sunk costs before yielding profits. The problem was not helped by the fact that projectors had a reputation for draining money from investors. It was accordingly vital to make sure that investors continued to believe in the feasibility of the scheme and its future profitability, and drawing on their investment, to pay contractors, workmen, and creditors in a timely fashion so that their credit would not be stretched too far. That some of the Stour navigation work remained unfinished due to 'want of Money' seems to suggest that these were no easy tasks. We need to ask how far the suspicion of projecting may have affected Yarranton's and others' capacity to secure the financial credit so vital for translating the project into reality.

Money and expert competence were not the only key factors. It was also vital to dig riverbanks and gardens, and to remove mills, bridges, and dams built on the

---

[40] Staff.RO, D(W)1788/P37/B8, an article of agreement, 27 January 1677/8. See also Lewis, *Early Wooden Railways*, p. 246.

[41] Yarranton, *England's improvement*, pp. 65–6 (italics added).

river. Compensation might not always be agreed upon or be paid as arranged. Extending a navigable river could alter trading routes; goods and money could start flowing in other directions, creating both winners and losers. Just like other kinds of projects, therefore, river navigation schemes could stir up complaints and grievances by infringing upon what was deemed to be subject's rights to labour and property. This was precisely what happened under the early Stuarts. While drainage schemes and ensuing social tensions before the Civil Wars have attracted sustained scholarly attention, relatively little has been done to consider inland navigation within the broader history of projecting.[42] We shall therefore turn to a short survey so that we can appreciate the heavy burden of history under which the Stour navigation bill was negotiated in and outside Westminster.

INLAND NAVIGATION PROJECTS UNDER THE EARLY STUARTS

Like many other schemes for economic innovations and improvement, river navigation schemes required support from a higher authority. This is because, in common law, public rights of navigation and its improvement existed only in tidal rivers. A great part of the two major tidal rivers, the Thames and the Severn, was navigable by the end of the sixteenth century. So during the seventeenth and early eighteenth centuries the effort to make rivers navigable was largely directed at non-tidal sections of rivers. Both the bank and the bed of such non-tidal rivers (over which water flowed) were the private property of riparian landowners. If such landowners were unwilling to make a river navigable, then it would remain impassable until some authority obliged them to work on it, or let others do it.[43] Governmental support was required, then, not primarily for protecting under-takers' rights for improvement, but for permitting privileged access to, and work upon, others' private property for the public good. This explains why safeguarding or disregarding riparian rights and interests becomes a vital issue.[44]

---

[42] An exception is a short article by Keith Fairclough, 'A Successful Elizabethan Project: The River Lea Improvement Scheme', *Journal of Transport History*, 3rd ser., 11 (1998), 54–65. For fen drainage, see Clive Holmes, 'Drainage Projects in Elizabethan England: The European Dimension', in Salvatore Ciriacono, *Eau et développement dans l'Europe moderne* (Paris: Éditions de la Maison des Sciences de l'Homme, 2004), 87–102; Piet van Cruyningen, 'Dealing with Drainage: State Regulation of Drainage Projects in the Dutch Republic, France, and England during the Sixteenth and Seventeenth Centuries', *EcHR*, 68 (2015), 420–40; Ash, *Draining of the Fens*.

[43] For a thorough legal discussion, including definitions of private and public streams, see H. J. W. Coulson and Urquhart A. Forbes, *The Law Relating to Waters, Sea, Tidal, and Inland* (3rd edn, London: Sweet & Maxwell, 1910), ch. 2, esp. pp. 81, 116–17. A useful overview is Frank A. Sharman, 'River Improvement Law in the Early Seventeenth Century', *Journal of Legal History*, 3 (1982), 222–45. See also Jackman, *Development of Transportation*, p. 157; Willan, *River Navigation*, p. 22.

[44] Focusing on *undertakers'* right to dig, its 'protection' and 'violation' thus risk neglecting the legal weight of *riparian property rights* in the history of inland navigation in the seventeenth century. This chapter, therefore, qualifies the approach adopted by Dan Bogart, 'Did the Glorious Revolution Contribute to the Transport Revolution? Evidence from Investment in Roads and Rivers', *EcHR*, 64 (2011), 1073–112, pp. 1078–84, 1087.

There were three types of legal support available: patent, commission of sewers, and act of parliament. The general impression is of a state of flux giving way to parliamentary supremacy.[45] All three methods were used up to the mid-seventeenth century; promoters often combined them for working on a single river. The use of statutes became dominant by the post-Restoration period. Between 1500 and 1660, only five acts were passed for extending inland navigation; during the 1660s alone six acts were passed for improving fourteen rivers, with twenty-five more bills which were submitted but failed. Another fifty-three bills would be passed by 1750. Obtaining acts of parliament would later become a standard method for launching canal schemes.[46]

Until parliamentary authorization became the dominant method, however, commissioners of sewers and patents provided the main channels. In Henry VIII's reign, the Statute of Sewers was passed with clauses that authorized local commissions to 'clense and purge the trenches[,] sewers and diches in all places necessarie' for 'the avauncynge of the common p[ro]fitte welthe and com[m]oditie of this his Realme'.[47] Drawing on this passage, local commissioners of sewers, appointed by privy councillors, improved the navigation of rivers including the Medway, the Dee, the Wye, and the Lea.[48] Yet, because the legal power of commissioners of sewers to make *new* trenches was often questioned by both lawyers and local opponents of particular schemes,[49] the early Stuart regimes also promoted inland navigation schemes by granting patents. At least eight patents with a monopoly of carriage were issued for making rivers navigable, covering rivers such as the Bristol Avon (1619), the Great Ouse (1628), the Soar (1634), the Warwickshire Avon (1636), the Lark (1637), and the Tone (1638).[50] Between 1616 and 1642, ten more patents were granted for protecting purported 'inventions' for engines for draining, cutting, and dredging rivers—possibly a pretext for authorizing the monopoly of carriage.[51]

---

[45] Willan, *River Navigation*, pp. 16–30; Sharman, 'River Improvement', *passim*; C. W. Chalklin, 'Navigation Schemes on the Upper Medway, 1600–1665', *Journal of Transport History*, 5 (1961), 105–15, p. 105.

[46] I have arrived at the figures for the bills that reached the statute book by comparing the lists given in Willan, *River Navigation*, pp. 28, 152–5 and Jackman, *Development of Transportation*, p. 164, and checking them against *Statutes of the Realm*; *A&O*; *Chronological Table of Private and Personal Acts 1539–1997* (London: HMSO, 1999). The numbers include acts for reappointing undertakers to complete the work begun by others, but exclude those concerning the repair of ports and of already navigable rivers. For the failed bills, see Julian Hoppit (ed.), *Failed Legislation, 1660–1800: Extracted from the Commons and Lords Journals* (London: Hambledon, 1997), pp. 587–8.

[47] 23 Hen. VIII, *c.* 5, preamble and section 1.

[48] Willan, *River Navigation*, pp. 16–23. See also H. G. Richardson, 'The Early History of Commissions of Sewers', *EHR*, 34 (1919), 385–93.

[49] See, for example, *The English Reports* (178 vols., Edinburgh: W. Green & Son, 1900–32), vol. 77, pp. 1141–2 (10 Co. Rep. 142b); BL, Harley MS 2003, 'The humble petition of the Mayor Aldermen Citizens and Inhabitantes of the Citie of Chester', fol. 227v. For background, see Clive Holmes, 'Statutory Interpretation in the Early Seventeenth-Century: The Courts, the Council, and the Commissioners of Sewers', in J. A. Guy and H. G. Beale (eds.), *Law and Social Change in British History: Papers Presented to the British Legal History Conference, 14–17 July 1981* (London: Royal Historical Society, 1984), 107–17; Willan, *River Navigation*, p. 18.

[50] Sharman, 'River Improvement Law', p. 227.

[51] Patent nos. 9, 13, 14, 19, 55, 64, 66, 105, 122, 125; Sharman, 'River Improvement Law', p. 228.

Importantly, these grants were linked with Crown finance. In the case of the Warwickshire Avon, Charles I encouraged the promoter William Sandys by granting him and his partners a duty of one shilling per cauldron on Newcastle coal.[52] In other cases, undertakers suggested that their schemes would benefit the Crown. In 1607 one Thomas Proctor proposed to James I to bring the 'Thames too or neare unto Severne, or from Severne to or near unto Thames', and do the same for several other rivers in order to facilitate the carrying of bulky goods such as coal, iron, corn, flax, hemp, and woollen and linen cloths.[53] Crucially, Procter suggested that 'a custome or rent may growe unto his Majesty' by levying tolls.[54] The patentee Thomas Skipwith also offered to pay the Exchequer one-tenth of the profit to be raised from the tolls upon the River Soare; patentees like John Cason, Arnold Spenser, and Robert Chiver made similar promises.[55]

Commissioners of sewers and patentees *could* advance the good of the king and of his subjects by facilitating carriage, reinvigorating trade up and down the river, creating employment, and even contributing to Crown revenues. Yet, as in the promotion of other kinds of projects and 'inventions', promoters' ambitions often colluded with royal interests and 'reasons of state', and thereby caused grievances under the guise of promoting beneficial 'improvement'. It is well known that such perversions were permitted in Lincolnshire fen drainage schemes, some backed by commissioners of sewers. One staunch local opponent, Robert Barkham, for example, was committed to Fleet prison in late 1637 by a Privy Council order issued in favour of commissioners close to the court. Barkham was prevented from seeking legal redress in common law courts.[56] A similarly heavy-handed approach was adopted towards inland navigation, as the case of the Upper Medway navigation illustrates.

In July 1627, the local commissioners of sewers contracted with one Michael Cole of Westminster to make a section of the Medway navigable between Maidstone and Penshurst within three years, in return for an exclusive use of water carriage there for thirty-three years. The scheme was backed primarily by those involved in iron manufacture and timber-growing, who would benefit from cheaper access to the London market.[57] In order to procure extra authority, a bill was also submitted

---

[52] See *CSPD 1638–1639*, p. 507; B. D. Henning (ed.), *House of Commons 1660–1690* (3 vols., Woodbridge: Boydell, 2006), vol. 3, p. 390.

[53] Thomas Procter, *A vvorthy vvorke profitable to this vvhole kingdome concerning the mending of all high-vvaies, as also for vvaters and iron vvorkes* (1607), sig. [D3v].

[54] Procter, *A vvorthy vvorke*, sig. [D3v]. A search into *CSPD*, *CTP*, *CTB* seems to suggest that a proposal was never executed.

[55] Thomas Rymer, *Foedera* (20 vols., 1704–35), vol. 19, p. 599. See also patent nos. 3, 14, 36, 105.

[56] Even in January 1639 Barkham had his petition for release rejected by the Privy Council. TNA, SP 16/409, fol. 384; Keith Lindley, *Fenland Riots and the English Revolution* (London: Heinemann, 1982), pp. 90–1. More broadly, see H. C. Darby, *The Draining of the Fens* (2nd edn, Cambridge, 1956); Lindley, *Fenland*, ch. 2; Clive Holmes, *Seventeenth-Century Lincolnshire* (Lincoln: History of Lincolnshire Committee, 1980), pp. 121–30; Clive Holmes, 'Drainers and Fenmen: The Problem of Popular Political Consciousness in the Seventeenth Century', in Anthony Fletcher and John Stevenson (eds.), *Order and Disorder in Early Modern England* (Cambridge: Cambridge University Press, 1985), 166–95; Ash, *Draining of the Fens*, pp. 151–2, 168, 177–8, 183–204, 215.

[57] For a useful overview, see Chalklin, 'Navigation Schemes on the Upper Medway'; Sharman, 'River Improvement Law', pp. 239–40.

to the Lords to procure an act. Although it was approved there, the Commons select committee then rejected it, declaring that 'it is a Monopoly'.[58] Despite this setback, the navigation work went ahead under the local commissioners' authority. Cole's workmen reportedly 'pulled down the weires' of riparian landowners that obstructed the flow; Cole even 'threatened som of the inhabitants' to 'make th[e]m pay 10s for ev[e]ry bush growing on the banke of the River'.[59] On 16 February 1629, riparian inhabitants in turn petitioned the Commons, reminding MPs that the scheme had been 'by this honourable house...noted to be a Monopolie'. Echoing the popular antipathy which would explode in the 1640s and continue to haunt the post-Restoration regime, the petition accused 'Michael Cole a projector' of 'the great Misdemeano[u]r', and prayed for the 'the restraining of his intended & threatned p[ro]ceding'.[60]

Both sides had by then launched several lawsuits. Charles I, however, dissolved parliament in March 1629; the commencement of his Personal Rule decidedly favoured Cole and the commissioners. The Privy Council now intervened, and decreed that local inhabitants' lawsuits against Cole be suspended, and the promoters continue 'the said worke of improveing the said Navigacion'. The council judged that no advance compensation was required; the order concluded with a threat of 'censure' in case inhabitants 'shall presume to oppose or interrupt the present execution' of the navigation work.[61]

Charles's government had a vested interest in suppressing local opposition. From the late Elizabethan period onwards, the government had been informed that connecting the Weald and Chatham via the Upper Medway would afford a cheaper timber supply for the navy.[62] By the late 1620s, strengthening the navy had become an urgent issue under the pressure of the Thirty Years War on the continent.[63] In fact, soon after the river was made navigable from Maidstone to Yalding upstream, the treasurer of the navy had commissioned a local purveyor in Kent to carry timber to a wharf near there, presumably so that it could be shipped down the river under Cole's supervision.[64] It is also probable that, like Skipwith and Sandys, Cole offered to pay the Crown.

Despite a degree of success in extending the navigable part of the river, the scheme remained highly contentious. One of the local petitioners, Robert Scole,

[58] *LJ*, vol. 3, p. 743; *CJ*, vol. 1, p. 914. The original bill does not seem to survive.
[59] BL, Add. MS 33923, fols. 35–54, 'To the right worshipful her Ma[jes]ties Commissio[ners] of Sewers for the Countie of Kent' [n.d.], fol. 42v.
[60] PA, HL/PO/JP/10/1/38, the petition of George Carpenter and Robert Scoles, 16 February 1629.
[61] *APC*, vol. 45, p. 49 (12 June 1629). The Privy Council promised to order compensation for damages if local inhabitants could either show that the commission exceeded their 'just power', or legally prove the uninterrupted use of particular mills or weirs at least since Edward I's accession (i.e. November 1272). Winning compensation was unlikely, though not impossible in theory.
[62] BL, Add. MS 34218, 'Reasons why the Weavers should stande [navigable]' [1600?], fol. 40; Chalklin, 'Navigation Schemes on the Upper Medway', p. 110.
[63] K. R. Andrews, *Ships, Money and Politics: Seafaring and Naval Enterprise in the Reign of Charles I* (Cambridge: Cambridge University Press, 1991), pp. 140–50 (esp. p. 148); Michael J. Braddick, *State Formation in Early Modern England c. 1550–1700* (Cambridge: Cambridge University Press, 2000), p. 208.
[64] TNA, SP 16/171/18.

who held land adjoining the Medway, arrested two of Cole's boatmen, and the matter was brought to the Privy Council again. Only after Scole's and others' complaints did the council order the local commissioners of sewers to 'set down' compensation for damaged trees, weirs, and towpaths before resuming the work further.[65]

What happened to the Medway scheme in the early 1640s is not clear, but the Long Parliament denounced promoters of inland navigation and commissioners of sewers alongside other kinds of projectors and monopolists. For his role in the Avon navigation, for example, William Sandys was stripped of his membership of the Commons along with other 'Monopolist[s] and Projector[s]'; the Commons also declared Barkham's 1637 imprisonment to have been illegal, and ordered the courtier-drainers behind the matter, William Killigrew and Anthony Thomas, to pay compensation.[66] Grievances made their way into the Grand Remonstrance of 1641, no doubt echoing numerous local complaints arising from the actions of coercive promoters such as Cole: 'Large quantities of common and several grounds hath been taken from the subject... by abuse of the Commission of Sewers, without their consent, and against it.'[67]

The 1640s and 1650s saw only one act passed for inland navigation—one for the River Wey, promoted by Richard Weston. Given the wars, constitutional change, and ideological divisions, actually reconciling competing local interests must have been harder than calling, as Hartlib and others did, for technical inventions or agricultural improvement.[68] Yet there were some calls for extending navigable rivers. In 1641 Lewes Roberts mentioned river navigation as the first among diverse 'points... conducing to the facilitating, ease and augmentation of Traffike' at home and abroad, including the improvement of ports, beacons, highways, and other infrastructures.[69] Francis Mathew urged both parliament and the Council of State to take up his navigation projects.[70] Commentators continued to stress the vital importance of river navigation. In 1652, Henry Robinson highlighted the importance of emulating the United Provinces, which 'have Navigable Rivers or Ditches from one to another, and so into the Sea':

[thanks to waterways] they have not onely all manner of Victualls brought so much cheaper unto them, but also all manner of Raw or unwrought Commodities,

---

[65] *APC*, vol. 45, p. 309 (12 March 1630). The phrasing does not make it clear if cash payment was required before further damage. See evidence of further troubles at *CSPD 1631–1633*, p. 480; *CSPD 1635–36*, p. 64.

[66] For Sandys, see *CJ*, vol. 2, p. 71; *House of Commons 1660–1690*, vol. 3, pp. 389–90; *CSPD 1638–1639*, p. 507. For Killigrew and Thomas, see John P. Ferris and Andrew Thrush (eds.), *House of Commons, 1604–1629* (6 vols., Cambridge: Cambridge University Press, 2010), vol. 5, p. 24; Lindley, *Fenland*, pp. 46–56, 114. For subsequent parliamentary handling of fen drainage, see a short summary in Holmes, *Seventeenth-Century Lincolnshire*, pp. 208–12.

[67] *Constitutional Documents*, pp. 212 (quotation), 214, 221.

[68] There is only a passing reference to inland navigation in Webster, *Great Instauration*, p. 357.

[69] Lewes Roberts, *The treatise of traffike or a discourse of forraine trade* (1641), pp. 43–50 (quotation from p. 44).

[70] Francis Mathew, *Of the opening of rivers for navigation: the benefit exemplified by the two Avons of Salisbury and Bristol* (1655); Francis Mathew, *Of the opening of rivers for navigation: the benefit exemplified by the two Avons of Salisbury and Bristol* (1656).

whereby their People are set a work, and by this meanes can afford all sorts of Manufactures, and Artificers work, so much cheaper as is the difference between Land and Water carriage.

Thus he urged the Rump Parliament 'To make all Rivers Navigable as much as may be, and cut navigable Ditches in all places'.[71] This was how inland navigation remained high on the agenda. In 1664, the speaker of the Commons, Edward Turnor, compared 'pleasant Rivers' with 'Veins in the Natural Body', and thereby highlighted the various benefits of inland navigation for the body politic, which were by then very well established:

> it easeth the People of the great Charge of Land Carriages; preserves the Highways... it breeds up a Nursery of Watermen, which, upon Occasion, will prove good Seamen; and with much Facility maintain Intercourse and Communion between Cities and Countries.[72]

Note that this grandiose vision said nothing of the chequered history of inland navigation, or how to reconcile the indisputable benefits of water carriage with the rights and interests of those affected by the work. For the Cavalier Parliament, the Stour navigation scheme provided a testing ground to work out precisely this challenging question. Its successful implementation hinged upon a careful balancing of competing claims, as much as it did upon the maintenance of credit lines, to which we shall turn later.

ADJUSTING THE STOUR NAVIGATION BILL: THE PARLIAMENTARY SESSION, MAY 1661–MAY 1662

The Stour navigation bill was submitted as a private bill to the Lords by Bristol, Windsor, and Smyth in May 1661. The *Commons'* and *Lords' Journals* for this period tend to be laconic about debates concerning such private bills—those concerned specifically with certain localities, individuals, or their possessions. For the present case, however, we have a draft bill that Bristol and others originally submitted, an engrossed bill created at the end of the Lords' deliberation, several petitions, committee minutes, and the printed act that resulted from the process. Juxtaposing these with other references relating to the debate, we can explore how the Stour navigation bill was debated in Westminster, critiqued by a range of stakeholders in and outside parliament, vigorously defended by its promoters, and altered in the course of negotiation. A close look into this process reveals that parliament took pains to render what appeared to its opponents a dangerous 'project' less harmful and more legitimate. One result was a move away from the heavy-handed intervention characteristic of the early Stuarts' reign.

---

[71] Henry Robinson, *Certain proposals in order to the peoples freedome and accommodation in some particulars* (1652), pp. 8, 9.

[72] *LJ*, vol. 11, p. 675. For another example, see also Mathew, *Of the opening of rivers* (1656), pp. 3–5.

We must begin by paying attention to regional economic contexts, as the difficult problem of compensating damage was compounded by the operation of local industries near the Stour. Along the river stood the watermills of Worcester clothiers, as well as mills and furnaces of the powerful Foley family.[73] To cut the river, some of their mills—indispensable for pounding or 'fulling' cloths and blowing bellows—might have to be removed or relocated; widening and diverting the stream might hinder their operation by lessening the flow of water. Extending the navigable part of the Stour farther upstream could affect other coal-producing regions such as Coalbrookdale and Madeley up the Severn that sold coal down the river. Should parliament push the scheme, as Charles' Privy Council had done for the Medway, local grievances might escalate into a more general criticism of the restored government.

The debate in the Lords, though brief, drew attention to some of the potential harm of the proposed scheme: ruining the existing coal trade up the Severn near Shrewsbury. On 15 May 1661, four days after the bill was first presented, it was committed to a second reading committee of twenty-one peers, five being quorate.[74] Their meetings were dominated by two outsiders, however: the earl of Bristol and Thomas Smyth. Bristol was a peer but not listed as a committee member; Smyth was not even a peer.[75] In their presence some Shropshire coal workers were invited and allowed to testify 'what they have to object ag[ain]st the bill'.[76] Among such opponents was Francis Woolf of Madeley, a small Severn-side parish in Shropshire; he managed the iron and coal business of the Catholic Brooke family, which produced more than 10,000 tonnes of coal a year through four shafts driven into the hillside of Madeley Wood.[77] Woolf argued that 'If wee cannot sell a sufficient quantitiy wee cannot defray the charge of draining our workes, & therefore pits must drowne'. Against such concerns, a burgess of Worcester gave assurances that coal pits 'of a greate depth' in the region were 'not likely to fail'. Bristol presented 'a petition [for the bill] signed with very many hands' from Worcester, Kidderminster, and elsewhere. The navigation scheme, Smyth promised, would employ 'workemen liv[ing] all below Bewdly' (twenty miles downstream of Madeley), and provide the region with coal at a cheaper rate. Smyth concluded that the scheme would only 'prejudice some proprietors whose designe [it] is to set [higher] rate on coales and

[73] R. G. Schafer (ed.), *A Selection from the Records of Philip Foley's Stour Valley Iron Works 1668–74*, 2 vols., Worcestershire Historical Society, new ser., 9, 13 (1982, 1990), vol. 1, p. xii. See also *VCH Worcestershire*, vol. 3, p. 293–4.

[74] *LJ*, vol. 11, pp. 250, 255.

[75] PA, HL/PO/CO/1/1, Manuscript Committee Minutes 1, fols. 1, 14–15, 18, 22. Those not listed as committee members often played an important role. See Chris R. Kyle, 'Attendance, Apathy and Order? Parliamentary Committees in Early Stuart England', in Kyle and Peacey (eds.), *Parliament at Work*, 43–58, p. 54.

[76] PA, HL/PO/CO/1/1, Manuscript Committee Minutes 1, fols. 1, 18.

[77] John Hatcher, *The History of the British Coal Industry, Volume I: Before 1700: Towards the Age of Coal* (Oxford: Clarendon, 1993), p. 146; G. C. Baugh, (ed.), *VCH, Shropshire, Volume 11* (Oxford: Oxford University Press, 1985), pp. 46–9, 60 n. 95. There is little indication that religious affiliations affected the parliamentary debate over the Stour bill.

so oppress the countrey'—a typical insinuation of monopolizing a trade and raising prices, which was to be repeated on both sides.[78]

Outside parliament, too, the bill and its potential adverse consequences drew attention. On 25 May, the Staffordshire landowner Sir Richard Leveson received a report about the progress of the committee:

> There is a bill now in the Lords House for the making a brook in Worcestershire navigable betwixt Seaverne and Shirbrige [i.e. Severn and Stourbridge], that the coals there may be brought cheaper to Worcester, Gloucester, and these Lower Countreys, which will absolutely destroy all the water-sale of coals out of Shropshire, the trade of Bridgnorth and in part of Shrewsbury[.][79]

So the potential damage to the Shropshire coal industry was well understood outside parliament. Yet the select committee and the Lords approved the bill with few amendments; the bill was then ordered to be engrossed, and passed to the Commons, where more rigorous scrutiny took place after the second reading of 5 July 1661.[80]

The bill was then committed to a large committee, including all members from eight Midland counties, including Worcestershire, Shropshire, and Staffordshire.[81] It received petitions and addresses for and against it from Worcestershire, Staffordshire, Warwickshire, and Shropshire.[82] Although the committee's minutes do not survive, we have five petitions and counter-petitions examined by the Commons' second reading committee, three of them collated and printed together, probably for committee members and other concerned parties.[83] Combined with other sources, these petitions afford us a closer look into the escalating controversy that the Commons now had to arbitrate. As the question of funding was left to the promoters themselves, parliamentary debate was not over whether money could be trusted to the experts involved. It instead revolved around the future of the region: what were the consequences of interregional competition; would the price of key commodities such as coal rise; what would become of riverside lands, ponds, and mills?

The debate can be examined in three stages: before the session adjourned for the summer on 30 July 1661, after the session resumed on 20 November, and after

---

[78] PA, HL/PO/CO/1/1, Manuscript Committee Minutes 1, fols. 14–15. Section 24 of the 1641 Grand Remonstrance, for example, complained of the 'engrossing [of] all the gunpowder into one hand' and thereby 'setting so high a rate upon it'. *Constitutional Documents*, p. 211.

[79] HMC, *Fifth Report of the Royal Commission on Historical Manuscripts* (2 parts, London: HMSO, 1876), pt. 1, p. 160, Andrew Newport to Sir Richard Leveson, 25 May 1661.

[80] *LJ*, vol. 11, p. 291; *CJ*, vol. 8, p. 284. This engrossed bill was later amended, added provisos or 'riders', and thereby became an official manuscript act kept in PA, HL/PO/PB1/1662/14C2n46, An Act for making navigable of the Rivers of Stower and Salwerp [hereafter cited as the 'Engrossed Stour Act'].

[81] *CJ*, vol. 8, p. 291. The other five are Herefordshire, Oxfordshire, Nottinghamshire, Warwickshire, and Gloucestershire.

[82] Ibid., vol. 8, pp. 371, 379.

[83] This compilation is at Staff.RO,D(W) 1788/P59/B3, among the business papers of Samuel Baldwyn, who became a prominent backer of the scheme from the end of 1665. The three addresses contained will be cited separately; two more related addresses have been found at the British Library.

the Commons' second reading committee was revived on 20 February 1662. Three of the five extant addresses seem to have been submitted at the first stage, before the adjournment. *Reasons for making Navigable the Rivers of Stower and Salwerp* enumerated the well-established economic benefits of inland navigation. Making the Stour navigable would stimulate the trading of commodities such as coal, iron, lead, glass, earthenware, apples, and cider. Once river transport was well established, manpower employed in land carriage would be 'converted to the improvement of Husbandry'—an argument designed to forestall the typical criticism that inland navigation projects would ruin carters, waggoners, and their families.[84]

To this standard argument was added a specific point. Ironworks near Worcester had virtually exhausted local forests to fuel their furnaces, and their search for alternatives doubled, or even trebled, the price of Shropshire coal carried from up the Severn—an argument based on local experience and observations, probably those of Yarranton.[85] The petition declared that the Stour navigation was timely because it would 'supply Worcester, Tewksbury, and Glocester' down the Severn with cheaper coal produced near Stourbridge, while allowing Shropshire coal producers to 'supply their own Country more plentiful and cheaper then now'.[86]

Instead of marshalling economic counterarguments, *Reasons against the making of the River Stower navigable* claimed to expose the 'main pretence of the Undertakers'.[87] Rejecting the alleged increase in coal prices down the Severn, it asserted that Shropshire coal works could provide affordable coal to all regions down the river 'if not forced to be neglected and destroyed by this new intended project'.[88] The address repeated the objection, raised earlier by Woolf at the Lords committee, that a loss of profit 'but of a fourth or fifth part' would interrupt expensive draining work and hence devastate the operation.[89] Now, the address went on to spell out the consequences—the virtual monopoly of the coal supply by the Stour promoters:

> What ever the Undertakers may now pretend (the *Shropshire* Works being once destroyed) it rest in their power to sell their Coals at what Rates they please, there being then no possibility of being furnished otherwise.[90]

The insinuation of a monopoly, something that the Stour promoters and Smyth had hinted at during a Lords committee meeting, had backfired. The introduction of a competitor was presented as a recipe for social and economic disaster; 'poor Colliers and Barge-men' dealing with Shropshire coal would 'be utterly ruined, undone, and forced to beg for a Livelihood', becoming further burdens on local poor relief. The inland water trade via the Severn 'from and to Bristol (as to other

---

[84] *Reasons for making Navigable the Rivers of Stower and Salwerp, and the rivlets and brooks running into the same, in the counties of Worcester and Stafford* [1661], p. 1.

[85] Ibid., p. 1.

[86] Staff.RO,D(W) 1788/P59/B3, *Reasons wherefore the making the rivers of Stower and Salwerp navigable*. For the perceived scarcity of timber in this period, see Lindsay Sharp, 'Timber, Science, and Economic Reform in the Seventeenth Century', *Forestry*, 48 (1975), 51–79.

[87] Staff.RO,D(W) 1788/P59/B3, *Reasons against the making of the River Stower navigable*, p. 3.

[88] Ibid., p. 3. It was claimed that 100,000 tonnes of coal would be produced yearly, the base coal sold for 4s 6d, the best coal for 6s 6d per ton.

[89] Ibid., p. 3.   [90] Ibid., pp. 3–4.

parts) will be lost' too, because those barges carrying Shropshire coals downstream were the principal means of bringing 'up the River all sorts of Merchandizes for the supply of the Towns of *Bridgenorth* and Shrewsbury, and all *North-Wales*'.[91] Thus, having presented the protection of the Shropshire coal works as a major *public* concern, the address prayed that the passage of the bill be suspended until a special commission was set up and its members visited Shropshire and Worcestershire to examine the issue at first hand, 'without respect to the Interest of particular persons'.[92]

The accusations of monopolizing trade, engrossing commodities, and manipulating prices 'as they please', were hardly unique. Similar complaints had been current at least since the fourteenth century,[93] and were often voiced against inland navigation schemes in the early modern period.[94] What was particularly alarming this time, however, was how these addresses induced responses in print form, and how the controversies thereby rapidly became acrimonious. The most disturbing signs began to emerge once the parliamentary session resumed in November 1661. The second reading committee was then ordered to consider 'the petitions of the several Inhabitants of the several Counties'.[95] One of them came from those promoting the Stour scheme; it reveals they took the blame game further. It claimed that the counter-address exaggerated the geographical spread of the inland coastal trade along the Severn, and overstated the potential damage from interregional competition. Given the 'great decay of Wood, [and] the now general approved use of Coal', the situation was not a zero-sum game. Rather, 'in all probability both places might finde Customers sufficient for their Coals'.[96] On this account, the Stour promoters reversed the accusation of a de facto monopoly once again:

> The Authors [i.e. Shropshire coal producers] have now the sole power in their hands (which they are loth to lose) to abuse the Countries, and therefore from experience of themselves conclude, that the Undertakers may abuse them also[.][97]

This replication to the counter-address provoked a rejoinder from those who opposed the bill.[98] Significantly, although the addresses hitherto submitted had

---

[91] Ibid., p. 4.   [92] Ibid., p. 4.

[93] James Davis, *Medieval Market Morality: Life, Law and Ethics in the English Marketplace, 1200–1500* (Cambridge: Cambridge University Press, 2012), pp. 254–63; Buchanan Sharp, *Famine and Scarcity in Late Medieval and Early Modern England: The Regulation of Grain Marketing, 1256–1631* (Cambridge: Cambridge University Press, 2016), pp. 17–18, 107. For the related notions of avarice and covetousness, see Sharp, *Famine*, pp. 49–55; David Harris Sacks, 'The Greed of Judas: Avarice, Monopoly, and the Moral Economy in England, ca. 1350 – ca. 1600', *Journal of Medieval and Early Modern Studies*, 28 (1998), 263–307.

[94] See Record Office for Leicestershire, Leicester, and Rutland, DG 7/3/104, *Reasons for opposing proposal to make the Derwent navigable from Derby to River Trent*, [n.d.], printed handbill not listed in the *ESTC*. See also Willan, *River Navigation*, p. 44; Ben Travers, 'Trading Patterns in the East Midlands, 1660–1800', *Midland History*, 15 (1990), 65–82, pp. 71–2; Mark Knights, 'Regulation and Rival Interests in the 1690s', in Perry Gauci (ed.), *Regulating the British Economy, 1660–1850* (Farnham: Ashgate, 2011), 63–81, pp. 72–3.

[95] *LJ*, vol. 11, p. 327.

[96] Staff.RO,D(W) 1788/P59/B3, *Further reasons for making the River of Stower navigable*, p. 2.

[97] Ibid., p. 2.

[98] *Answer as well to a paper, entituled Reasons wherefore the making navigable of the rivers Stower and Salwerp...As also to another paper, intituled, An answer to some partiall pretences, called, reasons dispersed by some Shropshire coal masters* [1661?], one-page handbill.

avoided blaming opponents by name, this rejoinder singled out Windsor for criticism, and asked, 'If this project be of that benefit to the Countrey as is pretended, and doth not rather respect the private Interest of the Undertakers thereof.'[99] As Jason Peacey has suggested, the use of printed petitions as a means of participatory politics reached maturity during the 1640s and 1650s; it even permitted the discreet escalation of public intervention in parliamentary procedure.[100] Available evidence does not allow us to ascertain how far disputants over the Stour bill controlled their language with tactical precision. Yet the present case clearly shows how the thriving public print politics intervened in parliamentary procedure with worrying rhetoric. The controversy was thereby bordering on the dangerous question of which side was promoting a destructive 'project' to monopolize the Severn-side coal trade.

Disturbingly for the members of the Cavalier Parliament, this was not an isolated case. By the time the Stour bill was approved by the Lords and passed to the lower house in July 1661, Killigrew and other drainers were also seeking to win Commons' backing for a bill for confirming their (disputed) possession of 14,000 acres of fenlands in the so-called Lindsey Level, Lincolnshire.[101] Landowners and commoners who stood to lose by this opposed it vehemently. They petitioned to protect what they deemed their 'undoubted right and Title in the Law'; in the process, the petitions invoked Barkham's imprisonment and release in the 1630s, and reminded the Commons of the local riots directed at Killigrew and other Caroline commissioners of sewers in the 1640s. The petitioners even slyly threatened that they 'know not' what 'oppressions constrained poor people to do, or may constrain them unto in the future'.[102]

Tumult and disorder were never notional. In September 1661, it was reported that 'a greate many countrey men who were concerned' about the Stour project gathered in front of Windsor's house in Kidderminster, 'cry[ing] out mightily at the prejudice they thinke they shall sustain by it'. Despite local concerns and the escalating opposition, Windsor was said to have been 'resolvd to proceede, it being a publike act, to get an act passe for it'.[103] As studies on early modern river navigation, fen drainage, enclosure, and turnpike legislation demonstrate,

---

[99] Ibid. Smyth was also named earlier in the address.

[100] Jason Peacey, *Print and Public Politics in the English Revolution* (Cambridge: Cambridge University Press, 2013), pp. 282–6, 322–8. Lobbying practices had a longer history, of course. A useful starting point includes Hannes Kleineke, 'Lobbying and Access: The Canons of Windsor and the Matter of the Poor Knights in the Parliament of 1485', *Parliamentary History*, 25 (2006), 145–59; Matthew Davies, 'Lobbying Parliament: The London Companies in the Fifteenth Century', *Parliamentary History*, 23 (2004), 136–48.

[101] *CJ*, vol. 8, pp. 285, 288, 291; William Killigrew, *The late earle of Lindsey his title, by which himself, and his participants, do claim 24000. acres of lands in the fennes in Lincoln-shire* (1661).

[102] *The case of the lords, owners, and commoners of 22. townes in the soake of bullingbrooke* [n.d., late 1661 or early 1662]; *The Earl of Exeter with divers other lords and gentlemen are proprietors and owners in possession* [n.d., late 1661 or early 1662]. For comparable examples of local politics regarding improvement reaching central government, see Heather Falvey, 'Custom, Resistance and Politics: Local Experiences of Improvement in Early Modern England' (2 vols., PhD thesis, University of Warwick, 2007), vol. 2, pp. 366, 387, 393–4.

[103] Edward Maunde Thompson (ed.), *Correspondence of the Family of Hatton, vol. I, 1601–1704* (Camden Society, 1878), pp. 23–4.

large-scale improvement schemes often provoked reactions ranging from formal petitioning and informal lobbying to tactical silence, blackmailing, and violent protests.[104] What is significant about the present case of 1661 is the timing, however. Charles II had just been crowned at Westminster Abbey in April 1661. Then, as soon as the Cavalier Parliament sat the next month, the Stour bill was submitted, its progress was reported far beyond Westminster, informal protests took place in Kidderminster, and the cross-petitioning escalated back in London. Opponents' petitions even betrayed a sense of frustration with the legislative process. Why, one petition asked, did the Commons fail to appoint special commissioners to visit key sites in Shropshire and Worcestershire? How could parliament otherwise secure judicious consideration?[105]

The Commons under the restored monarchy could not afford to adopt the heavy-handed approach of Charles I's Privy Council. The drainage bill backed by Killigrew never reached the statute book. The threatening petitions would have helped discredit the bill, but parliamentary records do not spell out exactly on what grounds it was dropped.[106] Members' underlying concerns were partially revealed in June 1661, when the House handled complaints from Plymouth, Hull, and other port towns. Upon the 'Pretence of a Patent touching Ballast', merchants had been forced to pay 'new Duties and Fees, that were never known before'. In less than two weeks, one John Walter was summoned to Westminster, and ordered to produce the patent. It turned out that the grant so produced included a clause to bar 'any evil Use thereof'. On this evidence the Commons swiftly condemned him, concluding that 'Walter was the Projector and prime Agent therein'. The grant was cancelled, with Walter being apprehended and ordered to return the money that he had levied. The House knew full well that it could not be seen to countenance such projectors reminiscent of Caroline fiscal exactions. The Commons wasted no time in acting upon 'so great a Grievance' and 'to put a Mark of their Displeasure upon it'.[107]

Removing sources of grievance was probably much easier, however, than promoting large-scale improvement without vexation. The case of the Stour navigation is especially significant because it shows us under what conditions the Cavalier

---

[104] In addition to Willan, *River Navigation*, pp. 28–51, see also John Walter, *Crowds and Popular Politics in Early Modern England* (Manchester: Manchester University Press, 2006), pp. 208–11; Matthew Clark, 'Resistance, Collaboration and the Early Modern "Public Transcript": The River Lea Disputes and Popular Politics in England, 1571–1603', *Cultural and Social History*, 8 (2011), 297–313, pp. 303–4; Lindley, *Fenland*, pp. 258–9; J. M. Neeson, *Commoners: Common Right, Enclosure and Social Change in England, 1700–1820* (Cambridge: Cambridge University Press, 1993), pp. 262, 272; Michael Freeman, 'Popular Attitudes to Turnpikes in Early Eighteenth-Century England', *Journal of Historical Geography*, 19 (1993), 33–47, esp. pp. 33, 44–5; Eric Pawson, *Transport and Economy: The Turnpike Roads of Eighteenth-Century Britain* (London: Academic Press, 1977), pp. 118–19.

[105] Staff.RO, D(W) 1788/P59/B3, *Reasons against the making of the River Stower navigable*, p. 4. The drainage bill that Killigrew promoted may well have prompted similar questions about parliament's credibility.

[106] Killigrew subsequently resubmitted bills, but never managed to win parliamentary backing in this regard. To recover his fortune, he turned to playwriting. See *House of Commons 1604–1629*, vol. 5, p. 25.

[107] *CJ*, vol. 8, pp. 272, 281.

Parliament passed the Stour bill at a time when a controversy over a small river *could* provoke the resentment and grievances which it was so anxious to eliminate.

How did the Commons proceed? On 20 February 1662, the Commons' second reading committee for the Stour bill was revived; it then reported to the House 'several Amendments to be made' along with 'several Provisoes to be added'.[108] Close reading of these provisos and amendments reveals how Commons MPs steered through the dangerous waters to pass the bill. These additions ensured extra protection for key riparian stakeholders, specified the undertakers' liability, and placed a cap on local commodity prices to prevent 'engrossing'. Upon such calibration, and amid political risk and echoes of distrust, hinged the passing of the bill, the scheme's implementation, and, to an extent, the future career of Yarranton as well as the subsequent economic development of the region.

The Commons first took steps to protect riparian properties, especially the mills of Worcester clothiers. Some of these town weavers established fulling mills by the Stour, presumably because the town was already crowded with mills and water power was more readily available in the Stour valley.[109] Setting up mills away from the city seems hardly surprising given that these clothiers formed the most numerous occupational group in the Severn-side city of Worcester. Clothiers, weavers, and walkers comprised more than half of those admitted to the Freedom of the City of Worcester during the 1660s and 1670s.[110] Their trade was protected by a charter granted in 1590, and the company successfully had its charter confirmed by the Cavalier Parliament in July 1661 just as the Stour bill was being considered; the Worcester clothiers thus represented a strong stakeholder in the bill.[111]

Prudently, the Stour promoters approached them prior to parliamentary debate; the draft bill originally submitted to the Lords already contained a proviso assuring that the promoters 'shall not...make any Trench or River for conveying of any Water from a place called Hucks Pound', a riverside pond which provided water vital for the clothiers' mills. As one of the petitions submitted to defend the bill proudly announced, the original Stour bill thus incorporated the 'provision' to protect fulling mills, as 'directed by the Clothiers of *Worcester*'—a reminder that negotiations outside Whitehall were just as vital even at the planning stage.[112] In order to fuel the clothiers' anxiety and undermine the bill, however, Shropshire coal producers reiterated the risk in their petition: 'What prejudice may redound to the Trade of Clothing in *Worcester*...if their many Fulling-Mills upon the River *Stower* shall

---

[108] Ibid., vol. 8, pp. 369, 371, at p. 371.

[109] Such relocation was common and played a role in the diffusion of fulling mills. John Reynolds, *Windmills & Watermills* (New York: Praeger, 1970), p. 116.

[110] Gwen Talbut, 'Worcester as an Industrial and Commercial Centre, 1660–1750', *Transactions of the Worcestershire Archaeological Society*, 3rd ser., 10 (1986), 91–102, at p. 92.

[111] *CJ*, vol. 8, p. 282; *LJ*, vol. 11, pp. 308, 331.

[112] PA, HL/PO/JO/10/1/303, Draft of an Act for making navigable of the rivers of Stower and Salwarpe (read 11 May 1661); Staff.RO,D(W) 1788/P59/B3, *Further reasons for making the River of Stower navigable*, p. 2.

suffer from want of Water'?[113] Hucks Pond would have been just one of the many key sites for clothiers that were vulnerable to such potential damage.

The Commons' committee thus responded by inserting an extra clause for protection. Not only were the promoters prevented from lessening the water of Hucks Pond, but the bill now stipulated that they 'shall not'

> [*insertion begins*] do any other Act or Acts, thing or things whatsoever that may be prejudicial unto or hinder any Clothier or Clothiers of the City of Worcester, or others, in the scowring or thickning of any Cloath or Cloathes at any or either of the Fulling Mills upon the said River of Stower [*insertion ends*] without the consent of... the Incorporated Company of Clothiers of the City of Worcester or the major part of them[.][114]

The kind of 'prejudice' and 'hinderance' foreseen was no longer limited to physical damage or the loss of water at a particular location, but now extended to include a broader range of eventualities. Accordingly, the committee went on to specify promoters' liability with greater precision. In the engrossed bill composed at the end of the Lords' session, the promoters were made liable only for the damage caused to riparian proprietors 'by the cutting or other wayes damnifying of their lands or tenements'—no mention of mills or the loss of profit.[115] This original phrasing, however, received extensive emendation. By the time the Commons' committee reported back to the whole house, the undertakers' liabilities extended to

> the cutting or other wayes damnifying [*insertion begins*] or abating the present value profitts or advantages [*insertion ends*] of their lands or tenements, [*insertion begins*] or farmes, cournmills, ironmills, and other mills, forges, and other things whatsoever, or in any prejudice obstruction or losses that may happen in fulling white cloathes to any person or persons whatsoever imployed or trading therein [*insertion ends*].

These insertions won Commons' approval, and made their way to the printed act of parliament.[116] Instead of retrospectively ordering compensation after local complaints (as Charles I's Privy Council had done for the Upper Medway navigation), the Cavalier Parliament inserted clauses for extra protections and thereby minimized the risk of local grievances in advance. The Commons conceded so far as to make the Stour promoters liable even for future lost profits of inhabitants and the Worcestershire clothiers who operated farms, mills, and forges by the river. The liability clauses inserted between the lines stand as conspicuous evidence of public politics that was informed by the memory of early Stuart precedents.

---

[113] Staff.RO,D(W) 1788/P59/B3, *Reasons against the making of the River Stower navigable*, p. 4. In common law of this period, water for a mill, like woods growing on land, was understood as 'an intergral part' of one's possession of land. See Joshua Getzler, *A History of Water Rights at Common Law* (Oxford: Oxford University Press, 2004), pp. 119–22, at p. 122.

[114] 'Engrossed Stour Act', membrane 6; Staff.RO, D(W)1788/P45/B14, *An Act for making navigable of the Rivers of Stower and Salwerpe* [printed], sig. [D2] [hereafter cited as *the Printed Stour Act*].

[115] 'Engrossed Stour Act', membrane 2.

[116] 'Engrossed Stour Act', membrane 2; *Printed Stour Act*, sig. [B2].

The safeguarding of riparian stakeholders, however, was part of broader concerns. What about the Shropshire coal producers' allegation that the Stour promoters might end up establishing a de facto monopoly of regional coal supply? One might expect that it would suffice to prohibit the Stour undertakers from selling coal above a certain price. The Wye navigation act of 1651 had earlier adopted such a price cap.[117] Perhaps in response to the heated controversies, however, the post-Restoration Commons went further. The provisos added to the bill now banned the Stour undertakers from buying coal from the Amblecote Works up the Stour 'in case the price of Coals' near the production site, i.e the wholesale price, 'shall hereafter be raised above the rate that Coals are now sold at'.[118] In so far as the coal trade was vital for the Stour promoters—they hoped to raise £3,000 yearly by it—they were therefore given an incentive not only to observe the current wholesale price themselves, but also to keep others in line.

Yet who was to determine the 'usual' rate? What about the selling price that the Stour promoters would set down the Severn? These questions were asked on the Commons' floor. When this proviso was read twice on 22 February, the House resolved that an independent local committee 'shall from time to time have power hereby to settle and appoint' the wholesale price. The proviso was 'so amended at the Table'.[119] On 27 February, a similar proviso was added to prevent 'the unreasonable rates of Coal' at the promoters' wharfs to be erected farther downstream.[120] Only after these extensive revisions did the Commons finally approve the bill and send it up to the Lords for confirmation the following month.

In the end, the Commons did not act upon the allegation made by Shropshire coal producers—that introducing competitors up the Stour would irrecoverably ruin them. After all, the manifold benefits of inland navigation had been known to the point of being commonplace; the Commons was therefore unwilling to discourage navigation schemes. Yet representatives could not afford to be held responsible for endorsing projects that might turn out to be locally disastrous. The Commons thus ended up taking on board many—perhaps too many—of the points advanced by local stakeholders. Previous inland navigation acts rarely (if ever) had comparable protection of key riparian industries, extensive specifications of liabilities, or price caps to prevent 'engrossing'.[121] We shall come back to the long-term legacies of the Stour act at the end of this chapter. For now, these emendations remind us how, through the participatory politics of petitioning, the underlying suspicion and memory of destructive projecting was brought to Westminster, and thereby subtly influenced the making of the first inland navigation act authorized after the Restoration (Illustration 4.2).

---

[117] The cap concerned how much the undertakers could levy from boats carrying coal. See *A&O*, vol. 2, pp. 515–16.

[118] 'Engrossed Stour Act', membrane 7; *Printed Stour Act*, sig. E.

[119] *CJ*, vol. 8, p. 371; *Printed Stour Act*, sig. E–[Ev].

[120] *CJ*, vol. 8, p. 374; *Printed Stour Act*, sig. [Ev]–[E2].

[121] Samples of the pre-1660 acts that I have examined for comparison are HL/PO/PU/1/1514/6H8n18 (6 Hen VIII, *c.* 17, Kentish Stour); HL/PO/PB/1/1571/13Eliz1n13 (13 Eliz I, *c.* 1, Welland); HL/PO/PU/1/1571/13Eliz1n35 (13 Eliz I, *c.* 18, Lea); HL/PO/PU/1/1623/21J1n32 (21 Jac I, *c.* 32, Thames); *A&O*, vol. 2, pp. 514–17 (An act for making navigable the river of Wye, 1651).

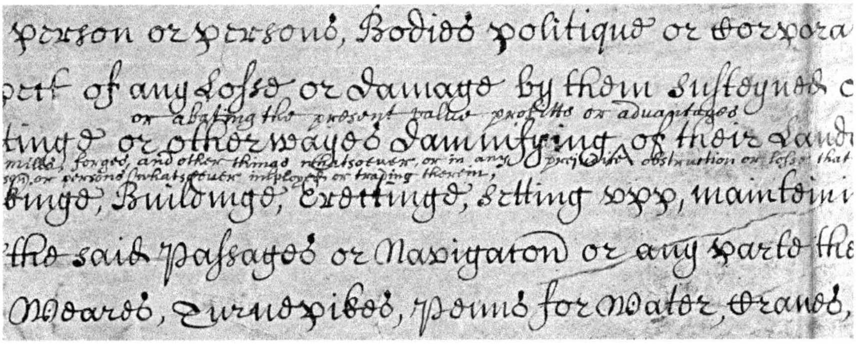
person or persons, Bodies politique or Corpora
of any losse or damage by them susteyned
or abating the present value profitts or advantages
tinge or otherwayes damnifying of their Land
inge, Buildinge, Erectinge, setting upp, maintaini
the said passages or Navigation or any parte the
Weares, Turnepikes, poundes for water, Cranes,

Illustration 4.2. PA, HL/PO/PB1/1662/14C2n46, An Act for making navigable of the Rivers of Stower and Salwerp [Engrossed Stour Act], membrane 2 (detail)

Notice the inserted clause on future profitability: 'other wayes damnifying [*insertion begins*] or abating the present value profitts or advantages [*insertion ends*] of their lands or tenements'. Insertions like this testify to the mature print politics that post-Restoration England inherited from the revolutionary decades; equally crucially, they suggest that, by invoking the fresh memory of destructive 'projects', such participatory politics ensured that England's emerging culture of improvement—in this case the extension of navigable rivers vital for regional specialization—did not exacerbate social tensions as it did under the early Stuarts. Courtesy of The Parliamentary Archives, London

FINANCING THE STOUR PROJECT

Winning parliamentary backing was, however, just a step towards turning a project into reality. As the Cavalier Parliament did not consider the feasibility of the scheme, its financial arrangement, or the technical skills of those involved, these had to be negotiated among the promoters themselves. Given the subsequent reputation of Yarranton as a proven expert in improvement, it might be tempting to suppose that his partners were able to entrust their money to him with relative confidence. So far, few accounts have examined the interface between the two kinds of credibility implicit here: credibility about experts' technical competence, and their creditworthiness in social and economic contexts.[122] Simon Schaffer's works are notable exceptions.[123] Yet the existing remarks give us an overall impression that trustworthiness in experimental philosophy and credit in the commercial sphere were more or less interchangeable. As a result, it has not been entirely clear how well trusting experts' knowledge and competence might translate into trusting

[122] For the former, see the publications by Ash and Johnston cited earlier. For the latter, the best overviews are Wrightson, *Earthly Necessities*, ch. 13 (esp. pp. 293–5, 300–3); Craig Muldrew, *Economy of Obligation: The Culture of Credit and Social Relations in Early Modern England* (London: Macmillan, 1998), chs. 5–6; Alexandra Shepard, *Accounting for Oneself: Worth, Status, and the Social Order in Early Modern England* (Oxford: Oxford University Press, 2015), pp. 35–7, 277–9, 287–302.

[123] Simon Schaffer, 'Defoe's Natural Philosophy and the Worlds of Credit', in John Christie and Sally Shuttleworth (eds.), *Nature Transfigured: Science and Literature, 1700–1900* (Manchester: Manchester University Press, 1989), 13–44, esp. p. 28; Simon Schaffer, 'A Social History of Plausibility: Country, City and Calculation in Augustan Britain', in Adrian Wilson (ed.), *Rethinking Social History: English Society 1570–1920 and its Interpretation* (Manchester: Manchester University Press, 1993), 128–57, pp. 137–41; Simon Schaffer, 'The Show that Never Ends: Perpetual Motion in the Early Eighteenth Century', *BJHS*, 28 (1995), 157–89, pp. 160–1, 181–3, 188–9.

money to them. Fortunately, the available evidence about the Stour scheme is so rich that it enables us to move beyond its *initial negotiation* to tackle this question. Backers did recognize Yarranton's expert competence; but, as we shall see, they did not readily trust their money to him. A brief look into the financing of the Stour scheme and other comparable projects explains why.

Large-scale schemes such as the Stour navigation required large expenditure before achieving profit. The navigation work involved making locks, removing mills and forges, bypassing some by widening the river, and making trenches in neighbouring lands.[124] Carpenters, labourers, and merchants providing goods had to be paid. Within a few years, all this came to cost more than £1,000.[125] Added to this was the compensation to riparian landowners. In a rather demanding proviso, the act stipulated that the promoters pay a minimum compensation of twenty years' purchase for the lands and properties to be damaged (that is, twenty times their annual rental value).[126] The phrasing of the Stour act elsewhere meant that the promoters did not have to pay compensation up front; they were instead permitted to start removing mills and weirs once their owners and occupiers agreed to accept compensation out of the money to be raised from tolls upon newly navigable sections of the river. Even so, arrears of more than £100 were due to a single riparian landowner, Sir Ralph Clare, by 1667—undoubtedly the tip of an iceberg.[127] Yet regular and timely cash injection was difficult to secure because of the chronic lack of specie—a pervasive problem in early modern England.[128] Money was also hard to come by, because backers were careful not to waste money on 'projects' that might turn out to be unsuccessful or even deceitful. Their caution was evident even before the navigation work began, as the initial contract of 1661 reveals.

The deed of agreement shows that Windsor's and Bristol's investment was conditional upon performance, only to be paid retrospectively in instalments. Only after Smyth and his undertakers, including Yarranton, first made three miles of the Stour and two miles of the Salwarpe navigable, were Windsor and Bristol then to pay one-sixth of the total investment of £1,500 for the first instalment (i.e. £250). As for the second instalment, each backer was to pay £500 after two-thirds of the Stour and one more mile of the Salwarpe were finished.[129] Windsor and Bristol did not have to pay the rest of the agreed sum (£750) themselves; it was to be deducted

[124] Skempton et al. (eds.), *Dictionary of Civil Engineers*, vol. 1, p. 810.
[125] See Staff.RO, D(W)1788/P61/B7(f), 'A particular of the Expenses laid out in discharging of the Rents and damages due upon the River Stower', n.d. 'Scouring and Enlarging Hafcut Trench', for example, cost £150; 'Hafcutt & Locks and Trench below', £90; 'Sturton Locke', £40.
[126] The Wye and Lug act of 1696, for example, specified the *maximum* at sixteen years' purchase, thus limiting the undertakers' liability. Compare Willan, *River Navigation*, pp. 48–9, 53–5 with *Printed Stour Act*, sig. D.
[127] *Printed Stour Act*, sig. D; Staff.RO, D(W)1788/P59/B3, Haycox and Leregoe to Baldwyn, 5 November 1667.
[128] For the interlocking issues of money supply and the heavy reliance upon credit, see B. A. Holderness, 'Credit in English Rural Society before the Nineteenth Century, with Special Reference to the Period 1650–1720', *Agricultural History Review*, 24 (1976), 97–109, pp. 101–2; N. J. Mayhew, 'Population, Money Supply, and the Velocity of Circulation in England, 1300–1700', *EcHR*, 48 (1995), 238–57, pp. 244, 253–5; Muldrew, *Economy of Obligation*, pp. 25–6, 96–103.
[129] Staff.RO, D(W)1788/P43/B10, 'Article for the River Stower &c', 10 May 1661.

from future profits raised from tolls and the sale of coal.[130] Windsor and Bristol sought to limit the amount of cash to be disbursed from their coffers; they did not have to raise a farthing up front.

It is not clear how far this initial agreement was in fact honoured. Little evidence is available on works that may have been carried out on the Salwarpe; Bristol in any case opted out by 1665. But this legal document does reveal investors' caution, which partly derived from their encounter with large-scale undertakings and projecting culture more broadly. For example, the Wey navigation was initiated by a correspondent of Hartlib, Richard Weston, in the 1630s and eventually completed by his son and his associates in 1653. This was accomplished, in Willan's assessment, 'by the simple method of not paying for it'. When chief justices and the chief baron of the Exchequer intervened to settle the disputes in the early 1670s, the total claims for unpaid debts amounted to £67,478.[131] The backer Windsor must have been familiar with another expensive case, that of the Avon navigation work, as he was seeking to take over its ownership at the time when the Stour navigation bill was being debated in parliament. William Sandys, who began the work in the late 1630s, spent over £40,000 in his own estimation, and borrowed a 'great part' of it from various investors. Some of the debts remained even after 1660. This, Sandys argued, was partly because his agent embezzled 'some thousands of pounds' by underestimating the profits from the river.[132]

Throughout the seventeenth century, river navigation schemes and other large-scale enterprises such as fen drainage and the vending of drinking water often led to financial disaster. This was one of the reasons why backers were usually reluctant to hand over their money up front. While river navigation was sometimes funded by local assessments, promoters themselves often paid from their own purse or borrowed upon credit to their ruin.[133] Profits from tolls were often dwarfed by the cost of removing gravel, widening the river, making trenches, and making locks and sluices using expensive timbers. In his *Worthies of England* (1662), Thomas Fuller related that John Morton, bishop of Ely (1479–85), and later archbishop of Canterbury, 'almost wasted his estate, by cutting a *water-passage*, (known by the name of the *New Leam*) & welnigh beggared himself'.[134] The reader was reminded that even competent and sincere promoters could fail in their projects when lacking '*assistants*, or *purses*, *performance of pay* to people imployed therein'.[135]

Arguably, for some wealthy aristocrats, the loss of several hundred (even a few thousand) pounds did not mean immediate bankruptcy. Yet we must guard against too readily equating aristocratic investment with gambling. As the Shropshire landowner Sir John Weld advised his son, it was vital not to ruin the family by

[130] Staff.RO, D(W)1788/P43/B10, 'Article for the River Stower &c', 10 May 1661.

[131] Willan, *River Navigation*, pp. 69–70 (quotation from p. 69). See ibid., ch. 4, for more examples of financial disasters.

[132] TNA, SP 29/66/160, 'Petition of William Sandys esq., against Lord Windsor's move to make the Avon navigable', [1662?].

[133] Willan, *River Navigation*, p. 66.

[134] Thomas Fuller, *The history of the University of Cambridge* (1655), p. 70.

[135] Ibid.

'searching for coals', or by being 'led away by colliers or miners or projectors, whose fair speech is but to get themselves money'.[136] Wasting money on abortive projects—like wasting money on gaming—was hardly a commendable form of conspicuous consumption.[137] Honour was to be established, but not upon one's financial ruin. The practical consequence was clear to Thomas Smyth when he negotiated with the earl of Bristol in 1661; as Smyth told Yarranton, the earl had 'a deate eare to monie and faime; hee would have them but not pay for them'.[138]

Accordingly, as in the case of technical inventions promoted by the likes of Wheeler and Dymock, the piecemeal demonstration of feasibility and technical competence was crucial. Smyth and Yarranton had to proceed 'att their proper Costs and Charges' in the first instance, paying workmen by themselves or borrowing from others, upon the promise that their backers would discharge the money as arranged—no easy task to accomplish with sceptical investors in a period of chronic cash shortage. Such were the broad contexts in which elements of caution about unreliable projects and deceitful experts came to affect the flow of money and the web of credit in the West Midlands, both indispensable for successful execution.

'THE WANT OF MONIES': SUSPECTING COMPETENT EXPERTS

When those involved failed to pay creditors and workers on time, far-reaching consequences followed. Contractors were imprisoned; the traffic of boats was obstructed; backers' reputations were blemished; new partners refused to join. We will explore the unfolding of these events, paying close attention to the two years from December 1665, for which we have rich evidence thanks to Baldwyn's family papers. These letters reveal that the caution of backers—and hence the lack of ready money—persisted despite the fact that Yarranton's experience and expertise were found to be indispensable.

When Baldwyn joined the enterprise at the end of 1665, the remaining task was to complete the unfinished 4.5-mile section from Kidderminster down to Lower Mitton. For this purpose, Baldwyn swiftly invested £1,500, which was not part of the original 1661 agreement. Even so, the undertaking had outstanding debt of at least £300 in 1667.[139] Windsor and Baldwyn were probably requested to disburse further sums so that Yarranton and other lesser partners could complete the

---

[136] Quoted in Felicity Heal and Clive Holmes, *The Gentry in England and Wales, 1500–1700* (Basingstoke: Macmillan, 1994), pp. 120–1.

[137] Nicholas Barry Tosney, 'Gaming in England, c. 1540–1760' (PhD thesis, University of York, 2008), pp. 265–6.

[138] TNA, SP 29/44/21, Thomas Smyth to Andrew Yarranton, 7 November 1661. The evidence presented here qualifies the view that a gambling mentality drove aristocratic investment on infrastructure. Cf. Lawrence Stone, *The Crisis of the Aristocracy, 1558–1641* (Oxford: Clarendon, 1965), pp. 381–4.

[139] See Staff.RO, D(W)1788/P61/B7, 'Mr Yarrantons note of moneys due upon the account of the navigation to workemen', 25 March 1667.

navigation and start raising profits to repay debts owed to creditors and offer compensation to riparian landowners and the owners of mills. This did not happen smoothly at all, because Windsor, one of the key backers, came to suspend further payments.

One reason was organizational. In early 1667 Baldwyn reported that 'Windsor doth now refuse to lay out any more money to finish the River Stower and to make a trade upon the same unlesse the other Partners will agree to make a division & Partition of the River' so that 'each Partner may know his p[ar]ticular division upon that River'.[140] This was not surprising given the virtual lack of organizational structure. Transactions with a range of stakeholders, from coal masters, timber merchants, wagon men, and carpenters to wage labourers and those entitled to compensation, generated a great number of deeds and articles of agreement. Of course, systematic accounting practices, such as the double-entry system, were becoming widespread. The Foleys used double-entry accounting to keep track of their tinplate manufacture, which was associated with the Stour navigation.[141] By contrast, the Stour navigation had no overall account. It instead relied on the standard practice of charge and discharge, sending pieces of paper of various sizes as receipts of money.[142] The task was further complicated because each partner assigned and sold off part of their agreement to others, and because shares of future profits were offered as payment and compensation. The web of debts, liabilities, and obligations was so complex that, in 1670, Yarranton proposed to tidy up the partnership in order 'to p[re]vent Confusion for the future'.[143] In the absence of an organized method, backers and undertakers struggled to understand where and how debts were incurred, when the money had to be paid to whom, and who should be responsible for paying it.[144] Windsor was becoming unwilling to invest more unless the web of partnerships was better organized.

Crucially for our discussion, however, Windsor had another reason to delay timely payment: suspicion towards the key player, Yarranton. Windsor seems to have accepted his technical and managerial competence, and initially paid him a fixed salary. Yet, by the end of 1666, Windsor refused to pay him on a regular basis: 'hee should have the conduct of the whole Trade, but I would grant no more certaine salaries, but allow him so much oute of each pound of the Cleer proffitts'.[145] Windsor insisted on suspending the regular salary because he had discovered from one of his partners that Yarranton might have deliberately neglected his supervisory role for a while so that other partners 'att last finde a necessity of taking him to manage the whole trade, which hee would doe for a good salary'.[146] Inflating the

---

[140] Staff.RO, D(W)1788/P59/B3, 'Mr Baldwyns Case' [February–July 1667?].

[141] Schafer (ed.), *Philip Foley's Stour Valley Iron Works*, vol. 1, pp. xi–xv, 34–8.

[142] These receipts and periodical summaries are now scattered across different bundles in Staff.RO, D(W)1788.

[143] Staff.RO, D(W)1788/P61/B5(a), 'Cap. Yarr proposal', March [1670?].

[144] Staff.RO, D(W)1788/P61/B5, 2 December 1671.

[145] Staff.RO, D(W)1788/P59/B3, Windsor [to Baldwyn?], 26 December 1666. See also Staff.RO, D(W)1788/P61/B7(f), Windsor to Baldwyn, 2 February 1667, where Windsor admitted that 'I am contented that Mr Yarington should mannage the River'.

[146] Staff.RO, D(W)1788/P59/B3, Windsor [to Baldwyn?], 26 December 1666.

value of one's expertise was a common strategy.[147] In the present case, it led Windsor to demand that Yarranton perform his duty first, a caution that Robert Cecil, for example, had exercised when backing Walter Morrell's New Drapery scheme.[148]

Strikingly, moreover, Windsor was also unwilling to take Yarranton's words at face value. Windsor told Baldwyn:

> Sir, I have received yo[u]r letter where in you designe to incourage mee to lett Mr Yarrington mannage the River, from whence I perceive his faire words hath once more gained credit with you, but I am so consatisfied [dissatisfied?] with his Dealing[.][149]

Yarranton and his business partners frequently tried to reassure investors that bearing financial 'incumbrances' would later lead to a healthy return. In 1670 Windsor sceptically commented on just such 'faire words':

> that the river is free from all incumbrances except the rents [to the landowners], and the rent charges [i.e. periodic payments] to Mr Streets Mr white and yarrington [and William] lerego, is to[o] easy to be believed because no person as I know of would venture mony upon it but ourselves[.]

Windsor hesitated to believe this because of the real possibility of cheating. Speaking of the equal distribution of the profit from tolls between partners, Windsor pointed out that Yarranton and his partners promised 'They will finde all boats et[c] . . . but who shall judge of the number'.[150] Windsor suspected that Yarranton and his workers who levied tolls on the river might embezzle the profit by underestimating the number of boats. Underrating the real profit was precisely how Sandys's contractor had defrauded him in the Avon navigation scheme. Given the parallels we have found with other cases, Windsor was not unusual in exercising such caution when investing his money.

Windsor also had more specific reasons to be wary. Yarranton accused him of committing 'great erers in the management', and pointed out that 'the Countrey are not satisfied in his late Actinges and his bad pay'.[151] Yarranton even secretly tried to persuade Baldwyn to rearrange the complex partnership so as to marginalize Windsor and oust him from his managerial role.[152] Windsor had come to know

---

[147] We have seen Cressy Dymock skilfully present his 'special secrets' to make advantageous contracts. See pp. 123–4.

[148] Michael Zell, 'Walter Morrell and the New Draperies Project, c. 1603–1631', *HJ*, 44 (2001), 651–75, p. 658. See also William Cecil's administration of patents discussed in Deborah E. Harkness, *The Jewel House: Elizabethan London and the Scientific Revolution* (New Haven, CT: Yale University Press, 2007), p. 153. For similar examples from the Stour case, see Staff.RO, D(W)1788/P59/B3, Windsor to [Baldwyn?], [1670?]; Staff.RO, D(W)1788/P61/B7(a), George Skyppe to Baldwyn, 16 January 1680.

[149] Staff.RO, D(W)1788/P61/B7(f), Windsor to Baldwyn, 2 February 1667.

[150] Staff.RO, D(W)1788/P59/B3, Windsor to [Baldwyn?], [1670?].

[151] Staff.RO, D(W)1788/P59/B3, Yarranton to Baldwyn [n.d., between 30 November and 8 December 1666?].

[152] Staff.RO, D(W)1788/P61/B7(a), Yarranton to Baldwyn, 30 November 1666. A postscript by another partner 'intreat[ed]' Baldwyn to 'keepe this private by you and I will asiste Mr Yarranton'.

about this from one of the partners,[153] and this would surely have reinforced Windsor's suspicions.

Windsor's misgivings, symptomatic of underlying doubts about projecting, but also fuelled by organizational challenges and internal rivalry, resulted in a serious lack of liquidity. Lord Windsor was, Yarranton fumed on 30 November 1666, causing 'great Confusion for want of monies' by 'not payinge any until yestaday and then but £60'.[154] It is not clear whether Windsor was accused of not paying the agreed sum or extra 'contingency' funds Yarranton and others found wanting. In any case, for Yarranton it was clear that the lack of cash was causing serious trouble: 'as to the erers of the Footrayle[,] it is in the bad management and I have provided the remedy and can put it into order when... there may be monies constantly to pay the Collyers'.[155] Yarranton predicted that the lack of a cash injection and Windsor's bad management would cause Baldwyn to 'rune in dept and lost by Christmas at least £50'.[156]

LOCAL CONSEQUENCES OF DISTRUST: LOSING CREDIT LINES, REPUTATION, AND NERVES

The lack of a timely cash injection forced Smyth, Yarranton, and other undertakers on the ground to depend heavily on their own credit, with far-reaching consequences. When debts could not be repaid fully and on time, the liability was often compensated by an offer of future profit. Yarranton, for example, paid only a proportion of what was due to his business partners, making them 'take the rest out of the [forthcoming] proffits'.[157] The technique was probably used when buying timber and bricks from local merchants, employing workmen to cut the river and make boats and wooden trams, and paying compensation to riparian landowners. In order to compensate them for damage to their fulling mills the clothiers John and Robert Willmott were asked to accept forty pounds annually to be 'raised by two pence p[er] tunne for every tunn that shall goe through the first lock below Hookes pound'.[158] It is hard to estimate the exact scale of such practices in this and other business undertakings. Yet, clearly, the shortage of ready cash was such that the project could not have been set in motion without an extensive network of personal credit, or without turning creditors into a web of de facto

---

[153] Staff.RO, D(W)1788/P59/B3, Windsor [to Baldwyn?], 26 December 1666.

[154] Staff.RO, D(W)1788/P61/B7(a), Yarranton to Baldwyn, 30 November 1666.

[155] Staff.RO, D(W)1788/P59/B3, Yarranton to Baldwyn, 8 December 1666.

[156] Staff.RO, D(W)1788/P59/B3, Yarranton to Baldwyn [n.d., between 30 November and 8 December 1666?].

[157] See for example, Staff.RO, D(W)1788/P59/B3, Yarranton to Baldwyn, 30 December 1667. Such a deal was possible presumably because others needed Yarranton's experience and expertise.

[158] Staff.RO, D(W)1788/P59/B3, A copy of the agreement with John and Robert Willmott, 2 October 1666. See also Staff.RO, D(W)1788/P61/B5, Windsor's note to Mr. Street, 1 July 1670.

investors. Here, we begin to explore an interface between the world of projecting and that of everyday credit relations.

As Keith Wrightson noted, 'Loss of reputation entailed loss of the trust which was fundamental to the capacity to do business effectively'.[159] In the present case, the backers' slow payment led to a vicious circle of loss of reputation, interruption of business, and further insolvency. Samuel Whyle, who had replaced the lawyer Thomas Smyth as a treasurer for the scheme, urged Baldwyn to 'set matters in some bett[e]r posture'. In January 1667, he warned that 'till it be in bett[e]r credit noe body will medle w[i]th it'. Whyle hinted that he himself came to doubt the future of the scheme, noting he would 'willingly leave it up to any th[a]t will manage it well for I knowe not howe'.[160] A few months later, Whyle reported to Baldwyn how the operation had halted because of the lack of liquidity. Few people were willing to work for the scheme and there were 'but 3 or 4 or 5 barges goeing' on the Stour. There was probably a small cash injection, but when such money was made available with the goal of continuing the navigation work, business partners who had hitherto been forced to accept a share of future profits in lieu of payment took the money to satisfy the outstanding debts owed to them. 'Because the Nav[ivation] in theire debt, I see noe accompt given of any of our last moneys', Whyle explained. In the absence of further investment, then, the operation was suspended and the credibility of the project severely undermined.

More than the project's credibility was at stake. Two partners, William Leregoe and Francis Haycox, had some timber and ironware delivered for building locks, and employed some workmen upon credit. They soon failed to meet their obligations, and were sued by their creditors by the end of 1666. While Windsor and others hesitated to supply the cash required, Leregoe had been 'arrested' due to insolvency.[161] By May 1667, the timber merchant Haycox had also been embroiled in 'several su[i]ts' and twice arrested for the money he owed. He wrote that he had 'enlarg[e]d the reach of my credit beyond its usual extent for Tymber[,] Iron worke[,] wages & other things for the Navigation…I beeing the possesor of continual Hazards and disadvantages'.[162] Thus he directly appealed to Baldwyn for more money:

> now being by all of you totali neglegted…there beeing not any person that will accept of Imploym[en]t…so th[a]t the Busines is quite at a stand…I pray S[i]r bee pleased to let mee hear from you when you will order us some mony[.][163]

The plea was not all rhetorical. Yarranton's financial memorandum in fact reveals that, by March 1667, Haycox had accumulated debts of more than £100 for the

[159] Wrightson, *Earthly Necessities*, p. 301.
[160] Staff.RO, D(W)1788/P61/B7(a), Whyle to Baldwyn, 2 January 1667.
[161] Staff.RO, D(W)1788/P61/B7(f), Whyle to Baldwyn, [after March 1667?] (quotation); Staff. RO, D(W)1788/P59/B3, Windsor to Baldwyn, 4 May 1667.
[162] Staff.RO, D(W)1788/P61/B7(a), Haycox to Baldwyn, 7 May 1667.
[163] Ibid.

navigation scheme.[164] On this basis Haycox argued that prominent backers like Baldwyn had every reason to keep the scheme moving forward:

> you knowe th[a]t proverb w[hi]ch I to my Greif see to much fullfiled (viz: not to go forward is to goe bakward)[,] so is it with the river…haveing bin for theis 2 years but slenderly supported by the Masters who had greatest reason to defend theyr own Intrest[.][165]

Unless speedy action was taken, Haycox hinted, all the time and money Baldwyn and other backers had poured in would come to nothing. When partners like Haycox and Whyle made transactions on credit, it was often unclear upon whose accounts agreements were made.[166] This meant that Balwyn's and Windsor's reputation was constantly at stake, even when they did not give explicit consent to each transaction. Haycox accordingly made it clear that the 'Intrest' that he urged Baldwyn to look after was not simply an economic one: 'were you in the Contry to heer those clamors w[hi]ch are dayly dispersed it would sertainly spur you on to revive the credit of yo[u]r names'.[167] Because contractual bargaining was often described as a mutual benefit, the word 'interest' was 'not used in the sense of self-interest, but rather referred to the mutual advantage, benefit or profit of two or more parties'.[168] Baldwyn's interest likewise had both personal and interpersonal dimensions. It was in Baldwyn's interest to revive the credit of his name by prompt repayment; upon that speedy repayment also hinged the credibility and survival of their partners like Haycox.

Other letters sent to Baldwyn hinted that his hesitation was causing grievances, with his name becoming odious in the locality. Whyle told Baldwyn that 'people p[ro]test[ed] they would petic[i]on the Parliam[en]t'.[169] As the proverb pithily put it, 'He that hath lost his credit is dead to the world.'[170] Leregoe suggested that some workmen were not quite dead but 'in disorder': 'Some are turned out of doors,…some of them begginge and intreatinge, others Swearinge and Cursing desiringe nothinge may thrive until they are payde'.[171] Haycox even juxtaposed the assurance of Christian salvation with Baldwyn's unreliable promise of payment: 'I think, if Christians had no better assurance of Celestial promises [than Baldwyn's

---

[164] Staff.RO, D(W)1788/P61/B7(a), 'Mr Yarrantons note of moneys due upon the account of the navigation to workemen'.

[165] Staff.RO, D(W)1788/P61/B7(a), Haycox to Baldwyn, 7 May 1667.

[166] See, for example, Staff.RO, D(W)1788/P61/B5, a memorandum concerning the Stour navigation, 2 December 1671.

[167] Staff.RO, D(W)1788/P61/B7(a), Haycox to Baldwyn, 7 May 1667.

[168] Muldrew, *Economy of Obligation*, p. 140 (quotation); Craig Muldrew, 'From Commonwealth to Public Opulence: The Redefinition of Wealth and Government in Early Modern Britain', in Steve Hindle, Alexandra Shepard, and John Walter (eds.), *Remaking English Society: Social Relations and Social Change in Early Modern England* (Woodbridge: Boydell, 2013), 317–39, pp. 334–5.

[169] Staff.RO, D(W)1788/P61/B7(f), Whyle to Baldwyn, [after March 1667?].

[170] The proverb is quoted by Natasha Glaisyer, *The Culture of Commerce in England, 1660–1720* (Woodbridge: Boydell, 2006), p. 38. On the vital importance of keeping one's words, see also Grassby, *The Business Community*, p. 297–301; Ceri Sullivan, *The Rhetoric of Credit: Merchants in Early Modern Writing* (Madison, NJ: Fairleigh Dickinson University Press, 2002), pp. 26–8.

[171] Staff.RO, D(W)1788/P61/B6, Leregoe to Baldwyn, 3 February 1668; D(W)1788/P59/B3, Leregoe to Baldwyn, 7 May 1667.

promises], none could ever have liv[e]d by faith'.[172] Like so many other tradesmen of this period, partners such as Haycox were 'relying on their trust in God, and in their neighbours, to provide for their needs rather than on capital accumulation on their own hands'.[173] In large-scale projects like the Stour scheme, however, such reliance upon the web of credit was rendered even more precarious by the scale of the undertaking, by the intricate coordination required, and, not least, by backers' suspicion of cheating and embezzlement.

The loss of a credit line was never about financial breakdown alone, therefore. As a middleman of the scheme, Whyle probably witnessed this development at first hand, while owing himself 'a great deale of mony in the country to worke men and others for land and Damages'.[174] Thus, he wrote to Baldwyn, 'I am soe harrassed for money…th[a]t I am ready to run away, And you write of taking up money on the River'.[175] This, Whyle claimed, was far too optimistic: 'you cannot thinke any one or any Interest will lend 4 d.' Whyle concluded: 'I weary my selfe with meluncholy, & shall infect you'.[176]

There is something theatrical, not to say tragicomic, about the body of letters presented here. After all, they were written by local partners in the Stour valley in order to solicit money from the London-based Baldwyn. The impression of desperation and melancholy needs be read with caution. Yet the loss of credibility was hardly a mere rhetorical construction. Switching perspective and looking into Baldwyn's and Windsor's responses now reveals how their (understandable) hesitation to offer timely investment backfired and threatened to undermine their own credibility and reputation.

In 1667, Baldwyn told the earl of Bristol that he was considering withdrawing from the scheme altogether, because of 'the very great Inconveniencies which he hath allready suffered & is like to suffer'.[177] Windsor's reply was striking, probably because he often stayed on his estate near Kidderminster, and presumably travelled along the river: 'all the Clamours of the whole Countrey comes to mee sayinge I wronge them and owe them great summe of money'.[178] Even a deputy lieutenant of Worcestershire, it seems, was not entirely immune from the adverse impacts of running up debts, or from the danger of losing his reputation.

The most striking evidence in this regard, however, comes from Windsor's abortive attempt to find a new partner. In early 1667 Yarranton travelled to Saxony to learn tinplate making, and the Worcestershire clothier Robert Willmott came to be seen as a potential candidate for his replacement. A draft article of agreement suggests that the backers preferred to leave 'the whole management of the navigation

---

[172] Staff.RO, D(W)1788/P61/B7(a), Haycox to Baldwyn, 7 May 1667.

[173] Muldrew, *Economy of Obligation*, p. 144 (quotation). Cf. Brodie Waddell, *God, Duty and Community in English Economic Life, 1660–1720* (Woodbridge: Boydell, 2012), pp. 49–50, 57–9, 157–8.

[174] Staff.RO, D(W)1788/P61/B7(f), Windsor to Baldwyn, 2 February 1667.

[175] That is, to borrow upon the security of future profits from the river. See, *OED*, s.v. take, *v.* 93, take up.

[176] Staff.RO, D(W)1788/P61/B7(f), Whyle to Baldwyn, [after March 1667?].

[177] Staff.RO, D(W)1788/P59/B3, Mr Baldwyns Case, [n.d., probably mid-1667].

[178] Staff.RO, D(W)1788/P59/B3, Windsor to Baldwyn, 4 May 1667.

upon the River' to Willmott. As in the May 1661 agreement, Willmott was to lay out his own money first for 'repaireing and amendinge of any thinge belonginge' to the river navigation, and later have his investment repaid with interest.[179]

Willmott responded with the utmost caution. The ironmaster Thomas Foley, who mediated the deal, told Baldwyn:

> he is ready and willing to doe you the best Service he cann about the navigac[i]on…
> But to engage to layout money in it or to Seale Article, that he will mannage it to the
> best advantage when there are soe many p[ar]tners concerned in it[,] he seys he is not
> willing to doe.[180]

According to Foley, Willmott alleged that the scheme in total owed a 'great many hundreds [of] pounds more then the pr[e]sent £300' which Baldwyn had acknowledged.[181] Willmott was concerned that he could be sued by the scheme's creditors should he seal the contract and become a proprietor. Accordingly, Willmott told Baldwyn that he would not agree to engage unless he 'shall not bee blamed for any abuse to bee donne by any that have been formerly hyred for any worke about the navigation'.[182] He explained he was being cautious because 'my secryty is small… and [I] have noe estate'. He thus concluded: 'I feare to borrowe: albeyt my Creddit would doe yt'.[183] Willmott's concern was amplified by his family members. His 'wife & Children', as Foley related, were 'utterly against it in case he were willing to it'.[184] The Willmotts' anxiety must be read in a broader context. Daily commercial transactions in early modern England depended heavily upon household credibility and reputation. The danger of losing that reputation and of the ensuing downward mobility was so pervasive that there was something of 'competitive piety' among middling households to underline their financial probity and creditworthiness.[185] In the later seventeenth century, when Willmott was being urged to step in, 'informal credit relations not only continued but also became *more heavily reliant* on judgements about reputation and character' partly because of the spread of the conspicuous consumption that in turn blurred traditional hierarchies based on lineage and occupation.[186] Willmott was therefore faced with the dangerous task of choosing either taking part in an onerous project or disappointing wealthier partners by refusing to take part. In the precarious economy of obligations ever dependent upon others' opinion and good will, both options could end up undermining his reputation. Willmott's hesitation

---

[179] Staff.RO, D(W)1788/P61/B6, draft article of agreement between Windsor, Baldwyn, Smith, Whyle and Willmott, 11 April 1667.
[180] Staff.RO, D(W)1788/P61/B6, Thomas Foley to Baldwyn, 25 April 1667.
[181] Ibid.
[182] Staff.RO, D(W)1788/P61/B7(f), Willmott to Baldwyn, [April 1667?].
[183] Ibid.
[184] Staff.RO, D(W)1788/P61/B6, Thomas Foley to Baldwyn, 25 April 1667.
[185] Muldrew, *Economy of Obligation*, pp. 148–9.
[186] Shepard, *Accounting for Oneself*, pp. 279–85, 301–2, 312 (quotation at p. 302). For the rise of consumerism, see publications cited at pp. 218–19 below.

thus testifies to the palpable impact of England's projecting culture upon the everyday credit relations of a middling clothier.

Given the growing importance of reputation in the late seventeenth century, it is perhaps not surprising that Windsor ultimately failed to make Willmott seal the contract. On 15 April 1667, Windsor wrote to Baldwyn: 'This morning, Mr Wilmott came to mee and truly I have pressed him very earnestly to have sealed to the agreem[en]t'. Windsor tried to reassure Willmott and even suggested a new advantageous contract. Yet, Windsor continued, he 'could not prevaile with him to doe it'.[187] It was upon such a tangible loss of credibility that, in September 1667, Windsor, Baldwyn, and others finally agreed to advance £360: 'therew[i]th the Arreares of rent, wages, Charges, and other debts shalbe paid, boates built and repaired, and the said River of Stower put in order as farr as the same [sum of money] will extend'.[188]

Even this was not enough to pay off all the debts, however. Sir Ralph Clare, one of the riparian landowners, then came to obstruct traffic on the river. More than £100 had been overdue to him, and on 5 November 1667 he reportedly declared that 'hee will Chaine up the River in his owne grounde [so] that noe Barges shall passe up until hee is payd his damages'.[189] 'This day wee cam downe with seaven Barges', reported Yarranton on the same day. '[B]ut when wee cam unto Kiderminster Sir Ralph Clare had chained up the lock nere his garden and would not let the Bargis pas'. It was 'about 12 of the Clock', and because 'the towne [was] full of Countrey people that take much Advantage by the passage of barges', Yarranton 'cause[d] the chaine to be brocke and put threw two barges'. Sir Ralph was apparently 'very angrey and threaten[e]d hard'. But, Yarranton said, by way of excuse, 'I thought that if I did not Clere theier passage that all would be nought'.[190]

Clare's anger, as well as Willmott's hesitation, encapsulates the repercussions of the backers' own caution and unwillingness to trust their money even to competent partners. The lack of liquidity exacerbated the problems of maintaining and synchronizing credit; consequently, some partners had to work to the limits of their credit and even beyond them. Thus, the negotiations between Windsor and Willmott focused primarily on the possibility of finding a way to bring Willmott in without exposing him to liability for others' debts. The situation was so grave that even the future earl of Plymouth could not persuade the Worcestershire clothier with no estate. The incident with Sir Ralph Clare also reminds us that the promoters faced opposition and interventions not only during the parliamentary debate in Westminster, but also during the scheme's implementation in the West Midlands. Yarranton's daring response to Clare highlights that the partners could

---

[187] Staff.RO, D(W)1788/P59/B3, Windsor to Baldwyn, 15 April 1667. The following month Willmott declared that 'he will not undertake or signe the Articles'. Staff.RO,D(W)1788/P59/B3, Windsor at Kidderminster to Baldwyn, 4 May 1667.

[188] Staff.RO, D(W)1788/P61/B5, 'Articles w[i]th the Lord Windsor & Mr While', 13 September 1667.

[189] Staff.RO, D(W)1788/P59/B3, Haycox and Leregoe to Baldwyn, 5 November 1667.

[190] Staff.RO, D(W)1788/P61/B7(a), Yarranton to Baldwyn, 5 November 1667.

not afford to be obstructed if they were to raise profit, pay for the completion of the works, and avoid cutting their losses.

The navigation work had to be sustained despite those financial, reputational, and societal setbacks. However grudging it may have been at times, Windsor and Baldwyn did not altogether withdraw their support. It was recounted in the early eighteenth century that Baldwyn (and his brother) had spent £4,000; and including Windsor and other investors, £8,000 in total.[191] Why did backers continue to pay for the undertaking despite the fact that Yarranton and other undertakers were only partially trusted? As has been seen, in 1661 Windsor pushed the legislation on the Stour as a 'public' cause. In 1666, speaking of Baldwyn's intention to withdraw from the scheme, Windsor upbraided him not to—because, Windsor argued, 'the country sees tis done and they Judge nothing can bee made of it, for they say If wee who aught best to understand it, can make no proffitts how should any other'?[192] This may suggest that Windsor continued to invest in the scheme in order to demonstrate its feasibility and profitability to the wider public.

A more mundane, and probably more plausible, reason is that backers like Windsor and Baldwyn tried to avoid cutting their losses and to recoup the sunk cost. As Haycox warned, the backers had to keep investing their money and complete the works, or risk losing the money they had spent for nothing. In this respect, like canal builders in the eighteenth century and proprietors of gas companies in the nineteenth, the backers of the Stour navigation were essentially 'economic' investors, those who were ready to bear large overheads because they were interested in long-term returns.[193] As long as backers like Windsor and Baldwyn committed to the scheme in this way, they had ultimately few alternatives but to keep supporting undertakers such as Yarranton who had the necessary skills to complete the scheme.

The backers also opted to continue the work because by exuding confidence they could bring in more investors. George Skyppe of Herefordshire, a lawyer and an excise officer, invested £500 in the navigation works in the mid-1670s, but later told Baldwyn that he had 'relinquished my concerne in the River'. Skyppe's complaint reveals that Baldwyn was playing a kind of 'confidence game'. He had withdrawn because 'it was not likely to turne to that profitable account as I hoped it would by the encouragement I had from you & others before I was concerned in it'.[194]

Trusting experts' technical competence did not automatically translate into trusting them with one's money. The implementation of the Stour project consequently

---

[191] HMC, *Manuscripts of the House of Lords, 1692–1693*, p. 389; Staff.RO, D(W)1788/P59/B3, *The Earl of Plymouth's Case* [early C18?], [one-page broadsheet not in the *ESTC*].

[192] Staff.RO, D(W)1788/P59/B3, Windsor [to Baldwyn?], 26 December 1666.

[193] J. R. Ward, *The Finance of Canal Building in Eighteenth-Century England* (Oxford: Oxford University Press, 1974), p. 126; John F. Wilson, *Lighting the Town: A Study of Management in the North West Gas Industry* (London: Paul Chapman, 1991), pp. 84–91.

[194] Staff.RO, D(W)1788/P61/B7(a), Skyppe to Baldwyn, 16 January 1680. On Skyppe, see T. W. M. Johnson, 'The Diary of George Skyppe of Ledbury', *Transactions of the Woolhope Naturalists' Field Club*, 34 (1952), 54–62.

accompanied tremendous troubles among those involved, who found themselves piling up debts, risking their reputations, confronting hostile stakeholders, and even facing imprisonment and enduring acute anxiety. Upon collective toil, amid echoes of distrust, rested the partial realization of the Stour navigation project. On such cooperative processes equally lay the subsequent recognition of Yarranton as a credible expert with which this chapter started.

CONCLUSION: INDIVIDUAL, ECONOMIC, AND INSTITUTIONAL OUTCOMES

The Stour scheme went ahead despite initial controversies in and outside parliament, and despite the fact that its backers only grudgingly bestowed their money upon the undertakers. The scheme was supported by the Cavalier Parliament and several thousand pounds was subsequently poured into it. Its promoters failed to meet the initial goal of making the river entirely navigable within two years; Yarranton subsequently had to make an excuse about this.

The scheme, however, had more direct implications for Yarranton's career, regional economic development, and the future framing of inland navigation acts. As noted by Wharton and Hooke, Yarranton was able to travel to the continent thanks to the tinplate business linked with the Stour navigation scheme. For him, the scheme became not only a source of income, but also an important career step towards establishing his credibility as a competent promoter of improvement. More importantly, the scheme contributed to local economic development. The wooden railway built near Stourbridge to carry coal was the first of its kind authorized by an act of parliament. The Stour scheme also set in motion the first organized attempt in England at producing tinplate in large quantities.[195] Capel Hanbury was employed in the Stour-side tinplate experiment during the 1660s and 1670s; in the early eighteenth century, his son John would establish the first commercial production of tinplate in Britain in southern Wales.[196] The Stourbridge canal, finished in the later eighteenth century, incorporated a part of the trenches that Yarranton cut on a difficult stretch of the river.[197] Admittedly, the hydrostatic techniques used in the navigation work may not have been path-breaking. Yet the Stour scheme did achieve tangible economic improvements amid pervasive distrust affecting virtually every step of the way.

The case of the Stour navigation left institutional as well as economic legacies. As Joanna Innes has observed, once parliament legislated in a particular field, such 'legislation might operate to encourage further legislation both positively

---

[195] Lewis, *Early Wooden Railways*, pp. 242–4; P. W. King, 'Wolverley Lower Mill and the Beginnings of the Tinplate Industry', *Historical Metallurgy*, 22 (1988), 104–13.

[196] Peter J. Brown, 'Andrew Yarranton and the British Tinplate Industry', *Historical Metallurgy*, 22 (1988), 42–8, p. 45. See also King, 'Wolverley Lower Mill', p. 110; F. W. Gibbs, 'The Rise of the Tinplate Industry: III. John Hanbury (1664–1734)', *Annals of Science*, 7 (1951), 43–61.

[197] G. H. C. Burley, 'Andrew Yarranton: A Seventeenth-Century Worcestershire Worthy', *Transactions of Worcestershire Archaeological Society*, new ser., 38 (1961), p. 30.

(by providing a model) and negatively (by instilling anxiety)'.[198] This is what happened in the present case. Following the 1652 Wey navigation act, the Stour navigation introduced a cap on the local price of coal. Subsequent inland navigation acts did not follow the exact formulation of the Stour act in making undertakers liable for maintaining the commodity price. Yet price caps of some description were included in eleven out of the thirteen other inland navigation bills that were passed between 1660 and 1700.[199] The underlying rationale is well captured by the proviso that the Commons added to the Avon navigation bill of 1664. It required justices of assize and other authorities 'to take speciall care' in supervising business in havens and wharfs so 'that all opportunity for the undertakers or any other to engrosse the Comodityes of the said Country, or impose upon the marketts may be prevented'.[200] The Commons also added a proviso to the Medway act of the same year to prevent promoters from removing or damaging 'any the now dwelling Houses, outhouses, Gardens or Orchards of any person or persons whatsoever w[i]thout their consent in writeing under hand and Seale first had and obteyned'.[201] Such protection of riparian sites by the addition of clauses and provisos, rarely seen before the Stour act, also became a regular feature thereafter. The legislative outcomes for the Stour act—its greater specification of riparian rights and the introduction of price caps to prevent engrossing—provided something of a model for how to promote improvement with minimum disruption to the local economy.

Finally, the case highlights the overriding need for a better organizational arrangement for raising investment capital when undertaking large-scale projects. Once the technology of public subscription became widespread during Defoe's Projecting Age, transport schemes would also come to be funded overwhelmingly by joint-stocks and by trusts based on public subscription. If their diffusion was complete and irreversible by the 'canal age' of the late eighteenth century, it was partly because of the earlier difficulty that beset undertakers like Yarranton and his partners caught in a tangled web of partnerships.[202]

---

[198] Joanna Innes, *Inferior Politics: Social Problems and Social Policies in Eighteenth-Century Britain* (Oxford: Oxford University Press, 2009), p. 95.

[199] Subsequent navigation acts came to place caps on the maximum toll that could be imposed on the goods transported. See PA, HL/PO/PB/1/1662/14C2n47, Private Act, 14 Charles II, *c.* 15; HL/PO/PB/1/1664/16&17C2n16, Private Act, 16 & 17 Charles II, *c.* 6; HL/PO/PB/1/1664/16&17C2n22, Private Act, 16 & 17 Charles II, *c.* 11; HL/PO/PB/1/1664/16&17C2n23, Private Act, 16 & 17 Charles II, *c.* 12; HL/PO/PB/1/1664/16&17C2n24, Private Act, 16 & 17 Charles II, *c.* 13; HL/PO/PB/1/1670/22C2n29, Private Act, 22 Charles II, *c.* 16; HL/PO/PB/1/1678/30C2n21, Private Act, 30 Charles II, *c.* 20; HL/PO/PU/1/1695/7&8W3n29, Public Act, 7 & 8 William III, *c.* 14; HL/PO/PU/1/1697/9&10W3n43, Public Act, 9 William III, *c.* 19; HL/PO/PU/1/1698/10&11W3n12, Public Act, 10 William III, *c.* 8; HL/PO/PU/1/1698/10&11W3n40, Public Act, 10 William III, *c.* 25; HL/PO/PU/1/1698/10&11W3n41, Public Act, 10 William III, *c.* 26; HL/PO/PU/1/1698/11&12W3n12, Public Act, 11 William III, *c.* 22.

[200] PA, HL/PO/PB/1/1664/16&17C2n22, An act for making the river Avon navigable from Christchurch to the City of New Sarum [Salisbury], an additional strip of parchment sewn at the upper end of membrane 7.

[201] PA, HL/PO/PB/1/1664/16&17C2n23, An act for making the river Medway navigable, the second proviso on the additional strip of parchment added to membrane 10.

[202] Ward, *Canal Building*, pp. 16, 169–71; Ron Harris, *Industrializing English Law: Entrepreneurship and Business Organization, 1720–1844* (Cambridge: Cambridge University Press, 2000), pp. 90–100; Dan Bogart 'The Transport Revolution in Industrialising Britain', in Roderick Floud, Jane Humphries,

This 'project' achieved what it did and left economic and institutional legacies, however, not because of a robust trusting relationship between participants, but despite doubts and suspicion lingering from Westminster to the West Midlands. This chapter has shown that tangible improvement of the River Stour hinged upon the difficult tasks of protecting regional interests, and upon maintaining credibility in all its forms. It has demonstrated that these tasks were made even more difficult due to deep-seated anxieties and the allegations that projects for improvement might induce insolvency and permit fraud, breach riparian rights, and at worst even destroy the regional economy. Expert competence was, of course, indispensable. Yet we can now be sure that on its own it could hardly turn a project into reality.

Those concerned with the Stour navigation scheme rarely acknowledged the tortuous processes of negotiation that we have uncovered, and this probably helps explain why the episode has not been revealed before. As noted at the beginning of this chapter, Yarranton did acknowledge 'want of money' to be a cause for the non-completion of the navigation work up to the Severn. Significantly, in his *England's improvement*, he never spoke of his difficult relationship with Windsor, partners like Whyle, or creditors like Clare. In its dedicatory preface, Yarranton just thanked Windsor for 'those indefatigable Pains you have taken in the Survey of several Rivers, and contriving with me effectually which way these might be rendred so far Navigable, that the Publick might thereby receive a general Advantage'.[203] Where both of them could be presented as champions of improvement and the public good, there was perhaps little point in publicizing the lack of trust between them, or the consequences that followed Windsor's hesitation to trust him with his money.

What went on behind the scenes to turn the Stour project into reality was therefore never acknowledged in *England's improvement*, in its positive review in *Philosophical Transactions*, or in manuscripts such as Hooke's diary and Wharton's letter. As Shapin has argued, Boyle's laboratory work was fundamentally collaborative, made possible thanks contributions by many 'laborants' and 'assistants'.[204] Yet Boyle rarely acknowledged others behind the experiments, and this was how he acquired the reputation as *the* credible author of these experiments. Inland navigation was extended, and Yarranton's reputation paraded, by similarly setting aside the contributions and hardships of partners such as Whyle, Leregoe, and Haycox. Economic historians would do well to bring such contributions back into the analysis of England's economic development, just as historians of science have put Boyle's assistants back into the narrative of the scientific revolution.

The other struggle—the safeguarding of local interests—was also soon to be forgotten. Windsor's grandson, the second earl of Plymouth, petitioned parliament in order to resume the navigation scheme. To this end, he portrayed the original undertakers as unsung heroes, and the 1662 act as a credible piece of legislation.

and Paul Johnson, *The Cambridge Economic History of Modern Britain* (2 vols., Cambridge: Cambridge University Press, 2014), vol. 1, 368–91, pp. 370–3.

[203] Yarranton, *England's improvement*, sig. b.

[204] Shapin, *Social History of Truth*, pp. 361–72, 405–7.

Windsor (and others) had expended about £8,000; he had died without completing the work that had 'so great an Advantage' to the public. The navigation scheme could be revived 'without any alteration [to] the said former Act'. For, the second earl continued, it 'was obtained upon hearing all parties, and due consideration had of the Rights and Properties of all Persons interested'.[205] There was perhaps little need for the second earl to find out that the protection of these local interests was secured only narrowly, after the heated debates and escalating cross-petitioning, in the form of provisos and insertions added to the original bill.

It is vital, however, to recover what went on behind the impression of harmony. For, upon the laborious negotiations in Westminster and in the West Midlands depended not only the subsequent rise of Yarranton as a renowned expert, but also the tangible extension of inland navigation—a crucial vehicle for market integration and regional specialization. Equally important for the purpose of this book, uncovering the arduous transactions in Worcestershire and Staffordshire enables us to clarify the social 'reach' of distrust: whom the distrust of projecting affected, and in what ways. Earlier in 1641, the self-appointed 'philosophical heir' to Bacon, Thomas Bushell, explained why his partners in Welsh mining had 'moved to presse me for more speedy payme[n]t, then my present abilities were able to make good'; for, some saw his '*Minerall adventures* to be but the fabricke of a fantasticke braine, others alledging that the greatnesse of my charge would ruine both me, and those who gave me credit'.[206] Were we to study Hartlib and his circle of reformers in isolation, were we to focus on promotional rhetoric alone, we would never be able to establish whether suspicion fell especially upon those who appeared dubious like Bushell, or upon Hartlibeans, who left numerous proposals but implemented few.

Having reconstructed the Stour navigation scheme within the broader history of projecting, we can now suggest with confidence that the damaging impacts of distrust were hardly reserved for the dubious or the unsuccessful. Windsor's suspension of timely investment, Leregoe's insolvency, Haycox's frustration, Whyle's melancholy, and Willmott's fear have all shown in telling detail how the distrust of projecting socially and financially affected the credibility of those involved in the scheme in the Stour valley. Even experts like Yarranton had to get things done amid the underlying suspicion of projecting.

Another crucial finding is the way the distrust of projecting subtly informed parliamentary debate. We have found that, when confronted with the threatening invocation of what had gone wrong in the 1630s, the Cavalier Parliament could not afford to repeat the heavy-handed practices characteristic of the Caroline Privy Council. In order to turn a potentially beneficial inland navigation project into reality, it was vital to move away from the controversial imposition of 'improvement' reminiscent of the early Stuarts' reign. Note that the outcome was neither automatic nor guaranteed; the emendations on the Stour bill would not have been made

[205] HMC, *Manuscripts of the House of Lords, 1692–1693*, p. 389; Staff.RO, D(W)1788/P59/B3, *The Earl of Plymouth's Case*.

[206] Thomas Bushell, *A iust and true remonstrance of his maiesties Mines-Royall in the principality of Wales* (1641), pp. 35–6.

without the escalating cross-petitioning evocative of earlier, destructive projects. More research into draft bills and related documents is needed to elucidate the exact mechanism through which legislative conventions developed. Yet the subsequent river navigation acts do seem to suggest that the intervention made in the Stour bill did lead to a significant change in the subsequent legislative routine towards greater protection of riparian rights.

The challenging question of typicality remains, however. How typical was the escalation of rhetoric that we have found? How often were memories of dangerous and destructive projects invoked in the post-Restoration period? Is it possible that, as in the Stour case, the social circulation of distrust, and its invocation at critical junctures, affected the promotion of other kinds of projects? Did memories of what had gone wrong earlier shape the practices of projecting after the Restoration more generally—how actors and institutions such as savants, inventors, opponents, statesmen, the Privy Council, and parliament interacted when promoting improvement? We shall now move from the River Stour once again to the bustling metropolis of London, to which Charles II returned in 1660. Did the Restoration of the monarchy amount to a return to the 1630s? In Chapter 5 we shall find out how choices and adjustments made haphazardly, yet repeatedly, in the environment of ideological uncertainty played a decisive role in the further evolution of projecting culture towards Defoe's Projecting Age.

5

Memories, Propriety, and Emulation

By the end of the 1670s, England's culture of projecting had undergone a significant development: power and profit were now to be augmented not only by producing new goods or improving manufactures and transport, but also by tapping into the infinite desire for comfort, consumption, and emulation among the population at large. Only two decades previously, at the end of the 1650s, royalists looked to the Restoration of the monarchy as a catalyst for improvement. Blaming the Cromwellian regime for the 'decay of trade', one author declared that the health of the body politic would not be restored without the restoration of its 'head': 'our Trades are generally lost...we are lessened in our Manufactures...because, alas, we have no *King*'.[1] Upon the king's return, John Evelyn proclaimed, 'the Merchant will be secure, Trades immediately recover'.[2] Within two decades, by contrast, we find a strikingly different prospect of improvement, dictated neither by a virtuous king nor by his ingenious projectors seeking royal patronage. In 1678, Nicholas Barbon made a most striking pronouncement:

> Emulation provoaks a continued Industry, and will not allow no Intervals or be ever satisfied: The Cobler is always indeavouring to live as well as a Shoomaker, and the Shoomaker as well as any in the Parish; so every Neighbour and every artist is indeavouring to outvy each other, and all Men by a perpetual Industry, are strugling to mend their former condition: and thus the People grow rich, which is the great advantage of a Nation[.]

Note that we are not dealing with a linear change from one frame of reference to another. The process of historical change is arguably more complex. Yet the case remains: in Barbon's writing we find the precocious vision of economic development that would later be elaborated by Bernard Mandeville and more fatefully by thinkers of the Scottish Enlightenment.[3] Here we come back to Adam Smith, with

---

[1] 'Awake o England: or the people's invitation to king Charles' (1660), in *Harleian Miscellany*, ed. William Oldys (8 vols., 1744–6), vol. 1, 267–70, p. 269.

[2] John Evelyn, *An apology for the royalist party* (1659), p. 11. See also *T&C*, pp. 374–5. For the importance of commercial prosperity for the restored monarchy, see Steve Pincus, 'Neither Machiavellian Moment nor Possessive Individualism: Commercial Society and the Defenders of the English Commonwealth', *AHR*, 103 (1998), 705–36, pp. 729–32; Blair Hoxby, 'The Government of Trade: Commerce, Politics and the Courtly Art of the Restoration', *ELH*, 66 (1999), 591–627, pp. 597–9.

[3] [Nicholas Barbon], *Discourse shewing the great advantages that new-buildings, and the enlarging of towns and cities do bring to a nation* (1678), p. 5. See also [John Houghton], *England's great happiness* (1677), p. 7. These two pamphlets and their significance are discussed expertly in Paul Slack, 'The

whom we began this book. In *The Theory of Moral Sentiments*, Smith spoke of 'the beauty of that accommodation which reigns in the palaces and oeconomy of the great'. He was clear that 'the real satisfaction which all these things are capable of affording, by itself and separated from the beauty of that arrangement...will always appear in the highest degree contemptible and trifling'. Yet, in a way that echoed Barbon's analysis of 'continued Industry', Smith suggested that the perceived 'pleasures of wealth and greatness' had far-reaching economic implications: 'this deception...rouses and keeps in continual motion the industry of mankind', inducing 'them to cultivate the ground, to build houses...and to invent and improve all the sciences and arts'.[4] This is the line of thinking that Smith later developed in a qualified form in his *Wealth of Nations*.[5]

The history of projecting throws fresh light on the underlying transformation: the fateful vision of improvement encapsulated by Barbon (and subsequently elaborated in the eighteenth century) took shape during the two decades after the Restoration of Charles II as a result of the *collective taming of England's projecting culture*, something that was dangerously close to returning to the early Stuart model. Albert Hirschman and others surveyed the attendant *intellectual* reappraisal of 'interest';[6] the history of projecting enables us to explore the concrete *social processes* that went with it.

We are dealing with two strands of inquiry. The first is about the evolution of England's culture of improvement during the post-Restoration period. What role did the restored Crown play in promoting improvement? Would Charles II revive the kind of projecting promoted under his father, something that turned out to be awfully vexatious? The general picture is clear enough. Charles II did not carry out the ambitious proposal for improving London's air that John Evelyn dedicated to him. When London suffered the Great Fire in 1666, John Evelyn, Valentine Knight, Robert Hooke, and Christopher Wren failed to convince the public authorities radically to alter the cityscape based on their geometrically

---

Politics of Consumption and England's Happiness in the Later Seventeenth Century', *EHR*, 122 (2007), 609–31; Paul Slack, *Invention of Improvement*, pp. 143–7.

⁴ Adam Smith, *The Theory of Moral Sentiments*, ed. D. D. Raphael and A. L. Macfie (Indianapolis, IN: Liberty Fund, 1976), p. 183 (pt. IV, sec. i, 9).

⁵ In *Wealth of Nations*, Smith introduced a distinction between the wasteful conspicuous consumption (of the elite) that diverts capital away from productive investments and the more desirable consumption of 'conveniencies' by the public that could invigorate home industries. Smith now commended the latter as a 'universal opulence which extends itself to the lowest ranks of the people'. See Adam Smith, *An Inquiry into the Nature and Causes of the Wealth of Nations*, ed. R. H. Campbell and A. S. Skinner (2 vols., Indianapolis, IN: Liberty Fund, 1976), vol. 1, p. 22 (bk I, ch. i, 10). See also Maxine Berg and Elizabeth Eger, 'The Rise and Fall of the Luxury Debates', in Maxine Berg and Elizabeth Eger (eds.), *Luxury in the Eighteenth Century: Debates, Desires and Delectable Goods* (Basingstoke: Palgrave, 2003), 7–27, pp. 11–12; Samuel Fleischacker, *On Adam Smith's Wealth of Nations: A Philosophical Companion* (Princeton, NJ: Princeton University Press, 2004), pp. 107–11; Dennis C. Rasmussen, *The Problems and Promises of Commercial Society: Adam Smith's Response to Rousseau* (University Park, PA: Pennsylvania State University Press, 2008), pp. 133–6.

⁶ Albert O. Hirschman, *The Passions and the Interests: Political Arguments for Capitalism before its Triumph* (Princeton, NJ: Princeton University Press, 1977). See also J. A. W. Gunn, *Politics and the Public Interest in the Seventeenth Century* (London: Routledge, 1969); Pincus, 'Neither Machiavellian', 705–36. A notable work here is Vera Keller, *Knowledge and the Public Interest, 1575–1725* (Cambridge: Cambridge University Press, 2015), esp. pp. 199–207, 213–24.

ordered street plan; speculative builders sprang up in their stead.[7] The Restoration regime displayed a marked disinclination to support schemes that amounted to de facto monopolies or to push schemes that required extensive mechanisms of coercion. Existing accounts provide some tentative explanations. The 'restoration of the monarchy had not restored confidence in the prerogative'; promoters of grandiose projects might have failed to grasp 'the reality' of post-Restoration England—'the cut-throat competition between different economic interests'.[8] These accounts agree that there was a notable shift 'from a politics of speedy reformation towards one of gradual enlightenment'.[9]

The second, related strand is about the rise of the consumer society. As Thomas Smith's *Discourse*, first written in 1549, reminds us, demand for consumer luxuries had of course taken root in England by the mid-sixteenth century. The Elizabethan and the early Stuart reigns saw numerous schemes to answer such consumer demand by producing (rather than importing) consumer articles.[10] What has been of great scholarly interest is how this society morphed into the world inhabited by the likes of Barbon and Mandeville, a consumer society of aspiring ladies and the beau monde sporting the latest fashions.[11] The emulation that Barbon spoke of has been predominantly studied in this latter context, with a special emphasis on the 1690s as the crucial moment in the rise of the consumer society in England.[12] Paul Slack's recent book has revised this chronology: the power of consumer appetite and emulation came to be reappraised thanks to the spectacular urban reconstruction after the 1666 Great Fire of London and the relative peace and prosperity during much of the 1670s and 1680s. In his account, due regard is also given to demographic stability and the rising spending power among middling sorts, and to the influence of Epicurean philosophy revived in France that reappraised the power of human desire and pleasure.[13] Taken together, the two lines of inquiry seem to suggest an

[7] Slack, *Reformation to Improvement*, pp. 88–9; Mark S. R. Jenner, 'The Politics of London Air: John Evelyn's *Fumifugium* and the Restoration', *HJ*, 28 (1995), 535–51; T. F. Reddaway, *The Rebuilding of London after the Great Fire* (London: Jonathan Cape, 1940), ch. 2.

[8] Slack, *Reformation to Improvement*, p. 88; John Spurr, *England in the 1670s: 'This Masquerading Age'* (Oxford: Blackwell, 2000), p. 144.

[9] Slack, *Invention of Improvement*, p. 102.

[10] Linda Levy Peck, *Consuming Splendor: Society and Culture in Seventeenth-Century England* (Cambridge: Cambridge University Press, 2005), ch. 2.

[11] Hannah Greig, *The Beau Monde: Fashionable Society in Georgian London* (Oxford: Oxford University Press, 2013); John Brewer, *The Pleasures of the Imagination: English Culture in the Eighteenth Century* (New York: Farrar, Straus, and Giroux, 1997), pp. 57–122.

[12] Joyce Appleby, 'Ideology and Theory: The Tension between Political and Economic Liberalism in Seventeenth-Century England', *AHR*, 81 (1976) 499–515, p. 509 (the 'idea of man as a consuming animal with boundless appetites, capable of driving the economy to new levels of prosperity, arrived with economic literature of the 1690s'); Neil McKendrick, John Brewer, and J. H. Plumb, *The Birth of a Consumer Society: The Commercialization of Eighteenth-Century England* (London: Europa Publications, 1982), p. 13 ('If we seek the intellectual origins of the revolution in consumption we will find them in the 1690s'). Cf. John Brewer and Roy Porter (eds.), *Consumption and the World of Goods* (London: Routledge, 1993); Maxine Berg, *Luxury and Pleasure in Eighteenth-Century Britain* (Oxford: Oxford University Press, 2005).

[13] Slack, *Invention of Improvement*, pp. 145–68. See also Frank Trentmann, *Empire of Things: How We became a World of Consumers, from the Fifteenth Century to the Twenty-First* (New York: Harper, 2016), pp. 97–8.

intriguing historical conjuncture: the *consumer-driven* vision of abundance came to emerge at a time when the economy was booming but confidence was being eroded regarding the possibility of implementing draconian schemes for forcefully improving *the supply side* of England's economy.

The goal of this chapter is to examine this conjunction by bringing together the findings of the preceding chapters. Given that the Hartlib circle and even Andrew Yarranton were affected by public distrust of the projector, and given that places like Westminster and the West Midlands were hardly impervious to the memories of early Stuart projectors and monopolists, it is striking that neither studies of consumer culture nor accounts of post-Restoration improvement have taken much notice of the burden of distrust. We must redress this imbalance all the more because it was vital for post-Restoration promoters to distance themselves from the projecting of preceding decades. The Royal Society, first chartered in 1662, chose to downplay its debts to the Hartlib circle. John Beale, one of its Fellows, was a former associate of Hartlib. Yet he in fact recommended supressing Hartlibean publications as 'very cheats' that 'ought to be laid aside', as we shall see in what follows. Even more fundamental for our purpose is the fact that Charles II's Restoration was itself predicated upon the due protection of subjects' rights, liberties, and happiness, something so self-righteously encroached upon by his royal father. A vital cornerstone was laid down even before Charles II entered London, as we can see in the king's letter presenting the Declaration of Breda to his embattled subjects in London. In this letter of 4/14 April 1660, Charles II highlighted

> How desirous wee are to contribute to the obtainning the Peace and Happinesse of our Subjects, w[i]thout further effusion of blood, and how farr wee are from desiring to recover what belongs to Us by a warr (if it can bee otherwise done) will appeare to you by the enclosed Declarac[i]on.[14]

The Restoration of the monarchy was thus accomplished with the public declaration that Charles II could have invaded but he did not, because the exiled king cared about the peace and happiness of his subjects so much. This was how the declaration promised 'the Restauration, both of King, Peers, and People, to their just, antient, and fundamental Rights'.[15] Together with this declaration, in other words, distancing from the early Stuart style of governance was deeply embedded in the very foundation of the post-Restoration regime.

We can push our analysis further if we now extend the notion of distrust to include elements of suspicion and anxieties engendered by *memories* of Charles I's Personal Rule, of vexatious projects, and of the ensuing wars, the regicide, and the reforming fervour of preceding decades. The analysis of memory, hitherto developed in the context of religious, political, and social history, can be profitably brought to bear upon the history of improvement and political economy in this

---

[14] LMA, COL/RMD/PA/01/009, Remembrancia, vol. IX, fol. 9, Charles II's declaration to Lord Major, Aldermen and Common Council of the City of London, 4/14 April 1660. See also the letters sent to the Speaker of the Commons and to Monck, *CJ*, vol. 8, pp. 5–6.

[15] *CJ*, vol. 8, p. 5. The declaration is ably analysed by N. H. Keeble, *The Restoration: England in the 1660s* (Oxford: Blackwell, 2002), pp. 68–70.

period.[16] If we thereby criss-cross different avenues for promoting projects, and if we attend to the disturbing presence of the 'troubled past' in post-Restoration petitions, letters, songs, manuscript proposals, and printed 'discourses on trade', then we can begin to unravel how far such memories were not only present, but at times even strategically invoked in the processes of negotiation over particular schemes. The haunting memory of the 'troubled' times laid bare the undesirability of nationwide improvement that required the imposition of penalties as a means of enforcement.

This was why, it will be shown, promoters of improvement began, from the 1660s, to give fresh attention to the power of micro-level incentives for achieving nationwide macro improvements in ways that anticipated Smith's account of the 'pleasures of wealth and greatness'. The desires and interests of ordinary subjects had now to be better understood, their appetite for comfort, consumption, and emulation to be more explicitly mobilized alongside the interests of the sovereign and his projectors. Subjects' private interests, if wisely directed towards domestic and colonial products, would be more capable than the enforcement of grandiose plans of generating wealth and achieving prosperity and abundance. This economic thinking (exemplified by Barbon's view) never emerged by accident or by a combination of fortunate circumstances alone. Instead, it emerged out of haphazard processes of trial and error, negotiation, and consultation, involving a range of actors and institutions from the courtiers of Charles I, former associates of Hartlib, artisans, savants, and wealthy farmers to the Privy Council, the Commons, the Mint, and the Royal Society. The collective taming of England's projecting culture in the post-Restoration period had far-reaching consequences. The potent vision of consumer society forged and projected in this period would soon realize its full potential in Defoe's Projecting Age, a society in which the avid consumption of company shares, rumours, and news about their rise and fall would in turn drive the economy.

CHANNELS AND STIMULI FOR POST-RESTORATION PROJECTS

Hartlib, who had backed parliamentarians and regicides in the preceding decades, was deprived of his state pension after the Restoration; some of his papers were lost in a fire, and he died in 1662. Although some of his reformist agendas survived into the 1660s, with his demise one of the most significant channels for projecting was lost. Neither the *ESTC* nor the patent records seem to indicate a significant level of activity (see Fig. 1.1 and Fig. 1.2). Little wonder that we have relatively few studies of post-Restoration projects compared to those of the early Stuart

[16] Studies of memories in post-Restoration England include Matthew Neufeld, *The Civil Wars after 1660: Public Remembering in Late Stuart England* (Woodbridge: Boydell, 2013); Andy Wood, *The Memory of the People: Custom and Popular Senses of the Past in Early Modern England* (Cambridge: Cambridge University Press, 2013); Edward James Legon, 'Remembering Revolution: Seditious Memories in England and Wales, 1660–1685' (PhD thesis, University College London, 2015).

reigns and the age of the financial revolution. There are, however, traces of new economic schemes that were stimulated by Restoration legal and political settlements, wars, and imperial competition, aided more broadly by the growth of overseas trade and favourable economic and demographic changes. Mapping out these channels and stimuli will enable us to start exploring the projecting culture as it was embedded in post-Restoration politics and religion, especially collective searches for legitimacy and propriety.

Charles II returned to London on 29 May 1660; even before he was formally crowned the next year, he invited merchants of trading companies to discuss with privy councillors how to 'rend[e]r this Nac[i]on, more p[ro]sperous & flourishing in Trade & Com[m]erce'.[17] Soon the king ordered the setting up of a Council of Trade,[18] sponsored a street clean-up campaign,[19] and encouraged the Lord Mayor and Aldermen of the City of London to employ the parish poor in making fishing nets and wooden barrels.[20] The king further urged the City to ensure the uninterrupted operation of 'a Corporac[i]on for the reliefe & Imploym[en]t of the Poore of our Citty of London' that caused 'many Hundreds of poore people' to be 'imployed & releived'.[21] Responding perhaps to such encouragement, books that contained ambitious projects were presented to the king alongside petitions and addresses. To give but a few examples, Thomas Bushell, who financed the king's army during the Civil Wars, dedicated his mining proposals to Charles. An obscure engineer, Francis Mathew, dedicated his inland navigation proposals to the monarch, while John Evelyn presented to him his *Fumifugium* (1661), which contained proposals for improving London air and cultivating fruit trees across the metropolis.[22]

A stream of proposals also emerged as petitions and addresses to the king.[23] In April 1661, Balthazar Gerbier, styled Baron D'Ouvilly, presented to the Privy Council a series of proposals to raise revenues, including a land bank and projects for 'cleansing and beautifying London' and improving Devonshire and Cornish tin mines.[24] Sir Edward Ford, who had operated the waterworks at Strand Bridge and elsewhere in London, petitioned the Treasury in November 1661 for a one-hundred-year lease of the site.[25] The following month, Sir Samuel Morland successfully petitioned the king for a patent for his water-raising engine.[26] About a year later, one James Street procured a patent for his corn-grinding mill, which would

---

[17] LMA, COL/RMD/PA/01/009, Remembrancia, vol. IX, fol. 12v, 17 August 1660.
[18] TNA, SP 29/21, fols. 47–8. [19] Slack, *Reformation to Improvement*, p. 88.
[20] LMA, COL/RMD/PA/01/009, Remembrancia, vol. IX, fols. 11v-12, 23 July 1660.
[21] Ibid., fol. 14v, 8 October 1660.   [22] See pp. 184, 186.
[23] The following cases are not included in Woodcroft's *Chronological Index*, and hence in my patent database. This is because these cases are culled from the State Papers and the Treasury Papers, both at the National Archives. Woodcroft used 'docket books' (now at TNA, C 233) and did not consult these sources when he complied the *Index*.
[24] *CSPD 1661–1662*, p. 78–9. See also Jason Peacey, 'Print, Publicity, and Popularity: The Projecting of Sir Balthazar Gerbier, 1642–1662', *JBS*, 51 (2012), 284–307, esp. p. 305.
[25] *CTB, vol. 1, 1660–1667*, pp. 167–8. Ford's waterworks are documented by Mark S. R. Jenner, 'Liquid Schemes, Solid Gold' (unpublished manuscript, n.d.), no pagination.
[26] *CSPD 1661–1662*, pp. 175, 199. See also J. R. Ratcliff, 'Samuel Morland and his Calculating Machines c.1666: The Early Career of a Courtier-Inventor in Restoration England', *BJHS*, 40 (2007), 159–79.

operate without using wind, water, horses, or men.[27] It is worth noting that, unlike early Stuart ones, few of these patents granted monopoly power over the industry to which the patented inventions were related.[28]

'In the midst of many and great Undertakings let not a Settlement for the *Poor* be forgotten,' one pamphlet said in 1660 by way of appeal to parliament—another channel for promoting new projects.[29] Inventors who applied for patents sometimes sought to obtain private acts for extra protection.[30] After the Restoration, private acts of parliament became an important means for promoting the cultivation of cash crops as well as inland navigation.[31] In early 1665, for example, Ralph Austen sought to petition parliament with a proposal for encouraging the planting of fruit and timber trees.[32] There was probably no coherent guideline to determine what types of schemes were to be considered by parliament and what by the royal executive. But members of parliament in principle represented the interests of each region, and as such the legislature was probably deemed more capable than the Crown of arbitrating between promoters and opposing parties over controversial schemes such as river navigation and enclosure that often involved the expropriation of private properties.

The Royal Society became one of the key institutions for promoting economic and technological projects.[33] Upon the Society's direction, Evelyn published his influential *Sylva* (1664) to redress the perceived decline of the timber supply.[34] In 1663 the Society set up a committee to consider the Somerset gentleman John Buckland's project for 'preventing famine, by dispersing potatoes throughout all parts of England'. Other committees were also formed to consider Thomas Toogood's water-raising engine, and John Beale's proposal for promoting cider production.[35] The Mechanical Committee met in an 'attempt to use the skills of its members to produce inventions which might be of immediate utility';[36] another committee met specifically to improve coaches;[37] there were some, largely abortive attempts to compile a 'history of trades'.[38] Many of these activities were interrupted by the

---

[27] *CSPD 1661–1662*, pp. 247, 425, 465. See also a patent granted to Tim Fulthorpe, ibid., p. 178.

[28] We shall come back to this later in the chapter.

[29] *An appeal to the parliament concerning the poor that there may not be a beggar in England* (1660), p. 1.

[30] MacLeod, *Patent*, pp. 49, 73.   [31] *AHEW Vii*, pp. 387–8; see pp. 142, 146 above.

[32] Michael Hunter, *Establishing the New Science: The Experience of the Early Royal Society* (Woodbridge: Boydell, 1989), p. 87. See also my discussion of Austen's writings later in this chapter.

[33] Another important institution was the Ordnance Office, for which, see Frances Willmoth, 'Mathematical Science and Military Technology: The Ordinance Office in the Reign of Charles II', in J. V. Field and Frank A. J. L. James (eds.), *Renaissance and Revolution: Humanists, Scholars, Craftsmen, and Natural Philosophers in Early Modern Europe* (Cambridge: Cambridge University Press, 1993), 117–31.

[34] Lindsay Sharp, 'Timber, Science, and Economic Reform in the Seventeenth Century', *Forestry*, 48 (1975), pp. 51–2, 63–8.

[35] Hunter, *Establishing the New Science*, pp. 77–8, 76.

[36] Ibid., pp. 87–91, at p. 89.

[37] Rob Iliffe, '"Meteorologies and Extravagant Speculations": The Future Legends of Early Modern English Natural Philosophy', in A. Brady and E. Butterworth (eds.), *The Uses of the Future in Early Modern Europe* (New York: Routledge, 2009), 192–228, at p. 226.

[38] Walter E. Houghton Jr, 'The History of Trades: Its Relation to Seventeenth-Century Thought: As Seen in Bacon, Petty, Evelyn, and Boyle', *Journal of the History of Ideas*, 2 (1941), 33–60; K. H. Ochs,

Great Plague of the summer of 1665. One exception was the 'Georgical Committee', convened to help improve agriculture. Before its meetings stopped due to the plague, the committee published 'Enquiries concerning Agriculture' in *Philosophical Transactions*—an ingenious measure which, despite the interruption, enabled them to keep calling for information from across the country about local practices and novelties.[39] Ultimately, the Society had neither the legal power to sanction particular schemes nor the ready purse to fund them. Yet its Fellows promoted projects for economic and technological improvement not only through its meetings and committees, but also by using its *Transactions*, by advising non-Fellows, or by lobbying parliament.[40]

The schemes backed by the Royal Society should be studied as a vital chapter of the history of projecting because its Fellows tacitly, yet *knowingly*, set their activities against Hartlibean schemes. A little-noticed letter of 1664 from John Beale to the Society is revealing in this regard. The former associate of Hartlib commented on agricultural pamphlets promoted by the reformer. Beale was particularly harsh on those that were hyperbolic or did not take effect as promised. Dymock's 1651 pamphlet, calling for the establishment of a college of husbandry, 'left the undertakers in Famine'. In Beale's view, the pamphlet 'is to be extinguish'd as a notorious cheate'.[41] His assessment of Gabriel Plattes was equally damning: Plattes 'had more of vapour and conceited projections. And tho no Man chid more against Mountebanks, yet his Stile and Titles [of his books] have much of that savour.'[42] The general conclusion was that Hartlib, a 'plain Man being a stranger in such matters, was apt to be abused'; accordingly, many of the pamphlets published under his tutelage 'were very cheats, and ought to be laid aside'. These were bad examples not to be emulated: 'It will be much our shame if we shall be like the Dog catching at the shadow, very busy about impossibilities.'[43] It is unclear whether Beale's strong disapproval of his former associates was due to genuine disappointment, or indicative instead of his tactical move to distance himself from the deceased supporter of the republican experiment. In any case, the letter is significant. Those who became Fellows of the Society rarely spoke of their former links with Hartlib. Yet, in this letter, we learn that the Society was specifically urged not to emulate Hartlibean 'projections' when developing its own programmes. How, then, should improvement be promoted? We can begin to unravel Beale's and others' responses once we put their activities back into their proper historical setting.

'The Royal Society of London's History of Trades Programme: An Early Episode in Applied Science', *NRRS*, 39 (1985), 129–58.

[39] *PT* (1665–78), 1 (1665–6), pp. 91–4; Reginald Lennard, 'English Agriculture under Charles II: The Evidence of the Royal Society's "Enquiries"', *EcHR*, 4 (1932), 23–45, esp. pp. 37–8; Hunter, *Establishing the New Science*, pp. 84–101, 105–14 (Agricultural Committee (a) Minutes).

[40] See pp. 191–3, 220–2 below; Lennard, 'English Agriculture', pp. 37–8; Hunter, *Establishing the New Science*, pp. 94–5, 98–101.

[41] RS, LBO/27, p. 350, discussing Dymock, *An essay for advancement of husbandry learning* (1651). This and the following quotations are drawn from the Society's official transcription of the letter. Beale's original letter is RS, EL/B1/43, 27 January [June?] 1664.

[42] RS, LBO/27, p. 352. See also pp. 55–6, 112–13 above.　　　　[43] RS, LBO/27, p. 353.

Projects—be they backed by the restored Crown or by the newly founded Royal Society—operated within a broader set of legal, political, economic, and international contexts. To begin with, the Restoration political settlement included legal and political arrangements conducive to projecting. The 1660 Statute of Tenure (12 Car. 2, *c.* 24) ruled that great landowners no longer had to pay feudal incidents to the Crown, a policy that afforded aristocrats some extra revenue.[44] Furthermore, lucrative governmental posts and grants were offered to ex-royalists. For example, Thomas Bushell was granted £2,000 for his role in royalist war finance and was made a gentleman of the Privy Chamber.[45] In August 1660, the royalist earl of Bristol obtained grants to sell off or enclose Broyle Park in Sussex, Lancaster Great Park, and Ashdown Forest.[46] Another royalist, Thomas Windsor, future earl of Plymouth, had his barony restored in 1660. He was also made lord lieutenant of Worcestershire and appointed the governor general of Jamaica, a lucrative post with an annual salary of £2,000.[47] These preferments help explain why ex-royalists such as Bristol and Windsor could afford to invest heavily on the Stour river navigation scheme after the return of the king. The Restoration settlement did not altogether disfavour parliamentarians either. During the Interregnum, commissioners of sequestration and purchasers of sequestered Crown and royalist lands had made handsome profits by sales, investment, and corruption; they were not forced after the Restoration to return their gains or compensate the original owners for profit so raised.[48] This enabled parliamentarians of lesser means such as Yarranton, as we have already seen, to launch small-scale enterprises and even to venture into publishing pamphlets on husbandry and trade.

Fires and wars stimulated certain kinds of schemes too. The Great Fire of 1666, which burnt down nearly two-thirds of the City within its walls, nevertheless triggered a series of projects for surveying, planning, and rebuilding the city, while, in the long term, stimulating the fire insurance industry and further improvement in urban water supply.[49] The mounting tension with the United Provinces, which led to the Second Anglo-Dutch War from March 1665, encouraged a series of initiatives. Within weeks, the Royal Society set up committees on 'the improvement of artillery' and 'experiments for improving chariots'. The first meeting of its Mechanical Committee after the outbreak of the war focused on gunnery.[50] The post-Restoration period also saw a series of attempts to improve naval vessels and military weapons.[51]

---

[44] For background, see Joan Thirsk, *The Rural Economy of England: Collected Essays* (London: Hambledon, 1984), ch. 8.

[45] *CTB, vol. 1, 1660–1667*, pp. 512, 528; *CSPD 1663–4*, p. 90.

[46] *CSPD 1661–1662*, p. 78.

[47] Stephen Sanders Webb, *The Governors-General: The English Army and the Definition of the Empire, 1569–1681* (Chapel Hill, NC: University of North Carolina Press, 1979), pp. 214, 478.

[48] Ronald Hutton, *The Restoration: A Political and Religious History of England and Wales, 1658–1667* (Oxford: Clarendon, 1985), pp. 139–42; Keeble, *Restoration*, pp. 81–2.

[49] Scott, *Joint-Stock*, vol. 3, p. 372; Reddaway, *Rebuilding of London*, pp. 168, 282–3; Mark S. R. Jenner, 'Print Culture and the Rebuilding of London after the Fire: The Presumptuous Proposals of Valentine Knight', *JBS*, 56 (2017), 1–26.

[50] Hunter, *Establishing the New Science*, pp. 88, 117–18 (Mechanical Committee minutes).

[51] Sarah Barter Bailey, *Prince Rupert's Patent Guns* (Leeds: Royal Armouries Museum, 2000); Marika Keblusek, '"Keeping it Secret": The Identity and Status of an Early-Modern Inventor', *History of Science*, 43 (2005), 37–56; Willmoth, 'Ordinance Office', pp. 117–31.

If the 1660s saw a good deal of projecting activities, the modest rise of the number of patents (sixty-nine of them) granted in the 1670s, from the fifty-seven patents in the previous decade, should warn us that there was perhaps a corresponding surge of activities outside the realm of patenting (Fig. 1.2). In fact, the 1670s saw a boom of pamphlets on economic improvement. The number of books and pamphlets with the words 'improve' and 'improvement' in their titles doubled from the 1660s. Among them were the reprint of Samuel Fortrey's *England's interest and improvement* (second edition 1673), Roger Coke's *England's improvement* (1675), and Yarranton's *England's improvement by sea and land* (1677).[52] These authors advised the king and politicians to learn from the Dutch and compete against them, and for that purpose offered a variety of recommendations, some concentrating on the 'balance of trade', others covering specific industries and ways to improve them.[53]

This literature flourished amid favourable changes in the economy—another important stimulus. As population growth subsided by mid-century, agricultural productivity continued rising; by the 1670s, the falling price of staple commodities and rising real wages gave middling sorts of people more purchasing power.[54] It was probably no coincidence that *Philosophical Transactions* started publishing reviews of the improvement literature that could accelerate such a favourable cycle.[55] Although the Fellows' attitudes towards inventions and useful knowledge were never homogeneous, they wished to see themselves (as a review in the *Transactions* put it) as 'concerned to take notice of those . . . who shew their Love to their Country by devising, proposing and soliciting the best Expedients for the Improvement of *England* and other his Majesties Dominions, by Trade, Agriculture, or any Commerce, Artifice, or Manufacture'.[56] In the 1670s and 1680s, as we shall see later, its Fellows also backed various promoters of economic innovations and improvement outside the Society by soliciting political support for them.

Stimulated by the king's return, lucrative grants, and the abolition of feudal tenure, and given further impetus by wars and favourable economic trends, projects for improvement thrived well into the 1670s, circulating in print and manuscript form, and clustering around the restored king and his government, parliament,

---

[52] The increase is from twenty-three to forty-four for 'improvement', and from seventy-six to 145 for 'improve' and its derivatives. In particular, the three years after the Dutch War ended in 1674 saw an unusual concentration of sixty titles, a three-year total that was not to be matched until the height of the early financial revolution (sixty-seven titles; 1692–4). The figures are based on the *ESTC* search results with title keywords 'improvement' and 'improve'. Cf. Slack, *Invention of Improvement*, p. 115; Slack, *Reformation to Improvement*, p. 96 n. 89.

[53] Spurr, *England in the 1670s*, pp. 135–41.   [54] See p. 54.

[55] Reviews, many of them celebratory, included *PT* (1665–78), 7 (1672), p. 5002, on Richard Sharrock's *History of the propagation and improvement of vegetables* (1660, 1666, 1672); *PT* (1665–78), 9 (1674), p. 252, on Richard Haines, *The prevention of poverty* (1674); *PT* (1665–78), 10 (1675), pp. 320–6, on John Blagrave, *Epitome of the whole art of husbandry* (1669, 1670, 1675, 1685). Mayling Stubbs suggests that John Beale penned many of these reviews. Mayling Stubbs, 'John Beale, Philosophical Gardener of Herefordshire, Part II. The Improvement of Agriculture and Trade in the Royal Society (1663–1683)', *Annals of Science*, 46 (1989), 323–63, pp. 349–52.

[56] *PT* (1665–78), 9 (1674), p. 19, a brief 'recommendation' of Fortrey's *England's interest and improvement*, and Roger L'Estrange's *A discourse of the fishery* (1674, 1695). See also Thomas Sprat, *The History of the Royal Society* [1667] (London: Routledge, 1959), pp. 401–2.

and the Royal Society, among others.[57] Just like projects in the ages of Hartlib and Defoe, those launched in the post-Restoration period deserve our critical attention. They are important particularly because they tell us how the millenarian enthusiasm of the Hartlibeans was eventually transformed into the commercial energies of Defoe's Projecting Age.

PROJECTING AND THE KING'S RETURN

One aspect of projecting culture predictably persisted before and the after the Restoration: the emphasis on public service. In dedicating his mining scheme to the king, Bushell ranked himself among '*persons of known integrity, abhorring all self-interest, and aiming soly at the Glory of God, promoting great designs for the publick good*'.[58] 'There is', Francis Mathew declared, 'nothing of greater advantage to a Land, than the opening of Rivers'. By dedicating a pamphlet to the king, then, Mathew presented himself as a champion of 'such great and publick Works'.[59] When Ford petitioned the Treasury, he stressed his 'great expense in inventing, contriving, and maintaining the waterworks for the public good, to serve the inhabitants with water and the prevention of fire'.[60] In offering proposals, then, projectors highlighted how they would contribute to the public good, just as the coteries of Hartlib had done during the 1640s and 1650s.

Yet, after the king's return, promoters across the ideological spectrum had reasons to exercise the utmost caution against uncertainty and vengeance. The *Act of Free and General Pardon Indemnity and Oblivion*, given royal assent on 29 August 1660, declared that criminal or treasonous deeds committed between 1637 and 1660 were to be 'Pardoned Released Indempnified Discharged and put in utter Oblivion', making any evocation of the issue (in speech or in print) subject to fines.[61] This was the legislative foundation upon which reconciliation was to be built. Yet ex-royalist officers had reasons to be resentful. Few of them received full payment for former military service to the Crown, while regicide army officers—key players who made the Restoration possible—had been handsomely paid, and some even promoted and rewarded with government posts. The act was thus resented as an Act of Indemnity for the King's enemies and Oblivion for his friends. As the act did not tolerate present disloyalty, dissatisfied royalists bent their anger by accusing ex-parliamentarians of plotting to subvert the restored monarchy.[62] Ex-royalists

---

[57] Coffeehouses also played an important role as venues in which projects were promoted and discussed. See pp. 132, 239, 241.

[58] Thomas Bushell, *An extract by Mr. Bushell of his late abridgement of the Lord Chancellor Bacons Phbilosophical Theory in mineral prosecutions* (1660), sig. A2–[A2v], 'Dread Soveraign'.

[59] Francis Mathew, *Of the opening of rivers for navigation: the benefit exemplified by the two Avons of Salisbury and Bristol* (1660), 'To the Most High and Mighty Monarch' [no signature], p. 2.

[60] *CTB, vol. 1, 1660–1667*, pp. 167–8.

[61] 12 Car. 2, *c.* 11. Paul Seaward, *The Cavalier Parliament and the Reconstruction of the Old Regime, 1661–1667* (Cambridge: Cambridge University Press, 1989), ch. 8 offers an excellent in-depth discussion of the Act and contestations over its scope, on which this paragraph has drawn. See also Hutton, *Restoration*, pp. 132–8; Keeble, *Restoration*, pp. 70–6.

[62] Hutton, *Restoration*, pp. 135–6.

were not entirely safe either. During the Interregnum, networks of one-time Cavalier projectors like Ford and John Lanyon cut across religious and ideological boundaries; even royalists like Evelyn and Ford had had contacts with Hartlib and parliamentarians.[63] Even after the passage of the Act of Indemnity and Oblivion, the precise extent of that pardon remained ambiguous and subject to manoeuvre. In fact, military officers, local officials, and others who had levied taxes for the regicide government—even royalists who had relented to avoid molestation by the republican government—came to be sued for alleged 'arrears' by the restored regime between 1662 and 1664 as 'defaulting accountants'. For Warwickshire alone, such debts allegedly amounted to £50,000.[64] For those who witnessed the dramatic return of the king in May 1660, then, the threat of retribution thus seemed still imminent, and the future of the Restoration settlement by no means settled.

Practices of projecting after the Restoration evolved under this wider context of uncertainty. During the 1650s authors such as John Dryden and Edmund Waller eulogized Cromwell; after the Restoration they eulogized the king, carefully trimming the Cromwellian tropes.[65] So did writers of alchemical treaties such as George Starkey and Henry Stubbe who had written against the established church and monarchy in the 1650s. Come the Restoration, the vast economic potential of alchemy was promoted as a means to strengthen the restored monarchy, and the restored Charles was lauded as capable of transmuting the Crown and its subjects into a harmonious whole in an alchemical fashion.[66] Defaulting accountants, too, facing charges in the Exchequer Court, appealed by stressing their 'royalist' past.[67] Doing so allowed them to present themselves as loyal, obedient, and pardonable subjects.

These were the tactics also adopted by promoters of economic and technological improvement. Upon the king's return, many of them chose to highlight whatever relation they had had with the royalist cause, passing over their associations with the previous regime. Although a royalist, Bushell received a grant from the Cromwellian government to search for silver and gold mines, with a promise to pay proceeds to the Exchequer. So, when dedicating his proposals to the restored king in 1660, he was careful to downplay his link with the republicans, and instead highlight that he had been 'loyal to Your Royal Father'.[68] In June, a surveyor of the

[63] Mark S. R. Jenner, '"Another *Epocha*"? Hartlib, John Lanyon and the Improvement of London in the 1650s', in *Universal Reformation*, 343–56, pp. 351–2.

[64] Ann Hughes, *Politics, Society and Civil War in Warwickshire, 1620–1660* (Cambridge: Cambridge University Press, 1987), p. 340. As we shall see in the next section, there were also harsh reactions to alleged religious 'fanatics' intent upon overthrowing the restored monarchy.

[65] James Grantham Turner, 'From Revolution to Restoration in English Literature', in David Loewenstein and Janel Mueller (eds.), *The Cambridge History of Early Modern English Literature* (Cambridge: Cambridge University Press, 2003), 790–833, esp. p. 796.

[66] J. Andrew Mendelsohn, 'Alchemy and Politics in England 1649–1665', *P&P*, 135 (1992), 30–78, pp. 63–7, 70–1, 74.

[67] Matthew Neufeld, 'Recollections of an Indemnified Past in Restoration England: The Answers of Defaulting Accounts to the Court of Exchequer' (unpublished paper, 2015); Stephen K. Roberts, 'Public or Private? Revenge and Recovery at the Restoration of Charles II', *Bulletin of the Institute of Historical Research*, 59 (1986), 172–88.

[68] J. W. Gough, *The Superlative Prodigall: A Life of Thomas Bushell* (Bristol: Bristol University Press, 1932), pp. 96–7; Thomas Bushell, *An extract by Mr. Bushell* (1660), sig. A2 (quotation).

Bedford Levels, Jonas Moore, presented an edition of his *Arithmetick* to prospective new patrons. He had to do this even more cautiously than Bushell because, shortly after the execution of Charles I, Moore dedicated an earlier edition of the book to three parliamentarians, showing '*thankefullnesse* of their great *Curtesies*'.[69] Now, Moore dedicated the new one to Charles II's brother, the Duke of York, and Sir Edward Montague (whose switch of allegiance ensured the navy's support for the king's return), and recounted a story he had not mentioned in the 1650 edition. Recalling an earlier encounter with Charles I in Durham, Moore suggested that he would not have devoted himself to mathematics and engineering without the king's encouragement.[70] During the 1650s, Mathew dedicated to Cromwell and the Rump his proposals for inland navigation, obeying '*divine Providence thus advancing you and your affairs*'.[71] Upon the king's return he put all this aside. An engraving of Charles II and a dedication to him accompanied the 1660 proposal. Mathew now emphasized his support of the royalist cause during the war, presenting himself as a '*Captain of a Troop of Horse in His late Majesties Service; as by his Commissions doth appear*'.[72] As late as 1668, Cressy Dymock, a protégé of Hartlib, styled himself '*a* *Gentleman* . . . a Col. of Horse in his late Majesties Armies; [who] Hath been several times undone by, or for his Fidelity'.[73] For the first few years after the king's return, then, highlighting one's 'royalist past', alongside public-spiritedness, became a pragmatic commonplace.

Historians have shown that seemingly 'popular' support at the king's return was not a spontaneous outburst of public opinion, but rather a result of a deliberate effort to orchestrate support.[74] The careful self-presentation of promoters such as Bushell, Mathew, Moore, and Dymock was integral to this fabrication of consensus. By selectively remembering the late 'troubled times', post-Restoration projectors across the ideological spectrum downplayed the extent to which the country was divided, obscured how often they had supported, or compromised with, the regicide governments, and thereby helped consolidate the legitimacy of the new regime that had just been pulled together. Their promotional writings, like the bells and bonfires celebrating the king's return, helped propagate the somewhat deceptive

---

[69] Jonas Moore, *Moores arithmetick discovering the secrets of that art, in numbers and species* (1650), sig. A3, 'To the Honourable Sir William Persall, Kt. Edmund Wild, Esq. and Nicholas Shuttleworth, Esq.'.

[70] Jonas Moore, *Moores arithmetick in two books* (1660), sig. A4–[A4v], 'To the Illustrious Prince James Duke of York'. See also Frances Willmoth, *Sir Jonas Moore: Practical Mathematics and Restoration Science* (Woodbridge: Boydell, 1993), pp. 78, 122.

[71] Francis Mathew, *Of the opening of rivers for navigation: the benefit exemplified by the two Avons of Salisbury and Bristol* (1655), sig. [A2v]. See also the 1656 edition with an additional preface, Francis Mathew, *Of the opening of rivers for navigation: the benefit exemplified by the two Avons of Salisbury and Bristol* (1656), sig. A2.

[72] Mathew, *Of the opening of rivers* (1660), 'To the Most High and Mighty Monarch' [no signature].

[73] Cressy Dymock, *The new and better art of agriculture* [1668], one-page handbill. This corrects Mark Greengrass's comment that Dymock 'apparently died shortly thereafter'. M. Greengrass, 'Dymock, Cressy (fl. 1629–1660)', *Oxford DNB*, vol. 17, 500–1 (at p. 501).

[74] Phil Withington, 'Views from the Bridge: Revolution and Restoration in Seventeenth-Century York', *P&P*, 170 (2001), 121–51, p. 123; Mark S. R. Jenner, 'The Roasting of the Rump: Scatology and the Body Politic in Restoration England', *P&P*, 177 (2002), 84–120, p. 109.

impressions of 'One Harmony, one Mirth, one Voice' for the restored regime.[75] The promoters' role in the collective making—or projecting—of Restoration society is important. Precisely because of their complicity, their schemes were promoted in ways that would not undermine the regime's legitimacy, its religious orthodoxy, or its precarious relationship with the subjects who had been tormented by the Civil Wars and ensuing political upheavals. Memories of the grievous project, and of the ensuing 'troubled times', were all too vivid. Only by fully appreciating the haunting presence of such memories can we begin to appreciate why improvement had to be reinvented in the way it was in post-Restoration England. Religious dimensions are examined first, before turning to the administration of patents, and to the promotion of improvement more broadly.

CHANGING FACES OF MILLENARIANISM

The promoters' adaptation to the new regime shaped how they expressed religious aspirations. It was a risky time for those who did not tightly attach themselves to the restored Anglican orthodoxy. After 1660, much of the radical views about the millennium went 'underground'.[76] There were numerous rumours of an imminent armed uprising by religious radicals; in January 1661 some Fifth Monarchists led by Thomas Venner did take up arms in order to bring down the restored church and state and prepare for the imminent arrival of the millennium.[77] Though hardly a serious military threat, it fuelled the denunciation of, and search for, 'fanatics' and 'phanatic parties' up and down the country. Religious fanatics were, according to Thomas Fuller, possessed by 'Apparitions, which they either saw or fancied themselves to have seen'; 'in their fits and wild raptures [they] pretended to strange predictions'.[78]

Even moderate nonconformists and ex-parliamentarians were molested because it was all too easy to collapse the distinction between them and genuine militant millenarians.[79] Benjamin Worsley, a protégé of Hartlib, for example, suffered imprisonment in the aftermath of Venner's rising with other alleged members of 'this Rebellious and bloody Crew'; his former parliamentarian patron Sir Henry Vane was arrested in July 1660 and executed in June 1662. Worsley even contemplated moving to New England to secure employment and to escape religious tension.[80] Yarranton, who was a Presbyterian and had fought for the Long Parliament, was also imprisoned in November 1660 for allegedly plotting a rebellion with other local

---

[75] The quotation is from Charles Cotton's 'To Alexander Brome' as in Turner, 'From Revolution to Restoration', p. 791.

[76] Richard L. Greaves, *Deliver Us from Evil: The Radical Underground in Britain, 1660–1663* (Oxford: Oxford University Press, 1986), pp. 49, 61, 207. See also Richard L. Greaves, *Enemies under His Feet: Radicals and Non-Conformists in Britain, 1664–1667* (Stanford, CA: Stanford University Press, 1990).

[77] Greaves, *Deliver Us from Evil*, pp. 10, 49; Hutton, *Restoration*, pp. 150–1.

[78] Thomas Fuller, *Mixt contemplations in better times* (1660), p. 78.

[79] Greaves, *Deliver Us from Evil*, p. 228.   [80] Leng, *Worsley*, pp. 139, 141.

Presbyterians.[81] In 1668, when the Bawdy House Riots broke out in London, the government was convinced that rioters were not apprentices, but ex-Cromwellian soldiers 'nursed in the late rebellion', still longing for the coming of the new millennium.[82] Fanaticism and enthusiasm continued to preoccupy Restoration churchmen to such an extent that they could unite against these common threats despite their doctrinal differences.[83]

Of course, being accused of 'fanaticism' did not completely ruin one's career. Thanks to his knowledge of colonial affairs, Worsley eventually secured an official post. Likewise, as we saw in Chapter 4, Yarranton's proposals for national improvement, published in the 1670s, were indeed taken seriously and promoted by the Royal Society. Nevertheless, like the image of the projector, the figure of the religious 'fanatick' became something best not to be associated with. In fact, a mock utopian tract was dedicated to Hartlib immediately after the Restoration, and he wrote: 'I confess I was not well pleased', for the book made it seem 'as if I were a refined Quaker, or a fanatick'.[84]

Did economic improvement become more secular as a result? Some accounts suggest it did. Joyce Appleby viewed the economic writings of the later seventeenth century as a step towards the essentially secular economic liberalism which she argued would culminate in the writing of Adam Smith.[85] Charles Webster also suggested that Whig radicals and their reforming allies precipitated 'a world of Leviathan political economy' in which provision to the poor was conceptualized less in religious terms than 'in terms of economic exploitation'.[86] While Spurr's account is more nuanced, it also suggests that '"Improvement" had lost some of its Utopian and religious associations' after the Restoration.[87] Steve Pincus has also argued that the language of 'interest' and 'reason of state had replaced promotion of the true religion as the language of public political discourse' in the later seventeenth century.[88]

---

[81] TNA, SP 29/21/87. For details, see Greaves, *Deliver Us from Evil*, pp. 72–7. Greaves suggests that the alleged plot 'had no solid evidential foundation' (ibid., p. 77).

[82] Tim Harris, 'The Bawdy House Riot of 1688', *HJ*, 29 (1986), p. 550. For legislative and 'popular' responses, see Turner, 'From Revolution to Restoration', p. 793; Hutton, *Restoration*, ch. 2 (esp. pp. 162–3). Those who sat in the Cavalier Parliament had conflicting and heterogeneous views on toleration and indemnity. See Seaward, *Cavalier Parliament*, chs. 7–8.

[83] John Spurr, *The Restoration Church of England, 1646–1689* (New Haven, CT: Yale University Press, 1991), ch. 6, esp. p. 328.

[84] John Worthington, *The Diary and Correspondence of Dr. John Worthington*, ed. James Crossley et al., Camden Society, old ser., 13, 36, 114 (3 vols., 1847, 1855, 1886), vol. 1, pp. 250–1, Hartlib to Worthington, 17 December 1660.

[85] Joyce Oldham Appleby, *Economic Thought and Ideology in Seventeenth-Century England* (Princeton, NJ: Princeton University Press, 1978), pp. 257, 278. Cf. Gunn, *Politics and the Public Interest*, pp. 205–65, 277–86.

[86] Webster, *Great Instauration*, pp. 244–5.

[87] Spurr, *England in the 1670s*, p. 135.

[88] Steve Pincus, 'From Holy Cause to Economic Interest: The Study of Population and the Invention of the State', in Alan Houston and Steve Pincus (eds.), *Nation Transfigured: England after the Restoration* (Cambridge: Cambridge University Press, 2001), 272–98, p. 292.

Ideas about 'interest' did play a vital role in the post-Restoration period, as we shall see. Yet suggestions of secularization need firm qualification. The 'Protestant and civic ideals', which had informed the Hartlib circle in the 1640s and 1650s, later inspired initiatives for social reform in urban centres like Bristol.[89] Millenarian thinking hardly died out after the Restoration either. Anglican divines (such as Henry More and Gilbert Burnet) continued to express apocalyptic ideas in ways that were compatible with the post-Restoration church and state.[90] While attacks upon 'enthusiasm' helped shape 'what was publicly acceptable', Boyle, too, privately took an interest in millenarian ideas.[91] Promoters of economic improvement operated under just such constraints after the Restoration. They took a spectrum of positions; some, like Boyle, kept aspects of their religious beliefs from public view.

The publicity of the Royal Society's 'Georgical Committee' epitomized the clear dissociation from millenarian language. When *Philosophical Transactions* advertised 'Enquiries concerning Agriculture' in 1665, the committee's aim was to encourage readers to 'impart their knowledg [*sic*] herein, for the *common* benefit of their Countrey', a goal closely resembling that of Hartlib, whose books the committee consulted.[92] Nothing was mentioned of the spiritual significance of husbandry or of communicating information. In his letter to Evelyn, Henry Oldenburg described the Buckland potato scheme as 'new propositions tending to universall good', a depiction reminiscent of the millenarian aspirations of Hartlib and his close allies. But no similar phrase was recorded in the minutes of the Georgical Committee in which the scheme was discussed.[93] Collectively, this was a significant shift. Just fourteen years before, Hartlib published Dymock's secret method of husbandry by telling the reader that husbandry was '*the most profitable* Industry *unto* Humane Society; *wherein the* Providence, *the* Power, *the* Wisdom *and the* Goodness of God, *appears unto man more eminently then in any other way of* Industry *whatsoever*'.[94]

Worsley continued to conceptualize his intellectual and economic pursuits in somewhat unorthodox millenarian terms, but refrained from expressing them publicly.[95] The Somerset clergyman John Beale argued that fruit trees were 'the Monum[en]ts of Eternity', and the orchard the God-given 'Paradyse for man'.

---

89 Jonathan Barry, 'The "Great Projector": John Cary and the Legacy of Puritan Reform in Bristol, 1647–1720', in Margaret Pelling and Scott Mandelbrote (eds.), *The Practice of Reform in Health, Medicine and Science, 1500–2000* (Aldershot: Ashgate, 2005), 185–206, pp. 185, 197–8 (at p. 185).

90 Warren Johnston, 'The Anglican Apocalypse in Restoration England', *Journal of Ecclesiastical History*, 55 (2004), 467–501.

91 Michael Hunter, *Robert Boyle (1627–92): Scrupulosity and Science* (Woodbridge: Boydell, 2000), pp. 223–4 (quotation), 236–7, 238; Michael Hunter, *Boyle Studies: Aspects of the Life and Thought of Robert Boyle* (Farnham: Ashgate, 2015), p. 52. I thank Professor Hunter for discussion on this point.

92 *PT* (1665–78), 1 (1665–6), pp. 91–4 (quotation from p. 92).

93 Compare Henry Oldenburg, *The Correspondence of Henry Oldenburg*, ed. and tr. A. R. Hall and M. B. Hall (9 vols., Madison, WI: University of Wisconsin Press, 1965–73), vol. 2, p. 30, Oldenburg to Evelyn, 9 March 1963; Hunter, *Establishing the New Science*, pp. 102–3 (minutes of the Buckland Committee).

94 [Samuel Hartlib and Cressy Dymock], *The reformed husband-man, or, A brief treatise of the errors, defects, and inconveniences of our English husbandry* (1651), sig. [A2v], 'To the reader'.

95 See Leng, *Worsley*, pp. 182–4.

Yet this was in a manuscript treatise. It was well received by the Royal Society, and transcribed verbatim for their records. Yet neither Beale nor the Society published it.[96] While these were by no means coherent religious beliefs or doctrines, together they highlight some common 'Discretion' (as Boyle put it) as to what one might express in public.[97]

The royalist and Anglican Evelyn did not publish his 'Elysium Britannicum, or the Royal Gardens', an 'encyclopaedic history of gardens and gardening practices' that he kept developing from the 1650s onwards, and in which he mused about 'an imminent restoration of paradise'.[98] But Evelyn did express some of his religious visions in public. In the 1670 edition of *Sylva*, Evelyn interpreted the current want of timber trees in England as evidence of the degeneration since Adam's Fall; he thus 'track[ed] the Religious esteem of *Trees* and *Woods*' in '*Holy Writ*', and argued that 'from the very Infancy of the *World*', Abraham 'receiv'd his Divine Guests, not in his *Tent*, but under a *Tree*, an *Oak*'.[99] In the 1702 edition, Evelyn even referred to the Apocalypse and mused about the coming of the time when God would be pleased 'to transplant me into those glorious Regions above, Coelestiall Paradise, planted with Perennial Groves, bearing Immortall Fruit'.[100] Forestry was thus presented as a potential means to restore Adam's innocence. Even in this published treatise 'the earthy business of forestry is carried on in a highly imaginative atmosphere'.[101]

Similar millenarian language can be found in pamphlets related to technological and economic innovations. In his *Micrographia* (1665), Hooke presented his innovative microscopes as 'artificial organs', 'a means, albeit imperfect, of seeking to recover that natural view of the world God intended for man in his innocence in Eden'.[102] Matthew Stevenson, a minor Yorkshire-born poet, used the prospective liberation from original sin as a motif to praise the 'Inimitable, Water-Commanding Engine' of the Marquis of Worcester:

> With the expence of Purse, and Brain, both great
> He buyes off from Mans brow the curse of sweat;
> His study travels to procure us rest,

---

[96] RS, EL/B1/65, Beale to Oldenburg, 22 September 1673, fol. 136v. The fair copy of the same treatise, without foliation, is at RS, MS/366/2/4; the table of contents for the same is at *Oldenburg Correspondence*, vol. 10, pp. 239–45. See also Michael Leslie, 'The Spiritual Husbandry of John Beale', in *Culture and Cultivation*, 151–72, pp. 156, 158–62, 168–9; P. Woodland, 'Beale, John (bap. 1608, d. 1683)', *Oxford DNB*, vol. 4, 513–16, pp. 514–15.

[97] Hunter, *Scrupulosity and Science*, p. 231.

[98] D. C. Chambers, 'Evelyn, John (1620–1706)', *Oxford DNB*, vol. 18, 770–5, at p. 772; Graham Parry, 'John Evelyn as Hortulan Saint', in *Culture and Cultivation*, 130–50, p. 144.

[99] John Evelyn, *Sylva, or a discourse of forest-trees, and the propagation of timber in his majesties dominions* (2nd edn, 1670), ch. 35 (at p. 227). Subsequent references to *Sylva* are to this edition.

[100] Quoted in Parry, 'John Evelyn', pp. 144–3.

[101] Parry, 'John Evelyn', p. 142. Note, however, that Evelyn did not present this millenarian vision as something to be imposed upon the public; it was something his readers might pursue by planting trees themselves. See p. 210.

[102] Jim Bennett, 'Instrument and Ingenuity', in Michael Cooper and Michael Hunter (eds.), *Robert Hooke: Tercentennial Studies* (Aldershot: Ashgate, 2006), 65–76, pp. 66–7, 72, 76 (quotation from pp. 66–7).

And gives a Sabbath to the weary Beast [Breast?];
In what more could he Mortals gratifie,
Ease to the hand, and pastime to the eye?[103]

Yarranton also stressed both the spiritual and temporal benefits of clover cultivation: 'With what delight and pleasure have I seen | The barren pasture cloathed all in green!...It fills each Sense with Joy, our Purse with Money | Our Land (like *Canaan*) flows with milk and hony'.[104]

Other promoters of economic improvement used religious language, but provided reassurance that their schemes would buttress king and country. In offering his mining project to Charles II, for example, Bushell related (as Bacon's opinion) that '*such hidden* [mineral] *Treasures...may, and will most probably be recovered*' when '*being freely devoted by Religious Princes, to holy and charitable uses and ends...for the publick good of his Church and People*'.[105] The Baptist Richard Haines's proposal for building poorhouses was designed to exploit his patented 'Spinning Engine' in order to provide the idle poor and street children with jobs, bibles, and a place to live. The scheme was, he declared, to advance 'the Glory of God, the Prosperity of the whole Nation, and the Welfare and happy Reformation of all poor distressed People'.[106] Rather than presenting individual schemes as part of the imminent universal reformation of mankind (through strong state-led action), these promoters now focused on the spiritual virtue of the king, or the spiritual improvement of sections of society (like the poor), or the spiritual benefit of technological innovations.

The incidental lack of religious language in some of the published writings on improvement thus tells us not so much about the general decline of religious aspirations as the changing sense of propriety in print culture: millenarian aspirations for state-led reform—something Hartlib, Dury, and others expressed in many pamphlets—became less publicly acceptable after the Restoration.

This changing code of conduct is not a revealed preference. Some promoters *chose* to drop spiritual themes in order to follow the changing sense of propriety, as the case of Ralph Austen shows. A Puritan whose mother was a cousin of the parliamentarian Henry Ireton, Austen was well known for his fruit tree cultivation and cider making, and published *A treatise of fruit-trees* in three editions (1653, 1657, and 1665). Although not university-educated, he was connected with virtuosi like Boyle and Hartlib.[107] It is worth investigating at some length the *process of*

---

[103] Matthew Stevenson, *Poems* (1665), pp. 2–3. Cf. Jenner, 'Liquid Schemes', no pagination. For Worcester's life and inventive activities in general, see the somewhat whiggish account of Henry Dircks, *The Life, Times, and Scientific Labours of the Second Marquis of Worcester* (London: Bernard Quaritch, 1865).

[104] Andrew Yarranton, *The Improvement improved, by a second edition of the great improvement of lands by clover* (Worcester, 1663), sig. [A7].

[105] Bushell, *An extract by Mr. Bushell*, pp. 2–3.

[106] Richard Haines, *A model of government for the good of the poor and the wealth of the nation* (1678), pp. 2, 8; Patent no. 202, granted on 18 April 1678. For his life and writings, see Charles R. Haines, *A Complete Memoir of Richard Haines (1633–1685), A Forgotten Sussex Worthy* (London: Harrison, 1899). On another dissenter projector Thomas Firmin, see H. W. Stephenson, 'Thomas Firmin, 1632–1697' (PhD thesis, University of Oxford, 1949).

[107] J. G. Turner, 'Austen, Ralph (c. 1612–1676)', *Oxford DNB*, vol. 2, 979–80.

negotiation that led Austen to adjust his religious expressions, because similar negotiations were repeatedly undertaken over non-religious matters. Reconstructing
such adjustments at the micro level is the first step towards understanding the
collective evolution of projecting culture in the post-Restoration period.[108]

In the first two editions, Austen presented plant cultivation as part of the pan-
sophic reform. Under government supervision, fruit tree cultivation was to be
spread across the country. Enclosing land, planting fruit trees in '*Fields and Hedges*',
and producing cider would bring a range of social and economic benefits, from
'setting on worke, very many *Poore People*' to preventing English money from being
wasted on French wines.[109] The project would confer spiritual benefit too. 'Adam
in time of his Innocency *was imployed in this part of* Husbandry', but 'when he had
sinned, he was put away from this worke to till the ground'. Thus, the project was
an attempt to reverse the Fall of Adam by turning England into 'another *Canaan*',
a place with '*Fruit-trees in abundance*' (Nehemiah 9:25).[110]

The much-expanded second edition of 1657 went further. Austen developed
the spiritual part of his argument into an accompanying tract, *The spirituall
use of an orchard, or garden of fruit-trees*. Here Austen examined fruit trees as 'a
TEXT from which may be raised many profitable *Doctrines*, and *Conclusions*' that
would be 'obvious and familiar to every mans Capacity'.[111] His conclusions
were radical indeed. By juxtaposing the high productivity of small trees with the
barrenness of bulky old trees, Austen declared that preachers of lower rank
could bring forth 'more profitable fruits than' those of eminent ranks '*adorned
with eminent Gifts, Humane learning*, and other *externall qualifications*'.[112]
Husbandmen made use '*of ordinary, and common Tooles*' and '*not of Gold, silver,
or costly mettles*' to achieve great work in their gardens. So too in God's work:
'God did not use some *great Monarch* as his Instrument', but shepherds and
plowmen such as Moses and Elisha. Austen thus asked whether, 'even before
our eyes', church and state had not been 'subdued by a handfull of men' by
divine intervention.[113] Austen dedicated the two editions of 1653 and 1657 to
Hartlib and presented them as an addition to the agricultural tracts of Hartlib
and 'our deceased friend Mr [Walter] *Blith*'. Thus, the dissemination of apple
trees was integral to the circle's religious vision, educating planters via 'plaine,
and pregnant SIMILITUDES', thereby turning England into the God-ordained
paradise on earth abounding in fragrant trees.[114]

---

[108] The following discussion extends those of James Grantham Turner, 'Ralph Austen, an Oxford
Horticulturalist of the Seventeenth Century', *Garden History*, 6 (1978), 39–45; Stubbs, 'Part II',
pp. 333–4; Vittoria di Palma, 'Drinking Cider in Paradise: Science, Improvement, and the Politics
of Fruit Trees', in Adam Smyth (ed.), *A Pleasing Sinne: Drink and Conviviality in Seventeenth-
Century England* (Cambridge: Brewer, 2004), 161–77, pp. 165, 175–6.

[109] Ralph Austen, *A treatise of fruit-trees* (1653), sig. [¶v].

[110] Ibid., sig. [¶4], [¶2v]. Turner, 'Ralph Austen', p. 43. See also *AHEW Vii*, p. 560.

[111] Ralph Austen, *A treatise of fruit-trees* (2nd edn, 1657); Ralph Austen, *The spirituall use of an
orchard, or garden of fruit-trees* (1657), sig. [†4v], ††.

[112] Austen, *Spirituall use*, pp. 144–5.   [113] Ibid., pp. 114, 115, 117.

[114] Ibid., sig. [††3].

The third edition, dedicated to Boyle, appeared in 1665. Austen was now corresponding with the Royal Society; though not a Fellow, he was invited in 1664 to sit on its 'Georgical Committee', which read and considered his proposals.[115] Prior to publication Austen asked Boyle's opinion about the plan to publish 'only the first part' of his *Treatise*:

> As for the [second] spirituall part...I conceive it best, upon some Accompts, to let it rest (*at present*) both what hath beene made publique formerly, & what I have prepared to add thereunto[.][116]

As Boyle later told Oldenburg, he had advised Austen 'to leave out many things w[hi]ch though for ought I know good in themselves were of a Theologicall not a rurall nature'.[117]

As a result the 1665 edition of Austen's *Treatise* became a curious remnant of millenarian aspirations which omitted most obvious calls for universal reform. It first of all dropped *The spirituall use of an orchard* with its discussion of similitude as 'the most plaine way of Teaching'. It retained the schematic 'Analysis' in the text that combined four 'Humane' arguments (from 'Presidents', 'Praise', 'Profit', and 'Pleasures') with 'Eight Divine Arguments of the dignity & value of Fruit-trees and Art of Planting'. But it dropped the conspicuous frontispiece used for the two previous editions that visualized the idea that fruit tree cultivation was the means to restore the 'Garden inclosed' depicted in *Solomon's Song* (Solomon 4:12–15). It also omitted the original dedication to Hartlib. The 1665 edition continued to highlight that '*Adam in time of his Innocency* was imployed in this part of *Husbandry*'.[118] But its new dedication to Boyle no longer spoke of 'making *a Spirituall use of Natural things*' in order to 'turne Earth (as it were) into heaven',[119] or turn England into 'another *Canaan*'. So the previous emphasis on radical teaching and the imminence of universal reformation was replaced by an emphasis on support of the restored regime:

> a work Pregnant with Profits, Real and Substantiall to all people all their life long... A Work that will enrich the Poor, and adorn the Rich: A Work that will Encrease the Kings Revenues, and the Substance of all his Subjects[.]...In a word, It is a Royal Work, and worthy [of] the most serious Considerations and Endeavours of the Royal Society.[120]

Assiduous readers would have deciphered hints of millenarian aspirations in corners of the revised edition. But for inattentive readers, the book read more like a mundane agricultural proposal by a pious would-be royalist. In the post-Restoration

---

[115] Hunter, *Establishing the New Science*, p. 87, Transcription of the 'Georgical Committee' (pp. 107, 111–14). Austen was to gather information for the 'history of agriculture' along with other Fellows like Evelyn and Lord Brereton.

[116] *Boyle Correspondence*, vol. 2, p. 450, Austen to Boyle, 14 January 1665 (my italics). Cf. Hunter, *Boyle Studies*, p. 52.

[117] Oldenburg, *Correspondence*, vol. 2, p. 509, 16 September 1665.

[118] Ralph Austen, *A treatise of fruit-trees* (3rd edn, 1665), sig. [A8], 'To the Reader'.

[119] Austen, *Spirituall use*, sig. [†2v].

[120] Austen, *A treatise of fruit-trees* (3rd edn, 1665), sig. [A6v]-[A7].

edition of *A treatise*, therefore, Austen's scheme lost some of the features that had most clearly made it a Hartlibean manifesto. Like Worsley, Boyle, and Beale, who withheld aspects of their religious views, Austen did not recant his religious beliefs, but worked out temporal adjustments suitable 'at present', an indication that he may have hoped to publish the second part with additions one day.

Neither apocalyptic language nor religious expressions in general lost currency in post-Restoration projecting culture, therefore. Like the alchemists Starkey and Stubbe, who adeptly continued to practise alchemy by adjusting their language, reformers like Austen carefully chose what to express in public, taking care to imply that their schemes would not affect, let alone challenge, the precarious political status quo after the Restoration. In the process, one of the most significant aspects of mid-century millenarianism—the radical rethinking of church and state—lost its pre-eminence as a public discourse. As Edmund Ludlow observed, many arguably 'thought it prudence [*sic*] to swim with the stream'.[121]

PATENTS AND MONOPOLIES AFTER 1660

Promoters of improvement thus went so far as to highlight their 'royalist past' and even adjust their religious utterances in order to follow the current. Yet the direction of that stream was by no means clear where the nature of the restored monarchy was concerned. If Charles II's return marked the Restoration of the Stuart monarchy, did it also restore the style of projecting and improvement characteristic of his royal father, Charles I? We know that this was not the case as far as the administration of patents was concerned. As Christine MacLeod has found, the Restoration regime 'held rigidly to the principle that a patent for an invention should not confer monopoly power over the whole industry to which it related'.[122] A closer look into post-Restoration patents suggests that the government ceased to have a large financial stake in granting them. Out of eighty-two patents for invention granted in the 1660s and the 1670s, only eleven promised to pay the Exchequer on a fixed-sum or pro-rata basis (see Fig. 1.5). Why did the restored monarchy not restore the old practices of fiscal exaction through the granting of patents?

This was not a foregone conclusion. Nor was it a result of new legislation or the uniform application of existing statutes. Charles II and his government did not inaugurate a concerted policy either, in order to move away from his father's use of patents for fiscal exploitation. A succinct statement about the government's position is, of course, hard to find. Yet if the government did tackle the issue at all, it did so through a mechanism of 'counsel'—a well-worn tradition, at least a century old by the 1660s.[123] The fittingly named Council of Trade illustrates the process well.

---

[121] Edmund Ludlow, *A Voyce from the Watch Tower: Part Five: 1660–1662*, ed. A. B. Worden, Camden 4th Series, vol. 21 (1978), p. 149.

[122] MacLeod, *Patent*, p. 27.

[123] John Guy, *Tudor England* (Oxford: Oxford University Press, 1988); John Cramsie, *Kingship and Crown Finance under James VI and I, 1603–1625* (Woodbridge: Boydell, 2002); Jacqueline Rose,

When it was revived in November 1660, the Council was commissioned 'to receive and prosecute' plans and proposals 'as shalbe offered to them by any other person or persons' for the better 'regulac[i]on and benefit of Trade and Navigac[i]on'.[124] The council accordingly proposed 'to invite and encourage all Such p[er]sons as are concerned in the matters...to apply themselves to your Ma[jes]ties Councell of Trade'.[125] We now need to move beyond the analysis of promoters' self-presentation to explore how the government's position on patenting took shape through numerous, haphazard consultations.

The process of counsel helped strike the difficult balance between risks and benefits. On the one hand, in the wake of the Restoration, many asked the restored king for the restitution of former monopolies and other grants, and for the introduction of new ones. Numerous petitions were submitted, for example, for discovering 'concealed crown lands'—a notorious project that stirred controversies under Elizabeth I and the early Stuarts.[126] Thomas Bushell had been granted a patent 'for reforming abuses in dyeing of silks' from Charles I, and was one of the patentees of the controversial Westminster soap monopoly (as we saw in Chapter 2). Upon the return of Charles II, Bushell was again asking for similar grants.[127] Richard Bagnall, a gentleman usher to Charles I, also petitioned his son for a grant regarding 'the sole making of saltpetre', a commodity that Thomas Brugis had attacked in 1641 as the 'stinking business'.[128] The goldsmith John Garill claimed to have invented a new way of minting coins, and as a reward for his invention sought a monopoly for drawing gold and silver into wire (which was then to be minted). The wire-drawing monopoly led by Sir Giles Mompesson was one of the controversial monopolies that sparked outrage in the 1621 Parliament.[129] Given the importance of consolidating supporters, the restored government had ample reasons to consider rewarding petitioners by granting requested patents.

Yet there were risks to be taken into account, as the fervour of the Restoration hardly dissipated public suspicion of the projector. While receiving requests for patents that could be controversial, the government was given no excuse to ignore this. A song published anonymously in 1662, *The new projector*, satirized monopolists who procured patents for 'discovery of all that I knew...with Dice, Drink, and Drabb [salt-making]'. Its satirical power was directed squarely at petitioners like Bushell, who, having cooperated with the regicides, later fell on their knees for royal protection:

Godly Kingship in Restoration England: The Politics of the Royal Supremacy, 1660–1688 (Cambridge: Cambridge University Press, 2011).

[124] TNA, SP 29/21, fol. 48.

[125] TNA, SP 29/23, fol. 144 (quotation); SP 29/24, fol. 38. See also a copy of the letter of appointment for the Council of Trade of 1668 sent to the Earl of Bridgewater, HEH, EL 8509, fol. 2.

[126] *CSPD 1660–1661*, pp. 289, 374–8, 452.

[127] *CSPD 1629–1631*, p. 466; *CSPD 1660–1661*, pp. 384, 391; *CTB, vol. 1, 1660–1667*, p. 31. See also Gough, *Bushell*, pp. 19–20, 22.

[128] *CSPD 1660–1661*, p. 385; Thomas Brugis, *The discovery of a proiector* (1641), p. 20 [*recte* p. 26].

[129] MacLeod, *Patent*, p. 32; Scott, *Joint-Stock*, vol. 1, p. 176.

> I am a Projector that alwaies have thriv'd
> by Sideing with every Faction; ...
> The Bonfires and Ringing, did usher the King in,
> which alter'd the *Zealots* complexion;
> Thought I, the Kings Party will be very strong
> And therefore Ile turn and be for him ding dong,
> For I by my subtlety ere it be long,
> *shall get me a cheating protection.*[130]

Earlier records and writings against the projector also continued to circulate while Jacobean plays were being staged. Pepys owned the first volume of John Rushworth's *Historical Collections*, published in 1659, which included records about the Parliament of 1621 and the condemnation of Mompesson over patents for inns and silver thread; on Christmas Day 1663, Pepys found himself absorbed by the volume, noting in his diary that it was 'a most excellent collection of the beginning of the late quarrels in this kingdom'.[131] The naval officer later acquired subsequent volumes of *Collections* (published from 1680 onwards), which contained the parliamentary speeches of November 1640 against Caroline projectors.[132] Thanks to his diary we also know that Pepys read Jonson's *The Devil is an Ass* on his way to Deptford in July 1663; a year and a half later, he went to King's House in Drury Lane to see Jonson's *Volpone*, which he noted was 'a most excellent play—the best I think I ever saw'. The latter play, in fact, had been performed at Charles II's court in October 1662. The two plays offer comical, yet critical depictions of projectors.[133] In 1665, borrowing heavily from Thomas Brugis's *Discovery of the proiector* (1641), John Wilson published a play entitled *The projectors*—another play that Pepys added to his library.[134] The Oxford antiquarian and historian Anthony Wood too had a copy of Brugis's *Discovery*, and made a good use of it. He used it as the first item for binding his pamphlets on improvement, including Evelyn's *Fumifugium* (1661) and Haines's *A method of government for...publick working almshouses* (1670). This was the result of his 'elaborate care in bringing together items on similar topics'. Evelyn and Haines would have been disturbed to find this.[135]

---

[130] *The new projector; or the privileged cheat* [1662?]. Compare this with John Taylor, *The complaint of M. Tenter-hooke the proiector, and Sir Thomas Dodger the patentee* (1641).

[131] His copy of the first volume of *Collections* is Pepys Library, Magdalene College, Cambridge, PL 2386 (pp. 27–8 on Mompesson); the diarist's reading experience is discussed by Kate Loveman, *Samuel Pepys and his Books: Reading, Newsgathering, and Sociability, 1660–1703* (Oxford: Oxford University Press, 2015), pp. 114–16 (quotation at p. 116).

[132] Pepys Library, PL 2387–2393.

[133] Samuel Pepys, *The Diary of Samuel Pepys*, ed. Robert Latham and William Matthews (11 vols., London: Bell, 1970), vol. 4, p. 240, 22 July 1663; ibid., vol. 6, p. 10, 14 January 1665; John Evelyn, *The Diary of John Evelyn*, ed. E. S. de Beer (6 vols., Oxford: Clarendon, repr. 2000), vol. 3, p. 341, 16 October 1662. See also pp. 82–3 above for my analysis of Jonson's *The Devil is an Ass*.

[134] John Wilson, *The projectors. A comedy* (1665); Pepys's copy is Pepys Library, PL 1604(6). The play is discussed by Jessica Ratcliff, '"Art to Cheat the Common-weal": Inventors, Projectors, and Patentees in English Satire, ca. 1630–70', *Technology and Culture*, 53 (2012), 337–65, pp. 351–6.

[135] Bodl., Wood, D. 27(5), Anthony Wood's bound pamphlets; Nicholas K. Kiessling (ed.), *The Library of Anthony Wood* (Oxford: Oxford Bibliographical Society, 2002), pp. xxv (quotation), 678. Binding practices of this kind were not uncommon. Hartlibean *A design for plenty* and other improvement literature published before 1660 were bound together with a polemical tract against the

With earlier writings, bitter memories of early Stuart projectors and monopolies continued to circulate. As Paulina Kewes has suggested, 'from the early 1660s onward the slightest hint of political unrest immediately provoked cries from loyalists that "1641 is come again" '.[136] The same memory was invoked to issue warnings to the government. Even a royalist propagandist did not shrink from reminding Charles II that 'we remember' how his father had caused 'Cries' by breaching 'our free-born Interest':

> We remember, that in the Beginning of our late transcendent [Long] Parliament ... how high the Cries went against Ship-money, Patents, Monopolies, illegal Imprisonments, and such other Breaches into our free-born Interests[.][137]

Others went further. *Vox et lacrimae anglorum; or the true Englishmen's complaints to their representatives in parliament* made a problematic link between the granting of controversial patents and the outbreak of 'that Domestic War':

> Tread all monopolies into the earth
> And make provision that no more get birth,
> In this a prince's danger chiefly lies,
> That he is forced to see with others' eyes,
> From hence our troubles rose in Forty One
> When that Domestic War at first began.

Though addressed to parliament, a copy of this pamphlet has been found among the state papers; it was perhaps sent to the government as a potentially subversive warning.[138] The restored government probably received more of such warnings than they would have liked, and some of these were unsettling. In 1664, when several applications for monopolies were being considered, the government received an anonymous letter. It warned against covetous courtiers 'under your majesties wing', who 'sell all places of Trust ... [being] Earnest for projects patents & new inventions till the kingdome bee impoverisht & the Prince hated'.[139] Julius Caesar, the letter added, was assassinated because he ignored a letter of warning coming into his hand. Would the restored king repeat the same mistake by ignoring *this* letter of warning? The anonymous author was drawing here on the climax of Plutarch's *Life of Caesar*—an influential story repeatedly reprinted during the seventeenth century.[140] Even a ballad, printed to praise the king's

---

Westminster Soap monopoly, *A short and trve relation concering the Soap-busines* (1641). See Wren Library, Trinity College, Cambridge, VI.9.111[14–17], and the inner board with a table of contents in a seventeenth-century hand.

[136] Paulina Kewes, 'History and its Uses: Introduction', in Paulina Kewes (ed.), *The Uses of History in Early Modern England* (Berkeley, CA: University of California Press, 2006), 1–30, p. 18.

[137] 'Awake o England', p. 269.

[138] TNA, SP 29/234/85, *Vox et lacrimae anglorum; or the true Englishmen's complaints to their representatives in parliament* (1668), p. 11.

[139] TNA, SP 29/99, fols. 24–24v (at fol. 24v). See also a similar warning at University of London Special Collection, MS 202, fol. 1v.

[140] See Plutarch, *The lives of the noble Grecians & Romans compared together*, tr. Thomas North (1657), p. 614. For background, see Freyja Cox Jensen, *Reading the Roman Republic in Early Modern England* (Leiden: Brill, 2012).

return, voiced a similar warning by singing that 'We[']l toil no more to maintain Patentees | That feed upon poor peoples trade…How joyful shall we be.' 'Englands Joy' was conditional, it was implied, upon careful management of courtiers and would-be patentees.[141] Now we are in a position to establish the typicality of the petitionary appeals against the Stour river navigation bill of 1661, which we studied in Chapter 4. Despite the Act of General Pardon and Oblivion, the spectre of early Stuart projecting continued to circulate through theatre plays, songs, pamphlets, and manuscripts, reminding the government that it was in its interest to avoid restoring old, vexatious practices.

While facing a flood of requests for reviving monopolies and other projects, then, the restored regime had good reasons to reject them. Some statesmen offered just such advice. Shortly after the Third Anglo-Dutch War (1672–4), a proposal was submitted to the government propounding 'Reasons for his Ma[jes]tie's ingrossing the Newcastle Coale trade'. It proposed to appoint a commissioner on the king's behalf to buy and selectively introduce Dutch flyboats currently not used in the English coal trade in order 'to worke others out of the trade' by selling coals 'so cheap'. This technology transfer and its competitive use would enable the king to 'quickly rayse him what mony he pleases' to the value of £250,000 yearly. On the back of the proposal is a hand written note by the Thomas Osborne, then the Lord High Treasurer: 'Coale trade. A Proposall made to the King of w[hi]ch I show'd him both the inconvenience & the danger wherupon itt was reiected.' Here we see clearly how a statesman counselled the king and had him reject a scheme for setting up a de facto monopoly because of its political danger (see Illustration 5.1).[142] As Anthony Ashley Cooper put it, it was crucial to 'manage the King's Justice and Revenue, as the King have most *Profit*, and the Subject least *Vexation*'.[143]

It was not always easy, however, to achieve the balance—to evaluate potential fiscal benefits of the requested grant and the need to reward particular petitioners, while weighing such factors against the political risks involved. In such cases, the monarch and his Privy Council took pains to gather information, solicit advice, weigh up alternatives, and evaluate eventualities. Such a process of counsel 'in action' is well captured in the richly documented case of John Garill's abortive application for a patent on silver wire drawing.

Garill's scheme emerged in response to the long-standing concern of the government about 'scarcity of money', an issue which was underlined by a proclamation of 1661 alongside 'many irregularities and abuses' practised in the making of 'Gold and Silver Wyer, Gold and Silver Threed, Spangles, Ones, Purles and Lace, &c'.[144]

---

[141] *Englands joy for the coming in of our gracious soveraign King Charles the second to the tune of, a joyful sight to see* [1660].

[142] Beinecke Library, Yale University, OSB MSS 6, Box 2, folder 30, 'Reasons for his Ma[jes]tie's ingrossing the Newcastle Coale trade, with the Method for doeing it' [n.d., 1674–5?], endorsement.

[143] *The lord chancellor's speech in the Exchequer, to Baron Thurland at the taking of his oath, 24 Jan 1672/3* (1673), pp. 3–4. Cooper's counsel was later copied and published in 1691. See T[homas] H[ale], *An account of several new inventions and improvements now necessary for England* (1691), pp. lxxiii–lxxiv.

[144] *By the king. A proclamation against exportation, and buying and selling of gold and silver at higher rates then in our Mint* (1661).

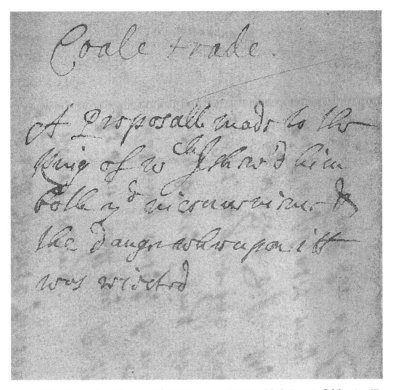

Illustration 5.1. Beinecke Library, Yale University, OSB MSS 6, Box 2, folder 30, 'Reasons for his Ma[jes]tie's ingrossing the Newcastle Coale trade, with the Method for doeing it' [n.d., 1674–5?], endorsement

Courtesy of The Beinecke Rare Book and Manuscript Library, Yale University

Garill was one of those who petitioned on this issue in 1663 to prevent abuses and waste in the production of silver and gold wire.[145]

What Garill asked for was not an overt monopoly covering the whole industry of wire drawing, but protection, for fourteen years, of his invention for 'Casting and preparing Gold and Silver Ingotte', designed for better 'preservac[i]on and increase of the Bullion'. This application was reported favourably by Lord Treasurer Southampton: Garill's invention 'would preserve and increase bullion', and thus 'redound to the public profit'.[146] A warrant for his patent was accordingly drawn in December 1663.[147] The government might have found attractive Garill's promise to reduce the loss of silver in the manufacturing process, and to pay the Exchequer 5 per cent of the value of all the silver and gold wire he would draw.[148]

---

[145] Garill's petition, 23 October 1663, TNA, SP 29/82, fol. 45; other petitions are filed at TNA, SP 29/68, fols. 216–17. For background, see Horace Stewart, *History of the Worshipful Company of Gold and Silver Wyre-Drawers* (London: Leadenhall Press, 1891), pp. 48–56.

[146] TNA, SP 29/82, fols. 45–45v. Southampton's report is written on the back of Garill's petition.

[147] Ibid., fol. 30.   [148] TNA, PC 2/57, p. 204.

Yet, before the Great Seal of the monarch was granted, the government received reports about one wire-drawer, Simon Urlin, living in Gutter Lane near St Paul's, 'reputed a very honest Man'. Urlin reportedly held a 'publique meeting in the said lane' and demanded that others of the same trade 'should stand to oppose the same', proclaiming 'in passion' that 'Granting Such Patents was the Cause…that the last King lost his head'.[149] The government faced a striking invocation, by an artisan, of Caroline projects and their alleged consequence.

Several petitions against the proposed patent followed. The Privy Council soon summoned Garill and the other parties concerned, including the Mint, the Company of Goldsmiths, and the 'same Wyre drawers who did formerly oppose his Patent'— an allusion perhaps to Urlin and his fellow wire-drawers. Garill was required to send 'Copies of his Petic[i]on' to those who objected to the move so that they would 'have timely notice to prepare' their counterarguments.[150]

Their petitions and memoranda, recorded in Privy Council minutes in unusual detail, reveal that the history of earlier projects loomed large in the consultation process that took place in the council chamber.[151] One memorandum, coming probably from Urlin and his fellow wire-drawers, likened Garill's patent to that of Sir Giles Mompesson's wire-drawing monopoly four decades earlier. It was alleged that Garill's proposed invention might well be 'the same [as what] Mompesson practiced'. Mompesson and his patents, it added, were condemned by the 1621 parliament. The memorandum further opposed Garill's application by citing Chapter 85 of Coke's influential *Third part of the institutes of the laws of England* (1644), a short chapter on the 1624 Statute of Monopolies that was entitled 'Against Monopolists, Propounders, and Projectors'. The ambiguous wording of Garill's proposed patent, it was alleged, could be used as a pretext to 'Ingrosse the whole Trade of Wyre drawing; w[hi]ch will be hartfull to Trade, & deprive many hundreds of their Labour and Livelyhood; and is therefore within the Stat[ute] of Monopolies: Cooke 3 Inst: 184'.[152] Another 'Representac[i]on of the Gold & Silver Wyre drawers' made the implication very clear:

> the sole buying, selling, making, working or using of any thing, whereby any of his Ma[jes]t[y']s Subjects are restrayned of the Freedome or Liberty they had before, or hindered in their Lawfull Trade, Is against Magn[a] Chart[a]; Vide Cooke upon the Statute of Monopolies Cap 85, fol:181[.][153]

Notice that the same section of Coke's *Third part of the institutes of the laws of England*, originally published in 1644, was cited once again. Did petitioners mention Coke to Charles II's Privy Council with the full knowledge that his royal father had once had the lawyer's papers seized, only to be later retrieved and printed by parliamentarians? Was the restored monarch duly reminded that the Long

---

[149] TNA, SP 29/93, fols. 82, 83. Two reports, one of them dated 27 February 1664.

[150] TNA, PC 2/57, p. 174 (3 August 1664); p. 181 (10 August 1664).

[151] Ibid., pp. 204–13 (31 August 1664).

[152] Ibid., p. 210; the edition mentioned is Edward Coke, *The third part of the institutes of the laws of England* (1660), pp. 181, 184.

[153] TNA, PC 2/57, p. 212.

Parliament voted for the publication of Coke's *Institutes* on 12 May 1641, on the very day his father's closest advisor, Thomas Wentworth, was beheaded?[154] Some of these connections might have been accidental, but their significance might not have escaped some privy councillors then attending the restored monarch. One of them, the Duke of Ormond, worked in the 1630s under Wentworth, then lord deputy of Ireland. Another councillor present, the earl of Clarendon, sat in the Commons during the Long Parliament; he might well have been the 'Mr Hide' who had been appointed by the Long Parliament on 5 December 1640 to rescue Coke's papers.[155] In the council chamber in Whitehall—a stone's throw from the Banqueting House, in front of which Charles I had been publicly executed—the recent past invoked by Urlin and many other petitioners was truly a *lived* experience. Historians seeking to explore the unfolding of post-Restoration political economy in its context must be alive to such disconcerting layers of significance.

Of course, we do not have to assume that early Stuart precedents and the memory of the recent past were the sole factors taken into royal consideration. Technical objections raised by the Mint and the Goldsmiths' Company about the feasibility of Garill's proposed invention probably mattered as much. Even after receiving these, moreover, a special committee appointed by the Privy Council asked Garill 'to reveale his Secret unto them, under their Oath of Secrecy'. The government thus did not immediately dismiss an application that *could* prove fiscally beneficial; yet the negotiations seem to have failed, as Garill refused to divulge his invention, demanding that the Great Seal be passed first.[156] The following year we find Garill harassing his opponents, 'not resting in his Ma[jes]ties Judgment and determination concerning his Project of Silver Wyer'.[157] The case of Garill reminds us that the restored government had a keen interest in augmenting revenue, and for that purpose was not averse to considering granting patents that could turn out to be monopolistic. Yet, instead of turning a blind eye to opposition, the Privy Council went a long way towards weighing up the fiscal benefits against the political risks involved. Upon receiving technical advice from the Mint and the Goldsmiths' Company, and upon facing vocal criticisms invoking Mompesson, the Statute of Monopolies, Coke's commentary, Charles I's Personal Rule, and his eventual demise, the restored regime stopped short of granting the requested patent.

Garill's case epitomizes a pattern of consultation more broadly. The Restoration government restored and, upon request, even extended monopolies and other privileges granted to trading companies for overseas trade. Yet, when the government received a petition complaining of the abuse of a patent on steel-making, the Privy

---

[154] *CJ*, vol. 2, p. 144; Thomas Wentworth, *The last speeches of Thomas Wentworth* (1641).

[155] TNA, PC 2/57, p. 195 (a list of attendees for the council meeting of 31 August 1664); *CJ*, vol. 2, p. 45.

[156] We can also take another factor into account. Among the special committees for the Garill case were Prince Rupert and the Duke of Buckingham. Rupert was interested in gunnery and metallurgy, and soon to be a FRS, and 'censured.... [for] giving encouragements to projectors'. Buckingham was at that time covertly involved in a monopoly for glass production. No wonder they were mindful of the risks involved in granting the requested patent. See John Campbell, *Lives of the British Admirals* (4 vols., London: Murray, 1785), vol. 2, p. 250 (quotation); MacLeod, *Patent*, pp. 25–6.

[157] TNA, PC 2/58, p. 152, 26 May 1665.

Council summoned and questioned the patentees; the patent was then revoked.[158] Other potentially controversial cases were treated with similar caution.[159] In general, the restored monarch was ready, or at least keen to appear ready, to judge upon considering petitions and grievances, and to reassure the country that 'the king would not sacrifice economic well-being to the whims and pockets of his courtiers'.[160] The Restoration administration of patents was, then, neither dictated by concerted policies imposed from above nor determined by collective memories of the previous decades alone. Nor was the overall trend decided by independent institutional changes taking place outside the administrative procedures. Garill's and others' requests might well have passed the Great Seal were it not for the vociferous interventions of likes of Urlin, wire-drawers, and the Mint. The politics of public interventions that we have found in the case of the Stour navigation bill were hardly unique or limited to the parliamentary sphere. If the patent system ultimately did not revert to the situation before the Civil Wars despite the restoration of prerogative, it owed much to numerous visible hands intervening in the politics of counsel, processes negotiated by petitioners and their opponents as well as by the privy councillors, mediated by multimedia circulation of the memories about, and judgements passed upon, early Stuart projectors.

PROJECTS OUTSIDE THE PATENT SYSTEM: FOUR CASE STUDIES

The changing priorities that we have found in inland navigation (in Chapter 4) and the patent system (in the preceding section) were symptomatic of a wider pattern across other spheres of projecting. Not only did applications for monopolistic patents fail; so did other kinds of proposals that appeared to involve avoidable infringements upon subjects' rights, liberties, and properties. The restored regime's extreme sensitivity on this issue is encapsulated in the ill fate of Valentine Knight's proposal in the immediate aftermath of the 1666 Great Fire of London. The disaster necessitated the extensive rebuilding of the City, and Knight responded with an audacious rebuilding plan.[161] Instead of restoring the narrow streets that had spread across the City, he proposed to rebuild 'stately with large Streets, [and] the Houses not in danger of Fire'. Moreover, Knight proposed to raise £223,517 'towards the maintenance of his [majesty's] Forces by Sea and Land' by imposing fines on defaulters.[162] Thus, in both town planning and the imposition of penalties, he would

---

[158] MacLeod, *Patent*, pp. 32, 27. See also a case of framework knitters and the importation of the laxative senna in Brian Weiser, *Charles II and the Politics of Access* (Woodbridge: Boydell, 2003), pp. 128–9; Leng, *Worsley*, pp. 143–5.

[159] See Weiser, *Politics of Access*, pp. 126–7 and *passim*; MacLeod, *Patent*, p. 28.

[160] Weiser, *Politics of Access*, p. 121. On this point, see also an earlier observation by F. J. Fisher, 'Some Experiments in Company Organization in the Early Seventeenth Century', *EcHR*, 4 (1933), 177–94, at pp. 180–1.

[161] For background, see Walter George Bell, *The Great Fire of London in 1666* (London: John Lane, 1920), pp. 241–2.

[162] Valentine Knight, *Proposals of a new model for re-building the City of London* (1666), one-page handbill. Knight was to collect rent and fines and keep an 8 per cent premium for himself.

have required extensive authority and mechanisms of enforcement. Knight showed this proposal to privy councillors. They apparently 'seemed to like the same' and Knight was 'encouraged to print some of them for his friend'.[163]

Knight's fortune plunged when one stationer 'Unadvisedly' published it, perhaps very widely. As a result, Knight was imprisoned for his 'misdemeano[u]rs'.[164] Probably being aware of the handbill's wide circulation, the official *London Gazette* publicized Knight's imprisonment, and thereby distanced the king from the proposal. Knight was punished, the paper announced, because his proposal promised 'considerable advantages to His Majesties Revenue', and thereby made it seem 'as if…his Majesty would draw a benefit from so public a calamity of his people, of which his Majesty is known to have so deep sense, that he is please to seek rather by all means to give them ease under it [i.e. his reign]'. Knight was released before long, but he seems to have never ventured into the world of printing again.[165] The privy councillors had shown interest, perhaps because of the royal debts piling up from Charles I's reign.[166] But such an interest ought not to be made public, for the restored king had to be 'known to have so deep sense' of his subjects' peace and happiness, true to his Declaration of Breda. Knight's imprisonment thus tells us more than his personal disaster: as in the administration of royal patents, the king and his government could not afford to be seen as imposing their authority to levy fines, let alone for extracting Crown revenues.

Given this striking readiness of the restored government to distance itself from the potentially divisive imposition of fines, it is little wonder that Dymock, the former protégé of Hartlib, failed to find a ready supporter when he proposed a project for nationwide agricultural improvement that could cause vexation. In 1668, he printed and distributed a handbill appealing for investors for his 'New and better ART of AGRICULTURE'. It was probably his first publication after the Restoration. He still seemingly remained convinced of his capacity to achieve a *cornucopia*. If his method was applied nationwide, he proclaimed, 'in all Submission to Gods Will…the Kingdom would be enriched [£] 24,000,000 every year more than in the common way'.[167] In order to realize it, Dymock would have had to enforce his method upon all the tilled land across the country, something that would be controversial.

Hartlib and Dury would have entertained such a scheme lest God's will should manifest through the improbable. But with Hartlib being dead and Dury in exile, Dymock was no longer well connected after the Restoration. In 1661 he helped Lord Brereton, later a member of the Royal Society's 'Georgical Committee', to survey his estate in Cheshire, but Dymock did not become a Fellow or a close contributor to the committee's activity, as Austen did.[168] As we saw earlier, Beale recommended to the Society not to republish Dymock's earlier writing. John Evelyn, too, received a rather negative report on the projector. In 1667, Dymock was in

---

[163] TNA, PC 2/59, fol. 189.
[164] Ibid., fol. 189. Jenner, 'Print Culture and the Rebuilding', pp. 14–15.
[165] *London Gazette*, 91, 27 September 1666; Jenner, 'Print Culture and the Rebuilding', pp. 15–16 (n. 75).
[166] See p. 36.   [167] [Dymock], *New and better art of agriculture*.
[168] *AHEW Vii*, p. 562.

Oxford, apparently offering a course on experimental philosophy 'to the young gentlemen in 15 days'. Ralph Bohun of Trinity College, who tutored John Evelyn the younger, was hardly impressed. He noted that Dymock was 'decry[ing] Aristotle & pretend[ing] as [if] it were to inspiration in philosophy'. Bohun reassured Evelyn that 'I play not thus the mountebank with y[ou]r Sonn...since I believe you [to be] too knowing in natural philosophy to be impos'd upon by any such artifice.'[169] Dymock's 1668 proposal reflected his relative isolation. Instead of dedicating the proposal to specific patrons or to the Royal Society, his handbill appealed indiscriminately to the king and parliament, knights, bishops, merchants, and to 'all others whatsoever that shall think fit to be concerned therein any way'—evidently without much success.

Among the Boyle Papers at the Royal Society is Dymock's petitionary memorandum of 1678—ten years after the handbill of 1668—which captures the difficulty and frustration that Dymock had faced over the years. Emphasizing '37 yeares faithful services' to 'my King and Country', Dymock beseeched:

> Now if after all this it bee the will of God, any my Soveraingne & my Native countrye, that the reward of all my ever faithfull services...must bee *not to bee understood and believed*, but to bee lost to perish and [sterve?], God will be done, I must submitt thereto[.][170]

Here, then, was a somewhat exaggerated grievance of a projector who went on airing grandiose schemes despite the absence of his former millenarian supporters. Unlike Boyle, Austen, and others, this former Hartlibean did not swim as well with the stream—an indication that the direction of historical change was in no way evident to all.

Even exalted natural philosophers could face similar disappointment and frustration, as is shown in the case of William Petty. This might come as a surprise, given his career and the lasting legacy of his ideas. For sure, Petty did ply his trade in more mundane technical inventions such as the 'double-writing engine', as we have already seen; in February 1664, Charles II was famously reported 'laughing at' another of Petty's inventions, the 'double-bottomed' boat.[171] Yet, by the 1670s, grander ideas came to emerge—what Petty called 'political arithmetic'. Under this rubric, he became the first to calculate the national annual income and expenditure of any nation by combining population estimates, wage rates, and tax returns among other key variables. Such macroeconomic analysis was combined with the consideration of

---

[169] BL, Add. MS 78314, fols. 16–21v 'Mr Bohune Concerning the Institution of my Son', [22 April?] 1667, at fol. 16. Aristotelian philosophy continued to play a vital role in natural philosophy training in this period. On this and Bohun's position, see Mordechai Feingold, 'The Mathematical Sciences and New Philosophies', in Nicholas Tyacke (ed.), *The History of the University of Oxford, Volume VI: Seventeenth-Century Oxford* (Oxford, 1997), 359–449, esp. pp. 401, 432; Dmitri Levitin, *Ancient Wisdom in the Age of New Science: Histories of Philosophy in England, c. 1640–1670* (Cambridge: Cambridge University Press, 2015), pp. 313–28, esp. p. 326 n. 494.

[170] RS, RB/1/40/28, fol. 92, Dymock to [?], 16 January 1678 [my emphasis]. No response has been found to this appeal.

[171] Pepys, *Diary*, vol. 5, pp. 25 n. 1, 32. For a detailed discussion of the episode, see McCormick, *Petty*, pp. 152–6.

the division of labour, household consumption, and the long-term impact on national wealth. His more specific proposals, ranging from trade, manufacture, a land registry, and taxation to ecclesiastical government, became part of the wider programme for transforming England and its overseas possessions.[172] The sheer scale and ambition of Petty's writings have certainly made him much more than a 'superintendent of Manufacturs, & improvement of Trade', as Evelyn once called him.[173]

Petty's genius, however, hardly extricated him from contemporary norms and expectations. To understand why, we only have to look into his proposals for mass migration, which proved just as controversial as they were crucial for his grand designs. Drawing on earlier thinking by Bacon and Hobbes, Petty viewed population increase as a taproot of national strength.[174] Never being an abstract thinker, he developed his views on population as a means to promote his policy interventions, especially on Ireland. Of particular importance during the 1670s was an ambitious scheme, inspired partly by alchemy, for 'transmuting' the Irish into the English. It was a plan that involved forced migration of English Protestant women to Ireland, who, by marrying poor Catholic Irish men, would turn future generations of Irish into more civilized, obedient, English subjects.[175] After the accession of the Catholic James II in 1685, Petty came to promote another set of mass migration schemes, this time of Irish inhabitants into England in order to increase the Catholic population in line with the confessional identity of the new monarch.[176] The most extensive of these proposals, 'A Treatise of Ireland' (1687), promised thereby to effect the 'Natural Union of both Kingdoms and Peoples'.[177]

These were ambitious schemes, and Petty sought to win support by circulating manuscript proposals through friends like Robert Southwell to a handful of powerful patrons. This was a conscious shift from the publication of his writings that he had tried in the late 1640s, and again between the Restoration and the mid-1670s.[178] By the end of that decade, his preference was to send his potential patrons short 'heads' of topics; indeed, about 75 per cent of the Petty Papers written under James II were of between one and two folio pages (300 out of 400 items dated 1685–7).[179]

---

[172] For overviews of Petty's political arithmetic, see Adam Fox, 'Sir William Petty, Ireland, and the Making of a Political Economist, 1653–87', *EcHR*, 62 (2009), 388–404; Slack, *Invention of Improvement*, pp. 116–28; on Petty's natural philosophy, see McCormick, *Petty*, pp. 175–85, 218–23; for a longer exposition of Petty's proposals under James II, see Sue Dale, 'Sir William Petty's "Ten Tooles": A Programme for the Transformation of England and Ireland during the Reign of James II', (PhD thesis, Birkbeck, 2014), chs. 4–7.

[173] Evelyn, *Diary*, vol. 4, p. 58. Cf. Slack, *Invention of Improvement*, p. 128.

[174] Fox, 'Petty', p. 394; Slack, *Invention of Improvement*, pp. 120, 124, 198.

[175] McCormick, *Petty*, pp. 185–205.

[176] Dale, 'Petty', pp. 299–312; McCormick, *Petty*, pp. 256–8.

[177] William Petty, *The Economic Writings of Sir William Petty*, ed. Charles Henry Hull (2 vols., Cambridge: Cambridge University Press, 1899), vol. 2, pp. 545–621, at p. 557.

[178] For his positions in the 1650s and 1660s, see William Petty, *A treatise of taxes and contributions* (1662), sig. [A3]; McCormick, *Petty*, p. 261; Koji Yamamoto, 'Reformation and the Distrust of the Projector in the Hartlib Circle', *HJ*, 55 (2012), 375–97, pp. 394–5.

[179] The percentage is based on the Petty Papers held at the British Library, excluding letters, estate papers, and survey maps. See Dale, 'Petty', p. 94, 104. The locations of Petty's other papers are set out in Rhodri Lewis, *William Petty on the Order of Nature: An Unpublished Manuscript Treatise* (Tempe, AZ: Arizona Center for Medieval and Renaissance Studies, 2012), pp. viii–ix.

Upon patrons' request, Petty would then expound these 'heads' in person at greater length, tailoring his proposals to suit his patrons' interests.[180]

Even this change of tactics did not win him sustained support for the mass migration schemes. Responding to his 1687 proposal, one reader pointed out that, in order to integrate Irish settlers, landowners in England 'must bee forced to sell' their lands at a price not advantageous to them.[181] Noticing the risk of expropriation in England, the perceptive reader pithily noted: 'How practicable?'[182] Elsewhere, Petty presented his 1687 proposal as a means to 'take away all the Evils arising from Differences' that existed across the Irish Channel, 'of Births, Extractions, Languages, Manners, Customs, Religion, and Laws, and Pretence whatsoever'. To achieve this, he suggested that Irish immigrants, as well as place names in Ireland, might 'have English Names put upon them'. The foregoing commentator was not convinced: 'The transplantees will not take English names—No Nation was ever contented to lose it selfe by relinquishing the name, distinction &c'.[183] Unlike Dymock, then, Petty (who began as a clothier's son) became so well connected by the 1670s that he was able to seek patronage without printing or publishing his proposals. Even so, it was not possible to implement the kind of social engineering that required drastic interventions in demographic structure on both sides of the Irish Sea.[184]

This was not, however, how Petty explained the limited success of his proposals. While Petty saw himself standing above the flock of common projectors, he was acutely aware that his proposals might be dismissed just like other, lesser projects. Such concerns about distrust were already visible when he first approached the Duke of Ormond shortly after the Restoration. Note how confident self-presentation betrayed undertones of anxiety:

> I do not appear a projector to shark for my necessities nor because the newness of my thoughts hath intoxicated me, but because I have so often slept with them...I have the courage to venture being laughed at once more.[185]

The lack of support could be accordingly attributed to the misconception of those who, taking the negative stereotype at face value, laughed at his proposals as mere conjectures typical of projectors. When Petty wrote a manuscript note 'Of Ridicule', he might well have been reflecting upon his own experience of distrust:

> Men of adventitious [i.e. incidental] & contingent eminence do fear...intrinsick & inherent vertue, and doe express their hatred by counterfeiting contempt, their contempt

---

[180] For the 'scribal publication' of Petty's writing, see McCormick, *Petty*, ch. 7, esp. pp. 269–72; Lewis, *Petty*, pp. 13–19.

[181] BL, Add. MS 72886, f.86.

[182] Ibid., f.86.

[183] Petty, *Economic Writing*, vol. 2, p. 568; BL, Add. MS 72886, f.86. His earlier 'The Political Anatomy of Ireland' (1672, published 1691) also attracted a critical response: see BL, Add. MS21127, fols. 53–4v; Dale, 'Petty', pp. 281–2.

[184] On the failure of Petty's recommendations, see also McCormick, *Petty*, p. 276; Dale, 'Petty', pp. 319–22; Toby Barnard, *Improving Ireland? Projectors, Prophets and Profiteers, 1641–1786* (Dublin: Four Courts Press, 2008), pp. 42, 69–70.

[185] HMC, *Calendar of Manuscripts of the Marquis of Ormonde*, vol. 3, p. 11. My reading here nuances that of McCormick, *Petty*, p 280, which foregrounds Petty's confidence and disinterestedness.

by counterfeit laugher, & the laugher of many together makes the thing laught at Ridicule [i.e. ridiculous][.][186]

Far from surrendering drastic policy interventions, Petty thus continued his efforts, tirelessly answering objections while privately venting his anger upon those who failed to appreciate the inherent virtue of his proposals. Even in 1687, just months before his death, Petty fiercely defended his transplantation scheme, adding sarcastically that it 'will Confirm the world in the opinion…that he is a person excessively Phantasticall and very drunk with his own Imaginations'.[187] His 'propensity to self-pity', which many scholars have noted, was most probably indicative of the subtle influence of distrust. Like many others, Petty read ridicule and stereotyping into others' reservations; in doing so, Petty misconstrued the nature of his own failure: his transplantation schemes were never implemented not so much because of the unthinking, envious mistrust of his chosen audience, but rather because such policies would have required radical social engineering that was no longer deemed feasible in the climate of post-Restoration England.[188] His intellectual rigour and his networks, backed by a comforting misattribution of blame, enabled him to swim against the emerging pattern of practices that we have been exploring in this chapter. This was how political arithmetic became a strong intellectual current in its own right. This 'art of reasoning by figures, upon things relating to government', as Charles Davenant succinctly defined it, would continue to thrive in the coming centuries, with profound consequences.[189]

An immediate question remained unresolved, however: how could potentially beneficial schemes be implemented without coercion or risking infringements upon subjects' rights and liberties? Parliamentary debates over hemp and flax cultivation are revealing in this regard. Bills to enforce the cultivation of these commercial crops were lodged in the Commons in 1662, 1663, 1664, and 1665, followed by yet another in 1670, and then in 1677 and 1678.[190] As in the Stour case, the *Commons Journals* do not contain much information about the actual debates that took place on the floor. Yet, for the bill considered in 1677, we have some records of lively discussion. Colonel Birch, the proposer of the bill, argued that it was vital to oblige subjects to plant these crops if profitable employment was to be created in the countryside to prevent rural depopulation and the decay of agriculture.[191] Yet striking opposition was voiced against the case for compulsion. Mr Swinfen

---

[186] *Petty Papers*, vol. 2, pp. 193–8, at p. 196. See also ibid., vol. 1, pp. 157–8; Lewis, *William Petty on the Order of Nature*, p. 120 n. 84.

[187] BL, Add. MS 72886, '17 Objections against the Essay about the Settlem[en]t of Ireland' [Petty's summary of others' objections], fols. 87–90, at fol. 90 (another copy of the same is at fols. 91–92v).

[188] McCormick, *Petty*, pp. 261, 263 (quotation); Lewis, *William Petty on the Order of Nature*, p. 17; Dale, 'Petty', p. 71. See pp. 26, 104, 223, 256–7, 260–1 (this book) for similar complaints.

[189] Slack, *Invention of Improvement*, p. 116 (quotation), 225–6; Joanna Innes, *Inferior Politics: Social Problems and Social Policies in Eighteenth-Century Britain* (Oxford: Oxford University Press, 2009), pp. 142–50, 172–5; Ted McCormick, 'Who Were the Pre-Malthusians?', in Robert J. Mayhew (ed.), *New Perspectives on Malthus* (Cambridge: Cambridge University Press, 2016), 25–51, pp. 33–41.

[190] *AHEW Vii*, pp. 339–40.

[191] William Cobbett (ed.), *Parliamentary History* (36 vols., London: Hansard, 1806–20), vol. 4, col. 835.

argued that 'If there be any profit in planting hemp and flax, there needs no law to compel men to it, but that of necessity, all ways else failing.... If it were for their advantage, men would turn all their lands to it.' If the statute was to compel plant-ing where no profit was forthcoming, then, he continued, the resulting act might end up being 'an universal penalty'—'Can this then help the poor, or the farmers, who, by this law, must groan under the penalties?' George Downing was more sympathetic to the tenor of the bill, but was 'utterly against the imposing the half acre in a 100 acres to be planted...under a penalty'. In a phrase that summarizes the underlying problem of so many of the projects for economic improvement, he demanded: 'Consider what this charitable pretence of relieving the poor has been.' Sir William Coventry agreed; his 'only material objection is, the compulsory parts of the bill'. He 'would have the committee think of an inducement and encourage-ment to do it, as well as compulsion'.[192] With no agreement on what such inducements would be, the bill lapsed.

Taken together, the failed legislation for disseminating hemp and flax cultivation, as well as the frustration, and even demise, of promoters such as Dymock, Knight, and Petty, bear witness to changing priorities in England's culture of projecting—what could and could not be permitted in the pursuit of improvement. Note that our findings are different from what Slack has described as the emergence in this period of the 'morality of cooperation' built around the ideology of improvement. According to this account, thanks largely to the economic growth after 1650, the collective belief in improvement was 'persuasively sustained'—a belief that 'it delivered benefits both to the nation and to every citizen' almost ad infinitum.[193] As Douglass North (cited by Slack) put it, such a conviction can 'acquire a moral force when almost everyone in the community follows it, and it is in the interests of each individual that people with whom he or she deals follow the rule'.[194] Notice that this choice-theoretic formulation does not encourage us to explore the power-laden processes of negotiation through which choices were made.

More pertinent here, I submit, is the work of French economists of convention such as Laurent Thévenot and François Eymard-Duvernary. Their work has called for an investigation of what they call *conventions constitutives*, patterns of justifiable action that inform (and hence cannot be reduced to) individual choices in eco-nomic transactions.[195] Because the modality of justifiable actions is embedded

---

[192]	Ibid., vol. 4, col. 836.

[193]	Slack, *Invention of Improvement*, pp. 240 (quotation), 253, 262.

[194]	Douglass C. North, *Institutions, Institutional Change and Economic Performance* (Cambridge: Cambridge University Press, 1990), p. 42 (quotation). Cf. Robert Sugden, *The Economics of Rights, Co-Operation and Welfare* (2nd edn, Basingstoke: Macmillan, 2004), pp. 172–4.

[195]	Laurent Thévenot, 'Équilibre et rationalité dans un univers complexe', *Revue Économique*, 40 (1989), 147–98, p. 170; François Eymard-Duvernay, *Économie politique de l'entreprise* (Paris: La Découverte, 2004), pp. 73–4, 98–9, 107. For its application to history, see Philippe Minard, 'Facing Uncertainty: Markets, Norms and Conventions in the Eighteenth Century', in Gauci (ed.), *Regulating the British Economy*, 177–94, pp. 187–8; William H. Sewell Jr, *Logics of History: Social Theory and Social Transformation* (Chicago: University of Chicago Press, 2005), pp. 73, 75. Cf. Luc Boltanski and Laurent Thévenot, *On Justification: Economies of Worth*, tr. Catherine Porter (Princeton, NJ: Princeton University Press, 2006) [French original published in 1991]. I thank Philippe Minard for drawing my attention to the concept of convention.

in the politics and culture of the time, this approach bodes well for the processes of negotiation under discussion, one that was heavily influenced by the haunting memories of early Stuart grievances. To adopt their language, then, the extensive social circulation and tactical invocation of distrust began to undermine the early Stuart model as a politically viable *convention* for improvement in post-Restoration England. Consequently, in the environment of distrust, promoters sought to adjust themselves to the changing sense of propriety; it was through their adjustments and misadjustments that constitutive conventions underlying England's improvement culture began to evolve away from practices that required extensive mechanisms of compulsion and penalties against established private interests. As Cheney Culpeper had already told Hartlib in 1647, 'if soe much good be like to be effected, to every particular man in his owne private concernements, every body will see that there will be noe neede of constraincte'.[196] This view gained firmer ground in the 1660s and 1670s. Fresh and greater attention was now given to identifying appropriate 'inducement and encouragement' for stimulating private initiatives, matched by measures to protect them. Herein we shall find a potent vision of wealth creation driven by private desire and interests.

EMULATION AS A PHILOSOPHER'S STONE

One of the most striking trends in the pursuit of improvement without state-led coercion is the reappraisal of 'emulation'. The moral status of the concept was rather ambiguous, since Aristotle coupled it with envy in his *Rhetoric*. Building on Aristotle, Hobbes thus defined emulation as a sort of '*Grief*, for the success of a Competitor in wealth, honour, or the good . . . joyned with Endeavour to enforce our own abilities to equall or exceed him', a competitive desire that could give rise to envy if joined with 'endeavour to supplant, or hinder a competitor'.[197] Yet contemporary writers were also alive to the productive potential of the human desire to emulate. Competitive emulation among early modern states, and among individuals, has been studied respectively in the contexts of international trade and of the rising consumer society.[198] Emulation is equally important for the history of projecting, for in the decades after the Restoration, writers began to suggest that agrarian improvement could be promoted with little coercion if subjects' desire for emulation and betterment was ignited.

The case of timber and fruit tree cultivation provides us with a series of well-documented case studies. This was one of the most frequently discussed topics of

---

[196] 'Culpeper Letters', p. 307 (13/194–5).

[197] Thomas Hobbes, *Leviathan*, ed. Richard Tuck (Cambridge: Cambridge University Press, 1991), pt. 1, ch. 6, p. 44. Cf. *OED*, s.v. emulation, *n.*; Christopher Tilmouth, *Passion's Triumph over Reason: A History of the Moral Imagination from Spenser to Rochester* (Oxford: Oxford University Press, 2007), pp. 226–7.

[198] Istvan Hont, *Jealousy of Trade: International Competition and the Nation-State in Historical Perspective* (Cambridge, MA: Harvard University Press, 2005), pp. 115–21; Slack, *Invention of Improvement*, pp. 153–8.

the early Royal Society. Between its establishment and the end of the 1670s, cider and cider-pressing engines alone were discussed at least thirty times.[199] The cultivation of fruit trees and shrubs, such as apples, pears, and berries, was one of the sectors for which, like the case of flax and hemp seen earlier, the imposition of government authority had often been deemed essential. Hartlib promoted just such *A design for plenty, by an universall planting of fruit-trees* (1653), a scheme to be 'enlivened and nourished by Authority and Law', overseen by a nationwide network of supervisors who would administer the 'penalty to be inflicted for the neglect'.[200] Ralph Austen, an Oxford-based promoter of fruit trees, who may have helped compose the tract, elsewhere 'much desired that the *Higher Powers* would by a *Law, or Injunction* set men to *this worke*'.[201] While Austen repeated this point after the Restoration, others looked for less controversial methods for improvement.

The shifting sense of propriety after the Restoration is most evident in Evelyn's *Sylva* and its accompanying tract *Pomona*, co-authored with Beale, both among the most influential books on horticulture in the early modern period, and first published just four years after the king's return. The bulk of these books was devoted to practical information, designed to teach readers different methods of growing timber and fruit trees and making cider that could compete with French or Spanish wine. Accordingly, they have been studied as examples of Baconian scientific collaboration, while literary aspects of *Sylva* have attracted some textual analysis.[202] The books' less frequently noticed aspect—their discussion of the role of government—deserves closer inspection, as it reveals the alternatives they proposed in order to realize improvement without nationwide mechanisms of enforcement.

Evelyn surveyed laws and regulations for the preservation and improvement of woods in ancient civilisations, as well as in contemporary Spain, France, and Germany.[203] He also commented on the Henrician and Elizabethan statutes, which required a proportion of timber to be fenced and protected, and prohibited the conversion of woodland into tillage; these statutes were, opined Evelyn, 'diligently to be consulted, revived, put in execution, and enlarg'd where any defect is

---

[199] For what it is worth, one might compare other industrial and agricultural topics: gunpowder and other explosives were mentioned at least fifty-three times during the 1660s and 1670s; wine, twenty times; saltpetre, sixteen; beer and ale, fifteen; salt, fourteen; alum and white lead, five; varnishes, five; tar and pitch, five. The numbers are drawn from Thomas Birch's *History of the Royal Society*. See Kathleen Helen Ochs, 'The Failed Revolution in Applied Science: Studies of Industry by Members of the Royal Society of London, 1660–1688' (PhD thesis, University of Toronto, 1981), pp. 150–1, 154, 157, 161, 168, 170, 173, 178, 184, 217.

[200] Samuel Hartlib, *A designe for plentie* (1653), pp. 3–6, 11–12, at pp. 3, 4.

[201] HP 41/1/40A, Austen to Hartlib, 25 July 1653; Austen, *A treatise of fruit-trees* (2nd edn, 1657), p. 127 (quotation). The same view is repeated in his undated letter to Hartlib at HP 41/1/144A, [n.d., 1650s?].

[202] Sharp, 'Timber', pp. 63–8, 80 n. 79; Michael Hunter, *Science and Society in Restoration England* (Cambridge: Cambridge University Press, 1981), pp. 91, 93, 99–101, 104, 109; William T. Lynch, *Solomon's Child: Method in the Early Royal Society of London* (Stanford, CA: Stanford University Press, 2001), pp. 37–43; Parry, 'John Evelyn', pp. 141–2; Douglas Chambers, '"Wild Pastorall Encounter": John Evelyn, John Beale and the Renegotiation of Pastoral in the Mid-Seventeenth Century', in *Culture and Cultivation*, 173–94.

[203] Evelyn, *Sylva*, ch. 33.

apparent'.²⁰⁴ *Pomona* suggested that parliamentary legislation might be devised to improve fruit tree cultivation, '*if already there be not effectual* provision *for it*'.²⁰⁵ The authors could have elaborated on how to enforce plant cultivation more effectively by drawing on justices of the peace, purveyors, or informers. Significantly, however, it was instead suggested that 'according to the old and best Spirit of true *English*, we ought to be more powerfully led by his *Majesties* Example, than have need of more cogent and violent *Laws*'.²⁰⁶ Fruit tree cultivation would likewise become widespread among public-spirited gentlemen, *Pomona* argued, '*when his* Majesty *shall once be pleas'd, to command the* Planting *but of some* Acres, *for the best* Cider-fruit, *at every of his Royal* Mansions, *amongst other of his most laudable* Magnificencies'.²⁰⁷ Not violent laws, but 'commendable emulation' among subjects, should drive improvement.²⁰⁸ Orchards and cider production could be spread across the nation by 'incit[ing] our Industry *to its utmost* effort'.²⁰⁹ This was how horticulture was to be improved and the inflow of continental wine to be replaced by domestic cider.

Accordingly, Beale was hardly enthusiastic when Austen repeated his argument for diffusion by compulsion and penalties. In December 1664, ten months after the publication of *Sylva* and *Pomona*, Austen presented to the Royal Society a proposal for promoting fruit trees. Revising his earlier argument, Austen argued that a law should be introduced to enforce the planting of fruit trees upon every piece of land that was newly enclosed. And 'because some p[er]sons will be negligent herein, notwithstanding many p[ro]fitts to themselves', it would be 'very necessary that some Overseers of the worke be chosen, & appoynted thereunto' by Justices of the Peace in every county, and granted the power to levy fines and to confiscate from defaulters. In order to ensure that 'none may plead ignorance in this matter', it was also requested that manuals 'of small Bulke & Price, yet containing plaine, experimentall instructions' should be published.²¹⁰ The third edition of his *Treatise of fruit-trees* (1665) repeated the need for compulsion by 'a *Law*, or *Injunction*, [to] set men to this *work*'.²¹¹ Commenting on Austen's proposals to 'promote Cider by lawes', Beale confessed to Boyle that 'I hope there is noe neede of such enforcement.'²¹²

Beale's own view was based on his broader vision of improvement via competitive emulation and consumption, something to be facilitated by networks of correspondents and their meetings, as well as by printed books, involving not only male landowners (who would manage their own properties), but also their wives, their tenants, poorer labourers, and planters across Britain, Ireland, and the West Indies.

²⁰⁴ Evelyn, *Sylva*, p. 206.
²⁰⁵ John Evelyn, *Pomona; or an appendix concerning fruit-trees in relation to cider* (2nd edn, 1670), p. 2. Subsequent references to *Pomona* are to this edition.
²⁰⁶ Evelyn, *Sylva*, p. 206. See also ibid., p. 208, where he sceptically commented on the penal statues for preventing the conversion of woods to pasture.
²⁰⁷ Evelyn, *Pomona*, pp. 5, 2.   ²⁰⁸ Evelyn, *Sylva*, p. 206.   ²⁰⁹ Evelyn, *Pomona*, p. 4.
²¹⁰ RS, Cl.P/10iii/7, 'Proposalls & Reasons for the improving, & advancing of Planting; Humbly tendered to the Lords & Com[m]ons in Parliament assembled', read on 14 December 1664.
²¹¹ Ralph Austen, *A treatise of fruit-trees* (3rd edn, 1665), pp. 238, 234–5, at p. 238.
²¹² *Boyle Correspondence*, vol. 2, p. 579, Beale to Boyle, 9 November 1665. See also RS, LBO/27, p. 354. Cf. Stubbs, 'Part II', p. 334.

This expansive vision was developed most fully in the series of his little-studied letters and manuscript tracts presented to the Royal Society.[213]

In the run-up to the publication of *Sylva* and *Pomona*, Beale praised the treatises as a wellspring of plenty, granaries on printed pages that were immune to harsh weather:

> when no granaries can preserve the plenty of abounding years from corruption, nor can deliver our fattest vales off corn and gras from blasts, meldews, storms, tempests, and inundac[i]ons[,] you have provided us a safe grannary, and a reserve of best viands under ground, and out of the reach of angry stars.[214]

Yet printed tracts represented only one of the available channels. For, as Beale explained later, 'the best books and writings in the world (tho the printing presse be the great wonder maker) are not of th[e]mselves the best conduit'. Networks of correspondence were to be developed further to find out 'what is best', 'what fruit yields the best Cyder, or how best it should be ordered'.[215] A closely related idea was the circulation of manuscripts undergoing successive additions and revisions. This was 'the characteristic early modern approach to natural and human history, in which new knowledge was continuously accreted through correspondence, conversation, observation, and reading'.[216] Beale in fact circulated his manuscript as a written response to one Mr Lewis's short essay on grafting methods. As he told Oldenburg, 'I do earnestly wish He would bestowe a better & more corrected Coppy [of Beale's manuscript] upon some Worthy Cantabrigian who would make the best uses of it.' Such a scribal communication, he wondered, 'may do more good then a huge Volum. Especially w[he]n many hands, & the assistance of the Multitudes are necessary to carry on the worke.'[217] These scribal networks were to be complemented by actual meetings of those sharing similar interests, such as gardeners and nursery men, to 'establish a correspondence of Free contributers'—a striking echo of the Hartlibean ideal of the uninterrupted communication of useful knowledge.[218]

---

[213] Beale's discussion of emulation has largely escaped critical attention. See Ochs, 'Failed Revolution', pp. 165–9; Ochs, 'History of Trades Programme', pp. 140–4; Stubbs, 'Part II', pp. 332–7; Di Palma, 'Cider in Paradise', pp. 167, 169, 171, 173; Keller, *Knowledge and the Public Interest*, pp. 238–40. Note that we cannot rely too heavily upon Thomas Birch's *The History of the Royal Society*, for it rarely quotes full papers presented to the Society, such as Early Letters [EL] or Classified Papers [Cl.P] that I have consulted alongside Letter Book Original [LBO], select fair copies of the letters sent to the Society. Birch's transcriptions are instead based largely on the Society's Journal Books Originals [JBO], volumes that only occasionally give footnote references to LBO. Birch's volumes accordingly do not quote Beale's extensive letters on husbandry written in 1664 and 1673 under discussion.

[214] RS, EL/B1/26, Beale to Evelyn, 6 April 1663, fol. [41]. See also *PT*, vol. 11, no. 131, 29 January 1676/7, p. 796 and no. 134, 23 April 1677, p. 849.

[215] RS, EL/B1/36, 3 May 1664, Beale to the Society. For examples of such correspondence on cider-making, see Bodl., Aubrey MS 12, fol. 211, John Hoskins to Aubrey, 16 March 1673; Aubrey MS 13, fol. 19, Andrew Paschall to Aubrey, 8 June 1677.

[216] Elizabeth Yale, *Sociable Knowledge: Natural History and the Nation in Early Modern Britain* (Philadelphia, PA: University of Pennsylvania Press, 2016), pp. 15–16, 250–1 (at p. 16).

[217] *Oldenburg Correspondence*, vol. 10, p. 240, 22 September 1673. Lewis's essay appeared in *PT*, vol. 8, no. 95, 23 June 1673, pp. 6067–8.

[218] John Beale, *Nurseries, orchards, profitable gardens, and vineyards encouraged* (1677), p. 14. Actual scribal collaborations tended to be less than ideal. See Yale, *Sociable Knowledge*, pp. 122–63.

But how do you get others involved in this corresponding network, or involve them in fruit tree cultivation in the first instance? Here, post-Restoration visions diverged visibly from their mid-century predecessors. Beale was confident that it could be accomplished with little legal compulsion. Most frequently invoked was the example of kings and notables. Noting that the example of ancient monarchs such as Solomon's in gardening were followed by many, Beale argued that

> there is <u>something better than any Law</u> before my Eye. For Laws we see many times…
> do fall to ground, and become void for want of due execution. But his majesties great
> example, and the example of the greatest Peers of the Realm, and in things of apparent
> utility to the People, is more sweetly, and also more powerfully binding to all good, &
> bad Men, than a Law; and carrieth more dispatch.[219]

More recently, Beale recounted, Charles I 'gave the Redstrake [cider] the precedence before any wine of the grape' when he stayed in Herefordshire. Local gentry soon started holding 'solemn meet[in]gs every yeare in Heref[or]d to trye' their produce. Cider in the region, Beale argued, underwent tremendous improvement thanks to just such 'fervent Emulation for Victory'—an insight drawn from his first-hand observations.[220]

In commending something of a local cider competition that could promote import substitution, Beale was sharply aware of the virtuous role of pleasure, even of drinking. As Christopher Tilmouth and others have shown, Epicurean philosophy had experienced a revival by the mid-seventeenth century. Passions and sensory pleasure were thereby reappraised as something not to be dismissed, but rather to be understood, tamed, and channelled towards virtues and desirable social ends.[221] Beale's case is significant because we know that he was familiar with some, if vulgarized, Epicurean tenets. While disapproving 'glottony & drunkenes' as 'the beastly prevayling Epicurisme', Beale in fact celebrated 'elegant Epicurisme', blessed with 'holy advantages'. His penchant for wholesome cider clearly belonged to the latter. In the same letter to Hartlib, Beale smugly proclaimed that 'Our Cider, if it bee brisky, will dance in the cup some good while'.[222]

Beale promoted horticultural improvement with such pleasure of fragrant trees and dancing bubbles in mind. Yet equal emphasis could be given to honour where

---

[219] RS, LBO/27, p. 412 (1 July 1664); underlining is in the original. Beale also sought to promote the cross-breeding of cattle and animals, displaying them in St James Park. BL, Add. MS 15948, fol. 138v, Beale to Evelyn, 14 June 1669.

[220] RS, EL/B1/64, Beale to Oldenburg, 22 September 1673, fol. 136v; *Oldenburg Correspondence*, vol. 10, p. 244 (quotation). For Beale's earlier cursory remarks about the benefits of emulation in horticulture, see his letters to Hartlib, HP 52/24A, 9 April 1658; HP 52/36B, 8 May 1658.

[221] Tilmouth, *Passion's Triumph*, pp. 244–80; Howard Jones, *The Epicurean Tradition* (New York: Routledge, 1989), pp. 186–205; Slack, *Invention of Improvement*, pp. 151–2; Trentmann, *Empire of Things*, p. 97.

[222] HP 62/24/2B, Beale to Hartlib, 1 February 1657. Beale also viewed cider as healthier than (often adulterated) ale. Similar language about health and pleasure featured prominently in the contemporary promotion of coffee and chocolate. See Brian Cowan, *The Social Life of Coffee: The Emergence of the British Coffeehouse* (New Haven, CT: Yale University Press, 2005), pp. 32, 54; Kate Loveman, 'The Introduction of Chocolate into England: Retailers, Researchers, and Consumers, 1640–1730', *The Journal of Social History*, 47 (2013), 27–46, pp. 29, 37.

required. 'Honor ali[gh]t[s] Artes', Beale declared. The way forward was to instil a traditional 'sense of honour, and honesty' in 'Our Nobility, Gentry and wealthy Tradesmen' and to encourage them to take up husbandry upon their retirement to rural mansions.[223] Beale even recommended that the Royal Society should enter into 'close correspondence w[i]th the heads of the Innes of Courts', those making 'their p[er]ambula[ti]on, and ruling w[i]th wit, language, authorety, example and activity in all parts'. If they were persuaded to practise horticulture and encourage others to do the same, the cultivation of fruit trees would be spread without the need of compulsion.[224] Upon Beale's request, Evelyn later asked John Hoskins and the Duke of Norfolk to develop just such a correspondence.[225]

If lawyers represented a powerful class for encouraging emulation, East Anglia stood as an important target region. The commercial vending of cider was probably still limited there. No licence seems to have been issued for the sale of cider in Cambridge until 1676; then it was only one Walter Carpenter who obtained a licence for this purpose.[226] Beale saw an opportunity for provoking emulation. Cider masters in Herefordshire, 'by sale & proofe for their own gaine may inspire the Champian Countryes [near Cambridge] to enrich & reform themselves, in purse & conscience'.[227] As Beale's associate, Anthony Lawrence, put it, 'when *both Universities* [Cambridge, in addition to Oxford,] shall be invested in a Golden Grove, it will have a good influence to allure the like improvements in all parts of *England*...for Ornament, Health, innocent Pleasure, and considerable Profit'.[228] Their hope was not unfounded. Writing to Oldenburg in September 1676, Newton suggested that Beale's campaign to spread fruit tree cultivation in East Anglia would 'prove a very reasonable one, considering the new humour of planting that begins to grow among them'. In fact, the architect Roger Pratt, who founded Ryston Hall thirty miles north of Cambridge in 1670, soon afterwards paid £3 16s for the total of forty-six apple and pear trees, with fifteen different varieties of each.[229] Fruit trees were not only bought, but also sent as presents.[230] Beale was promoting cider and fruit trees that were taking deep root in the gift, as well as the market economy.

The profitable cycle of emulation and pleasure was never to be confined within the walls of aristocratic gardens, or within England. Beale hoped that humbler sorts of people might be persuaded to plant fruit trees if they were told how a small investment in grafts would yield handsome profits within a few years.[231]

---

[223] RS, LBO/27, pp. 391–2, 402.

[224] RS, EL/B1/36, Beale to Society, 3 May 1664.   [225] Stubbs, 'Part II', p. 336.

[226] Cambridge University Library Special Collection, University/T.II.29, licences and excise certificates of persons selling coffee, chocolate, tea, etc. in Cambridge, 1663–99. Other licensees do not appear to have sold cider.

[227] RS, EL/B1/65, fol. 136v.

[228] Beale, *Nurseries*, p. 8, a letter from Anthony Lawrence. See also EL/B1/65, 22 September 1673, fol. 135.

[229] Isaac Newton, *The Correspondence of Isaac Newton*, ed. H. W. Turnbull (7 vols., Cambridge: Cambridge University Press, 1959–77), vol. 2, p. 93, 2 September 1676; Norfolk Record Office, MF/RO 220, Roger Pratt Estate Memoranda, 1672, not foliated.

[230] Beinecke Library, Osborn fb152, Henry Clarendon to Robert Clayton, 30 September 1676.

[231] Beale, *Nurseries*, p. 22.

His vision of nationwide improvement also had an imperial dimension: 'the Countenance of Engl[an]d may awaken Virginia, and seems more likely to rayse their Emulaci[on]'.[232] Beale's readers were also told that wives and daughters, as well as male heads of household, had a role to play in this expansive vision of horticultural improvement. Commending manuals written by John Worlidge and Kenelm Digby, Beale suggested that these books could 'instruct [them] in that practical devotion and charity, which obligeth our Country, and keeps the Poor from idleness and famine':

> [W]hen our Country-Ladies have taught one another the best way of drawing bush-wines or shrub-wines by the help of Sugar; it will be a sudden improvement of *England, Wales,* and *Ireland,* and a great kindness also to *Jamaica.*[233]

The suggestion was timely because the import of Caribbean sugar into London was growing significantly at the time. The recorded import of West Indian muscovado sugar into London in 1686 hit 403,911 hundredweight, and had more than doubled in two decades. By this time, sugar had become the single most important article among colonial imports, amounting to 60 per cent of the total value of imports into London, tobacco being next (17 per cent).[234] Making and consuming cider at home, following the recommended use of sugar for fermentation, were therefore an integral part of the imperial political economy, linked explicitly to the expansion of colonial trade, feeding back into incessant improvement across the empire. Seeds of different varieties could likewise be tested and exchanged across the Atlantic:

> It was but a step or two, and a gentle swing from *Whitehall-stairs* to *Barbadoes,* or to *Jamaica.* . . . One ingenious Nursery-man in each of the English Colonies, corresponding with ingenious Seedmen in *Lombard-street,* and in *Bristol,* and in all our chief Port Towns, (to try all the Seeds we could send them . . . and we doing the like to them,) by many returns upon trials, again and again, here and there, would make the work short, and wonderful, and (doubtless) exceeding profitable[.]

Household consumption and production of cider, promoted via print and manuscript, supported by a growing traffic of sugar, seeds, and letters across the empire, could at best replace schemes for enforcing the cultivation of crops.[235]

---

[232] RS, EL/B1/36, Beale to the Society, 3 May 1664.

[233] Beale, *Nurseries,* p. 20, 23.

[234] Nuala Zahedieh, *The Capital and the Colonies: London and the Atlantic Economy, 1660–1700* (Cambridge: Cambridge University Press, 2010), pp. 189, 210–26 (at p. 189); John J. McCusker and Russell R. Menard, *The Economy of British America, 1607–1789* (Chapel Hill, NC: University of North Carolina Press, 1985), p. 159.

[235] Beale, *Nurseries,* pp. 27–8. See also *Oldenburg Correspondence,* vol. 12, p. 230, Beale to Oldenburg, March–April 1676: producing shrub wines 'by the help of Sugar' across regions unfit for apple-trees 'may in a short time prove a great benefit to our Sugar-plantations'. A robust economic analysis of the cider-making industry is John Chartres, 'No English Calvados? English Distillers and the Cider Industry in the Seventeenth and Eighteenth Centuries', in John Chartres and David Hey (eds.), *English Rural Society, 1500–1800* (Cambridge: Cambridge University Press, 1990), 313–42, esp. pp. 332–3, 337–8, 341–2. For an excellent analysis of the technologies involved, see Eric Otremba, 'Inventing Ingenios: Experimental Philosophy and the Secret of Sugar-Makers of the Seventeenth-Century Atlantic', *History and Technology,* 28 (2012), 119–47.

In placing greater emphasis on emulation across the empire and across the social spectrum, Beale was clearly seeking to distinguish the Royal Society and its activities from previous patterns of projecting. In his manuscript treatises of 1673, Beale contrasted positions adopted by two Stuart kings: 'his Ma[jes]tyes Countenance in Hortulane advancem[en]t may by his Royall example, be more effectuall, then was K[in]g James his Letter (for the propagation of Mulberry-trees) to the L[or]ds Lieutenants'.[236] Under the auspices of the Society, the promotion of fruit tree cultivation might go beyond 'Gabriel Plats instrument of setting wheat or any other projects (that I could ever hear or read) . . . For they build Colleges, or Castles in the air.'[237] Neither correspondence networks nor emphasis on emulation was a novelty, of course. Hartlib and his allies accorded great importance to correspondence networks in the circulation of useful knowledge; Walter Blith developed by the early 1650s a vision of trial and error inducing the improvement of agricultural knowledge. In England and elsewhere, the ruling class was to set a good example to be followed up and down the social ladder.[238] Beale's argument in subsequent decades drew on these precedents, and shared their global ambitions to create wealth out of that which God had given unto them. Yet his vision underwent a subtle, yet profound shift of emphasis as he critically confronted the decades of projecting activities, and thereby faced the question of law and compulsion, a question that loomed even larger after the return of Charles II. Accordingly, Beale's promotion of agricultural improvement drew squarely upon the desires of the governed population at large. It was their adoption of horticulture, and their competitive production and consumption of cider, which would give jobs to the poor, develop the home production of cider, integrate regional economies across the expanding empire, and thereby strengthen England's imperial economic prowess against its continental rivals. The philosopher's stone for generating wealth was not to be found in the projector's brain, but in people's desire for pleasure, profits, honour, emulation, and consumption. Here, I submit, is an unmistakable case of the taming and remaking of England's projecting culture.

IMPROVEMENT AND THE PROJECTING OF A COMMERCIAL SOCIETY

The argument for emulation was hardly an intellectual conceit of virtuosi like Evelyn and Beale alone. Similar positions were also adopted by less privileged men of expertise writing about horticulture, echoed by writers on the 'discourse of trade', endorsed by the Royal Society, and even taken up by members of parliament. The thorny question of foreign luxuries remained, but there was a growing body of

---

[236] RS, EL/B1/65, fol. 133, Beale to the Society, 22 September 1673. Aaron Hill quoted extensively from the same letter when appealing to his investors in 1715. See p. 26.

[237] RS, LBO/27, pp. 389–90.

[238] Cf. Trinity College Dublin Special Collections, MS 842, fols. [180v]–181, 'Advertisements for Ireland', n.d. [early C17], which tasked Protestant settlers to set 'such a president [i.e. precedent] to the rest' in matters of civility and industry.

writers who found a powerful leverage for improvement in the public's desire for emulation and consumption.

Drawing on his thirty years of experience in forestry, John Smith dedicated his *England's improvement reviv'd* (two editions in 1670 and 1673) to William Brounker, the first president of the Royal Society, a commissioner of the navy, and comptroller of the treasurer's accounts. Evelyn offered a eulogy to the book, commending Smith as 'a Person of so great a Talent and Experience beyond me'.[239] John Rose was the royal gardener to Charles II, and published his *English vineyards* (1666) with the help of Evelyn. For experienced men like Rose and Smith who earned their living from their expertise, possible governmental support would have been attractive, for it could have given them employment opportunities as official supervisors. In fact Smith did admit that 'Authority should Constrain some men' where 'Wit and Providence will not'.[240] Yet, instead of elaborating the point further, he drew on his first-hand experience to discuss the relative costs of different timber cultivation methods. A quarter of the book was devoted to this cost–benefit analysis, which a historian has judged to be 'unusually competent and thorough'.[241] Smith would not have done this had it been his intention to push his schemes through legislation or to promote himself as an overseer for enforcement. Rather, his book was an attempt to convince his readers of the relative advantages of timber cultivation over widespread arable husbandry.[242]

Rose was even more explicit. If Charles accepted his pamphlet, he declared, 'Gentlemen shall be encourag'd to Plant those *sorts* of *Vines* which I here recommend, and to *Cultivate* them by my *Direction*'.[243] The king's encouragement, stirring emulation down the social ladder, would be followed by 'thousands of Your *Majesties* Subjects, whose glory it is to transcribe after your great *Example* for the good of the *Ages* to come'.[244] By the mid-1670s, even Ralph Austen set aside his earlier advocacy of legal compulsion: 'Grace in the heart of a Christian', rather than the force of law, was now to become the '*Phylosophers stone*; that turns *Earth, into Heaven*'.[245]

Comparable arguments can also be found in a wider discussion of political economy. In the course of a debate about tax-farming, one anonymous writer observed in 1662 that 'his Maj[es]ties most happy restauration', accompanied by 'Soe Splendid and Glorious a Court' attended by foreign dignitaries and returning royalist exiles, would 'occation a farr greater expence and Consumption of all com[m]odityes then formerly, whereby his maj[es]ties revenue (especially the Customs) will bee

---

[239] Smith, *England's improvement*, sig. [A3], 'To the Reader', sig. [A2v], 'The Report of John Evelyn Esquire'.

[240] Ibid., p. 8.

[241] Sharp, 'Timber', p. 61 (quotation); Smith, *England's improvement*, pp. 82–103, 106–59. For a broader analysis of Smith's book, see Lynch, *Solomon's*, p. 60–3.

[242] Sharp, 'Timber', p. 78, n. 61.

[243] John Rose, *The English vineyard vindicated* (1666), sig. [A5]–[A5v], dedication to Charles II.

[244] Rose, *English vineyard*, sig. A4–[A4v], dedication to Charles II.

[245] Ralph Austen, *A dialogue (or familiar discourse) and conference between the husbandman and fruit-trees* (1676), sig [*7] (quotation), pp. 27–9. Compare this with earlier mentions of the philosopher's stone in Austen, *A treatise of fruit-trees* (2nd edn, 1657), p. 124; Austen, *A treatise of fruit-trees* (3rd edn, 1665), pp. 232, 238. Cf. Palma, 'Cider in Paradise', pp. 176–7.

greatly Improved beyond the vallue att present Sett upon them'—a remark shrewdly articulating the economic implication of conspicuous consumption, in this case as practised by the luxurious, even promiscuous court of the 'merry monarch'.[246]

Others tended to focus on the leverage of consumer behaviour without commending imported luxuries. In his book *England's interest* (1663, republished 1673) Samuel Fortrey, a merchant of Flemish descent and at one time an investor and surveyor for the Bedford Levels, argued that England was yearly losing more than £1.5 million by the steady import of fans, hats, papers, wines, furniture, silk and linen textiles, and other commodities from France.[247] 'But', he added immediately, 'most of these evils would be easily prevented, if only his Majesty would be pleased to commend to his people, by his own example, the esteem and value he hath of his own commodities.' 'This alone, *without further trouble*, would be at least ten hundred thousand [i.e. one million] pounds a year to the advantage of his people.'[248] An anonymous author on 'the Promotion of Trade in England' concurred; it was vital that the 'prince is so obliging to his own Mechanicks that he dispises any person that wants and Effects the Manufactures of other Countries'. Fortrey articulated an underlying assumption: as long as 'we impoverish not our selves to enrich strangers', expense upon such consumer goods 'ought to be maintained, and encouraged'.[249]

By highlighting the leverage of emulation-driven consumption, these authors were developing a set of arguments that were not only in line with the political sensibilities of the post-Restoration regime, consistent with the intellectual reappraisal of pleasure and passion, but also capable of tapping into rising per capita income and spending power. Various estimates in fact tend to agree that per capita income in England increased by almost by 50 per cent in the second half of the seventeenth century. The growth of the cloth trade also meant that husbands' earnings were often supplemented by wives' and children's work in spinning. These favourable circumstances probably enabled middling households to spend more on items that enhanced ease and comfort. In London, for example, small paned windows were being replaced by sash windows; more chairs upholstered; linen cupboards filled with more and better-quality cloths; beds covered by better sheets and adorned by lighter bed curtains. The houses of Fortrey and other mercantile authors may well have been becoming more airy, comfortable, and luxurious.[250]

---

[246] Senate House Library Special Collection, MS 202, A series of fifteen queries directed against the farming out of the customs, [1662?], fol. 1v. For a brief depiction of Restoration court life, see Keeble, *Restoration*, pp. 171–82.

[247] Samuel Fortrey, *England's interest and improvement* (1663), pp. 22–5. The passage on French imports was copied out and kept among the Petty Paper, BL, Add. MS 72890, fols. 46–47v, 'Mr Fortrey's accompt of the French Trade', [n.d.]. For Fortrey's background, see his entry in *Oxford DNB*.

[248] Fortrey, *England's interest*, pp. 25–6 (my italics). The republication of 1673, identical to the first except for the preface, made the same point.

[249] Baker Library, Kress MS, E-13, 'A Manuscript concerning Promotion of Trade in England', n.d. [1675?], p. 75; Fortrey, *England's interest*, pp. 26–7.

[250] Slack, *Invention of Improvement*, pp. 12–13; Craig Muldrew, *Food, Energy and the Creation of Industriousness: Work and Material Culture in Agrarian England, 1550–1780* (Cambridge: Cambridge University Press, 2011), pp. 241–6, 257; Craig Muldrew, '"Th'ancient Distaff" and "Whirling Spindle":

Note, however, that the argument for emulation was much more than a simple reflection of rising consumer behaviour in urban centres. Beale's comment on the Herefordshire cider contest derived from his *rural* observations. Equally important, Fortrey's and others' pronouncements in the 1660s and 1670s predated the best-known phases in the rise of the consumer society. Studies of probate inventories suggest that items such as mirrors, upholstered chairs, and coffee- and tea-making equipment did not become widespread among middling Londoners until the beginning of the eighteenth century.[251] Even in Kent—a wealthy county close to the capital—these semi-luxury items were adopted with the time lag of a few decades. In provincial towns such as Sudbury (Suffolk) and Preston (Lancashire), it was predominantly local office-holders that adopted similar consumer items for achieving greater comfort and social distinction, with remoter areas in Cornwall and the Welsh border, for example, showing relatively little inclination to adopt them despite increasing affordability for and spending power among middling sorts.[252] Mercantile authors like Fortrey, writing in the 1660s or 1670s, may not have been aware of these emerging variegated patterns of consumption, as we are. Yet their arguments are significant, all the more because they foretold, or *projected*, the potential leverage of consumer behaviour before its imminent triumph. If they paid closer attention to the power of emulation, if they were alive to the economic potential of middling spending power and human desire for consumption and comfort, it was because these authors knew they could no longer rely on the draconian modes of improvement typical under the early Stuarts. This explains why the post-Restoration argument for consumption is so strikingly similar to the projecting literature concerned with the production side of the economy. As Fortrey declared, if rightly directed towards 'the art, manufacture and workmanship of the commodity made in our own country', then through consumer appetite 'ingenuity would be encouraged, the people employed, and our treasure kept at home'.[253]

These arguments for emulation did not mean the decline of governmental regulation, or the rise of a 'liberal' market economy. The navigation acts of 1660 and 1673, attempts at regulating England's shipping trade, are fitting reminders.[254]

Measuring the Contribution of Spinning to Household Earnings and the National Economy in England, 1550–1770', *EcHR*, 65 (2012), 498–526, pp. 517–22; Peter Earle, *The Making of the English Middle Class: Business, Society and Family Life in London, 1660–1730* (London: Methuen, 1989), pp. 292–3; David M. Mitchell, '"My Purple will be too Sad for that Melancholy Room": Furnishings for Interiors in London and Paris, 1660–1735', *Textile History*, 40 (2009), 3–28, esp. p. 7 (table 2), p. 9 (table 3).

[251] Earle, *Middle Class*, pp. 292–5, 386 nn. 40, 42, p. 387 n. 45.

[252] See Mark Overton, Jane Whittle, Darron Dean, and Andrew Hann, *Production and Consumption in English Households, 1600–1750* (Abingdon: Routledge, 2004), pp. 91, 99, 111; H. R. French, *The Middle Sort of People in Provincial England, 1600–1750* (Oxford: Oxford University Press, 2007), pp. 166–7. For Ludlow (Shropshire) and Hereford (Herefordshire), see Karen Banks, 'The Ownership of Goods and Cultures of Consumption in Ludlow, Hereford and Tewkesbury, 1660–1760' (PhD thesis, University of Wolverhampton, 2014), pp. 36–7, 116, 156, 158.

[253] Fortrey, *England's interest*, p. 27. See also *England's happiness improved* (1697), pp. 2, 174; Jonas Moore, *England's interest* (2nd edn, 1703), p. 13.

[254] For a balanced assessment of the Navigation Acts, see Zahedieh, *Capital and the Colonies*, pp. 36–8, 47, 182–3.

What we find instead is policy recommendations seeking to provide incentives to achieve given objectives. For example, Yarranton was perceptive regarding local interests when he discussed the exhaustion of timber supply in the West Midlands. His diagnosis was that the sum of the 'interests' of local landlords, bailiffs, clerks of ironworks, tanners, colliers, and woodsmen 'all ends in the destruction and cutting down [of] the Standals'.[255] Like Petty in the last years of his life, Yarranton only outlined his recommendations, perhaps in a bid to solicit enquiries from potential patrons. Yet he did suggest that the national demand for timber would be sufficiently met by the regional coppice woods alone if the 'evil combinations' of local private interests were properly understood, with the existing statutes accordingly 'amended with some small Addition'.[256] Likewise, in order to strengthen the fishing industry in coastal areas, the anonymous author of the 'Promotion of Trade in England' urged the government to grant temporary tax exemptions 'to all such as shall build, and inhabit on the sea Coast, and particularly in the best fishing Towns, and upon Navigable Rivers', while levying more on those building 'houses of pleasures' inland. The government was even urged to lend money with no interest for ten years to those English or foreign subjects settling in port towns.[257] The author was clear about the wider implications of such a policy:

> this would not only be a great Motive to ingage people to settle in the said ports but also, but also [*sic*] be a great incouragement to all public undertakings, for the Common Good of the Nation in restoreing Trade, when they shall see their benevolences are not diverted from their designed End.[258]

This passage is convoluted; yet it is also revealing. It shows how the provision of incentives was recommended as something capable of appealing to actors' desire for benevolence, thereby turning—or transmuting—private ends into the common good, towards the encouragement of 'all public undertakings'.[259]

The Royal Society's *Philosophical Transactions* reviewed and commended many of the tracts mentioned in this chapter, and in doing so propagated the emerging arguments for emulation and private incentives. The Society, or its secretary Oldenburg, probably published some reviews without the authors' permission—an action reminiscent of Hartlib, whose network they partly inherited. The *Transactions* published Beale's commentary of an anonymous tract, *Epitome of Husbandry*, for example. Specifying the pages in which the reader might find directions about the cultivation of fruit trees on 'barren Heaths', the review suggested that, thanks to such

---

[255] Andrew Yarranton, *England's improvement by sea and land. The second part* (1681), p. 75.
[256] Ibid., pp. 76, 72–3.
[257] Baker Library, Kress MS, E-13, 'Promotion of Trade in England', pp. 66, 68.
[258] Ibid., p. 68.
[259] On the importance of inducements, see also British Library of Political and Economic Science, Coll. Misc. 158, 'Considerations induceing to the revival of the Royall Fishery Company and Trade by a joint stock', 3 September 1691; National Library of Ireland, MS 258, 'Discourse on the Fishery of Great Brittain and in particular on the Herring Buss Trade', 1713: 'The most effectual method that Can be Taken to bring the Herring fishery of Great Britain to Perfection, must be by Granting such encouragements to it, as will render it the Interest of all private Persons to Engadge in' (Discourse V, no foliation).

instructions, 'any Gentleman by his own good example may lead on the multitude to drive away laziness, and poverty, and to enrich themselves, by turning our waste Grounds, Heaths…and Downs (which contain a great part of England) into Gardens, and Modern Vineyeards'.[260] The Society thus taught its readers how to encourage emulation across social strata, with clear implications for social order.

The reader of *Philosophical Transactions* was also reminded of wider, imperial implications of horticulture. In 1675, Oldenburg declared that ciders and fruit wines fermented with sugar 'may challenge, or excel, the richest wine of the Grape'. 'In this Testimony', he told the reader, 'my aim is for the benefit of *Jamaica*, and our other Sugar-Plantations.'[261] What awaited the West Indies was, of course, the rise of a sugar monoculture driven by slave labour that undermined the diversity of local ecologies and farming practices. Inhabitants' reliance on imported food and manufactured goods became such that it fuelled the growth and diversification of England's export trade.[262] If we turn to the metropolis, however, the tone remained almost cheerfully Epicurean. In 1673, Aphra Behn memorably addressed the reader of her comedy *The Dutch Lover* as 'Good, Sweet, Honey, Sugar-candied READER'.[263] Three years later, in *Philosophical Transactions*, Beale's review of Worlidge's *Vinetum Britannicum* offered to add 'refreshing liquors' to the 'Noble Tables' of his readers, naming among them 'a most delicious *Bonello* (or winy liquor extracted by infusion, and compounded with sugar) for the Summer heat'.[264] Such sugar-fortified drinks were promoted as 'exceeding good Husbandry'; for Beale, they proved that English fruit trees could be 'improved to bear more delicat and more wholsom Wines, than a *French Vineyard*; and also find good Employment of poor Widows and Children'.[265] The pleasure of tending fruit trees and consuming ciders and fruit wines, the reader was told, carried tremendous charitable and global implications. By publishing such reviews, the Royal Society promoted the sanguine vision of economic and colonial development, reliant on colonial slavery, but driven more prominently (in their view) by the virtuous alliance of profit, pleasure and emulation among the households of free-born Englishmen. The evidence presented here forces us to interrogate for whom the history of improvement can stand as a story of progress.

The Royal Society did more than use *Philosophical Transactions* to disseminate useful information for stimulating emulation among private households. It also served as a go-between, promoting a wide range of improvers to political circles. Here the relative success of those who stayed clear of blanket enforcement is unmistakable. For example, in February 1677, shortly after the first part of Yarranton's *England's improvement by sea and land* was licensed, Beale urged Evelyn to help

---

[260] *PT*, vol. 11, no. 124, 24 April 1676, p. 583.

[261] *PT*, vol. 10, no. 112, 25 March 1675, p. 256.

[262] McCusker and Menard, *British America*, p. 156. In 1686, when an inhabitant of New England and Chesapeake only spent the average of thirteen to fourteen shillings per year on goods shipped from London, the population in Barbados and Jamaica respectively spent on them more than £3 and £2 per capita per annum. See also Zahedieh, *Capital and the Colonies*, pp. 258–9.

[263] Aphra Behn, *The Dutch lover* (1673), sig. A2.

[264] *PT*, vol. 11, no. 124, 24 April 1676, pp. 584–5.

[265] Ibid., p. 583. See also Evelyn, *Diary*, vol. 4, p. 481; Di Palma, 'Cider in Paradise', pp. 163, 174–6.

circulate 'substantiall Breviats' of Yarranton's book among MPs, claiming that 'all those who have done excellently well for any maine branch of reall Improvem[en]ts' as well as 'the Favouring patrons', were now 'engaged in their Reputations, to embrace a fitt opportunityes to drive it on afresh':

> Sir y[o]u are concerned....His Ma[jes]ty is engaged as the Graicious Patron to the S[a]m[uel] Fortoryes Adresses. Pr[ince] Rup[ar]t to [Richard] Hayns Adresse. Lord Brouncker & y[ou]r self for John Smith....If substantiall Breviats [of Yarranton's proposals] be handsomely put into y[ou]r hands, I presume y[o]u can dispose them for the best advantage.[266]

Yarranton's schemes had been so well received in London that he was giving 'weekly lectures' from about 1678.[267] Fortrey was appointed to the office of clerk of deliveries of the ordnance in November 1680. In an anonymous memorandum signed the same month, Evelyn, Fortrey, Smith, Worlidge, and Yarranton were recommended as 'worthy persons' whom Commons MPs might wish to consult 'for the advancement of foreign commerce, domestic manufacturers and good culture'. It was suggested that appointing a parliamentary committee to hear from them 'wilbe very popular And acceptable to the whole kingdome'.[268] Citing liberally from *Philosophical Transactions*, the memorandum suggested its recipient 'may freely com[m]unicate to such members [of parliament] as will make the best use of it for the publique benefitt; and to satisfy the people who concern themselves for their owne gaines'.[269]

Was the memorandum written by Beale or circulated under his or the Society's direction? If so, it gives us a rare glimpse of the Society's lobbying for a wide range of experts beyond its institutional membership. If not, the manuscript then suggests that someone outside the Society referred to the *Transactions'* reviews to recommend agricultural authors for policy consultation—striking evidence of readership and the flow of information into the corridors of power. All the same, the manuscript first signed in 1680 was still borrowed and hand-copied three years later by a former MP, John Speke, and witnessed by five others, suggesting the manuscript continued to invite readers to consult certain authors via *Transactions*.[270] Equally notable is the relative success of writers such as Fortrey and Yarranton in contrast to the frustration and the failure of those promoters examined earlier, who continued to propose ambitious schemes that required sweeping mechanisms of enforcement. It is significant that promoters such as Petty, Knight, and Dymock were not mentioned among the 'worthy persons'. Even those who attracted a degree of support remained vulnerable to distrust, however. As will be seen in the next (penultimate) section, as England witnessed the first age of party, the promotion of economic improvement became embroiled in the politics of Nonconformity and religious toleration.

[266] RS, EL/B1/72, Beale to [Evelyn?], 10 February 1677. For identification, see Sharp, 'Timber', p. 60.
[267] See p. 132.
[268] TNA, SP 29/414, pp. 499–501, at p. 500, a copy letter from John Speke to an MP.
[269] Ibid., p. 501.   [270] Ibid., p. 501.

DISTRUST, THE EXCLUSION, AND THE
POLITICS OF TOLERATION

It is only to be expected that, despite all the subtle adjustments we have detected thus far, post-Restoration promoters of improvement, like those who came before and were to come after them, remained vulnerable to the general stereotype of the unreliable projector. Yarranton knew it very well when he dedicated his *England's improvement* to the earl of Anglesey, who was the Lord Privy Seal, and Sir Thomas Player, chamberlain of the City of London. Their patronage was indispensable, he argued, for it 'might not only obtain for it [his book] a free Access to his Majesty, but such also whose very smilings on its Design might be a sufficient Shield to guard it against all the Arrows of Obloquy and Envy, that are usually shot at the Projector'.[271] Richard Haines also complained of distrust, ironically counting himself among 'Projectors':

> I above all Projectors, have been most discouraged: And I know whoever will attempt any thing for publick Benefit, may expect these Three things.... viz. To be the Object of wise mens Censure, other mens Laughter, and ... Envies implacable displeasure[.][272]

The Royal Society was not entirely immune from similar suspicion either. In his *The History of the Royal Society*, Thomas Sprat complained of 'the ill *Treatment* which has bin most commonly given to *Inventors*' in England. Contrasting the successful promotion of profitable '*Projects*' by the Dutch, Sprat lamented 'the *English* avers from admitting of new *Inventions*, and shorter ways of labour, and from naturalising New-people':

> the *Discoverers* themselves have seldom found any any [*sic*] other entertainment than contempt and impoverishment.... The Common titles with which they are wont to be defam'd, are those of *Cheats* and *Projectors*.[273]

Even those who did not seek monopolies or sweeping imposition of their schemes by fines and confiscation could be stereotyped as conmen or promoters of impractical schemes.

There was, however, another layer of distrust and suspicion, one that was linked specifically with the post-Restoration politics of religion. Some writers, especially Nonconformist writers like Fortrey and William Penn, argued for a greater toleration for Protestant dissenters by highlighting their economic contribution.[274] The promotion of improvement accordingly became embroiled in the politics of toleration, and it in turn rendered promoters susceptible to suspicion. Samuel Parker, for example, not only attacked dissenters as 'fanatics', but also portrayed

---

[271] Andrew Yarranton, *England's improvement by sea and land* (1677), sig. [a3v].

[272] Richard Haines, *Proposal for building in every country a working-alms-house or hospital* (1677), p. 4.

[273] Sprat, *History of the Royal Society*, pp. 401–2 (italics are original). See also Petty, *Treatise of taxes and contributions*, p. 55.

[274] Fortrey, *England's interest and improvement*, 4–13; Baker Library, Kress MS E-13, 'Promotion of Trade in England', pp. 72–4; Richard Ashcraft, *Revolutionary Politics and Locke's 'Two Treatises of Government'* (Princeton, NJ: Princeton University Press, 1986), pp. 507–8.

the improvement of trade as a dangerous slogan for covering up the spread of sedi-
tion and political instability.[275]

The stakes were so high that projecting became an integral part of the politics of
royal succession on the eve of the Exclusion Crisis. In 1679 it was reported that
Yarranton had a proposal for 'Methodising' battleships 'tow 5ths [*sic*] cheaper than
now'.[276] The duke of York (the future James II), former lord high admiral, sent
agents to learn the details of the proposal. Yarranton, however, 'kept off from discovering the great secret' of his scheme, because 'the times [were] so uncertain' that
entrusting his proposal to the Catholic duke would make it 'more lickly to make
of this advantage to go [to] the French'. Yarranton instead imparted his project to
the mastermind of the Exclusion Bill, the earl of Shaftsbury.[277] This must have been
ripe for political interpretation. As Letwin has shown, the duke of York is known
to have been suspicious of the Council of Trade as 'being part of a conspiracy
organized by Buckingham and Shaftesbury' to promote religious dissent and 'make
Parliament master over the King, by first depriving him of money and then doling
it out only for purposes of which they approved'.[278]

Thus, it is hardly surprising that an anonymous pamphlet, *A coffee-house dialogue*,
soon attacked Yarranton as a Nonconformist supporting the exclusion of the duke
from the succession. The author did not refer specifically to Yarranton's refusal to
reveal his scheme to York; but the connection is likely. The author argued that the
Exclusionists' attempt 'to punish His [i.e. the duke's] particular person only, or that
he should be condemn'd unheard, are things...to be Dissentaneous both to right
Reason and Justice'. The author thus reproached Yarranton 'and all the Fanatic
Crew' for their 'blind Zeal'.[279] An anonymous pamphlet defended Yarranton as an
'honest Gentleman', and suggested that the author of *A coffee-house dialogue* 'has
been tram'd up for *French* Government, to bring Popery into Church, slavery upon
the Nation'.[280]

Little is known about what became of Yarranton's plan. Yet York's approach to
Yarranton, Yarranton's refusal, his preference for cooperating with Shaftsbury, and
the extant letter that reported the story illuminate the pursuit of improvement in
post-Restoration England, a pursuit that was at once dynamic and precarious.
Thanks to rich networks of information and patronage, the ex-parliamentary sol-
ider was able to establish himself so well that he even attracted the attention of
the king's brother, who had fought for the other side before 1660. Yet the pursuit

---

[275] Ashcraft, *Revolutionary Politics*, p. 72. Parker was not alone. See, for example, Roger North,
Examen: or an enquiry into the credit and veracity of a pretended complete history (1740), pp. 461–2. Cf.
William Letwin, *The Origins of Scientific Economics: English Economic Thought 1660–1776* (London:
Methuen, 1963), pp. 21–4; Leng, *Worsley*, pp. 170–1.

[276] Bodl., Carte MS, 233, fol. 293v, Goodwin [Wharton] to [Thomas Wharton?], 9 July 1679.

[277] Ibid., fols. 293–4, Goodwin [Wharton] to [Thomas Wharton?], 9 July 1679.

[278] Letwin, *Origins of Scientific Economics*, p. 21.

[279] *A coffee-house dialogue: or a discourse between Captain Y—and a young barrester of the Middle-
Temple; with some reflections upon the bill against the D. of Y.* [1679], pp. 3–4, 2. See also *A continuation
of the coffee-house dialogue* [1680?].

[280] *A coffee-house dialogue*, p. 2; *England's improvements justified; and the author thereof, Captain Y.
vindicated from the scandals in a paper called a coffee-house dialogue* [1679?], pp. 1, 2.

of improvement remained at best precarious, deeply woven into the political and religious fabric of the time. Nonconformist promoters of economic improvement, such as Fortrey and Yarranton, were acutely aware of the implications of their schemes for religion and politics. Ideological points were made by highlighting Nonconformists' contributions to the nation's improvement, or by choosing to collaborate or not with the Catholic heir at times of heightened political tension. Politics of toleration, by turn, shaped some of the ways in which promoters' reliability was questioned or defended in public arenas.

CONCLUSION

The post-Restoration promotion of improvement now needs to be considered as a chapter in the long-term history of projects and discourses about it. Although the 1660s and 1670s do not feature prominently in the *ESTC* or in the patent database, projects for economic improvement and innovations emerged in large number thanks to the opportunities afforded by the return of Charles II, the Great Fire, the establishment of the Royal Society, the Anglo-Dutch Wars, and increasing colonial trade and real wages amid a stabilizing population.

The evolution of projecting culture in this period was closely intertwined with the Restoration of the monarchy, its promises, and its uncertainties. Like poets such as Dryden and Waller, and alchemists such as Starkey and Stubbe, promoters of improvement carefully highlighted their 'royalist past' wherever possible. Cautious ones presented their schemes in ways that would not upset the precarious status quo, the regime's legitimacy, its religious orthodoxy, or its fraught relationship with the king's subjects in England. Charles II's government was expected to boost the economy, but it now had to promote improvement without defaulting on his commitment upon the Restoration to maintain his subjects' peace, happiness, and 'fundamental Rights'.

This chapter has paid much attention to ensuing episodes of adjustment and misadjustment. For it is in these episodes of individual choices, made across different industries, that we have discerned the subtle evolution of conventions underlying projects for improvement. Religious aspirations, even millenarian visions, hardly disappeared; yet some chose not to publish their unorthodox views, while others expressed their religious convictions in print, but in ways that explicitly endorsed the legitimacy of the restored monarchy; some, as in the case of Austen's third edition of *A treatise of fruit-trees* (1665), calibrated religious expression after careful consultation. In the administration of patents, too, the direction of change was not evident, and elements of caution prevailed accordingly. Here, we have found, processes of consultation or 'counsel' proved crucial. Faced with requests for monopolistic grants as well as with bitter public memories of Caroline monopolists and projectors, the restored regime had little choice but to weigh its fiscal needs carefully against the political risk of granting patents that could be deeply controversial. This was why Garill's bid for a wire-drawing patent was rejected upon advice from the Mint and the Goldsmiths, and, crucially, also upon stiff opposition from Urlin and the London wire-drawers. The restored regime was not immune to favouritism, of course; yet even the rising virtuoso Petty failed to win sustained support for his forced migration plans. To the frustration of men like Petty, Dymock, and Knight, projects that required sweeping mechanisms of coercion became far less likely to attract sustained governmental support, especially where vocal opponents existed.

The findings of this chapter should not be taken to imply the triumph of individual liberty and property rights. For within the British Isles, as in slave-dependent Barbados and Jamaica, it remained eminently feasible to force specific, especially vulnerable groups to work. A large number of proposals continued to appear for setting up workhouses and putting women, children, and vagabonds to work, thereby producing linen textiles, hemp ropes, toys, and other commodities that had relied on imports.[281] Similarly, there were numerous schemes that tried to procure cheap labour by putting imprisoned debtors and those convicted of misdemeanours to work on weaving, digging mines, or deepening rivers.[282] Landowners achieved selective compulsion by binding their tenants to implement certain improvements. Upon leasing his tenement in Kensington in 1684, Baptist Noel of Rutland, a younger son of Edward Noel, bound the tenant Francis Percevall to 'plant & sett ... good & best sort of fruite trees of all sorts' within seven years. Such a measure was no novelty; yet horticultural writers of this period now recommended this indirect method over a nationwide legal regime.[283] The exploitation of less-advantaged populations, promoted under the banner of England's improvement, thus continued to take place not only in the context of its colonies, Ireland, and later Scotland, but also in domestic settings.[284] Upon that fraught foundation the practices of projecting evolved away from industrial monopolies and blanket compulsion.

In the repetition of circumspection, frustration, and failure we have found fresh and greater attention being paid to the means to stimulate private initiatives and competitive emulation among the governed population. Horticultural writings in and outside the Royal Society, written by savants like Evelyn and Beale and also by less exalted experts such as John Smith and the Royal Gardener John Rose, all highlighted the importance of the ruling elites in setting desirable examples to be emulated across the social spectrum. In Beale's manuscript and published writings we have found one of its most expansive expressions. For him, the spread of cider production across humble rural households could at best help to reduce imports of French wines and stimulate sugar production in the Caribbean colonies. Writers of national improvement such as Fortrey likewise argued for fostering consumer taste for home-manufactured goods over foreign imports.

---

[281] Yarranton, *England's improvement*, p. 44–64, esp. p. 47. See also Haines, *Proposals*; Thomas Firmin, *Some proposals for the imployment of the poor* (1681).

[282] Richard Haines, *A method of government for such publick working alms-houses* (1670), p. 6; Daniel Defoe, *An essay upon projects* (1697), p. 103. See also Koji Yamamoto, 'Piety, Profit and Public Service in the Financial Revolution', *EHR*, 126 (2011), 806–34, pp. 819, 822.

[283] Record Office for Leicestershire, Leicester, and Rutland, DE3214/3533/1–2; Evelyn, *Pomona*, p. 2; Beale, *Nursery*, p. 3. See also Austen, *A treatise of fruit-trees* (1665), p. 233.

[284] See pp. 271–2.

The culture of post-Restoration projecting therefore reveals a link between the *supply-side* visions of economic improvement, to be promoted and executed by individual projectors, and those *demand-side* visions of abundance that drew upon the power of emulation and the appetite of middling consumers. The connection between the two lines of thinking is hardly surprising. After all, those who argued for the role of emulation—such as Beale, Barbon, and Houghton—were among the foremost promoters of schemes for improving domestic production. If arguments for emulation came to be adopted more prominently under the restored monarchy, a history of projecting shows that it owed much to the practical, political challenges of imposing supply-side programmes of nationwide economic regeneration from above in conditions of political uncertainty. The philosopher's stone was now to be found, as it were, in the power of emulation among the governed population at large. *Their* interests, not just the private interests of promoters or of needy monarchs, were to become essential ingredients for the powder of projection capable of transmutation.

Nicholas Barbon was, therefore, not breaking new ground when he declared that emulation, by provoking 'a continued Industry', would make the people grow richer and a nation stronger, as we saw at the beginning of this chapter. The author also suggested that this 'benefit ariseth solely from Cities; for in a Countrey Solitude there is little Emulation'.[285] As a promoter of building construction in the metropolis, Barbon had an obvious reason to single out cities as the unique drive for an improving economy. Having surveyed the rich seams of horticultural literature and the 'discourse of trade' in and outside the Royal Society, however, we can now establish that the argument for improvement via emulation was not pioneered by a few writers like Barbon (as Slack has indicated), but had been adopted by a broader range of authors and experts promoting rural, as well as urban, improvement. Public desire for betterment and emulation assumed a vital role in their argument because it was deemed capable of transmutation, turning barren ground into fertile gardens, and putting idle hands into profitable labour, thereby making England and its subordinate dominions into a potent empire. Defoe's Projecting Age, as will be seen in Chapter 6, would rest squarely upon such consuming desire, albeit in different forms: public consumption both of company shares and of news and rumours about them.

The findings of this chapter enable us to qualify Mokyr's account of useful knowledge: 'What counts is what the few who mattered knew, how they knew it, and what they did with this knowledge.'[286] I agree that enabling factors are not to be neglected. Yet this parsimonious statement looks almost simplistic once we take into account the decisive role played by a large number of post-Restoration promoters, statesmen, savants, craftsmen, petitioners, and even street protesters at this critical juncture. Their interventions, their trial and error, I submit, collectively amounted to what Jan de Vries has called 'structure-modifying acts'—'sequences

---

[285] [Barbon], *Discourse shewing the great advantages*, p. 5.
[286] Joel Mokyr, *The Gifts of Athena: Historical Origins of the Knowledge Economy* (Princeton, NJ: Princeton University Press, 2002), p. 291.

leading to path dependent outcomes'.[287] Their actions collectively gave rise to the new vision of abundance by invoking and confronting the 'troubled past', by preventing English society from restoring the vexatious early Stuart practices, and by reappraising the leverage of micro-level incentives in ways that were consistent with expanding Atlantic trade and rising spending power below the middling ranks. It was thanks to these numerous *visible hands* taming England's incipient capitalism that the precocious vision of consumption-driven improvement evolved in this period, a vision that would be elaborated in the eighteenth century.

---

[287] Jan de Vries, *The Return from the Return to Narrative* [Max Weber Lecture No. 2013/01] (Badia Fiesolana: European University Institute, 2013), p. 11. See p. 25 above.

6

Consuming Projects

In the summer of 1698, William Digby (bap. 1661/2–1752) was gathering information from a correspondent in London. Digby enquired about a new bill on gaming, the malt tax, and in September, about the Company of the Mine Adventurers of England (often called the Mine Adventure) that had started calling for investors. At the end of the month Digby told his London agent that the company's 'proposal seems rationall enough' and that it merited further inquiries: 'pray tell me what you hear of it; for tis hard to judg at this distance'. He was writing from his estate in Sherborne, Dorset. Digby soon received more news. Led by Sir Humphrey Mackworth, the Mine Adventure proposed to tap into the lead mines of the deceased Sir Carbery Price of Cardiganshire in western Wales, which were believed to be rich in silver. The plan was to form a company to reorganize the venture that Price had started, and to bring lead ore to Mackworth's estate in Neath (in south Wales) and smelt it with the coal from his own mines. After a week Digby concluded he had 'so good an opinion of the *project* as to accept of 5 shares for the 100lb you [owe?] me, if you think fit'.[1] This landed gentleman used the notion of a project when he became a shareholder of the company.

Now we have come full circle back to the world of Defoe, Cary, and Hill with which we began this book. Joint-stock companies driven by the incipient stock market, a precocious manifestation of *modern* financial capitalism, emerged as a climax of the *early modern* history of projecting. Conversely, it will be argued, assertions of public service and the pervasive distrust of such promises that we have encountered repeatedly in the preceding chapters provided a fundamental, bipartisan framework for corporate publicity and its public consumption in the age of the financial revolution.

Digby's encounter with the Mine Adventure encapsulates England's new projecting culture that was visibly different from that of his father's cousin, George Digby, the earl of Bristol (1612–77), who, as an MP in the Long Parliament, criticized early Stuart monopolists, and whose involvement in the Stour river navigation scheme from 1661 was representative of post-Restoration large-scale projects that rarely drew on public subscription.[2] Now in the 1690s, patenting boomed and unincorporated joint-stock companies mushroomed; there were many

---

[1] BL, Egerton 2540, fols. 115, 117, 123, 127, 132 (my italics). For Digby, see Howard Erskine-Hill, *The Social Milieu of Alexander Pope: Lives, Example and the Poetic Response* (New Haven, CT: Yale University Press, 1975), pp. 145–50; for Mackworth and the Mine Adventure, see Koji Yamamoto, 'Piety, Profit and Public Service in the Financial Revolution', *EHR*, 126 (2011), 806–34.

[2] See Chapter 4.

readers seeking information about potentially navigable rivers. John Houghton, FRS, knew this well when he published the issue of his *Collection for Improvement of Husbandry and Trade* for 3 March 1693. Naming eleven rivers, including the Humber, the Don, the Trent, and the Ouse, Houghton informed readers of the distance between 'the principal Towns' on these navigable rivers, 'reckoned by strait lines from one place to the other'; for example, 'The Ouse, which from the *Humber* bears ships by *Selby, Barleby,…Middlethorp*, &c to *York* seventeen and thirteen' miles.[3] 'I know these measures are not exact, neither was the first Dictionary, [nor] the first map,' wrote Houghton. Providing these figures would be particularly beneficial, he suggested, because they could be 'a ground for learning what trade already is, what may be improved upon these rivers', especially 'mines of *coal, lead, tinn, iron, copper*, or any other mineral not far from them; also for the easie carriage' of bulky goods like '*wood, charcoal*, [and] *corn*'.[4] But Houghton went on to underline a unique reason for publishing this kind of information 'especially at this time',

> when companies of men are so eager to enter into joint-stocks for improvement of anything that appears reasonable; witness our *linen* and *copper* companies, and the company that lately subscribed for *lead* mines in *Wales*, to which, to my knowledge, a subscription was made in one day of 2,500*l*.[5]

Stock trading became a crucial element of England's new projecting culture, which we shall explore in this chapter.

Like George Digby and other promoters of the Stour navigation scheme in the 1660s that we encountered in Chapter 4, Houghton was concerned with the exploitation of navigable rivers for improving inland trade and domestic industries. But during the financial revolution, a long process that culminated in Defoe's *Projecting Age* in the 1690s, schemes for economic innovations and improvements became relevant to the public in ways that they had not been before: new economic schemes were increasingly funded through 'joint-stocks' as Houghton observed. Of course, it had long been possible to buy East India Company shares or the stock of other chartered joint-stock companies and sell them to third parties. Yet both the number of shareholders and the scale of stock transfer were rather limited before the final decade of the seventeenth century. The Hudson Bay's Company oversaw an annual average of fewer than ten transfers for much of the 1670s, and fewer than thirty transfers during the 1680s. More transfers took place for the Royal African Company; yet for the same two decades its annual average share transfers were respectively about forty and then just under eighty. The volume of stock trading rose sharply in the early 1690s. In 1691, the number of stock transfers for the Royal African Company hit the height of 930; the Hudson's Bay Company, 149. The number of joint-stock companies also increased from eleven before 1688 to ninety-three in 1695, adding breadth to the range of shares traded.

---

[3] John Houghton, *A collection for improvement of husbandry and trade* (4 vols., 1727–8), vol. 1, no. 30, p. 85.
[4] Ibid., vol. 1, no. 30, pp. 86–7.   [5] Ibid., vol. 1, no. 30, p. 87.

As Anne Murphy's important study warns us, speculative investment tended to concentrate upon a handful of companies, and such interests were often short-lived. We need not assume that England was transformed into a nation of stock traders. Yet it is worth highlighting that the scale and the scope of stock trading visibly expanded in the final decade of the century.[6]

Accordingly, wealthy country gentlemen like William Digby, and many men and women below him, now sought and bought news, commentaries, and proposals about new economic schemes. They could even purchase shares in new companies and expect not only dividends but also capital gains by selling and reselling them in the emerging stock market. During the early financial revolution, in short, England's culture of improvement evolved into highly marketable commodities aimed at the wider public, to be traded in Exchange Alley, coffeehouses, printers' workshops, and beyond. The projectors' tortuous processes of promotion and implementation became tightly knitted into this market. Their efforts and failures would be reported, rumoured, ridiculed, and ultimately consumed by investors and wider publics willing to inform and entertain themselves.

This chapter revisits the early financial revolution as the climax of the history of projecting. As Henry Roseveare has argued, the word 'revolution' is 'one of the most overworked terms in the historian's vocabulary, glibly invoked to give some spurious drama and significance to developments which could be more fairly described as "evolution"'.[7] He has accordingly extended the chronology of the financial revolution by tracing the complex evolution of *governmental finance* since Charles II's reign. Carl Wennerlind has offered an equally important revision with regard to *earlier natural philosophical, often alchemical, ideas* that came to inform the discussion of banking and its economic potential in the 1690s.[8] Building upon these works, I argue that new *practices of projecting*—what Houghton called the new 'joint-stocks for improvement'—must likewise be considered from a long-term perspective. Even the South Sea Bubble might profitably be considered as part of the story.

Joint-stock companies that sprang up in large numbers in Defoe's Projecting Age were, like projects of earlier decades, obsessed with promises of piety and public service and mocked precisely for that reason. Yet such an obsession was now tied firmly to the burgeoning stock market and, equally importantly, to the contemporary religious movements, as is shown by the cases of the Mine Adventure and the little-known Cornish projector Samuel Weale. Like company stocks, the rise and fall of these projects were themselves rumoured, reported, and ultimately consumed in the burgeoning marketplace. The public scrutiny—we might say the

---

[6] The best account is Anne L. Murphy, *The Origins of English Financial Markets: Investment and Speculation before the South Sea Bubble* (Cambridge: Cambridge University Press, 2009), esp. pp. 16, 23, 143, 225. Note also that, for much of the seventeenth century, share transfers usually had to be approved at corporate meetings. See Edmond Smith, 'The Global Interests of London's Commercial Community, 1599–1625: Investment in the East India Company', *EcHR* (forthcoming). I thank Anne Murphy and Edmond Smith for advice.

[7] Henry Roseveare, *The Financial Revolution* (Harlow: Longman, 1991), p. 2.

[8] Carl Wennerlind, *Casualties of Credit: The English Financial Revolution, 1620–1720* (Cambridge, MA: Harvard University Press, 2011), pp. 67–85.

taming—of joint-stock projects became so closely entangled with this market that cautionary tales like Swift's *Gulliver's Travels* became commodities in their own right, *literary projects* sold seemingly for the public good.

Revisiting the financial revolution from a long-term perspective yields an unexpected dividend. Over the last three decades, studies of corporate social responsibility and its conceptual variables have become a thriving subfield of business and management studies. Yet these accounts rarely go beyond the nineteenth century.[9] The topic has remained peripheral to early modern economic history. The history of projecting provides us with a powerful way of connecting these fields without becoming too anachronistic.[10] In so far as Defoe's Projecting Age was driven by public consumption of stocks, financial news, and rumours, and to the extent that this period represents a crucial stage in the emergence of financial capitalism, England's projecting culture examined in this chapter stands as an unacknowledged antecedent of our culture, one in which the corporate promotion of public service continues to invite commendations, reappraisal, and even distrust. Then, as now, there were serious anxieties about the need for taming capitalism and rendering it serviceable and sustainable.[11]

PUBLIC CONSUMPTION OF PROJECTS

The patent boom that had begun in 1691 started subsiding by 1694 (see Fig. 1.2), and so did the volume of share trading by 1695. Although the Nine Years War initially helped trigger the boom of domestic investment, in the long run it damaged international trade and diverted credit towards army remittances to fund the war effort abroad. Many of the newly established companies did not survive these economic setbacks, exacerbated by debased English coins and the ensuing recoinage of 1696. The number of joint-stock companies, which reached a peak of ninety-three in 1695, had plunged to twenty-eight by 1698.[12]

Projecting did not go out of fashion, however. It is worth remembering that Defoe's *Essay upon projects* was published in 1697. Another case in point is

---

[9] Influential treatments include Milton Friedman, 'The Social Responsibility of Business is to Increase its Profit', *New York Times Magazine*, 13 September 1970, 32–3, 122–6; Peter Drucker, 'The New Meaning of Corporate Social Responsibility', *California Management Review*, 26 (1984), 53–63; Archie B. Carroll, 'Corporate Social Responsibility: Evolution of a Definitional Construct', *Business and Society*, 38 (1999), 268–95; David Henderson, *Misguided Virtue: False Notions of Corporate Social Responsibility* (London: The Institute of Economic Affairs, 2001). A more recent survey, which reflects the limited chronological scope of the field, is Archie B. Carroll, 'A History of Corporate Social Responsibility: Concepts and Practices', in Andrew Crane et al. (eds.), *The Oxford Handbook of Corporate Social Responsibility* (Oxford: Oxford University Press, 2008), 19–46, esp. pp. 20–1.

[10] I find the following reflections on anachronism particularly useful: Andre Wakefield, 'Butterfield's Nightmare: The History of Science as Disney History', *History and Technology*, 30 (2014), 232–51, esp. p. 235.

[11] Another path for opening up the dialogue would be to explore the history of corporations as intellectual and social constructs. See Henry S. Turner, *The Corporate Commonwealth: Pluralism and Political Fictions in England, 1516–1651* (Chicago: University of Chicago Press, 2016).

[12] Murphy, *Origins*, pp. 31–3, 36; Scott, *Joint-Stock*, vol. 1, pp. 347–9; D. W. Jones, *War and Economy in the Age of William III and Marlborough* (Oxford: Blackwell, 1988).

William Walcot's desalination engine. Walcot originally obtained a patent for his desalination engines in 1675, but Richard Fitzgerald, who claimed to have invented a better one, had it revoked in 1683. In February 1693, at the height of the patent boom, Walcot successfully reversed this revocation. Walcot died in 1699, but his scheme did not end with the patent boom. His nephew Humphrey Walcot took over the privilege. In 1702, shortly after the outbreak of the War of the Spanish Succession, Humphrey published a pamphlet and circulated a handbill announcing that the engine would help naval ships secure fresh water in war zones.[13] The proliferation of these and numerous other schemes discussed in this chapter may have owed something to the lapse of the licensing act in 1696. 'T''is true', an anonymous author declared in 1699:

> we live in a very Teeming Age: Never was the Press more guilty of Impertinent Productions, than since the Expiration of the Act of Licensing: The whole Nation seems to have run a Gadding, and every little Trifler sets up now for Wit, Politicks, or Projects.[14]

The author's impression warns us that the planning and promotion of improvement schemes proved resilient despite the relative decline in the number of companies, patents granted, and the volume of stock trading.

As Houghton observed, many of these new schemes called for investors through public subscription. Examples are numerous. When marketing his desalination engine, Walcot called for subscribers to a joint-stock company to realize a capital of £5,000, with one hundred shares valued at £50 each.[15] To exploit their patented invention 'to preserve ships from foundering' at sea, the merchant George Oldner and his partners proposed to set up an unincorporated joint-stock company with a capital of £60,000 by selling 6,000 shares valued at £10 each.[16] The White Paper Company was launched once a patent was granted in 1687; it raised funds by issuing 400 shares at £50 per share, making a nominal total of £20,000. The Royal Lustring Company, which made silk textiles using continental methods patented in 1688, expanded its operation in 1692, issuing 2,400 shares valued at £25 each, totalling £60,000 as nominal capital. The King's and Queen's Corporation for the Linen Manufacture in England (the Linen Company) was operating in 1690 with 340 shares at £10 each, with further issues of shares at £50 each.[17]

While some large-scale domestic schemes, especially inland navigation and turnpikes, continued to operate as trusts or partnerships, some natural resource management schemes came also to be funded by joint-stocks. An undertaking to improve the Hampstead Aqueducts operated from 1692 with 600 shares at a nominal value of £20 each, giving it a total capital of £12,000. Similarly, in 1703

---

[13] R. E. W. Maddison, 'Studies in the Life of Robert Boyle, F.R.S. Part II. Salt Water Freshened', *NRRS*, 9 (1952), pp. 211–12. See also MacLeod, *Patent*, pp. 36–7.

[14] *An epistle to a member of parliament, concerning Mr. George Oldner's invention* (1699), p. 3.

[15] Humphrey Walcot, *Sea-water made fresh and wholsome* (1702), pp. 6, 25–8.

[16] Patent no. 352, 24 September 1697; George Oldner, *Mr. George Oldner's invention to preserve ships from foundering, or sinking, at sea, &c* (1698), title-page, pp. 9–12. Details of the invention were kept secret.

[17] Scott, *Joint-Stock*, vol. 3, pp. 65, 75, 97.

the London Bridge Water Works was operating with 300 shares at £500 each, but later converted them into 1,500 shares at £100 each, giving it a nominal capital of £150,000.[18]

Schemes for poor relief, hospitals, and the like—some of the recurrent themes in the history of projecting—also began to adopt joint-stocks as a method of funding. Charles Davenant tried to set up a joint-stock for poor relief.[19] Hospitals were to be funded by public subscription to lotteries. Greenwich Hospital carried this out, and Defoe proposed a similar scheme to fund what he called a 'Fool-House'.[20] The notorious Charitable Corporation, established by a patent in 1707, was essentially 'a large scale corporate pawnbroker', empowered to lend out its funds 'for the relief of industrious poor, upon goods, wares, pawns, and pledges'. It had amassed a capital of about £50,000 by the time parliament investigated its mismanagement in 1733.[21] Some promoters explicitly called for mobilizing private interests for public purposes. In 1695, the Quaker reformer John Bellers proposed to set up what he called the College of Industry. While his call for employing and educating the poor echoed much of earlier proposals, he followed the emerging trend and began his campaign by calling for a 'General Subscription'.[22] 'Tho' it would be Toilsome for any one Man, or a few [to raise money], yet 'tis easily done by a great Number'. Notably, Bellers planned to provide dividends to shareholders by selling agricultural produce and goods manufactured by college members. 'A thousand Pound is easier raised where there is Profit' to be distributed, he declared.[23] The proposal did not live up to his original expectation. But a workhouse was in fact established in Clerkenwell in 1702, following the subscription of forty-five Friends to the 'joint Stock' in 1697, and official approval next year at the yearly London meeting.[24]

Experimental philosophy, heralded by the Royal Society, could now harness the private interests of numerous investors through the public offering of shares. Robert Hooke and Christopher Dodsworth obtained a patent for a new way of making glass in June 1691; this was followed by a move to incorporate the 'Company of Glass Makers in & about the Cittys of London and Westminster', which was to have the power 'to raise a Joint Stock... to any value whatsoever'.[25]

---

[18] Ibid., vol. 3, pp. 5, 15.   [19] Slack, *Reformation to Improvement*, p. 120.

[20] Daniel Defoe, *An essay upon projects* (1697), pp. 178–91 (esp. p. 184).

[21] A. J. G. Cummings, 'The York Buildings Company: A Case in Eighteenth-Century Corporation Mismanagement' (PhD thesis, University of Strathcyde, 1980), pp. 395, 449.

[22] See John Bellers, *John Bellers: His Life, Times and Writings*, ed. George Clarke (London: Routledge, 1987), pp. 62–3, 66.

[23] Bellers, *John Bellers*, pp. 67, 79.

[24] Library of the Society of Friends, London Yearly Meeting Minutes, vol. 2 (1694–1701), pp. 185, 187, 258–9; Wandsworth Monthly Meeting Minutes, 2nd day of 1st month, 6th day of 2nd month, 1698. For more, see Charles R. Simpson, 'John Bellers in Official Minutes', *Journal of the Friends Historical Society*, 12 (1915), 120–7, 165–71.

[25] Patent no. 268; TNA, SP 44/235, fol. 201; SP 44/341, fols. 197–201 (quotations at fols. 198, 201). The proposed company was attacked on the ground that the 'Things ... will in Effect be a Monopoly, and engross that Commodity into a few Hands'. See *The case of William Gutteridge, and other glass-makers* [n.d., *c*.1691]. Note that this Robert Hooke may have been a namesake of the experimental philosopher. See Hentie Louw, 'The "Mechanick Artist" in Late Seventeenth-Century English and French Architecture: The Work of Robert Hooke, Christopher Wren and Claude Perrault

The Huguenot Denis Papin applied the idea of joint-stock subscription to the systematic promotion of technical ingenuity more broadly. He proposed to erect a 'Company or Society for New Inventions, for which Subscriptions may be made for £1,000 Stock'.[26]

In short, joint-stock companies funded by public subscription emerged as a major outlet for projecting initiatives during the early financial revolution. It was for this reason that Thomas Baston fumed that 'the Modern Mode' of projecting aimed to fleece the '*Vulgar* sort of *People*' by 'Opening Books, Taking in Subscriptions, dividing it into Shares'.[27]

As we can infer from the increasing popularity of public subscription to joint-stocks, this mode of projecting drew in not only wealthy landed gentlemen like William Digby, but also investors from across the social strata. As Peter Earle has shown in his study of the London middling sort, shares in companies and public funds became major assets (47.6 per cent) in their personal investment portfolios for the three decades after 1690. This was an increase from 27.4 per cent for the previous twenty-five years.[28] Among the 'early adopters' were also women—not only wealthy ones, but also those from the gentry and middling ranks.[29] Clergymen held shares in companies, governmental bonds, and even lottery tickets.[30] Corporate bodies purchased shares too. Despite its ambiguous attitude to stock trading and economic schemes of immediate utility, the Royal Society purchased government bonds and company shares and committed their management to its Fellows and brokers.[31] Even charitable institutions such as the Society for Promoting Christian Knowledge (SPCK) and Christ's Hospital held investments in lottery tickets, public credits, and company shares.[32] Shareholding became a fact of life. 'Several Projects about this time began to run in my mind', wrote the Sussex trader Samuel Jeake in his diary in 1694. '[T]he war having spoiled all

---

Compared as Products of an Interactive Science/Architecture Relationship', in Michael Cooper and Michael Hunter (eds.), *Robert Hooke: Tercentennial Studies* (Aldershot: Ashgate, 2006), 181–99, pp. 193–4.

[26] Larry Stewart, *The Rise of Public Science: Rhetoric, Technology, and Natural Philosophy in Newtonian Britain, 1660–1750* (Cambridge: Cambridge University Press, 1992), pp. 25, 176. See also Michael Hunter, *Establishing the New Science: The Experience of the Early Royal Society* (Woodbridge: Boydell, 1989), pp. 89–90.

[27] Thomas Baston, *Thoughts on trade and a publick spirit* (1716), pp. 16, 13.

[28] Peter Earle, *The Making of the English Middle Class: Business, Society and Family Life in London, 1660–1730* (London: Methuen, 1989), pp. 145–8. Other investment assets in the analysis include loans and mortgages, leases, and shipping.

[29] Amy M. Froide, *Silent Partners: Women as Public Investors during Britain's Financial Revolution* (Oxford: Oxford University Press, 2017), esp. pp. 63, 67.

[30] For example, see C. F. Secretan, *Memoirs of the Life and Times of the Pious Robert Nelson* (London: John Murray, 1860), p. 283. See also the case of Thomas Bray mentioned later.

[31] Stewart, *Public Science*, pp. 167–8.

[32] For the SPCK's dealing in insurance, company shares, and lottery tickets, see Edmund McClure, *A chapter in English church history: being the minutes of the Society for Promoting Christian Knowledge for the years 1698–1704; together with abstracts of correspondents' letters during part of the same period* (London: SPCK, 1888), pp. 18–20, 31, 41, 194. For Christ's Hospital's shareholding, see my case study of the Mine Adventure later in this chapter.

my Trade at Rye', he hoped to 'advance my Income' by buying shares in the Bank of England, the East India Company, and the Million Adventure.[33]

Public subscriptions could never have penetrated a society this way without intensive public relations. A plethora of pamphlets promoted, defended, commented on, or satirized them. For example, at the height of banking experiments between 1695 and 1696, this subject alone produced no fewer than 260 pamphlets, almost one in ten of the books published in London during the period.[34] Specialist newspapers, mainly catering for those involved in foreign trade, listed the stock prices of joint-stock companies along with prices of commodities, bills of entry, and shipping lists.[35] Stock prices were also circulated by non-specialist papers catering for a wider audience. John Houghton's *Collection for Improvement of Husbandry and Trade* started listing the share prices of about a dozen companies when its publication was resumed in March 1692. Two years later it began to offer, for a surcharge, the stock prices of about forty more companies, both incorporated and unincorporated.[36] The Sun Fire Office's *British Mercury*, another non-specialist paper that took over Charles Povey's *General Remark on Trade* from 1710, also reported stock prices with other content such as foreign news.[37] Publicity about new economic projects had become so widespread by 1695 that the author of *Angliae tutamen* complained that 'the *Gazettes* and Public Papers are cramm'd with Advertisements, the fourth Column is entirely theirs'.[38] The *ESTC* search results discussed in Chapter 1, which show that the term 'project' came to be used more frequently from the 1690s as a relatively neutral term to discuss new economic and financial schemes, therefore reflect this emerging public consumption of projecting activities (see Fig. 1.3).

It is difficult to ascertain the extent and geographical scope of the circulation of such print media or readers' responses to them, but, as Houghton explained, he decided to list share prices for more companies because 'A great many desire[d]' them. The *British Mercury* sold about 3,000 copies or more each issue, matching the government's *London Gazette* and other major newspapers like the semi-weekly *Evening Post* and the tri-weekly *Post-Boy* and *Post-Man*.[39] Flourishing prints and newspapers never entirely replaced more private channels of circulation, of course.

---

[33] Samuel Jeake, *An Astrological Diary of the Seventeenth Century: Samuel Jeake of Rye 1652–1699*, ed. Michael Hunter and Annabel Gregory (Oxford: Clarendon, 1988), p. 233.

[34] The source is a chronological bibliography in J. Keith Horsefield, *British Monetary Experiments, 1650–1710* (Cambridge, MA: Harvard University Press, 1960), pp. 289–311, which lists 265 items published in London for 1695 and 1696. The corresponding total number of published titles for the two years is estimated to be 2,990. See John Barnard and D. F. McKenzie (eds.), *The Cambridge History of the Book in Britain, vol. IV, 1557–1695* (Cambridge: Cambridge University Press, 2002), Appendix 1, Statistical tables, Table 1, Annual book production 1475–1700.

[35] Natasha Glaisyer, *The Culture of Commerce in England, 1660–1720* (Woodbridge: Boydell, 2006), p. 143.

[36] Larry Neal, 'The Rise of a Financial Press: London and Amsterdam, 1681–1810', *Business History*, 30 (1988), 163–78, p. 167.

[37] Glaisyer, *Culture of Commerce*, pp. 156–71.

[38] *Angliae tutamen: or, the safety of England* (1695), p. 23. For a study of advertisements, see Jeffrey R. Wigelsworth, 'Bipartisan Politics and Practical Knowledge: Advertising of Public Science in Two London Newspapers, 1695–1720', *BJHS*, 41 (2008), 517–40.

[39] Glaisyer, *Culture of Commerce*, pp. 160–1, 171–82.

Walcot, for example, sent his 'papers' around through his network; while apologizing that 'I abhorrer the thoughts of Imposing on any one', he asked his niece's father-in-law Adam Ottley in Hereford to 'get me some subscriptions'.[40] Through private correspondence and through pamphlets and periodicals, information about new schemes circulated daily and reached interested parties in London and in the provinces.

When calling for investors, promoters of new schemes for economic innovations and improvements invoked a wide range of authorities, including acts of parliament, expert testimonies and legal affidavits, letters of recommendation, and lists of prominent gentlemen who agreed to patronize the proposed undertakings. These written authorities in turn were part of an intensive mobilization of various media, a process that drew on both 'visual languages (public shows, experiments, exhibitions) and print resources: advertisements, posters, tracts, how-to leaflets and users' books'.[41] So when George Oldner and his partners called for subscribers, they carried out a demonstration of their patented marine invention on the Thames using a miniature boat, and later published several testimonies along with details of how to subscribe.[42] In a bid to market the desalination engine in 1701, Walcot not only publicized it by circulating handbills, but also displayed engines of varying size, 'to be seen and ... to be sold at his Warehouse In Wool=Pack Ally in Houndsditch' in London.[43]

No longer an instrument of royal fiscal policy, letters patent became one of the main publicity tools that promoters could mobilize in order to lend credibility to their new economic schemes. The 1690s boom marked 'the development of a major new heterodox use' of patents; promoters increasingly came 'to recognize the publicity value of a patent. They liked to imply, or at least did not discourage the misconception, that a patent was a form of royal guarantee, that the product or project had been inspected and passed by officials, ministers, or even the king himself'.[44] In this respect, the patent boom in the early 1690s was integral to the increasing consumption of news about new enterprises, and thus needs to be distinguished from earlier booms in the 1670s and 1680s. Of course, just like earlier ones, some patents issued during the 1690s protected smaller business

---

[40] NLW, Ottley (Pitchford Hall) Correspondence/2189, 2190 (quotation from 2190, Humphrey Walcot to Adam Ottley, 8 November 1701). It is not clear whether the 'papers' were manuscripts or printed proposals. Both Walcot and Ottley were connected to James Brydges, later the first duke of Chandos. See John Richard Burton, *Some Collections towards the History of the Family of Walcot* (Shrewsbury: Brown & Brinnard, 1930), pp. 78–81; Eveline Cruickshanks, Stuart Handley, and David Hayton (eds.), *History of Parliament: The House of Commons, 1690–1715* (5 vols., Cambridge: Cambridge University Press, 2002), vol. 5, pp. 762–3; J. D. Davies, 'Ottley, Adam (bap. 1655, d. 1723)', *Oxford DNB*, vol. 42, 107–8. For the case of Samuel Weale's manuscript circulation, see pp. 253–4.

[41] Liliane Hilaire-Pérez and Marie Thébaud-Sorger, 'Les Techniques dans l'espace public: Publicité des inventions et littérature d'usage au XVIIIe siècle (France, Angleterre)', *Revue de Synthèse*, 5th ser., 2 (2006), 393–428, at p. 393.

[42] Oldner, *Mr. George Oldner's invention*, pp. 9–12.

[43] Humphrey Walcot, *Sea-water made fresh and wholsom* [1702], [a printed handbill], Kress, S.2260 (a handwritten note at the bottom).

[44] Christine MacLeod, 'The 1690s Patents Boom: Invention or Stock-Jobbing?', *EcHR*, new ser., 39 (1986), pp. 555–6.

partnerships, as in the case of John Lofting and his patents for fire engines and thimbles.[45] The 'heterodox' use was not unprecedented either. John Wells, for instance, obtained in 1673 a patent for a 'new engine for teaching to perform by articifial hourses, the usual exercises of a complete horseman'. He circulated a handbill proudly promising the 'most curious and most profitable Engine that ever was invented', to which 'the Kings Majesty hath given leave to *John Wells* to establish thorowout all *England*, by vertue of His Letters Patents sealed with the Great Seal of *England*'. In effect, the patent helped Wells promote his horse machine and the entertainment offered for one shilling a ride in the military ground near Soho an 'Entertainment and Divertisement' styled as the 'ACADEMY by the Kings Privilege' that would teach horsemanship, 'the Noble Employs of a true Gentleman'.[46] Such strategic use of patents became so conspicuous during the speculation boom of the early 1690s that, in 1695, the author of *Angliae tutamen* dismissed 'trifling Engines and Whims', and fumed that 'Oh, a Patent gives a Reputation to it, and cullies in the Company.'[47]

The South Sea Bubble of 1720 was in fact part of this new projecting culture that drew upon public appetite for shares and quick profits. As is well known, the financial crisis was closely connected with the British government's long-term debt, which rapidly increased due to its war against France. The Scotsman John Law offered the French government a comprehensive scheme to restructure government debt. Inspired partly by Law's 'System' of 1719, the South Sea Company, which conducted the slave trade to Spanish America, proposed to parliament a debt-conversion scheme. At the heart of the scheme was the public offering of subscriptions for South Sea shares in exchange for government bonds. So, the more people who gave up interest-bearing bonds to buy South Sea shares for the prospect of a quick profit, the higher the share price would become, and the better this would be for the government. This was in effect a debt-for-equity swap, fuelled by speculation in a secondary market. Note that the process, like other projects floated on the stock market, was to be driven by the private desire of many potential investors. As the archbishop of Dublin, William King, observed in May 1720: 'if the debts of the nation may be paid by the folly of particulars... it will be very well for the public, and I know no obligation on me to hinder it. Perhaps what would be spent this way would be spent on gaming or on luxury'.[48] The unfolding of the 1720 bubble is so rich a subject that it certainly deserves a separate investigation.[49]

[45] MacLeod, 'The 1690s Patents Boom', p. 556.

[46] *Academy. By the Kings privilege* [1674?]. The handbill bore an engraving of the king's Great Seal and a French translation of the advertisement.

[47] *Angliae tutamen*, pp. 22, 23, at p. 23.

[48] Trinity College Dublin Special Collections, MS 750/6, fol. 87. See also Simon Schaffer, 'The Show that Never Ends: Perpetual Motion in the Early Eighteenth Century', *BJHS*, 28 (1995), 157–89, pp. 183–4.

[49] My preliminary study on the subject, including a brief survey of recent historiography, is Koji Yamamoto, 'Beyond Rational and Irrational Bubbles: James Brydges the First Duke of Chandos during the South Sea Bubble', in Francesco Ammannati (ed.), *Le crisi finanziarie: gestione, implicazioni sociali e conseguenze nell'età preindustriale* (Florence: Fondazione Istituto internazionale di storia economica 'F. Datini', 2016), 327–57.

Yet King's comment underscores how the South Sea scheme drew upon the potent mobilization of private desire for public ends, which was characteristic of England's projecting culture at the time. This explains why the scheme was often compared to alchemical transmutation, and dubbed the South Sea 'project'.[50]

Financial speculation highlights a shady side of the new projecting culture: the proliferation of rumours and false news. In 1712, the *Spectator* offered a revealing tale of a man 'who used to divert himself by telling a Lie at *Charing-Cross* in the Morning' and then enjoyed observing its manifold repercussions elsewhere: 'what Censure it had at *Will's* in *Covent-Garden*, how dangerous it was believed to be at *Childs*, and what Inference they drew from it with Relation to Stock at *Jonathan's*'.[51] Note how false news was expected to affect stocks at Jonathan's coffeehouse, a venue, along with Garraway's, well known for stock trading. The author of the episode was Richard Steele, who invented and patented a 'fish-pool' vessel and a carriage that would 'bring Fish alive much better than at present' with the assistance of the Wiltshire mathematician Joseph Gillmore.[52] The tale indicates that those actively involved in the promotion of new schemes could be acutely aware of the damaging implications of false news about their activities. Such a concern was surely no novelty. The projecting activities of the Hartlib circle operated alongside its news-gathering, and we saw in Chapter 3 that Hartlib's allies, such as Blith, complained of 'heare-sayes' which had 'brought Ingenuity under greatest Scandall'. As early as the mid-1660s, an Italian visitor wrote that in English coffeehouses 'one hears what is or is believed to be new, be it true or false'.[53] News about Francis Mathew's project to connect the Thames and the Severn attracted much attention after it was presented to Charles II in 1660 and again in 1670. Yet 'some foolish Discourse at Coffee-house laid asleep that design as being a thing impossible and impracticable'.[54] The impacts of such news and rumours probably become even more substantial due to the expansion of stock trading. Upon receiving news and rumours, investors could now buy and sell stocks and exert immediate influence upon the operation of joint-stock companies.

A few examples suffice to illustrate how news about new schemes could circulate rapidly and affect (potential) stockholders. On 29 May 1711, Humphrey Mackworth wrote to his brother about the debate for setting up the South Sea Company, now 'goeing on in p[ar]liament'. He related that the 'New Corporac[i]on' was 'upon a good fund', and that it would offer 6 per cent interest for those who accepted the Company's shares to replace 'the Navy Bills, army debentures', and other government

---

[50] See, for example, BM, 1868,0808.3493, 'An Epilogue spoke to a Play call'd the Alchymist', 1721.

[51] *Spectator*, ed. Donald F. Bond (5 vols., Oxford: Clarendon, 1965), vol. 1, no. 521, pp. 355–6. At Jonathans, the goldsmith John Casting Sr had been buying and selling shares and lottery tickets. See Glaisyer, *Culture of Commerce*, p. 155

[52] Richard Steele and Joseph Gillmore, *An account of the fish-pool* (1718), pp. 4, 56–60. Patent no. 419. See also MacLeod, *Patent*, p. 77.

[53] Quoted in Brian Cowan, *The Social Life of Coffee: The Emergence of the British Coffeehouse* (New Haven, CT: Yale University Press, 2005), p. 172.

[54] Andrew Yarranton, *England's improvement by sea and land* (1677), pp. 64–5; T. S. Willan, *River Navigation in England, 1600–1750* (London: Frank Cass, 1964), pp. 9–10.

bonds and securities. Mackworth was reporting the latest amendments which MPs had just approved the day before.[55] Being a high Tory MP himself, Mackworth was perhaps able to gather first-hand information very quickly. He also told his brother the news that a fleet was being assembled to sail 'to the rich Gold Mines in the South Sea in America', where the French and the Dutch 'raise millions every year'. He had obtained the news 'privately', and reckoned that it would circulate soon, and in doing so would 'raise the [South Sea] stock to an high degree', a comment that smacked of his interest in short selling. Mackworth also remarked that 'Investors would have '7 1/2 p[er] cent certain & very probable Expectac[i]ons of real Profit by those trades & the Stock can never fall lower…w[hi]ch makes mee & my friends resolved to adventure in it'.[56]

The episode is significant, revealing not only that this high Tory gentleman was happy to speculate in the 'real Profit' from the company's shares, but that news could also spread within a matter of days, stir up 'Expectac[i]on', and trigger some 'to adventure' in a new scheme. So it is hardly surprising that the share price of the York Buildings Company rose sharply above its nominal price in 1730, even though it was hugely in debt and was in position to distribute profits. The price increase was triggered when the expectation of much-awaited dividends was fuelled by news of six ships on their way to fetch lead ore from the company's Scottish mines.[57]

Stock-jobbing was an extreme form of the manipulation of information that characterized the new projecting culture in the early financial revolution. People in the provinces as well as those in the capital became involved. Thomas Steers, engineer and freeman of Liverpool, and William Squire, once mayor of the city, submitted a bill to authorize their scheme for making the River Douglas navigable in 1719 and obtained an act in April 1720. In June 1720, just as speculation heated up during the summer that year, they issued 1,200 shares valued at £5 each. The share price went up with other shares during the bubble of the summer and reached £70, but had fallen to £3 3s by mid-August. It was alleged that the promoters obtained a handsome profit by selling their shares when the market was at its peak. Two shareholders, from London and from Beaconsfield, who bought fifty-nine shares and twenty-six shares respectively, alleged that the promoters only intended 'to make a Bubble thereof and to raise money from all such Unwary Persons as they could draw in'.[58] Stock-jobbing like this was repeatedly practised from the early 1690s, during the South Sea Bubble in 1720, and thereafter.[59]

---

[55] West Glamorgan Archive Service, Swansea, Royal Institution of South Wales [hereafter WGAS], Gnoll Estate Collection, RISW/Gn 4/552, Letter from Humphrey Mackworth to his brother, 29 May 1711; *CJ*, vol. 16, pp. 680–1. For background to the legislation, see P. G. M. Dickson, *The Financial Revolution in England: A Study in the Development of Public Credit, 1688–1756* (London: Macmillan, 1967), pp. 64–5.

[56] WGAS, RISW/Gn 4/552, Letter from Humphrey Mackworth to his brother, 29 May 1711.

[57] Cummings, 'York Buildings Company', pp. 250, 431–3, 576.

[58] Alfred P. Wadsworth and Julia De Lacy Mann, *The Cotton Trade and Industrial Lancashire, 1600–1789* (Manchester: Manchester University Press, 1931), pp. 214–17 (quotation from p. 215); Willan, *River Navigation*, pp. 59, 70; *An answer to the reasons for making the river Douglas navigable* [1720].

[59] K. G. Davies, *The Royal African Company* (London: Longman, 1957), p. 83; Scott, *Joint-Stock*, vol. 1, pp. 306–8. Contrast Davies's judgement with that of Baston, *Thoughts on trade*, pp. 3–4.

Jobbers and brokers were frequently associated with the Royal Exchange, Exchange Alley, and coffeehouses such as Jonathan's and Garraway's. Stock-jobbery was frequently condemned as the deed of a 'beast' or 'devil'.[60] Thomas Baston fumed: 'by *forging false News, raise* and *fall* the *Stocks*, all the Commodity they deal in, for when their Hands are full [with stocks], then they are pleas'd to afford the Nation very good News, and so raise them as high as ever they can, and then dispose of them'.[61] These authors even suggested that stock-jobbing was ruining the national economy.

Having surveyed projecting activities in the early financial revolution, it should now be possible to identify a subtle change of emphasis that was taking place in the negative stereotypes about the projector. In previous chapters we have seen that promoters in the early and mid-seventeenth century often sought to implement their purported economic 'improvement' by imposing governmental authority upon people's lives. Consequently, the image of the projector was specifically associated with some one who abused authority under the slogan of the public good, thereby encroaching upon people's livelihoods and properties. Like projectors and monopolists under the early Stuarts, projectors operating in the stock market were also alleged to 'have fatal and pernicious Consequences' for society.[62] As economic initiatives became objects of public consumption, however, the stereotype of the projector became more closely associated with the image of a dubious businessman who would, together with stockjobbers, fleece innocent and credulous investors.

Speaking of treasure-hunting 'projects', for example, the author of *Angliae tutamen* marvelled: 'what abundance of People have been drawn in and abus'd, of all Qualities, Gentle and Simple, Wise and Otherwise'.[63] Other commentators tended to focus on the harm the projector did to the foolish and the credulous. Defoe complained that 'projectors' so often 'advanc'd [their schemes only] in Notion, and talk'd up to great things to be perform'd when such and such Sums of Money shall be advanc'd, and such and such Engines are made':

> the Fancies of Credulous People [have been thus] rais'd to such height, that meerly on the shadow of Expectation, they have form'd Companies, chose Committees, appointed Officers, Shares, and Books, rais'd great Stocks, and cri'd up an empty Notion to that degree, that People have been betray'd to part with their Money for Shares in a *New-Nothing*[.][64]

Baston also complained that the 'weak and unthinking Part of Mankind', or the '*Vulgar* sort of *People*', had been 'gulled out of their money...by *knavish* and *ridiculous Projects* and *Stock-jobbing*'.[65] One of the best illustrations would be that of Edward Ward:

> All loose vain projects ought to be debarred
> Which are of evil to the public known,

---

[60] *Hickelty-pickelty: or, a medly of characters adapted to the age* (1710), pp. 55–6.
[61] Baston, *Thoughts on trade*, pp. 7–8.   [62] *Angliae tutamen*, p. 34.
[63] Ibid., pp. 20–1.   [64] Defoe, *Essay upon projects*, pp. 11–12.
[65] Baston, *Thoughts on trade*, pp. 12–13.

> Wherein projectors have a large reward
> For doing what had better ne'er been done....
> The knaves are vultures and the fools their prey.[66]

The projector stereotype did not become monolithic, of course. In Ben Jonson's *Volpone* (1607), each character pursued 'Mine own project' and 'my invention' to dupe others and deprive them of money, wife, and inheritance. Thomas Brugis's *Discovery of the proiector* (1641), and John Wilson's *The projector: A comedy* (1665), had poked fun at the stereotypical projector as a deluded dreamer and an ostentatious and foolish virtuoso.[67] Similar negative images were also present, for example, in Swift's *A Tale of a Tub* (1704) and *Gulliver's Travels* (1726).[68] The generic stereotypes of the projector thus remained multifaceted. Nor do we have to suppose that monopolies, the imposition of prerogative, and rent-seeking altogether disappeared. There were monopolies in overseas trade, parliamentary expropriation, and corrupt links between powerful merchants and the government affecting economic performance.[69] Even in the domestic sphere, the chemist Moses Stringer sought to restore monopolistic power to the Mines Royal and the Mineral and Battery Works, arguing erroneously that 'All *Minerals*, *Earths* and *Metals*, *Salts* and whatsoever is subterraneous, is the *Prerogative Royal*'. By the first decade of the eighteenth century, however, such a view had become little better than an anachronism.[70] The more specific concern about the 'Trade and Liberty-destroying Projectors',[71] something that had haunted the Interregnum and the Restoration periods, became a less pressing issue when new schemes for improving the domestic economy started calling for subscribers.

CORPORATE RESPONSIBILITY IN THE AGE OF THE MORAL AND FINANCIAL REVOLUTIONS

The vogue for joint-stock companies (both proposed and actually floated), the circulation of rumours, stock-jobbing, and the conspicuous fluctuation of public

---

[66] Edward Ward, *The London Spy*, ed. Paul Hyland (East Lansing, MI: Colleagues Press, 1993), p. 261. For more examples, see Aaron Hill, *An account of the rise and progress of the beech-oil invention* (1715), pp. 7–8; Francis Brewster, *Essays on trade and navigation* (1695), p. vii.

[67] Ben Jonson, *The Cambridge Edition of the Works of Ben Jonson*, ed. David Bevington et al., (7 vols., Cambridge: Cambridge University Press, 2012), vol. 3 (esp. Act 1 Scenes 1–2, 4–5; Act 2, Scenes 5–7; Act 3, Scene 7); Thomas Brugis, *The discovery of a proiector* (1641), pp. 20–9; John Wilson, *The projectors. A comedy* (1665), p. 5.

[68] Jonathan Swift, *The Prose Writings of Jonathan Swift, Vol. 1: A Tale of a Tub with Other Early Works 1696–1707*, ed. Herbert Davis (Oxford: Blackwell, 1939), pp. 165–76; Jonathan Swift, *The Prose Writings of Jonathan Swift, Vol. 11: Gulliver's Travels, 1726*, ed. Herbert Davis, (Oxford: Blackwell, 1941), pp. 179–92. See also pp. 62, 78–9, 82–3 above.

[69] Murphy, *Origins*, pp. 74–5; Philip J. Stern, *The Company-State: Corporate Sovereignty and the Early Modern Foundations of the British Empire in India* (New York: Oxford University Press, 2011); Julian Hoppit, 'Compulsion, Compensation and Property Rights in Britain, 1688–1833', *P&P*, 210 (2011), 93–128; Nuala Zahedieh, 'Regulation, Rent-Seeking, and the Glorious Revolution in the English Atlantic Economy', *EcHR*, 63 (2010), 865–90.

[70] Koji Yamamoto, 'Medicine, Metals and Empire: The Survival of a Chymical Projector in Early Eighteenth-Century London', *BJHS*, 48, (2015), 607–37, p. 630.

[71] *The soap-makers complaint for the losse of their trade* (1650), title page.

confidence and share prices might make it appear that we are describing a new age, the emergence of modern financial capitalism. Yet the financial revolution was not so much a break from the past as a dramatic manifestation of early modern practices, played out in the transforming setting of a thriving financial market. This is why Defoe called it the Projecting Age, drawing on a concept so redolent of historical precedents. In other words, strikingly *modern* forms of corporate enterprises emerged out of the *early modern* history of projecting. Pervasive promises of public service will be considered first. The analysis of religious elements, in particular the intersection between the financial revolution and the so-called 'moral revolution', will follow. Business and management scholars will find unexpected antecedents of corporate social responsibility. Historians might find an opportunity for making fresh connections between the early modern past and the present, and do so without being too anachronistic.

As in earlier decades, the emphasis placed upon public service was not an undifferentiated mentality but was anchored in a variety of conflicting visions, ideologies, and priorities about issues such as expensive wars and religious toleration. Attitudes to wars against France varied among entrepreneurs, but numerous projects for manufacture and commerce highlighted their public service by suggesting their contribution to imperial prowess. A particular way of sheathing ships, called 'milled lead sheathing', was advertised as superior to 'wood sheathing', which depended upon materials 'of foreign growth, often in times of War (when most wanted) not to be had, or at very dear rates'. Thus, milled lead, sourced domestically, would be more conducive to England's naval strength.[72] Oldner and his partners claimed that their invention, which involved an engine for pumping water out of the vessel, would 'preserve ships from foundering' at sea even if damaged 'by great Shot'—a point they highlighted even though the Nine Years War had just been concluded. With typical hyperbole, they further asserted that the invention would render great service to 'the King's Ships, of the *East-India*, *African*, *Levant*, and other Companies', and ultimately be 'so extensive and universal a Good and Benefit to all mankind'.[73] Promoting the desalination engine originally patented by his uncle, Humphrey Walcot argued that its 'Advantages will be very great, even in times of Peace'. It would help maritime trade and alleviate health risks during voyages, and thus 'tend to the Publick Benefits of this Nation...the Advantage of Trade, the Preservation of Mens Lives and Healths', and ultimately the 'Advancement of his Majesty's Customs' through increased commerce. But its value, he suggested, would be 'much more in War'. 'How great to the Navy, which will want Ports, may stay much longer abroad [by this invention] and need not Ships to tend them laden only with Water, very expensive, causing great delays, and often separated by Weather from Fleet?'[74] Timing was telling in this case. He was selling his invention in 1702, at the beginning of the War of the Spanish Succession.

---

[72] [Charles Hale], *Mill'd lead sheathing for ships against the worm* [n.d., 1696], p. 4.
[73] Patent no. 352, 24 September 1697; Oldner, *Mr. George Oldner's invention*, p. 3. Details of the invention were kept secret.
[74] Walcot, *Sea-water made fresh and wholsome*, p. 4; Walcot, *Sea-water made fresh and wholsom*, non-paginated handbill. For similar claims, see also a handbill by Humphry's uncle, William Walcot, *The case of Mr. Walcot* [1694].

Such concerns were not limited to those promoting technical inventions. Defoe, no doubt mindful of the prosecution of what he called the 'just and necessary War' against France, proposed among other things an insurance scheme for seamen and a nationwide system to register them for effective deployment and payment.[75] In 1715, Aaron Hill urged that a 'free and open Ear' be lent to 'all Pretences for the publick Good, or indeed towards bettering a Man's private Condition'. This granted, he argued, 'the War [of the Spanish Succession] we have so much complain'd of, had been found no Burthen'.[76]

Others emphasized their contribution to England's imperial prowess by other paths—trade and industry. The Company of White Paper Makers argued in 1689 that manufacturing printing paper would 'employ many Thousands of Poor People, and keep vast Sums of Money in the Nation, which have been sent over Yearly into *France*, to pay for the said Commodity'.[77] Promoters of the new Glassmakers Company similarly argued that they 'actually doe make finer...Glasse than Normandy Venice or any Forraigne Glasse', and that the enterprise, if incorporated, would be able to 'employ grat number of Artists & poor people that must otherwise have gone beyond sea'.[78] In the case of the Company of Mine Adventurers, we know that its deputy governor and mastermind Mackworth was a high Tory critical of Whig war finance.[79] This did not prevent the concern from highlighting its contribution to England's economic prowess against foreign rivals: it promised in 1698 to 'Employ the Poor, and improve our Manufactures; and consequently, to add considerably to the National Stock, and bring more Wealth to England than any Foreign Trade whatsoever.'[80] The Royal Lustring Company was even more explicit about its service to the state when lobbying for a duty exemption for imported raw silk in 1695. Its secretary told the Treasury that the company's activities would tend 'to the great benefitt of this Nation not only in ruining the French Trade but in Raising that of England'.[81] Indeed, it did more than promote domestic silk production; available evidence suggests that it actively spied into, and disrupted, the inflow of French silk smuggled into London, a contraband trade overseen by a group of Lyons merchants collaborating with factors in Calais and London. Offering 'a Clear Insight' into it was the first step towards 'the better Discovery, and Prevention, of this pernicious Trade'.[82] Two decades later, John Apletre repeated what by then had become standard arguments. Calling for investors in a joint-stock venture, he argued that producing raw silk in

[75] Defoe, *Essay upon projects*, pp. 10, 123–32, 312–34.   [76] Hill, *Rise and progress*, p. 14.

[77] *The case of the Company of White Paper-makers: Humbly presented to the consideration of this present parliament* (1689), sig. A.

[78] HEH, EL 8517, Case of the intended Corporation of Glassmakers about London, n.d. [1691?], unfoliated.

[79] Humphrey Mackworth, *The principles of a member of the black list* (1702), p. xxiii.

[80] [The Mine-Adventurers of England], *True copy of several affidavits* (1698), p. 4. See also [The Mine-Adventurers of England], *A new abstract of the mine-adventure* (1698).

[81] Baker Library, Kress MS, E-12, collection of documents relating to the woollen and silk trade, item no. 34, Lewis Gervaise to the Lords of the Treasury, 18 July 1695.

[82] Ibid., item no. 51, a report on intercepted French books and correspondence regarding the silk trade, fols. 1–3, 15 (quotations from fols. 1, 15). See also TNA, SP 44/274, fols. 61, 311–12; *CJ*, vol. 12, p. 210–35. A concise account of the incident is to be found in Scott, *Joint-Stock*, vol. 3, pp. 80–4.

England would 'have our own People employ'ed, immense Sums of Money kept at Home, with which we now purchase our Raw-Silk... but should Export great Quantities to *Holland*, *Germany* and other Places and return very great Sums of Money to the effectual turning [of] the Balance of Trade against our Neighbours, as well *Dutch* as *French*'.[83]

Elements of piety and religious aspirations, which featured in many projects of earlier decades, especially those of the Hartlib circle, saw something of a revival during the financial revolution. It was also the age of the so-called 'godly reformation' or a 'moral revolution'.[84] From the 1690s, Societies for the Reformation of Manners were established; the Sunday School movement grew; foundling hospitals and workhouses were erected; and special sermons funded by public subscriptions, so-called 'lectureships', thrived. Landed gentlemen as well as the middling sort of people took part from across the political and religious spectrums.[85] Preaching to the Levant merchants, Laurence Hacket urged that 'Riches, and Honour, and Power are given unto Mankind, for no other end, but to Do Good, and Shew Mercy, and he who frees the Poor and Oppressed... acts God-like in his Station.'[86] This ideal of *imitatio Christi* was often expressed from the later seventeenth century in the teaching of 'practical godliness' and 'sanctification'. According to John Spurr, many Anglican and dissenting clergymen argued that, in order for sinners to be accepted and saved as righteous on account of Christ's atonement, they would have to show some evidence of repentance and amendment first. That is to say, they would have to 'sanctify' their lives by doing good in this world for God's honour.[87] Economic opportunities opened up by the financial revolution thus could be taken up with religious zeal. As Mackworth pithily put it in his diary, one 'should adjust a due care of Temporall affairs & of Spirituall Togeather'.[88] Such a fusion of the moral and financial revolutions deserves a closer look, as it has so far received limited attention despite its prevalence.

For one thing, adopting practical godliness could enhance one's reputation. Speaking of his plan to publish hitherto concealed medical recipes, Robert Boyle declared: 'I should not think it mony mispent but employed to promote a publick good, if

---

[83] John Apletre, *Proposals for an undertaking to manage and produce raw-silk* [1718], p. 2. Directors' names are mentioned at p. 6.

[84] Tony Claydon, *William III and the Godly Revolution* (Cambridge: Cambridge University Press, 1996); John Spurr, 'The Church, the Societies and the Moral Revolution of 1688', in John Walsh, Colin Haydon, and Stephen Taylor (eds.), *The Church of England c.1689–c.1833: From Toleration to Tractarianism* (Cambridge: Cambridge University Press, 1993), 127–42.

[85] Mark Goldie, 'Voluntary Anglicans', *HJ*, 46 (2003), 977–90, pp. 989–90; Craig Rose 'Providence, Protestant Union and Godly Reformation in the 1690s', *TRHS*, 6th series, 3 (1993), 151–69. For the complex relationship between party politics and moral reform, see Claydon, *William III*, pp. 110–15; Craig Rose, 'The Origins and Ideals of the SPCK 1699–1716', in *The Church of England*, 172–90, p. 173; Tim Hitchcock, 'Paupers and Preachers: The SPCK and the Parochial Work-House Movement', in Lee Davison, Tim Hitchcock, Tim Keirn, and Robert B. Shoemaker (eds.), *Stilling the Grumbling Hive: The Responses to Social and Economic Problems in England, 1689–1750* (New York: St Martin's Press, 1992), 145–66, p. 149.

[86] Quoted by Glaisyer, *Culture of Commerce*, 97.

[87] John Spurr, *The Restoration Church of England, 1646–1689* (New Haven, CT: Yale University Press, 1991), chs. 5–6. Spurr suggests that this doctrine became widespread after the Restoration.

[88] NLW, 14362E, Diary of Sir Humphrey Mackworth, fols. 71–2, 27 September 1696.

upon reasonable terms I should redeem any valuable Receits or Processes, that... may relieve the sick'. It was 'a work of Charity... to do good'.[89] Some joint-stock companies adopted, or literally capitalized on, this ideal. The Mercers Company, which managed a life insurance scheme originally proposed by an Anglican clergyman, William Assheton, declared that:

> the *Company* of *Mercers*, by Accepting and Managing this Proposal, will do a greater and more Publick Good to the whole Nation, than they could pretend to do by founding an Hospital for Widows in every County of the Kingdom... Because it is a much Nobler Charity so to support any Person, as to prevent him from being Poor, than it is to Relieve the same Person when he is actually Poor.[90]

In a similar vein, the Company of London Insurers presented its schemes as 'more desirable' than 'a truly Charitable Work', for they would 'prevent' people from being 'driven into great Wants and Necessities'.[91] The Mine Adventure also underlined its charitable intention. It supported two charity schools chiefly for the children of mineworkers.[92] It was further said that 'all aged and impotent Miners and Labourers in their service, are to be maintained out of the Profits of the Mines'.[93] The company planned to donate 'as far as Ten thousand pounds' worth of the company's shares to Corporations for the Poor in London, Bristol, York, and elsewhere, so that they would be funded annually by dividends of the company.[94] In 1709 the Mineral Battery Works similarly promised charitable donations towards 'the Building and Reparing the houses of God' and also towards the establishment of hospitals, schools, and libraries.[95] The Mine Adventure even arranged for condemned criminals 'to be Transported over [the] *Severn* to work in the Mines' as indentured labourers for five years, a form of slavery that was given the charitable gloss of allowing the nation to 'reap the benefit of their Labour, and the poor penitent Criminals be able to make some Atonement for their Crimes in the Service of their Native Country'.[96]

Promoters did not simply try to sanctify their schemes; the same charitable aspirations were harnessed to attract investors. William Salmon's book of medical cures was advertised in the *Athenian Mercury* as 'A work of singular use' not only to physicians, but also to 'charitable and well-disposed gentlemen and ladies who

---

[89] Quoted by Michael Hunter, *Robert Boyle (1627–91): Scrupulosity and Science* (Woodbridge: Boydell, 2000), pp. 221, 215.

[90] William Assheton, *An account of Dr Assheton's proposal* (1699), p. 20. This is strikingly similar to the assertion of public service Gabriel Plattes made in 1639. See p. 56 n. 119 above.

[91] [William Adams], *The proposal of the Company of London Insurers* (1714), pp. 5, 6, 7.

[92] See Thomas Shankland, 'Sir John Philipps of Picton Castle, the Society for Promoting Christian Knowledge, and the Charity-School Movement in Wales 1699–1737', *Transactions of the Honourable Society of Cymmrodorion* (1904–5), 74–216, pp. 142, 211.

[93] William Shiers, *A familiar discourse or dialogue concerning the Mine- Adventure* (1700), p. 150.

[94] Shiers, *Familiar discourse*, pp. 11–14. This plan was later changed to the donation of 1/12 of yearly clear profit.

[95] Yamamoto, 'Medicine, Metals and Empire', p. 633.

[96] Shiers, *Familiar discourse*, pp. 141–50, at p. 142. The idea of using convicted criminals as cheap labourers was not uncommon. See p. 226 n. 282.

have espoused the afflictions of the poor and needy'.[97] Because stock in the Amicable Society would bear interest and dividends, the company suggested that the benefits arising from its insurance scheme 'may be employ'd in publick Charities and Benefactions': 'to the Augmentation of poor Livings; to the Propagation of Christianity in Foreign Parts; to Charity-Schools; the Relief of poor Debtors; and to any such excellent Design'.[98] A proposal for setting up an infirmary via public subscription captured the underlying assumption:

> many will, of their own Accord, send in of their Charity; particularly those who are in Conscience bound, as they value their Salvation, to make Restitution of their unjust Gains; and know not the Persons whom they have wronged, and to whom they are obliged to make Restitution.[99]

The Mine Adventure tapped into just such concerns about sanctification. In one of the promotional pamphlets a protagonist, a 'Learned Doctor of Divinity', explained why he had decided to subscribe to the venture:

> I thought it became every good Man to give a helping Hand to it, not only to bring this particular Undertaking to good Effect, but by the Success of this, to encourage all other Persons concerned in Mineral Works, to follow so good an Example; and to set apart some Share of the Profits thereof to Charitable Uses, if it were only to the Relief of such poor Miners, their Wives and Children, as may in time stand in need thereof.[100]

Prominent divines were in fact among the subscribers and directors. Thomas Bray, the founder of the SPCK, wrote that he had 'a considerable Interest' in the company.[101] The non-juror and Jacobite Robert Nelson, another member of the SPCK and praised for his 'Heroick Piety', held shares of more than £400, and acted twice as a director.[102] Its publicity did reach would-be investors. One observer marvelled that 'They propose to imploy above 6000 people & to support all [who] shall become unable to work by age or accident & to erect an Hopsitall for them & their families...a great, Gen[era]ll & Nationall Concern.'[103] By the time the company collapsed in 1710 and negotiations with creditors began, John Chamberlayne, FRS, a member of the SPCK, and a secretary to the Society for the Propagation of the Gospel in Foreign Parts (SPG), was owed £791 by the company,

---

[97] William Salmon, *Iatrica: seu praxis medendi* (1694), title page; *Athenian gazette or casuistical mercury*, 30 September 1693, issue 24.

[98] *A letter from a member of the Amicable Society for a perpetual assurance* (1706), pp. 6, 7.

[99] *The charitable society: or, a proposal for the more easy and effectual relief of the sick and needy* (1715), p. 17.

[100] Shiers, *Familiar discourse*, pp. 10–11.

[101] H. P. Thompson, *Thomas Bray* (London, 1954), pp. 43, 61, at p. 61.

[102] See [The Mine-Adventurers of England], *A list of all the adventurers in the mine-adventure* (1700). The praise came from David Humphreys, the Church of England clergyman. See Beinecke Library, Osborn MS File 7764, 'A poem presented to Robert Nelson Esq. on his birthday', 1713. Another manuscript copy of the poem is at National Library of Ireland, MS 41,576/2.

[103] Houghton Library, Harvard University, MS Eng 1358, 'Proposals made by Sir Humphrey Mackworth', a contemporary manuscript memorandum about the proposal of the Mine Adventure, n.d. [*c.*1698]. For the possible impact of its corporate publicity upon female investors, see Froide, *Silent Partners*, pp. 65–7, 167–8.

whereas one Thomas Nichol was owed more than £5,000 'in Trust for Christ Hospital'.[104] The case of the Mine Adventure, therefore, reminds us that joint-stock companies could operate in a state of symbiosis with charitable missions. Dividends were intended to help finance charitable organizations. The ideal of charity in turn helped lend prestige to the business, and perhaps even to subscribers: having one's name listed along with prominent aristocrats and well-known divines 'did one's social position little harm'.[105] Pious-looking projects thus appeared to offer alluring opportunities for dividends, public service, sanctification, and even atonement. In a letter written after the Mine Adventure's collapse, Nelson was indeed reminded that 'wee both were deceived by S[i]r H[umphrey] M[ackworth's] plausible discourses, I pray for our credulity'.[106] To some, then, promises of mundane and other-worldly rewards were quite irresistible. If the point is too starkly drawn, we can at least suggest that, during the early financial revolution, religious ideas that had long informed projecting came to serve as a powerful tool for public relations—a tool that not only lent credibility to the assertion of public service as before, but also was now capable through public subscriptions of bringing in wider, religiously minded segments of society.

When we discuss religion and publicity together, it might be tempting to discount pious pronouncements as an insincere veneer to snare investors. Mackworth's case is once again instructive, as it alerts us to a more complex picture. In 1698, while busy setting up the Mine Adventure, Mackworth helped found the SPCK; from 1701 he was a member of the SPG, making an annual donation of £10 to support its missions abroad.[107] His diary reveals how this company promoter conceptualized the joint-stock company as an opportunity for sanctification. In the first entry he wrote after he had set up the company, he declared to his 'Lord' that 'I began this Undertaking w[i]th a good designe soe I may Carry it on in such manner as may bee acceptable in thy light', 'doeing good to the poor for y[ou]r sole sake of my Blessed Saviour'.[108] He often had a long break in his diary writing; he was, he wrote to himself, almost failing to live up to his own expectation of godly living. His rich diary therefore reminds us that he was neither a saintly entrepreneur nor a complete cynic. Instead, he was a man of business alive not only to his religious duty but also to its marketing potential. The case warns us that we cannot simply side with Nelson's correspondent and equate the presentation of piety with a deceptive publicity exercise with no ideological commitment.[109]

---

[104] [The Mine-Adventurers of England], *An alphabetical list of the creditors of the Company of Mine-Adventurers of England* (1712), pp. 5, 14. For Chamberlayne, see also Lambeth Palace Library, SPG XIV/256, secretary [Chamberlayne] to Robinson and Reynolds, 30 June 1711.

[105] Stewart, *Public Science*, p. 181.

[106] Hoare's Bank, Nelson Papers, RN/1/32, Weymouth to Nelson, 6 August 1711.

[107] Rose, 'Origins', p. 173; Lambeth Palace Library, SPG VI, fols. 7, 14–15, 27, 35, 37, 63, 112. Mackworth also donated £3 4s 6d when the organization was set up. Rhodes House Library, Oxford, USPG, X 180, First Donation List, 1701.

[108] NLW, 14362E, Mackworth Diary, fol. 98, 30 July 1699.

[109] For an extended discussion, see Yamamoto, 'Piety, Profit and Public Service', pp. 820–4, 827–9. In contrast, the case of Samuel Weale, discussed later, shows an adept operator making a strategic choice to adopt a pious outlook.

Recent work has begun to show that the Royal African Company, the SPCK, and the SPG also fused charitable impulses with commercial ambitions in their activities. We also know that similar charitable language was adopted by Moses Stringer when selling medicines and metals. He was an Oxford-trained chemist who performed metallurgical experiments for the Russian Tsar Peter the Great during his London visit in 1698, and opened a 'Laboratory and Foundery' in Blackfriars in 1700.[110] It remains to be seen how far the joint pursuit of piety, profit, and public service was shared across the social hierarchy. The long-term history of projecting provides a useful vantage point. In the preceding chapters, we found abundant evidence of the remarkable social reach of England's projecting culture. As in local officeholding, participants were drawn from across the social spectrum; even songs and local protests and petitions had no hesitation in suggesting that promised public service could be easily perverted by private interests. It was within such a cultural landscape that even humbler folks took part in Defoe's Projecting Age, speaking confidently of the public good in ways that fitted their private interests. The little-known prison writings of a humble Cornish projector, Samuel Weale, throw new light on this aspect.

Little is known about Weale's early life, except that he was born before the Civil Wars. After the Restoration, he found employment as a servant at the customs house in Plymouth, later taking a post at Truro, and becoming a collector of customs at Fowey in 1672. Although the son of an Anglican clergyman, Weale had a dissenting tendency and was dismissed from the collectorship in 1676 'for several misdemeanours in execution of his trust, as also his disaffection to the established religion': he allegedly 'extort[ed] reward' from merchants, and used 'the King's Custome hous Boat every Sunday to carry factious p[er]sons to Conventicles'.[111] Still in Cornwall, he continued acting as an informer, petitioning the Treasury in 1688 for the 'restoration to his place [as a Customs officer], he having made several seizures [of smuggled or under-taxed items] and endeavoured the reformation of the port'.[112] By then he seems to have had some ideas about fiscal projects to 'Advance the Kings Revenue', by imposing a new tax on Jews, and by preventing the evasion of customs duties, nominating himself as an 'Authority to search the Warehouse books & the Excheq[ue]r office and compare them together'.[113]

Come the Revolution and the Nine Years War, however, we find him in London, right at the heart of the projecting boom. By no means a novice in projecting, he now obtained diverse patents with others: one for a diving engine, 'made of Timber with glass windows a door and severall Air pipes Leather Sleeves and Iron braces affixed thereunto'; another for 'a New Machine ... usefull for beating, pounding,

---

[110] William A. Pettigrew, *Freedom's Debt: The Royal African Company and the Politics of the Atlantic Slave Trade, 1672–1752* (Chapel Hill, NC: University of North Carolina Press, 2013), pp. 198–200; Brent S. Sirota, *The Christian Monitors: The Church of England and the Age of Benevolence, 1680–1730* (New Haven, CT: Yale University Press, 2014), pp. 96–8; Yamamoto, 'Medicine, Metals and Empire', pp. 630–4.

[111] TNA, PRO 30/32/38, Out-letters (custom), vol. 3, fol. 210; PRO 30/32/33, Treasury Minute Book, vol. 5, fol. 75. His short autobiographical account is in Bodl., Rawl. D 808, fol. 246.

[112] *CTB 1679–1680*, vol. 6, p. 658; *CTB 1685–1689*, vol. 8, pt. 3, p. 1782.

[113] Bodl., Rawl. A 336, fols. 1–1v, 3, quotation at fol. 1v.

or stamping' ores, hemp, and flax; yet another for a new method for dying silk and woollen and linen cloths.[114] He became one of the assistants for a company engaged in digging English and Welsh lead mines and for the Glassmakers Company; he was involved in treasure hunts, drawn to a land speculation in Tobago, and himself aired a plantation scheme for the island of St Christopher in the West Indies.[115] In 1694 he petitioned the Treasury for a government post, claiming himself to have been 'the first to propose raising money by way of tonnage'. A year later he and a partner became large shareholders in a commercial vending of water in Norwich, nominally worth £10,500.[116] Other speculators such as John Blunt, Craven Howard, and Captain John Tyzacke of dubious repute were among his associates. Thanks to the lead mining scheme, Weale may have interacted with the former English ambassador to the Ottoman Empire, James Lord Chandos, and the master of the Mint, Thomas Neale, and through the Glassmakers Company, possibly even with Robert Hooke.[117]

His fortune in the teeming metropolis was short-lived, however. He was soon sued for his alleged fraud in the water-supply scheme. The Glassmakers Company had stopped trading by 1695, within four years of its inception. John Poyntz's salvage scheme for Spanish treasures, for which Weale procured the patent, was never successful; at least two expeditions were carried out, but the ships suffered the 'misfortune of their falling into the hands of the French', which reduced 'the shares to a very low value' and piled up 'many Debts'.[118] Probably being unable to recover the loss, Weale launched further projects in the hope of their yielding profits. Failing to satisfy his creditors, however, he was confined to the Rules of Fleet sometime between 1702 and 1706.[119] Even then, within the Rules of Fleet Prison, he launched a plethora of projects to recover his fortune, repay his debts, and restore his freedom and reputation, until his death sometime after 1712. Neither his detailed financial accounts nor the relevant records of Fleet Prison seem to survive, but we do have his manuscript proposals and some copies of the letters he sent while incarcerated.[120] Although Weale was of middling status, a Nonconformist, and probably died in confinement and made little tangible impact on the economy, thick manuscript volumes of his now-forgotten projects afford us

---

[114] TNA, SP 44/235, fols. 185, 213; SP 44/236, fols. 343–4.

[115] TNA, SP 44/341, fols. 198, 579–80; Bodl., Rawl. D 916, fols. 196–7; Bodl., Rawl. A 336, fols. 34–5v.

[116] *CTP* 1556–1696, vol. 1, p. 364; TNA, C 6/311/62 Yarnold v Smith.

[117] Lord Chandos was a former English Ambassador to the Ottoman Empire and the father of James Bridges, the future duke of Chandos, who also supported a number of projects; Thomas Neale was the Master of the Mint before Newton. On Lord Chandos, see John-Paul Ghobrial, *The Whispers of Cities: Information Flows in London, Paris, and Istanbul in the Age of William Trumbull* (Oxford: Oxford University Press, 2013); for the duke of Chandos, see Stewart, *Public Science*; for Neale, see J. H. Thomas, 'Thomas Neale, A Seventeenth-Century Projector' (PhD thesis, University of Southampton, 1979).

[118] For the water supply project, see TNA, C 6/311/62 Yarnold v Smith. For the glass company, see Scott, *Joint-Stock*, vol. 3, pp. 111–12; Murphy, *Origins*, p. 21. For the Spanish salvage scheme, Bodl., Rawl. D 808, fol. 16 (quotation).

[119] On the Rules of Fleet, see p. 61 n. 149.

[120] Bodl., Rawl. A 336, *passim*; Rawl. D808. Fleet Prison Commitment Books do not survive for the period between 1701 and 1707.

a rare window into an interface between the financial and moral revolutions at the middling sections of English society, a milieu somewhat resembling the circle of Hartlib, in which men across different ranks took part, spilling a considerable amount of ink for promoting projects which promised to advance piety and public service as well as profit.

If anything, Weale was more unscrupulous than conscientious, more speculative than wisely cautious. When promoting the plantation scheme for St Christopher's in 1694, Weale stipulated that a quarter of the shares 'bee reserved for a Great Peer that the sayd Weale shall name who will bee exceeding Useful in Promoting the affair'. This was the 'crying up' of a project, a practice that Defoe and the author of *Angliae tutamen* strongly criticized.[121] While pious and charitable elements hardly featured in his schemes during the early 1690s,[122] Weale later started promoting schemes with explicitly pious overtones, perhaps prompted by his declining fortunes, by the recently established SPCK and the SPG, or by the pious publicity of companies such as the Mine Adventure.[123] He had been no stranger to charitable initiatives. In the 1670s, he helped collect donations to support poor local clergymen, and proposed (without success) a nationwide system of subscription for the cause, appointing himself as its supervisor.[124] It is hard to figure out the rationale for such actions because most of the surviving evidence about Weale is his promotional documents. Yet one draft proposal has been found in which he explained to himself why he proposed to donate shares of the Spanish salvage scheme to the SPG and the Royal Greenwich Hospital among other beneficiaries. Such charitable contributions were 'added' in order

> To make my Projection about the Spanish Wracks to bee more agreeable, and becoming the Solicitation of a Clergy man or Divine, and more acceptable to her most sacred Maj[es]ty, and also more secure to our selves, which otherwise may bee precarious.[125]

Did he also hope to make his schemes 'agreeable' to God, as Mackworth had aspired?[126] Whatever the case, it is highly likely that Weale's pious outlook was primarily intended to make his project 'agreeable' to potential supporters. The

---

[121] Bodl., Rawl. A 336, fol. 34; Defoe, *Essay upon Projects*, p. 13; *Angliae tutamen*, pp. 10, 20–1, 22.

[122] See, for example, Bodl., Rawl. D 916, fols. 200–1, 'Draught of the Articles with Cpt Poyntz', 1691; Rawl. D 808, fols. 4–5v, 'Copy of the Proposall sent Mr Campell by Ms Seagrave about the Spanish Wrecks', n.d.

[123] Among his projects with pious overtones was a scheme for setting up a fund for lending money for those imprisoned for small debts (Bodl., Rawl. A 336, fols. 52, 56–7), and a proposal for suppressing London theatres (BL, Add. 61546, Weale to Sunderland, 15 March 1708).

[124] Bodl., Rawl. D 808, fols. 115–16, 157–8.

[125] Ibid., fol. 13, 'A perticuler of the Publicke uses of our Patent. Additionall Charities being Added. Fowle Draught', n.d. [after 1701]. Out of the total of 2,000 shares, 600 were to be given gratis to 'my Lord or some others of the Queens Favorites'—the strategy he had adopted earlier for the Spanish salvage scheme. But now he also proposed to distribute 200 shares to 'the Governors of the Clergy Charity', another 200 to the Royal Hospital Greenwich, and fifty shares each to the SPG, a society for the reformation of manners, and for promoting charity schools, leaving one hundred shares for himself, and the rest to other proprietors.

[126] His own explanation was that he 'could not better Imploy my thoughts than in works of Charity during the time of my unhappy Confinement'. See ibid., fol. 96.

commercial potential of charitable rhetoric was appreciated not only by the high Tory landed gentleman Mackworth but also by the Cornish projector standing at the other end of the religious, political, and economic spectrums.

Among Weale's religiously inflected schemes, the most striking, and richly documented, is a scheme to find and work a gold mine in Scotland. By July 1706, he was busy sending letters and petitions to potential patrons ranging from the Whig-leaning clergyman White Kennet and the Whig duke of Marlborough to the moderate Tory peer, the eighth earl of Pembroke, the archbishop of Canterbury Thomas Tennison, and Queen Anne herself. Weale was at first viewed with suspicion because, without initially disclosing that his scheme had to do with gold mining, he started circulating grandiose claims of raising millions of pounds and advancing charitable missions at home and abroad. Yet his extant petitions to the Lord Keeper of the Great Seal and to Queen Anne provide us with details of his scheme.[127] It was based on the information that small grains of gold were known to occur on the ground near Crawford Moor, close to Wanlockhead in south-west Scotland. His plan was to find gold mines there—an undertaking which was extremely ambitious, yet not altogether without foundation. Here, the influence of Mackworth's business is unmistakable. Speaking favourably of the Mine Adventure and its Welsh lead mines, Weale suggested that, because it would work on the superior metal, gold, his company deserved to be 'distinguished in name, and incorporated' as the 'Royall Mine Adventure'. In a pious tone, of which Mackworth and even Hartlib or Dury would have approved, Weale declared:

> It is a Sinfull Neglect and unaccountable Ingratitude to divine Providence, that for our use hath Enriched the Bowells of the Earth with his Hid Treasures, and we seem to slight them, by taking no notice of them, nor applying them as we ought to his Glory & our own Good[.][128]

To keep the benefit for himself, Weale proposed to act as a transfer clerk for the company, taking the fee of 2s 6d for each transaction. He also proposed to divide the stake into 400 shares, keeping one-eighth for himself and his assignees.[129] Yet, true to the tradition of projecting, Weale's argument included extensive discussion of public service. The company would 'give Imploym[en]t to many Thousand Families that now want it'; it 'may also Imploy such of the disbanded Forces as have no Trades', who would be monthly mustered so that they 'be always ready for service' while preventing 'us from the Greivance & burthen of a Standing Army'. Weale also suggested that the opening of mines in Scotland would bring economic growth to the region not only through the production and refining of minerals, but also through miners' consumer behaviour:

> where so many men reside & eat & drink & Cloath themselves, all manner of provisions will sell at great Rates, & the Miners weekly or monthly wages, & all other Incident Charges expended about the Mines will so Circulate that there will not be any one Trade or shop in that Kingdom, but will in some Measure participate & share

---

[127] Ibid., fols. 37–54, 65–8.   [128] Ibid., fols. 38, 40.   [129] Ibid., fol. 40v.

in the profits thereof especially those that are Neighbouring to the Mines, whose Lands will be greatly Improved & advanced in their value by the plenty of money and Increase of Trade in these parts.[130]

The planned constitution of this company also reflected the desire to present the business as a charitable and pious undertaking. Weale asked for a charter to be granted to 'two or three persons' from the SPG and Queen Anne's Bounty. They were probably to serve as trustees or nominal directors—undoubtedly useful for drawing religiously minded investors. Once overhead investments were repaid, clear profits were to be liberally distributed: 2.5 per cent to those who helped procure the grant of a charter (an inducement for government officials to help realize the scheme), 5 per cent to the Crown, and another 5 per cent to various charities such as the SPG.[131]

Specific elements of public service and piety, however, were not identical to those of the high Tory Mackworth or others. While his Mine Adventure remained rather silent about its implications for the war against France—something that was pursued by Whig ministers, Weale declared his intention to raise 'a Million of money' to underpin 'the Just and necessary war wherein we are engaged', and do so 'without Imposition on any of her Maj[es]ties Subjects'.[132] The money was to be advanced out of 'the product of the Mines... and being reimburs[e]d the principall in some reasonable time after the War shall cease'.[133] Once the Union between England and Scotland was accomplished in 1707, Weale started calling his proposal the 'Union Corporation'. When explaining why, he revealed his religious preference as well as his business acumen. He renamed it, he said,

> not only because the word Union is in general acceptac[i]on, & some affected with the title, may the rather come into the interest, but because p[er]sons of all perswasions, Churchmen, Presbiterians, Independents, Anabaptists and Quakers, will be all united in this Corporac[i]on, both for the Publick benefit, and their own profit.[134]

Perhaps reflecting his background as a Nonconformist, his scheme thus embodied a Low Church vision. It was, declared Weale, 'more unit[ing] & cement[ing] our affections, then all... the advices given us from the Pulpits, or the Throne'. This 'noble Undertaking' and the mines 'seem, by speciall Providence, to be reserve'd from former ages, as a peculiar blessing on Yo[u]r Ma[jes]t[y']s propitious Reign'.[135]

In the 1670s, Weale's pious outlook had once been queried in Cornwall: 'he pretends to be Religious', it was said, '[for] ensnaring the Simple'.[136] Indeed, it is likely that his pious language was not always taken at face value. Yet fragmentary evidence suggests that Weale's mining proposal was by no means rejected outright. He probably sent a full proposal on 18 October 1706 to the SPG and asked the society to 'Print my papers' and collect one guinea per head towards the charge 'because it is very troublesome and Chargeable to get written so many Copies of

---

[130] Ibid., fols. 39v, 38v.   [131] Ibid., fols. 38, 39.
[132] Ibid., fol. 100, a copy proposal sent to Marlborough. On improvement 'without imposition', see also pp. 56–7, 108–9, 207–8, 211 above.
[133] Bodl, Rawl. D 808, fol. 19, a petition to Anne.   [134] Ibid., fol. 20.
[135] Ibid., fol. 20.   [136] TNA, PRO 30/32/33, fol. 75v.

my Papers as are necessary to make Publick for the service of this Society'.[137] Ten days later, the SPG committee members were presented with Weale's 'Secret papers'; in two subsequent meetings, 'abstracts' of these papers were read to the committee.[138] Although nothing more about Weale seems to have been recorded in the minutes, the SPG continued to send its members to the Rules of Fleet to discuss the matter with Weale. For example, he wrote an extensive defence of his original request to reserve one-eighth of the shares for himself.[139] He had probably been quizzed about it; among his papers survives a manuscript memorandum, not in Weale's hand, which asks how much of the forthcoming profit 'shall be allow'd . . . to compensate S.W. for this extraordinary & acceptable Service'.[140] His mining scheme thus provoked a conditional, yet serious response. Although leaning more towards religious toleration, and towards supporting the Whig-led war, Weale's schemes did display a striking resemblance to those of the high Tory Mackworth. Weale even called his mining scheme the 'Royal Mine Adventure'. They both claimed to pursue piety and public service through economic enterprises, and managed to attract attention and, in the Mine Adventure's case, tangible investments, from those who were religiously as well as financially interested. The joint pursuit of piety, profit, and public service served as a powerful template upon which different visions of England's economic prowess could be articulated along party and ideological lines.

Not surprisingly, this pious outlook was not universally shared. Promoters such as Hill, Walcot, and the purveyor of polite conversation Richard Steele spoke little of, or perhaps kept a meaningful silence about, pious and charitable elements, other than hinting that their schemes would employ the poor. Yet, when placed in the long-term history of projecting, it is their commonality that stands out among heterogeneous political, economic, and religious components. By launching publicity campaigns for economic projects via books, pamphlets, bills, and newspapers, their engagement with the emerging financial market looked like competitive pursuits—or pretentions—of corporate social responsibility.

PROJECTS: 'REALITIES', REPRESENTATIONS, AND CONSUMPTION

That the projecting culture cut across factional divisions can be confirmed by the fact that all sorts of promoters faced the same force of stereotyping. As the *ESTC* suggests, the notion of projecting came to be used from the 1690s more frequently in the context of promoting and discussing new schemes.[141] Such descriptive usage coexisted, however, with a strong undercurrent of negative stereotypes about projecting. Indeed, irrespective of promoters' identities and affiliations, public

---

[137] Bodl., Raw. D 808, fol. 85v.

[138] Lambeth Palace Library, SPG Minutes I, fols. 126, 127, 129v. Descriptions of the meetings are laconic.

[139] Bodl., Rawl. D 808, fols. 150–4.   [140] Ibid., fol. 217.   [141] See Figure 1.3.

responses to the rise and fall of new projects were often bluntly negative, and resembled contemporary forms of political and religious discourse, which was 'characterized by defamation rather than rationality'.[142] We need not assume irrationality on the part of the public, but it is important to highlight that public responses to new joint-stock companies rarely captured the intricacies involved in floating joint-stock companies in the emerging stock market. The long-standing public suspicion of projecting provided a crucial context for how corporate promises and business failure were depicted in print and consumed by the public in the age of the financial revolution.

The richly documented case of Mackworth's company can once again serve as a useful test case. Under different management some of the company's mines would produce more than a thousand tonnes of ore annually in the mid-nineteenth century.[143] So there was some material basis to this scheme. Yet the company perpetrated various types of mismanagement in order to repay debts and keep paying interest to shareholders; the Commons carried out an investigation in 1710 and voted through a motion that Mackworth was 'guilty of many notorious and scandalous Frauds'.[144] Mackworth was unanimously condemned as a mere cheat and greedy projector. If we take a closer look, however, we can move 'behind the scenes' and consider the actual circumstances of the company's failure, something that was much more complex than contemporary responses allowed for. The case, which came to be remembered as yet another 'project', exemplifies the experience of many promoters with different religious or political orientations.

The Mine Adventure initially promised that interest of 6 per cent would be 'paid every Second Wednesday in June Yearly'.[145] Yet, because the company underestimated the overhead costs and the time required to repay them, by January 1700 it became clear that it would not have enough capital to pay the annual interest the following June. Mackworth thus decided to fabricate reports from the mines. He told the head steward of the Company's mines, William Waller, what to write in his reports:

> the Water being strong upon you, and you cannot suddenly drain it, nor make room for many Men to work, but in time you shall double your Men, and raise Quantities, but much more, when... no water troubles you[.][146]

[142] Mark Knights, 'How Rational was the Later Stuart Public Sphere?', in Peter Lake and Steve Pincus (eds.), *The Politics of the Public Sphere in Early Modern England* (Manchester: Manchester University Press, 2007), 252–67, p. 258. See also Mark Knights, *Representation and Misrepresentation in Later Stuart Britain: Partisanship and Political Culture* (Oxford: Oxford University Press, 2005).

[143] W. J. Lewis, 'Lead Mining in Cardiganshire', in Geraint H. Jenkins and Ieuan Gwynedd (eds.), *Cardiganshire County History: Volume 3: Cardiganshire in Modern Times* (Cardiff: University of Wales Press, 1998), 160–81, pp. 168, 169, 178.

[144] *CJ*, vol. 16, p. 391. The verdict came out of the parliamentary investigation documented ibid., pp. 311, 322, 328, 358–69, 388–90. The list of malpractices was long. For example, false news was fabricated and accounts were 'cooked'; sometimes directors manipulated the share price; the select committee meetings run by directors were often held without being quorate and were frequently dominated by Mackworth, his cousin, and their associates.

[145] *A New Abstract*; Scott, *Joint-Stock*, vol. 2, p. 447.

[146] *CJ*, vol. 16, p. 360. See also an undated letter: 'I hope you will send us a particular Account of the Mines in yours, that may put Life into us, for we are all dead at present.' William Waller, *The Mine Adventure laid open* (1710), pp. 36–7.

Waller accordingly wrote letters excusing the delay; they were compiled and published as a series of *Abstracts*. In a report dated 2 April 1700, he wrote that 'we are troubled with Water and cannot raise much Oar [*sic*] yet'. At the same time, he promised that, once the drainage was finished, he would 'then double and treble our Men in raising Oar', an excuse that bore a striking resemblance to Mackworth's instruction.[147] In a report sent shortly afterwards, Waller again followed Mackworth's instruction closely and projected the 'Victory...in Prospect' while excusing the delay.[148] Such reports were 'confirmed' by other reports, and then endorsed as 'matters of fact' by the directors, in London who ordered them to be printed and published.[149] Such misinformation was repeatedly promulgated and helped sustain shareholder confidence until about the middle of 1708.

One of the few extant letters from Mackworth to Waller reveals that the manipulation of information was not primarily intended to fleece investors:

> As to [company mines at] Bwlchyr-Eskirhyr, give me leave to put in my foolish Thoughts, unless you can coffer out [i.e. drain] the Bog-Water into the Levels, or Curtis Drift, I could never imagine what good you could do in so wet a place.... We have given it all over the Town that you are raising Ore in two places, and now we shall be found Lyars....You cannot imagine the Cry against us in the Town. All my best Friends begin to forsake us. If there be no Prospect of Interest Money this *June*, neither Blanks, nor Shares, will be worth Picking up in the Streets; but, if we had a little Oar in the Banks, and were raising Oar in Two or Three Places, I could get the Committee, perhaps, to buy the company's Shares, and pay the Interest, at least to all the new Adventurers....The name of raising Oar in several Places will raise us Money, and keep our Credit, till the great Vein is found, and our Interest Money paid. Pray consider these things, and see what you can do.[150]

The letter suggests that Mackworth forged reports because he was primarily concerned to maintain the company's credit until the technical problems could be solved. His fear that the company's shares might no longer be 'worth Picking up in the Streets' speaks volumes about the intensified stock trading, a central feature of projecting culture in this period. Keeping the shareholders on board was in fact difficult. Investors, of course, sought a financial return from an investment, but were also wary of being cheated by joint-stock 'projects'. So, an imaginary character

---

[147] *The Second Abstract of the State of the Mines of Bwlchyr-Eskir-Hyr* (1700), p. 9.

[148] *The Second Abstract*, p. 13.

[149] The authentication of 'matters of fact' was a prevailing knowledge-making procedure in experimental philosophy, legal courts, and in novels. See pp. 106 n. 7, 128, and also Barbara J. Shapiro, *A Culture of Fact: England, 1550–1720* (Ithaca, NY: Cornell University Press, 2000); Simon Schaffer, 'A Social History of Plausibility: Country, City and Calculation in Augustan Britain', in Adrian Wilson (ed.), *Rethinking Social History: English Society 1570–1920 and its Interpretation* (Manchester: Manchester University Press 1993), 128–57.

[150] The quotation is reconstructed from two transcripts of the same letter, dated 23 January 1700, found in *CJ*, vol. 16, p. 360; Waller, *Mine Adventure laid open*, pp. 78–80. These transcripts cover largely different portions of this now lost letter, but where they overlap, the transcripts match word for word. Most of the extant business letters by Mackworth have survived only as transcriptions printed in Waller's polemics against Mackworth. The letter quoted here was reportedly transcribed from the original, which two of Mackworth's closest subordinates 'owned to be Sir *Humphry Mackworth's* Hand-writing' (*CJ*, vol. 16, p. 360).

in *A Familiar Discourse* (1700) announced: 'there hath been several Projects set on foot, which have either proved unsuccessful, or which is worse, meer Cheats'.[151] In 'all the late Projects that were not founded on an honest bottom, the principal Promoters of them sold out immediately'.[152] One of the pamphlets admitted that 'this Undertaking [was] so ridiculed', some 'malicious or designing Person shall spread a false Report in Town, which will soon be believed by a thousand such Inconsiderate Persons'.[153]

Paying the promised dividends would surely have been the best retort to these allegations. But the Mine Adventure could not do this because of the underlying problems of drainage and the slender profit margin. It is known that the Mine Adventure was using shafts for drainage called 'levels' and 'drifts', besides pumps and engines. The foregoing letter to Waller suggests these technologies failed to function as expected. Perhaps more than incompetence was at stake here. As cultural historians have told us, assessing risk and probability was often difficult for early modern businessmen and commentators, who drew heavily upon divine intervention to understand the world around them.[154] Predicting the cost of drainage was accordingly not easy, and the problem was exacerbated by local variations. The challenge of drainage thus frequently ruined mining entrepreneurs. As one commented in the 1660s, 'Instead of draining the water, their pockets are drained.'[155] In this respect, the Mine Adventure's struggle was not exceptional.

The letter also reveals that Mackworth was anxious about the prospect of paying 6 per cent interest (£2,700) in only six months.[156] Many entrepreneurs found it difficult to secure profits. For example, the New River Company, which began in James I's reign and survived into Victoria's, had to endure two decades of unprofitable operations with huge overhead charges.[157] It also took nearly two decades to yield a modest profit from the Newcomen steam engine, a device that later revolutionized power supply across Europe and beyond.[158] Likewise, the Mine Adventure suffered from producing only a slender profit margin at its inception.

---

[151] Shiers, *Familiar discourse*, p. 16. See also ibid., p. 45: 'they are resolved to make the *Mine-Adventure* to be a meer Cheat, right or wrong'.

[152] Ibid., p. 44.

[153] Ibid., pp. 2, 16. See also [The Mine-Adventurers of England], *An abstract of letters concerning the mines* (1706), p. 4.

[154] This began to change during the eighteenth century. See Lorraine J. Daston, 'The Domestication of Risk: Mathematical Probability and Insurance 1650–1830', in Lorenz Kruger, Lorraine J. Daston, and Michael Heidelberger (eds.), *The Probabilistic Revolution* (2 vols., Cambridge, MA: MIT Press, 1987), vol. 1, 237–60; Geoffrey Clark, *Betting on Lives: The Culture of Life Insurance in England, 1695–1775* (Manchester: Manchester University Press, 1999).

[155] Stephen Primatt, *The City and Country Purchaser and Builder* (1667), p. 29, as quoted in Lawrence Stone, *The Crisis of the Aristocracy, 1558–1641* (Oxford: Clarendon, 1965), p. 340. See also p. 159 n. 136 above.

[156] This sum represents the payment only for the 'New Adventurers' who joined the venture in 1698, and excludes interest due to the old partners who had been shareholders of Sir Carbery Price's concern.

[157] Mark S. R. Jenner, 'L'Eau changé en l'argent? Vendre l'eau dans les villes anglaises au dix-septième siècle, *Dix-Septième Siècle*, 55 (2003), 637–51, p. 650.

[158] For the episode, see Alan Smith, 'Steam and the City: The Committee of Proprietors of the Invention for Raising Water by Fire, 1715–1735', *Transactions of the Newcomen Society*, 49 (1977–8), 5–20. See also Stewart, *Public Science*, pp. 115–16.

Mackworth's forging of reports was, therefore, a possibly well-intentioned, but evidently ad hoc and dishonest response to the interlocking problems of drainage, realizing profits, and keeping corporate credit in the precarious financial market. Mackworth was in fact acutely aware that he was sanctioning dubious practices. In the aforementioned letter, he conceded: 'if you think the Mines will not answer' the expectation of great profit, 'we had better give them up'.[159] Viewing deliberate misinformation as a sin, Mackworth even used the diary to show his repentance and record his resolution to make amends.[160] It was by mixing facts and fiction that the company managed to keep up its share price until 1708.

Thanks partly to the fraudulent transactions, the company was able to operate long enough to diffuse new technologies and develop infrastructures in Wales. Mackworth brought skilled miners and smelters from his native Shropshire; instead of working on surface coal seams, he drove a 'level' into rising ground to assist drainage by pumps;[161] he cut a river to make 'a Docke', and installed 'Flood-Gates' so that larger ships could carry goods effectively;[162] by 1700, he was 'making an Artificial Waggon-way or Wooden-Rails' from 'the Canal to the Work-houses, and from the Work-Houses to the Canal'.[163] Robert Lydall, the chief operator of works in Neath, obtained patents in 1697, 1702, and 1705, including one for 'a new way of smelting and melting black tin into good merchantable white tin in a reverberatory furnace without the help of bellows'.[164] By 1708, the industrial complex in Neath boasted a smelting house 165 feet long and 78 feet wide, furnished with twenty-two furnaces, along with storehouses for ore, a counting house, and a lime kiln.[165]

The long-term benefits of those efforts, perhaps unevenly distributed across regions and social strata, are unmistakable. The tramway developed in Neath in Glamorganshire was the earliest wooden railway in Wales, while Lydall's invention, used in both Neath and Garreg (Cardiganshire), was the first coal-fired reverberatory furnace in Britain.[166] While smelting at Garreg 'was not a success', the company introduced to the region the use of gunpowder for blasting and coal for smelting ore.[167] The Mackworths maintained interests in the mining industry throughout the eighteenth century, and Neath became 'the earliest to achieve some

---

[159] Waller, *Mine-Adventure laid open*, p. 80.

[160] The malpractice involved in the joint-stock company was therefore not exogenous to the godly frame of mind. For further discussion on the complex interworking of Mackworth's piety, sin, and repentance, see Yamamoto, 'Piety, Profit and Public Service', pp. 827–9.

[161] Wiliam Rees, *Industry before the Industrial Revolution* (2 vols., Cardiff: Cardiff University Press, 1968), vol. 2, pp. 524–5.

[162] *Second Abstract*, pp. 14–15.

[163] [The Mine-Adventurers of England], *The Third Abstract of the State of the Mines of Bwlchyr-Eskir-Hyr* (1700); Clive Trott, 'Copper Industry', in Elis Jenkins (ed.), *Neath and District: A Symposium* (Neath: Published by the editor, 1974), 111–48, pp. 124–5.

[164] *CSPD 1697*, pp. 284, 322; *CSPD 1702–1703*, pp. 420, 488, at 420; *CSPD 1704–1705*, pp. 298, 302.

[165] Trott, 'Copper Industry', pp. 125–7.

[166] M. J. T. Lewis, *Early Wooden Railways* (London: Routledge, 1970), pp. 247–50; John Hatcher, *The History of the British Coal Industry, Volume I: Before 1700: Towards the Age of Coal* (Oxford: Clarendon, 1993), p. 211; Lewis, 'Lead Mining', p. 162; Geraint H. Jenkins, *The Foundations of Modern Wales, 1642–1780* (Oxford: Clarendon, 1987), p. 121.

[167] Lewis, 'Lead Mining', p. 161.

'prominence' among smaller Welsh port towns.[168] In a provincial context, then, Mackworth was one of the 'pioneering entrepreneurs' who pushed forward industrialization and long-term local economic development.[169]

Few contemporary commentators acknowledged that this godly landed gentleman was contributing to economic development in Wales while causing financial havoc in London. Stereotypical interpretations instead held sway. As early as June 1705, it was rumoured that 'S[i]r Humphreys projecting faculties are at worke how to ... p[re]vent the ill consequences of the Dammed Lye he told' to investors. 'It is the Subject of a great many Coffeehouses where you cann hardly step in for a Dish But some Prophet or other Foretels the Dissolution of that noble Company'.[170] Little wonder that Defoe soon listed the Mine Adventure among what he called all 'Sort of Enigmas' such as 'Salt-Peter Works; Linen Manufactures, Paper Companies, diving Engines, and the like'. They had, he told the reader, 'nothing material in them, but being merely imaginary in their Substance'; the investors 'were deceived with the Appearance'.[171] Once the Commons had voted against Mackworth, Defoe jubilantly went on to attack Mackworth's 'pious Shams, Pretences of Religion'. Even Tory-inclined Edward Ward mocked the company.[172]

Some truth there may have been in these remarks and rumours, but the company's collapse attracted very few sustained analyses of its business failure or critical reflections upon the working of godly aspirations or reappraisal of concrete achievements in Wales. This was no exception, as revealed by the case of the Linen Company, established in 1691, a short-lived business that Defoe condemned alongside the Mine Adventure as 'merely imaginary'.[173] A manuscript note written by a major investor in the company, Charles Howard, seems to support the impression that the two founders and patentees for a weaving invention, Nicolas Dupin and Henry Million, were incompetent projectors. Howard alleged that 'neither of them had any new Inventions or Misteryes at all of their own but feared they should appear Grand Cheates'. Even though Howard tells us he sought to rescue the venture, we know from other sources that transactions in the company's shares had ceased by the end of 1694, its manufacturing operations by 1696.[174] But because Howard was engaged in a dispute with Dupin and Million, he probably

[168] Philip Jenkins, *The Making of a Ruling Class: The Glamorgan Gentry, 1640–1790* (Cambridge: Cambridge University Press, 1983), pp. 59–60; Arthur H. John and Glanmor Williams (eds.), *Glamorgan County History* (5 vols., Cardiff: University of Wales Press, 1936–88), vol. 5, p. 481.

[169] John and Williams, *Glamorgan County History*, vol. 5, p. 489.

[170] NLW, P&M Muniments (2)/ L521, [William Phillipps?] to [Thomas Mansel?], 5 June 1705; Ibid., L526 Phillipps to Sir Edward Mansel, 30 June 1705.

[171] Daniel Defoe, *Defoe's Review* (9 vols., London: Pickering & Chatto, 2003–11), vol. 3, pt. 2, pp. 645–6.

[172] Ibid., vol. 7, pt. 1, pp. 21–2 (at p. 21). See also [Edward Ward], *The fourth part of vulgus Britannicus* (1710), p. 140.

[173] A balanced, detailed account of the English and Scottish Linen Companies remains Scott, *Joint-Stock*, vol. 3, pp. 90–7, 162–8, which is to be read against MacLeod, 'Patents Boom', p. 564; Murphy, *Origins*, p. 31.

[174] Bodl., Rawl. A 336, fols. 40–41v, Mr Charles Howard's Paper to the Corporation touching his Concerns with Mr Dupin & Mr Million', n.d. (quotation at fol. 40v); Murphy, *Origins*, p. 21; *T&C*, p. 576.

had reasons for exaggerating the promoters' ineptitude. In order to arrive at a more balanced assessment, we must turn to other manuscript sources. A petition submitted to the company suggests that the business declined because Dupin and Million had developed 'a separate Interest' in Ireland at the expense of the London-based company, and did so 'without Imparting their Arts and Misteries'.[175] We also know that, under Dupin's leadership, the parallel Scottish linen company was set up in 1694; a year earlier, the Scottish parliament had been told that 'none less then 700 persones are already imployed by us in this kingdom'.[176] While it is difficult to ascertain the veracity of these statements, these two pieces of evidence point not so much to Dupin's and his partners' lack of competence as to their interest in expanding the business to Ireland and Scotland even at the expense of the English branch. Seen in this context, we can better understand why Howard's effort to rescue the English company did not work out. As with the case of the Mine Adventure, then, we should caution ourselves against attributing the business failure to technical incompetence or the dishonesty of its projectors alone. Although neither Howard nor Defoe considered the reasons in depth, there was a combination of circumstances that led to the project's decline, including the founders' investment strategies across the three kingdoms, their (probably unscrupulous) practice of secrecy, and Howard's failure to rescue the venture.

These cases testify to a wider pattern of stereotyping and reductive discourse and tell us something of the nature and limitations of early modern public understanding of entrepreneurship. Indeed, like those of previous decades, the majority of the promoters discussed in this chapter, coming from different religious and political backgrounds, voiced strikingly similar complaints. Thomas Savery, FRS, protested in 1702 that 'it would be hard' if the public concluded that 'because some are knaves, therefore none are honest.'[177] In the same year, Walcot, a protégé of the Whig-leaning duke of Chandos, hoped to remove 'all Objections' that existed to the desalination engine 'except one only, which is, that People call this a Project'. Perhaps looking back at the patents boom of the early 1690s, he suggested that this 'very Name alone hath been of great Prejudice to it [his invention], because many have of late suffered by Ill-grounded and Ridiculous Undertakings, or Projects'.[178] Such prejudices did not seem to have subsided in the 1710s. Speaking of saltpetre works, the Linen Company, and the Mine Adventure, Hill complained of what he perceived as pervasive public hostility:

> They remember several Great *Pretentions*…and go on to reckon up *Salt-Petre-Works*, *Linnen-Manufacture*, *Mine-Adventure*, and endless Train of *unsuccessful Projects*, and then gravely conclude, That what they *were*, This *must be*.

---

[175] Bodl., Rawl. A 336, fol. 38, a petition submitted to the Linen Corporation, n.d.

[176] Robert Chambers, *Domestic Annals of Scotland* (3 vols., Edinburgh: Chambers, 1858–61), vol. 3, p. 86; National Archives of Scotland, PA 7/14/100, 'Memorandum for the Committie of Parliament anent Trade', 1693 (quotation).

[177] Thomas Savery, *The miners friend* (1702), pp. 79–80.

[178] Walcot, *Sea-water made fresh and wholsome*, pp. 1, 6, at p. 1.

In his view, 'every Thing that has been since propos'd, is presently rejected with a silly Grin, a Shake of the Head'.[179] Promoters' complaints quoted here were voiced in the context of persuading the audience to invest. As such, these remarks probably exaggerated public distrust. Yet in the case of Weale, in his confinement, we can perhaps detect a sense of real frustration. When petitioning the archbishop of Canterbury, he had to admit that 'I am ready on my part to perform', although 'perhaps by few or none believed'. In a letter sent to the SPG, he appealed that printing the proposals under the tutelage of the society would be 'for the better pr[e]serving of my Reputation'. This, he hoped, would demonstrate that 'All Projectors are not Imposters'.[180] *The Tatler*, too, used an entire issue in June 1710 to make a similar point. 'He in Civil Life whose Thoughts turn upon Schemes which may be of general Benefit, without further Reflection, is call'd a Projector'. 'The Ridicule among us runs strong against laudable Actions.'[181] Promoters' complaints, together with the complex circumstances behind the collapse of the Mine Adventure and the Linen Company, warn us that the language of projecting and the public distrust it nurtured rarely did adequate justice to the complex business of turning projects into tangible improvements. Of equal importance, the powerful discourse of projecting affected promoters across various religious, economic, and political divisions. Projecting activities had close ties with contemporary politics and religion, but it would be 'too simplistic', as Tim Harris reminds us, 'to argue that England polarized neatly into two camps of Whig and Tory'.[182] Projecting provided a basic framework by which schemes with heterogeneous visions of public service were launched, promoted, and consumed with a mixture of excitement, caution, mockery, and distrust.

CONCLUSION

In the early financial revolution, economic projects evolved into objects of intensive consumption. If taken separately, joint-stock companies, news mongering, and the diffusion of paper credits were not new innovations of the 1690s. Nor was it the case that other modes of projecting were completely phased out. Some economic initiatives were promoted without subscription or publicity in the stock market.[183] Even so, we have found that crucial symptoms of change surfaced concurrently in the 1690s: public subscription to joint-stocks flourished; the rise of newspapers and the use of patents for publicity added to the already existing print, manuscript, and oral channels for promoting projects for economic improvement;

[179] Aaron Hill, *Proposals for raising a stock of one hundred thousand pounds; for laying up great quantities of beech-mast for two years* (1714), p. 10; Hill, *Rise and progress*, p. 13.

[180] Bodl., Rawl. D 808, fols. 87v, 85–6.

[181] *The Tatler*, ed. Donald F. Bond (3 vols., Oxford: Clarendon, 1987), vol. 1, no. 183, pp. 491–2.

[182] Tim Harris, *Restoration: Charles II and his Kingdom, 1660–1685* (London: Penguin, 2006), pp. 324–8, at p. 324. For an account that highlights the division between 'a land-based Tory political economy and labor-centered Whig one', see Steve Pincus, *1688: The First Modern Revolution* (New Haven, CT: Yale University Press, 2009), pp. 366–99 (at p. 369).

[183] Stewart, *Public Science*, pp. 50–2.

and publics composed of different political and economic strata became consumers of their news, rumours, shares, and dividends. Without completely replacing other forms of projects, therefore, the public consumption of economic projects had become a conspicuous feature by the early eighteenth century.[184]

Accordingly, negative stereotypes about the projector also came to be reconfigured and associated closely with stock-jobbing. Although public responses to joint-stock projects often misrepresented the complex reality, public discourse about projecting was not simply inaccurate, nor something that can be dismissed as irrelevant for our understanding of early capitalism. By way of conclusion, we can consider why it made sense to early modern commentators to draw on the existing negative stereotype and invoke the built-in negative connotations already associated with it. For one thing, by highlighting the projector's greed and incompetence, one could undermine a rival's reputation. Defoe sharply disagreed with Mackworth about the treatment of Nonconformists, calling him 'famous for his Zeal for the persecuting Laws offer'd against the *Dissenters*'.[185] Thus, when the Commons, then dominated by Whigs, voted against Mackworth, Defoe brought his polemical point back home by declaring that the indictment 'let[s] us see, that all the Canting is not among the *Dissenters*, nor all the Hypocrisie among the *Occasional Conformists*'. Depicting him as the epitome of the projector was all too convenient an attack upon a political enemy.[186] John Dennis, who had quarrelled with Steele about the management of a London theatre, also mocked 'a certain Knight's Fish-Pool' by which 'Purses let out Gold, as the Fish-Pool does Water, as fast as they take it in'.[187] In the contexts of the 'rage of party' as well as of personal rivalry, ridiculing projectors proved a handy polemical weapon.

At the same time, denouncing projectors provided lessons for others. For Defoe, ridiculing companies such as the Linen Company and the Mine Adventure as merely imaginary 'projects' served as a warning to other schemers to be virtuous. As he boldly put it, the 'end of satyr is reformation'.[188] Drawing on existing stereotypes also served to admonish investors. For example, an anonymous author satirized Mackworth as 'an old *successful-projecting-Chevalier*' who had 'found in a corner of *Atlantis* the *Mines* of *Potosi*', a mock-reference to the company's publicity that invoked the Peruvian silver mines. Alluding to the Company's rhetorically dexterous 'Reports', the anonymous author jibed that Mackworth was 'destin'd to enjoy the *present Benefit*' by feeding the investors 'with *distant pretended Hopes*: No easy Task to *content* and *delay* (and by which he shows his vast Capacity)'. The

---

[184] In so far as presenting the consumption of projects as *one of the ways* in which publics had come to be involved in the projecting culture, my account parts with Stewart's. Projectors, entrepreneurs, and Newtonians, he suggests, had handed natural philosophy from private patrons to 'the public that would increasingly be the arbiter of the value of natural philosophy.' See Stewart, *Public Science*, pp. xv, xxii, 384, 392–3 (quotation from p. xv).

[185] Daniel Defoe, *A new test of the sence of the nation* (1710), p. 54.

[186] Defoe, *Defoe's Review*, vol. 7, pt. 1, p. 21. Was the Commons' accusation equally harsh on Mackworth? One might wish to consider the question without underplaying the mismanagement committed by the company under Mackworth's management.

[187] [John Dennis], *The characters and conduct of Sir John Edgar* (1720), p. 17.

[188] Daniel Defoe, *The true-born Englishman: a satyr* (1701), sig. A3v.

Mine Adventure, its deputy governor and his reports in particular, came to offer an enlightening and entertaining lesson for a '*Multitude*, stung with the quickest, the universalest of all Passions, the Desire and Prospect of becoming suddenly Rich.'[189]

Such entertaining lessons were offered at a price; they formed a veritable industry of their own, selling literary wit purportedly for the public good. This was no new invention: under the early Stuarts, playwrights such as Ben Jonson and James Shirley did just that. Yet, with the lapse of the licensing act and the advent of periodicals and newspapers, the commercialization of literary comments on the economy arguably arrived at a new height.[190] An extreme example would be the 'Bubble' playing cards sold by Thomas Bowles in the aftermath of the South Sea Bubble.[191] The customer was offered amusing warnings against the folly of speculative 'projects' depicted on a pack of cards—a major means of gambling at the time.[192] Such mingling of market and moral 'lessons' was not missed by Swift's *Gulliver's Travels*. Not only did he offer biting satires of contemporary projectors sporting their wit in the Royal Society or peddling their schemes in the Exchange Alley, but his satirical gaze in fact extended to his own act of publishing the *Travels*. As Mr Gulliver put it with hyperbole, the book's ultimate ambition was 'to correct every vice and folly', a reforming ambition, he feared, which had not lived up to his expectation. No visible reformation has been accomplished since the original publication in 1726. Mr Gulliver thus ended his introductory letter to the 1734 edition of his *Travels* by declaring that 'I should never have attempted so absurd a Project as that of reforming the *Yahoo* race [i.e. humankind] in this kingdom; but, I have now done with all such visionary Schemes for ever.'[193] Within months of its publication in October 1726, no fewer than 20,000 copies were circulating in London with its population of half a million—a staggering estimate of one copy

[189] *Secret memoirs and manners of several persons of quality, of both sexes* (1709), 257–8. For historians' accounts, see Scott, *Joint-Stock*, vol. 2, p. 452; Mary Ransome, 'The Parliamentary Career of Sir Humphrey Mackworth, 1701–13', *University of Birmingham Historical Journal*, 1 (1948), 232–54, p. 235 n. 16. For a more balanced view, see *House of Commons, 1690–1715*, vol. 4, pp. 731–4.

[190] For an overview, see James Raven, *The Business of Books: Booksellers and the English Book Trade, 1450–1850* (New Haven CT: Yale University Press, 2007), pp. 83–6; James Raven, 'Publishing and Bookselling 1660–1780', in John Richetti (ed.), *The Cambridge History of English Literature 1660–1780* (Cambridge: Cambridge University Press, 2004), 13–36. Literary studies that may be broadly classified as new economic criticism have tended to focus either on Renaissance literature or on the eighteenth century. Compare studies cited on pp. 69 n. 7, 97 n. 142; Michael Rotenberg-Schwartz (ed.), *Global Economies, Cultural Currencies of the Eighteenth Century* (New York: AMS Press, 2012); Natalie Roxburgh, *Representing Public Credit: Credible Commitment, Fiction, and the Rise of the Financial Subject* (London: Routledge, 2016).

[191] BM, Schreiber Collection, English 66, 'English Bubble Companies Playing Cards'.

[192] More than 300,000 packs of cards were stamped for duty in 1719 alone, at least one newly stamped pack for every seventeen people in England. See Nicholas Barry Tosney, 'Gaming in England, c. 1540–1760' (PhD thesis, University of York, 2008), p. 59; E. A. Wrigley and R. S. Schofield, *The Population History of England, 1541–1871: A Reconstruction* (paperback edn with new introduction, Cambridge: Cambridge University Press, 1989), 533.

[193] Swift, *Gulliver's Travels*, p. 8. This overlap between the literary and other kinds nof project is elegantly examined by J. M. Treadwell, 'Jonathan Swift: The Satirist as Projector', *Texas Studies in Literature and Language*, 17 (1975), 439–60. See also Jessica Ratcliff, '"Art to Cheat the Commonweal": Inventors, Projectors, and Patentees in English Satire, ca. 1630–70', *Technology and Culture*, 53 (2012), 337–65, at pp. 343–4.

per twenty-five inhabitants. Swift was on a publishing *project* of a grand scale.[194] In the preceding chapters, the taming of projects often took on a variety of forms, from theatrical performance to political interventions such as protesting, petitioning, and providing prudent counsels. Swift's reflexivity reminds us that, in the age of the financial revolution, the processes of taming became parasitic on the burgeoning marketplace.

Finally, promoters of economic innovations were themselves trapped in the very process of reproducing biases. The experimental philosopher J.T. Desaguliers complained of 'Projectors [who] contrive new Machines (new to them, tho' perhaps describ'd in old Books, formerly practised and then difus'd and forgot)', those who would hastily procure 'a Patent... then divide it into Shares, and draw in Persons more ignorant than themselves'. As Larry Stewart points out, by highlighting projectors' perceived incompetence and dishonesty, Desaguliers sought to consolidate his reputation as a reliable purveyor of technical ingenuities and natural philosophy.[195] Exercises of differentiation, which took various forms, were widespread. The inventor of a steam engine, Thomas Savery, published a detailed '*Draught* of my *Machine*' accompanied by a detailed explanation. By doing so he hoped to distance himself from 'the *Scandal* of a bare *Projector*' that 'I am not very fond of'.[196] Hill even attached to his proposal for the beech oil company a real beech mast from which oil was to be extracted. This he did in the hope of presenting his real 'discovery', something to be distinguished from mere projects that 'having no real or visible Existence... subsists at best upon a precarious Probability'.[197] Seen individually, these efforts were intended to enhance credibility. Seen collectively, however, such attempts drew upon and thereby reinforced, rather than dispelled, existing stereotypes.[198]

It was not that their early modern contemporaries were incapable of exploring complex issues behind the failure of projects. Yet, all too often, the image of the projector was used in public discourse to reduce complexities to the problem of personal moral deficiency; it hardly fostered a robust understanding of business failure or entrepreneurial culture. In this respect, the discourse that operated in the burgeoning world of print was not quite as 'rational' as it was socially meaningful. Just like shares traded on the market, the complex reality behind the rise and fall of particular projects was trimmed and consumed as yet another story about typical 'projects'.

If, during the early financial revolution, projecting came to look like the pursuit of incipient corporate social responsibility promoted through the thriving media, then public discourse about it operated in ways that anticipated the public image of the capitalist and the banker in subsequent decades, if not centuries. Talking about the projector—perhaps like talking about the City and Wall Street—provided

---

[194] J. Paul Hunter, '*Gulliver's Travels* and the Later Writings', in Christopher Fox (ed.), *The Cambridge Companion to Jonathan Swift* (Cambridge: Cambridge University Press, 2003), 216–40, at p. 216.

[195] See p. 106 n. 10 above. J. T. Desaguliers, *A course of experimental philosophy* (2nd edn, corrected, 1745), p. 138 (quotation).

[196] Savery, *Miners friend*, pp. 1–2.

[197] Hill, *Rise and progress*, pp. 112, 8. See also Hill, *An impartial account of the nature, benefit, and design of a new discovery and undertaking, to make a pure, sweet, and wholesome oil* (1714), appendix at p. 31.

[198] On the reproduction of biases, see also Yamamoto, 'Medicine, Metals and Empire', pp. 610, 637.

a powerful way of stigmatizing certain individuals or groups as unreliable, while enhancing the credibility of those who offered expert advice, and giving comforting clarity in an otherwise complex commercializing society, demarcating the pious and the sinful, the wise and the unwary, the virtuous and the greedy. What is currently discussed as *relatively recent responses* to traditional capitalism—corporate social responsibility, wealth creation, and social entrepreneurship—is rooted in the business 'projects' and public understanding of these projects that have been developing since at least since the end of the seventeenth century, if not earlier.

Conclusion
Visible Hands Taming Capitalism

> Projectors disturb nature in the course of her operations in human affairs; and it requires no more than to let her [i.e. nature] alone, and give her fair play in the pursuit of her ends, that she may establish her own designs.... Little else is requisite to carry a State to the highest degree of opulence from the lowest barbarism[.]
>
> Dugald Stewart, 'Account of the Life and Writings of Adam Smith, LL.D', ed. I. S. Ross, in Adam Smith, *Essays on Philosophical Subjects*, ed. W. P. D. Wightman and J. C. Bryce (Oxford: Clarendon, Oxford University Press, 1980), 263–351, p. 322.

These are 'Smith's earliest authentically recorded thoughts on political economy', from the 1750s. These thoughts proved foundational to the *Wealth of Nations* (1776), in which he cast aside 'those who affected to trade for the public good'.[1] The presumptuous projector, then, had little or no constructive role to play in Smith's magisterial vision of political economy or in those of his ardent admirers. The reader of this book will have little hesitation in suggesting that a robust historical revision is in order. If Smith built his political economy as a 'science of a statesman or legislator'[2] and highlighted the role of numerous individuals and their pursuit of benign private interest as the vital fuel for the wealth of nations, if Milton Friedman urged business communities to mind their own interests (rather than those of the public), as we saw earlier,[3] it was by setting aside the visible hands that we have recovered, of numerous promoters like Bushell, Dymock, Yarranton, and Weale who promised public service, and of those who expressed distrust of their flowery promises.

More prescient than Smith on this count was Joseph Hall, who authored *Characters of vertues and vices* (1608), the first English 'character book'. Among his characters were the 'ambitious' and the 'distrustfull', who launched nefarious

---

[1] Istvan Hont, *Jealousy of Trade: International Competition and the Nation-State in Historical Perspective* (Cambridge, MA: Harvard University Press, 2005), p. 358; Adam Smith, *An Inquiry into the Nature and Causes of the Wealth of Nations*, ed. R. H. Campbell and A. S. Skinner (2 vols., Indianapolis, IN: Liberty Fund, 1976), vol. 1, p. 456 (bk IV, ch. ii, 9).

[2] Smith, *Wealth of Nations*, vol. 1, p. 428 (bk IV, introduction).

[3] See p. v. See also F. A. Hayek, *The Collected Works of F. A. Hayek: Volume II: The Road to Serfdom*, ed. Bruce Caldwell (Abingdon: Routledge, 2008), p. 100.

'projects', one of the earliest stereotypes concerned with 'project'.[4] The book was an attempt 'to learne wit of Heathens' such as of Theophrastus, the pioneer of character writing. Hall argued that such writers 'were the Overseers of maners, Correctors of vices, Directors of lives, Doctors of virtue'. Character writing was, Hall declared, at best capable of 'drawing out the true lineaments of every vertue and vice, so lively, that . . . the ruder multitude might even by their sense learne to know vertue, and *discerne what to detest*'. Hall expected literary characters to have profound influence: 'I am deceived if any course could be more likely to prevaile; for herein the grosse conceit is led on with pleasure, and informed while it feeles nothing but delight'.[5] The character of the projector that Hall helped establish did in fact prevail for more than a century. It gained such a wide circulation that Smith came to inherit, rather than scrutinize, its negative connotations. It was not all about delight, however. Not only was the character of the projector staged for the pleasure of Charles I and Henrietta Maria, as in Shirley's *Triumph of Peace* in the winter of February 1634, but it was also invoked elsewhere with much suspicion, contempt, anger, and sardonic laughter. Hall's prediction, prophetic though it was, turned out to be too optimistic.

The specific goal of this book has been to historicize the pervasiveness of public distrust of the projector, and thereby understand how Defoe's Projecting Age came to emerge in the way in which it did—fascinated by projects' potential to serve the public, and yet obsessed with projectors' perceived vices, as Cary, Defoe, and Hill knew all too well. We thus began by placing their experience within the wider context of state-formation in early modern England, a context in which initiatives for improvement played an important, yet precarious role in relation to the areas of activity commonly studied in terms of mercantilism, the decline of a demesne state, and the financial and scientific revolutions.

By repositioning their anxious experience within these crucial developments in early modern England, I wanted to make a broad, historiographical point—to find a 'middle way' between grand syntheses highlighting the unique success of England's improvement culture, a 'growth-friendly' culture that allegedly conferred 'bourgeois dignity' on the endless pursuit of wealth, and more specialized case studies of particular periods or industries that stop short of replacing these whiggish narratives. I have sought to contribute to this rethinking of long-term narratives by showing that numerous visible hands played an indispensable role in the taming of incipient capitalism. Actors often drew upon the early modern concept of projecting when engaging with this process—hence the centrality of this concept to the present study.

Projects for economic improvement were first promoted en masse under the late Tudor monarchs by emulating European policies and products. This came about in response to long-term population rise, decreasing wages, and inflation, compounded by mounting political tensions within the realm and against continental rivals. Import substitution schemes, as well as schemes to relieve the poor, were

---

[4] Joseph Hall, *Characters of Vertves and vices* (1608), sig. A4. See also pp. 81–2.
[5] Hall, *Characters*, sig. [A4v]-[A5v] (emphasis added).

accordingly promoted for the 'commonweal' of England alongside the immigration of a skilled workforce. Belief in the power of economic projects had medieval origins. It stemmed from the increasing appreciation in medieval and Renaissance Europe of labour, technical knowledge, and mercantile skills as something at best capable of augmenting the greatness of polities, and of bettering the social conditions of their inhabitants. In early modern England, some schemes were accordingly given religious significance—the means to inculcate godliness into the disorderly poor, and even to reform the nation. By the first decade of the seventeenth century, the notion of the 'project' gained currency among privy councillors and their technocrats as a rallying cry for producing wealth, a heuristic concept for searching for useful precedents, analysing present problems, and planning future actions. Early modern projects for improvement stand as an early modern antecedent of Schumpeterian enterprises seeking 'new combinations'. Given that the proximity between early modern projecting and the Schumpeterian definition has rarely been noted, the early modern period represents a promising field for those seeking to renew a research agenda in business history and management studies.[6]

Promises of wealth creation were prone to perversion, however. Under Elizabeth I and the early Stuarts, many spurious schemes emerged under the colour of serving the commonwealth, such as procuring royal privileges to monopolize whole industries or pressing for controversial 'improvements' of forests, rivers, or fenland. While promising revenues to the Crown, they threatened to disrupt the local economy by imposing fines and confiscation. The pursuit of economic improvement and innovation was therefore prone to perversion, not only by the self-interest of entrepreneurs, but also by the financial necessities of ambitious monarchs. At stake was not just the ancient problem of morality in the market but people's rights and liberties as well as social and political stability. The pejorative image of the projector that emerged in the first decade of the seventeenth century captured precisely these problems.

Representations have thus proved crucial for the history that we have unearthed. Combining the analysis of literary texts with that of manuscripts and their circulation, we have accumulated a critical mass of evidence showing that the character of the early Stuart projector was elaborated in character writings, enacted in theatres, sung in songs, spread as rumours, invoked in petitions, and derided in visual satires. The character was subsequently recorded by London Puritan Nehemiah Wallington in his list of divine punishments, invoked with anger by inhabitants of the Forest of Dean, picked up by the Long Parliament against its members who profited from monopolies, alluded to by Coke's *Third Institute* as well by Plattes's utopian depiction in *Macaria*, subsequently linked with the beheading of Charles I (as by the wire-drawer Simon Urlin), and commemorated in songs celebrating Charles II's Restoration. Immediate contexts for particular productions and invocations were never identical, but the body of evidence is robust enough to make a

---

[6] These disciplines are yet to tap fully into studies of early modern England (let alone of Europe). See Geoffrey Jones and R. Daniel Wadhwani, 'Entrepreneurship and Business History: Renewing the Research Agenda', Harvard Business School Working Paper, No. 07–007, July 2006; Mairi Maclean, Charles Harvey, and Stewart R. Clegg, 'Conceptualizing Historical Organization Studies', *Academy of Management Review*, 41 (2016), 609–32.

case for extensive social circulation: the character of the projector, which only began to circulate in the first decade of the seventeenth century, became something of common parlance by the end of Charles I's Personal Rule, and continued to haunt promoters and statesmen well into the post-Restoration period as dark memories of the late 'troubled times'.

The underlying problem of distrust has provided us with an unusual prism for looking into different aspects of the early modern pursuit of improvement and wealth creation often studied separately: practices of collaboration and exclusion, as in the case of the Hartlib circle; the safeguarding of local interests in Westminster and the maintaining of credit lines in the West Midlands, as in the case of the Stour river navigation scheme; and the changing sense of propriety, as we found in the promotion of horticulture and patent administration under Charles II. The character of the projector, we have found, was hardly an object of mere literary consumption or a simple tool for partisanship or lobbying. Because most promoters pursued their interests and ambitions without dropping gestures of public-spiritedness, many of them still looked worryingly like unreliable or oppressive projectors. Accordingly, few promoters whom we have encountered were oblivious to the danger of being stereotyped; they tried to differentiate themselves from the undesirable image—what followers of Goffman would call *stigma consciousness* and ensuing attempts at *role-distancing*. The pejorative character thereby shaped promoters' identities and even conditioned their negotiations with the government and a wider range of stakeholders. Permeating public discourse and affecting private lives, the notion of projecting presented a point of reference from which to consider how to promote useful knowledge amid unreformed brethren yearning for remuneration, and how to pursue improvement and abundance without infringing upon citizens' rights and liberties. Imaginative literature and its artful appropriation not only *represented*, but also *shaped* England's culture of improvement—especially the self-identity of promoters, their promotional strategies, and their capacity to continue business on credit.

Crucially, repercussions of public distrust were never confined to *incidental* experience of distrust and role-distancing. They instead gave rise to *systemic* consequences. We have pursued this line of argument by moving from individual experience of distrust to the long-term evolution of collective economic conventions. Vital in this respect were interventions from stakeholders ranging from the Privy Council and parliament, to promoters such as Ralph Austen, John Beale, Cressy Dymock, Valentine Knight, and Andrew Yarranton, and other interested parties like the Royal Society, Shropshire coal masters, Worcestershire clothiers, and London wire-drawers. Individual responses to the problem of distrust varied. Yet, in the environment of pervasive distrust, promoters of economic improvement and innovation collectively moved away from the predatory projects and monopolies that characterized the early Stuarts' reigns. By the end of the 1670s, individual role-distancing added up to the renewing of conventions underlying the culture of improvement, whereby private desire for gain, comfort, emulation, and consumption were adeptly mobilized for the furtherance of national power and profit, as Barbon elegantly put it. Some of the illustrations in this book are the material evidence of what Jan de Vries has called 'structure-modifying' acts, of the visible hands taming incipient capitalism.

Of course, we need not assume that certain literary features or their social circulation had the single most decisive causal impact on England's overall economic development. As Tony Wrigley warns us, it is absurd to suppose that any one development of earlier times can serve to explain more than a part of it.[7] Atlantic trade grew substantially in the second half of the seventeenth century, while real wages also rose thanks in part to the stabilizing population. The underlying convention about projecting evolved in ways that were not only adjusted to the political uncertainty of the 1660s and 1670s (exacerbated by the haunting memory of early Stuart projects), but also well suited to rising purchasing power below the middling ranks and to expanding colonial trade. The burden of distrust and political uncertainty conditioned how actors and institutions collectively responded to these material circumstances.

Our findings enable us to qualify existing larger narratives of England's improvement culture in the early modern period. It evolved the way it did never simply because of a combination of fortunate circumstances or thanks to the success of those whom Mokyr has called 'cultural entrepreneurs', such as Bacon, Petty, Hartlib, and Newton. Neither did it evolve the way it did solely because improving economic conditions from the late seventeenth century gave rise to a collective 'morality of cooperation' (as Slack has put it), convincing almost everyone that they could adopt improvement culture and profit from it while delivering some benefits to the nation as a whole.[8] Such interpretations appear to bear a certain similarity to the extravagant hope of projectors for endless improvement.

It is worth remembering that the idea of improvement continued to serve as a powerful weapon for evicting poor labourers from common lands and for expanding more profitable enclosure; the slogan also helped justify interventions in what were deemed 'unimproved' territories inhabited by Irish Catholics, Scottish Highlanders, or Native American 'savages', all allegedly in need of spiritual and material betterment.[9] By the late eighteenth century, the ambitions of projects to coerce reformation and improvement 'for the public good' were directed not so much towards wealthy, vocal, English male citizens, as towards weaker 'others' around them or far from them, such as poor labourers in the English countryside, and Irish, Scottish, and Indian inhabitants on the fringes of the emerging empire.

---

[7] E. A. Wrigley, 'A Simple Model of London's Importance in Changing English Society and Economy', *P&P*, 37 (1967), 44–70, at p. 63. Cf. Joseph A. Schumpeter, *The Theory of Economic Development: An Inquiry into Profits, Capital, Credit, Interest, and the Business Cycle*, tr. Redvers Opie (Cambridge, MA: Harvard University Press, 1961) [first published in German in 1911], p. 58.

[8] See pp. 17, 66, 208.

[9] E. P. Thompson, *Customs in Common: Studies in Traditional Popular Culture* (New York: New Press, 1993), ch. 3, esp. p. 138; William Cronon, *Changes in the Land: Indians, Colonists, and the Ecology of New England* (New York: Hill & Wang, 1983); Richard Drayton, *Nature's Government: Science, Imperial Britain, and the 'Improvement' of the World* (New Haven, CT: Yale University Press, 2000), pp. 57–67, 104–5; Frederik Albritton Jonsson, *Enlightenment's Frontier: The Scottish Highlands and the Origins of Environmentalism* (New Haven, CT: Yale University Press, 2013).

Recall that Beale's cheerful promotion of sweet fruit wines took the slave production of sugar for granted. We should do well to reappraise the further unfolding of capitalism as a history accentuated by recurring promises of wealth creation and ever-changing modalities of their perversion.

Taming Capitalism, therefore, serves as an antidote to celebratory accounts of progress. Note that, once we attend to the distrust of the projector and its social circulation, anxieties about improvement can no longer be treated as occasional reservations about uneven, yet ultimately victorious material progress towards plenty and comfort. Instead, we have found that a *post-medieval* understanding of projecting informed the *early modern* processes in which numerous visible hands contributed to the taming of incipient capitalism. Even what looks like 'positive externalities'—acts of parliament, the protection of properties, collaboration in the republic of letters—was often outcomes of these incessant processes of negotiation unfolding in the transforming circumstances of early modern England. From these processes emerged recognizably *modern* elements, Defoe's Projecting Age, in which joint-stock schemes and news and rumours about them were offered for sale so that their public consumption could (like the consumption of semi-luxuries) now drive the economy forward. It was thanks to this process of taming that human passions and interests no longer threatened an *immediate* breakdown of social cohesion, but came to be studied and mobilized as a vital motor for improvement. Smith's political economy hinged upon, and took for granted, the outcome of this taming and remaking of incipient capitalism, and developed further the underlying vision of a commercial society—one driven by benign private desire for gain and comfort. Yet the economic reality was far from orderly. We should now be able to revisit the South Sea Bubble of 1720 and the ensuing social and cultural dislocation as a dramatic episode in the long-term history of projecting, in which private desire for short-term profit was mobilized to accomplish a (purportedly) public end: the radical restructuring of long-term government debt.[10]

It is at this point that we must engage with various conceptions of capitalism in order to bring the findings of this book into sharper relief. Following Butterfield's advice, we have first assumed unlikeness between projecting and modern capitalism. Yet, in so far as projecting anticipated Schumpeterian entrepreneurship, in so far as the evolution of projecting in the early modern period may be considered as an evolution of embryonic capitalism, it would be vital to juxtapose the history of projecting with broader studies of capitalism so that we can start making fresh connections while exploring the limits of such comparisons.[11]

Let us begin with Marx, because, while he used the term capitalism only occasionally, his discussions have nonetheless left indelible marks on subsequent accounts. Two aspects are of particular relevance—his deterministic view of material circumstances, and the possibility that he indicated of latent critique and

---

[10] This will be the theme of my next monograph.

[11] In addition to Butterfield's dictum quoted at the end of the Introduction, I have drawn inspiration from Roger Chartier's reflection upon the multi volume *History of Private Life*. See Pierre Bourdieu and Roger Chartier, *Le Sociologue et l'historien* (Marseilles: Agone, 2010), pp. 32–3.

transformation. In his *A Contribution to the Critique of Political Economy* (1859), Marx famously declared that 'men inevitably enter into definite relations, which are independent of their will, namely relations of production appropriate to a given stage' in the unfolding of capitalism.[12] His writings also had less deterministic aspects. In the preface to the second edition of *Capital*, he suggested that after the upheaval of 1848, workers in Germany arrived at a clear 'theoretical awareness' of the capitalist mode of production and its antagonistic character—that in Germany the unfolding of capitalism did not prevent its 'critique'.[13]

Following Marx, many accounts highlight the autonomous aspects of capital accumulation. For example, Wallerstein and others have recently defined capitalism as 'a particular historical configuration of markets and state structures where private economic gain by almost any means is the paramount goal and measure of success'.[14] Other accounts have viewed the 'basic objective of the capitalist system' as 'the production and self-expansion of capital', a historically distinctive system whereby 'both production and consumption are freed from the limits set by traditional cultural constraints', a system in which workers are said to be 'creating profits for those who buy their labour-power'.[15]

This study has brought to light the taming of capitalism, a historical process that seems rarely captured by these standard definitions. In this historical process human interventions were neither materially determined nor inevitable. The amendments the Cavalier Parliament made to the Stour navigation act in 1662 were the result of the escalating polemical print politics invoking the memory of controversial projects of preceding decades. Interventions like this then could become a precedent, and make a difference to the long-term trajectory. *Taming Capitalism* thus supports the calls from historians such as Sven Beckert, Patrick Fridenson, Frank Trentmann, and Mark Bevir for developing research into the political economy of capitalism, into markets and businesses as they were embedded in historical contexts.[16] *Taming Capitalism* has shown one way of exploring the shifting negotiation of power among various social groups and the ensuing shaping and reshaping of economic conventions through such power-laden processes.

The nature of our findings can be further clarified if we juxtapose them with the seminal approaches to capitalism advocated by Weber and Schumpeter.[17] Defying

---

[12] Karl Marx and Friedrich Engels, *Collected Works* (50 vols., Moscow: Progress, 1975–2004), vol. 29, p. 263. See also Karl Marx, *Capital, Vol. 1*, tr. Ben Fowkes (London: Penguin, 1976), pp. 90–1.

[13] Marx, *Capital, Vol. 1*, pp. 98 (quotation), 929.

[14] Immanuel Wallerstein et al., *Does Capitalism Have a Future?* (Oxford, Oxford University Press, 2013), p. 7.

[15] Ellen Meiksins Wood, *The Origin of Capitalism: A Longer View* (New York: Monthly Review Press, 1999), p.3; Geoffrey Ingham, *Capitalism* (Cambridge: Polity, 2008), p. 60. Cf. Jürgen Kocka, 'Introduction', in Jürgen Kocka and Marcel van der Linden (eds.), *Capitalism: The Reemergence of a Historical Concept* (London: Bloomsbury, 2016), 1–10, pp. 4–5.

[16] See pp. 19–20.

[17] For concise accounts of Marx, Weber, Polanyi, and Schumpeter, see Ingham, *Capitalism*, pp. 15–43, 113; Sjoerd Beugelsdijk and Robbert Maseland, *Culture in Economics: History, Methodological Reflections, and Contemporary Applications* (Cambridge: Cambridge University Press, 2011), pp. 36–44, 97–103; Jürgen Kocka, *Capitalism: A Short History* (Princeton, NJ: Princeton University Press, 2016) [German original published in 2014], pp. 7–20.

Marxist determinism, Weber highlighted the role of culture and belief in the unfolding of capitalism. My research—like that of many others after Weber—has likewise given close attention to cultural values and assumptions as expressed by early modern actors. Yet in Weber's account a cultural component—in his case Calvinist asceticism—is given weight because of its putative role in lending legitimacy to the rational maximization of profit.[18] By contrast, the history of projecting has shown (among other things) the negative image of the projector, its social circulation, and its subtle impact on economic practices. Cultural assumptions thus played a role in *taming* and *reformulating*, as much as in *legitimating*, the pursuit of profit and power.

The historical process we have uncovered is also different from Schumpeter's account of innovative entrepreneurship and its role in development. He defined economic development as 'such changes in economic life as are not forced upon it from without but arise by its own initiatives, from within'. He placed entrepreneurs making 'new combinations' as the driving force behind 'spontaneous and discontinuous change in the channels of the flow' that alters and displaces existing equilibriums.[19] The story of projecting in early modern England helps us to clarify the historical relationship between enterprises and society in early modern England. Projectors were certainly entrepreneurial in that they sought to tap into neglected resources (such as dormant statutes, uncultivated lands, and idle hands) to generate wealth. Yet, especially during the early seventeenth century, they did not bring about discontinuous change via the success of their enterprises. Rather, it was their relentless rent-seeking in the guise of 'reforming' abuses and—this is crucial—the subsequent collective processes of taming that led to a path-dependent change. If the entrepreneurial efforts of Hill, Mackworth, Weale, and other promoters in Defoe's Projecting Age were no longer directed to the reformation of alleged abuses, it was thanks to the earlier processes of taming that we have uncovered. At least in this respect, the taming of capitalism facilitated the pursuit of creative destruction without the immediate destruction of the social and political order.

Fundamental to the process of taming were elements of criticisms based on the distrust of the projector and its appropriation. Our findings enrich the idea of 'critique', one that was indicated by Marx, and developed much further by Polanyi and Schumpeter. Polanyi famously dated the take-off of capitalism in the nineteenth century, and argued that this process was accentuated by a kind of 'double movement'—not only by the expansion of market activities freed from traditional morality, but also by 'protective' responses to counterbalance their destructive consequences. In this view, these 'counter-measures', such as Robert

---

[18] Max Weber, *The Protestant Ethic and the Spirit of Capitalism*, tr. Talcott Parsons (Mineola, NY: Dover Publications 2003) [German original published in 1904], pp. 180–2: Max Weber, *Economy and Society*, ed. Guenther Roth and Claus Wittich (2 vols., Berkeley, CA: University of California Press, 1978), vol. 1, pp. 164–6, 586, 630, vol. 2, pp. 1198–200.

[19] Schumpeter, *Theory of Economic Development*, pp. 57–78 (quotations from pp. 63, 64); Schumpeter, 'The Creative Response in Economic History', *Journal of Economic History*, 7 (1947), 149–59, pp. 149–50, 155. Cf. Schumpeter, *Capitalism, Socialism, and Democracy* (3rd edn, New York: Harper, 1950), pp. 121–8; Schumpeter, 'An Economic Interpretation of Our Time: The Lowell Lectures', in Schumpeter, *The Economics and Sociology of Capitalism*, ed. Richard Swedberg (Princeton, NJ: Princeton University Press, 1991), 339–400, pp. 359–61.

Owen's New Lanark and Chartist movements, served to re-embed economic relations in social, cultural, and spiritual fabrics.[20] Inspired in part by Polanyi, Luc Boltanski and Eve Chiapello have 'assign[ed] critique the role of a motor in changes in the spirit of capitalism'.[21] They have argued that the 'dangers capitalism runs when it can deploy itself unconstrained, destroying the social substratum on which it thrives, have a palliative in its ability to listen to criticism'. In Boltanski and Chiapello's view, it was this ability that has ensured the endurance of capitalism and its transformation since the nineteenth century well into the 1990s.[22]

The history of projecting enables us to qualify these accounts. Incipient capitalism prompted vehement responses from rhymesters, playwrights, petitioners, and statesmen at least since the early seventeenth century, well before the age of Robert Owen and Chartism, to which Polanyi gave special attention. Some elements of 'critique' existed at least since the seventeenth century, if not earlier. More importantly, the resulting public image of the projector was never antithetical to capitalism in the way Polanyi and Boltanski and Chiapello respectively depicted 'protective responses' and 'critique'.[23] The figure of the projector was often staged and published as a literary *commodity* as in Jonson's plays; satirical songs relishing the demise of Caroline projectors were sold as cheap print ballads; in Defoe's Projecting Age rumours about joint-stock companies featured in newspapers and periodicals; promoters from Petty to the more humble Weale all co-opted the negative image in order to suggest that their schemes were no mere 'projects' and hence to be trusted; and others who petitioned against a proposed monopoly could in the next petition ask for a similar grant for stamping out allegedly rampant abuses. It is therefore not enough to hint that critique 'shares "something" with what it seeks to criticize'.[24] Critique of incipient capitalism and its social circulation were long *symptomatic* of its expanding operations. It was within this parasitic condition that the public distrust of the projector helped shape the unfolding of capitalism.

Schumpeter in fact captured this element of symbiosis in his *Capitalism, Socialism, and Democracy*. The 'coincidence of the emergence of humanism with the emergence of capitalism is striking', he observed.[25] Seeds of critique were sown in his view during the Renaissance. The invention of print and the ensuing advent of the print industry helped undermine the authority of the Catholic Church. The print industry, coupled with the rise of the bourgeoisie, came by the late eighteenth century to create a host of intellectuals who had 'nothing to work with but the socio-psychological mechanism called Public Opinion'. This 'intellectual group' lived off criticism, and soon escalated their scathing scrutiny into 'criticism of

[20] Karl Polanyi, *The Great Transformation: The Political and Economic Origin of Our Time* (Boston, MA: Beacon Press, 2001) [1944], p. 136.

[21] Luc Boltanski and Eve Chiapello, *The New Spirit of Capitalism*, tr. Gregory Elliott (Verso: London, 2005) [French original, 1999], pp. xiv, 27–41, 408, 486–98 (at p. 27). Their work also draws on the French theories of *convention* and *justification*, and Albert Hirschman's discussion of 'voice'. See also pp. 208–9 above.

[22] Boltanski and Chiapello, *New Spirit*, p. 514.

[23] See Polanyi, *The Great Transformation*, pp. 175–82.

[24] Boltanski and Chiapello, *New Spirit*, p. 40.

[25] Schumpeter, *Capitalism, Socialism, and Democracy*, pp. 147–8.

classes and institutions'.[26] This is an intriguing overview, and seems consistent with our finding in so far as the projector stereotype was in fact sold as literary 'projects', something, as Swift admitted, that claimed to serve consumers while profiting its producers.

Our findings refine Schumpeter's overview, however, because his sweeping discussion is cast within his view of capitalism as 'the propelling force of the rationalization of human behaviour'.[27] Close attention to the post-medieval notion of projecting has enabled us to show that distrust of the projector was in fact rooted in the traditional complaint of avarice and covetousness, anchored with the notion of alchemical projection, and personified through the revived genre of Theophrastian character writing. In this respect, there is little or nothing inherently rationalistic about the critique based on public distrust of the projector. If anything, it was embedded as much in early modern *moral economies* as in the emerging market economy.

Yet it is clear that the history of incipient capitalism that begins to emerge from this study is not entirely coterminous with E. P. Thompson's classic account of the pre-industrial moral economy, 'a consistent traditional view of social norms and obligations, of the proper economic functions of several parties within the community'.[28] Thompson presented the unfolding of capitalism as the decline of the traditional moral economy by the end of the eighteenth century, and its eventual replacement by a capitalist market economy.[29] This 'transitional' interpretation has now been questioned as being too linear and teleological. Early modern commercial culture was infused with cultural values ranging from reputation, creditworthiness, and industriousness to charity, hospitality, patriarchy, and politeness; expanding markets facilitated poor labourers' and especially women's access to credit.[30] What has been more difficult is to examine how moral concerns shaped the unfolding of capitalism.

Taming Capitalism has shown the contradictory role that moral impulses played in the process. On the one hand, the very ideas about commonwealth, public good, reformation, and Christian charity lent themselves to the pursuit of wealth creation—or projection. We have found plenty of examples, from Tudor and early Stuart ones like Thomas Smith, Thomas Trollop, Robert Payne, and Thomas Bushell, via Hartlibeans like Ralph Austen, Cressy Dymock, and John Beale, all the way to post-Restoration writers and those in Defoe's Projecting Age such as John Rose, Richard Haines, Andrew Yarranton, Aaron Hill, and Samuel Weale. Yet, on the other hand, the making and breaking of such promises rendered promoters liable to derision, laughter, and criticism, as these promoters knew all too

---

[26] Ibid., pp. 145–51 (quotations from pp. 149, 151).   [27] Ibid., p. 125.

[28] Thompson, *Customs in Common*, p. 188.

[29] Ibid., pp. 95, 249–53. See also Buchanan Sharp, *Famine and Scarcity in Late Medieval and Early Modern England: The Regulation of Grain Marketing, 1256–1631* (Cambridge: Cambridge University Press, 2016), p. 235.

[30] Brodie Waddell, *God, Duty and Community in English Economic Life, 1660–1720* (Woodbridge: Boydell, 2012); Laurence Fontaine, *L'Économie morale: Pauvreté, crédit et confiance dans l'Europe préindustrielle* (Paris: Gallimard, 2008), pp. 152–63; Laurence Fontaine, *Le Marché: Histoire et usages d'une conquête sociale* (Paris: Gallimard, 2014), pp. 196–7, 201–6.

well. Pre-industrial moral economies thus lent themselves to the legitimation, as well as to the taming, of capitalism. If the notion of general morality that Mokyr speaks of has any purchase in the context of our discussion, it is not so much in discouraging opportunistic behaviours (as Mokyr's account implies), as in exposing promoters and their backers to potential scrutiny.[31]

By combining a range of sources and analytic concepts, *Taming Capitalism* has shown one way of exploring such critiques in concrete settings and measuring their repercussions. The underlying element of agency, not just of intellectual giants and of influential 'cultural entrepreneurs', but also of a much wider assortment of actors and institutions informed by the early modern moral economy, needs to be rescued from the whiggish condescension of posterity. One irony is that the role of visible hands taming incipient capitalism has long become rather invisible once Smith's vision was taken for granted. It was perhaps not a coincidence that Schumpeter, who reappraised the role of entrepreneurs, was an astute reader of early modern writers who were often dubbed projectors.[32] The present study thus raises new questions: moral economies were perhaps more successfully mobilized in taming certain aspects of capitalism than others (as in the decline of family farming and the turning of small farmers into a landless proletariat). What factors and contexts contributed to their different outcomes? In what ways does the history of collective taming by numerous visible hands relate to the subsequent story of the visible hand of the corporate manager, pioneered by Alfred Chandler?[33]

This study also provides us with a departure point to look into subsequent developments. The terms 'project' and 'projector' began to appear less frequently on title pages by the 1740s. One reason may have been the steady rise of the term 'improvement' as a more cogent and palatable slogan for economic development.[34] Yet, far from declining, concerns about public service and public scepticism in fact survived well beyond the late eighteenth century. As MacLeod has suggested, James Watt, who was to be enshrined as the heroic inventor of the Industrial Revolution, 'could describe himself ironically as a "projector"'.[35] The Scottish chemist Joseph Black was concerned about his brother James: 'I always fear this hunting after Schemes and Projects will get him the Character of a Projector...when they [the

---

[31] This finding can be profitably compared with the case of English 'freedom' in relation to the slave trade. Will Pettigrew has shown how the idea helped deregulate the transatlantic slave trade, and later came to inspire abolitionist arguments. See William A. Pettigrew, *Freedom's Debt: The Royal African Company and the Politics of the Atlantic Slave Trade, 1672–1752* (Chapel Hill, NC: University of North Carolina Press, 2013), pp. 180, 187–8, 191, 205–9.

[32] See pp. 52, 66–7.

[33] Alfred D. Chandler Jr, *The Visible Hand: The Managerial Revolution in American Business* (Cambridge, MA: Harvard University Press, 1977).

[34] Yamamoto, 'Thesis', p. 359; David Hancock, *Citizens of the World: London Merchants and the Integration of the British Atlantic Community, 1735–1785* (Cambridge: Cambridge University Press, 1995), ch. 9; Paul Langford, *A Polite and Commercial People: England, 1727–1783* (Oxford: Clarendon, 1998), ch. 9.

[35] Christine MacLeod, *Heroes of Invention: Technology, Liberalism and British Industry, 1750–1914* (Cambridge: Cambridge University Press, 2007), p. 40.

public] find his Projects are unsuccessful or impracticable'.[36] Writing to Erasmus Darwin, the medical practitioner Thomas Beddoes also spoke of 'the danger to which I am exposing my reputation': 'It is impossible to engage in a new and arduous undertaking without incurring ridicule and obloquy: Of course I must expect to be decried by some as a silly projector'.[37] It is possible that the image of projectors in the later eighteenth century became more of 'over-ambitious and unrealistic visionaries' than of unskilled fools or calculating cheats and swindlers. Samuel Johnson in fact tried to 'conciliate' his readers with projectors, suggesting that 'the folly of projection is very seldom the folly of a fool... it proceeds often from the consciousness of uncommon powers, from the confidence of those who, having already done much, are easily persuaded that they can do more'. Inventors may well have come to be glorified by the Victorian era.[38] Yet, crucially, Victorian Britons still had serious concerns about the compatibility of morality and the market, of Christianity and the pursuit of gain.[39] Even the free trade movement—what might look like a paragon of capitalist modernity—was defended in Edwardian England by moral language. The complete absence of tariffs on imported goods, with the attendant competition with foreign markets, was hailed as capable of promoting thrift, independence, and industriousness at home, interdependence and harmonious international relationships abroad.[40] Political economy emerged as an intellectual discipline amid these value-laden perspectives; it did not replace them.

Once we conceptualize the unfolding of capitalism in terms of changing modalities of operations and their imminent perversions, once we attend to the conceptual frameworks that lent themselves to the taming of capitalism in a given context, once, finally, we overcome scholarly specialization and equip ourselves with the appropriate tools, then it should be possible to start connecting the early modern past with the present and thereby asking new questions without falling into dire anachronism. Have we outlived the projecting culture and its characteristic promise of wealth creation? Or are we living under its globalizing descendants? Future studies of early capitalism need to take into account projectors' and their heirs' visions of abundance, their presumption of public service and public distrust and critique of such promises (which may well be spread as marketable commodities).

---

[36] William Ramsey, *Life and Letters of Joseph Black* (London: Constable, 1918), p. 104. For background, see Jan Golinski, *Science as Public Culture: Chemistry and Enlightenment in Britain, 1760–1820* (Cambridge: Cambridge University Press, 1992), pp. 29–30, 31, 34–6, 40.

[37] Thomas Beddoes, *A letter to Erasmus Darwin, M.D. on a new method of treating pulmonary consumption* (1793), p. 4.

[38] MacLeod, *Heroes of Invention*, p. 39; Vera Keller and Ted McCormick, 'Towards a History of Projects', *Early Science and Medicine*, 21 (2016), 423–44, at pp. 436–7. For subsequent developments into the nineteenth century, see also Frédéric Graber, 'Du Faiseur de projet au projet régulier dans les travaux publics (XVIIIe–XIXe siècles): Pour une histoire des projets', *Revue d'Histoire Moderne et Contemporaine*, 58(3) (2011), 7–33, pp. 19–28.

[39] Boyd Hilton, *The Age of Atonement: The Influence of Evangelicalism on Social and Economic Thought, 1795–1865* (Oxford: Oxford University Press, 1988); G. R. Searle, *Morality and the Market in Victorian Britain* (Oxford: Oxford University Press, 1998); James Taylor, *Creating Capitalism: Joint-Stock Enterprise in British Politics and Culture, 1800–1870* (Woodbridge: Boydell, 2006).

[40] Frank Trentmann, *Free Trade Nation: Commerce, Consumption, and Civil Society in Modern Britain* (Oxford: Oxford University Press, 2007), p. 64.

Such historical research might at best help us to rethink how we might tame, sustain, and thereby ultimately transform the capitalism that we have inherited. This line of inquiry is sorely needed, not just because private businesses continue to affect public lives around the globe. It is also needed because, as William H. Sewell Jr once put it, 'the dynamics of capitalism have demonstrated a renewed ability to disrupt profoundly and refigure fundamentally our own social, political, cultural lives'.[41] We have found that, for all its limits and complicity, the taming of incipient capitalism was conducive to its transformation in early modern England. Whether that holds true also for the twenty-first century depends largely on our future dialogues and actions—both scholarly and civic, official and mundane. We still have much to learn from history.

---

[41] William H. Sewell Jr, *Logics of History: Social Theory and Social Transformation* (Chicago: University of Chicago Press, 2005), p. 77.

Bibliography

MANUSCRIPTS AND UNIQUE COPIES

Baker Library, Harvard University, Cambridge, MA
Kress MS, E-12
Kress MS, E-13
Kress MS 85
Kress MS 106

Beinecke Rare Book and Manuscript Library, Yale University, New Haven, CT
Osborn fb152
Osborn fb158
OSB MSS 6
Osborn MS File 7764

Bibliothèque Nationale, Paris
Français 23355

Bodleian Library, Oxford
Aubrey MSS 12, 13
Bankes MS 11/39
Carte MS 233
Rawlinson MS A 336
Rawlinson MSS D 808, 916
Wood D 27(5)

British Library, London
Add. MS 15948
Add. MS 21935
Add. MS 33923
Add. MS 34218
Add. MS 61546
Add. MS 72886
Add. MS 72890
Add. MS 78314
Cotton MS, Cleopatra F VI
Egerton MS 1140
Egerton MS 2540
Egerton MS 3352
Harley MS 2003
Harley MS 4931
Stowe MS 354

British Library of Political and Economic Science, London School of Economics, London
Coll. Misc. 158

British Museum, London
1856,0815.48
1868,0808.3493
Schreiber Collection, English 66

Brotherton Library Special Collection, University of Leeds, Leeds
MS Lt q 50

Cambridge University Library Special Collection, Cambridge
University/T.II.29

Chetham's Library, Manchester
MUN Mun.A.6.17

Harvard Law School, Harvard University, Cambridge, MA
Small Manuscript Collection, 'A coppie of a wrytten discourse by the Lord Chauncellor Elsemere, concerning the Royal Prerogative', n.d. [April 1628]

Henry E. Huntington Library, San Marino, CA
EL 8509
EL 8517
HA, Parliament Box 2(11)

Hoare's Bank, London
RN/1, Robert Nelson Papers

Houghton Library, Harvard University, Cambridge, MA
MS Eng 243.50
MS Eng 600
MS Eng 1358

Lambeth Palace Library, London
SPG VI, SPG Financial Records, 1702–96
SPG XIV, SPG Correspondence
SPG Minutes I, 1701–8

Library of the Society of Friends, London
London Yearly Meeting Minutes, vol. 2 (1694–1701)
Wandsworth Monthly Meeting Minutes, 1698

London Metropolitan Archives, City of London (* = items held at Guildhall Library)
CLC/L/SD/A/003/MS04600, Shipwrights Company Ordinance and memorandum book*
CLC/L/SD/D/001/MS04597/001, Shipwrights Company Account Book 1621–1726*
CLC/L/WC/B/001/MS04655/001, Court Minutes of Weavers Company*
COL/RMD/PA/01/009, Remembrancia, vol. IX

National Archives, Kew
C 6/311/62

C 66/2842/1
PC 2/43, 48, 57, 58, 59
PRO 30/32/33, 38
SP 14/26, 71
SP 16/171, 260, 338, 363, 393, 409, 456, 535
SP 17/C
SP 18/2
SP 20/251B
SP 29/21, 23, 24, 44, 66, 68, 82, 85, 93, 99, 171, 234, 414
SP 44/235, 236, 274, 341

National Archives of Scotland, Edinburgh
NAS, PA 7/14/100

National Library of Ireland, Dublin
MS 258
MS 41,576/2

National Library of Scotland, Edinburgh
Adv. MS 33.1.1 [Denmilne], vol. 13, no. 69

National Library of Wales, Aberystwyth
14362E, Diary of Sir Humphrey Mackworth
Ottley (Pitchford Hall) Correspondence/2189, 2190
P&M 4A, 5555 Penrice and Margam Estate Records
P&M Muniments (2)/L521, Penrice and Margam Muniments

National Maritime Museum, Greenwich
SER/77, Sergiston Papers

Norfolk Record Office, Norwich
MF/RO 220, Roger Pratt Estate Memoranda

Nottingham University Manuscripts and Special Collections, Nottingham
Mi 5/165/124
Pw2 Hy 164

Parliamentary Archives, London
HL/PO/CO/1/1
HL/PO/JO/10/1/52
HL/PO/JO/10/1/58
HL/PO/JO/10/1/303
HL/PO/JP/10/1/38
HL/PO/PB/1/1571/13Eliz1n13
HL/PO/PB/1/1662/14C2n46
HL/PO/PB/1/1662/14C2n47
HL/PO/PB/1/1664/16&17C2n16
HL/PO/PB/1/1664/16&17C2n22

HL/PO/PB/1/1664/16&17C2n23
HL/PO/PB/1/1664/16&17C2n24
HL/PO/PB/1/1670/22C2n29
HL/PO/PB/1/1678/30C2n21
HL/PO/PU/1/1514/6H8n18
HL/PO/PU/1/1571/13Eliz1n35
HL/PO/PU/1/1623/21J1n32
HL/PO/PU/1/1695/7&8W3n29
HL/PO/PU/1/1697/9&10W3n43
HL/PO/PU/1/1698/10&11W3n12
HL/PO/PU/1/1698/10&11W3n40
HL/PO/PU/1/1698/10&11W3n41
HL/PO/PU/1/1698/11&12W3n12

Pepys Library, Magdalene College, Cambridge
PL 1604(6)
PL 2386
PL 2387–93

Record Office for Leicestershire, Leicester, and Rutland
11D53/XIII/6
DE3214/3533/1–2
DG 7/3/104

Rhodes House Library, Oxford
USPG, X 180, First Donation List, 1701

Royal Society, London
Cl.P/10iii, Classified Papers, Agriculture, 1662–1730
EL/B1, Early Letters, 1659–75
LBO/27, Fair copy of letters, 1664–77
MS/92
MS/238
MS/366/2
RB/1/40, Boyle Papers Miscellaneous
RB/3/1
RB/3/7

Sheffield University, Sheffield
The Hartlib Papers, (2 CD-ROMs, 2nd edn, Sheffield: HR Online, 2002).

Staffordshire Record Office, Stafford
Aqualate Paper, Baldwyn Papers
D(W)1788/P3/B78
D(W)1788/P43/B10
D(W)1788/P45/B14
D(W)1788/P59/B3
D(W)1788/P61/B5, B6, B7

Surrey History Centre, Woking
Loseley Manuscripts, LM/1777

Trinity College Dublin Special Collections, Dublin
MS 750/6
MS 842

University of London Special Collection, Bloomsbury, London
MS 195
MS 202
MS 260
MS 308
MS 581

West Glamorgan Archive Service, Swansea
Royal Institution of South Wales, RISW/Gn 4/552

Wren Library, Trinity College, Cambridge
VI.9.111[14–17]

GOVERNMENT AND OTHER OFFICIAL PUBLICATIONS

Acts and Ordinances of the Interregnum, ed. C. H. Firth and R. S. Rait (3 vols., London: Wyman, 1911).
Acts of the Privy Council of England.
Analytical Index to the Series of Records Known as the Remembrancia (London: E. J. Francis, 1878).
Calendar of State Papers, Domestic.
Calendar of Treasury Books.
Calendar of Treasury Papers.
Chronological Table of Private and Personal Acts 1539–1997 (London: HMSO, 1999).
Cobbett, William (ed.), *Parliamentary History* (36 vols., London: Hansard, 1806–20).
Commons Debates 1621, ed. Wallace Notestein, Frances Helen Relf, and Hartley Simpson (7 vols., New Haven, CT: Yale University Press, 1935).
Commons Debates 1628, ed. Robert C. Johnson et al. (4 vols., New Haven, CT: Yale University Press, 1977–8).
The Constitutional Documents of the Puritan Revolution, 1625–1660, ed. Samuel Rawson Gardiner (3rd edn, Oxford: Clarendon, 1906).
The English Reports (178 vols., Edinburgh: W. Green & Son, 1900–32).
Hartley, T. E. (ed.), *Proceedings in the Parliaments of Elizabeth I* (3 vols., Leicester: Leicester University Press, 1981).
HMC, *Calendar of Manuscripts of the Marquis of Ormonde*, new ser., 3–7 (London: HMSO, 1905–12).
HMC, *Fifth Report of the Royal Commission on Historical Manuscripts* (2 parts, London: HMSO, 1876).
HMC, *Manuscripts of the Earl Cowper* (3 vols., London: HMSO, 1888–9).
HMC, *Manuscripts of the House of Lords, 1692–1693* (London: HMSO, 1984).
HMC, *Sixth Report, Part 1 (Report and Appendix)* (London: HMSO, 1877).
Journals of the House of Commons.
Journals of the House of Lords.
Statutes of the Realm (11 vols., London: George Eyre and Andrew Strahan, 1810–28).
Stuart Royal Proclamations, ed. James F. Larkin and Paul L. Hughes (2 vols., Oxford: Clarendon, 1973, 1983).

Woodcroft, Bennet. *Alphabetical Index of Patentees of Invention* (2nd edn, London: Evelyn, Adams & MacKay, 1969).

Woodcroft, Bennet. *Subject Matter Index of Patents of Invention: From March 2, 1617 (14 James I) to October 1, 1852 (16 Victoriae)* (2 vols., London: Queen's Printing Office, 1854).

Woodcroft, Bennet. *Titles of Patents of Invention, Chronologically Arranged, from March 2, 1617 (14 James I) to October 1, 1852 (16 Victoriae), Part I. Nos. 1 to 4,800* (London: Queen's Printing Office, 1854).

PERIODICALS

Athenian gazette or casuistical mercury.

Flying post or the post master.

Houghton, John. *A collection for improvement of husbandry and trade* (4 vols., 1727–8).

London gazette.

Philosophical transactions.

Post boy.

Post man and the Historical account.

The Spectator, ed. Donald F. Bond (5 vols., Oxford: Clarendon, 1965).

The Tatler, ed. Donald F. Bond (3 vols., Oxford: Clarendon, 1987).

Ward, Edward. *The London Spy*, ed. Paul Hyland (East Lansing, MI: Colleagues Press, 1993).

DICTIONARIES

Blaise, Albert. *Dictionnaire latin-français des auteurs chrétiens* (Paris: Librairie des Méridiens, 1954).

Du Cange, Charles et al., *Glossarium Mediae et Infimae Latinitatis* (10 vols., Niort: L. Favre, 1883–7).

Godefroy, Frédéric. *Dictionnaire de l'ancienne langue française et de tous ses dialectes du IXe au XVe siècle* (10 vols., Paris: F. Vieweg, 1891–1902).

Huguet, Edmond. *Dictionnaire de la langue française du seizième siècle* (7 vols., Paris: E. Champion, 1925–73).

Kurath, Hans (ed.), *Middle English Dictionary* (128 parts, Ann Arbor, MI: University of Michigan Press, 1955–2001).

Latham, R. E., D. R. Howlett, and R. K. Ashdowne (eds.), *Dictionary of Medieval Latin from British Sources* (2 vols., Oxford: British Academy, 1975–2013).

Matsumura, Takeshi. *Dictionnaire du français médiéval* (Paris: Les Belles Lettres, 2015).

Wartburg, Walther von et al., *Französisches etymologisches Wörterbuch* (25 vols., Bonn: Schroeder, 1922–2002).

OTHER PRINTED PRIMARY SOURCES

Academy. By the Kings priviledge [1674?].

Angliae tutamen: or, the safety of England (1695).

The Anonymous Life of William Cecil, Lord Burghley, ed. Alan G. R. Smith (Lewiston, NY: Edwin Mellen, 1990).

Answer as well to a paper, entituled Reasons wherefore the making navigable of the rivers Stower and Salwerp…As also to another paper, intituled, An answer to some partiall pretences, called, reasons dispersed by some Shropshire coal masters [1661?].

An answer to the reasons for making the river Douglas navigable [1720].

The anti-projector or the history of the fen project (1646).

An appeal to the parliament concerning the poor that there may not be a beggar in England (1660).

By the king. A proclamation against exportation, and buying and selling of gold and silver at higher rates then in our Mint (1661).

By the King. A proclamation conteyning his Maiesties royall pleasure, concerning the proiect of dying and dressing of broad cloathes within the kingdome, before they be exported (1614).

Camiltons discoverie, of devilish designes and killing projects of the Society of Jesuites of later yeares (1641).

The case of the Company of White Paper-makers: Humbly presented to the consideration of this present parliament (1689).

The case of the lords, owners, and commoners of 22. townes in the soake of bullingbrooke [n.d., late 1661 or early 1662].

The case of William Gutteridge, and other glass-makers [n.d., c.1691].

The charitable society: or, a proposal for the more easy and effectual relief of the sick and needy (1715).

The charter of the Royal Lustring Company (1697).

A coffee-house dialogue: or a discourse between Captain Y—and a young barrester of the Middle-Temple; with some reflections upon the bill against the D. of Y. [1679].

Conscience by scruples, and money by ounces; or, new fashioned scales for old fashioned money (1697).

A continuation of the coffee-house dialogue [1680?].

The copie of a letter sent from the roaring boyes in Elizium (1641).

A dialogue or accidental discourse betwixt Mr. Alderman Abell, and Richard Kilvert, the two maine projectors for wine (1641).

The Earl of Exeter with divers other lords and gentlemen are proprietors and owners in possession [n.d., late 1661 or early 1662].

England's improvements justified; and the author thereof, Captain Y. vindicated from the scandals in a paper called a coffee-house dialogue [1679?].

Englands joy for the coming in of our gracious soveraign King Charles the second to the tune of, a joyful sight to see [1660].

An epistle to a member of parliament, concerning Mr. George Oldner's invention (1699).

The French rogue: or the life of Monsieur Ragour de Versailles (1694).

Hickelty-pickelty: or, a medly of characters adapted to the age (1710).

A letter from a member of the Amicable Society for a perpetual assurance (1706).

A looking-glasse for sope-patentees (1646).

The lord chancellor's speech in the Exchequer, to Baron Thurland at the taking of his oath, 24 Jan 1672/3 (1673).

The new projector; or the priviledged cheat [1662?].

'A Relation of a Short Survey of the Western Counties', ed. L. G. Wickham Legg, in *Camden Miscellany*, 3rd ser., vol. 52 (1936).

Secret memoirs and manners of several persons of quality, of both sexes (1709).

A short and trve relation concerning the soap-busines (1641).

The soap-makers complaint for the losse of their trade (1650).

Sport upon sport; or, the Jacobite tos'd in a blanket [1692].

Vox et lacrimae anglorum; or the true Englishmen's complaints to their representatives in parliament (1668).

The Wars of Alexander: An Alliterative Romance, ed. Walter W. Skeat (London: Early English Text Society, 1886).

Witt's recreations augmented (1641).

[Adams, William] *The proposal of the Company of London Insurers* (1714).

Apletre, John. *Proposals for an undertaking to manage and produce raw-silk* [1718].

Aquinas, Thomas. *Summa Theologiae: Latin Text and English Translation*, ed. T. Gilby et al. (61 vols., London, 1964–80).

Assheton, William. *An account of Dr Assheton's proposal* (1699).

Aubrey, John. *Brief Lives, with an Apparatus for the Lives of our English Mathematical Writers*, ed. Kate Bennett (2 vols., Oxford: Oxford University Press, 2015).

Austen, Ralph. *A treatise of fruit-trees* (1653).

Austen, Ralph. *The spirituall use of an orchard, or garden of fruit-trees* (1657).

Austen, Ralph. *A treatise of fruit-trees* (2nd edn, 1657).

Austen, Ralph. *A treatise of fruit-trees* (3rd edn, 1665).

Austen, Ralph. *A dialogue (or familiar discourse) and conference between the husbandman and fruit-trees* (1676).

Bacon, Francis. *The Oxford Francis Bacon, Volume XV: The Essayes or Counsels, Civill and Morall*, ed. Michael Kiernan (Oxford: Clarendon, 1985).

[Barbon, Nicholas] *Discourse shewing the great advantages that new-buildings, and the enlarging of towns and cities do bring to a nation* (1678).

Baston, Thomas. *Thoughts on trade and publick spirit* (1716).

Beale, John. *Nurseries, orchards, profitable gardens, and vineyards encouraged* (1677).

Becon, Thomas. *The catechism of Thomas Becon*, ed. John Ayre (Cambridge: Cambridge University Press, 1844).

Beddoes, Thomas. *A letter to Erasmus Darwin, M.D. on a new method of treating pulmonary consumption* (1793).

Behn, Aphra. *The Dutch lover* (1673).

Bellers, John. *John Bellers: His Life, Times and Writings*, ed. George Clarke (London: Routledge, 1987).

Bentham, Jeremy. *Defense of usury* (1790).

The Bible: Authorized King James Version, ed. Robert Carroll and Stephen Prickett (Oxford: Oxford Paperbacks, 2008).

Birch, Thomas. *History of the Royal Society of London* [1757] (4 vols., Brussels: Culture et Civilisation, 1968).

Blith, Walter. *The English improver* (1649).

Blith, Walter. *The English improver improved* (1652).

Boyle, Robert. *The Correspondence of Robert Boyle*, ed. Michael Hunter, Antonio Clericuzio, and Lawrence M. Principe (6 vols., London: Pickering & Chatto, 2001).

Brewer, J. S. and Richard Howlett (eds.), *Monumenta Franciscana* (2 vols., Cambridge: Cambridge University Press, 1858–82).

Brewster, Francis. *Essays on trade and navigation* (1695).

Brugis, Thomas. *The discovery of a proiector* (1641).

[Burton, Henry] *A divine tragedie lately acted* (1636).

Bushell, Thomas. *The first part of youths errors* (1628).

Bushell, Thomas. *A iust and true remonstrance of his maiesties mjnes-royall in the principality of Wales* (1641).

Bushell, Thomas. *An extract by Mr. Bushell of his late abridgment of the lord chancellor Bacons philosophical theory of mineral prosecutions* (1660).

Butler, Samuel. *Samuel Butler 1612–1680: Characters*, ed. Charles W. Daves (Cleveland, OH: Press of Case Western Reserve University, 1970).

Byfield, Nicholas. *Paterne of wholsome words* (1618).

Cary, John. *An essay on the state of England in relation to its trade, its poor, and its taxes for carrying on the present war* (1695).

Cawdry, Robert. *A table alphabeticall contayning and teaching the true writing and vnderstanding of hard vsuall English wordes* (1609).

Chambers, Ephraim. *Cyclopaedia: or an universal dictionary of art and science* (2 vols., 1728).

Cicero. *Marcus Tullius Ceceroes thre bokes of duties to Marcus his sonne*, tr. Nicholas Grimalde (1556).

Clarendon, Edward Hyde, Earl of, *A history of the rebellion and civil wars in England* [published 1702–4, but composed from 1646 onwards] (8 vols., Oxford, 1826).

Cockeram, Henry. *The English dictionarie: or, An interpreter of hard English words* (1623).

Coke, Edward. *The third part of the institutes of the laws of England* (1660).

Coles, Elisha. *An English dictionary explaining the difficult terms* (1692).

Cotrugli, Benedetto. *Della mercatura et del mercante perfetto* (Brescia, 1602) [composed originally in 1458].

[Cotton, Robert] *An abstract out of the records of the Tower, touching the Kings revenue* (1642).

[Cotton, Robert] *Cottoni posthuma: divers choice pieces of that renowened antiquary Sir Robert Cotton* (1651).

Culpeper, Cheney. 'The Letters of Sir Cheney Culpeper (1641–1657)', ed. M. J. Braddick and M. Greengrass, *Camden Miscellany*, 33, 5th ser., 7 (1996), 105–402.

Culpeper, John. *Sir Iohn Cvlepeper his speech in Parliament concerning the grievances of the Church and common-wealth* [1641?].

Defoe, Daniel. *An essay upon projects* (1697).

Defoe, Daniel. *The true-born Englishman: a satyr* (1701).

Defoe, Daniel. *A new test of the sence of the nation* (1710).

Defoe, Daniel. *Defoe's Review*, ed. John McVeagh (9 vols., London: Pickering & Chatto, 2003–11).

[Dennis, John] *The characters and conduct of Sir John Edgar* (1720).

Desaguliers, J. T. *A course of experimental philosophy* (2nd edn, corrected, 1745).

Dury, John. *A motion tending to the publick good of this age, and of posteritie* (1642).

Dury, John. *Considerations tending to the happy accomplishment of Englands Reformation in church and state* (1647).

Dury, John. *A seasonable discourse written by Mr John Dury* (1649).

Dymock, Cressy. *An essay for advancement of husbandry-learning; or propositions for the erecting a colledge of husbandry* (1651).

Dymock, Cressy. *An invention of engines of motion lately brought to perfection* (1651).

Dymock, Cressy. *The new and better art of agriculture* [1668].

Ellis, Henry (ed.), *Original Letters, Illustrative of English History*, 2nd ser., (4 vols., London, 1827).

Erasmus. *Collected Works of Erasmus, Vol. 27, Panegyricus, Moria, Julius Exclusus, Institutio Principis Christiani, Querela Pacis*, ed. A. H. T. Levi (Toronto: University of Toronto Press, 1986).

Erasmus. *Collected Works of Erasmus, Vol. 66, Spiritualia. Enchiridion, de Contemptu Mundi, de Vidua Christiana*, ed. John W. O'Malley (Toronto: University of Toronto Press, 1988).

Evelyn, John. *An apology for the royalist party* (1659).

Evelyn, John. *Pomona; or an appendix concerning fruit-trees in relation to cider* (2nd edn, 1670).

Evelyn, John. *Sylva, or a discourse of forest-trees, and the propagation of timber in his majesties dominions* (2nd edn, 1670).

Evelyn, John. *Navigation and commerce, their original and progress* (1674).

Evelyn, John. *The Diary of John Evelyn*, ed. E. S. de Beer (6 vols., Oxford: Clarendon, reprint 2000).

Firmin, Thomas. *Some proposals for the imployment of the poor* (1681).

Fish, Simon. *A supplicacyon for the beggers* ([Antwerp?], [1529?]).

Fortrey, Samuel. *England's interest and improvement* (1663).

Fuller, Thomas. *The history of the University of Cambridge* (1655).

Fuller, Thomas. *Mixt contemplations in better times* (1660).

Fuller, Thomas. *The history of the worthies of England* (1662).

Gentleman, Tobias. *Englands vvay to vvin vvealth, and to employ ship and mariners* (1614).

Gerbier, Balthazar. *The none-such Charles his character* (1651).

Haines, Richard. *A method of government for such publick working alms-houses* (1670).

Haines, Richard. *The prevention of poverty* (1674).

Haines, Richard. *Proposal for building in every country a working-alms-house or hospital* (1677).

Haines, Richard. *A model of government for the good of the poor and the wealth of the nation* (1678).

Haines, Richard. *Aphorisms upon the new way of improving cyder* (1684).

[Hale, Charles] *Mill'd lead sheathing for ships against the worm* [n.d., 1696].

H[ale], T[homas] *An account of several new inventions and improvements now necessary for England* (1691).

Hall, Joseph. *Characters of virtues and vices in two bookes* (1608).

Harleian Miscellany, ed. William Oldys (8 vols., 1744–6).

Hartlib, Samuel. *Further discoverie of the office of publick addresse for accommodations* (1648).

Hartlib, Samuel. *Samuel Hartlib his legacie* (1651).

[Hartlib, Samuel?] *Cornu copia, a miscellanium of lucriferous and most fructiferous experiments, observations and discoveries immethodically distributed to be really demonstrated and communicated in all sincerity* (1652).

Hartlib, Samuel. *A designe for plentie* (1653).

Hartlib, Samuel (ed.), *Chymical, medicinal, and chirurgical addresses* (1655).

Hartlib, Samuel (ed.), *Samuel Hartlib his legacy of husbandry* (3rd edn, 1655).

Hartlib, Samuel (ed.), *The compleat husband-man: or, A discourse of the whole art of husbandry; both forraign and domestick* (1659).

[Hartlib, Samuel and Cressy Dymock] *The reformed husband-man, or, A brief treatise of the errors, defects, and inconveniences of our English husbandry* (1651).

[Hartlib, Samuel and Cressy Dymock] *A discoverie for division or setting out of land, as to the best form* (1653).

Heywood, Thomas. *Machiavel. As he lately appeared to his deare sons, the moderne projectors* (1641).

Hill, Aaron. *An impartial account of the nature, benefit, and design of a new discovery and undertaking, to make a pure, sweet, and wholesome oil* (1714).

Hill, Aaron. *Proposals for raising a stock of one hundred thousand pounds; for laying up great quantities of beech-mast for two years* (1714).

Hill, Aaron. *An account of the rise and progress of the beech-oil invention* (1715).

Hobbes, Thomas. *Leviathan*, ed. Richard Tuck (Cambridge: Cambridge University Press, 1991).

Hooke, Robert. *Diary of Robert Hooke, 1672–1680*, ed. Henry W. Robinson and Walter Adams (London: Taylor and Francis, 1935).

Hoppit, Julian (ed.), *Nehemiah Grew and England's Economic Development: The Means of Most Ample Increase of the Wealth and Strength of England 1706–7* (Oxford: Oxford University Press, 2012).

[Houghton, John] *Englands great happiness* (1677).

Jeake, Samuel. *An Astrological Diary of the Seventeenth Century: Samuel Jeake of Rye 1652–1699*, ed. Michael Hunter and Annabel Gregory (Oxford: Clarendon, 1988).

Johnson, Samuel. *A Dictionary of the English Language* (2 vols., 1756).

Jonson, Ben. *The Cambridge Edition of the Works of Ben Jonson*, ed. David Bevington et al. (7 vols., Cambridge: Cambridge University Press, 2012).

J. R. *Trades increase* (1615).

Kem, Samuel. *The king of kings his privie marks for the kingdoms choyce of new members Remarques upon the new project of association: in a letter to a friend* [1646].

Killigrew, William. *The late earle of Lindsey his title, by which himself, and his participants, do claim 24000. acres of lands in the fennes in Lincoln-shire* (1661).

Knight, Valentine. *Proposals of a new model for re-building the City of London* (1666).

Krünitz, Johan Georg, et al. (eds.), *Oekonomische Encyklopädie* (242 vols., Berlin, 1773–1858).

Locke, John. *Correspondence of John Locke*, ed. Edmund de Beer (8 vols., Oxford: Clarendon, 1976–89).

Loxley, James, Anna Groundwater, and Julie Sanders (eds.), *Ben Jonson's Walk to Scotland: An Annotated Edition of the 'Foot Voyage'* (Cambridge: Cambridge University Press, 2015).

Ludlow, Edmund. *A Voyce from the Watch Tower: Part Five: 1660–1662*, ed. A . B. Worden, Camden 4th Series, vol. 21 (1978).

Luttrell, Narcissus. *A Brief Historical Relation of State of Affairs from September 1678 to April 1714* (6 vols., Oxford: Oxford University Press, 1857).

McClure, Edmund. *A chapter in English church history: being the minutes of the Society for Promoting Christian Knowledge for the years 1698–1704; together with abstracts of correspondents' letters during part of the same period* (London: SPCK, 1888).

Mackworth, Humphrey. *England's glory* (1694).

Mackworth, Humphrey. *The principles of a member of the black list* (1702).

Marx, Karl. *Capital, Vol. 1*, tr. Ben Fowkes (London: Penguin, 1976).

Marx, Karl and Friedrich Engels, *Collected Works* (50 vols., Moscow: Progress, 1975–2004).

Mathew, Francis. *Of the opening of rivers for navigation: the benefit exemplified by the two Avons of Salisbury and Bristol* (1655).

Mathew, Francis. *Of the opening of rivers for navigation: the benefit exemplified by the two Avons of Salisbury and Bristol* (1656).

Mathew, Francis. *Of the opening of rivers for navigation: the benefit exemplified by the two Avons of Salisbury and Bristol* (1660).

[The Mine-Adventurers of England] *A new abstract of the mine-adventure* (1698).

[The Mine-Adventurers of England] *A true copy of several affidavits* (1698).

[The Mine-Adventurers of England] *A list of all the adventurers in the mine-adventure* (1700).

[The Mine-Adventurers of England] *The Third Abstract of the State of the Mines of Bwlchyr-Eskir-Hyr* (1700).

[The Mine-Adventurers of England] *An abstract of letters concerning the mines* (1706).

[The Mine-Adventurers of England] *An alphabetical list of the creditors of the Company of Mine-Adventurers of England* (1712).

Moore, Jonas. *Moores arithmetick discovering the secrets of that art, in numbers and species* (1650).

Moore, Jonas. *Moores arithmetick in two books* (1660).

More, Thomas. *A fruteful, and pleasant worke of the beste state of a publyque weale, and of the newe ysle called Vtopia*, tr. Ralphe Robynson (1551).

Mousnier, Roland (ed.), *Lettres et mémoire adressés au Chancelier Séguier (1633–1649)* (2 vols., Paris: Presses Universitaires de France, 1964).

Nash, T. Russell. *Collections for the history of Worcestershire* (2 vols., 1781–2).

Nelson, Robert. *An address to persons of quality and estate* (1715).

Newton, Isaac. *The Correspondence of Isaac Newton*, ed. H. W. Turnbull (7 vols., Cambridge: Cambridge University Press, 1959–77).

Noddle, Daniel. *To the parliament of the commonvvealth of England, and every individual member thereof* (1654).

North, Roger. *Examen: or an enquiry into the credt and veracity of a pretended complete history* (1740).

Oldenburg, Henry. *The Correspondence of Henry Oldenburg*, ed. and tr. A. R. Hall and M. B. Hall (9 vols., Madison, WI: University of Wisconsin Press, 1965–73).

Oldner, George. *Mr. George Oldner's invention to preserve ships from foundering, or sinking, at sea, &c* (1698).

Olivi, Pierre de Jean. *Traité des contrats*, ed. and tr. Sylvain Piron (Paris: Les Belles Lettres, 2012).

Pepys, Samuel. *The Diary of Samuel Pepys*, ed. Robert Latham and William Matthews (11 vols., London: Bell, 1970).

Petty, William. *The advice of W. P. to Mr. Samuel Hartlib for some particular parts of learning* (1647 [1648]).

Petty, William. *A declaration concerning the newly invented art of double writing* (1648).

Petty, William. *Double writing* [1648].

Petty, William. *A treatise of taxes & contributions* (1662).

Petty, William. *The Economic Writings of Sir William Petty*, ed. Charles Henry Hull (2 vols., Cambridge: Cambridge University Press, 1899).

Phillips, Edward. *The new world of words: or, universal English dictionary* (6th edn, 1706).

Plattes, Gabriel. *A discovery of infinite treasure, hidden since the worlds beginning* (1639).

Plattes, Gabriel. *A discovery of subterraneal treasure* (1639).

Plattes, Gabriel. *Certaine new inventions and profitable experiments* (1640).

Plattes, Gabriel. *A description of the famous kingdome of Macaria* (1641).

Plattes, Gabriel. *The profitable intelligencer, communicating his knowledge for the generall good of the common-wealth and all posterity* (1644).

Plutarch. *The lives of the noble Grecians & Romans compared together*, tr. Thomas North (1657).

Procter, Thomas. *A vvorthy vvorke profitable to this vvole kingdome concerning the mending of all high-vvaies, as also for vvaters and iron vvorkes* (1607).

Prynne, William. *An humble remonstrance to his maiesty, against the tax of ship-money* (1641).

Rabelais, François. *Le cinquiesme et dernier livre...du bon Pantagruel* ([Lyons], 1564).

Ramsey, William. *Life and Letters of Joseph Black* (London: Constable, 1918).

Roberts, Lewes. *The treatise of traffike or a discourse of forraine trade* (1641).

Robinson, Henry. *Certain proposals in order to the peoples freedome and accommodation in some particulars* (1652).

Rose, John. *The English vineyard vindicated* (1666).

Rushworth, John. *Historical collections* (8 vols., 1721).

Rymer, Thomas. *Foedera* (20 vols., 1704–35).

Salmon, William. *Iatrica: seu praxis medendi* (1694).

Savery, Thomas. *The miners friend* (1702).

Schafer, R. G. (ed.), *A Selection from the Records of Philip Foley's Stour Valley Iron Works 1668–74*, 2 vols., Worcestershire Historical Society, new ser., 9, 13 (1982, 1990).

Scott, Thomas. *The proiector* (1623).

Shiers, William. *A familiar discourse or dialogue concerning the Mine- Adventure* (1700).

Shirley, James. *Triumph of peace* (1634).

Skinner, Stephen. *A new English dictionary shewing the etymological derivation of the English tongue, in two parts* (1691).

Smith, Adam. *An Inquiry into the Nature and Causes of the Wealth of Nations*, ed. R. H. Campbell and A. S. Skinner (2 vols., Indianapolis, IN: Liberty Fund, 1976)

Smith, Adam. *The Theory of Moral Sentiments*, ed. D. D. Raphael and A. L. Macfie (Indianapolis, IN: Liberty Fund, 1976).

Smith, John. *England's improvement reviv'd* (1670).

Smith, Thomas. *A Discourse of the Commonweal of This Realm of England*, ed. Mary Dewar (Charlottesville, VA: University Press of Virginia, 1969).

Spicker, Paul (ed.), *The Origins of Modern Welfare: Juan Luis Vives, De Subventione Pauperum, and City of Ypres, Forma Subventionis Pauperum* (Oxford: Peter Lang, 2010).

Sprat, Thomas. *The history of the Royal Society* [1667] (London: Routledge, 1959).

Steele, Richard and Joseph Gillmore, *An account of the fish-pool* (1718).

Stevenson, Matthew. *Poems* (1665).

Stewart, Dugald. 'Account of the Life and Writings of Adam Smith, LL.D', ed. I. S. Ross, in Adam Smith, *Essays on Philosophical Subjects*, ed. W. P. D. Wightman and J. C. Bryce (Oxford: Clarendon, Oxford University Press, 1980), 263–351.

Stoughton, William. *An assertion for truee and Christian church-policie* (1604).

Swanton, Michael (ed.), *Anglo-Saxon Prose* (London: Dent, 1975).

Swift, Jonathan. *The Prose Writings of Jonathan Swift, Vol. 1: A Tale of a Tub with Other Early Works 1696–1707*, ed. Herbert Davis (Oxford: Blackwell, 1939).

Swift, Jonathan. *The Prose Writings of Jonathan Swift, Vol. 11: Gulliver's Travels, 1726*, ed. Herbert Davis (Oxford: Blackwell, 1941).

Tawney, R. H. and Eileen Power (eds.), *Tudor Economic Documents* (3 vols., London: Longmans, 1924).

Taylor, John. *The carriers cosmographie* (1637).

Taylor, John. *The complaint of M. Tenter-hooke the proiector, and Sir Thomas Dodger the patentee* (1641).

Thirsk, Joan and J. P. Cooper (eds.), *Seventeenth-Century Economic Documents* (Oxford: Clarendon, 1972).

Thomas, John. *Liberality in promoting the trade and interest of the publick display'd: A sermon preach'd at St. Mary's in Chester September 1733 on occasion of obtaining an act of parliament for making the river Dee navigable* [1733?].

Thompson, Edward Maunde. (ed.), *Correspondence of the Family of Hatton, vol. I, 1601–1704* (Camden Society, 1878).

Vaughan, Rowland. *Most approued, and long experienced water-workes* (1610).

Walcot, Humphrey. *Sea-water made fresh and wholsom* [1702], [a printed handbill].

Walcot, Humphrey. *Sea-water made fresh and wholsome* (1702).

Waller, William. *An essay on the value of the mines* (1698).

Waller, William. *Mine-Adventure laid open* (1710).

[Ward, Edward] *The fourth part of vulgus Britannicus* (1710).

Webster, Charles (ed.), *Samuel Hartlib and the Advancement of Learning* (Cambridge: Cambridge University Press, 1970).

Weldon, Anthony. *The court and character of King James whereunto is now added the court of King Charles* (1651).

Weldon, Anthony. *A cat may look upon a king* (1652).

Wentworth, Thomas. *The last speeches of Thomas Wentworth* (1641).

Wentworth, Thomas. *The Earl of Strafforde's letters and dispatches*, ed. W. Knowler (2 vols., 1739).

Weston, Richard. *A discourse of husbandrie used in Brabant and Flanders* (1650).

Wheeler, William. *Mr William Wheeler's case from his own relation* (1645).

Whitelocke, Bulstrode. *Memorials of the English affairs* (1682).

Wildman, John. *Putney proiects. Or the old serpent in a new forme* (1647).

Wilson, John. *The projectors. A comedy* (1665).

Winthrop, Robert C. (ed.) with introduction, *Correspondence of Hartlib, Haak, Oldenburg, and others of the founders of the Royal Society, with Govenor Winthrop of Connecticut: 1661–1672* (Boston, MA: Press of John Wilson and Son, 1878).

[Worsley, Benjamin] *The advocate: or, a narrative of the state and condition of things between the English and Dutch nation, in relation to trade* (1651).

Worsley, Benjamin. *Free ports, the nature and necessitie of them stated* (1652).

Worthington, John. *The Diary and Correspondence of Dr. John Worthington*, ed. James Crossley et al., Camden Society, old ser., 13, 36, 114 (3 vols., 1847, 1855, 1886).

Yarranton, Andrew. *The Improvement improved, by a second edition of the great improvement of lands by clover* (Worcester, 1663).

Yarranton, Andrew. *England's improvement by sea and land* (1677).

Yarranton, Andrew. *England's improvement by sea and land. The second part* (1681).

SECONDARY SOURCES

Alff, David. 'Swift's Solar Gourds and the Rhetoric of Projection', *Eighteenth-Century Studies*, 47 (2014), 245–60.

Alff, David. *The Wreckage of Intentions: Projects in British Culture, 1660–1730* (Philadelphia, PA: University of Pennsylvania Press, 2017).

Allen, Martin. *Mints and Money in Medieval England* (Cambridge: Cambridge University Press, 2012).

Allen, Robert C. *The British Industrial Revolution in Global Perspective* (Cambridge: Cambridge University Press, 2009).

Alsop, J. D. 'The Age of the Projectors: British Imperial Strategy in the North Atlantic in the War of Spanish Succession', *Acadiensis*, 21 (1991), 30–53.

Andrews, Kenneth R. *Trade, Plunder and Settlement: Maritime Enterprise and the Genesis of the British Empire, 1480–1630* (Cambridge: Cambridge University Press, 1984).

Andrews, Kenneth R. *Ships, Money and Politics: Seafaring and Naval Enterprise in the Reign of Charles I* (Cambridge: Cambridge University Press, 1991).

Appleby, John C. 'War, Politics, and Colonization, 1558–1625', in Nicholas Canny (ed.), *The Oxford History of the British Empire, Volume 1: The Origins of Empire* (Oxford: Oxford University Press, 1998), 55–78.

Appleby, Joyce Oldham. 'Ideology and Theory: The Tension between Political and Economic Liberalism in Seventeenth-Century England', *AHR*, 81 (1976), 499–515.

Appleby, Joyce Oldham. *Economic Thought and Ideology in Seventeenth-Century England* (Princeton, NJ: Princeton University Press, 1978).

Archer, Ian. 'The London Lobbies in the Later Sixteenth Century', *HJ*, 31 (1984), 17–44.

Archer, Ian. *The History of Haberdashers' Company* (Chichester: Phillimore, 1991).

Asch, Ronald G. 'The Revival of Monopolies: Court and Patronage during the Personal Rule of Charles I, 1629–40', in Ronald G. Asch and Adolf M. Birke (eds.), *Princes, Patronage, and the Nobility: The Court at the Beginning of the Modern Age* (Oxford: Oxford University Press, 1991), 357–92.

Ash, Eric H. *Power, Knowledge, and Expertise in Elizabethan England* (Baltimore, MD: Johns Hopkins University Press, 2004).

Ash, Eric H. *The Draining of the Fens: Projectors, Popular Politics, and State Building in Early Modern England* (Baltimore, MD: Johns Hopkins University Press, 2017).

Ashcraft, Richard. *Revolutionary Politics and Locke's 'Two Treatises of Government'* (Princeton, NJ: Princeton University Press, 1986).

Ashworth, William J. 'The Ghost of Rostow: Science, Culture and the British Industrial Revolution', *History of Science*, 46 (2008), 249–74.

Ashworth, William J. *The Industrial Revolution: The State, Knowledge and Global Trade* (London: Bloomsbury, 2017).

Aylmer, G. E. 'Attempts at Administrative Reform', *EHR*, 72 (1957), 229–59.

Aylmer, G. E. *The King's Servants: The Civil Service of Charles I, 1625–1642* (New York: Columbia University Press, 1961).

Aylmer, G. E. 'Buckingham as an Administrative Reformer?', *EHR*, 105 (1990), 355–62.

Aylmer, G. E. *The Crown's Servants: Government and Civil Service under Charles II, 1660–1685* (Oxford: Oxford University Press, 2002).

Bailey, Mark. 'The Commercialisation of the English Economy, 1086–1500', *Journal of Medieval History*, 24 (1998), 297–311.

Barnard, John and D. F. McKenzie (eds.), *The Cambridge History of the Book in Britain, vol. IV, 1557–1695* (Cambridge: Cambridge University Press, 2002).

Barnard, Toby. *Improving Ireland? Projectors, Prophets and Profiteers, 1641–1786* (Dublin: Four Courts Press, 2008).

Barry, Jonathan. 'Publicity and the Public Good: Presenting Medicine in Eighteenth-Century Bristol', in W. F. Bynum and Roy Porter (eds.), *Medical Fringe and Medical Orthodoxy, 1750–1850* (London: Croom Helm, 1987), 29–39.

Barry, Jonathan. 'Civility and Civic Culture in Early Modern England: The Meanings of Urban Freedom', in Peter Burke, Brian Harrison, and Paul Slack (eds.), *Civil Histories: Essays Presented to Sir Keith Thomas* (Oxford: Oxford University Press, 2000), 181–96.

Barry, Jonathan. 'The "Great Projector": John Cary and the Legacy of Puritan Reform in Bristol', in Margaret Pelling and Scott Mandelbrote (eds.), *The Practice of Reform in Health, Medicine and Science, 1500–2000* (Aldershot: Ashgate, 2005), 185–206.

Barter Bailey, Sarah. *Prince Rupert's Patent Guns* (Leeds: Royal Armouries Museum, 2000).

Baugh, G. C. (ed.), *Victoria County History, Shropshire, Volume 11* (Oxford: Oxford University Press, 1985).

Baxter, Stephen B. *The Development of The Treasury, 1660–1702* (London: Longman, 1957).

Bayard, Françoise. 'L'Image littéraire du financier dans la première moitié du XIIe siècle', *Revue d'Histoire Moderne et Contemporaine*, 33 (1986), 3–20.

Beckert, Sven. 'History of American Capitalism', in Eric Foner and Lisa McGirr (eds.), *American History Now* (Philadelphia, PA: Temple University Press, 2011), 314–35.

Beckett, J. V. *The Aristocracy in England 1660–1914* (Oxford: Blackwell, 1986).

Belich, James, John Darwin, and Chris Wickham. 'Introduction: The Prospect of Global History', in James Belich et al. (eds.), *The Prospect of Global History* (Oxford: Oxford University Press, 2016), 3–22.

Bell, Walter George. *The Great Fire of London in 1666* (London: John Lane, 1920).

Bellany, Alastair. *The Politics of Court Scandal in Early Modern England: News Culture and the Overbury Affair, 1603–1660* (Cambridge: Cambridge University Press, 2002).

Bennett, Jim. 'Instrument and Ingenuity', in Michael Cooper and Michael Hunter (eds.), *Robert Hooke: Tercentennial Studies* (Aldershot: Ashgate, 2006), 65–76.

Beresford, M. W. 'The Common Informer, the Penal Statutes and Economic Regulation', *EcHR*, new ser., 10 (1957), 221–38.

Berg, Maxine. *Luxury and Pleasure in Eighteenth-Century Britain* (Oxford: Oxford University Press, 2005).

Berg, Maxine. 'The Genesis of "Useful Knowledge"', *History of Science*, 45 (2007), 123–33.

Berg, Maxine and Elizabeth Eger, 'The Rise and Fall of the Luxury Debates', in Maxine Berg and Elizabeth Eger (eds.), *Luxury in the Eighteenth Century: Debates, Desires and Delectable Goods* (Basingstoke: Palgrave, 2003), 7–27.

Berrogain, Jean Vilar. *Literatura y economía: la figura satírica del arbitrista en el Siglo de Oro* (Madrid: Revista de Occidente, 1973).

Beugelsdijk, Sjoerd and Robbert Maseland, *Culture in Economics: History, Methodological Reflections, and Contemporary Applications* (Cambridge: Cambridge University Press, 2011).

Bevir, Mark and Frank Trentmann, 'Markets in Historical Contexts: Ideas, Practices and Governance', in Mark Bevir and Frank Trentmann (eds.), *Markets in Historical Contexts: Ideas and Politics in the Modern World* (Cambridge: Cambridge University Press, 2004), 1–24.

Biagioli, Mario. 'From Print to Patents: Living on Instruments in Early Modern Europe', *History of Science*, 44 (2006), 139–86.

Bogart, Dan. 'Did the Glorious Revolution Contribute to the Transport Revolution? Evidence from Investment in Roads and Rivers', *EcHR*, 64 (2011), 1073–112.

Bogart, Dan. 'The Transport Revolution in Industrialising Britain', in Roderick Floud, Jane Humphries, and Paul Johnson, *The Cambridge Economic History of Modern Britain* (2 vols., Cambridge: Cambridge University Press, 2014), vol. 1, 368–91.

Boltanski, Luc and Eve Chiapello, *The New Spirit of Capitalism*, tr. Gregory Elliott (Verso: London, 2005) [French original, 1999].

Boltanski, Luc and Laurent Thévenot, *On Justification: Economies of Worth*, tr. Catherine Porter (Princeton, NJ: Princeton University Press, 2006) [French original, 1991].

Boon, George C. *Cardiganshire Silver and the Aberystwyth Mint in Peace and War* (Cardiff: National Museum of Wales, 1981).

Bottomley, Sean. *The British Patent System during the Industrial Revolution: From Privilege to Property* (Cambridge: Cambridge University Press, 2014).

Bottomley, Sean. 'Mansell v Bunger (1626)', in Jose Bellido (ed.), *Landmark Cases in Intellectual Property Law* (London: Bloomsbury, 2017), 1–20.

Boulton, Jeremy. 'Food Prices and the Standard of Living in London in the "Century of Revolution", 1580–1700', *EcHR*, 53 (2000), 455–92.

Bourdieu, Pierre and Roger Chartier, *Le Sociologue et l'historien* (Marseilles: Agone, 2010).

Boyce, Benjamin. *The Theophrastan Character in England to 1642* (Cambridge, MA: Harvard University Press, 1947).

Boyce, Benjamin. *The Polemic Character 1640–1661* (Lincoln, NE: University of Nebraska Press, 1955).

Braddick, Michael J. *The Nerves of State: Taxation and the Financing of the English State, 1558–1714* (Manchester: Manchester University Press, 1996).

Braddick, Michael J. *State Formation in Early Modern England c. 1550–1700* (Cambridge: Cambridge University Press, 2000).

Braddick, Michael J. *God's Fury, England's Fire: A New History of the English Civil Wars* (London: Allen Lane, 2008).

Braddick, Michael J. and John Walter (eds.), *Negotiating Power in Early Modern Society: Order, Hierarchy and Subordination in Britain and Ireland* (Cambridge: Cambridge University Press, 2001).

Brakensiek, Stefan. 'Projektemacher: Zum Hintergrund ökonomischen Scheiterns in der Frühen Neuzeit', in Stefan Brakensiek and Claudia Claridge (eds.), *Fiasko—Scheitern in der Frühen Neuzeit: Beiträge zur Kulturgeschichte des Misserfolgs* (Bielefeld: Transcript, 2015), 39–58.

Braunstein, Philippe. *Travail et entreprise au Moyen Âge* (Brussels: De Boeck, 2003).

Brewer, John. *Sinews of Power: War, Money and the English State, 1688–1783* (London: Unwin Hyman, 1989).

Brewer, John. *The Pleasures of the Imagination: English Culture in the Eighteenth Century* (New York: Farrar, Straus, and Giroux, 1997).

Brewer, John and Roy Porter (eds.), *Consumption and the World of Goods* (London: Routledge, 1993).

Brioist, Pascal. ' "Familiar Demonstrations in Geometry": French and Italian Engineers and Euclid in the Sixteenth Century', *History of Science*, 47 (2009), 1–26.

Broadberry, Stephen et al., *British Economic Growth, 1270–1870* (Cambridge: Cambridge University Press, 2015).

Brooks, Christopher W. *Law, Politics and Society in Early Modern England* (Cambridge: Cambridge University Press, 2008).

Brooks, Colin. 'Projecting, Political Arithmetic and the Act of 1695', *EHR*, 97 (1982), 31–53.

Brown, Peter J. 'The Early Industrial Complex at Astley, Worcestershire', *Post-Medieval Archaeology*, 16 (1982), 1–19.

Brown, Peter J. 'Andrew Yarranton and the British Tinplate Industry', *Historical Metallurgy*, 22 (1988), 42–8.

Brown, Peter J. 'The Military Career of Andrew Yarranton', *Transactions of Worcestershire Archaeological Society*, 3rd ser., 13 (1992), 193–202.

Bulman, William J. *Anglican Enlightenment: Orientalism, Religion and Politics in England and its Empire, 1648–1715* (Cambridge: Cambridge University Press, 2015).

Buning, Marius. 'Between Imitation and Invention: Inventor Privileges and Technological Progress in the Early Dutch Republic (c.1585–1625)', *Intellectual History Review*, 24 (2014), 415–27.

Burke, Peter. 'The Microhistory Debate', in Burke (ed.), *New Perspectives on Historical Writing* (2nd edn, University Park, PA: Pennsylvania State University Press, 2001), 115–17.

Burley, G. H. C. 'Andrew Yarranton: A Seventeenth-Century Worcestershire Worthy', *Transactions of Worcestershire Archaeological Society*, new ser., 38 (1961), 25–36.

Burton, John Richard. *Some Collections towards the History of the Family of Walcot* (Shrewsbury: Brown & Brinnard, 1930).

Butler, Martin. *Theatre and Criticism 1632–1642* (Cambridge: Cambridge University Press, 1984).

Butler, Martin. 'Politics and the Masque: *The Triumph of Peace*', *Seventeenth Century*, 2 (1987), 117–41.

Butler, Martin. *The Stuart Court Masque and Political Culture* (Cambridge: Cambridge University Press, 2008).

Butterfield, Herbert. *The Whig Interpretation of History* (New York: Norton, 1965) [originally published, 1931].

Campbell, John. *Lives of the British Admirals* (4 vols., London: Murray, 1785).

Cannadine, David. 'The Present and the Past in the English Industrial Revolution 1880–1980', *P&P*, 103 (1984), 131–72.

Cantrill, Thomas Crosbee and Marjory Wight. 'Yarranton's Works at Astley', *Transactions of the Worcestershire Archaeological Society*, 2nd ser., 7 (1929), 92–115.

Carroll, Archie B. 'Corporate Social Responsibility: Evolution of a Definitional Construct', *Business and Society*, 38 (1999), 268–95.

Carroll, Archie B. 'A History of Corporate Social Responsibility: Concepts and Practices', in Andrew Crane et al. (eds.), *The Oxford Handbook of Corporate Social Responsibility* (Oxford: Oxford University Press, 2008), 19–46.

Carruthers, Bruce G. *City of Capital: Politics and Markets in the English Financial Revolution* (Princeton, NJ: Princeton University Press, 1996).

Carus-Wilson, E. M. and Olive Coleman, *England's Export Trade, 1275–1547* (Oxford: Clarendon, 1963).

Cavert, William M. *The Smoke of London: Energy and Environment in the Early Modern City* (Cambridge: Cambridge University Press, 2016).

Cavill, P. R. 'Anticlericalism and the Early Tudor Parliament', *Parliamentary History*, 34 (2015), 14–29.

Cavillac, Michel. 'Miquel Giginta et la délinquance urbaine', in Alexandre Pagès (ed.), *Giginta: de la charité au programme social* (Perpignan: Presses Universitaires de Perpignan, 2012), 107–22.

Chalklin, C. W. 'Navigation Schemes on the Upper Medway, 1600–1665', *Journal of Transport History*, 5 (1961), 105–15.

Chambers, Douglas. '"Wild Pastorall Encounter": John Evelyn, John Beale and the Renegotiation of Pastoral in the Mid-Seventeenth Century', in Leslie and Raylor (eds.), *Culture and Cultivation*, 173–94.

Chambers, Robert. *Domestic Annals of Scotland* (3 vols., Edinburgh: Chambers, 1858–61).

Chandaman, C. D. *The English Public Revenue, 1660–1688* (Oxford: Clarendon, 1975).

Chandler Jr, Alfred D. *The Visible Hand: The Managerial Revolution in American Business* (Cambridge, MA: Harvard University Press, 1977).

Chartres, John. 'No English Calvados? English Distillers and the Cider Industry in the Seventeenth and Eighteenth Centuries', in John Chartres and David Hey (eds.), *English Rural Society, 1500–1800* (Cambridge: Cambridge University Press, 1990), 313–42.

Chrimes, S. B. *Henry VII* (New Haven, CT: Yale University Press, 1972).

Christie, John. 'Laputa Revisited', in Christie and Shuttleworth (eds.), *Nature Transfigured*, 45–60.

Christie, John and Sally Shuttleworth (eds.), *Nature Transfigured: Science and Literature, 1700–1900* (Manchester: Manchester University Press, 1989).

Clark, Geoffrey. *Betting on Lives: The Culture of Life Insurance in England, 1695–1775* (Manchester: Manchester University Press, 1999).

Clark, Gregory. 'The Condition of the Working Class in England, 1209–2004', *Journal of Political Economy*, 113 (2005), 1307–40.

Clark, Gregory. 'The Long March of History: Farm Wages, Population, and Economic Growth, England 1209–1869', *EcHR*, 60 (2007), 97–135.

Clark, Matthew. 'Resistance, Collaboration and the Early Modern "Public Transcript": The River Lea Disputes and Popular Politics in England, 1571–1603', *Cultural and Social History*, 8 (2011), 297–313.

Claydon, Tony. *William III and the Godly Revolution* (Cambridge: Cambridge University Press, 1996).

Clucas, Stephen. 'Samuel Hartlib: Intelligencing and Technology in Seventeenth-Century Europe', in Robert Kretzschmar and Sönke Lorenz (eds.), *Leonardo da Vinci und Heinrich Schickhardt: Zum Transfer technischen Wissens im vormodernen Europa* (Stuttgart: Verlag W. Kohlhammer, 2010), 58–75.

Coffman, D'Maris. *Excise Taxation and the Origins of Public Debt* (Basingstoke: Palgrave, 2013).

Cogswell, Thomas. '"The Symptoms and Vapors of a Diseased Time": The Earl of Clare and Early Stuart Manuscript Culture', *Review of English Studies*, new ser., 57 (2006), 310–36.

Cogswell, Thomas. '"In the Power of the State": Mr Anys's Project and the Tobacco Colonies, 1626–1628', *EHR*, 123 (2008), 35–64.

Coleman, D. C. *The Economy of England, 1450–1750* (Oxford: Oxford University Press, 1977).

Coleman, D. C. 'Mercantilism Revisited', *HJ*, 23 (1980), 773–91.

Collinson, Patrick. *Elizabethan Essays* (London: Hambledon, 1994).

Collinson, Patrick. 'Ben Jonson's *Bartholomew Fair*: The Theatre Constructs Puritanism', in David L. Smith, Richard Strier, and David Bevington (eds.), *The Theatrical City: Culture, Theatre and Politics in London, 1576–1649* (Cambridge: Cambridge University Press, 1995), 157–69.

Cook, James W. 'The Kids Are All Right: On the "Turning" of Cultural History', *AHR*, 117 (2012), 746–71.

Coulson, H. J. W. and Urquhart A. Forbes, *The Law Relating to Waters, Sea, Tidal, and Inland* (3rd edn, London: Sweet & Maxwell, 1910).

Cowan, Brian. *The Social Life of Coffee: The Emergence of the British Coffeehouse* (New Haven, CT: Yale University Press, 2005).

Cramsie, John. 'Commercial Projects and the Fiscal Policy of James VI and I', *HJ*, 43 (2000), 345–64.

Cramsie, John. *Kingship and Crown Finance under James VI and I, 1603–1625* (Woodbridge: Boydell, 2002).

Cressy, David. *Saltpeter: The Mother of Gunpowder* (Oxford: Oxford University Press, 2013).

Cronon, William. *Changes in the Land: Indians, Colonists, and the Ecology of New England* (New York: Hill & Wang, 1983).

Cruickshanks, Eveline, Stuart Handley, and David Hayton (eds.), *History of Parliament: The House of Commons, 1690–1715* (5 vols., Cambridge: Cambridge University Press, 2002).

Cruyningen, Piet van. 'Dealing with Drainage: State Regulation of Drainage Projects in the Dutch Republic, France, and England during the Sixteenth and Seventeenth Centuries', *EcHR*, 68 (2015), 420–40.

Cruz, Anne J. *Discourses of Poverty: Social Reform and the Picaresque Novel in Early Modern Spain* (Toronto: University of Toronto Press, 1999).

Cunningham, W. *The Growth of English Industry and Commerce in Modern Times, Part 1, Mercantile System* (6th edn, Cambridge: Cambridge University Press, 1925).

Cust, Richard. *The Forced Loan and English Politics, 1626–1628* (Oxford: Oxford University Press, 1987).

Cust, Richard. 'Charles I and Providence', in Kenneth Fincham and Peter Lake (eds.), *Religious Politics in Post-Reformation England* (Woodbridge: Boydell, 2006), 193–208.

Cust, Richard. 'Reading for Magistracy: The Mental World of Sir John Newgate', in John McDiarmid (ed.), *The Monarchical Republic of Early Modern England: Essays in Response to Patrick Collinson* (Aldershot: Ashgate, 2007), 181–99.

Darby, H. C. *The Draining of the Fens* (2nd edn, Cambridge, 1956).

Daston, Lorraine J. 'The Domestication of Risk: Mathematical Probability and Insurance 1650–1830', in Lorenz Kruger, Lorraine J. Daston, and Michael Heidelberger (eds.), *The Probabilistic Revolution* (2 vols., Cambridge, MA: MIT Press, 1987), vol. 1, 237–60.

Daston, Lorraine J., and H. Otto Sibum, 'Introduction: Scientific Personae and Their Histories', *Science in Context*, 16 (2003), 1–8.

Daunton, M. J. *Progress and Poverty: Economic and Social History of Britain 1700–1850* (Oxford: Oxford University Press, 1995).

Davies, K. G. 'Joint-Stock Investment in the Later Seventeenth Century', *EcHR*, new ser., 4 (1952), 283–301.

Davies, K. G. *The Royal African Company* (London: Longman, 1957).

Davies, Matthew. 'Lobbying Parliament: The London Companies in the Fifteenth Century', *Parliamentary History*, 23 (2004), 136–48.

Davis, James. *Medieval Market Morality: Life, Law and Ethics in the English Marketplace, 1200–1500* (Cambridge: Cambridge University Press, 2012).

Davis, Ralph. *English Overseas Trade 1500–1700* (London: Macmillan, 1973).

Dear, Peter. *Discipline and Experience: The Mathematical Way in the Scientific Revolution* (Chicago: University of Chicago Press, 1995).

Deaux, Kay and Gina Philogène (eds.), *Representations of the Social: Bridging Theoretical Traditions* (Oxford: Blackwell, 2001).

Desan, Christine. *Making Money: Coin, Currency, and the Coming of Capitalism* (Oxford: Oxford University Press, 2014).

Dessert, Daniel. 'Le "Laquais-financier" au Grand Siècle: Mythe ou réalité?', *Dix-Septième Siècle*, 122 (1979), 21–36.

Dessert, Daniel. *Argent, pouvoir et société au Grand Siècle* (Paris: Fayard, 1984).

Dessert, Daniel. *L'Argent du sel: Le Sel de l'argent* (Paris: Fayard, 2012).

De Vivo, Filippo. 'Prospect or Refuge? Microhistory, History on the Large Scale', *Cultural and Social History*, 7 (2010), 387–97.

Dickson, P. G. M. *The Financial Revolution in England: A Study in the Development of Public Credit, 1688–1756* (London: Macmillan, 1967).

Dietz, Frederick C. *English Public Finance, 1558–1641* (2nd edn, London: Frank Cass, 1964).

DiMeo, Michelle. 'Openness vs Secrecy in the Hartlib Circle: Revisiting "Democratic Baconianism" in Interregnum England', in Elaine Leong and Alisha Rankin (eds.), *Secrets and Knowledge in Medicine and Science, 1500–1800* (Farnham: Ashgate, 2011), 105–21.

Di Palma, Vittoria. 'Drinking Cider in Paradise: Science, Improvement, and the Politics of Fruit Trees', in Adam Smyth (ed.), *A Pleasing Sinne: Drink and Conviviality in Seventeenth-Century England* (Cambridge: Brewer, 2004), 161–77.

Dircks, Henry. *The Life, Times, and Scientific Labours of the Second Marquis of Worcester* (London: Bernard Quaritch,1865).

Drayton, Richard. *Nature's Government: Science, Imperial Britain, and the 'Improvement' of the World* (New Haven, CT: Yale University Press, 2000).

Drucker, Peter. 'The New Meaning of Corporate Social Responsibility', *California Management Review*, 26 (1984), 53–63.

Duke, Alastair. 'The Ambivalent Face of Calvinism in the Netherlands, 1561–1618', in Menna Prestwich (ed.), *International Calvinism, 1541–1715* (Oxford: Clarendon, 1985), 109–34.

Dunn, Kevin. 'Milton among the Monopolists: *Areopagitica*, Intellectual Property and the Hartlib Circle', in Greengrass, Leslie, and Raylor (eds.), *Samuel Hartlib and Universal Reformation*, 177–92.

Dutton, Richard. 'Jonson's Satiric Styles', in Richard Harp and Stanley Stewart (eds.), *The Cambridge Companion to Ben Jonson* (Cambridge: Cambridge University Press, 2000), 58–71.

Dyer, Christopher. 'Work Ethics in the Fourteenth Century', in James Bothwell, P. J. P. Goldberg, and W. M. Ormrod (eds.), *The Problem of Labour in Fourteenth-Century England* (Rochester, NY: York Medieval Press, 2001), 21–41.

Dyson, Jessica. *Staging Authority in Caroline England: Prerogative, Law and Order in Drama, 1625–1642* (Farnham: Ashgate, 2013).

Eamon, William. *Science and the Secrets of Nature: Books of Secrets in Medieval and Early Modern Culture* (Princeton, NJ: Princeton University Press, 1994).

Earle, Peter. *The Making of the English Middle Class: Business, Society and Family Life in London, 1660–1730* (London: Methuen, 1989).

Early Modern Research Group, 'Commonwealth: The Social, Cultural, and Conceptual Contexts of an Early Modern Keyword', *HJ*, 54 (2011), 659–87.

Edgerton, David. *The Shock of the Old: Technology and Global History since 1900* (London: Profile Books, 2006).

Emery, Frank. 'The Mechanics of Innovation: Clover Cultivation in Wales before 1750', *Journal of Historical Geography*, 2 (1976), 35–48.

Epstein, Steven A. *An Economic and Social History of Later Medieval Europe, 1000–1500* (Cambridge: Cambridge University Press, 2009).

Erskine-Hill, Howard. *The Social Milieu of Alexander Pope: Lives, Example and the Poetic Response* (New Haven, CT: Yale University Press, 1975).

Evans, R. C. 'Contemporary Contexts of Jonson's "*The Devil is an Ass*"', *Comparative Drama*, 26 (1992), 140–76.

Eymard-Duvernay, François. *Économie politique de l'entreprise* (Paris: La Découverte, 2004).

Fairclough, Keith. 'A Successful Elizabethan Project: The River Lea Improvement Scheme', *Journal of Transport History*, 3rd ser., 11 (1998), 54–65.

Feingold, Mordechai. 'The Mathematical Sciences and New Philosophies', in Nicholas Tyacke (ed.), *The History of the University of Oxford, Volume VI: Seventeenth-Century Oxford* (Oxford, 1997), 359–449.

Feingold, Mordechai. '"Experimental Philosophy": Invention and Rebirth of a Seventeenth-Century Concept', *Early Science and Medicine*, 21 (2016), 1–28.

Feingold, Mordechai. 'Projectors and Learned Projects in Early Modern England', *Seventeenth Century*, 32 (2017), 63–79.

Ferguson, Arthur B. *The Articulate Citizen and the English Renaissance* (Durham, NC: Duke University Press, 1965).

Ferris, J. P. 'The Saltpetreman in Dorset, 1635', *Proceedings of the Dorset Natural History and Archaeological Society*, 85 (1963), 158–63.

Ferris, John P. and Andrew Thrush (eds.), *House of Commons, 1604–1629* (6 vols., Cambridge: Cambridge University Press, 2010).

Finkelstein, Andrea. *Harmony and the Balance: An Intellectual History of Seventeenth-Century English Economic Thought* (Ann Arbor, MI: University of Michigan Press, 2000).

Fisher, F. J. 'Some Experiments in Company Organization in the Early Seventeenth Century', *EcHR*, 4 (1933), 177–94.

Fleischacker, Samuel. *On Adam Smith's Wealth of Nations: A Philosophical Companion* (Princeton, NJ: Princeton University Press, 2004).

Fletcher, Anthony. *Reform in the Provinces: The Government of Stuart England* (New Haven, CT: Yale University Press, 1986).

Fontaine, Laurence. *L'Économie morale: Pauvreté, crédit et confiance dans l'Europe préindustrielle* (Paris: Gallimard, 2008).

Fontaine, Laurence. *Le Marché: Histoire et usages d'une conquête sociale* (Paris: Gallimard, 2014).

Forman, Valerie. *Tragicomic Redemptions: Global Economics and the Early Modern English Stage* (Philadelphia, PA: University of Pennsylvania Press, 2008).

Foster, Elizabeth Read. 'The Procedure of the House of Commons against Patents and Monopolies', in W. A. Aiken and B. D. Henning (eds.), *Conflict in Stuart England* (New York: Jonathan Cape, 1960), 59–85.

Fox, Adam. *Oral and Literate Culture in England, 1500–1700* (Cambridge: Cambridge University Press, 2000).

Fox, Adam. 'Sir William Petty, Ireland, and the Making of a Political Economist, 1653–87', *EcHR*, 62 (2009), 388–404.

Freedman, Paul. *Images of the Medieval Peasant* (Stanford, CA: Stanford University Press, 1999).

Freeman, Michael. 'Popular Attitudes to Turnpikes in Early Eighteenth-Century England', *Journal of Historical Geography*, 19 (1993), 33–47.

French, H. R. *The Middle Sort of People in Provincial England, 1600–1750* (Oxford: Oxford University Press, 2007).

Fridenson, Patrick. 'Is there a Return of Capitalism in Business History?', in Jürgen Kocka and Marcel van der Linden (eds.), *Capitalism: The Reemergence of a Historical Concept* (London: Bloomsbury, 2016), 107–31.

Friedman, Milton. 'The Social Responsibility of Business is to Increase its Profit', *New York Times Magazine*, 13 September 1970, 32–3, 122–6.

Friis, Astrid. *Alderman Cockayne's Project and the Cloth Trade: The Commercial Policy of England in its Main Aspect* (Copenhagen: Levin & Munsgaard, 1927).

Fritschy, Wantje. 'The Efficiency of Taxation in Holland', in Oscar Gelderblom (ed.), *The Political Economy of the Dutch Republic* (Farnham: Ashgate, 2009), 55–84.

Froide, Amy M. *Silent Partners: Women as Public Investors during Britain's Financial Revolution* (Oxford: Oxford University Press, 2017).

Fusaro, Maria. *Political Economies of Empire in the Early Modern Mediterranean: The Decline of Venice and the Rise of England, 1450–1700* (Cambridge: Cambridge University Press, 2015).

Gadd, Ian Anders and Patrick Wallis, 'Reaching beyond the City Wall: London Guilds and National Regulation, 1500–1700', in S. R. Epstein and Maarten Prak (eds.), *Guilds, Innovation and the European Economy, 1400–1800* (Cambridge: Cambridge University Press, 2008), 288–315.

Garnsey, Peter. 'The Generosity of Veyne', *Journal of Roman Studies*, 81 (1991), 164–8.

Gauci, Perry. (ed.), *Regulating the British Economy, 1660–1850* (Farnham: Ashgate, 2011).

Gelderblom, Oscar and Joost Jonker, 'Public Finance and Economic Growth: The Case of Holland in the Seventeenth Century', *Journal of Economic History*, 71 (2011), 1–39.

Gentilcore, David. *Medical Charlatanism in Early Modern Italy* (Oxford: Oxford University Press, 2006).

Gerrard, Christine. *Aaron Hill: The Muse's Projector 1685–1750* (Oxford: Oxford University Press, 2003).

Getzler, Joshua. *A History of Water Rights at Common Law* (Oxford: Oxford University Press, 2004).

Ghobrial, John-Paul. *The Whispers of Cities: Information Flows in London, Paris, and Istanbul in the Age of William Trumbull* (Oxford: Oxford University Press, 2013).

Gibbs, F. W. 'The Rise of the Tinplate Industry: III. John Hanbury (1664–1734)', *Annals of Science*, 7 (1951), 43–61.

Glaisyer, Natasha. *Culture of Commerce in England 1660–1720* (Woodbridge: Boydell, 2006).

Glăveanu, Vlad and Koji Yamamoto, 'Bridging History and Social Psychology: What, How and Why', *Integrative Psychological and Behavioural Science*, 46 (2012), 431–9.

Goffman, Erving. 'Role Distance', in Goffman, *Encounters: Two Studies in the Sociology of Interaction* (London: Penguin, 1961), 75–134.

Goffman, Erving. *Stigma: Notes on the Management of Spoiled Identity* (Englewood Cliffs, NJ: Prentice Hall, 1963).

Goldie, Mark. 'The Unacknowledged Republic: Officeholding in Early Modern England', in Tim Harris (ed.), *The Politics of the Excluded, c.1500–1850* (Basingstoke: Palgrave, 2001), 153–94.

Goldie, Mark. 'Voluntary Anglicans', *HJ*, 46 (2003), 977–90.

Goldthwaite, Richard A. *The Economy of Renaissance Florence* (Baltimore, MD: Johns Hopkins University Press, 2009).

Golinski, Jan. *Science as Public Culture: Chemistry and Enlightenment in Britain, 1760–1820* (Cambridge: Cambridge University Press, 1992).

Gough, J. W. *The Superlative Prodigall: A Life of Thomas Bushell* (Bristol: Bristol University Press, 1932).

Gough, J. W. *Sir Hugh Myddelton: Entrepreneur and Engineer* (Oxford: Clarendon, 1964).

Gough, J. W. *The Rise of the Entrepreneur* (London: Batsford, 1969).

Graber, Frédéric. 'Du Faiseur de projet au projet régulier dans les travaux publics (XVIIIe–XIXe siècles): Pour une histoire des projets', *Revue d'Histoire Moderne et Contemporaine*, 58(3) (2011), 7–33.

Graham, Aaron and Patrick Walsh, 'Introduction', in Aaron Graham and Patrick Walsh (eds.), *The British Fiscal-Military States, 1660–c.1783* (Abingdon: Routledge, 2016).

Grassby, Richard. *The Business Community of Seventeenth-Century England* (Cambridge: Cambridge University Press, 1995).

Grav, Peter F. 'Taking Stock of Shakespeare and the New Economic Criticism', *Shakespeare*, 8 (2012), 111–36.

Greaves, Richard L. *Deliver Us from Evil: The Radical Underground in Britain, 1660–1663* (Oxford: Oxford University Press, 1986).

Greaves, Richard L. *Enemies under His Feet: Radicals and Non-Conformists in Britain, 1664–1667* (Stanford, CA: Stanford University Press, 1990).

Greengrass, Mark. 'Samuel Hartlib and the Commonwealth of Learning', in Barnard and McKenzie (eds.), *Cambridge History of the Book in Britain, vol. IV, 1557–1695*, 304–22.

Greengrass, Mark, Michael Leslie, and Timothy Raylor (eds.), *Samuel Hartlib and Universal Reformation: Studies in Intellectual Communication* (Cambridge: Cambridge University Press, 1994).

Greig, Hannah. *The Beau Monde: Fashionable Society in Georgian London* (Oxford: Oxford University Press, 2013).

Grove, J. M. 'The Initiation of the "Little Ice Age" in Regions round the North Atlantic', *Climatic Change*, 48 (2001), 53–82.

Grove, Richard. 'Cressey Dymock and the Draining of the Fens: An Early Agricultural Mode', *Geographical Journal*, 147 (1981), 27–37.

Gunn, J. A. W. *Politics and the Public Interest in the Seventeenth Century* (London: Routledge, 1969).

Guy, John. *Tudor England* (Oxford: Oxford University Press, 1988).

Hailwood, Mark. *Alehouses and Good Fellowship in Early Modern England* (Woodbridge: Boydell, 2014).

Haines, Charles R. *A Complete Memoir of Richard Haines (1633–1685), A Forgotten Sussex Worthy* (London: Harrison, 1899).

Hancock, David. *Citizens of the World: London Merchants and the Integration of the British Atlantic Community, 1735–1785* (Cambridge: Cambridge University Press, 1995).

Harkness, Deborah. *The Jewel House: Elizabethan London and the Scientific Revolution* (New Haven, CT: Yale University Press, 2007).

Harris, Jonathan Gil. *Sick Economies: Drama, Mercantilism, and Disease in Shakespeare's England* (Philadelphia, PA: University of Pennsylvania Press, 2003).

Harris, Ron. *Industrializing English Law: Entrepreneurship and Business Organization, 1720–1844* (Cambridge: Cambridge University Press, 2000).

Harris, Tim. 'The Bawdy House Riot of 1668', *HJ*, 29 (1986), 537–56.

Harris, Tim. *Restoration: Charles II and his Kingdom, 1660–1685* (London: Penguin, 2006).

Harrison, Peter. 'Adam Smith and the History of the Invisible Hand', *Journal of the History of Ideas*, 72 (2011), 29–49.

't Hart, Marjolein. *The Dutch Wars of Independence: Warfare and Commerce in the Netherlands, 1570–1680* (London: Routledge, 2014).

Hatcher, John. *The History of the British Coal Industry, Volume I: Before 1700: Towards the Age of Coal* (Oxford: Clarendon, 1993).

Hayek, F. A. *The Collected Works of F. A. Hayek: Volume II: The Road to Serfdom*, ed. Bruce Caldwell (Abingdon: Routledge, 2008).

Hayton, David. 'Moral Reform and Country Politics in the Late Seventeenth-Century House of Commons', *P&P*, 128 (1990), 48–91.

Heal, Felicity and Clive Holmes, *The Gentry in England and Wales, 1500–1700* (Basingstoke: Macmillan, 1994).

Heal, Felicity and Clive Holmes, 'The Economic Patronage of William Cecil', in Pauline Croft (ed.), *Patronage, Culture and Power: The Early Cecils* (New Haven, CT: Yale University Press, 2002), 199–229.

Heijnders, Miriam and Suzanne Van Der Meij, 'The Fight against Stigma: An Overview of Stigma-Reduction Strategies and Interventions', *Psychology, Health & Medicine*, 11 (2006), 353–63.

Henderson, David. *Misguided Virtue: False Notions of Corporate Social Responsibility* (London: The Institute of Economic Affairs, 2001).

Henning, B. D. (ed.), *House of Commons 1660–1690* (3 vols., Woodbridge: Boydell, 2006).

Hilaire-Pérez, Liliane. *L'Invention technique au siècle des Lumières* (Paris: Albin Michel, 2000).

Hilaire-Pérez, Liliane and Marie Thébaud-Sorger, 'Les Techniques dans l'espace public: Publicité des inventions et littérature d'usage au XVIIIe siècle (France, Angleterre)', *Revue de Synthèse*, 5th ser., 2 (2006), 393–428.

Hilaire-Pérez, Liliane and Catherine Verna, 'Dissemination of Technical Knowledge in the Middle Ages and the Early Modern Era: New Approaches and Methodological Issues', *Technology and Culture*, 47 (2006), 536–65.

Hill, Christopher. *The Century of Revolution 1603–1714* (2nd edn, London: Routledge, 1980).

Hilton, Boyd. *The Age of Atonement: The Influence of Evangelicalism on Social and Economic Thought, 1795–1865* (Oxford: Oxford University Press, 1988).

Hindle, Steve. *The State and Social Change in Early Modern England, 1550–1640* (Basingstoke: Palgrave, 2000).

Hindle, Steve. *On the Parish? The Micro-Politics of Poor Relief in Rural England, 1550–1750* (Oxford: Clarendon, 2004).

Hindle, Steve, Alexandra Shepard, and John Walter (eds.), *Remaking English Society: Social Relations and Social Change in Early Modern England* (Woodbridge: Boydell, 2013).

Hindle, Steve, Alexandra Shepard, and John Walter, 'The Making and Remaking of Early Modern English History', in Hindle, Shepard, and Walter (eds.), *Remaking English Society*, 1–40.

Hirschman, A. O. *The Passions and the Interests: Political Arguments for Capitalism before its Triumph* (Princeton, NJ: Princeton University Press, 1977).

Hirst, Derek. *Authority and Conflict: England 1603–1658* (London: Edward Arnold, 1986).

Hitchcock, Tim. 'Paupers and Preachers: The SPCK and the Parochial Work-House Movement', in Lee Davison, Tim Hitchcock, Tim Keirn, and Robert B. Shoemaker (eds.), *Stilling the Grumbling Hive: The Responses to Social and Economic Problems in England, 1689–1750* (New York: St Martin's Press, 1992), 145–66.

Holderness, B. A. 'Credit in English Rural Society before the Nineteenth Century, with Special Reference to the Period 1650–1720', *Agricultural History Review*, 24 (1976), 97–109.

Holderness, B. A. *Pre-Industrial England: Economy and Society 1500–1750* (London: Dent, 1976).

Holmes, Clive. *Seventeenth-Century Lincolnshire* (Lincoln: History of Lincolnshire Committee, 1980).

Holmes, Clive. 'Statutory Interpretation in the Early Seventeenth-Century: The Courts, the Council, and the Commissioners of Sewers', in J. A. Guy and H. G. Beale (eds.), *Law and Social Change in British History: Papers Presented to the British Legal History Conference, 14–17 July 1981* (London: Royal Historical Society, 1984), 107–17.

Holmes, Clive. 'Drainers and Fenmen: The Problem of Popular Political Consciousness in the Seventeenth Century', in Anthony Fletcher and John Stevenson (eds.), *Order and Disorder in Early Modern England* (Cambridge: Cambridge University Press, 1985), 166–95.

Holmes, Clive. 'Drainage Projects in Elizabethan England: The European Dimension', in Salvatore Ciriacono, *Eau et développement dans l'Europe moderne* (Paris: Éditions de la Maison des Sciences de l'Homme, 2004), 87–102.

Hont, Istvan. *Jealousy of Trade: International Competition and the Nation-State in Historical Perspective* (Cambridge, MA: Harvard University Press, 2005).

Hont, Istvan and Michael Ignatieff, 'Needs and Justice in the *Wealth of Nations*: An Introductory Essay', in Hont and Ignatieff (eds.), *Wealth and Virtue: The Shaping of Political Economy in the Scottish Enlightenment* (Cambridge: Cambridge University Press, 1983), 1–44.

Hope, Jonathan and Michael Whitmore, 'The Very Large Textual Object: A Prosthetic Reading of Shakespeare', *Early Modern Literary Studies*, 9 (2004), 1–36.

Hoppit, Julian. *Risk and Failure in English Business, 1700–1800* (Cambridge: Cambridge University Press, 1987).

Hoppit, Julian. 'Attitudes to Credit in Britain, 1680–1790', *HJ*, 33 (1990), 305–22.

Hoppit, Julian. (ed.), *Failed Legislation, 1660–1800: Extracted from the Commons and Lords Journals* (London: Hambledon, 1997).

Hoppit, Julian. *The Land of Liberty? England 1689–1727* (Oxford: Clarendon, 2000).

Hoppit, Julian. 'The Contexts and Contours of British Economic Literature, 1660–1760', *HJ*, 49 (2006), 79–110.

Hoppit, Julian. 'Compulsion, Compensation and Property Rights in Britain, 1688–1833', *P&P*, 210 (2011), 93–128.

Horsefield, J. Keith. *British Monetary Experiments, 1650–1710* (Cambridge, MA: Harvard University Press, 1960).

Hoselitz, Bert F. 'The Early History of Entrepreneurial Theory', *Explorations in Entrepreneurial Theory*, 3 (1951), 193–220.

Hotson, Howard. *Johann Heinrich Alsted, 1588–1638: Between Renaissance, Reformation, and Universal Reform* (Oxford: Clarendon, 2000).

Houghton Jr, Walter E. 'The History of Trades: Its Relation to Seventeenth-Century Thought: As Seen in Bacon, Petty, Evelyn, and Boyle', *Journal of the History of Ideas*, 2 (1941), 33–60.

Howell, Martha C. *Commerce before Capitalism in Europe, 1300–1600* (Cambridge: Cambridge University Press, 2010).

Hoxby, Blair. 'The Government of Trade: Commerce, Politics and the Courtly Art of the Restoration', *ELH*, 66 (1999), 591–627.

Hoyle, Richard. 'The Masters of Requests and the Small Change of Jacobean Patronage', *EHR*, 126 (2011), 544–81.

Hughes, Ann. *Politics, Society and Civil War in Warwickshire, 1620–1660* (Cambridge: Cambridge University Press, 1987).

Hughes, Ann. 'Men, the "Public" and the "Private" in the English Revolution', in Lake and Pincus (eds.), *Politics of the Public Sphere*, 191–212.

Hughes, Edward. *Studies in Administration and Finance, 1558–1825* (Manchester: Manchester University Press, 1934).

Hulme, E. Wyndham. 'The History of the Patent System under the Prerogative and at Common Law', *Law Quarterly Review*, 12 (1896), 141–54.

Hulme, E. Wyndham. 'The History of the Patent System under the Prerogative and at Common Law. A Sequel', *Law Quarterly Review*, 16 (1900), 44–56.

Hunt, Arnold. 'Book Trade Patents, 1603–1640', in Arnold Hunt, Giles Howard Mandelbrote, and Alison E. M. Shell (eds.), *The Book Trade and its Customers, 1450–1900* (Winchester: St Paul's, 1997), 27–54.

Hunt, Arnold. *The Art of Hearing: English Preachers and their Audiences, 1590–1640* (Cambridge: Cambridge University Press, 2010).

Hunt, Lynn. *Writing History in the Global Era* (London: Norton, 2014).

Hunter, J. Paul. 'Gulliver's Travels and the Later Writings', in Christopher Fox (ed.), *The Cambridge Companion to Jonathan Swift* (Cambridge: Cambridge University Press, 2003), 216–40.

Hunter, Michael. *Science and Society in Restoration England* (Cambridge: Cambridge University Press, 1981).

Hunter, Michael. *Establishing the New Science: The Experience of the Early Royal Society* (Woodbridge: Boydell, 1989).

Hunter, Michael. *Robert Boyle (1627–92): Scrupulosity and Science* (Woodbridge: Boydell, 2000).

Hunter, Michael. *Boyle Studies: Aspects of the Life and Thought of Robert Boyle* (Farnham: Ashgate, 2015).

Hussey, David. *Coastal and River Trade in Pre-Industrial England: Bristol and its Region, 1680–1730* (Exeter: Exeter University Press, 2000).

Hutchinson, Steven. 'Arbitrating the National *Oikos*', *Journal of Spanish Cultural Studies*, 2 (2001), 69–80.

Hutton, Ronald. *The Restoration: A Political and Religious History of England and Wales, 1658–1667* (Oxford: Clarendon, 1985).

Iliffe, Robert. 'Material Doubts: Hooke, Artisan Culture and the Exchange of Information in 1670s London', *BJHS*, 28 (1995), 285–318.

Iliffe, Robert. *Newton: A Very Short Introduction* (Oxford: Oxford University Press, 2007).

Iliffe, Robert. ' "Meteorologies and Extravagant Speculations": The Future Legends of Early Modern English Natural Philosophy', in A. Brady and E. Butterworth (eds.), *The Uses of the Future in Early Modern Europe* (New York: Routledge, 2009), 192–228.

Iliffe, Robert. *Priest of Nature: The Religious Worlds of Isaac Newton* (Oxford: Oxford University Press, 2017).

Ingham, Geoffrey. *Capitalism* (Cambridge: Polity, 2008).

Ingram, Martin. 'Ridings, Rough Music and Mocking Rhymes in Early Modern England', in Barry Reay (ed.), *Popular Culture in Seventeenth-Century England* (London: Croom Helm, 1985), 166–97.

Innes, Joanna. *Inferior Politics: Social Problems and Social Policies in Eighteenth-Century Britain* (Oxford: Oxford University Press, 2009).

Ito, Seiichiro. 'The Making of Institutional Credit in England, 1600–1688', *European Journal of the History of Economic Thought*, 18 (2011), 487–519.

Ito, Seiichiro. 'Registration and Credit in Seventeenth-Century England', *Financial History Review*, 20 (2013), 137–62.

Jackman, W. T. *The Development of Transportation in Modern Britain* (3rd edn, London: Frank Cass, 1966).

Jacob, Margaret C. *The First Knowledge Economy: Human Capital and the European Economy, 1750–1850* (Cambridge: Cambridge University Press, 2014).

Jacob, Margaret C. and Larry Stewart, *Practical Matter: Newton's Science in the Service of Industry and Empire, 1687–1851* (Cambridge, MA: Harvard University Press, 2004).

Jenkins, Geraint H. *The Foundations of Modern Wales, 1642–1780* (Oxford: Clarendon, 1987).

Jenkins, Philip. *The Making of a Ruling Class: The Glamorgan Gentry, 1640–1790* (Cambridge: Cambridge University Press, 1983).

Jenkins, Rhys. 'The Protection of Inventions during the Commonwealth and Protectorate', *Notes & Queries*, 11th ser., 12 (1913), 162–3.

Jenner, Mark S. R. ' "Another *Epocha*"? Hartlib, John Lanyon and the Improvement of London in the 1650s', in Greengrass, Leslie, and Raylor (eds.), *Samuel Hartlib and Universal Reformation*, 343–56.

Jenner, Mark S. R. 'The Politics of London Air: John Evelyn's *Fumifugium* and the Restoration', *HJ*, 38 (1995), 535–51.

Jenner, Mark S. R. 'The Roasting of the Rump: Scatology and the Body Politic in Restoration England', *P&P*, 177 (2002), 84–120.

Jenner, Mark S. R. 'L'Eau changé en l'argent? Vendre l'eau dans les villes anglaises au dix-septième siècle', *Dix-Septième Siècle*, 55 (2003), 637–51.

Jenner, Mark S. R. 'Print Culture and the Rebuilding of London after the Fire: The Presumptuous Proposals of Valentine Knight', *JBS*, 56 (2017), 1–26.

Jensen, Freyja Cox. *Reading the Roman Republic in Early Modern England* (Leiden: Brill, 2012).

John, Arthur H. and Glanmor Williams (eds.), *Glamorgan County History* (5 vols., Cardiff: University of Wales Press, 1936–88).

Johns, Adrian. *The Nature of the Book: Print and Knowledge in the Making* (Chicago: University of Chicago Press, 1998).

Johns, Adrian. 'Identity, Practice, and Trust in Early Modern Natural Philosophy', *HJ*, 42 (1999), 1125–45.

Johns, Adrian. 'Miscellaneous Methods: Authors, Societies and Journals in Early Modern England', *BJHS*, 33 (2000), 159–86.

Johnson, T. W. M. 'The Diary of George Skyppe of Ledbury', *Transactions of the Woolhope Naturalists' Field Club*, 34 (1952), 54–62.

Johnston, Warren. 'The Anglican Apocalypse in Restoration England', *Journal of Ecclesiastical History*, 55 (2004), 467–501.

Jones, D. W. *War and Economy in the Age of William III and Marlborough* (Oxford: Blackwell, 1988).

Jones, E. L. *Agriculture and Economic Growth in England 1650–1815* (Oxford: Blackwell, 1974).

Jones, Geoffrey and R. Daniel Wadhwani, 'Entrepreneurship and Business History: Renewing the Research Agenda', Harvard Business School Working Paper: 07-007 (2006), 1–48.

Jones, Howard. *The Epicurean Tradition* (New York: Routledge, 1989).

Jones, Whitney R. D. *The Tudor Commonwealth, 1529–1559: A Study of the Impact of the Social and Economic Developments of Mid-Tudor England upon Contemporary Concepts of the Nature and Duties of the Commonwealth* (London: Athlone Press, 1970).

Jonsson, Fredrik Albritton. *Enlightenment's Frontier: The Scottish Highlands and the Origins of Environmentalism* (New Haven, CT: Yale University Press, 2013).

Jonsson, Fredrik Albritton. 'The Origins of Cornucopianism: A Preliminary Genealogy', *Critical Historical Studies*, 1 (2014), 151–68.

Jovchelovitch, Sandra. 'Social Representations, Public Life, and Social Construction', in Deaux and Philogène (eds.), *Representations of the Social*, 165–82.

Jovchelovitch, Sandra. *Knowledge in Context: Representation, Community and Culture* (London: Routledge, 2007).

Kamen, Henry. *The Iron Century: Social Change in Europe 1550–1660* (London: Cardinal, 1976).

Kane, Bronach. 'Social Representations of Memory and Gender in Later Medieval England', *Integrative Psychological and Behavioural Science*, 46 (2012), 544–58.

Kaye, Joel. *Economy and Nature in the Fourteenth Century: Money, Market Exchange and the Emergence of Scientific Thought* (Cambridge: Cambridge University Press, 1998).

Kaye, Joel. *A History of Balance, 1250–1375: The Emergence of a New Model of Equilibrium and its Impact on Thought* (Cambridge: Cambridge University Press, 2014).

Keblusek, Marika. '"Keeping it Secret": The Identity and Status of an Early-Modern Inventor', *History of Science*, 43 (2005), 37–56.

Keeble, N. H. *The Restoration: England in the 1660s* (Oxford: Blackwell, 2002).

Keeler, Mary Frear. *The Long Parliament, 1640–1641: A Biographical Study of its Members* (Philadelphia, PA: American Philosophical Society, 1954).

Keibek, Sebastian A. J. and Leigh Shaw-Taylor, 'Early Modern Rural By-Employments: A Re-Examination of the Probate Inventory Evidence', *Agricultural History Review*, 61 (2013), 244–81.

Keller, Vera. 'Mining Tacitus: Secrets of Empire, Nature and Art in the Reason of State', *BJHS*, 45 (2012), 189–212.

Keller, Vera. 'Air Conditioning Jahangir: The 1622 English Great Design, Climate, and the Nature of Global Projects', *Configurations*, 21 (2013), 331–67.

Keller, Vera. 'The "Framing of a New World": Sir Balthazar Gerbier's "Project for Establishing a New State in America," ca. 1649', *William and Mary Quarterly*, 70 (2013), 147–76.

Keller, Vera. *Knowledge and the Public Interest, 1575–1725* (Cambridge: Cambridge University Press, 2015).

Keller, Vera, and Ted McCormick, 'Towards a History of Projects', *Early Science and Medicine*, 21 (2016), 423–44.

Keller, Vera, and Leigh T. I. Penman, 'From the Archives of Scientific Diplomacy: Science and the Shared Interests of Samuel Hartlib's London and Frederick Clodius's Gottorf', *ISIS*, 106 (2015), 17–42.

Kewes, Paulina. 'History and its Uses: Introduction', in Paulina Kewes (ed.), *The Uses of History in Early Modern England* (Berkeley, CA: University of California Press, 2006), 1–31.

Kiessling, Nicholas K. (ed.), *The Library of Anthony Wood* (Oxford: Oxford Bibliographical Society, 2002).

King, P. W. 'Wolverley Lower Mill and the Beginnings of the Tinplate Industry', *Historical Metallurgy*, 22 (1988), 104–13.

Kirk, Thomas Allison. *Genoa and the Sea: Policy and Power in an Early Modern Maritime Republic, 1559–1684* (Baltimore, MD: Johns Hopkins University Press, 2005).

Kitch, Aaron. *Political Economy and the States of Literature in Early Modern England* (Farnham: Ashgate, 2009).

Kitching, C. J. 'The Quest for Concealed Lands in the Reign of Elizabeth I', *TRHS*, 5th ser. 24 (1974), 63–78.

Kleineke, Hannes. 'Lobbying and Access: The Canons of Windsor and the Matter of the Poor Knights in the Parliament of 1485', *Parliamentary History*, 25 (2006), 145–59.

Knights, Mark. *Representation and Misrepresentation in Later Stuart Britain: Partisanship and Political Culture* (Oxford: Oxford University Press, 2005).

Knights, Mark. 'How Rational was the Later Stuart Public Sphere?', in Lake and Pincus (eds.), *Politics of the Public Sphere*, 252–67.

Knights, Mark. 'Regulation and Rival Interests in the 1690s', in Gauci (ed.), *Regulating the British Economy*, 63–81.

Knights, Mark. 'Historical Stereotypes and Histories of Stereotypes', in Christian Tileagă and Jovan Byford (eds.), *Psychology and History: Interdisciplinary Explorations* (Cambridge: Cambridge University Press, 2014), 242–67.

Knowles, James. *Politics and Political Culture in the Court Masque* (Basingstoke: Palgrave, 2015).

Kocka, Jürgen. *Capitalism: A Short History* (Princeton, NJ: Princeton University Press, 2016) [German original, 2014].

Kocka, Jürgen. 'Introduction', in Jürgen Kocka and Marcel van der Linden (eds.), *Capitalism: The Reemergence of a Historical Concept* (London: Bloomsbury, 2016), 1–10.

Kyle, Chris R. ' "But a New Button to an Old Coat": The Enactment of the Statute of Monopolies, 21 James I cap.3', *Journal of Legal History*, 19 (1998), 203–23.

Kyle, Chris R. 'Attendance, Apathy and Order? Parliamentary Committees in Early Stuart England', in Kyle and Peacey (eds.), *Parliament at Work*, 43–58.

Kyle, Chris R. and Jason Peacey (eds.), *Parliament at Work: Parliamentary Committees, Political Power and Public Access in Early Modern England* (Woodbridge: Boydell, 2002).

Kyle, Chris R. and Jason Peacey, ' "Under Cover of So Much Coming and Going": Public Access to Parliament and the Political Process in Early Modern England', in Kyle and Peacey (eds.), *Parliament at Work*, 1–23.

Lake, Peter. 'Anti-Popery: The Structure of a Prejudice', in Richard Cust and Ann Hughes (eds.), *Conflict in Early Stuart England: Studies in Religion and Politics, 1603–1642* (London: Longman, 1989), 72–106.

Lake, Peter. 'Anti-Puritanism: The Structure of a Prejudice', in Kenneth Fincham and Peter Lake (eds.), *Religious Politics in Post-Reformation England* (Woodbridge: Boydell, 2006), 80–97.

Lake, Peter and Steve Pincus (eds.), *The Politics of the Public Sphere in Early Modern England* (Manchester: Manchester University Press, 2007).

Lake, Peter and Steve Pincus (eds.), 'Rethinking the Public Sphere in Early Modern England', in Lake and Pincus (eds.), *Politics of the Public Sphere*, 1–30.

Landreth, David. *The Face of Mammon: The Matter of Money in English Renaissance Literature* (Oxford: Oxford University Press, 2012).

Langford, Paul. *A Polite and Commercial People: England, 1727–1783* (Oxford: Clarendon, 1998).

Langholm, Odd Inge. *Economics in the Medieval Schools: Wealth, Exchange, Value, Money, and Usury according to Paris Theological Tradition 1200–1350* (Leiden: Brill, 1992).

Lazardzig, Jan. ' "Masque der Possibilität": Experiment und Spektakel barocker Projektemacherei', in Helmar Schramm, Ludger Schwarte, and Jan Lazardzig (eds.),

Spektakuläre Experimente: Praktiken der Evidenzproduktion im 17. Jahrhundert (Berlin: De Gruyter, 2006), 176–212.

Lears, Jackson. *Fables of Abundance: A Cultural History of Advertising in America* (New York: Basic Books, 1994).

Le Goff, Jacques. *Money and the Middle Ages* (Cambridge: Polity, 2012) [French original, 2010].

Leinwand, Theodore. *Theatre, Finance and Society in Early Modern England* (Cambridge: Cambridge University Press, 1999).

Leng, Thomas. *Benjamin Worsley (1618–1677): Trade, Interest and the Spirit in Revolutionary England* (Woodbridge: Boydell, 2008).

Leng, Thomas. '"A Potent Plantation Well Armed and Policeed": Huguenots, the Hartlib Circle, and British Colonization in the 1640s', *William and Mary Quarterly*, 66 (2009), 173–94.

Lennard, Reginald. 'English Agriculture under Charles II: The Evidence of the Royal Society's "Enquiries"', *EcHR*, 4 (1932), 23–45.

Leslie, Michael. 'The Spiritual Husbandry of John Beale', in Leslie and Raylor (eds.), *Culture and Cultivation in Early Modern England*, 151–72.

Leslie, Michael and Timothy Raylor (eds.), *Culture and Cultivation in Early Modern England* (Leicester and London: Leicester University Press, 1992).

Letwin, William. *The Origins of Scientific Economics: English Economic Thought 1660–1776* (London: Methuen, 1963).

Levitin, Dmitri. *Ancient Wisdom in the Age of New Science: Histories of Philosophy in England, c.1640–1670* (Cambridge: Cambridge University Press, 2015).

Lewis, M. J. T. *Early Wooden Railways* (London: Routledge, 1970).

Lewis, Rhodri. *William Petty on the Order of Nature: An Unpublished Manuscript Treatise* (Tempe, AZ: Arizona Center for Medieval and Renaissance Studies, 2012).

Lewis, W. J. 'Lead Mining in Cardiganshire', in Geraint H. Jenkins and Ieuan Gwynedd (eds.), *Cardiganshire County History: Volume 3: Cardiganshire in Modern Times* (Cardiff: University of Wales Press, 1998), 160–81.

Linden, Stanton J. *Darke Hierogliphicks: Alchemy in English Literature from Chaucer to the Restoration* (Lexington, KY: University Press of Kentucky, 1996).

Lindley, Keith. *Fenland Riots and the English Revolution* (London: Heinemann, 1982).

Link, Bruce G. and Jo C. Phelan, 'Conceptualizing Stigma', *Annual Review of Sociology*, 27 (2001), 363–85.

Long, Pamela O. *Openness, Secrecy, Authorship: Technical Arts and the Culture of Knowledge from Antiquity to the Renaissance* (Baltimore, MD: Johns Hopkins University Press, 2001).

Long, Pamela O. *Artisan/Practitioners and the Rise of the New Sciences, 1400–1600* (Corvallis, OR: Oregon State University Press, 2011).

Louw, Hentie. 'The "Mechanick Artist" in Late Seventeenth-Century English and French Architecture: The Work of Robert Hooke, Christopher Wren and Claude Perrault Compared as Products of an Interactive Science/Architecture Relationship', in Michael Cooper and Michael Hunter (eds.), *Robert Hooke: Tercentennial Studies* (Aldershot: Ashgate, 2006), 181–99.

Love, Harold. *Scribal Publication in Seventeenth-Century England* (Oxford: Clarendon, 1993).

Loveman, Kate. 'The Introduction of Chocolate into England: Retailers, Researchers, and Consumers, 1640–1730', *The Journal of Social History*, 47 (2013), 27–46.

Loveman, Kate. *Samuel Pepys and his Books: Reading, Newsgathering, and Sociability, 1660–1703* (Oxford: Oxford University Press, 2015).

Luu, Lien Bich. *Immigrants and the Industries of London, 1500–1700* (Aldershot: Ashgate, 2005).

Lynch, William T. *Solomon's Child: Method in the Early Royal Society of London* (Stanford, CA: Stanford University Press, 2001).

McCabe, Richard A. *Joseph Hall: A Study in Satire and Meditation* (Oxford: Clarendon, 1982).

McCabe, Richard A. 'Ben Jonson, Theophrastus, and the Comedy of Humours', *Hermathena*, 146 (1989), 25–37.

McCloskey, Deirdre Nansen. *Bourgeois Dignity: Why Economics Can't Explain the Modern World* (Chicago: University of Chicago Press, 2010).

McCloskey, Deirdre Nansen. *Bourgeois Equality: How Ideas, Not Capital or Institutions, Enriched the World* (Chicago: University of Chicago Press, 2016).

McCormick, Ted. *William Petty and the Ambitions of Political Arithmetic* (Oxford: Oxford University Press, 2009).

McCormick, Ted. 'Who Were the Pre-Malthusians?', in Robert J. Mayhew (ed.), *New Perspectives on Malthus* (Cambridge: Cambridge University Press, 2016), 25–51.

McCusker, John J. and Russell R. Menard, *The Economy of British America, 1607–1789* (Chapel Hill, NC: University of North Carolina Press, 1985).

Macfarlane, Stephen. 'Social Policy and the Poor in the Later Seventeenth Century', in A. L. Beier and Robert Finlay (eds.), *London 1500–1700: The Making of the Metropolis* (London: Longman, 1986), 252–77.

McGee, C. E. '"Strangest Consequence from Remotest Cause": The Second Performance of *The Triumph of Peace*', *Medieval and Renaissance Drama in England*, 5 (1991), 309–42.

McGee, C. E. 'The Presentment of Bushell's Rock: Place, Politics, and Theatrical Self-Promotion', *Medieval and Renaissance Drama in England*, 16 (2003), 31–80.

McIntosh, Marjorie Keniston. *Poor Relief in England 1350–1600* (Cambridge: Cambridge University Press, 2011).

McKendrick, Neil, John Brewer, and J. H. Plumb, *The Birth of a Consumer Society: The Commercialization of Eighteenth-Century England* (London: Europa Publications, 1982).

Maclean, Mairi, Charles Harvey, and Stewart R. Clegg, 'Conceptualizing Historical Organization Studies', *Academy of Management Review*, 41 (2016), 609–32.

McLean, Matthew. *The Cosmographia of Sebastian Münster: Describing the World in the Reformation* (Abingdon: Routledge, 2007).

MacLeod, Christine. 'The 1690s Patents Boom: Invention or Stock-Jobbing?', *EcHR*, new ser., 39 (1986), 549–71.

MacLeod, Christine. *Inventing the Industrial Revolution: The English Patent System, 1660–1800* (Cambridge: Cambridge University Press, 1988).

MacLeod, Christine. 'The Paradoxes of Patenting: Invention and its Diffusion in Eighteenth- and Nineteenth-Century Britain, France, and North America', *Technology and Culture*, 32 (1991), 885–910.

MacLeod, Christine. *Heroes of Invention: Technology, Liberalism and British Industry, 1750–1914* (Cambridge: Cambridge University Press, 2007).

McRae, Andrew. 'Husbandry Manuals and the Language of Agrarian Improvement', in Leslie and Raylor (eds.), *Culture and Cultivation*, 35–62.

McRae, Andrew. *God Speed the Plough: The Representation of Agrarian England, 1500–1660* (Cambridge: Cambridge University Press, 1996).

McRae, Andrew. *Literature, Satire and the Early Stuart State* (Cambridge: Cambridge University Press, 2004).

Maddison, R. E. W. 'Studies in the Life of Robert Boyle, F.R.S. Part II. Salt Water Freshened', *NRRS*, 9 (1952), 196–216.

Magnusson, Lars. *Mercantilism: The Shaping of an Economic Language* (London: Routledge, 1994).

Maifreda, Germano. *From Oikonomia to Political Economy: Constructing Economic Knowledge from the Renaissance to the Scientific Revolution* (Farnham: Ashgate, 2012).

Malcolm, Noel. *The Origins of English Nonsense* (London: Fontana Press, 1998).

Malcolm, Noel. *Agents of Empire: Knights, Corsairs, Jesuits and Spies in the Sixteenth-Century Mediterranean World* (London: Penguin, 2016) [originally published, 2015].

Marshall, Peter. 'Anticlericalism Revested? Expressions of Discontent in Early Tudor England', in Clive Burgess and Eamon Duffy (eds.), *The Parish in Late Medieval England* (Donington: Shaun Tyas, 2006), 365–80.

Martin, Evelyn H. 'History of Several Families Connected with Diddlebury. I. The Baldwyns: Part III', *Transactions of the Shropshire Archaeological and Natural Historical Society*, 4th ser., 2 (1912), 327–47.

Martz, Linda. *Poverty and Welfare in Habsburg Spain: The Example of Toledo* (Cambridge: Cambridge University Press, 1983).

Mascuch, Michael. 'Social Mobility and Middling Self-Identity: The Ethos of British Autobiographers, 1600–1750', *Social History* [Hull], 20 (1995), 45–61.

Mayhew, N. J. 'Population, Money Supply, and the Velocity of Circulation in England, 1300–1700', *EcHR*, 48 (1995), 238–57.

Mayhew, N. J. 'Prices in England, 1170–1750', *P&P*, 219 (2013), 3–39.

Mazzaoui, Maureen Fennell. 'The Emigration of Veronese Textile Artisans to Bologna in the Thirteenth Century', *Atti e memorie dell'Accademia di Agricoltura, Scienze e Lettere di Verona*, 6th ser. 19 (1967–68), 275–319.

Mendel, Michael. 'De Facto Freedom, De Facto Authority: Press and Parliament, 1640–1643', *HJ*, 38 (1995), 307–32.

Mendelsohn, J. Andrew. 'Alchemy and Politics in England 1649–1665', *P&P*, 135 (1992), 30–78.

Meneghin, Vittorino. *I monti di pietà in Italia dal 1462 al 1562* (Vicenza: LIEF Edizioni, 1986).

Menning, Carol Bresnahan. *Charity and State in Late Renaissance Italy: The Monte di Pietà of Florence* (Ithaca, NY: Cornell University Press, 1993).

Michell, A. R. 'Sir Richard Weston and the Spread of Clover Cultivation', *Agricultural History Review*, 22 (1974), 160–1.

Millgate, Michael. *Testamentary Acts: Browning, Tennyson, James, Hardy* (Oxford: Clarendon, 1992).

Millstone, Noah. *Manuscript Circulation and the Invention of Politics in Early Stuart England* (Cambridge: Cambridge University Press, 2016).

Minard, Philippe. *La Fortune du colbertisme: État et industrie dans la France des Lumières* (Paris: Fayard, 1998).

Minard, Philippe. 'Facing Uncertainty: Markets, Norms and Conventions in the Eighteenth Century', in Gauci (ed.), *Regulating the British Economy*, 177–94.

Minchinton, W. E. *The British Tinplate Industry: A History* (Oxford: Clarendon, 1957).

Mitchell, David M. ' "My Purple will be too Sad for that Melancholy Room": Furnishings for Interiors in London and Paris, 1660–1735', *Textile History*, 40 (2009), 3–28.

Mokyr, Joel. *The Lever of Riches: Technological Creativity and Economic Progress* (Oxford: Oxford University Press, 1990).

Mokyr, Joel. 'Editor's Introduction: The New Economic History and the Industrial Revolution', in Joel Mokyr (ed.) *The British Industrial Revolution: An Economic Perspective* (2nd edn, Boulder, CO: Westview Press, 1999), 1–127.

Mokyr, Joel. *The Gifts of Athena: Historical Origins of the Knowledge Economy* (Princeton, NJ: Princeton University Press, 2002).

Mokyr, Joel. 'Knowledge, Enlightenment, and the Industrial Revolution: Reflections on *The Gifts of Athena*', *History of Science*, 45 (2007), 185–96.

Mokyr, Joel. *The Enlightened Economy: Britain and the Industrial Revolution, 1700–1850* (London: Penguin, 2011) [originally published, 2009].

Mokyr, Joel. *A Culture of Growth: The Origins of the Modern Economy* (Princeton, NJ: Princeton University Press, 2017).

Molà, Luca. *The Silk Industry of Renaissance Venice* (Baltimore, MD: Johns Hopkins University Press, 2000).

Molà, Luca. 'State and Crafts: Relocating Technical Skills in Renaissance Italy', in Michelle O'Malley and Evelyn Welch (eds.), *The Material Renaissance* (Manchester: Manchester University Press, 2007), 133–53.

Mormando, Franco. *The Preacher's Demons: Bernardino of Siena and the Social Underworld of Early Renaissance Italy* (Chicago: University of Chicago Press, 1999).

Morrill, John. *The Nature of the English Revolution: Essays* (London: Longman, 1993).

Moscovici, Serge. 'Notes towards a Description of Social Representations', *European Journal of Social Psychology*, 18 (1988), 211–50.

Moxham, N. 'Fit for Print: Developing an Institutional Model of Scientific Periodical Publishing in England, 1665–ca. 1714', *NRRS*, 69 (2015), 241–60.

Muchmore, Lynn. 'The Project Literature: An Elizabethan Example', *Business History Review*, 45 (1971), 474–87.

Muldrew, Craig. *Economy of Obligation: The Culture of Credit and Social Relations in Early Modern England* (London: Macmillan, 1998).

Muldrew, Craig. *Food, Energy and the Creation of Industriousness: Work and Material Culture in Agrarian England, 1550–1780* (Cambridge: Cambridge University Press, 2011).

Muldrew, Craig. '"Th'ancient Distaff" and "Whirling Spindle": Measuring the Contribution of Spinning to Household Earnings and the National Economy in England, 1550–1770', *EcHR*, 65 (2012), 498–526.

Muldrew, Craig. 'From Commonwealth to Public Opulence: The Redefinition of Wealth and Government in Early Modern Britain', in Hindle, Shepard, and Walter (eds.), *Remaking English Society*, 317–39.

Muldrew, Craig. 'The "Middling Sort": An Emergent Cultural Identity', in Keith Wrightson (ed.), *A Social History of England, 1500–1750* (Cambridge: Cambridge University Press, 2017), 290–309.

Muldrew, Craig. 'Self-Control and Savings: Adam Smith and the Creation of Modern Capital', in James Shaw and Simon Middleton (eds.), *Market Ethics and Practices, 1300–1850* (Abingdon: Routledge, 2017) 63–86.

Murphy, Anne L. 'Lotteries in the 1690s: Investment or Gamble?', *Financial History Review*, 12 (2005), 227–46.

Murphy, Anne L. *The Origins of English Financial Markets: Investment and Speculation before the South Sea Bubble* (Cambridge: Cambridge University Press, 2009).

Murphy, Gwendolen. *A Bibliography of English Character-Books, 1608–1700* (Oxford: Bibliographical Society, 1925).

Nash, Michael. 'Barge Traffic on the Wey Navigation in the Second Half of the Seventeenth Century', *Journal of Transport History*, 7 (1965–6), 218–24.

Neal, Larry. 'The Rise of a Financial Press: London and Amsterdam, 1681–1810', *Business History*, 30 (1988), 163–78.

Neal, Larry. *The Rise of Financial Capitalism: International Capital Markets in the Age of Reason* (Cambridge: Cambridge University Press, 1990).

Neeson, J. M. *Commoners: Common Right, Enclosure and Social Change in England, 1700–1820* (Cambridge: Cambridge University Press, 1993).

Neufeld, Matthew. *The Civil Wars after 1660: Public Remembering in Late Stuart England* (Woodbridge: Boydell, 2013).

Newman, William R. *Gehennical Fire: The Lives of George Starkey, an American Alchemist in the Scientific Revolution* (Cambridge, MA: Harvard University Press, 1994).

Newman, William R. *Promethean Ambitions: Alchemy and the Quest to Perfect Nature* (Chicago: University of Chicago Press, 2004).

Newman, William R. and Lawrence M. Principe, *Alchemy Tried in the Fire: Starkey, Boyle, and the Fate of Helmontian Chymistry* (Chicago: University of Chicago Press, 2002).

Newton, Diana. *The Making of the Jacobean Regime: James VI and I and the Government of England* (Woodbridge: Boydell, 2005).

Nigro, Giampiero (ed.), *Francesco di Marco Datini: The Man the Merchant* (Florence: Firenze University Press, 2010).

Noonan, John T. *The Scholastic Analysis of Usury* (Cambridge, MA: Harvard University Press, 1957).

North, Douglass C. *Institutions, Institutional Change and Economic Performance* (Cambridge: Cambridge University Press, 1990).

Novak, Maximillian E. (ed.), *The Age of Projects* (Toronto: University of Toronto Press, 2008).

Novak, Maximillian E. 'Introduction', in Novak (ed.), *Age of Projects*, 3–25.

Nummedal, Tara E. *Alchemy and Authority in the Holy Roman Empire* (Chicago: University of Chicago Press, 2007).

O'Brien, Patrick K. 'Fiscal Exceptionalism: Great Britain and its European Rivals from Civil War to Triumph at Trafalgar and Waterloo', in Donald Winch and Patrick O'Brien (eds.), *The Political Economy of British Historical Experience, 1688–1914* (Oxford: Oxford University Press, 2002), 245–65.

O'Brien, Patrick K. and Philip A. Hunt, 'The Rise of a Fiscal State in England 1485–1815', *Historical Research*, 66 (1993), 129–76.

Ochs, K. H. 'The Royal Society of London's History of Trades Programme: An Early Episode in Applied Science', *Notes & Records of the Royal Society*, 39 (1985), 129–58.

Ormrod, David. *The Rise of Commercial Empires: England and the Netherlands in the Age of Mercantilism, 1650–1770* (Cambridge: Cambridge University Press, 2003).

Ormrod, David. 'Agrarian Capitalism and Merchant Capitalism: Tawney, Dobb, Brenner and Beyond', in Jane Whittle (ed.), *Landlords and Tenants in Britain, 1440–1660: Tawney's Agrarian Problem Revisited* (Woodbridge: Boydell, 2013), 200–15.

Otremba, Eric. 'Inventing Ingenios: Experimental Philosophy and the Secret of Sugar-Makers of the Seventeenth-Century Atlantic', *History and Technology*, 28 (2012), 119–47.

Overton, Mark, Jane Whittle, Darron Dean, and Andrew Hann. *Production and Consumption in English Households, 1600–1750* (Abingdon: Routledge, 2004).

Parry, Graham. 'John Evelyn as Hortulan Saint', in Leslie and Raylor (eds.), *Culture and Cultivation*, 130–50.

Pastorino, Cesare. 'The Mine and the Furnace: Francis Bacon, Thomas Russell, and Early Stuart Mining Culture', *Early Science and Medicine*, 14 (2009), 630–60.

Pawson, Eric. *Transport and Economy: The Turnpike Roads of Eighteenth-Century Britain* (London: Academic Press, 1977).

Peacey, Jason. 'Print, Publicity, and Popularity: The Projecting of Sir Balthazar Gerbier, 1642–1662', *JBS*, 51 (2012), 284–307.

Peacey, Jason. *Print and Public Politics in the English Revolution* (Cambridge: Cambridge University Press, 2013).

Pearl, Valerie. *London and the Outbreak of the Puritan Revolution: City Government and National Politics, 1625–43* (Oxford: Oxford University Press, 1961).

Pearsall, Derek. '*Piers Plowman* and the Problem of Labour', in James Bothwell, P. J. P. Goldberg, and W. M. Ormrod (eds.), *The Problem of Labour in Fourteenth-Century England* (Rochester, NY: York Medieval Press, 2001), 123–32.

Peck, Linda Levy. *Court Patronage and Corruption in Early Modern England* (London: Unwin Hyman, 1990).

Peck, Linda Levy. *Consuming Splendor: Society and Culture in Seventeenth-Century England* (Cambridge: Cambridge University Press, 2005).

Pesciarelli, Enzo. 'Smith, Bentham, and the Development of Contrasting Ideas on Entrepreneurship', *History of Political Economy*, 21 (1989), 521–36.

Pettigrew, William A. *Freedom's Debt: The Royal African Company and the Politics of the Atlantic Slave Trade, 1672–1752* (Chapel Hill, NC: University of North Carolina Press, 2013).

Pettigrew, William A. 'The Failure of the Cloth Trade to Surat and the Internationalisation of English Mercantilist Thought, 1614–1621', in William A. Pettigrew and Mahesh Gopalan (eds.), *The East India Company, 1600–1857: Essays on Anglo-Indian Connection* (Abingdon: Routledge, 2017), 21–43.

Pfister, Christian and Rudolf Brázdil, 'Climatic Variability in Sixteenth-Century Europe and its Social Dimension: A Synthesis', *Climatic Change*, 43 (1999), 5–53.

Phillips, D. Rhys. *The History of the Vale of Neath* (Swansea: published by the author, 1925).

Phillipson, Nicholas. *Adam Smith: An Enlightened Life* (New Haven, CT: Yale University Press, 2010).

Pincus, Steve. 'Neither Machiavellian Moment nor Possessive Individualism: Commercial Society and the Defenders of the English Commonwealth', *AHR*, 103 (1998), 705–36.

Pincus, Steve. 'From Holy Cause to Economic Interest: The Study of Population and the Invention of the State', in Alan Houston and Steve Pincus (eds.), *Nation Transfigured: England after the Restoration* (Cambridge: Cambridge University Press, 2001), 272–98.

Pincus, Steve. 'A Revolution in Political Economy?', in Novak (ed.), *The Age of Projects*, 115–40.

Pincus, Steve. *1688: The First Modern Revolution* (New Haven, CT: Yale University Press, 2009).

Pincus, Steven and Alice Wolfram, 'A Proactive State? The Land Bank, Investment and Party Politics in the 1690s', in Gauci (ed.), *Regulating the British Economy*, 41–62.

Plummer, Alfred. *The London Weavers' Company 1600–1970* (London: Routledge, 1972).

Pocock, J. G. A. *The Machiavellian Moment: Florentine Political Thought and the Atlantic Republican Tradition* (Princeton, NJ: Princeton University Press, 1975).

Pocock, J. G. A. *Virtue, Commerce, and History: Essays on Political Thought and History, Chiefly in the Eighteenth Century* (Cambridge: Cambridge University Press, 1985).

Polanyi, Karl. *The Great Transformation: The Political and Economic Origin of Our Time* (Boston, MA: Beacon Press, 2001) [1944].

Poliakov, Léon. *Jewish Bankers and the Holy See: From the Thirteenth to the Seventeenth Century*, tr. Miriam Kochan (London: Routledge, 1977) [French original, 1965].

Porter, Roy. *Quacks: Fakers and Charlatans in English Medicine* (Stroud: Tempus, 2000).

Prestwich, Menna. *Cranfield: Politics and Profits under the Early Stuarts* (Oxford: Clarendon, 1966).

Price, William Hyde. *The English Patents of Monopoly* (Boston, MA: Houghton, Mifflin & Co., 1906).

Priestley, Margaret. 'Anglo-French Trade and the "Unfavourable Balance" Controversy, 1660–1685', *EcHR*, 4 (1951), 37–52.

Principe, Lawrence M. 'Boyle's Alchemical Secrecy: Codes, Ciphers, and Concealments', *Ambix*, 39 (1992), 63–74.

Principe, Lawrence M. *The Aspiring Adept: Robert Boyle and his Alchemical Quest* (Princeton, NJ: Princeton University Press, 1998).

Principe, Lawrence M. *The Secrets of Alchemy* (Chicago: University of Chicago Press, 2013).

Pumfrey, Stephen and Frances Dawbarn, 'Science and Patronage in England, 1570–1625: A Preliminary Study', *History of Science*, 42 (2004), 137–88.

Puttevils, Jeroen. '"Eating the Bread Out of their Mouth": Antwerp's Export Trade and Generalized Institutions, 1544–5', *EcHR*, 68 (2015), 1339–64.

Rabb, Theodore K. *Enterprise and Empire: Merchant and Gentry Investment in the Expansion of England, 1575–1630* (Cambridge, MA: Harvard University Press, 1967).

Rampling, Jennifer M. 'The Catalogue of the Ripley Corpus: Alchemical Writings Attributed to George Ripley (d. ca. 1490)', *Ambix*, 57 (2010), 125–201.

Ransome, Mary. 'The Parliamentary Career of Sir Humphrey Mackworth, 1701–13', *University of Birmingham Historical Journal*, 1 (1948), 232–54.

Rasmussen, Dennis C. *The Problems and Promises of Commercial Society: Adam Smith's Response to Rousseau* (University Park, PA: Pennsylvania State University Press, 2008).

Ratcliff, J. R. 'Samuel Morland and his Calculating Machines c.1666: The Early Career of a Courtier-Inventor in Restoration England', *BJHS*, 40 (2007), 159–79.

Ratcliff, J. R. '"Art to Cheat the Common-weal": Inventors, Projectors, and Patentees in English Satire, ca. 1630–70', *Technology and Culture*, 53 (2012), 337–65.

Raven, James. 'Publishing and Bookselling 1660–1780', in John Richetti (ed.), *The Cambridge History of English Literature 1660–1780* (Cambridge: Cambridge University Press, 2004), 13–36.

Raven, James. *The Business of Books: Booksellers and the English Book Trade, 1450–1850* (New Haven CT: Yale University Press, 2007).

Ravid, Benjamin. 'A Tale of Three Cities and their *Raison d'État*: Ancona, Venice, Livorno, and the Competition for Jewish Merchants in the Sixteenth Century', *Mediterranean Historical Review*, 6 (1991), 138–62.

Raylor, Timothy. 'Samuel Hartlib and the Commonwealth of Bees', in Leslie and Raylor (eds.), *Culture and Cultivation*, 91–129.

Raymond, Joad. *Pamphlets and Pamphleteering in Early Modern Britain* (Cambridge: Cambridge University Press, 2003).

Reddaway, T. F. *The Rebuilding of London after the Great Fire* (London: Jonathan Cape, 1940).

Redlich, Fritz. 'The Origin of the Concepts of "Entrepreneur" and "Creative Entrepreneur"', *Explorations in Entrepreneurial History*, 1(2) (1949), 1–7.

Rees, William. *Industry before the Industrial Revolution* (2 vols., Cardiff: Cardiff University Press, 1968).

Reinert, Sophus A. *Translating Empire: Emulation and the Origins of Political Economy* (Cambridge, MA: Harvard University Press, 2011).

Reyerson, Kathryn L. 'Commerce and Communications', in David Abulafia (ed.), *The New Cambridge Medieval History Volume V, c.1198–1300* (Cambridge: Cambridge University Press, 1999), 50–70.

Reynolds, John. *Windmills & Watermills* (New York: Praeger, 1970).

Reynolds, Susan. *Before Eminent Domain: Toward a History of Expropriation of Land for the Common Good* (Chapel Hill, NC: University of North Carolina Press, 2010).

Richardson, H. G. 'The Early History of Commissions of Sewers', *EHR*, 34 (1919), 385–93.

Roberts, Lissa, Simon Schaffer, and Peter Dear (eds.), *The Mindful Hand: Inquiry and Invention from the Late Renaissance to Early Industrialisation* (Amsterdam: Koninkliijke Nederlandse Akademie van Wetenschappen, 2007).

Roberts, Peter R. 'The Business of Playing and the Patronage of Players at the Jacobean Courts', in Ralph Houlbrooke (ed.), *James VI and I: Ideas, Authority, and Government* (Aldershot: Ashgate, 2006), 81–106.

Roberts, Stephen K. 'Public or Private? Revenge and Recovery at the Restoration of Charles II', *Bulletin of the Institute of Historical Research*, 59 (1986), 172–88.

Robertson, H. M. 'Sir Bevis Bulmer: A Large-Scale Speculator of Elizabethan and Jacobean Times', *Journal of Economic and Business History*, 4 (1932), 99–120.

Robertson, H. M. *Aspects of the Rise of Economic Individualism: A Criticism of Max Weber and his School* (New York: Kelley Millman, 1959) [first published, 1933].

Rose, Craig. 'The Origins and Ideals of the SPCK 1699–1716', in Walsh, Haydon, and Taylor (eds.), *The Church of England*, 172–90.

Rose, Craig. 'Providence, Protestant Union and Godly Reformation in the 1690s', *TRHS*, 6th ser., 3 (1993), 151–69.

Rose, Jacqueline. *Godly Kingship in Restoration England: The Politics of the Royal Supremacy, 1660–1688* (Cambridge: Cambridge University Press, 2011).

Rosen, Christine Meisner. 'What is Business History?', *Enterprise and Society*, 14 (2013), 475–85.

Roseveare, Henry. *The Financial Revolution* (Harlow: Longman, 1991).

Rössner, Philipp R. 'New Inroads into Well-Known Territory? On the Virtues of Re-Discovering Pre-Classical Political Economy', in Philipp R. Rössner (ed.), *Economic Growth and the Origins of Modern Political Philosophy* (Abingdon: Routledge, 2016), 3–25.

Rotenberg-Schwartz, Michael (ed.), *Global Economies, Cultural Currencies of the Eighteenth Century* (New York: AMS Press, 2012).

Rothschild, Emma. 'Smith and the Invisible Hand', *American Economic Review*, 84 (1994), 319–22.

Rothschild, Emma and Amartya Sen, 'Adam Smith's Economics', in Knud Haakonssen (ed.), *The Cambridge Companion to Adam Smith* (Cambridge: Cambridge University Press, 2006), 319–65.

Roxburgh, Natalie. *Representing Public Credit: Credible Commitment, Fiction, and the Rise of the Financial Subject* (Abingdon: Routledge, 2016).

Ruellet, Aurélien. *La Maison de Salomon: Histoire du patronage scientifique et technique en France et en Angleterre au XIIIe siècle* (Rennes: Pressese Universitaires de Rennes, 2016).

Sacks, David Harris. *The Widening Gate: Bristol and the Atlantic Economy, 1450–1700* (Berkeley, CA: University of California Press, 1991).

Sacks, David Harris. 'The Countervailing of Benefits: Monopoly, Liberty, and Benevolence in Elizabethan England', in Dale Hoak (ed.), *Tudor Political Culture* (Cambridge: Cambridge University Press, 1995), 272–91.

Sacks, David Harris. 'The Greed of Judas: Avarice, Monopoly, and the Moral Economy in England, ca. 1350–ca. 1600', *Journal of Medieval and Early Modern Studies*, 28 (1998), 263–307.

Sacks, David Harris. 'Richard Hakluyt's Navigation in Time: History, Epic, and Empire', *Modern Language Quarterly*, 67 (2006), 32–62.

Sanders, Julie. *Ben Jonson's Theatrical Republics* (Basingstoke: Macmillan, 1998).

Sanders, Julie. *The Cultural Geography of Early Modern Drama, 1620–1650* (Cambridge: Cambridge University Press, 2011).

Schaffer, Simon. 'Defoe's Natural Philosophy and the Worlds of Credit', in Christie and Shuttleworth (eds.), *Nature Transfigured*, 13–44.

Schaffer, Simon. 'The Consuming Flame: Electrical Showmen and Tory Mystics in the World of Goods', in John Brewer and Roy Porter (eds.), *Consumption and the World of Goods* (London: Routledge, 1993), 489–526.

Schaffer, Simon. 'A Social History of Plausibility: Country, City and Calculation in Augustan Britain', in Adrian Wilson (ed.), *Rethinking Social History: English Society 1570–1920 and its Interpretation* (Manchester: Manchester University Press, 1993), 128–57.

Schaffer, Simon. 'The Show that Never Ends: Perpetual Motion in the Early Eighteenth Century', *BJHS*, 28 (1995), 157–89.

Schumpeter, Joseph A. *Business Cycles: A Theoretical, Historical and Statistical Analysis of the Capitalist Process* (2 vols., New York: McGraw-Hill, 1939).

Schumpeter, Joseph A. 'The Creative Response in Economic History', *Journal of Economic History*, 7 (1947), 149–59.

Schumpeter, Joseph A. *Capitalism, Socialism, and Democracy* (3rd edn, New York: Harper, 1950).

Schumpeter, Joseph A. *Economic Doctrine and Method: An Historical Sketch*, tr. R. Aris (London: Unwin, 1954) [German original, 1914].

Schumpeter, Joseph A. *History of Economic Analysis* (New York: Oxford University Press, 1954).

Schumpeter, Joseph A. *The Theory of Economic Development: An Inquiry into Profits, Capital, Credit, Interest, and the Business Cycle*, tr. Redvers Opie (Cambridge: MA: Harvard University Press, 1961) [German original, 1911].

Schumpeter, Joseph A. 'The Crisis of the Tax State', in Schumpeter, *The Economics and Sociology of Capitalism*, ed. Richard Swedberg (Princeton, NJ: Princeton University Press, 1991), 99–140.

Schumpeter, Joseph A. 'An Economic Interpretation of Our Time: The Lowell Lectures', in Schumpeter, *The Economics and Sociology of Capitalism*, ed. Richard Swedberg (Princeton, NJ: Princeton University Press, 1991), 339–400.

Scott, Jonathan. ' "Good Night Amsterdam." Sir George Downing and Anglo-Dutch Statebuilding', *EHR*, 118 (2003), 334–56.

Scott, William Robert. *The Constitution and Finance of English, Scottish and Irish Joint-Stock Companies to 1720* (3 vols., Cambridge: Cambridge University Press, 1910–12).

Scranton, Philip and Patrick Fridenson, *Reimagining Business History* (Baltimore, MD: Johns Hopkins University Press, 2013).

Searle, G. R. *Morality and the Market in Victorian Britain* (Oxford: Oxford University Press, 1998).

Seaward, Paul. *The Cavalier Parliament and the Reconstruction of the Old Regime, 1661–1667* (Cambridge: Cambridge University Press, 1989).

Sebek, Barbara. 'Global Traffic: An Introduction', in Barbara Sebek and Stephen Deng (eds.), *Global Traffic: Discourses and Practices of Trade in English Literature and Culture from 1550 to 1700* (Basingstoke: Palgrave, 2008), 1–15.

Secretan, C. F. *Memoirs of the Life and Times of the Pious Robert Nelson* (London: John Murray, 1860).

Sewell Jr, William H. *Logics of History: Social Theory and Social Transformation* (Chicago: University of Chicago Press, 2005).

Shagan, Ethan. *Popular Politics and the English Reformation* (Cambridge: Cambridge University Press, 2003).

Shankland, Thomas. 'Sir John Philipps of Picton Castle, the Society for Promoting Christian Knowledge, and the Charity-School Movement in Wales 1699–1737', *Transactions of the Honourable Society of Cymmrodorion* (1904–5), 74–216.

Shapin, Steven. 'Who was Robert Hooke?', in Michael Hunter and Simon Schaffer (eds.), *Robert Hooke: New Studies* (Woodbridge: Boydell, 1989), 253–85.

Shapin, Steven. '"A Scholar and a Gentleman": The Problematic Identity of the Scientific Practitioner in Early Modern England', *History of Science*, 29 (1991), 279–327.

Shapin, Steven. *A Social History of Truth: Civility and Science in Seventeenth-Century England* (Chicago: University of Chicago Press, 1994).

Shapin, Steven and Simon Schaffer, *Leviathan and the Air-Pump: Hobbes, Boyle, and the Experimental Life* (Princeton, NJ: Princeton University Press, 1985).

Shapiro, Barbara J. *A Culture of Fact: England 1550–1720* (Ithaca, NY: Cornell University Press, 2000).

Sharman, Frank A. 'River Improvement Law in the Early Seventeenth Century', *Journal of Legal History*, 3 (1982), 222–45.

Sharp, Buchanan. *Famine and Scarcity in Late Medieval and Early Modern England: The Regulation of Grain Marketing, 1256–1631* (Cambridge: Cambridge University Press, 2016).

Sharp, Lindsay. 'Timber, Science, and Economic Reform in the Seventeenth Century', *Forestry*, 48 (1975), 51–79.

Sharpe, Kevin. *The Personal Rule of Charles I* (New Haven, CT: Yale University Press, 1992).

Shaw-Taylor, Leigh. 'The Rise of Agrarian Capitalism and the Decline of Family Farming in England', *EcHR*, 65 (2012), 26–60.

Shaw-Taylor, Leigh and E. A. Wrigley, 'Occupational Structure and Population Change', in Roderick Floud, Jane Humphries, and Paul Johnson (eds.), *The Cambridge Economic History of Modern Britain* (2 vols., Cambridge: Cambridge University Press, 2014), vol. 1, 53–88.

Shepard, Alexandra. *Meanings of Manhood in Early Modern England* (Cambridge: Cambridge University Press, 2003).

Shepard, Alexandra. *Accounting for Oneself: Worth, Status, and the Social Order in Early Modern England* (Oxford: Oxford University Press, 2015).

Simpson, Charles R. 'John Bellers in Official Minutes', *Journal of the Friends Historical Society*, 12 (1915), 120–7, 165–71.

Sirota, Brent S. *The Christian Monitors: The Church of England and the Age of Benevolence, 1680–1730* (New Haven, CT: Yale University Press, 2014).

Sivasundaram, Sujit. *Nature and the Godly Empire: Science and Evangelical Mission in the Pacific, 1795–1850* (Cambridge: Cambridge University Press, 2005).

Skempton, Alec W. 'Engineering on the English River Navigations to 1760', in M. Baldwin and A. Burton (eds.), *Canals: A New Look* (Chichester: Phillimore, 1984), 23–44.

Skempton, Alec W. et al. (eds.), *Biographical Dictionary of Civil Engineers in Great Britain and Ireland: 1500–1830* (2 vols., London: Thomas Telford, 2002).

Skinner, Quentin. *Liberty before Liberalism* (Cambridge: Cambridge University Press, 1998).

Slack, Paul. *Poverty and Policy in Tudor and Stuart England* (London: Longman, 1988).

Slack, Paul. *From Reformation to Improvement: Public Welfare in Early Modern England* (Oxford: Clarendon, 1998).

Slack, Paul. 'Great and Good Towns, 1540–1700', in Peter Clark (ed.), *The Cambridge Urban History of Britain, Volume II, 1540–1840* (Cambridge: Cambridge University Press, 2000), 347–76.

Slack, Paul. 'The Politics of Consumption and England's Happiness in the Later Seventeenth Century', *EHR*, 122 (2007), 609–31.

Slack, Paul. *The Invention of Improvement: Information and Material Progress in Seventeenth-Century England* (Oxford: Oxford University Press, 2015).

Smith, Alan. 'Steam and the City: The Committee of Proprietors of the Invention for Raising Water by Fire, 1715–1735', *Transactions of the Newcomen Society*, 49 (1977–8), 5–20.

Smith, David Chan. *Sir Edward Coke and the Reformation of the Laws* (Cambridge: Cambridge University Press, 2014).

Smith, Pamela H. *The Business of Alchemy: Science and Culture in the Holy Roman Empire* (Princeton, NJ: Princeton University Press, 1994).

Smith, Pamela H. 'Science on the Move: Recent Trends in the History of Early Modern Science', *Renaissance Quarterly*, 62 (2009), 345–75.

Smith, R. S. 'A Woad Growing Project at Wollaton in the 1580s', *Transactions of the Thoroton Society of Nottinghamshire*, 65 (1961), 27–46.

Smith, Simon. 'Determining the Industrial Revolution', *HJ*, 54 (2011), 907–24.

Spufford, Peter. 'Trade in Fourteenth-Century Europe', in Michael Jones, *The New Cambridge Medieval History Volume VI, c. 1300–1415* (Cambridge: Cambridge University Press, 2000), 155–208.

Spufford, Peter. *Power and Profit: The Merchant in Medieval Europe* (London: Thames & Hudson, 2002).

Spufford, Peter. 'From Antwerp and Amsterdam to London: The Decline of Financial Centres in Europe', *De Economist*, 154 (2006), 143–75.

Spurr, John. *The Restoration Church of England, 1646–1689* (New Haven, CT: Yale University Press, 1991).

Spurr, John. 'The Church, the Societies and the Moral Revolution of 1688', in Walsh, Haydon, and Taylor (eds.), *Church of England*, 127–42.

Spurr, John. *England in the 1670s: 'This Masquerading Age'* (Oxford: Blackwell, 2000).

Stein, Tristan. 'Passes and Protection in the Making of a British Mediterranean', *JBS*, 54 (2015), 602–31.

Stern, Philip J. *The Company-State: Corporate Sovereignty and the Early Modern Foundations of the British Empire in India* (New York: Oxford University Press, 2011).

Stern, Philip J. and Carl Wennerlind, 'Introduction', in Stern and Wennerlind (eds.), *Mercantilism Reimagined*, 3–22.

Stern, Philip J. and Carl Wennerlind (eds.), *Mercantilism Reimagined: Political Economy in Early Modern Britain and its Empire* (New York: Oxford University Press, 2014).

Stevenson, Laura Caroline. *Praise and Paradox: Merchants and Craftsmen in Elizabethan Popular Literature* (Cambridge: Cambridge University Press, 1984).

Stewart, Horace. *History of the Worshipful Company of Gold and Silver Wyre-Drawers* (London: Leadenhall Press, 1891).

Stewart, Larry. *The Rise of Public Science: Rhetoric, Technology, and Natural Philosophy in Newtonian Britain, 1660–1750* (Cambridge: Cambridge University Press, 1992).

Stewart, Larry. 'Experimental Spaces and the Knowledge Economy', *History of Science*, 45 (2007), 155–77.

Stone, Lawrence. *The Crisis of the Aristocracy, 1558–1641* (Oxford: Clarendon, 1965).

Straker, Ernest. *Wealden Iron* (London: Bells and Sons, 1931).

Stubbs, Mayling. 'John Beale, Philosophical Gardener of Herefordshire, Part II. The Improvement of Agriculture and Trade in the Royal Society 1663–1683', *Annals of Science*, 46 (1989), 323–63.

Sturgess, H. A. C. (ed.), *Register of Admissions to the Honourable Society of the Middle Temple* (3 vols., London: Middle Temple, 1949).

Suarez, Michael F. 'Towards a Bibliometric Analysis of the Surviving Record, 1701–1800', in Michael F. Suarez and Michael L. Turner (eds.), *The Cambridge History of the Book in Britain, vol. V, 1695–1830* (Cambridge: Cambridge University Press, 2009), 39–65.

Sugden, Robert. *The Economics of Rights, Co-Operation and Welfare* (2nd edn, Basingstoke: Macmillan, 2004).

Sullivan, Ceri. *The Rhetoric of Credit: Merchants in Early Modern Writing* (Madison, NJ: Fairleigh Dickinson University Press, 2002).

Supple, B. E. *Commercial Crisis and Change in England, 1600–1642: A Study in the Instability of a Mercantile Economy* (Cambridge: Cambridge University Press, 1959).

Surkis, Judith. 'When Was the Linguistic Turn? A Genealogy', *AHR*, 117 (2012), 700–22.

Talbut, Gwen. 'Worcester as an Industrial and Commercial Centre, 1660–1750', *Transactions of the Worcestershire Archaeological Society*, 3rd ser., 10 (1986), 91–102.

Tarlow, Sarah. *The Archaeology of Improvement in Britain, 1750–1850* (Cambridge: Cambridge University Press, 2007).

Taylor, James. *Creating Capitalism: Joint-Stock Enterprise in British Politics and Culture, 1800–1870* (Woodbridge: Boydell, 2006).

Tazzara, Corey. 'Managing Free Trade in Early Modern Europe: Institutions, Information, and the Free Port of Livorno', *Journal of Modern History*, 86 (2014), 493–529.

Thévenot, Laurent. 'Équilibre et rationalité dans un univers complexe', *Revue Économique*, 40 (1989), 147–98.

Thirsk, Joan. (ed.), *The Agrarian History of England and Wales, Volume IV, 1500–1640* (Cambridge: Cambridge University Press, 1967).

Thirsk, Joan. *Economic Policy and Projects: The Development of a Consumer Society in Early Modern England* (Oxford: Clarendon, 1978).

Thirsk, Joan. 'Plough and Pen: Agricultural Writers in the Seventeenth Century', in T. H. Aston et al. (eds.), *Social Relations and Ideas: Essays in Honour of R. H. Hilton* (Cambridge: Cambridge University Press, 1983), 295–318.

Thirsk, Joan. *The Rural Economy of England: Collected Essays* (London: Hambledon, 1984).

Thirsk, Joan. (ed.), *The Agrarian History of England and Wales, Volume Vii, 1640–1750: Agrarian Change* (Cambridge: Cambridge University Press, 1985).

Thirsk, Joan. 'The Crown as Projector on its Own Estates, from Elizabeth I to Charles I', in R. W. Hoyle (ed.), *The Estates of the English Crown, 1558–1640* (Cambridge: Cambridge University Press, 1992), 297–352.

Thirsk, Joan. 'Making a Fresh Start: Sixteenth-Century Agriculture and the Classical Inspiration', in Leslie and Raylor (eds.), *Culture and Cultivation*, 15–34.

Thirsk, Joan. *Alternative Agriculture: A History* (Oxford: Oxford University Press, 1997).

Thomas, Keith. *The Ends of Life: Roads to Fulfilment in Early Modern England* (Oxford: Oxford University Press, 2009).

Thomas, Nicholas. 'Sanitation and Seeing: The Creation of State Power in Early Colonial Fiji', *Comparative Studies in Society and History*, 32 (1990), 149–70.

Thompson, E. P. *Customs in Common: Studies in Traditional Popular Culture* (New York: New Press, 1993).

Thompson, H. P. *Thomas Bray* (London: SPCK, 1954).

Thrupp, Sylvia L. *The Merchant Class of Medieval London* (Ann Arbor, MI: University of Michigan Press, 1962) [first published, 1948].

Tilmouth, Christopher. *Passion's Triumph over Reason: A History of the Moral Imagination from Spenser to Rochester* (Oxford: Oxford University Press, 2007).

Todeschini, Giacomo. *I mercanti e il tempio: la società cristiana e il circolo virtuoso della ricchezza fra Medioevo ed età moderna* (Bologna: Il Mulino, 2002).

Todeschini, Giacomo. *Ricchezza francescana: dalla povertà volontaria alla società di mercato* (Bologna: Il Mulino, 2004).

Todeschini, Giacomo. 'Theological Roots of the Medieval/Modern Merchants' Self-Perception', in Margaret C. Jacob and Catherine Secretan (eds.), *The Self-Perception of Early Modern Capitalists* (New York: Macmillan, 2008), 17–46.

Todeschini, Giacomo. 'Usury in Christian Middle Ages: A Reconsideration of the Historiographical Tradition (1949–2010)', in Francesco Ammannati (ed.), *Religion and Religious Institutions in the European Economy, 1000–1800* (Florence: Firenze University Press, 2012), 249–60.

Travers, Ben. 'Trading Patterns in the East Midlands, 1660–1800', *Midland History*, 15 (1990), 65–82.

Treadwell, J. M. 'Jonathan Swift: The Satirist as Projector', *Texas Studies in Literature and Language*, 17 (1975), 439–60.

Trentmann, Frank. *Free Trade Nation: Commerce, Consumption, and Civil Society in Modern Britain* (Oxford: Oxford University Press, 2007).

Trentmann, Frank. *Empire of Things: How We became a World of Consumers, from the Fifteenth Century to the Twenty-First* (New York: Harper, 2016).

Trevor-Roper, H. R. 'Three Foreigners: The Philosophers of the Puritan Revolution', in H. R. Trevor-Roper, *Religion, the Reformation and Social Change and Other Essays* (New York: Harper, 1968), 237–93.

Trott, Clive. 'Copper Industry', in Elis Jenkins (ed.), *Neath and District: A Symposium* (Neath: Published by the editor, 1974), 111–48.

Turnbull, G. H. *Hartlib, Dury and Comenius: Gleanings from Hartlib's Papers* (London: University Press of Liverpool, 1947).

Turner, Henry S. *The Corporate Commonwealth: Pluralism and Political Fictions in England, 1516–1651* (Chicago: University of Chicago Press, 2016).

Turner, James Grantham. 'Ralph Austen, an Oxford Horticulturalist of the Seventeenth Century', *Garden History*, 6 (1978), 39–45.

Turner, James Grantham. 'From Revolution to Restoration in English Literature', in David Loewenstein and Janel Mueller (eds.), *The Cambridge History of Early Modern English Literature* (Cambridge: Cambridge University Press, 2003), 790–833.

Unwin, George. *The Guilds and Companies of London* (London: Methuen, 1908).

Unwin, George. *Studies in Economic History: The Collected Papers of George Unwin* (London: Macmillan, 1927).

Unwin, George. *Industrial Organization in the Sixteenth and Seventeenth Centuries* (2nd edn, London: Frank Cass, 1957).

Vassberg, David E. *The Village and the Outside World in Golden Age Castile: Mobility and Migration in Everyday Rural Life* (Cambridge: Cambridge University Press, 1996).

Vérin, Hélène. 'Rédiger et réduire en art: Un Projet de rationalisation des pratiques', in Pascal Dubourg Glatigny and Hélène Vérin (eds.), *Réduire en art: La Technologie de la Renaissance aux Lumières* (2008), 17–58.

Veyne, Paul (ed.), *A History of Private Life I: From Pagan Rome to Byzantium*, tr. Arthur Goldhammer (Cambridge MA: Harvard University Press, 1987).

Vries, Jan de. *The Return from the Return to Narrative* [Max Weber Lecture No. 2013/01] (Badia Fiesolana: European University Institute, 2013).

Vries, Jan de. and Ad van der Woude, *The First Modern Economy: Success, Failure, and Perseverance of the Dutch Economy, 1500–1815* (Cambridge: Cambridge University Press, 1997).

Waddell, Brodie. *God, Duty and Community in English Economic Life, 1660–1720* (Woodbridge: Boydell, 2012).

Wadsworth, Alfred P. and Julia De Lacy Mann, *The Cotton Trade and Industrial Lancashire, 1600–1789* (Manchester: Manchester University Press, 1931).

Wagner, Wolfgang and Nicole Kronberger, 'Killer Tomatoes! Collective Symbolic Coping with Biotechnology', in Deaux and Philogène (eds.), *Representations of the Social*, 147–64.

Wakefield, Andre. 'Butterfield's Nightmare: The History of Science as Disney History', *History and Technology*, 30 (2014), 232–51.

Wallerstein, Immanuel et al., *Does Capitalism Have a Future?* (Oxford, Oxford University Press, 2013).

Walsh, John, Colin Haydon, and Stephen Taylor (eds.), *The Church of England c. 1689–c. 1833: From Toleration to Tractarianism* (Cambridge: Cambridge University Press, 1993).

Walsham, Alexandra. *Providence in Early Modern England* (Oxford: Oxford University Press, 1999).

Walsham, Alexandra. 'Inventing the Lollard Past: The Afterlife of a Medieval Sermon in Early Modern England', *Journal of Ecclesiastical History*, 58 (2007), 628–55.

Walter, John. *Crowds and Popular Politics in Early Modern England* (Manchester: Manchester University Press, 2006).

Walzer, Michael. *Revolution of the Saints: A Study in the Origins of Radical Politics* (Cambridge, MA: Harvard University Press, 1965).

Wanklyn, Malcolm. 'The Severn Navigation in the Seventeenth Century: Long-Distance Trade of Shrewsbury Boats', *Midland History*, 13 (1988), 34–58.

Wanklyn, Malcolm. 'The Impact of Water Transport Facilities on the Economies of English River Ports c. 1660–c.1760', *EcHR*, 2nd ser., 49 (1996), 20–34.

Ward, J. R. *The Finance of Canal Building in Eighteenth-Century England* (Oxford: Oxford University Press, 1974).

Ward, Joseph P. *Metropolitan Communities: Trade Guilds, Identity, and Change in Early Modern London* (Stanford, CA: Stanford University Press, 1997).

Warde, Paul. 'The Idea of Improvement, 1520–1720', in Richard Hoyle (ed.), *Custom, Improvement and the Landscape in Early Modern Britain* (Farnham: Ashgate, 2011), 127–48.

Warde, Paul. 'Global Crisis or Global Coincidence?', *P&P*, 228 (2015), 287–301.

Webb, Stephen Sanders. *The Governors-General: The English Army and the Definition of the Empire, 1569–1681* (Chapel Hill, NC: University of North Carolina Press, 1979).

Weber, Max. *Economy and Society*, ed. Guenther Roth and Claus Wittich (2 vols., Berkeley, CA: University of California Press, 1978).

Weber, Max. *The Protestant Ethic and the Spirit of Capitalism*, tr. Talcott Parsons (Mineola, NY: Dover Publications 2003) [German original, 1904].

Webster, Charles. 'The Authorship and Significance of *Macaria*', *P&P*, 56 (1972), 34–48.

Webster, Charles. 'Benjamin Worsley: Engineering for Universal Reform from the Invisible College to the Navigation Act', in Greengrass, Leslie, and Raylor (eds.), *Samuel Hartlib and Universal Reformation*, 213–46.

Webster, Charles. *The Great Instauration: Science, Medicine and Reform 1626–1660* (2nd edn with new preface, Oxford: Peter Lang, 2002).

Weiser, Brian. *Charles II and the Politics of Access* (Woodbridge: Boydell, 2003).

Wennerlind, Carl. *Casualties of Credit: The English Financial Revolution, 1620–1720* (Cambridge, MA: Harvard University Press, 2011).

Westeijn, Arthur. *Commercial Republicanism in the Dutch Golden Age: The Political Thought of Johan and Pieter de la Court* (Leiden: Brill, 2012).

Whitted, Brent. 'Street Politics: Charles I and the Inns of Court's *Triumph of Peace*', *Seventeenth Century*, 24 (2009), 1–25.

Wigelsworth, Jeffrey R. 'Bipartisan Politics and Practical Knowledge: Advertising of Public Science in Two London Newspapers, 1695–1720', *BJHS*, 41 (2008), 517–40.

Willan, T. S. *Studies in Elizabethan Foreign Trade* (Manchester: Manchester University Press, 1959).

Willan, T. S. *River Navigation in England 1600–1750* (London: Frank Cass, 1964).

Williams, A. R. 'The Production of Saltpetre in the Middle Ages', *Ambix*, 22 (1975), 125–33.

Willis Bund, J. W. et al. (eds.), *Victoria County History, Worcestershire* (4 vols., London: Constable, 1901–24).

Willmoth, Frances. 'Mathematical Science and Military Technology: The Ordinance Office in the Reign of Charles II', in J. V. Field and Frank A. J. L. James (eds.), *Renaissance and Revolution: Humanists, Scholars, Craftsmen, and Natural Philosophers in Early Modern Europe* (Cambridge: Cambridge University Press, 1993), 117–31.

Willmoth, Frances. *Sir Jonas Moore: Practical Mathematics and Restoration Science* (Woodbridge: Boydell, 1993).

Wilson, Charles. *England's Apprenticeship 1603–1763* (2nd edn, Harlow: Longman, 1984).

Wilson, John F. *Lighting the Town: A Study of Management in the North West Gas Industry* (London: Paul Chapman, 1991).

Winch, Donald. *Adam Smith's Politics: An Essay in Historiographic Revision* (Cambridge: Cambridge University Press, 1978).

Winch, Donald. *Riches and Poverty: An Intellectual History of Political Economy in Britain, 1750–1834* (Cambridge: Cambridge University Press, 1996).

Winch, Donald. 'Adam Smith's Problems and Ours', *Scottish Journal of Political Economy*, 44 (1997), 384–402.

Withington, Phil. 'Views from the Bridge: Revolution and Restoration in Seventeenth-Century York', *P&P*, 170 (2001), 121–51.

Withington, Phil. *The Politics of Commonwealth: Citizens and Freemen in Early Modern England* (Cambridge: Cambridge University Press, 2005).

Withington, Phil. 'Public Discourse, Corporate Citizenship, and State Formation in Early Modern England', *AHR*, 112 (2007), 1016–38.

Withington, Phil. *Society in Early Modern England: Vernacular Origins of Some Powerful Ideas* (Cambridge: Polity, 2010).

Wood, Andy. *The Memory of the People: Custom and Popular Senses of the Past in Early Modern England* (Cambridge: Cambridge University Press, 2013).

Wood, Diana. *Medieval Economic Thought* (Cambridge: Cambridge University Press, 2002).

Wood, Ellen Meiksins. *The Origin of Capitalism: A Longer View* (New York: Monthly Review Press, 1999).

Wood, Neal. *Foundations of Political Economy: Some Early Tudor Views on State and Society* (Berkeley, CA: University of California Press, 1994).

Worden, Blair. 'Providence and Politics in Cromwellian England', *P&P*, 109 (1985), 55–99.

Wrightson, Keith. *English Society 1580–1680* (London: Routledge, 1982).

Wrightson, Keith. ' "Sorts of People" in Tudor and Stuart England', in Jonathan Barry and Christopher Brooks (eds.), *The Middling Sort of People: Culture, Society and Politics in England, 1550–1800* (Basingstoke: Macmillan, 1994), 28–51.

Wrightson, Keith. *Earthly Necessities: Economic Lives in Early Modern Britain, 1470–1750* (London: Penguin Books, 2002).

Wrigley, E. A. 'A Simple Model of London's Importance in Changing English Society and Economy 1650–1750', *P&P*, 37 (1967), 44–70.

Wrigley, E. A. *Poverty, Progress, and Population* (Cambridge: Cambridge University Press, 2004).

Wrigley, E. A. *The Path to Sustained Growth: England's Transition from an Organic Economy to an Industrial Revolution* (Cambridge: Cambridge University Press, 2016).

Wrigley, E. A. and R. S. Schofield, *The Population History of England, 1541–1871: A Reconstruction* (paperback edn with new introduction, Cambridge: Cambridge University Press, 1989)

Yale, Elizabeth. *Sociable Knowledge: Natural History and the Nation in Early Modern Britain* (Philadelphia, PA: University of Pennsylvania Press, 2016).

Yamamoto, Koji. 'Piety, Profit and Public Service in the Financial Revolution', *EHR*, 126 (2011), 806–34.

Yamamoto, Koji. 'Reformation and the Distrust of the Projector in the Hartlib Circle', *HJ*, 55 (2012), 375–97.

Yamamoto, Koji. 'Medicine, Metals and Empire: The Survival of a Chymical Projector in Early Eighteenth-Century London', *BJHS*, 48 (2015), 607–37.

Yamamoto, Koji. 'Beyond Rational and Irrational Bubbles: James Brydges the First Duke of Chandos during the South Sea Bubble', in Francesco Ammannati (ed.), *Le crisi finanziarie: gestione, implicazioni sociali e conseguenze nell'età preindustriale* (Florence: Fondazione Istituto internazionale di storia economica 'F. Datini', 2016), 327–57.

Yamamoto, Koji. 'Early Modern Business Projects and a Forgotten History of Corporate Social Responsibility', in André Spicer and Grietje Baars (eds.), *The Corporation: A Critical, Multi-disciplinary Handbook* (Cambridge: Cambridge University Press, 2017), 226–37.

Yeo, Richard. *Notebooks, English Virtuosi, and Early Modern Science* (Chicago: University of Chicago Press, 2014).

Youings, Joyce. *The Dissolution of the Monasteries* (London: Allen, 1971).

Young, John T. *Faith, Medical Alchemy and Natural Philosophy: Johan Moriaen, Reformed Intelligencer, and the Hartlib Circle* (Aldershot: Ashgate, 1998).

Zahedieh, Nuala. *The Capital and the Colonies: London and the Atlantic Economy, 1660–1700* (Cambridge: Cambridge University Press, 2010).

Zahedieh, Nuala. 'Regulation, Rent-Seeking, and the Glorious Revolution in the English Atlantic Economy', *EcHR*, 63 (2010), 865–90.

Zaret, David. *Origins of Democratic Culture: Printing, Petitions, and the Public Sphere in Early-Modern England* (Princeton, NJ: Princeton University Press, 2000).

Zell, Michael. 'Walter Morrell and the New Draperies Project, c. 1603–1631', *HJ*, 44 (2001), 651–75.

UNPUBLISHED THESES AND MANUSCRIPTS

Banks, Karen. 'The Ownership of Goods and Cultures of Consumption in Ludlow, Hereford and Tewkesbury, 1660–1760' (PhD thesis, University of Wolverhampton, 2014).

Bretthauer, Isabelle and Yohann Guffroy, 'Patents and Exclusivity in Seventeenth-Century England: Was Invention at Stake?' (conference paper presented at the World Economic History Congress, Kyoto, 3–7 August 2015).

Brooks, Colin. 'Taxation, Finance, and Public Opinion, 1688–1714' (PhD thesis, University of Cambridge, 1970).

Cummings, A. J. G. 'The York Buildings Company: A Case Study in Eighteenth Century Corporation Mismanagement' (PhD thesis, University of Strathclyde, 1980).

Dale, Sue. 'Sir William Petty's "Ten Tooles": A Programme for the Transformation of England and Ireland during the Reign of James II' (PhD thesis, Birkbeck, 2014).

Duncan, G. D. 'Monopolies under Elizabeth I, 1558–1585' (PhD thesis, University of Cambridge, 1976).

Evans, S. 'An Investigation of Sir Humphrey Mackworth's Industrial Activities (MA thesis, University of Wales, Cardiff, 1953).

Falvey, Heather. 'Custom, Resistance and Politics: Local Experiences of Improvement in Early Modern England' (2 vols., PhD thesis, University of Warwick, 2007).

Greengrass, Mark. 'The Projecting Culture of Samuel Hartlib and his Circle' (unpublished conference paper for 'Publicists and Projectors in Seventeenth-Century Europe', Wolfenbüttel, 1996).

Healey, Simon. 'Crown Revenue and the Political Culture of Early Stuart England' (PhD thesis, Birkbeck, University of London, 2015).

Jenner, Mark S. R. 'Liquid Schemes, Solid Gold' (unpublished manuscript, n.d.).

Johnston, Stephen. 'Making Mathematical Practice: Gentlemen, Practitioners and Artisans in Elizabethan England' (PhD thesis, University of Cambridge, 1994).

Legon, Edward James. 'Remembering Revolution: Seditious Memories in England and Wales, 1660–1685' (PhD thesis, University College London, 2015).

MacLeod, Christine. 'Patents for Invention and Technical Change in England, 1660–1753' (PhD thesis, University of Cambridge, 1983).

Nasu, Kei. 'Heresiography and the Idea of "Heresy" in Mid-Seventeenth-century English Religious Culture' (PhD thesis, University of York, 2000).

Neufeld, Matthew. 'Recollections of an Indemnified Past in Restoration England: The Answers of Defaulting Accounts to the Court of Exchequer' (unpublished paper, 2015).

Ochs, Kathleen Helen. 'The Failed Revolution in Applied Science: Studies of Industry by Members of the Royal Society of London, 1660–1688' (PhD thesis, University of Toronto, 1981).

Smith, Edmond. 'The Global Interests of London's Commercial Community, 1599–1625: Investment in the East India Company', *EcHR* (forthcoming).

Stephenson, H. W. 'Thomas Firmin, 1632–1697' (PhD thesis, University of Oxford, 1949).

Thomas, J. H. 'Thomas Neale, A Seventeenth-Century Projector' (PhD thesis, University of Southampton, 1979).

Tosney, Nicholas Barry. 'Gaming in England, c. 1540–1760' (PhD thesis, University of York, 2008).

Yamamoto, Koji. 'Distrust, Innovation and Public Service: "Projecting" in Early Modern England' (PhD thesis, University of York, 2009).

Young, John T. 'Utopian Artificers: Hartlib's Promotion of German Technology in the English Commonwealth' (unpublished paper).

Index